URSYN

NEW STORYTELLING

LEARNING THROUGH METAPHORS

URSYN.COM

URSYN.COM

First published 2026
by CRC Press
2385 NW Executive Center Drive, Suite 320, Boca Raton FL 33431

and by CRC Press
4 Park Square, Milton Park, Abingdon, Oxon, OX14 4RN

CRC Press is an imprint of Taylor & Francis Group, LLC

ISBN: 9781032972558 (hbk)
ISBN: 9781032970608 (pbk)
ISBN: 9781003592945 (ebk)

DOI: 10.1201/9781003592945
Typeset in Times New Roman and Herculanum

Publisher's note: This book has been prepared from printer-ready copy provided by the author.

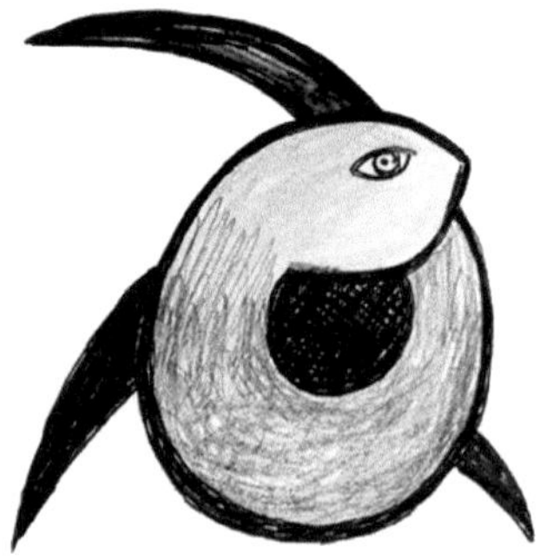

For M and M, with Much Love.

A SERIES OF BOOKS: KNOWLEDGE THROUGH THE ARTS
PLAYFUL BOOKS ABOUT SERIOUS THINGS

This series consists of the following volumes:

- Dance Code: Dance Steps as a Code, Taylor & Francis
- New Storytelling: Learning through Metaphors, Taylor & Francis
- Code Appreciation: Reshaping Knowledge, Taylor & Francis
- Nature Appreciation: Knowledge as Art, Taylor & Francis

Several common themes are woven throughout these books. They provide crucial insights into coding and the ongoing connections between programming and various fields of knowledge, areas of specialization, courses of study, and a diverse range of subjects. The books playfully explore knowledge domains and technologies within the framework of everyday situations faced by characters who endeavor to express their challenges through coding. These volumes also examine a collective understanding of nature. In each book, text and illustrations are accompanied by artworks from the author and other artists, visual outputs from computer programs, and sketches of imaginary characters.

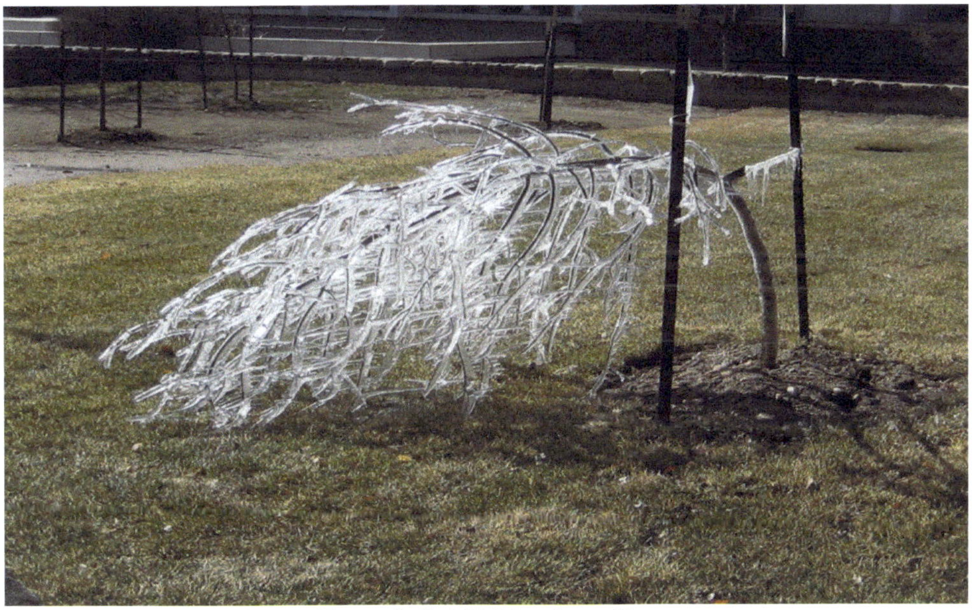

Frozen Fractal. © 2025 by Anna Ursyn

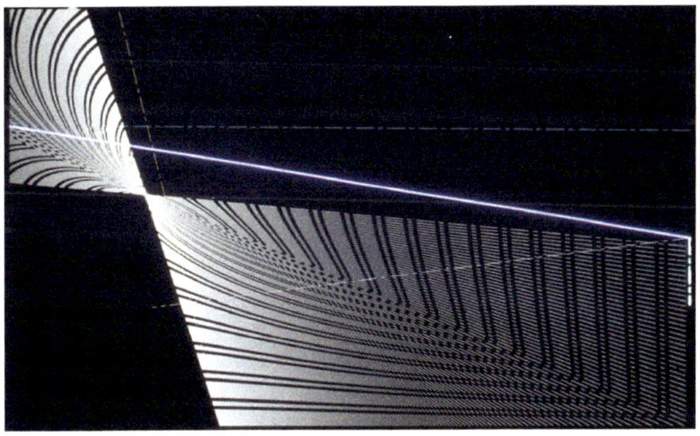

Swirl. Output from the computer code. © 2025 by Anna Ursyn

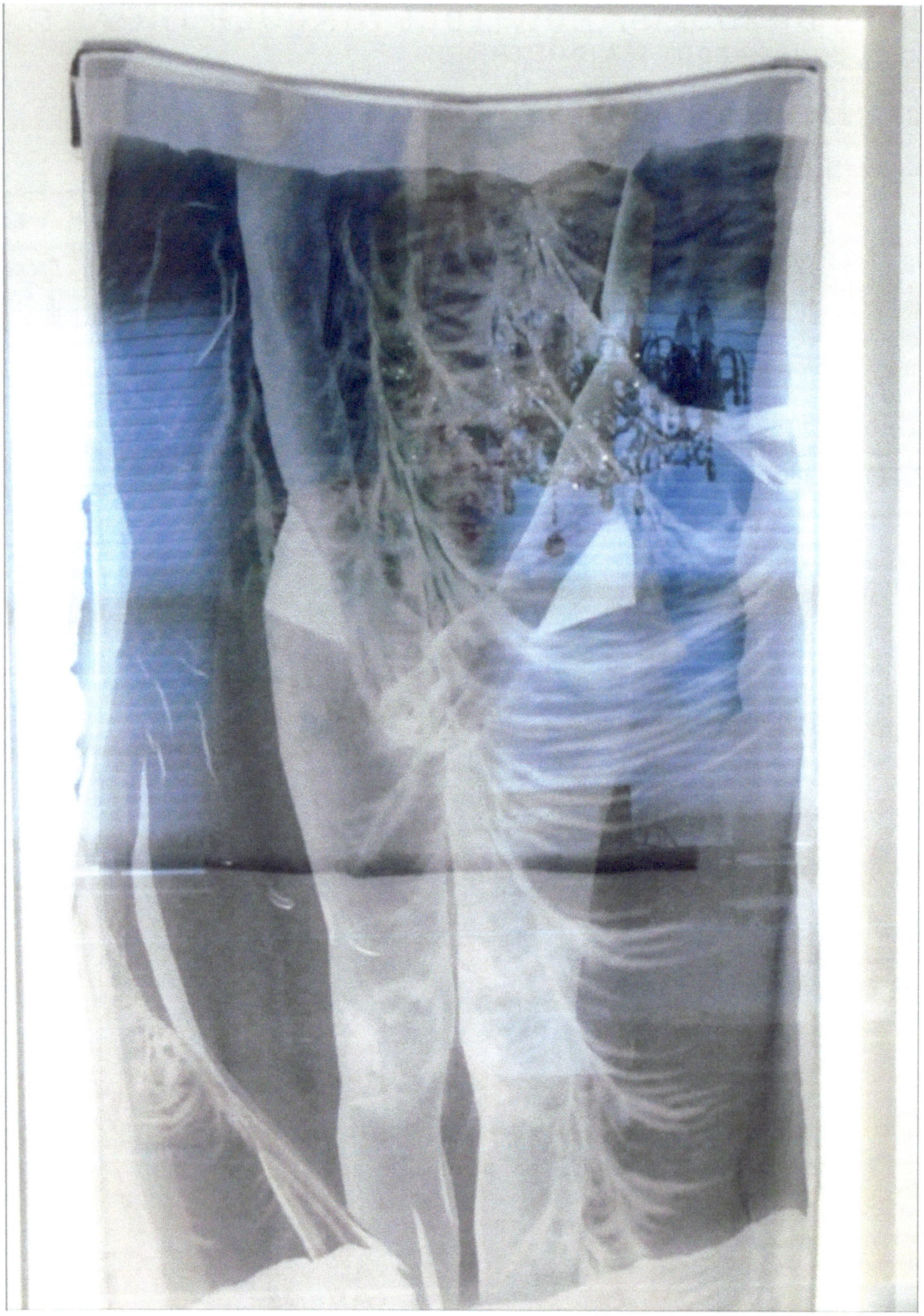

Artwork © by Joohyun Pyune. (Used with permission).

KEYWORDS

Storytelling, Art, Coding, Programming, Music, Dance, Choreography, Video, Mathematical Art, Stage Design, Art and Science Connection, Professions, Computer Graphics, Digital Media, Knowledge Visualization, Knowledge Transfer through Art, Character Creation, Concept Art and Digital Illustration, Cognitive and Abstract Thinking, Talents.

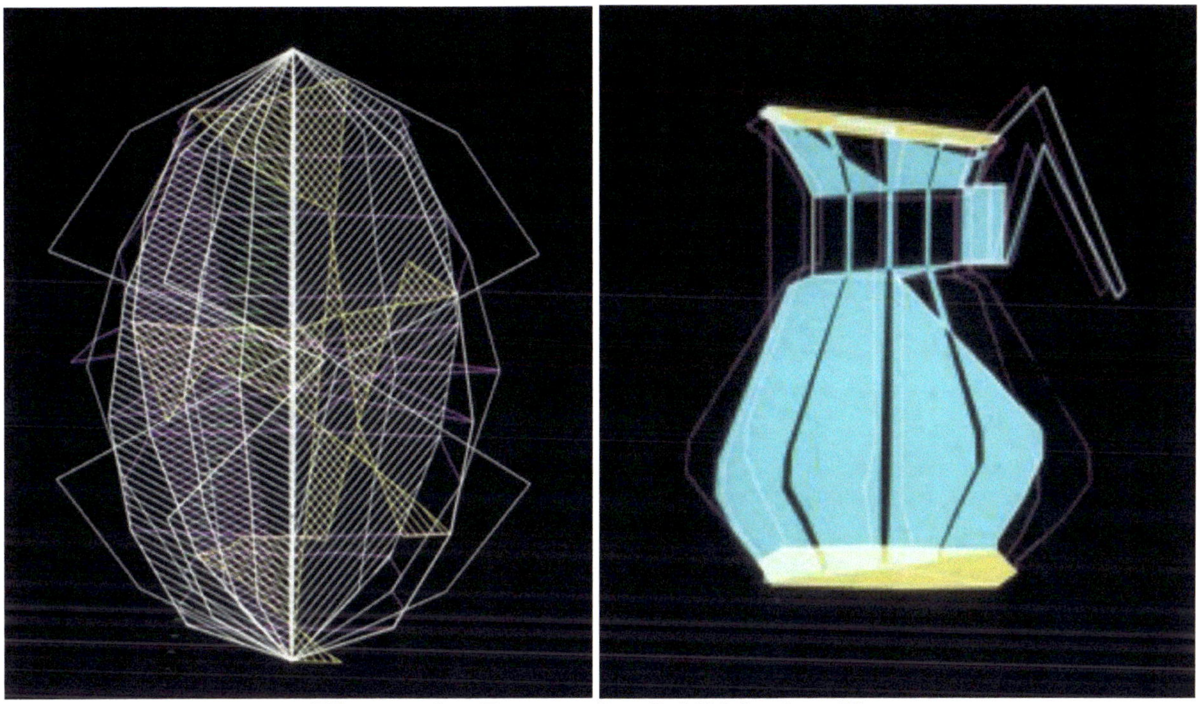

An Ellipse and its Functionality. © 2025 by Anna Ursyn.

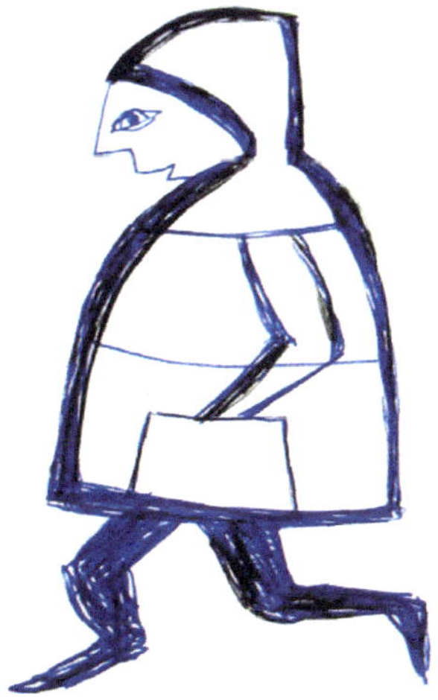

Tacho: keeps it all in his pocket.

Tacho: keeps it all in his pocket.

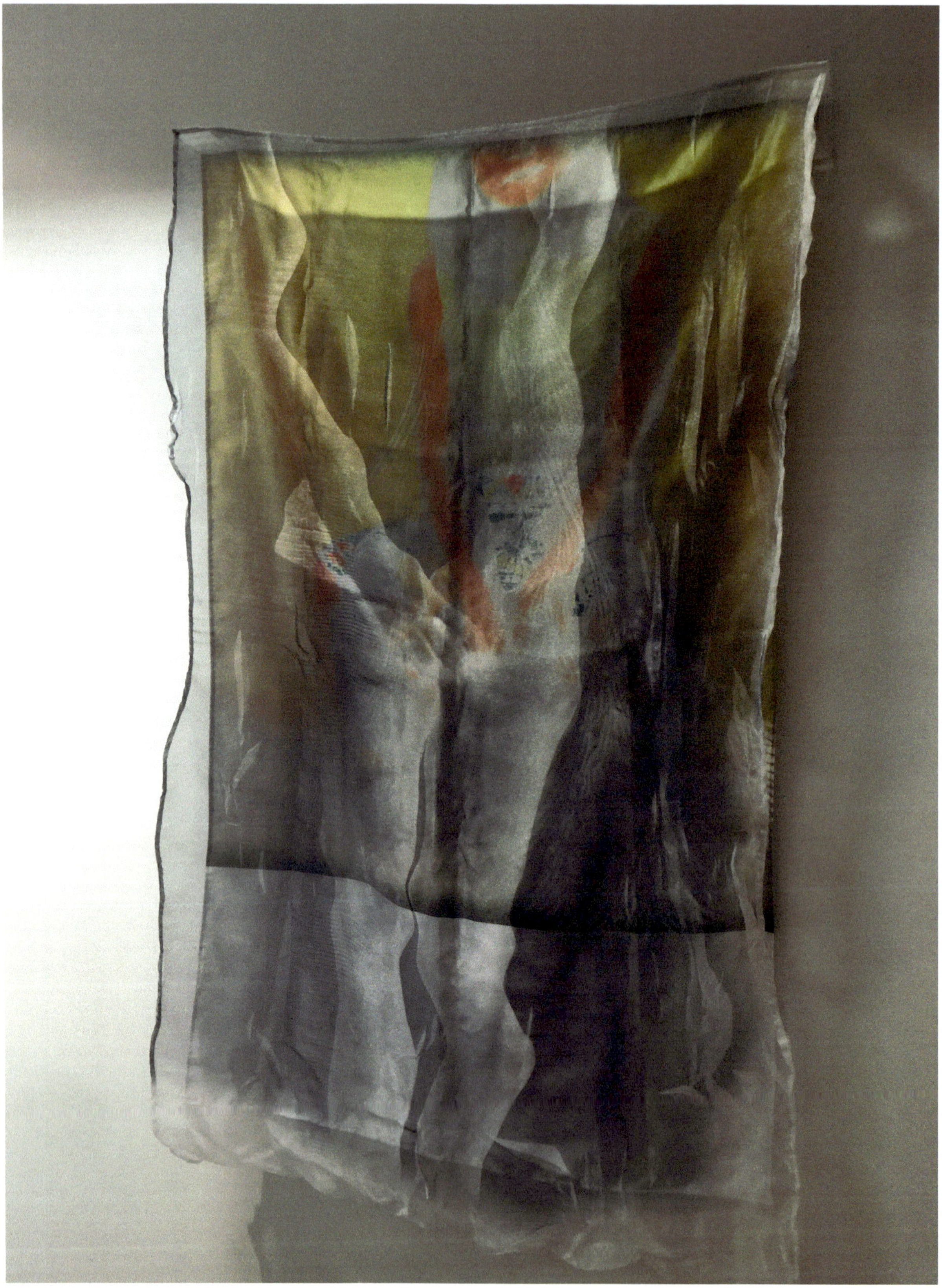

Artwork © by Joohyun Pyune. (Used with permission).

TABLE OF CONTENTS

This book comprises the following chapters, each telling a story. Some of the stories were converted to videos and then performed on the theater stage to explore the impact of technology on our daily lives.

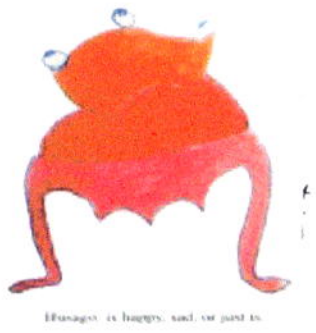

Hutago: is happy, sad, or just is.

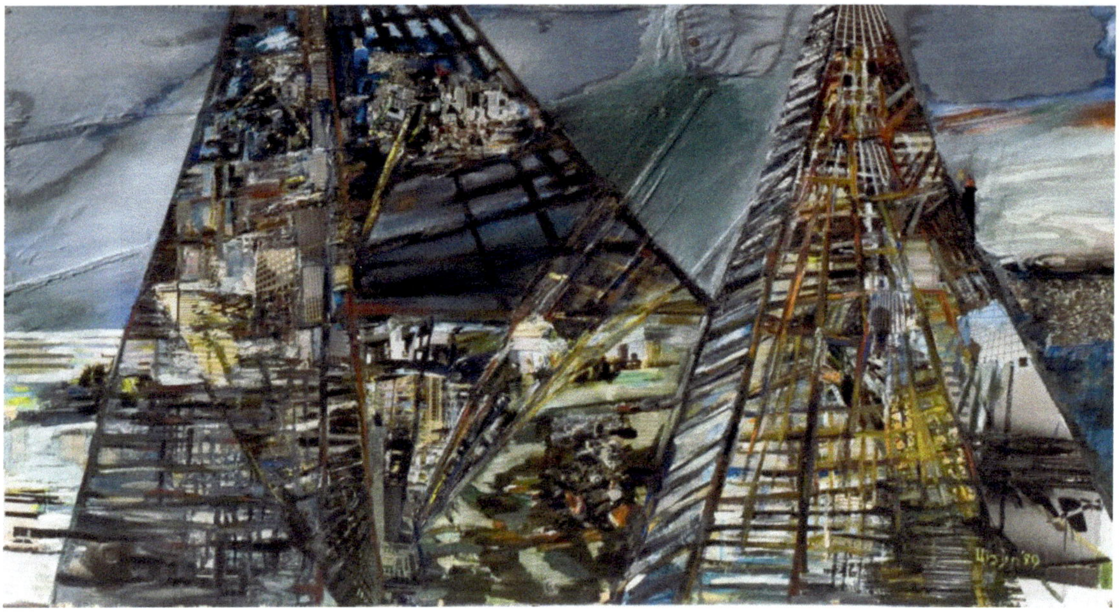

Landscape with a Blue Jeans Sky, © 2025 by Anna Ursyn

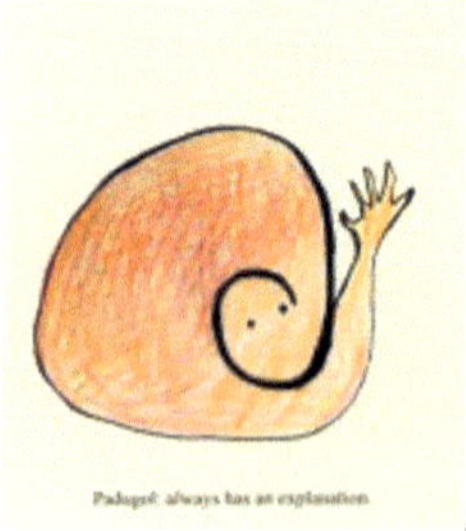

Padugol: always has an explanation.

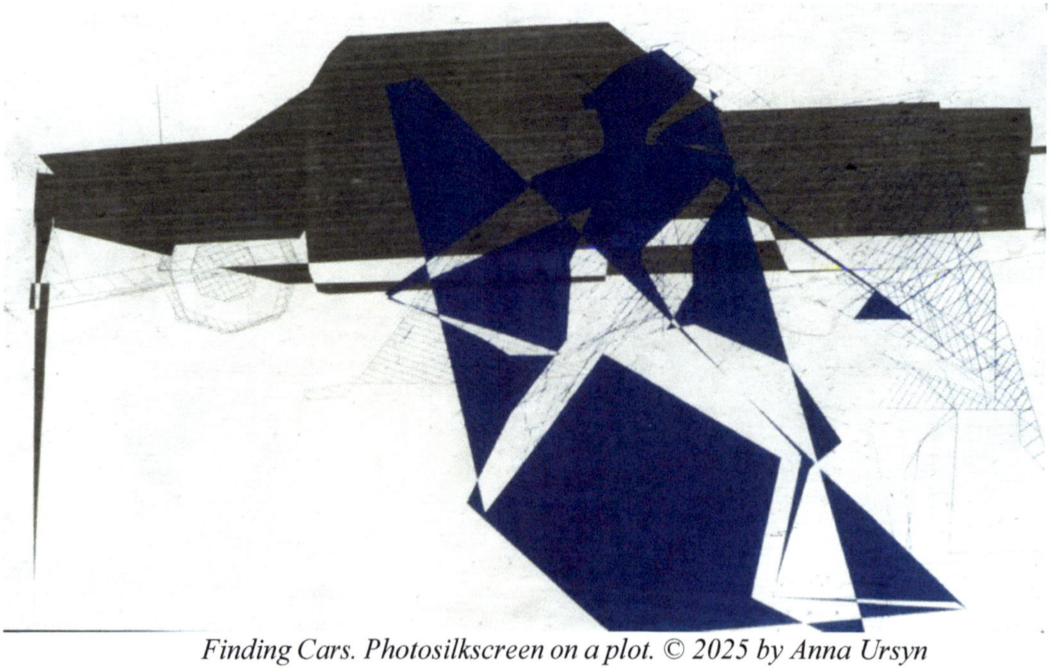

Finding Cars. Photosilkscreen on a plot. © 2025 by Anna Ursyn

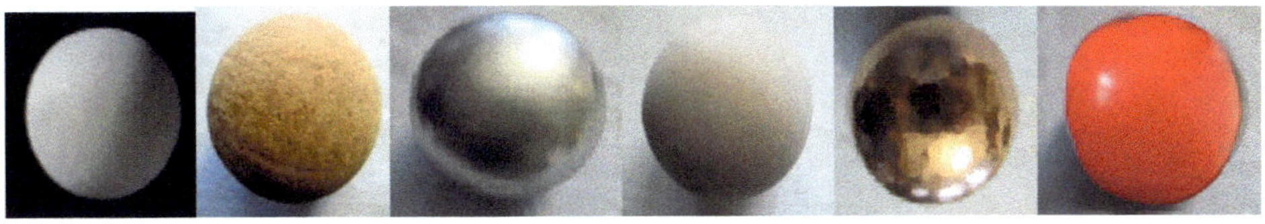

HELLO WORLD!

My name is Moil. You may call me Task. Moi is fine, as well. I am perfect, but I am not a Platonic Object. I wish, but I cannot belong to that group. That makes me less superb, but still, I am flawlessly objective. I think.

I take orders – my way. I'll make your tasks disappear. I do not do it physically. Just tell me what you need; it's not like you'd ask your phone, watch, or any device you can talk to. I will connect all the materials, tools, and procedures according to what it takes to fulfill your wishes. I am not a Genie, and I am not anthropomorphized. No need for that. They say I look like a Moon, which pleases me. They also tell me I roll, which I like because I do.

Let me bring you up to what is happening. It will unfold in the following chapters, with the last ones summarizing the topics covered and some ideas about what technologies might bring us.

THROUGHOUT THIS BOOK:

Dialog is in this font.
Characters and some directions are in italics.
`Exposition is in this font (Information for the audience's benefit).`

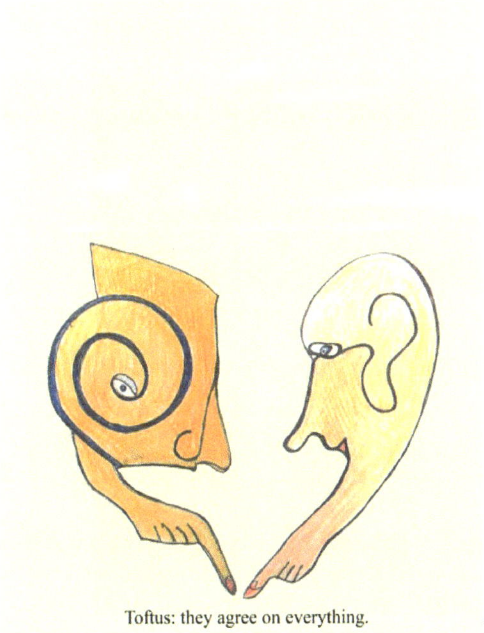

Toftus: They usually agree on almost everything

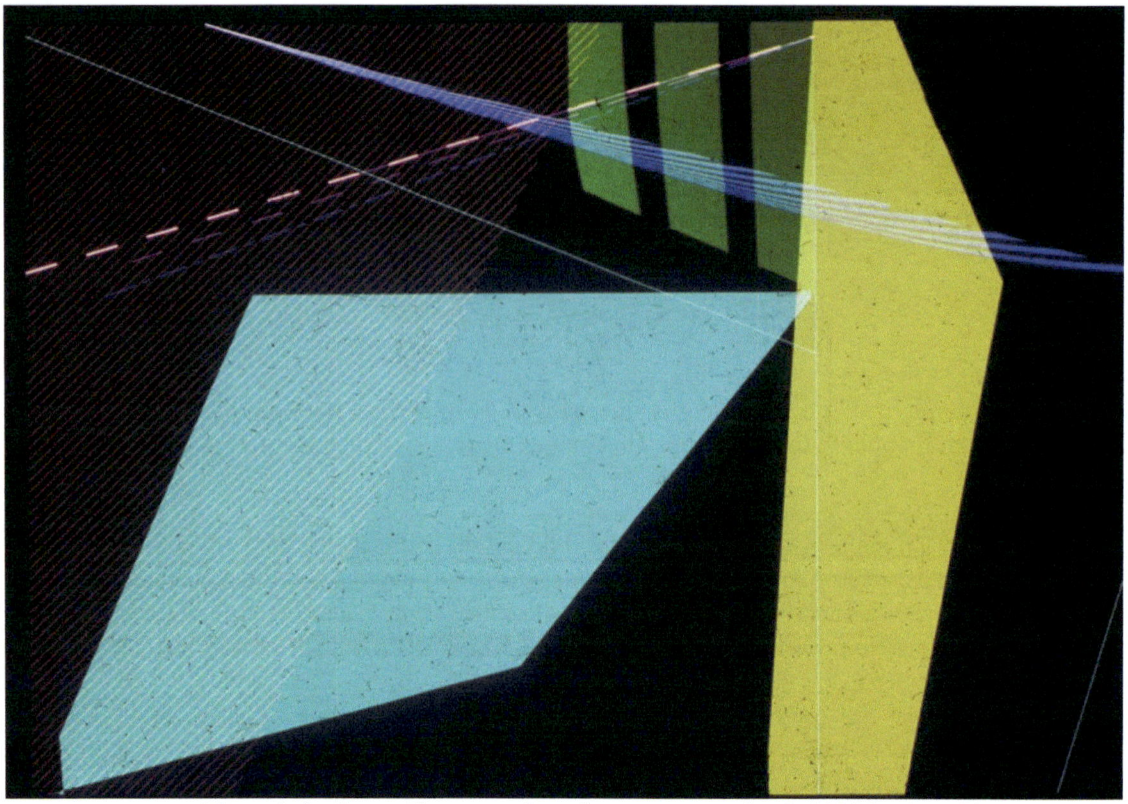

Through the Space. The output from the computer code. © 2025 by Anna Ursyn

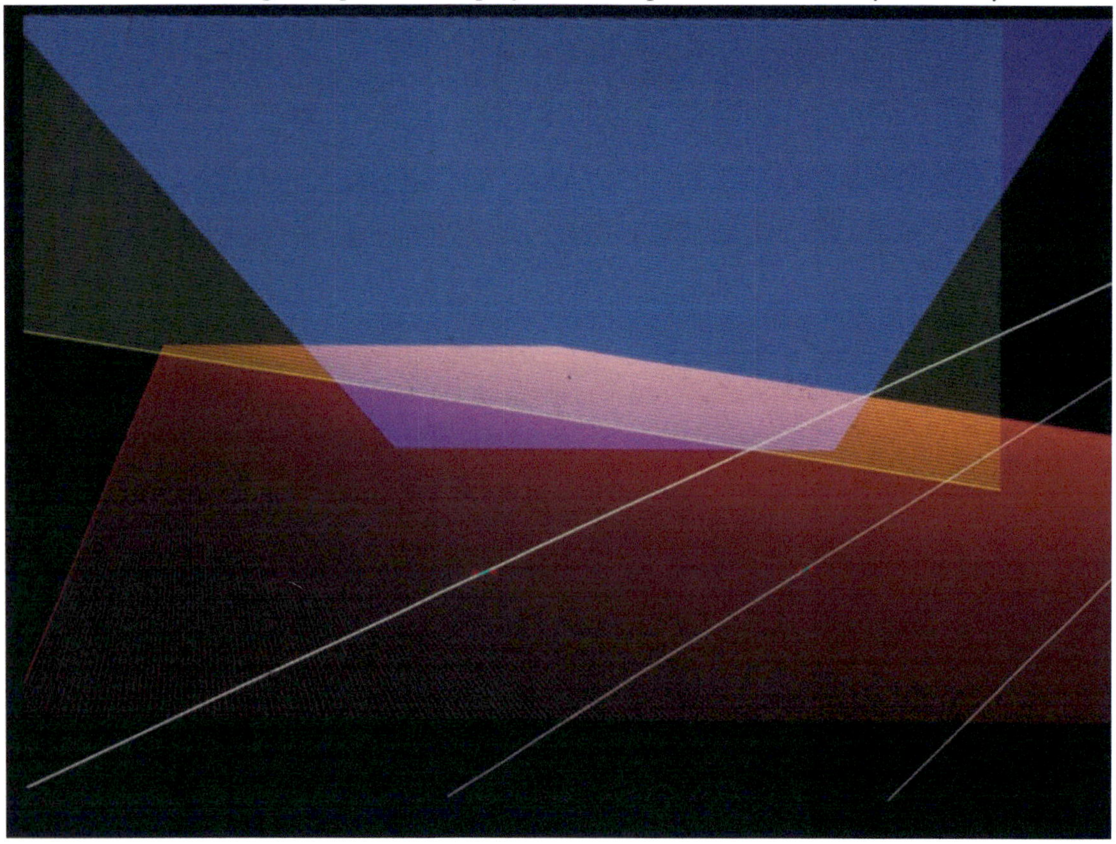

Morning Light. The output from the computer code, © 2024. by Anna Ursyn

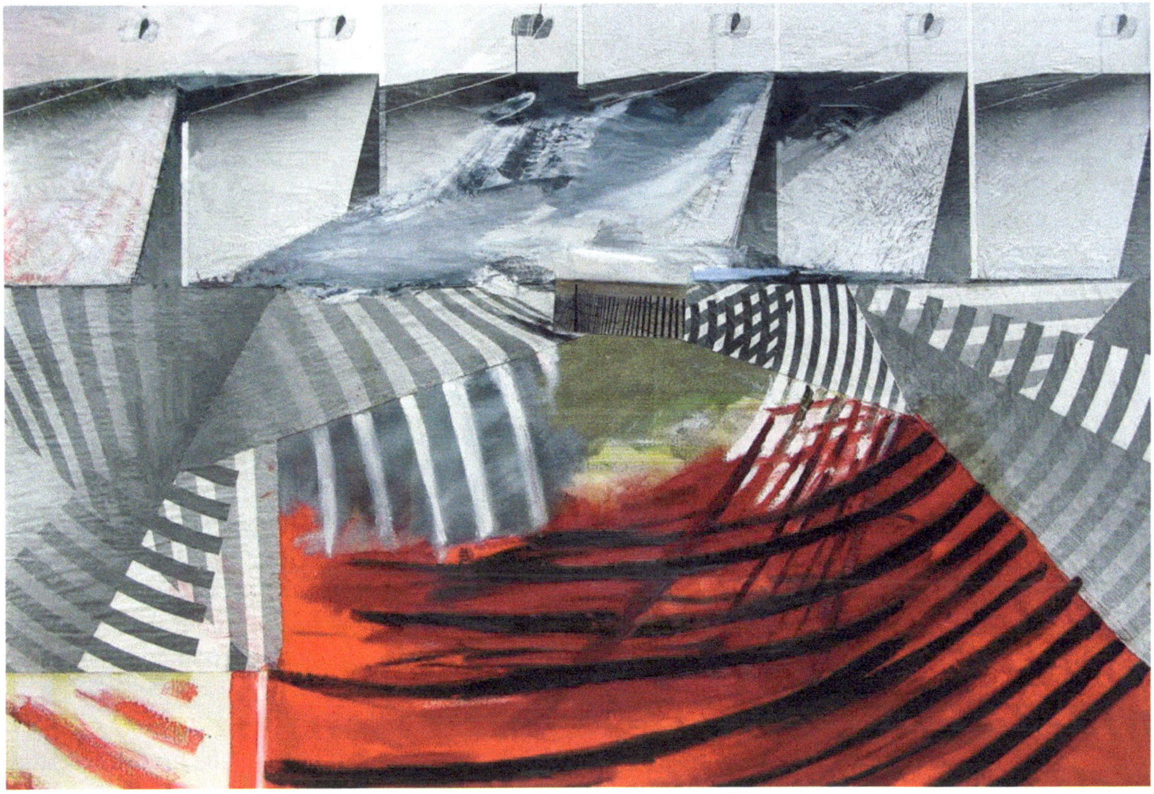

Two Skies. © *2025 by Anna Ursyn*

INTRODUCTION

ABOUT THIS BOOK

We live in a fast-changing environment ruled by coding. The *New Storytelling: Learning through Metaphors* is a collection of texts that help people perceive coding as less feared and show how programming appears in various disciplines. The goal is to set a different, more comfortable way of learning about technology through dramatized or choreographed stories that display information. Many professions encompass different approaches to communication, which are technical, theoretical, historical, multicultural, analytical, critical, and performative, with the underlying technology, media, and art. Issues described in these stories inspire new ways to look at visually presented knowledge through performing or choreographed movements. Hence, the audience learns often without knowing that they do. Learn without studying.

This book involves innovative ways of transferring knowledge to technology-based instruction by using storytelling, dance, music, and performance as an analogy, thus showing how technologies affect various disciplines. It introduces the audience to the ideas behind basic concepts in technology through metaphors, with movement in mind. These stories show how coding is important and related to most fields. This set provides materials for people involved in Computer Graphics, Media, Digital Media, Dance, Music, and Theater to familiarize them with principles that link arts with coding, thus understanding and meeting some requirements of the contemporary job market. It also might help some readers to find their niche.

ENHANCEMENT OF VARIOUS CAREERS

Many people shy away from programming as they perceive it as difficult math, while coders with high math skills often see it as a language. A student once commented that if they knew about coding as a language, they would not be so afraid of it. Many find coding difficult, stressful, and beyond their interests, even though some basic understanding of how programming works speeds up communication between coworkers and thus enhances both the company's production and professional careers. Experimentation and exploration in multimedia inform and enrich our learning, teaching, service, and community outreach.

Employers value candidates who understand the mechanics, basic jargon, terminology, and coding logistics. This knowledge enables better contact with the coders on the job; a better grasp of what other coworkers are doing speeds up the process. Leading entertainment companies inform and train computer graphics educators on what they expect from their prospective employees and how to prepare students for the job. All agreed that beyond a high-quality artistic portfolio, students should be able to write, play, understand, and/or enjoy music, and have experience in sports or performing on the stage to know how characters can deliver stories better. Moreover, prospective employees should have collaborative skills and some experience with programming, not to be turned into coders but to communicate better with programmers on the job. Most tasks are created through cooperative efforts, and coding is involved in many parts of production processes.

Understanding basic concepts about coding helps people write prompts to obtain the most interesting solutions. This research-based project introduces programming through the visual and performing arts, by offering basic ideas behind coding and showing how art and data overlap in science and nature.

ONLINE LEARNING MATERIALS

This book mixes experiences in art, coding, music, dance, choreography, video, mathematical art, stage design, and Nature. Some chapters in this book were used as a basis for collaborative, international, and interdisciplinary theatrical performances, which involved colleagues, multidisciplinary worldwide collaborators, faculty, staff, and students from the Computer Science, Music, Dance, and the Arts, and were performed by faculty and student dancers at the University of Northern Colorado (UNC). Also, contributions from various specialists resulted in artistic videos that visualize ideas behind programming and connect coding with visual and performing arts. Art students contributed to preparatory animated videos with their research, voices, characters, and art projects. Some codes and videos with credits are on a website that complements the book:

https://ursyn.com/art-and-programming

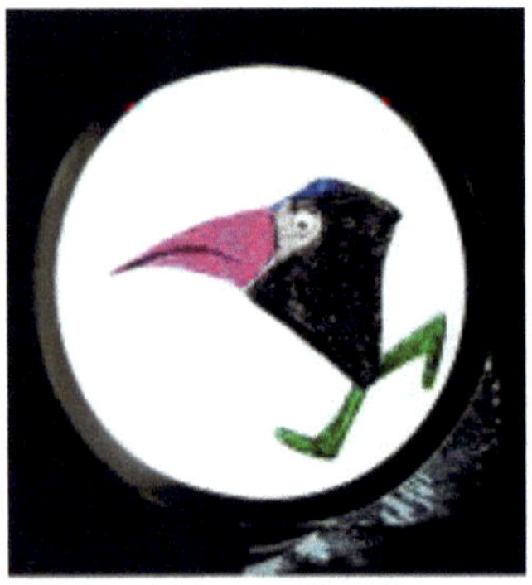

Radikun: remembers his first dinner.

COLLABORATIVE WORK

The current workspace involves cross-disciplinary collaborative efforts. Even if someone creates alone, the technology involved in the process has already been developed by somebody else or needs more expertise. Collaborations often happen online with participants living across seas, oceans, mountains, or forests. The concept of using coding for artistic creation is not a new one. Many artists started creating art with computers by writing codes before any software for art was available. Computers allow for exploration beyond space and time. Technology allows us to output our multisensory experiences in visual ways. This work aims to help people learn about programming for graphical outputs. Intended as open-ended, it can be approached from any direction and fit anyone's interests, passions, fun time, etc.

METAPHORS AS A TOOL FOR KNOWLEDGE TRANSFER

The visual approach to coding uses metaphors to link codes to other disciplines. Everyday activities or tasks may impact new media-focused communication modes to unleash technology in various disciplines. For example, rules in Nature can be shown through visual moves based on the dance rules provided. The stories explore techniques behind various occupations and pursuits. They symbolically introduce basic concepts beyond computing. They evolve through stories, dance, performance, codes, and comments.

EDUCATIONAL APPROACH: LEARNING CODING IN A VISUAL WAY

This method involves innovative knowledge transfer to the instructional strategies with the STEAM (with S for science, T for technology, E for education, A for art, and M for mathematics). It follows the current educational trend: STREAM (Science, Technology, Reading, Engineering, Art, and Math).

To summarize, this set of story-based learning projects links dance performances, music, tasks, ideas, and topics for discussion with computing codes. There is a worldwide need to help students become fearless of coding, as it improves communication between the artists and the coders by bridging a gap between them on the job. The resulting materials serve students in Computer Graphics, Digital Media, or anyone interested in understanding and becoming familiar with principles and the logic behind coding, which hiring companies often request, and help understand how machines are set when writing a prompt.

MEASURES AND SOLUTIONS

Knowledge-based stories can serve as learning projects, as they visualize ideas behind programming through connections with visual and performing arts through storytelling. The information provided with explanatory power as time-based and graphical data offers visual tools for grasping ideas beyond programming. The scope of this work fits the spectrum of knowledge-based learning projects that take the form of visual stories that involve several programming languages to make one feel more at ease with coding. Using metaphors is a powerful and relatively easy way for a novice to comprehend. Some codes were translated into other programming languages.

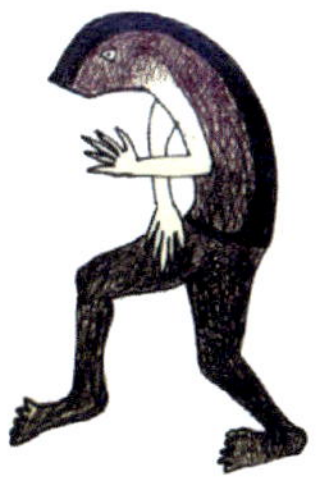

Gendowe: composes music while walking.

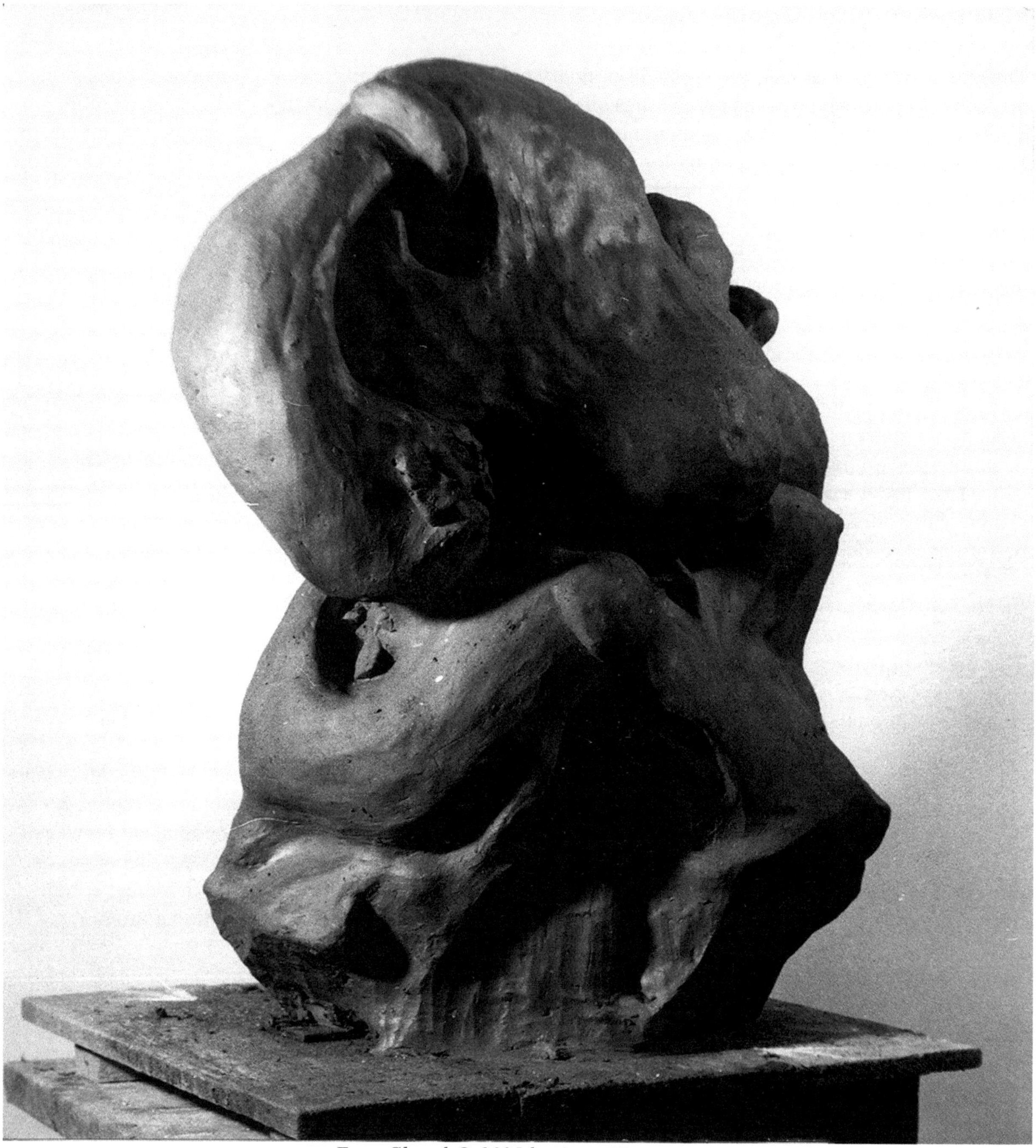

Form Closed. © 2025 by Anna Ursyn

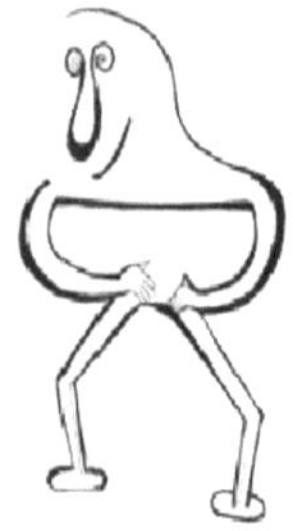

Baklash: never leaves the water.

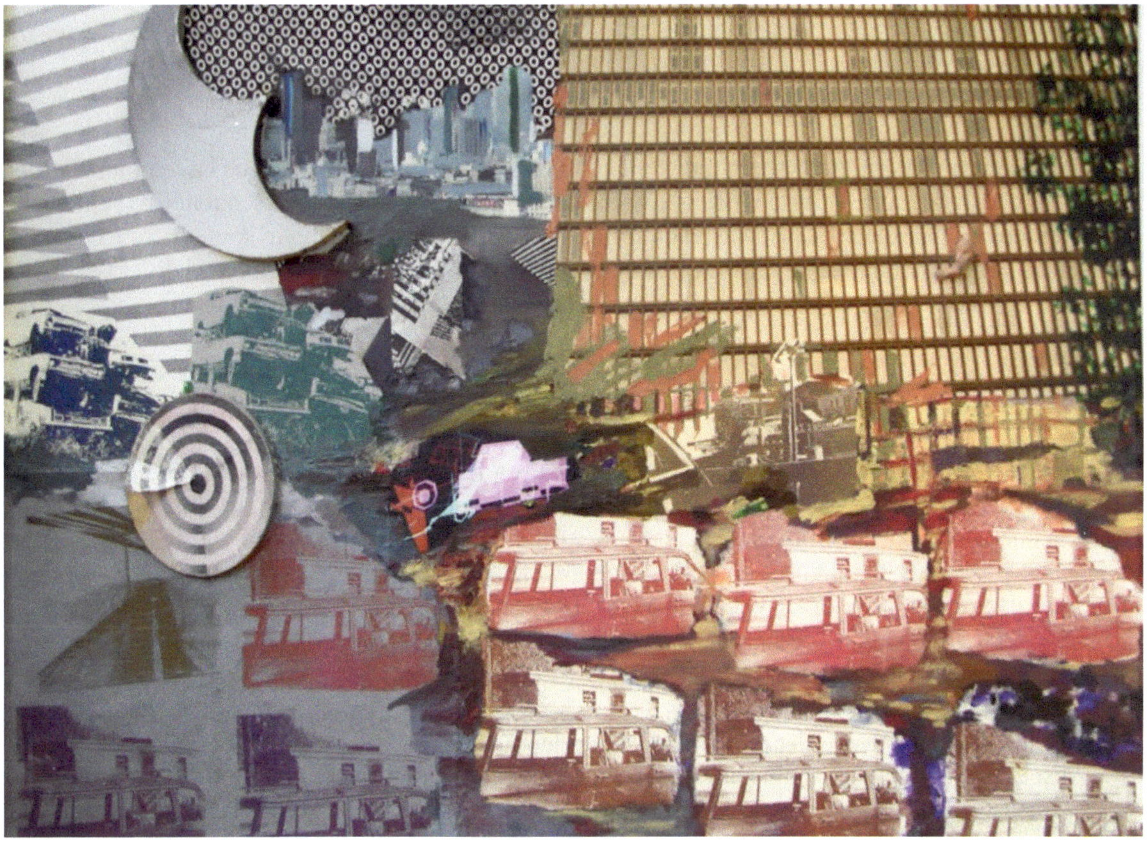

Two Moons. © *2025 by Anna Ursyn*

CHAPTER 1
DANCE CODE

AN INTERNET EXCHANGE

INTRODUCTION

This chapter aims to make coding look easier and encourage the audience to become more open to it rather than teach coding. The goal of this project is to use dance as a metaphor for programming so as a result, a dancer feels ready to code, and the coder feels ready for dancing. Hopefully, readers and viewers will start thinking about coding as something doable. This chapter's objectives focus on general ideas behind programming in several languages, creating informative Metaphors, and showing a script for animated videos and performances. Thus, the project aims to facilitate learning how to comprehend programs by translating selected dance performances into computing codes. This may support an understanding of writing computer codes through dance-step metaphors. Many people are active, love sports, and enjoy dancing. Several performances and dances are introduced in the following text, with various forms, steps, rules, and conditions juxtaposed with steps in coding. It simplifies the process of introducing a particular language to someone unfamiliar with coding. Conditions, restrictions, and ideas related to coding and dance are introduced. For the resulting performance, several programs and music compositions were served for the selected dances. Coding, music, acting, dancing, and other video and performance-related credits can be found along with resulting products at the accompanying website. This different, more comfortable way of understanding programming uses metaphors. One may start with a dance following the code, and then the code will somehow evolve out of the dance.

THE ANALOGY BETWEEN CODING AND DANCING

There are some similarities between the work of the coders and dancers. Dances have unique structures, and so do computer codes. Code writing involves applying certain steps to a sequence to achieve a goal. Dancing a particular dance is also based on following sequences according to some patterns. Dances can be seen as very structured. They have rules that obey conditions. Both disciplines deliver beauty and elegance combined with emotions.
What is Coding: https://www.bitdegree.org/tutorials/what-is-coding/

SYNOPSIS (A PLOT)

Dramata, a well-recognized, self-assured dancer, reads a letter from Kalizuko, a timid computer programmer who has recently watched her dance, which made him aware of parts missing in his life to be a whole one. Kalizuko, a timid, modest coder, is afraid that the famous prima-ballerina could ignore him; thus, he acts strongly to schedule an online meeting. They discuss them, as they initially thought, as very different disciplines, as both are based on steps. They soon discover that they have a lot in common. Dramata, a bit spoiled by fame and her success, begins to understand Kalizuko's ideas, so they compare the guiding rules, restrictions, and norms in their respective disciplines while explaining them one to each other. Self-aware Kalizuko becomes more secure after including arts, while somewhat bossy, rule-driven Dramata finds her interest in learning and discovering new ideas. They keep comparing and contrasting their disciplines, which helps the audience explore the hidden nature behind the rules that shape each field. The dance-based codes are provided on the website in the Introduction chapter for the audience's further explorations.

SUMMARY

After watching her perform, a coder demands an online meeting with a prima ballerina. They discuss what their different disciplines have in common, resulting in mutual learning of their disciplines. Prima ballerina starts appreciating programming while the coder grasps some dancing.

CAST OF CHARACTERS

Kalizuko, the coder
Dramata, the dancer

STAGE DIRECTIONS

Kalizuko sits on a blue-lit cube in front of his laptop, while Dramata sits on a red-lit cube on the right side of the stage with the grand piano. Both corners of the stage are decorated with lights reacting with reflective surfaces. Their rooms are filled with typical props. Kalizuko has maps, clocks, computers with multiple screens, neon signs, an aquarium, an oversized black stuffed teddy bear, LED lights, sport-related props, messy shoes, shirts, etc. There is a large workshop-style mirror hanging above him. Balls and balloons are shaped like our planet, and a large crescent silver moon hangs above Kalizuko. Dramata's space is organized. There are flowers, a jellyfish aquarium, masks, a teacup, instruments, a dressed-up dog, and her silver and gold

purse with matching very high heels shoes. A butterfly-shaped balloon hangs above Dramata's space. Cloud-shaped balloons connect the space between the two actors.

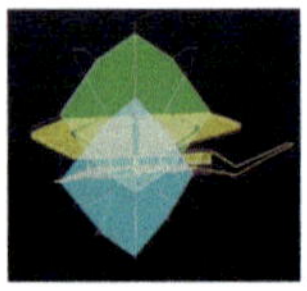
A Top of a Teapot. The output from the computer code.

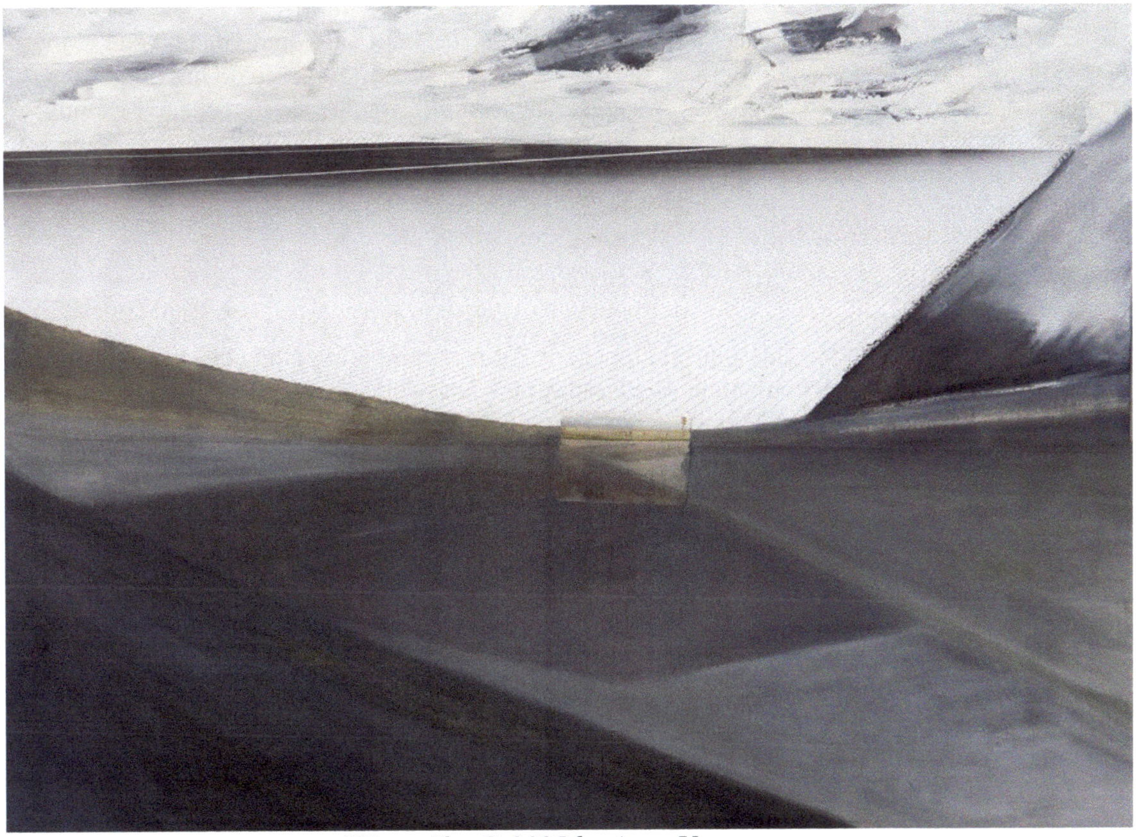

Winter Sky. © 2025 by Anna Ursyn

THE SCRIPT FOR THE DANCE CODE

Kalizuko: "Dear Dramata,

Please forgive me for writing to you. I know it comes as unexpected, but I am simply urged to share my strong senses with you, so please read it unless you want me to stay alert, nervous, unhappy, and destructed. I am in your hands: I saw you on TV dancing one night and cannot shake the feeling off. The rhythm and structure caused some consequences and conditions embedded into your movement; it was all like some instructions would come up to you from above, causing you to create new solutions, an environment, and very special air to breathe. This night was such a multisensory experience, and I saw the arts in a totally new light, causing my brain to function on a new level. I cannot lose that experience; I cannot forget the unique organization my brain went through, which created a new order for me to cope with information, knowledge, beauty, and all connecting movements. I used to think about the word as 2-D, flat, 3D, sculptural, and 4D, time-based. I used to enjoy looking at images by changing my distance to see less to focus or more to appreciate and connect. I used to walk around sculptures to see their different dimensions, structures, or variations, or I enjoyed architecture by seeing it from all around, from the inside, or from above. I used to appreciate work based on time, from reading a book to listening to music. I enjoyed musicals combining images, voices, and motions.

I cannot name the number of "Ds" you added to my world last night just by dancing. Now, I can see it all in 4D, 5D, and even more. What I felt during your performance is hard to describe; elation might be the closest word, and I only experienced that once before, when I saw a butterfly for the first time. I am begging you to meet with me via video conferencing so we can talk, and all my questions, excitement, and anxiety can be resolved one way or another. I do realize that you are a talented, well-known artist, and I am but an unknown coder, yet it causes me to think about your art and craft, pushing me to write

this letter and beg you for a virtual meeting. We live so far apart, but I am hoping that when I explore some options with you, you yourself will ask me for yet another meeting. Please do not think of me as callous or self-important. I am the opposite. It is just that something happened to me, and I cannot resist contacting you and risking going on with my life without losing my sleep. We all know that might lead to some special conditions we would all be less appreciative of, so please take it as a social duty to release my tensions."
Sincerely,
Kalizuko"

Dramata: "Dear Kalizuko,
I surely appreciate your letter, and despite coding or any form of computing going beyond my passions, I feel I simply have to meet with you online. Wednesday at 3 a.m. works for me. You need to set it up, as for me computers are for typing and answering excessively long and demanding messages. The same applies to the other arts: I cannot draw a stick figure.
Sincerely,
Dramata."

Kalizuko: "Dear Dramata,
Wednesday at 3 a.m.- oops, this is Wednesday at 3 a.m. already, so I am connecting us now. Bear with me. It will take just a minute.
P.S. I cannot dance. I never could, but I enjoy watching people dance very much.
Sincerely,
Kalizuko."

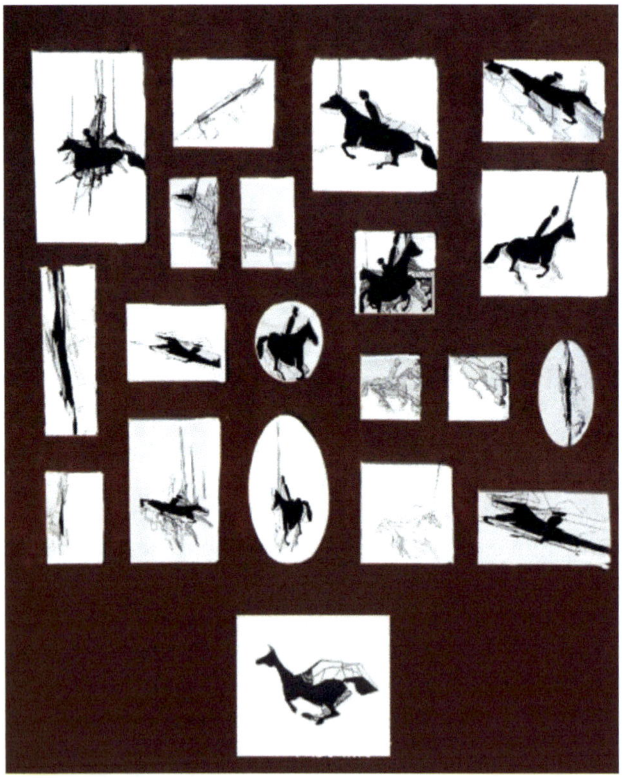

All the Horses. Outputs from the computer codes. © 2025 by Anna Ursyn.

Kalizuko and Dramata began interacting online via video conferencing, which Kalizuko had just set up for them. Their faces are projected on the big screen.

Kalizuko, "Hello"
Dramata, "Hello"
Kalizuko, "How are you"

Dramata, "I'm fine. And you?"
Kalizuko, "Fine. Thank you for asking. Have you read my letter?"
Dramata, "Oh, yes. Therefore, I must be here."
Kalizuko, "Oh, that is such a relief. I am a simple coder."
Dramata, "A coder?"
Kalizuko, "A programmer. It is not so simple. I mean, it is quite complicated, but people are so afraid of my profession that it makes me feel smaller and less important. I do many good things that you benefit from daily …"
Dramata, "Enough, I know, but it does not interest me. I am a dancer and only function in a step-by-step-based world. I think in steps. My life consists of steps, routines, tempos, values, and more. I need to know music and, of course, all the elements and principles of design. I need to know literature, as they often want me to sing texts while dancing, but I am a dancer. I always was, and I will always be!"
Kalizuko, "I know, but when you dance, why do I feel so connected to you and so involved? My job and passion are the routines, steps, conditions, and all the resulting consequences. I also think in steps. Maybe I am losing my sleep because I can see it all in your craft."
Dramata, "My craft is art! Do not offend me."
Kalizuko, "There is nothing wrong with craft. You sleep under a cover and have a keychain on your car keys."
Dramata, "Nope. I have a manufactured weighted blanket and open every door with my phone."
Kalizuko, "So nice to hear. You are immersed in technology, then."
Dramata, "I did not make it. I bought it, and my dancing provided for it."
Kalizuko, "So, I see, we have much more in common."
Dramata, "What?"
Kalizuko, "We both follow steps, routines, and conditions. We create new content or make the old content more appealing. We are both structured and organized but playful and imaginative."
Dramata, "But I only can think in a linear fashion."
Kalizuko, "Even when you improvise?
Dramata, "Well…."
Kalizuko, "See?"
Dramata, "Pardon me?"
Kalizuko, "Well, we are the same thinkers. We are both creators and developers, often bending the rules but guided by some rules."
Dramata, "Oh, I see."
Kalizuko, "Would you describe your biggest challenges for me, please?"
Dramata, "Yes, there is a tango or a waltz. Tango originated in Buenos Aires, Argentina, in the 19th century. Working-class women danced it and then became partner dancers. Argentine tango is highly improvisational; there is also an International Ballroom style. The American Ballroom basic step consists of a slow 1,2, slow 3,4, quick 5, quick 6, and slow 7,8 in an 8-count pattern where the lead begins forward on their left and the follow steps back on their right. They often have me dance it, but I simply do not follow it well. There are steps and all, but it does not appeal to me altogether."
Kalizuko, "Which way?"
Dramata, "The turns."
Kalizuko, "Here is a sequence of how they could be defined through visually recorded steps:"

`A photograph of a sequence with still frames of the dancers dancing tango appears.`

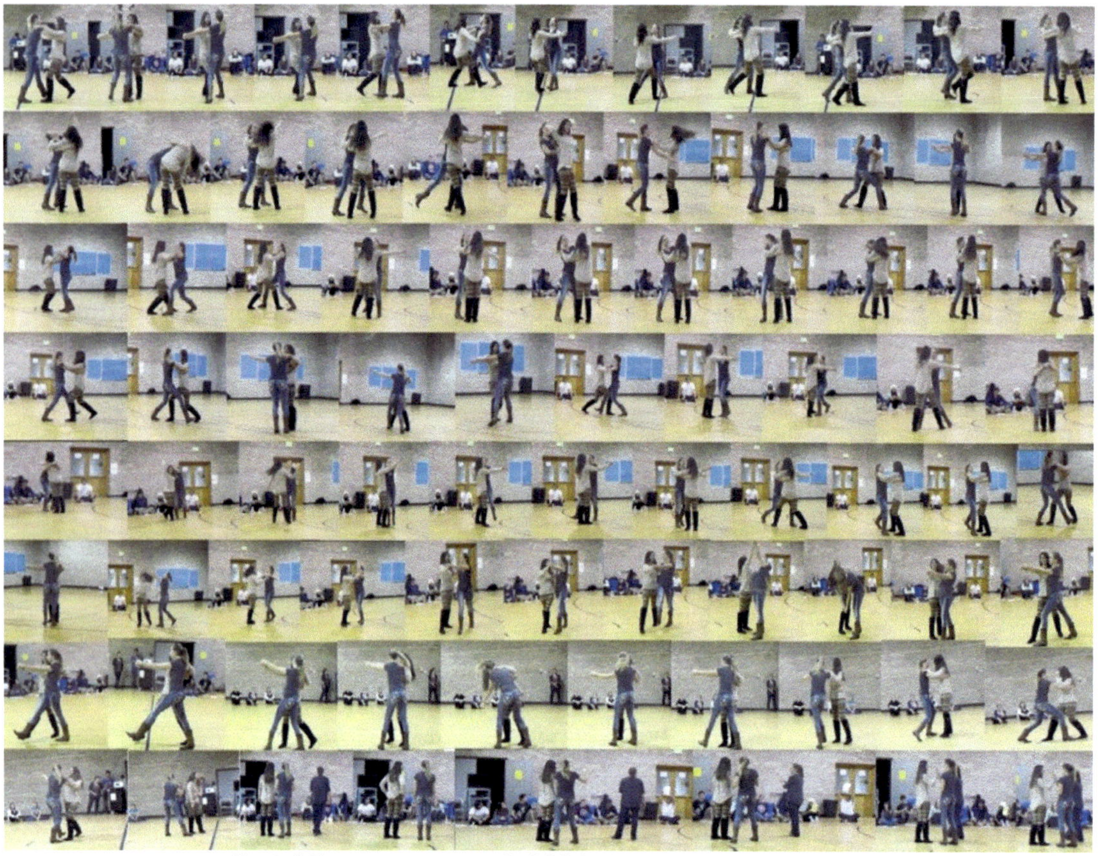

Social Dance: a tango. © 2024, Anna Ursyn

Dramata, "I know what the dance looks like!"

Kalizuko, "I can simplify it for you, let's look at a graph: "

`A graph of an output from a computer code appears on the screen.`

Dramata, "But it is an abstract!"

Kalizuko, "There is nothing wrong with abstracts, but let me do it for you: I'll show you how the codes work."

Kalizuko, "Typically, you'd need a partner to dance it with, so perhaps we can solve it by looking at a code. Give me a second. Make yourself a nice cup of tea, and I will show you a code. "

`A dancer enters the stage carrying a giant teapot and tries to pour some tea into an oversized teacup, but the dancer with the teacup runs away from the teapot-carrying dancer.`

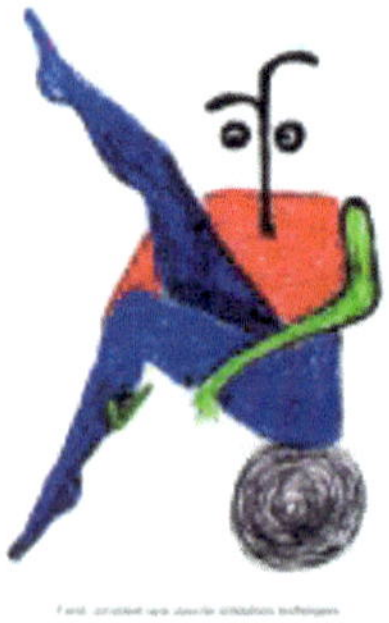

Farul: Developed a new muscle relaxation technique.

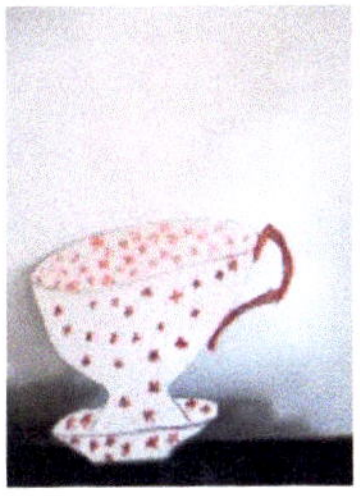
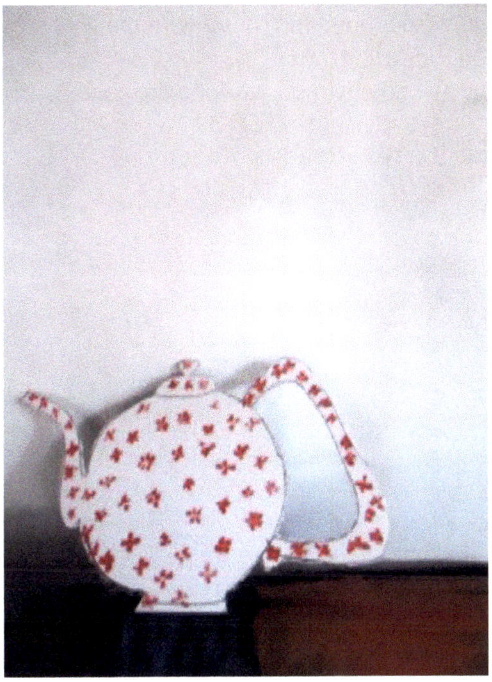

Dramata drinks her tea while Kalizuko works on a program to show her code in Python. The output of basic tango dance steps and the respective musical notes appear on the screen.

Dramata, "I cannot understand a single line."
Kalizuko, "It's all in English… And this is how it looks like when outputted as a visual outcome."

An animation of dance steps (from a code) appears on the screen.

Dramata, "This I can refer to."
Kalizuko, "This is what coding is about!"
Kalizuko, "Here's another example of a tango, but in a different language: C # (C Sharp) in Visual Studio."
Dramata, "Oh, I see."
Kalizuko, "Can we dance it now?"

Six dancers dressed in black outfits dance. (tango).

Dramata, "Now I get it.
OOOO, I made it. I made proper turns."
Kalizuko, "Can you make some unproper ones now?"
Dramata, "Beg your pardon?"
Kalizuko, "Oh, well, try to release your tension in old patterns and relax the rules a bit. Keep in tune with the general rules, but try to listen to and focus on the music more and see what happens."

Dramata makes a big, indescribable sound.

Kalizuko, "See?"
Dramata, "See! Now, the waltz, please.
Waltz is an 18th-century Bohemia, Bavaria, and Austrian word derived from the German word Walzer (to roll or revolve). Dancers perform it in the closed position in ¾ time. Steps include a basic box step,

natural turn, and reverse turn danced counterclockwise around the room, with the lead stepping forward on the left foot and the follower stepping back on their right."
Kalizuko, "All right, have some freshly brewed coffee now while I work on the code."

A dancer carrying an oversized coffee maker chases another who carries a coffee mug across a scene. Six dancers dressed in black dance (waltz).

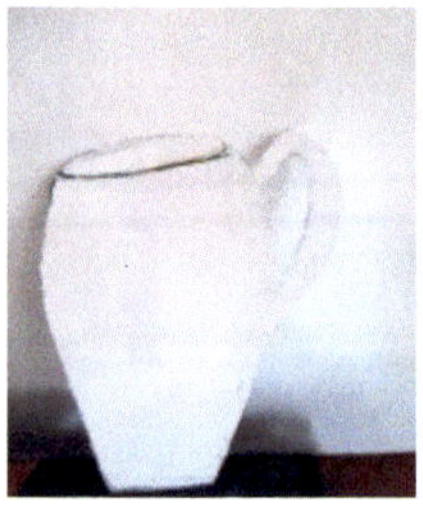
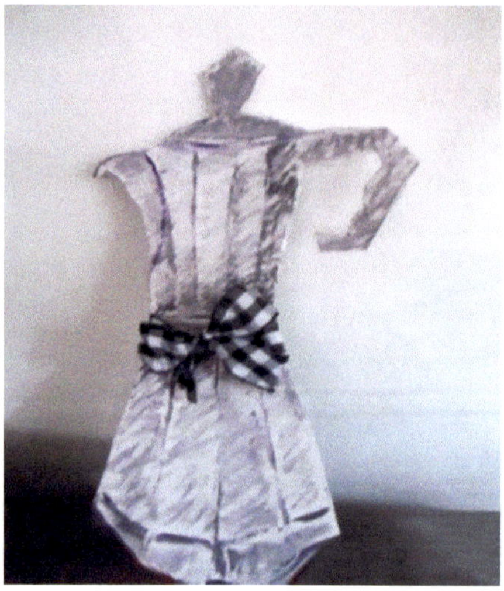

Kalizuko, "Here it is."

A set of photographs showing still frames of dancers waltzing.

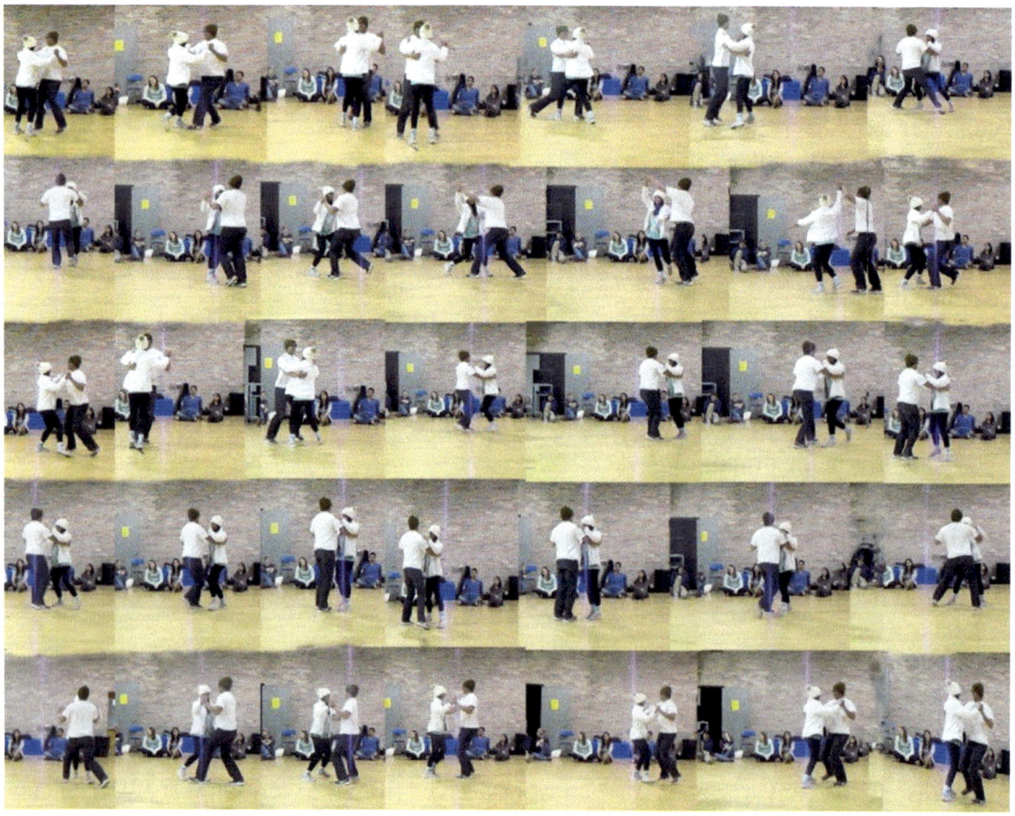

Social Dance: Waltz. © *2025 by Anna Ursyn*

Dramata, "I know what the dance looks like, but the code?"

A waltz code is projected along with the musical notes.

Kalizuko, "Now, we'll work. Make yourself a nice cup of..."
Dramata, "I cannot possibly drink that much!"
Kalizuko, "Eat an apple!"

An actor carrying an apple crosses the stage in a dignified way.
Six dancers dressed in black dance (cha-cha).

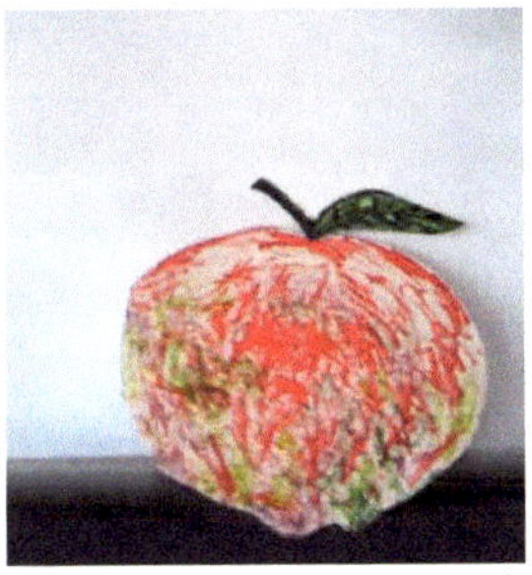

Dramata, "Can I see the rumba now?"
Kalizuko, "Sure. Make yourself a cup of cacao, and I'll be right back with the code. "

Two actors carrying two cacao pitchers approach from the two sides of the stage, trapping the cacao cup as it tries to run away.

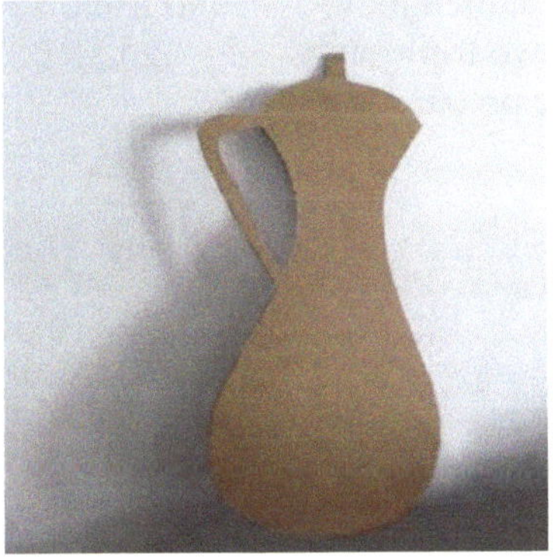
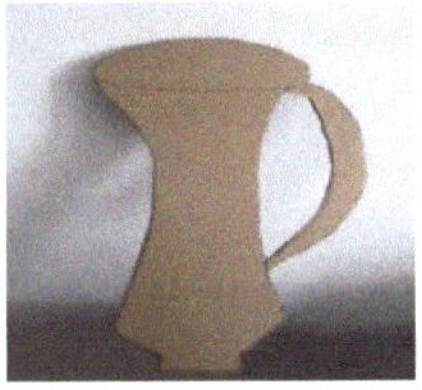
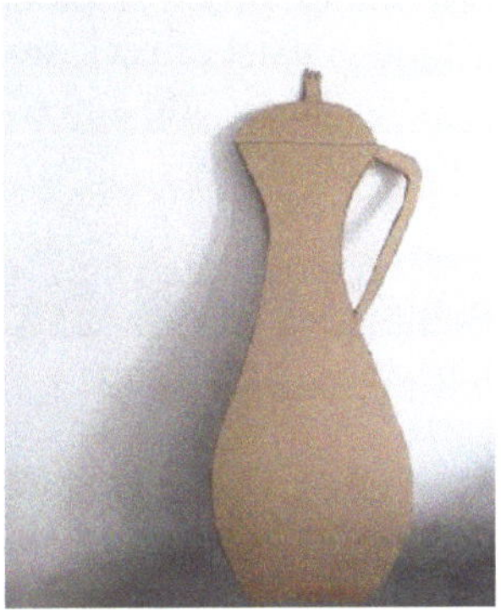

Kalizuko, "Here it is, the graphical output, then rumba when danced simultaneously. Here is the code for you."

Rumba output from the computer code and the musical notes appear on the screen. Six dancers dressed in black dance (rumba).

Dramata, "That makes sense. How about the foxtrot?"
Kalizuko, "Yes, of course. Please pour yourself a glass of water while I come up with a code."

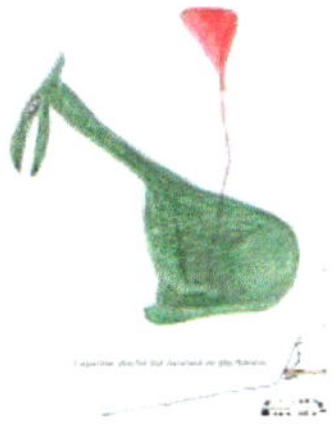

Lagaccha: playful but focused on playfulness.

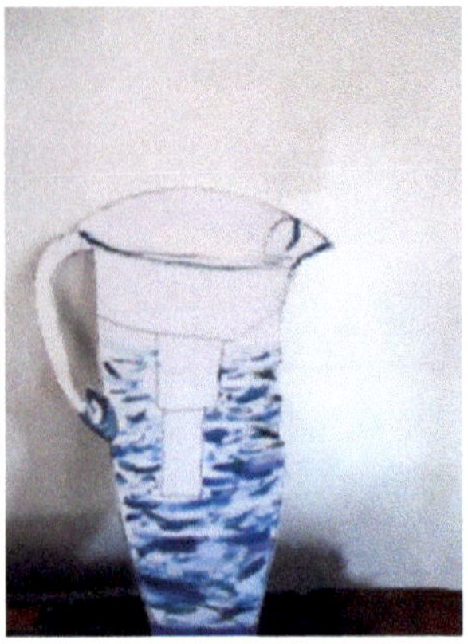 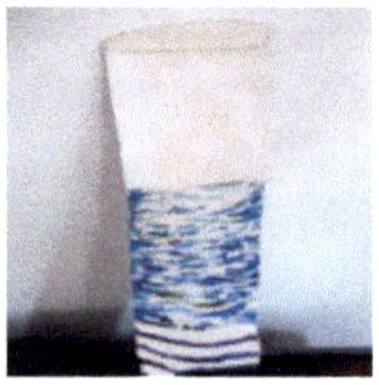

A water pitcher is chasing a water glass which lovingly accepts the liquid. The graph, the code, and the musical notes are projected. Six dancers dressed in black dance (foxtrot).

Dramata, "I feel ready to become a coder!"

Kalizuko, "Sure, you are."

Dramata, "So, how do I know which dance to code and how? Which language to use?"
Kalizuko, "For that, you will need a simulator: waltz, foxtrot, cha-cha, salsa, tango, rumba, samba, jive, and swing."
Dramata, "Yes, swing (Lindy Hop). This dance originated in Harlem in the 1920s in the Savoy Ballroom. Inspired by aviator Charles Lindbergh, who 'hopped 'the Atlantic Ocean in 1927. The dance consists of 6- and 8-count patterns to 4/4 music, with the lead starting on their left foot and the follow starting on their right. An 8-count basic would consist of a rock step on 1,2, triple steps 3&4, then rock, 5, 6, and triple steps 7&8. The 6-count basic would consist of rock step 1,2, followed by two triple steps, 3&4 and 5&6.
Kalizuko, "I will explore how to translate it into any other language. Please prepare some juice while I make it available for you."

Two dancers carrying juice pitchers run towards one carrying a juice glass to compete over who will fill it. Codes and music notations appear (swing). Six dancers dressed in black dance (swing).

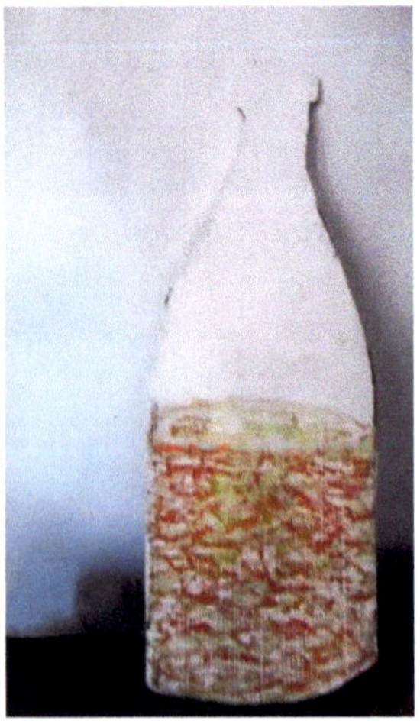 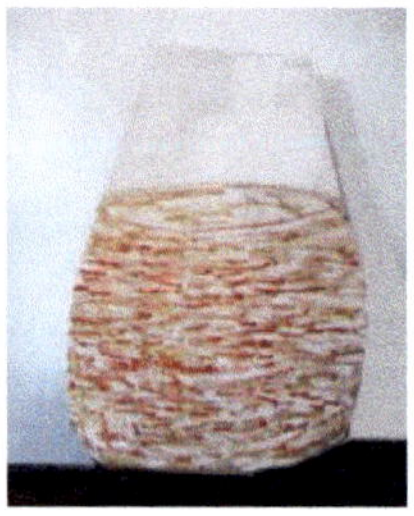 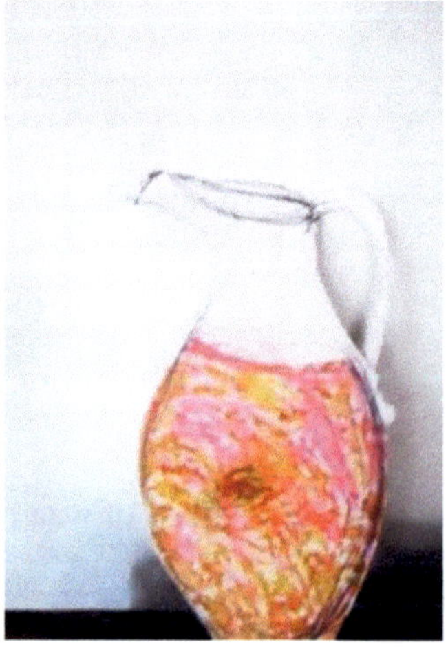

Dramata, "Would you describe your own challenges for me, please?"
Kalizuko, "That would be the conditions. I never know what to expect."
Dramata, "That should be easy; just dance a tango with two partners."

Three dancers dressed in black dance (tango) while changing/alternating partners.

Kalizuko, "I feel ready for a dancing career!"
Dramata, "I can code!"
Kalizuko, "I can dance!"
Kalizuko + *Dramata (together),* "Let's do both!"

Dramata sings to a projected computer code while Kalizuko dances with a large stuffed bear.

Dramata, "You made me curious!"
Kalizuko, "You made me dance!"

The End.
The curtain goes down (or closes).

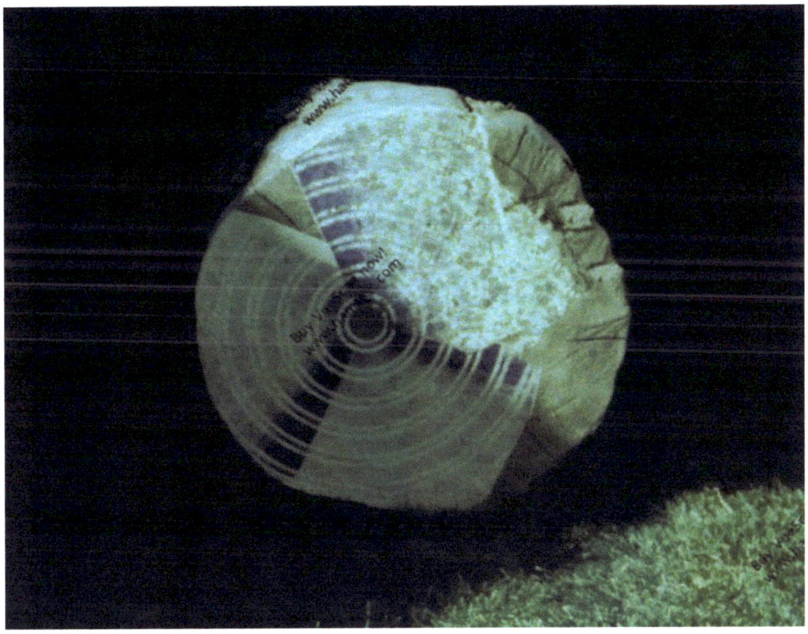

Logical Log. An output from the computer code photosilkscreens on the cut tree trunk. © 2025 by Anna Ursyn

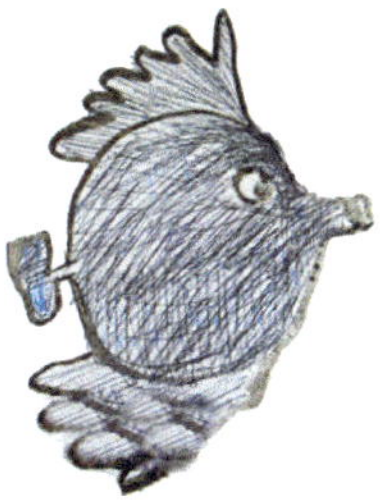

Tuskio: goes around the globe.

Tuskio: goes around the globe.

Projects resulting from this script:

Collaborative video

A video and performance resulting from this text involved multidisciplinary, international collaboration and included programmers, our students, faculty, and staff. Many talents combined to visualize ideas behind programming by applying connections between visual and performing arts. It facilitates learning how to write programs by translating dance performances into computing codes. This knowledge-based learning project provides metaphors between the dance steps and steps in coding – lists of instructions written to tell a computer task it should perform.

Collaborative stage performance

With five Musical Theater students, the UNC dance professor danced traditional dances to coding during the performance. Videos and graphics served as visual tools for explaining basic parts of programming: to carry information with explanatory power. After the end of performing traditional dances, the performers improvised in distinctive colors of their costumes following the six-color arrows resulting from the code. Music-based Videos and graphics serve as visual tools for apprehending programming developed by international experts. They carry information with explanatory power. The lists of instructions written to tell a computer what task it should perform were translated back into dance performances. The animated videos and performances create an initial environment for understanding generic ideas and rules behind coding, and the actual codes and credits are provided on the accompanying website listed at the beginning and the end of the book so that anyone can see their structure and try them.

During the performance that followed this story, the two characters sit on red and blue-lit cubes in front of their laptops, interacting online. At the same time, a well-lit, colorful space on the stage allows the dancers to explain major coding and dance-related ideas in front of projected programs, musical notations, visuals, and props. This performance involves art, coding, music, dance, choreography, video, mathematical art, stage design, and web development. Many talents contributed to this enterprise with their research, codes, music, voices, characters, and art projects. Please see their credits and the funding units listed on the website that hold the codes, music, videos, and performances.
Following the performance and on this website, there is singing to the code on display and dancing to a poem about a coder who taught a dancer about coding and the dancer teaching a coder about dancing. The miscommunication occurs when two different disciplines are discussed, resulting in the unintentional breaking of the rules in coding and those in dancing.

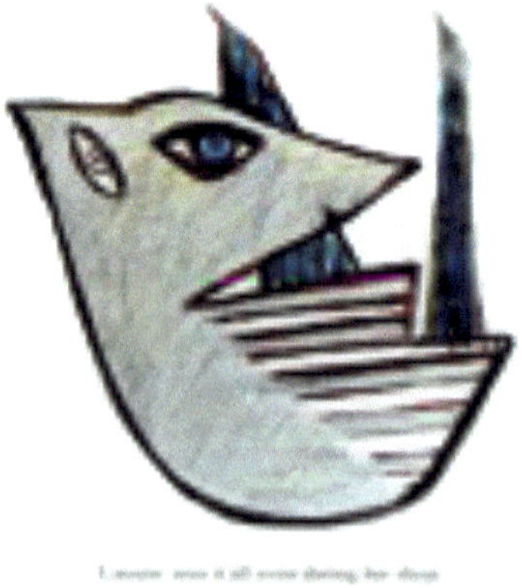

Laxura: Sees it all, even during his sleep.

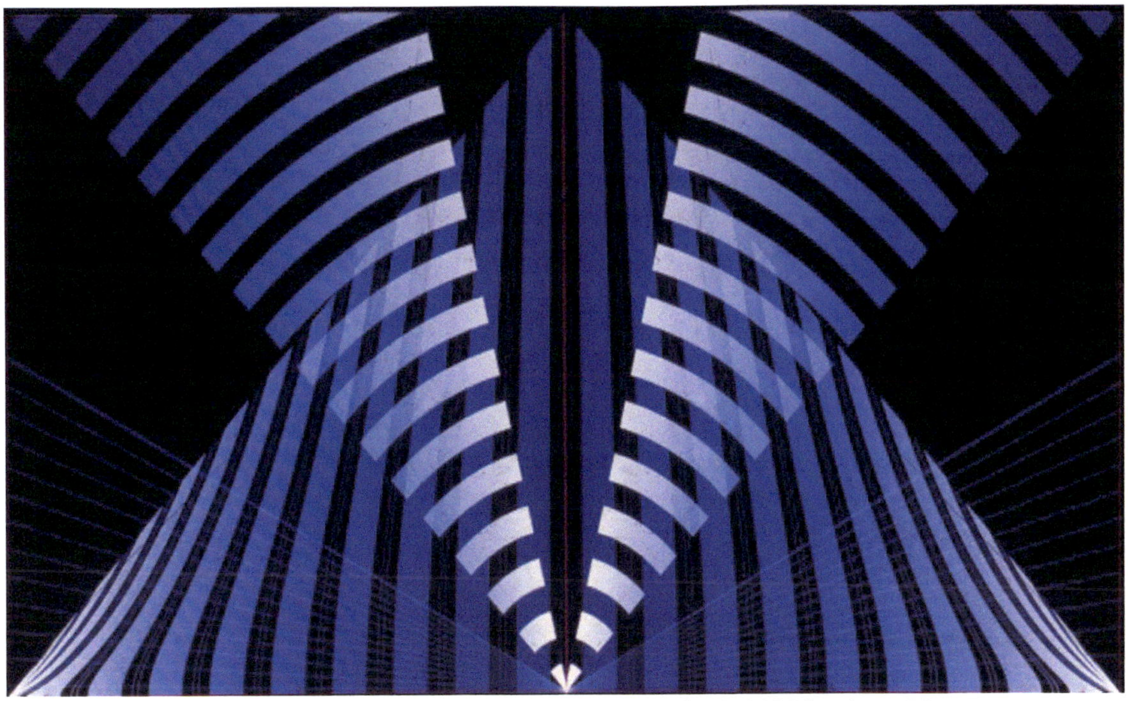

The Flow. The output from the computer code. © 2025 by Anna Ursyn

DANCE CODE VIDEO:

https://www.youtube.com/watch?v=0YED8KkB7wE

CODING THROUGH DANCE METAPHORS VIDEO:

https://www.youtube.com/watch?v=pNRIIVzRHEE

RULE BREAKING VIDEO:

https://www.youtube.com/watch?v=dsb-p7fFo_o

Based on:

RULE-BREAKING POEM:

He introduced her to performing functions, accurate guiding, path planning, and following trajectories, automatic avoidance of objects, version interface, autonomous navigation, and replication of movements. She used hard coding with messy formatting code, several things in one function, variables with magic numbers and strings, and no comments.

She told him about the principles: centering, gravity, alignment, contraction, release, breath use, falling, then recovering, balancing, and then off-balancing, opposition, succession, tension, relaxation, spiral, swing, and momentum.

He crossed his arms and put them on his hips when listening.
He told her about safety, security, reliability, testability, maintainability, and portability.
Those she applied to her work, respectively.

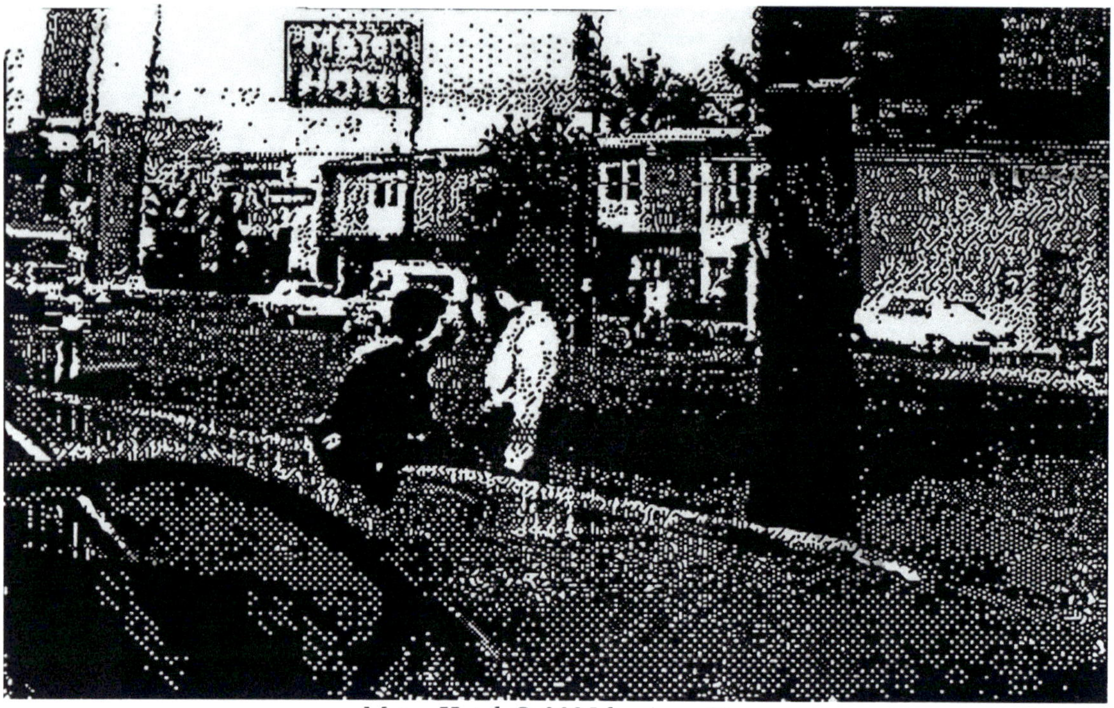

Motor Hotel. © 2025 by Anna Ursyn

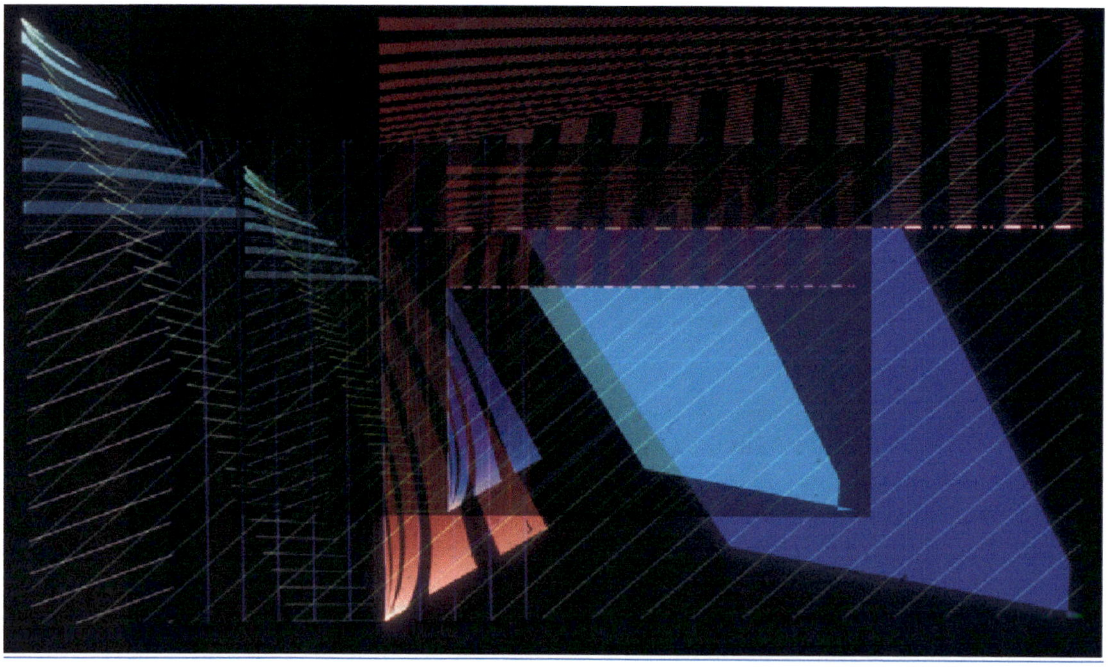

Repetition. © 2025 by Anna Ursyn

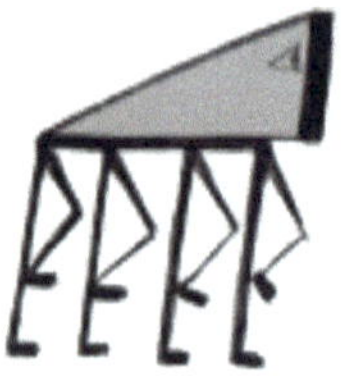

Masala: goes rhythmically whenever he goes.

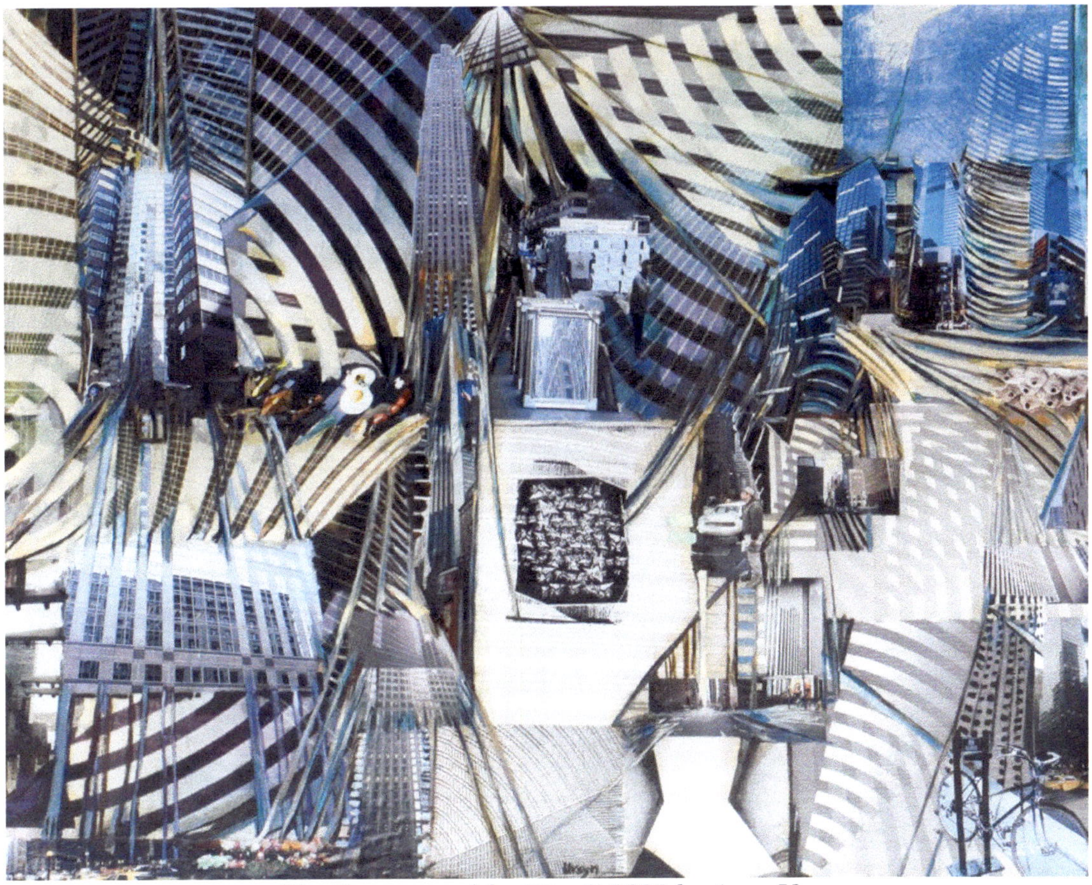

The Grammar of the City. © 2025 by Anna Ursyn

CHAPTER 2
MUSIC CODE: LIVE COSMIC BOOK THEATER

STORYTELLING AS KNOWLEDGE TRANSFER THROUGH METAPHORS

INTRODUCTION

This work explores connections between music and programming with various types of communication in mind. The content is delivered through acting, movements, and animation with props and lights. It attempts to convert a classic comic book format into a live cosmic book through a dance and theater performance. This work is set along the STEAM and STREAM movements. (STEM uses an S for science, T for technology, E for education, and M for mathematics), STEAM adds an A for Art, and STREAM has an R for reading/writing).

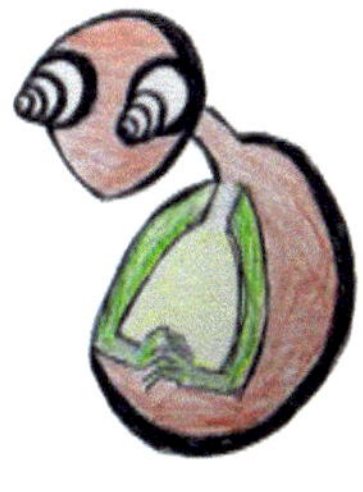

Varaga: keeps it all together.

SYNOPSIS

Henry, a university student, is not happy with the assigned simple but tedious homework. What he enjoys doing is coding. He sits in his room, resigned. He hears someone trying to connect and interprets it as an alien trying to communicate via sounds and musical notations. As a coder, Henry responds with codes in Python. He soon realizes that the alien is another boy, presumably also sitting in his room staring at his assigned homework rather than doing what he wants to do: to compose music. While both think they communicate with extraterrestrials, the boys exchange their respective codes: Henry writes in Python, and the other boy uses music notations. This way, the coder learns some codes used in the music field, and the musician grasps programming. Two narrators, who happen to be the Spatians, comment on the boys' efforts; thus, they explain the structure behind coding, just like the comments serve programmers. Then, the roles reverse, as the Spatians start translating their codes by learning and sharing, while Henry, as the Narrator, comments on the Spatians' codes.

SUMMARY

This work attempts to convert a classic comic book format into a live cosmic book through theater performance. This life cosmic book provides an entertaining background through the two boys' communication in the context of the history of alien movies, then sharing their passions of coding and music. The two Spatian creatures serve as the narrators in the way of the Greek Theater Chorus while commenting on the codes' structure and meaning as the programmers do it for future reference, and other coders, which the computer ignores. Then, the roles reverse: the Spatians code, Henry narrates.

A CAST OF CHARACTERS

Henry, a university student, a coder
The Other Boy, a boy across the street
Henry-Binary, a university student, a musician
Henry-Two, a university student, a coder
The Spatian-Narrator One
The Spatian-Narrator Two
The Spatian-Coder One
The Spatian-Coder Two
The Earthsians = the Audience

STAGE DIRECTIONS

Henry is sitting in his dorm (filled with electronic and computer gear, with many LEDs, alien posters, bedsheets, books, movies on a shelf, screens, graphic displays, and a telescope). He thinks about aliens and wonders what they would look like. (Do aliens call humans the Earthsians?). A sizeable wooden rectangle frame in front of Henry suggests a window. Two large frames represent two windows on the same level across the street as the two tall risers face each other. Another student is visible in a window across the street, marked by a glittery fabric. The set of iconic Manhattan buildings is hung like a laundry between the two windows the boys sit behind. The two Spatian- creatures are shown as manikins dressed in graduation togas (or two white sheets of fabric with projected images) and comment on the boys' efforts; thus, they explain the structure behind coding, just like the comments are widely used in coding practices by programmers. Then, the Spatians start translating their codes by learning and sharing, while Henry becomes the narrator to comment on the codes of the Spatians. Henry picks the Spatian's oversized graduation toga and puts it on, while the Spatians, now wear Roman-style togas. What the Spatians say is projected on the large, 72" or smaller balloons: white, green, blue, yellow, silver, or transparent. Spatians use AI-based spoken by-computer voice – text-to-speech to communicate. Spatians use strange sounds while thinking and using sophisticated language while talking. A comic book-style grid is projected on them all. This way, a comic book becomes a 3D time-based cosmic book. A video of a pianist improvising music on a piano references silent movies.

TIMELINE

Act I	30	minutes	= 1.8E+12 in nanoseconds
Break	7.3	minutes	= 4.38E+11 in nanoseconds
Act II	20	minutes	= 1.2E+12 in nanoseconds
Break	2	minutes	= 1.2E+11 in nanoseconds
Act III	15	minutes	= 9E+11 in nanoseconds
Act IV	5	minutes	= 3E+11 in nanoseconds

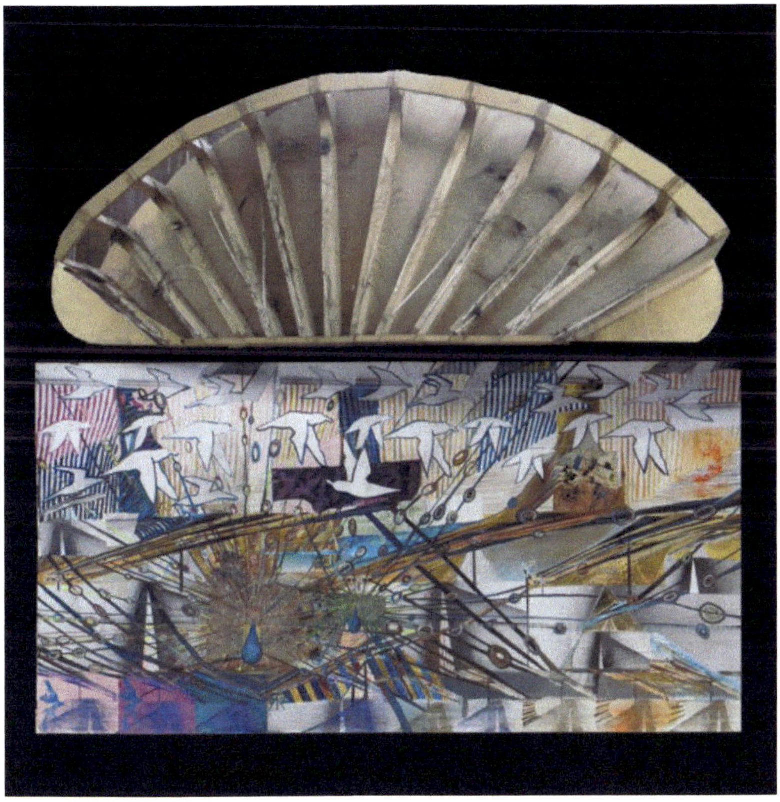

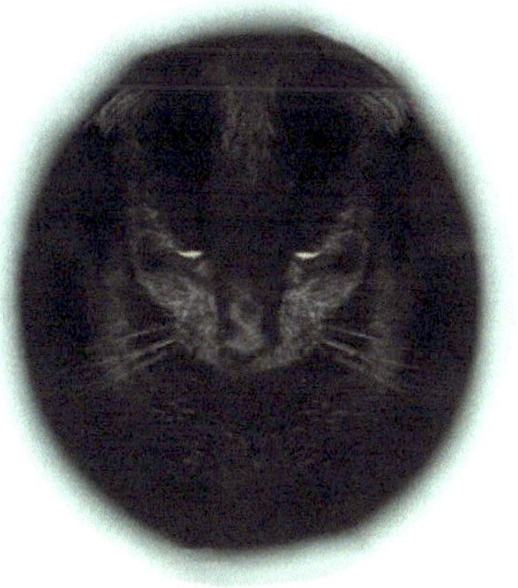

Power Lines. © *2025 by Anna Ursyn*

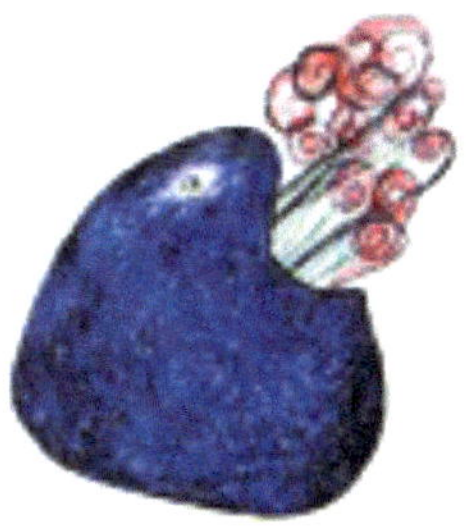

Atuzebo: always filled out with.

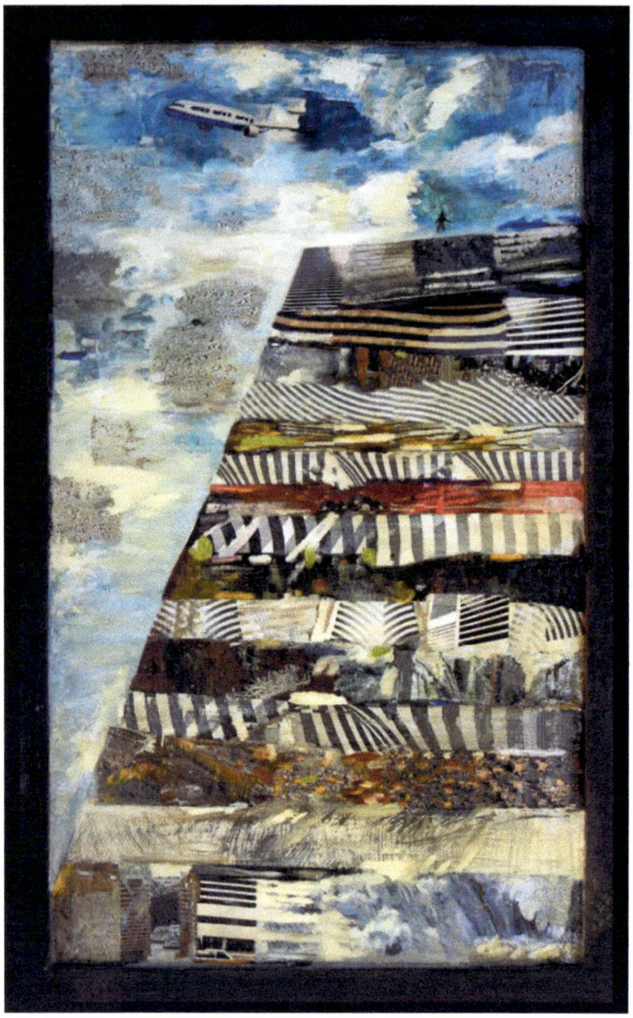

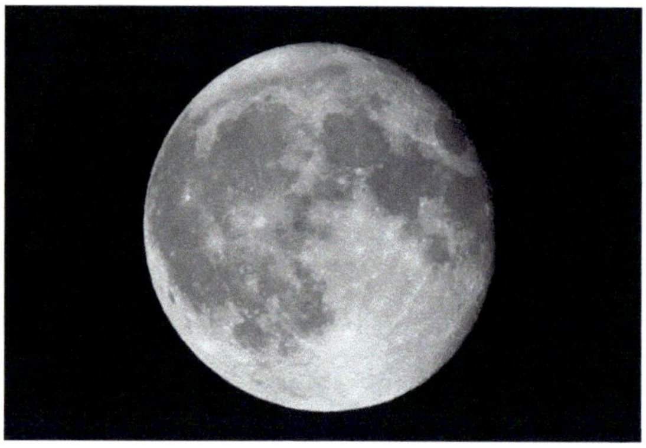

Lake City.© 2025 by Anna Ursyn

Act I
The Curtain goes up (or opens).

Spatian-Narrator- One, "Odoo, who's here, a little Earthsian trying to concentrate."
*Spatian -Narrator-Two, "*In a cluster marked by them as la Gran Manzana."
Spatian-Narrator -One, "That is the tourists' name of this place."
Spatian- Narrator-Two, "We are Tourists."
*Spatian Narrator-One, "*There is the Chrysler Building, the Empire State Building, The Statue of Liberty, One World Trade Center, the Flatiron Building, The Plaza New York, the Guggenheim Museum, 30 Rockefeller Plaza, VIA 57 West, 432 Park Avenue, the tallest one.
Henry, "Why do they make me do this vicissitudinous homework when I already gave all the answers in class? The teacher knows that I know and that my passion is coding. Yawjo! Why do they want us all to be the same? I see futility when it occurs. Are we that annoying to our teachers? Why do gifted students have to take all those general electives? I want to focus on my research and my coding. Is it that hard to see that we need more, but not less, education to follow our passions? The school system puts all those who are different, gifted, talented and those with problems and needs under special education. This is the best way to raise a hacker! Oh, that's cosmic!"

Henry, daydreaming, wonders aloud, "How would aliens communicate with humans? All must be done telepathically. What message would they possibly send? Probably, 'Take care of your planet.'"
Spatian Narrator-Two, "Start by stopping your fighting."

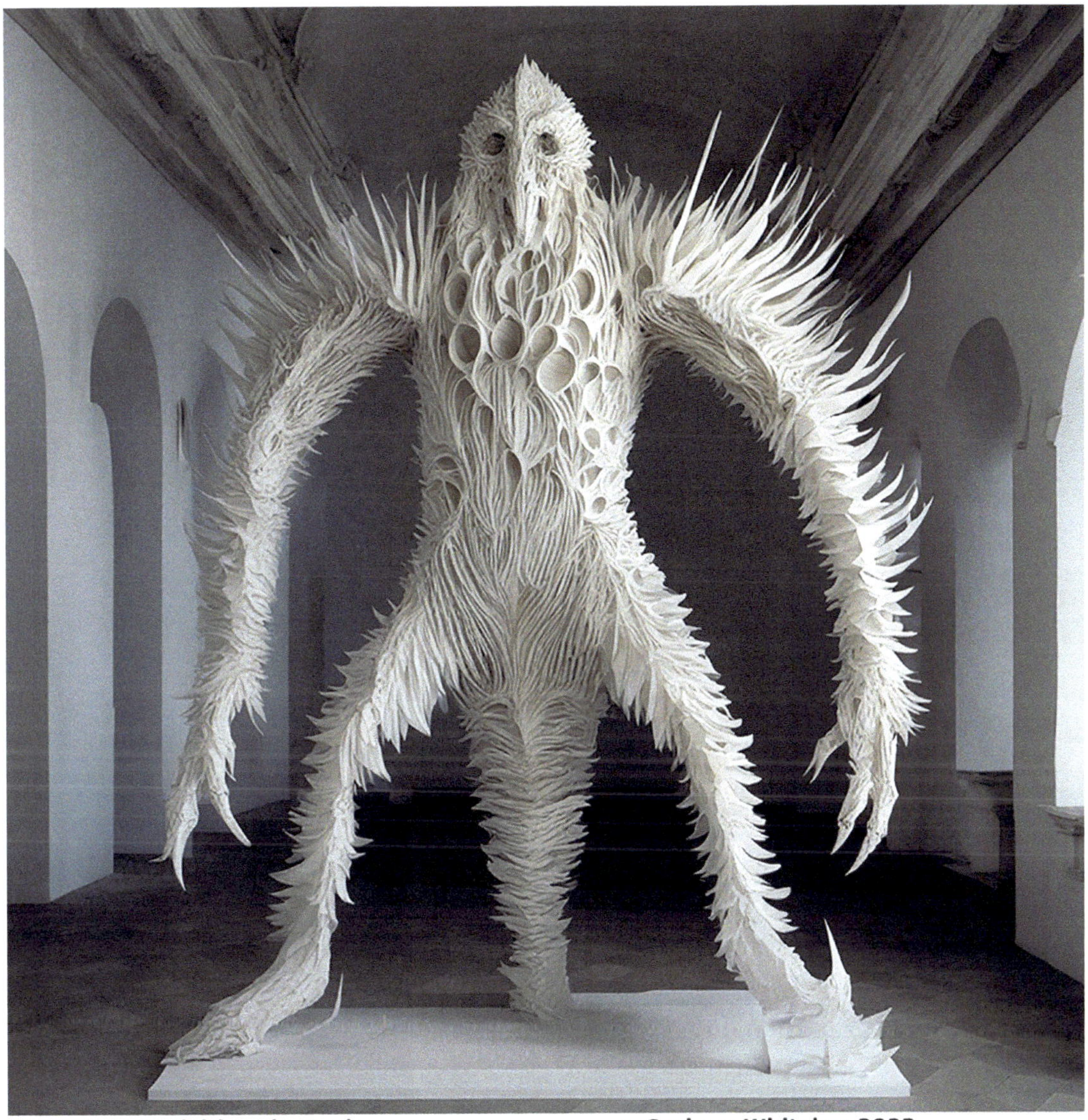

Revisiting the Body **c. Corinne Whitaker 2023**

Henry continues, "It would be awesome to communicate with an alien. They say you'd understand them without words. I'd like to see their codes. Would extraterrestrials from different galaxies use the same code? My teachers would not get it."

Spatian-Narrator One: "The Earthsian must have heard about how machine learning software algorithms search for transmissions in the background noise of the cosmos, to follow with disturbances corrections of radio frequency interference, and measure voltage time-series data and time-frequency spectrogram data."

Henry, "No tools for searching, no radio telescope available.

Now, Henry hears some strange music.

Henry says, "What's that? Where is it coming from?"
He looks over the gear in his room, trying to find the source. Meanwhile, the "alien" continues to send random four-note combinations of C, D, E, F, and G (sounds, notes) with a few seconds' pause between combinations. Henry looks again over his electronic gear to see where the music is coming from.

Henry, "Aha!"
He sits at his desktop computer and launches a program displaying incoming music as waves and standard musical notation.

Henry, "It must be a hacker. I need to tell him to get lost."

The music codes keep coming in. After listening to a few repetitions, *Henry says,* "It sounds like whoever is sending it is communicating something. Hmm, it might be an unknown source. After watching many outer space-related movies, I have some ideas about communicating with aliens."

Henry says, "Hello out there. Can you understand me?"

Henry Sends Einstein's mass-energy equivalence equation," $E=mc^2$ mass, speed of light."

Henry thinks," Nothing again. The world is all about waves," He sends a sinusoid graph: $y = A \sin(B(x - C)) + D$.

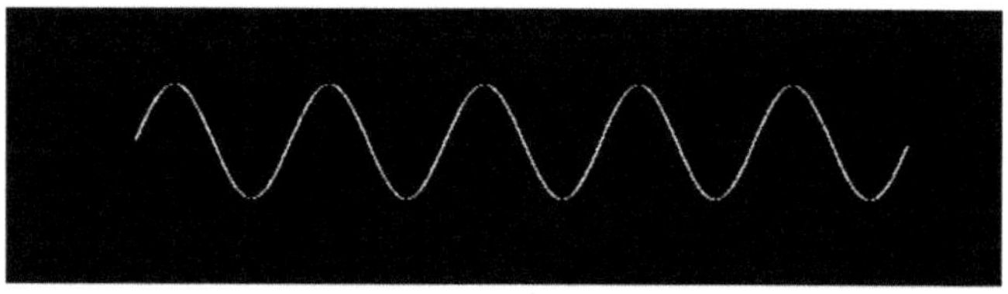

Spatian Narrator-One, "Those include wind waves, sound waves, and light waves, such as monochromatic radiation."

Henry continues: "A sine wave can be shown as a graph of the sine function. They occur in mathematics, sciences, and engineering. I read about sine-wave signals used in the search for extraterrestrial intelligence (SETI) and using multi-beam observations at UC Berkeley with libraries and databases.

Bryan Brzyski, a Ph.D. student in astronomy, developed this method."

Nothing. He sends Python codes out, "I'm Henry," while holding a picture of himself.

```
print "I'm Henry!"

class Window {

  public static void main(String[] args) {

    System. out.printlng("I'm Henry!");

  }

  }
```

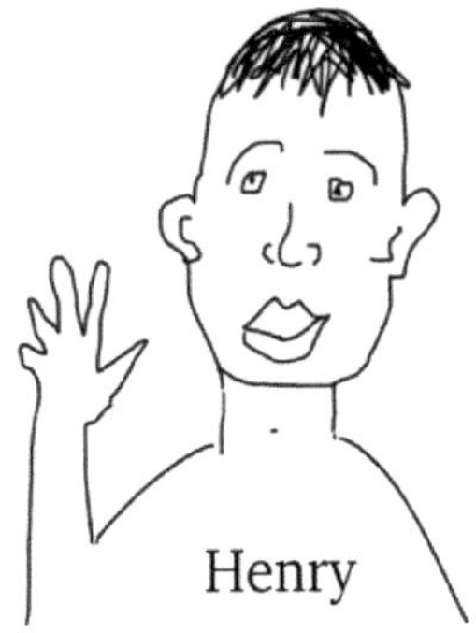

This time, he creates his self-portrait with zeros and ones.

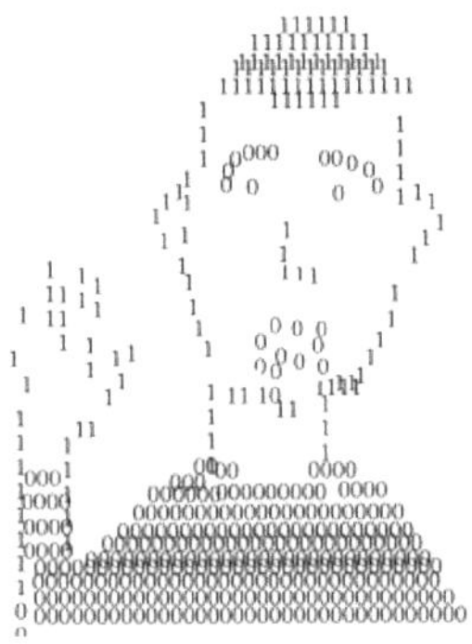

Not a signal comes in.

Spatian-Narrator One, "That's not binary! Using binary or a data type gives a different output."

Spatian-Narrator Two, "Give him some time."

Henry, "Let's try the American Standard Code for Information Interchange system, which uses characters, numbers, and operations for electronic communication. Binary *01101000* means 104, *01101001* means 105, and they mean 'HI" in ASCII." Or let's try what every programmer learns first: "Hello world' which in binary is: 01101000 01100101 01101100 01101100 01101111 00100000 01110111 01101111 01110010 01101100 01100100, and in ASCII will look like:

Hello World 72 101 108 108 111 32 119 111 114 108 100

Nothing

Henry corrects himself: "Oops, that is a binary me!

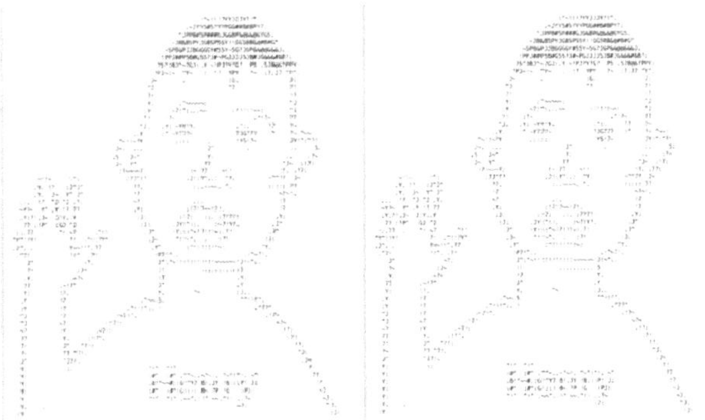

This is the corrected system. It looks nice when doubled."

Henry hears some signals.

Henry, "Yes, those signals must be coming from an alien."

Henry tries the Morse code with the following:
https://morsecode.me/#/rooms/1

He types: "Is there anybody out there?"

.. ... / - .... . .-. . / .- -. -.-- -... --- -.. -.-- / --- ..- - / - .... . .-. . .

Henry tries sending some light-based signals with his glowing gloves:

"Is there anybody out there?" Replies keep coming as gibberish.

Henry gets too many confusing answers. "Not for me," he *remarks*.

.. ... / - .... . .-. . / .- -. -.-- -... --- -.. -.-- / ---
..- - / - .... . .-. . ..--.. .-..-.

Nothing.

Henry continues, "Let's try chemistry; if they are Martians, they will get it:
Oxygen, O_2, 21% on Earth, and 0.16 % on Mars.
Hmm, what other elements can define us? Carbon! Everything is made of Carbon!
0.03% of the Earth and 18.5 % of the human body.
Let's send both together, C+O_2 = Carbon Dioxide CO_2, 0.04 % on Earth, and 95% on Mars."

Henry sends out three symbols: O_2, C in various bonds, and CO_2.

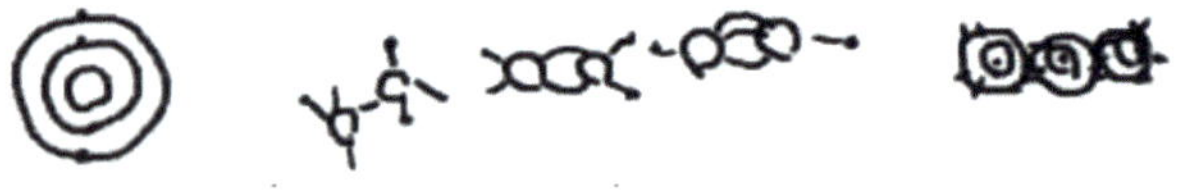

Nothing.

Henry, "The graph does not help either".

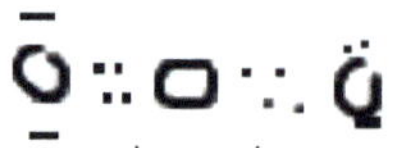

Henry needs to imagine outer space. Projections of abstract images fill out the stage. Nothing!

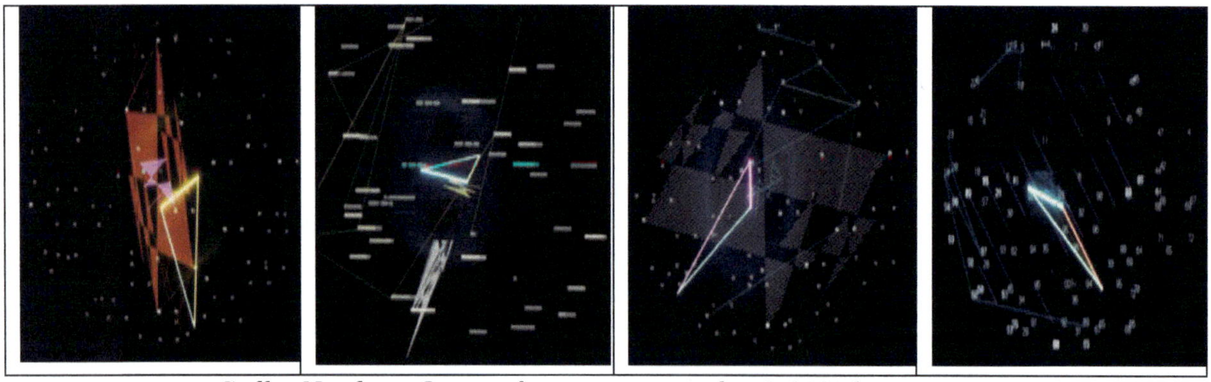

Stellar Numbers. Outputs from computer codes. © 2025 by Anna Ursyn

Two Spatian-Narrators show their outer space faces and bodies in togas, and a projection of two aliens shows up on the two manikins.

The first Spatian's appearance 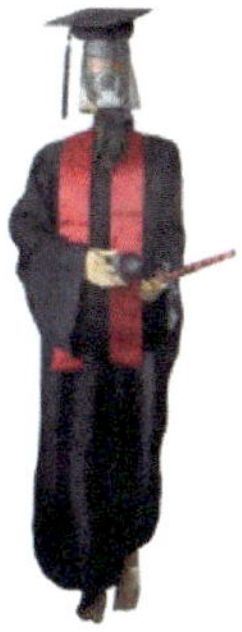 then 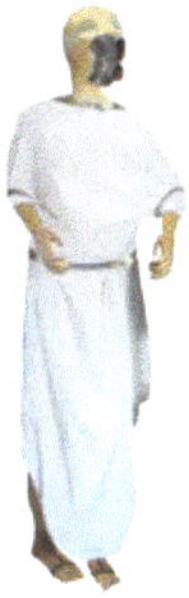

The Spatian Narrators are shown in the graduation togas, and later, the Spatian Coders as commentators are shown in ancient togas.

Henry wonders, "How does it work to live in outer space? What would it look like? What would galactic space sound like? How would the ocean of emptiness smell like?

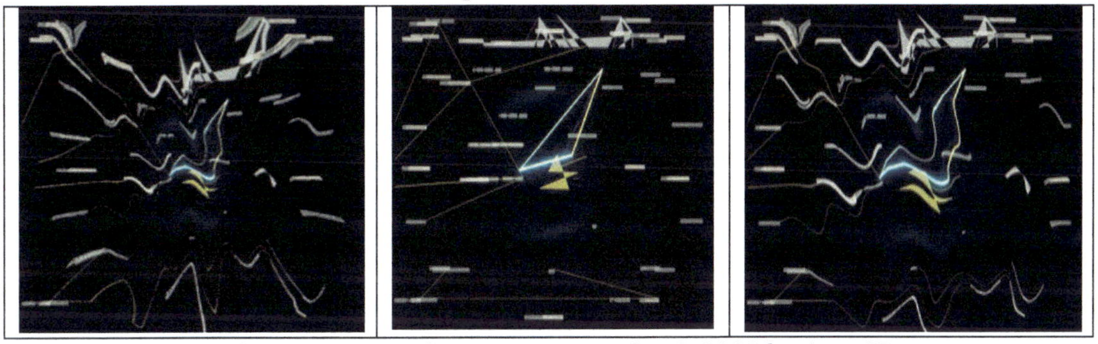

Stellar Problems. Outputs from computer codes. © 2025 by Anna Ursyn

Henry exclaims, "Anyone lives there?"

Projected images of space creatures fill the stage, representing Henry's ideas of outer space. Henry, then the Spatian-Narrator One, speaks, and soft music plays simultaneously. What Henry says can slightly overlap with what each of the Spatian-Narrator states.

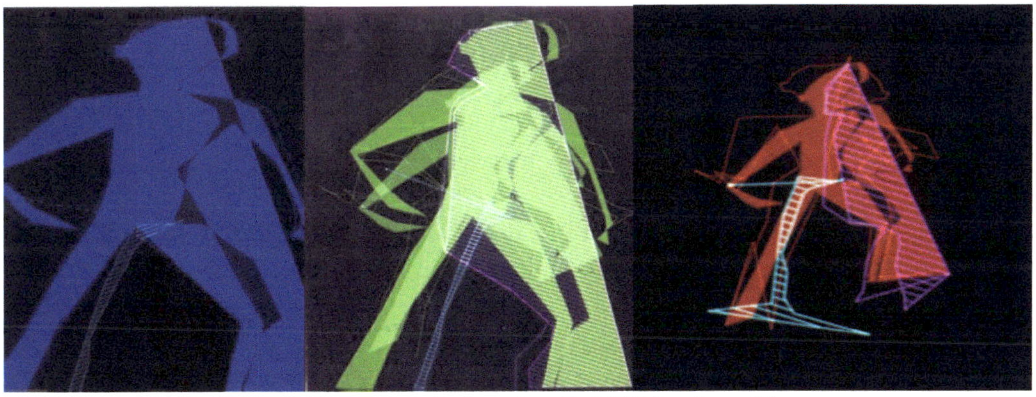

Men. Outputs from computer codes. © 2025 by Anna Ursyn

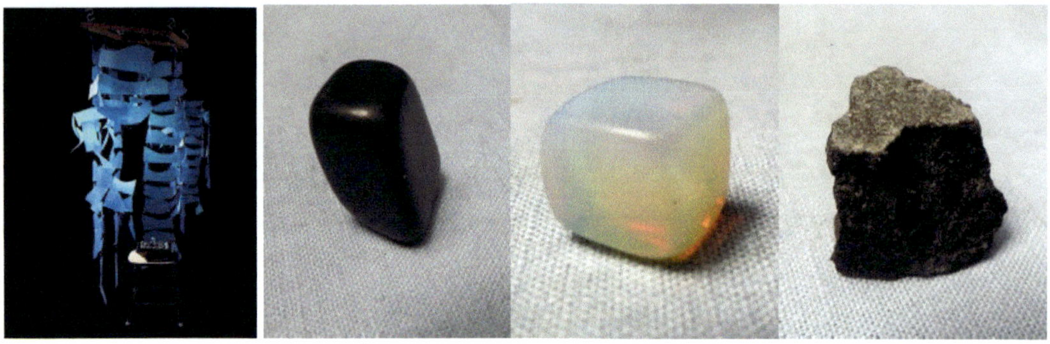

Water *Obsidian* *Opalite* *Basalt rock*

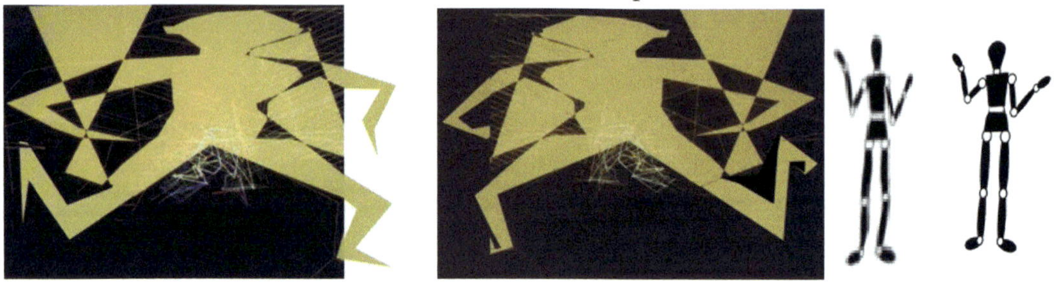

Men. Outputs from computer codes© 2025 by Anna Ursyn

Henry, "How do they travel*?"*

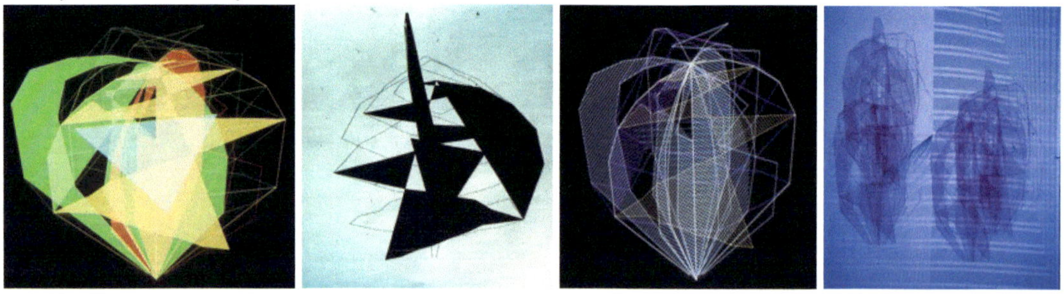

An Ellipse series. Outputs from computer codes. © 2025 by Anna Ursyn

*Henry keeps thinking, "*How do we look far from above?"

Henry states, "I vividly remember two movies that carried those ideas. In *Close Encounters of the Third Kind*, humans and aliens attempted to communicate via synthesized music. In another one, the scientists are receiving a signal from an unknown source, but they don't know how to respond. The kid, about my age, suggests while eating a pie, "Send pi (π)." So, they send 3.1416. Back comes 3.1416. After a couple of times, of getting the same response, one guy says, "Don't round it off." So, this time, they sent 3.14159. The alien's response is a torrent of further digits of this mathematical constant."

Spatian-Narrator One, "Most eloquently, it was in the *Red Planet Mars* (1952) by Harry Horner,

https://www.youtube.com/watch?v=4OXYLCVUaCc (21.10/1.27:18) or (22:11)

Spatian-Narrator Two, "Pi (π) is the ratio of the circumference of a circle to its diameter, which is 3.141592653589793238462643…."

Henry continues, "What is the structure of their communication? What are the techniques we'd use to teach various languages? What do they have in common? Do they all start similarly by introducing a single sentence as an output?"

Henry googles some alphabets: Latin, Korean, Japanese, Runic, Greek, and Sumerian, and Adinkra are projected on the screen.

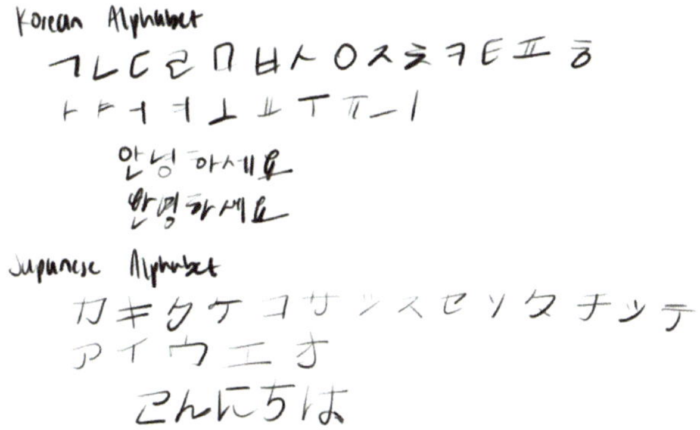

The Alphabets. © 2025 by Eunice Lee, iArt, NYC. (Used with permissions).

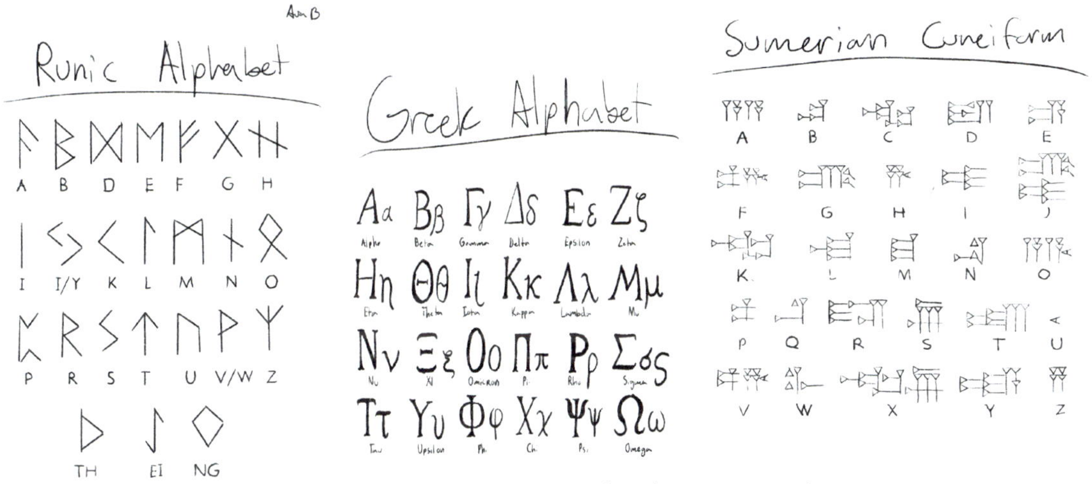

The Alphabets © Ava Becker, iArt Institute, NYC. (Used with Permissions).

Silence again.

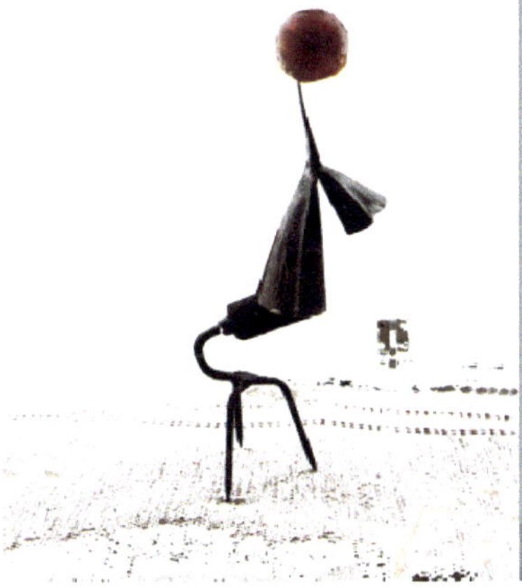
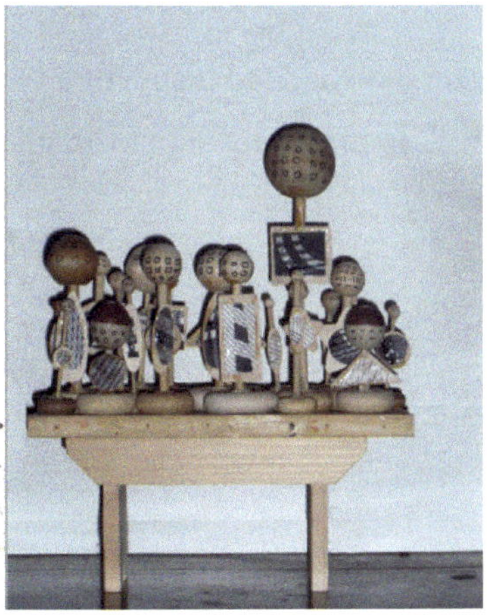

Spatian-Narrator One, “Those Earthsians are so indecisive.”

Henry wonders, "Maybe they know C++?”

Henry types in C++ code, “Hello World!” which is often used for the first coding assignment,

No reply.

```
#include

int main()

{

  std::cout << "Hello, world!"; //which is often used for the first coding assignment, the green color denotes comments

  return 0;

}

 }
```

Still no reply. Henry thinks for a while.

Henry tries, “How about Python?

Print(Hello, World)

Henry tries again, “Last chance: HTML, the languages of the World Wide Web!”

Henry, “HTML?”

HTML: <p>Hello, World!<p

Nothing

Henry, “JavaScript?”

```
document.write('Hello, World!');
```

Henry, “Nope! Silence.”

Spatian-Narrator Two, “Waouh, they sure have some ways.”

Spatian-Narrator One, “In the movie ‘Contact,’ aliens send plans for a vehicle to take a human to a distant place in the universe where humans can speak in their language to an alien presence designed to look like humans.”

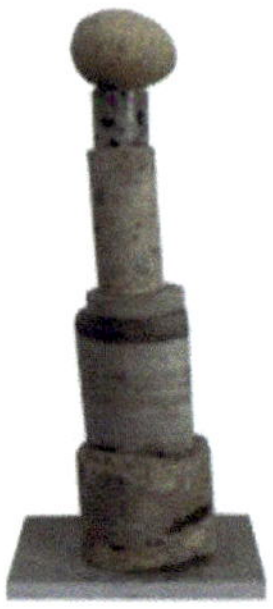

Colimur: understands hierarchy.

Spatian-Narrator Two, “The Earthsian did not learn from other Earthsians about Astrolinguistics or interstellar languages, such as artificial ‘Lingua Cosmica’ assumes receiving radio emissions Lincos.”
Henry says, “I wish I knew music notations. I can only recognize sounds. I have to find someone to help me understand music and the codes they use for music. But for now, let’s try math. It must be a universal language.”
Henry tries again, ”**1+1=3.”** Joseph Albers saw the space between the two lines as a space.” **||**
Nothing again.
Spatian-Narrator One, “The Earthsian is searching for hieroglyphs. His thoughts must have gone to another Earthsian movie, ”*Stargate:* ’The Air Force brings in an Egyptologist to interpret hieroglyphics on a structure it already knows to be of alien origin. They correctly translate the inscriptions, and the system is a portal to another world (which looks surprisingly like Earth!). Of course, all immediately go through the portal to an adventure awaiting them in the other world.”

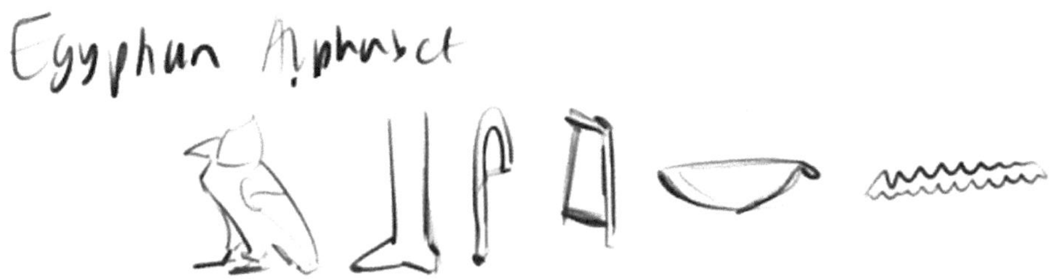

Egyptian Alphabet. © 2025 by Eunice Lee, iArt, NYC. (Used with permissions).

Spatian-Narrator Two, ”Ouoohooch, they use emojis!”

Henry tries again by sending a simple code for a graphical output: an image of an alien as he imagines one, as he wrote a code in Python:

```
#Import required library
From PIL import Image

#Open Image
Im=Image.open(Alien.png”)
#Image show
Im.show()
```

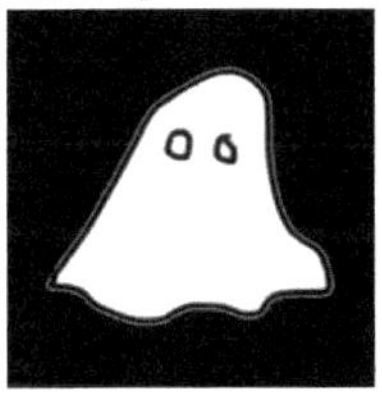

Spatian-Narrator One: “Hutoo, I look like a Pac-Man.”
Spatian-Narrator Two, “Most authoritatively, The Earthsian has heard of Quine's "Word and Object," a doctrine of "indeterminacy of translation," stating that at a minimum he needs agreement on "yes" and "no" even to begin the most basic conversation.”

This time, Henry's messages are in computer graphics programs, which show up as codes and resulting images.

Henry, "Since both parties must agree about the meaning of "yes" and "no" (or "agree" and "disagree"), without any further knowledge, I can indicate that the other side's response to a signal I sent is correct or appropriate. Then, if one side sends a gobbledygook signal to the other, the receiver can send back some signal that it might view as meaningless. But if the sender replies with "yes," the receiver now knows that its reply means something in the other party's language. For example, if I send them '1001100100010101', and they send me back '1', now I know that '1001100100010101' means something in their language. The challenge is to figure out what it is. The process could go much faster if we send images back and forth."

A white balloon for 'YES' and a red balloon for 'NO' appear.

No reply. Henry comes up with a new approach: "High pitch for 'YES,' and deep note for 'NO' in music notation.

Spatian Narrator One, "The Earthsian did not hear about the whistling languages that go ten times further as words."

Spatian Narrator Two, "Oh, like Silbo, but it would not reach us there."

Henry's messages keep coming in computer codes for graphics. They show up as a code and its resulting images.

Then, again thinking out loud, Henry says, "If I recognize a sequence of sounds, I'll send this"

(he types a code for a white rectangle using the Turtle module).

```
# draw square in Python Turtle # Turtles are used to draw a line
in a specified direction and length
import turtle

t = turtle.Turtle()
t.forward(100) #Forward turtle by 100 units
t.left(90) #Turn turtle by 90 degree
t.forward(100)
t.left(90)
t.forward(100)
t.left(90)
t.forward(100)
t.left(90)
```

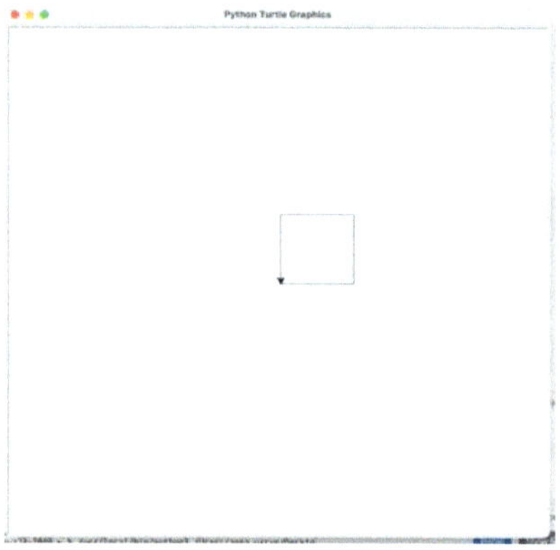

The right side shows an output of the code from the left one.

Henry continues, "Or the same can be achieved using loops:"

```
#Use loop for a square in Python Turtle
import turtle

t = turtle.Turtle()
for i in range(4): #Loop will run 4 times
  t.forward(100) #Move turtle by 100 units
  t.left(90) #Turn turtle by 90 degree
```

Henry states, “This program is shorter but runs the same output as above. If they don't recognize it, I'll send this:"

`Henry types of another Python code, this time using loops. A more straightforward approach appears on the screen with a black square.`

```
import turtle
t = turtle.Turtle()
t.fillcolor("black") #fill black
t.pencolor("red") #stroke red
t.begin_fill()
def draw_square(length, height):
  for i in range(0,4):
    if i % 2 == 0:
      t.forward(length)
      t.right(90)
    else:
      t.forward(height)
      t.right(90)
draw_square(100, 100)t.end_fill()
```

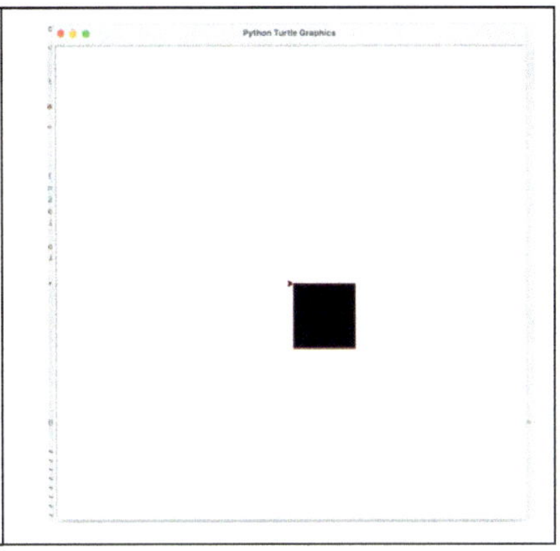

Henry thinks, “So how would the same image look when coded with a forward function?
Spatian-Narrator One, “This program creates a turtle object and then uses the forward() and left() methods to draw the square's four sides. The forward() method moves the turtle forward by 100 units, and the left() method turns it left by 90 units. The turtle.done() statement keeps the turtle graphics window open until the user closes it.

```
import turtle

t = turtle.Turtle()

t.forward(100)
t.left(90)
t.forward(100)
t.left(90)
t.forward(100)
t.left(90)
t.forward(100)

turtle.done()
```

Now with angles,

```
import turtle

# Create a turtle object
t = turtle.Turtle()

# Draw a square with sides of length 100
for i in range(4):
  t.forward(100)
  t.left(90)

# Keep the turtle window open until it is closed
turtle.done()
```

Spatian-Narrator Two, “This code uses a for loop to draw a square with the turtle. The turtle.done() function keeps the window open until the user closes it.

Henry continues, “Or I could signal a ‘YES’ with a white light and a ‘NO’ with a red beam of light.”
`'YES' with a tactical white light. 'NO'with a red laser pointer.`

Henry responds with his 'NO' signal until he receives a familiar sequence, such as CCDE ('Yankee Doodle'), EEFG (Beethoven), or CDEC ('Are you sleeping'), etc. So, he sends his 'YES' signal. The "alien" responds with Henry's 'YES' signal (which appears on Henry's screen precisely as he had just sent it) instead of a new note sequence.

Realizing that they've finally made contact, Henry exclaims, "Yes! Gotcha!"
Spatian-Narrator One, "Now, The Earthsian tries a new set of random sequences using the same five pitches. "

After several sequences, the "alien" sends the continuation of the first sequence Henry recognized (this could be CEDG for" Yankee Doodle)."

Spatian-Narrator Two, "The binary form (AABB), is sonata form (ABCAB'), rondo form (ABACADA), and modern song form (ABABCBB). It can exist in operas or sonatas, descending chromatic patterns shared by two outer movements in their second themes, which they call cyclic."
Spatian-Narrator One: " On their Knowledge Learning cover, they wrote, "A technique of the Cyclic Form in musical construction has sections or movements, theme, and melody."
Spatian-Narrator Two, "Or someplace else: The *Sonata Cycle* is the layout of a multi-movement composition for recognizing forms of the tradition of classical music."
Spatian-Narrator One, "That is music theory, but they do not realize their AI picked our waves."
Henry exclaims, "Wait a minute! An "Alien" knows 'Yankee Doodle? This guy must be human!"
"Just to make sure, *"Henry says,* "Let's try this."

He sends out the code for the first phase, and the correct completion CDEC comes back.

Henry says to himself, "OK, you're human!"

Spatial Music plays (very rhythmical). Henry looks out of the window and sees university buildings with various departments. He focuses on the physics department with its' sections in action.

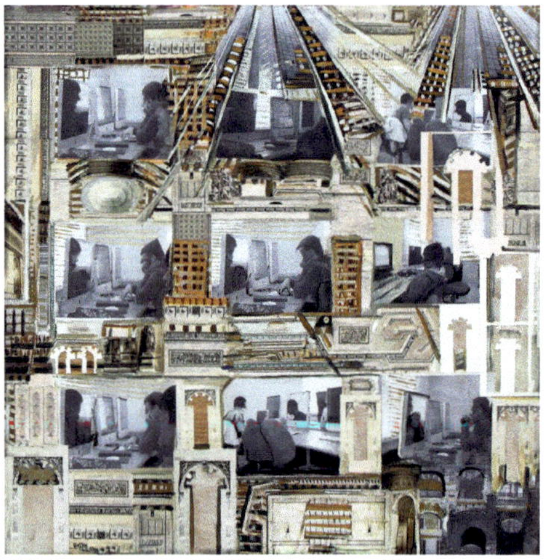

Solutions. © 2025 by Anna Ursyn

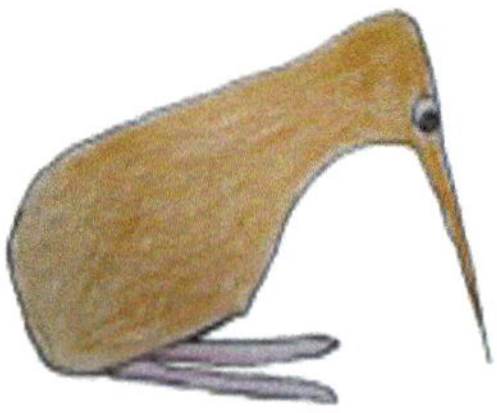

Judugas: types slowly but makes no mistakes.

Rhythmic music continues.

Spatian-Narrator Two: "It looks like the Earthsian's other passion is Entrainment, facts related to the daily rhythms of plants and animals during the day and night cycle. The Earth's rotation causes them. The Earthsians and other species react to music and dance. When a signal or motion produces a response with the same frequency, synchronization of different rhythms inherent in organisms starts making sense to the Earthsian. The Earthsian now sees that the coordination between people moving to music becomes synchronized."

Spatian-Narrator Two, "Spatianmathicians suggest that comparing Earthsians and Earthnimals with their tuning to a particular stimulus could offer new information about the origin of their music and dancing."

Spatian-Narrator One, "The observed rhythmic movement, so similar to his response to music, caught Earthsian's attention, to realize that it came from the window across the street on the same floor as his. This window faces his window with another Earthsian, focused on his phone but moving rhythmically, just as this Earthsian does."

Henry says, "While my body moves along with the sounds, another body is doing the same set of moves. Why is this boy sitting alone in his room? Why is he sending codes out? Why so alone? "He must be like me."

Henry exclaims, "Obviously, this boy tries to communicate with someone out there."

Henry says, "Let's use the phones to send our codes as signals, but what is his phone number?"

Henry concludes, "I am not alone! It feels more like a brotherhood than friendship. We are similar; we have the same problem but possess different skills. Could we do something together? Create something new? Share our different passions and learn from each other. But wait, it would still not solve our homework."

"Ha!" *Both Spatian's-Narrators exclaim.*

Henry, "I'm so glad I saw him swinging his body along the same rhythm as I. We could have had an interesting discussion about what we had just done and what we learned from it, but to talk, we probably both would feel guilty by not doing our homework."

Spatian-Narrator Two: "The tools and research have changed a lot. Some magic symbols and equations are becoming more common in Earthsians' minds. They can see outer space now, which is more than interesting. Artemis and SpaceX are sent to the Moon. War and space have been long and overused topics, but soon, space and communication will become important to them."

Spatian-Narrator One, "Yes, but they do not know about us as much as they think."

Spatian -Narrator Two, "Shell we tell them?"

Spatian-Narrator One, "Nooo! Let's teach ourselves OUR codes and thus exchange OUR languages; would you like that, Spatian-Narrator Two?"

Spatian -Narrator Two, "We, the Spatians, use different languages/codes, but we still want to communicate with others."

Spatian-Narrator Two to the Spatian-Narrator One, "Let me learn your code first."

Both Spatian-Narrators drop their togas off, showing their alien bodies as they start learning the codes no longer as Narrators but as Coders. The Spatians' skins appear in two color schemes. Henry assumes the role of a Narrator, so he bends down to pick up a toga dropped on the floor by one of the Spatians and puts it on. The toga is too large for Henry, but he continues regardless. They change their roles. The Spatians become learners, and Henry becomes their Narrator. The projections of the codes appear on the backdrop.

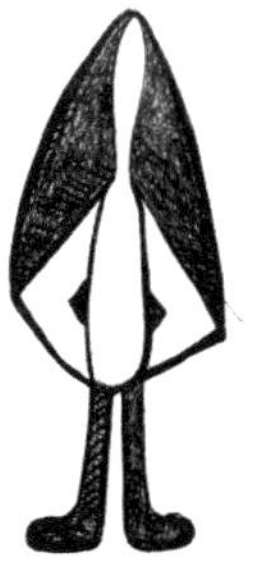

Munsta worries about the lost handkerchief.

```
import turtle

t = turtle.Turtle()

t.fillcolor("black") #fill black

t.pencolor("red") #stroke red

t.begin_fill()

def draw_square(length, height):
    for i in range(0,4):
        if i % 2 == 0:
            t.forward(length)
            t.right(90)
        else:
            t.forward(height)
            t.right(90)

draw_square(100, 100)

t.end_fill()
```

Henry, "Another coder using different coding structures, and I can see the codes! How cool it is!"

Alien music starts, which is aligned with the stars: velvet-like spatial tones to set the audience for the next part. Alien music can be inspired by any remote place or images from NASA's website.

Spatian-Coder One, "Let's try translating my code into the language of the other *Spatian*. Let's use the "Hello Cosmos" to translate my code into another one, callable from C."

Henry shows the Audience how the coding works so the learner can compare and contrast two languages. A new code is coming in C# (C Sharp).

Spatian-Coder Two, "Most eloquently, that is C Sharp! using System. That's like in their music!

The Spatian-Coder One follows using another language, but the output stays almost the same. Henry explains each line of Spatian's code so the audience can understand the first language and then the second language (translated from the first one). Both languages are commented on, and logic, structure, similarities, and differences are emphasized.
The translation follows. Subtle but rhythmical Cosmic Music continues.
Spatian-Coder One in Python:

import turtle # a turtle is used to draw lines with. Such a convenient feature in this particular language
Spatian-Coder Two, "It's like in LOGO, the Earthsian, Seymour Pappert created LEGO/LOGO with turtle Robot, for Nano-Earthsians to learn while playing."
Spatian-Narrator Two, "Oh la la, most movingly, they sure are playful."

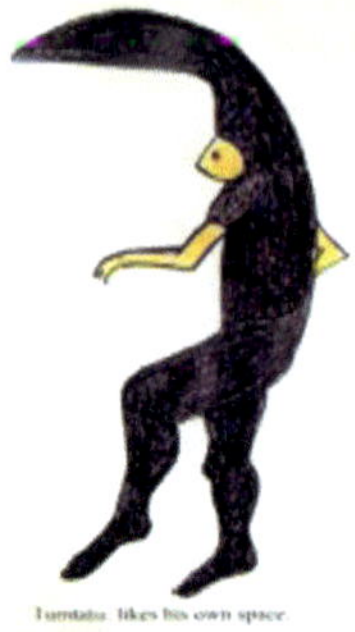

Tumtatu: likes his own space.

```
class Program

{

   public static void Main(string[] args)

   {

      Console.WriteLine("Hello, Cosmos!");

   }

}
```

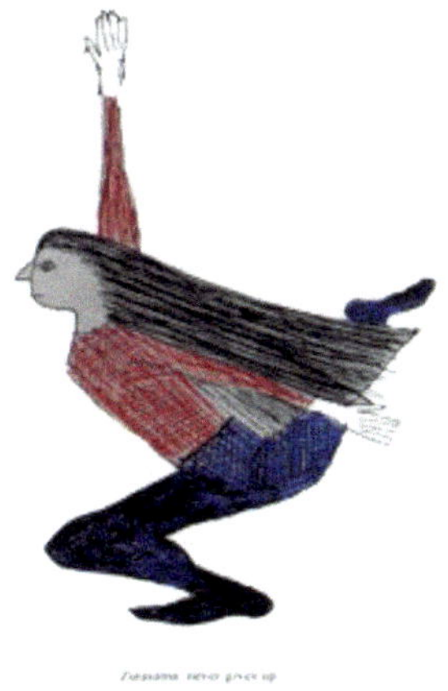

Zutasama never gives up.

Spatian Coder -Two, "Let's try translating my code into the language of the Spatian-One. Let's use the "Hello Space" to translate my code into another language."

It shows the audience how coding works so the learner can compare and contrast the two languages.

Henry-Narrator, "Now they are doing what I did. Just differently. Let's look at the two new languages while following them."

Henry can see the codes displayed by the Spatian-Coder One in C.

```
#include

int main(void)

{

  puts("Hello, Universe!");
```

Spatian-Coder One, "The Spatian-Coder Two sends a Python code that the Earthsian can relate to.

Henry, Narrator, "If one wants to make a comment that does not affect the code, a simple "//" will do. All languages should have comments applied so it is easier to return to the previous code or understand someone else's code. We use Python, where "#" is used as a comment, just like in C++. But there is more to it."

```
void setup(){
        size (720,720);
        background(255);
        }

void draw() // remember that the screen origin (0,0) is on the top left corner
{

  ellipse(350,470,350,400);//draw the oval for the body
  ellipse(300,450,55,65);//draw the first eye

  ellipse(400,450,55,65);//draw the second eye
  ellipse(390,440,25,35);//draw the first pupil
  ellipse(290,440,25,35);//draw the second pupil
```

```
line(219,600,240,670); //use lines to define a shape
line(240,670,250,629);
line(259,640,270,710);
line(267,710,300,660);
line(300,660,320,720);
line(320,720,350,670);
line(350,670,420,710);
line(420,710,430,644);
triangle(430,646,460,690,470,680);//or use ready to use shapes of the triangles

}
```

Henry-Narrator, "Shapes can be built with lines, like the first four triangles under the body of an alien. They can also be created with ready-to-use triangles, like the last one below on the right side of the body of an alien. The output will look like that:"

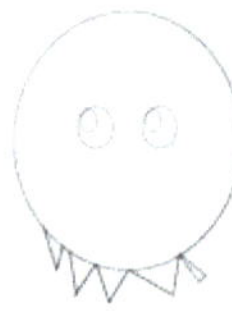

Henry-Narrator continues, "The color-coding improves understanding and organization of the code. With so much scrolling, its structure is crispier, more apparent, more consistent, and easier to understand and manage. When debugging a code, color lines of code or variables show errors or bugs. We use green or grey for making comments or to denote a string, orange for a number or a parameter, purple shows a keyword (for example, if, else, for, while, etc.), light blue denotes an operator (+, -, =, *,/,<, ==, etc., dark blue serves as a predefined function name, red for predefined classes, for code that has been deleted, or an error. The buttons on websites show their functionality through colors."
Spatian-Coder One, "One out of 200 coders cannot see at all."

Spatian-Coder Two, "It makes it harder for them to talk about colors."
Spatian-Coder One, "*They* use screen readers with hundreds of words per minute read to them.
https://www.freecodecamp.org/news/how-blind-people-code-fdb64e3bf5c/

```
screen = turtle.Screen()
screen.setup(720,720)

turtle.speed(6)

turtle.hideturtle()
def draw_oval(x,y,big_radius,small_radius,tilt):
    turtle.up()
    turtle.goto(x,y)
    turtle.down()
    turtle.seth(-45+tilt)
    turtle.color('black')
    turtle.circle(big_radius,90)
    turtle.circle(small_radius,90)
    turtle.circle(big_radius,90)
    turtle.circle(small_radius,90)

draw_oval(0,0,100,70,100)

from turtle import *

pensize(3)
color("black")
```

```
penup()
goto (-145, -15)
pendown()
turtle.speed(10)
# The lines
pensize(2)
right (65)
forward(20)
right (5)
forward(2)
right(40)
forward(10)
```

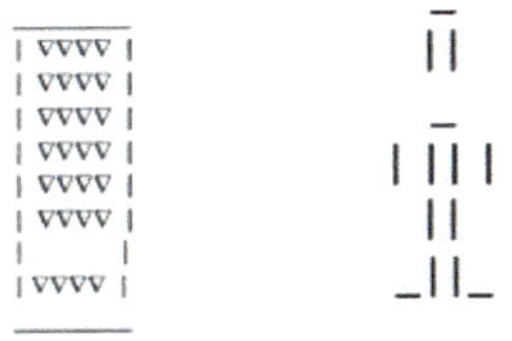

i

`Nothing again`

Henry thinks, "Let's try some flag semaphore communication of sign bearers: sign σῆμα *(sêma)* bearers: φόρος *(phóros),* sending distant messages through signals with their hands rotating flags according to the pattern, the method used in the old Greece. "

Spatian-Coder One, "Semaphore is a coding term now."

Spatian-Coder Two, "Can't you drop that Narrator habit, now, Spatian-Coder One?"

Henry sends his question:

http://semaphorify.info/?c=What%20is%20your%20phone%20number

`The animated semaphore signing appears.`

`This time, the Other Boy replies:`

http://semaphorify.info/?c=1%20010%20110%200110

`The animated semaphore signing appears.`

"Perfect!, *exclaims Henry.* "1 010 110 0110 is your phone number. "

`Henry sends a message,"` How is your music?"

`this time via text message.`

```
left (85)
forward(10)
left (85)
forward(2)
right(60)
forward(10)
back(10)
right (90)
forward(20)
right (-60)
forward(10)
right(90)
forward(10)
left (45)
forward(10)
left (45)
forward(10)
right(10)
forward(10)
back(10)
```

```
# Small Triangle

pendown()

x=turtle.Turtle()
x.forward(16)
x.left(90)
x.forward(16)
x.left(180-45)
x.forward(14.42)

# Eyes
import turtle

screen = turtle.Screen()
screen.setup(720,720)

turtle.speed(1)
turtle.hideturtle()

def draw_oval(x,y,big_radius,small_radius,tilt):
   turtle.up()
   turtle.goto(x,y)
   turtle.down()
   turtle.seth(-45+tilt)
   turtle.color('black')
   turtle.circle(big_radius,90)
   turtle.circle(small_radius,90)
   turtle.circle(big_radius,90)
   turtle.circle(small_radius,90)

draw_oval(-90,100,12,10,90)
draw_oval(-40,100,12,10,90)
# Pupils
draw_oval(-40,100,5,5,90)
draw_oval(-88,100,5,5,90)
```

Spatian-Coder Two, "The spellchecker does not like it, but we need to remember the Earthsians designed it."

Henry-Narrator, "The turtles are set to draw lines. They need to be called up and told which way and how to move."

Henry-Narrator, "The code works, but I could do it much simpler, I think."

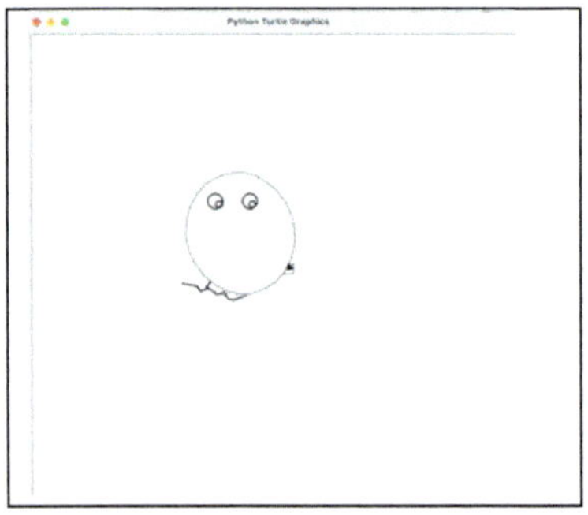

Henry-Narrator, "Just by changing white with black, we can have this self-portrait:

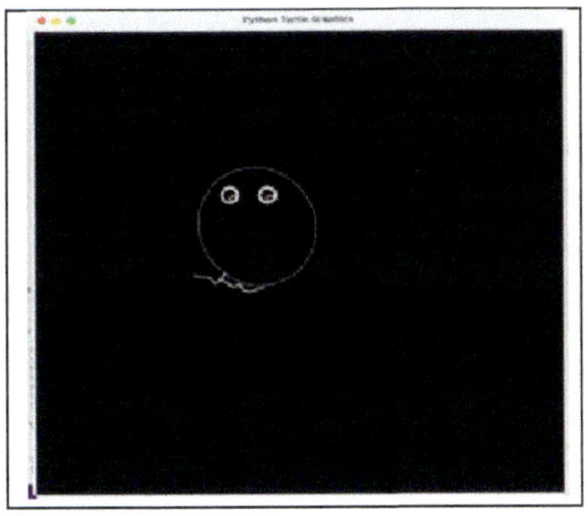

Henry-Narrator, “The Other Boy must have been watching as well. Did he learn to code? How to ask? By using a series of patterns, *he decides.* Electrical pulse transmitted via electrical wire is out of the question nowadays. The other boy must be a musician. He must understand codes.”

Henry sends a radio code via audio tones: “QTH” using zone and grid squares (What is your location*).”*

No reply. He tries using sign language.

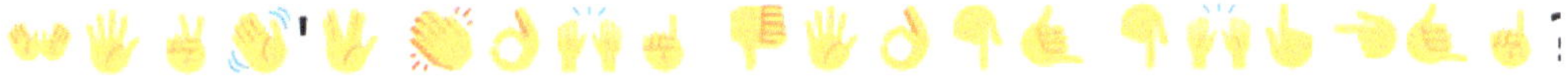

No answer

Henry-Narrator, “How about in the Morse code?”

.. ... / - .... . .-. . / .- -. -.-- -... --- -.. -.-- / --- ..- - / - .... . .-. .

Spatian-Coder Two, "I TERRA AND BOY?"

Spatian-Coder One, “You are not the Narrator anymore.”

Henry tries differently:

.-- .... .- - .----. ... / -.-- --- ..- .-. / .--. .... --- -. . / -. ..- -- -... . .-.

Henry-Narrator, “Maybe with emojis,” 絵文字, picture characters for pictographs for simplified faces, weather, objects, emotions, feelings, things, or activities, all following the Unicode Standard across platforms, programs, and languages. A U+1F600 is for the “grinning face” emoji, U+1F609 for the “winking” one, U+1F60F stands for the “smirking” emoji, etc., ☺ :-);-} :-]. The emoticons are different, and typefaces and fonts are not protected by copyright as they do not qualify as artistic works. While font styles represent letters, emojis' emotions also send a message.”

Henry states, “Let’s try the American Standard Code for Information Interchange for electronic communication. Here is my ASCII emoji for ‘Call me, Boy.’

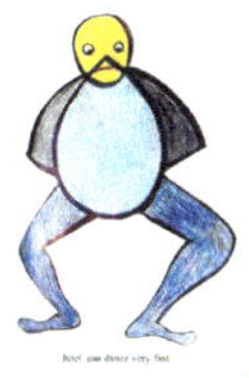

Juiel: can dance uphill.

The Break
The Curtain goes down (or closes).

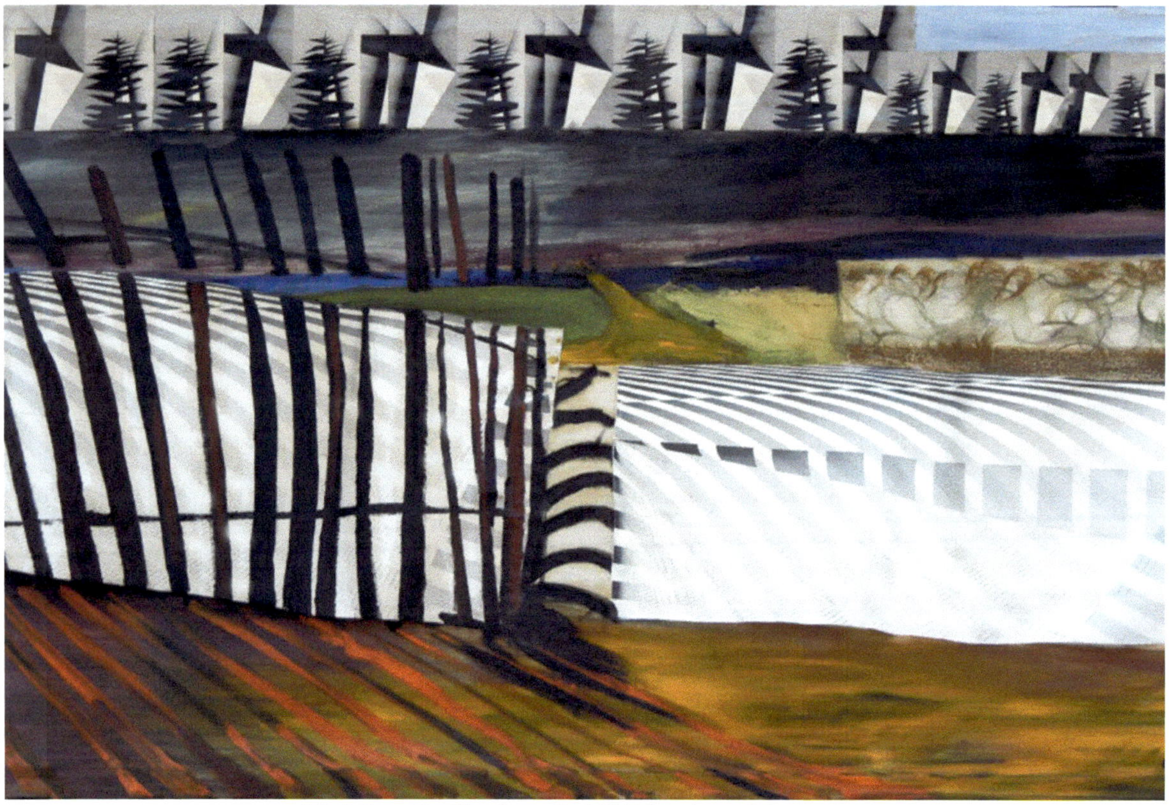

No Man, No Shadow. © *2025 by Anna Ursyn*

Act II
The Curtain goes up (or opens).

The Other Boy's Room.
Henry pays a visit to the Other Boy. There is a piano and a guitar in the Other Boy's room, but no gear or LED lights. Now, his own window with neon, LED lights, lighted gear, signs, and gadgets is visible across the street.

Henry asks the Other Boy, "What's your name, boy?"

The Other Boy replies, "My name is Henry; what's yours?"

Henry hesitating, "Henry, or Binary-Henry."

The Other Boy, "Henry! In that case, my name is Henry-Two, but not Henry-The-Second, mind you."

Henry-Two, "Let me show you how the music code works."

Henry, to himself, "I hope he'll make it fast as my attention span has been measured as 8 seconds."

Henry-Two explains, "Let's look at music notations using a piano."

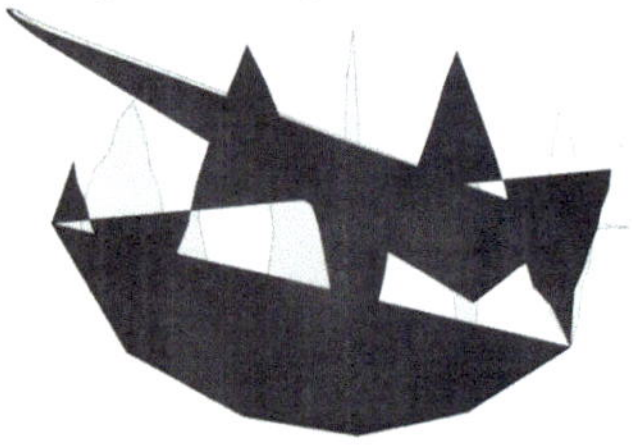

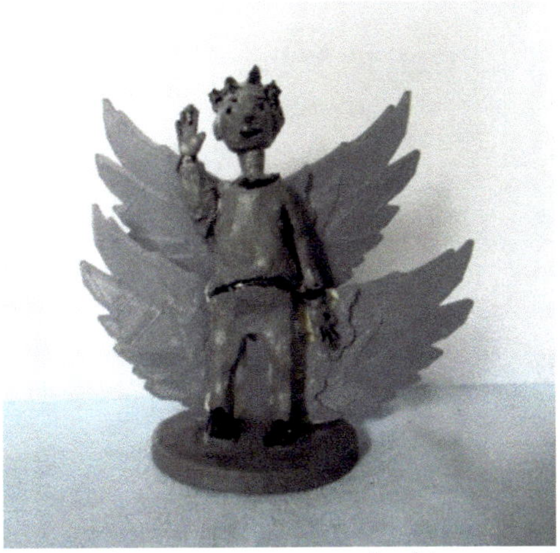

Henry-Two opens a website, and a large image of a keyboard on the phone appears on the stage.

Henry-Two continues, "Look at the white keys ABCDEFG, repeated seven times. There are fifty white keys, with seven C keys. The fourth from either side is a Middle C."

Henry, "That, I already know."

Henry-Two keeps going, "You'll find the black keys set as twos and threes. On your left are two black keys; on your right, white keys, C and E, can be found. The three black keys are F on the left and B on the right. Memorize this pattern to find each key on the keyboard. Middle C is the most crucial one. Any piano has seven octaves. That means a distance between two white notes with the same name, eight notes, from note A."

Henry, "The same pattern applies to the black notes."

Henry-Two continues, "On a music sheet with rows of two sets of five staves, horizontal parallel lines, the treble clef, for the right hand the G clef is on the upper stave, and the bass clef, the F clef on the lower stave, is for the left hand. Sounds of different heights or depths, of being higher or lower, are called pitch—as notes on the spaces between the lines, above or below each stave.
Memorize the notes on the lines and in the spaces of each stave:
Treble notes on the lines: EGBDF
Treble notes in the spaces: FACE
Bass notes on the lines: GBDFA
Bass notes in the spaces: ACEG."

Henry-Two, "Some artists share their visual music."

Henry thinks, "Hmmm, how would they look if we could see the sounds?

Henry-Two, "They can look like colorful lines and shapes. First, the waves,

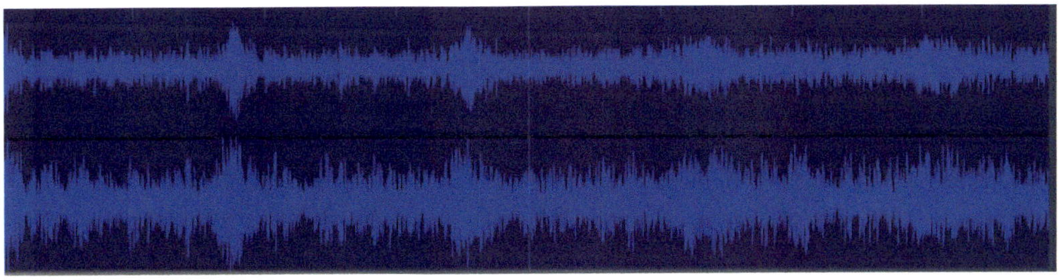

or more linear descriptions. Maybe not beautiful, but informational.

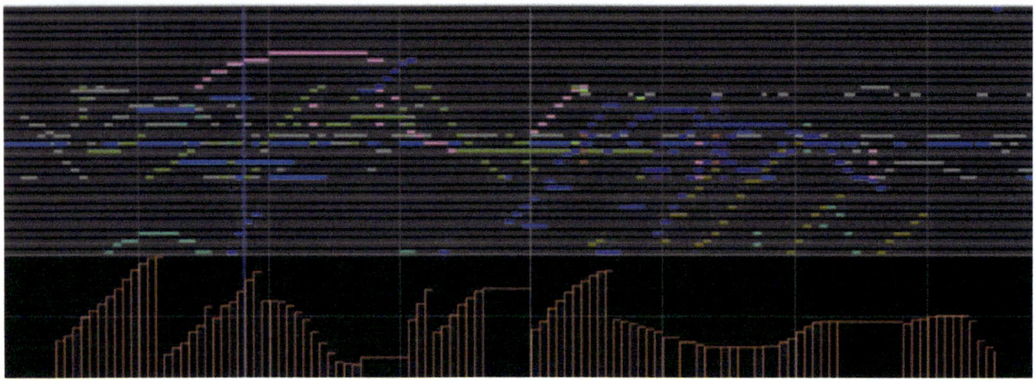

Or more artistic composition with lines

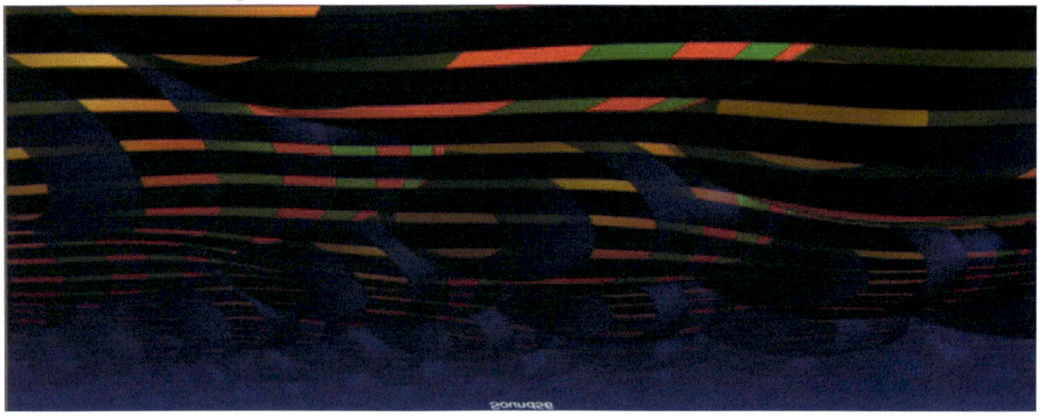

Music can follow the shapes one creates as geometrical forms-based composition.

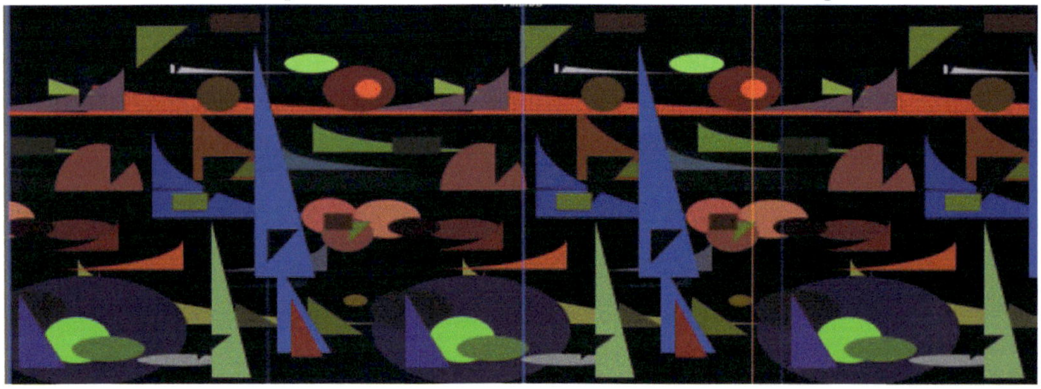

Or organic ones.

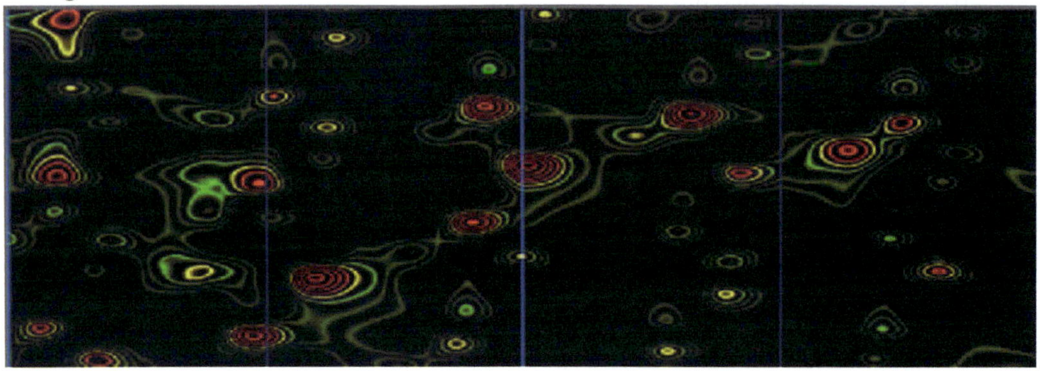

It can be based on textures.

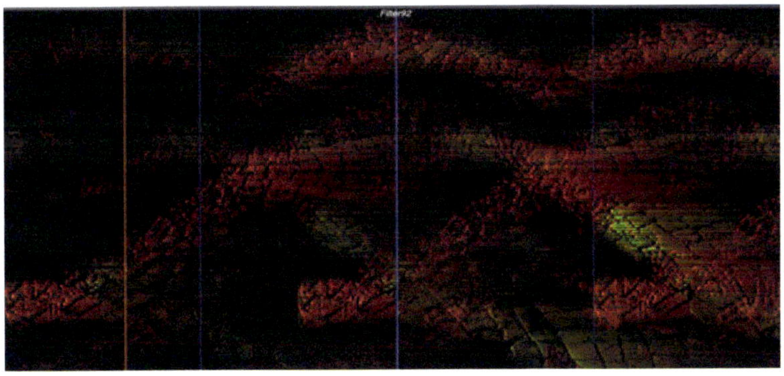

Or, by reading an existing image and following it through sounds

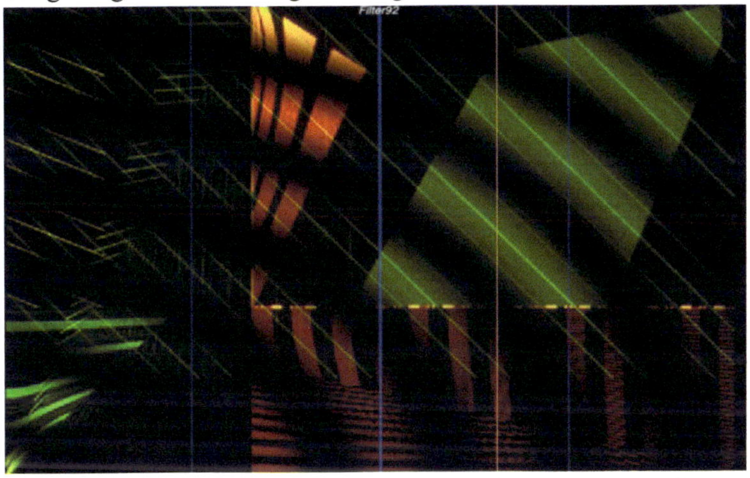

And this one converts a geometric shape of a man into a botany-based iconography.

From: 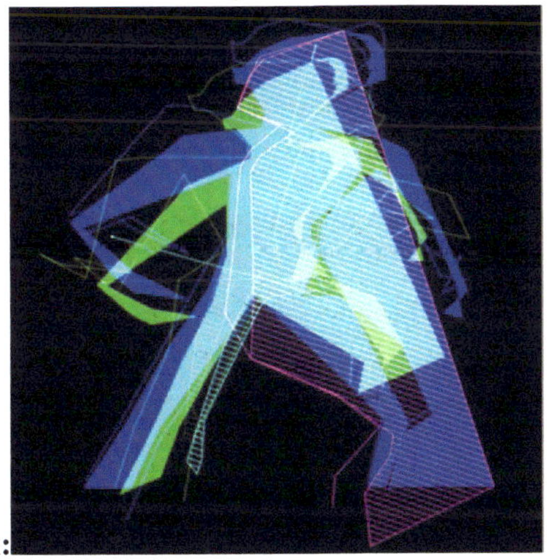 **To:** 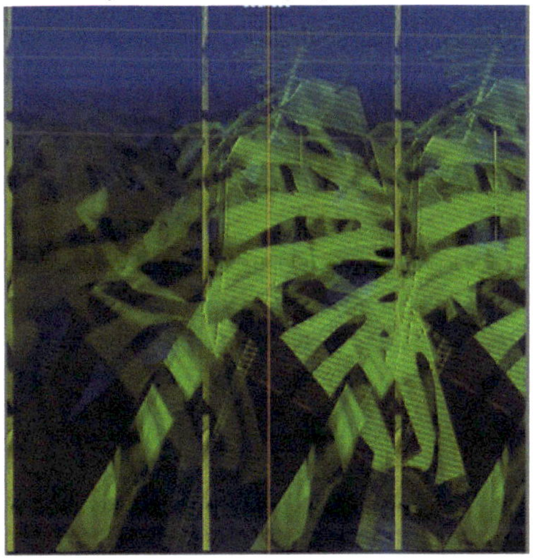

Spatian-Coder Two, "That is Organic!"
Spatian-Coder One, "They use software developed by other Earthsians, such as Eric Wenger.
https://uisoftware.com/MetaSynth/ or
https://tuneform.com/media/visualizers/

https://www.renderforest.com/
or there is free Audacity for audio editing.
https://www.audacityteam.org/

Spatian-Coder Two, "That's Synesthetic! "Some Earthsians give away their doings over their patchwork without wanting anything from anyone."
Spatian-Coder One, "Prominently spirited! "

Henry-Two keeps sending his instructions, "We can look at the composition that we are listening to, and it is shown in musical notation and as images or animated sequences."

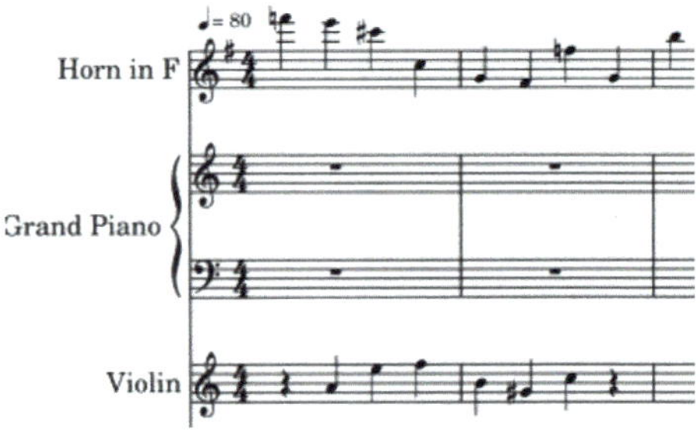

Spatian-Coder One, "What a nice surprise to learn something from an Earthsian."
Spatian-Coder Two, "Hacha, they plan first, then compose."

Henry exclaims, "I understand it now. I have no piano or any instrument to play. I'll have to use the first ever musical tool: my hands."

Binary Henry starts clapping to the musical notes displayed on the screen. The two Spatian Coders and Henry Two join in by following the melodic tunes. The musical notation changes, and the clapping modifications as well. The audience is given a chance to join in.
Clapping sound.

Exit.
The Curtain goes down (or closes).
The Break

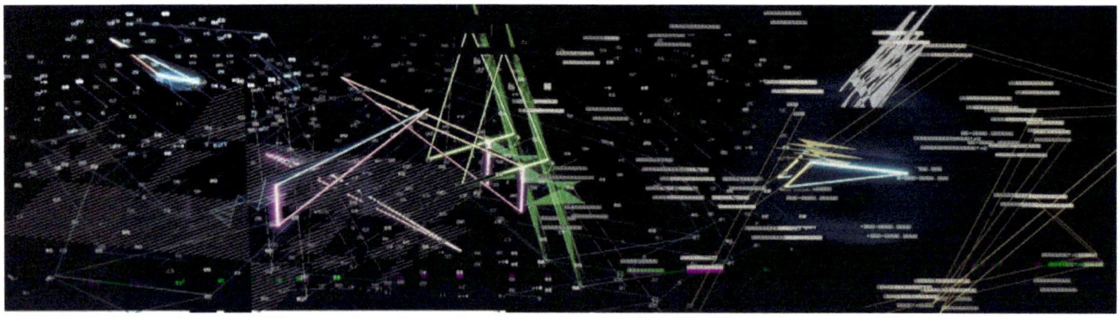

The Cosmos. The output from the computer code. © 2025 by Anna Ursyn

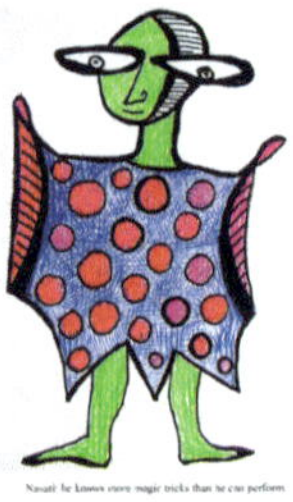

Nasati: knows more magic tricks that he can pewrformt.

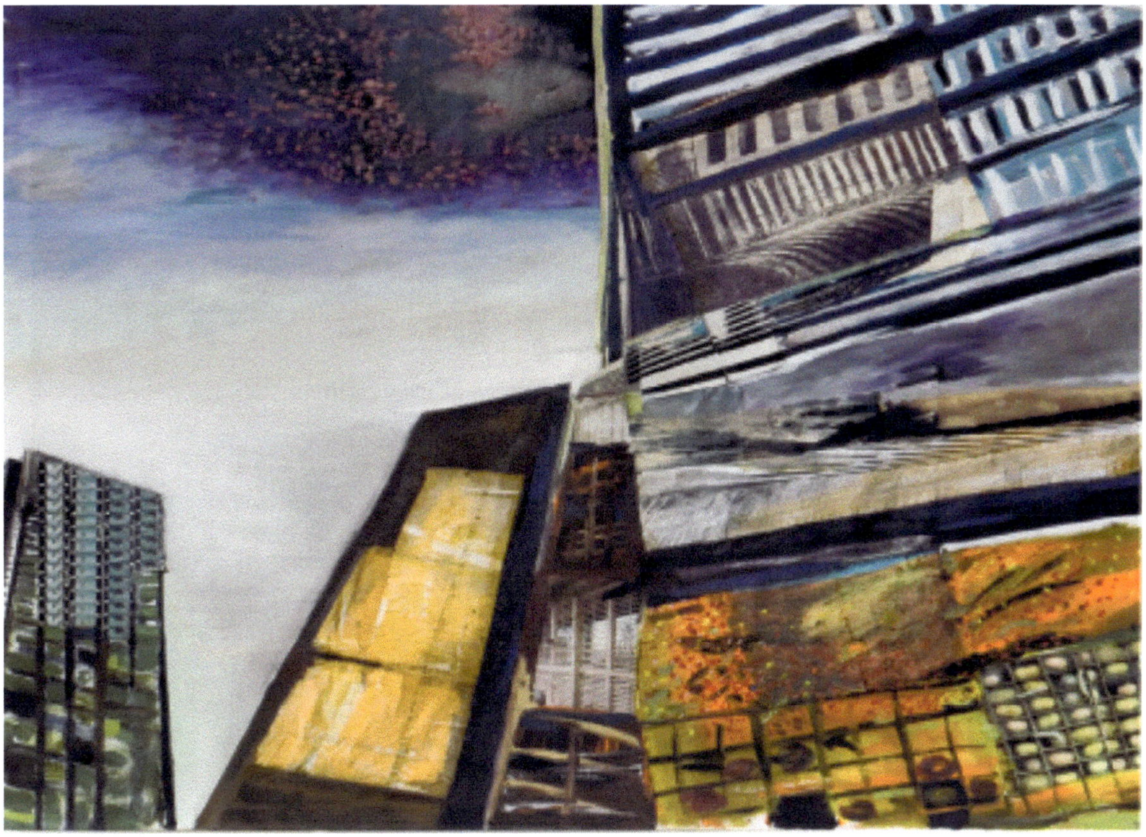

Small Window as a Part of a Big City. © *2025 by Anna Ursyn*

Act III
The Curtain goes up (or opens).

Henry says, "It looks like music uses the elements and principles of design just like people use it in art:"

A related projection illustrates each element and principle of design. The matching visuals accompany the descriptions.

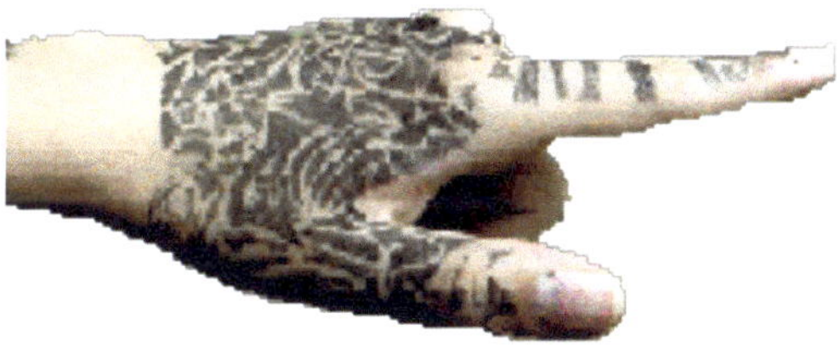

Henry-Two, "Ha?"

Henry continues:

Elements and Principles of Design in Art

The elements are line, color, values, forms and shapes, space, and textures. They refer to what is available for visual communication with people, while Principles of Design describe how the details could be used (e.g., a line can be repeated with symmetry, radial, or spiral, can be black or another color, straight, curved, etc.).

Principles of Design in Art define how in any form of a composition balance, emphasis, movement, variety, proportion, and unity are used."

Spatian-Coder Two, "It makes me want to make art, whatever it is…"

Henry-Two, "There must be a way to use Elements and Principles of Design in music!"

Henry adds, "Yes, but not only in music."

Henry-Two, "My passions are Harmony and Melody."

Henry wonders aloud, "How would those elements and principles of design look like in coding?"

Elements and Principles of Design in Coding

Elements of Design in Programming

Color and Value

Color sends information and speeds up reading and editing the code. Color structures lines of the code. Even the slightest typo, such as replacing a "." with a "," sends an error message in red, preventing the code from running, compiling, etc."

Spatian-Narrator One, "Whap, this cannot be cosmossy."

We are talking about light here, not pigment. Colors are displayed as numbers and letters.

The HEX number for color is the three primary colors: red, green, and blue. For example, there is no blue or green, but red is 00,00,255, all together in hex: 0x0000ff.

Examples RGB model	**Examples in Hex:**
Red - [255, 0, 0]	Red - 0xff0000
Green - [0,255,0]	Green - 0x00ff00
Blue - [0,0,255]	Blue - 0x0000ff

Spatian-Narrator Two, "Do they have a spell-checker for coding?"

Spatian-Narrator One, "Yup, it gives suggestions."

Form and Shape

- Some servers see lowercase and uppercase letters as different characters (a coder's problem).
- Coders use visual controls (buttons, text boxes, etc.) in their programs.
- Shapes with symbols for control: Round brackets: (), Curly:{}, Square: [], Angle: <>
- The Oval Shape is for the start/end,
- The Rectangle Shape, for a process,
- The Parallelogram Shape – the input/output of the information,
- The Diamond Shape – decision,
- The Arrow Shape – the flow of the sequence.
- The comments use different characters in various programming languages.

Space
- Memory space is essential to run an algorithm.
- The program uses memory to execute and is represented by its space complexity.
- Running a program requires memory to store input data and values.

Line
- Lines of source code involve writing instructions.
- One line may generate one or more instructions for a computer.
- Lines of code differ for various tasks and languages.
- One output can be written as a short or long list of instructions.
- We do not evaluate codes by the length of their instructions.

Texture
- Shaders have textures, a 1D/2D/3D grid of pixel values; there are different interpolation filters.
- Values can be sampled from the texture to provide data and commands to the computer.

Spatian-Narrator One, "The Earthsian is making the Earthsians-audience bored."

Spatian-Narrator Two, "Don't exacerbate, Spatian-Narrator One. They do not seem bored, just the opposite!"

Principles of Design in Programming

Balance
- Balanced code is accurate, consistent, readable, crisp, and maintainable for collaboration.
- Write codes with modules of the same parameters, complexity, and simplicity for flow.

Emphasis
- A program consists of a collection of classes.
- Objects are the minor units for communication.
- Data is more important than procedure.

Movement
- To make objects move through coding, keys are programmed to follow some path.
- Objects and paths can be set in motion.

Variety and Contrast
- Programming paradigms incorporate attributes or functions.
- Languages use a set of strings to support multiple paradigms with their own jargon.

Proportion
- A code converts values into proportions.
- The mathematical symbol is used (::).

Unity measures how each coding element works together for united communication.
- It is also the name of a 3D game engine combining skills for building a game.

Spatian-Narrator One, "The Earthsian is making their audience tired."

Spatian-Coder Two, "We do it another way:"

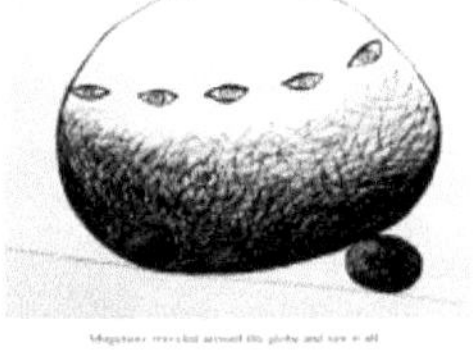

Mugeraso traveled around the world and saw it all.

The Elements and Principles of the Visuals in Ciphering

The Elements of the Visuals in Ciphering

They are components to create and organize codes.

Syntax: Rules and structure of a language telling how code is written and executed.
Variables: a named location in memory that stores a value or reference.
Data structures: Organize and store data in memory, such as arrays, lists, or maps.
Libraries and frameworks: Collections of code and tools to simplify development.
Data: Information used and manipulated in a program: variables, arrays, and objects.
Functions: the modular and reusable blocks of code that perform tasks within a program.
Control flow: Logic and sequencing of loops, conditionals, and branching statements.
Simplicity: using clear and concise code that is easy to understand and maintain.
Modularity: Separating the code into small components to be modified and combined.
Abstraction: Using concepts and structures to simplify code and hide complexity.
User interface: the visual parts allowing for interaction and control of the program.

The Principles of Visuals in Ciphering; for precise, efficient, maintainable code.
Consistency: using naming, formatting, and design patterns throughout a program.
Scalability: a program can handle complexity with performance or maintainability.
Security: the design of code and systems resistant to unauthorized access and attacks.
Testing: to ensure it works as intended and to identify and fix bugs and errors.
Accessibility: a code and user interface that is usable for different abilities and needs.
Henry-Two exclaims, "Yes, everything is connected. Let's see how they are applied to music!"
Spatian-Narrator One, "Heva, The Other Earthsian will now bore them…"
Spatian-Narrator Two, "Gruaa, let him be for a while."
Spatian-Narrator One, "Wooomh, All right. They sound exciting to me; I find it universy!"

Elements and Principles of Design in Music

Elements of Design in Music

Color
- Tone colors, timbres, waveforms, and harmonics as created by an instrument's sound.
- The basic waveform is the sine wave, graphed as pitch vs. time y=sin x.
- Recent synthesizers use recording sounds for more authentic sounds.

Value of Color
- Seen as volume, represented by the amplitude of the sound wave.
- Louder sounds require more energy. Two musicians can't produce identical sounds.
- A shorter string changes pitch in vibrating instruments (violin, guitar, harp, piano).

Form and Shape
- The envelope is the timbre of a particular sound.
- The musical piece uses a binary form for the sonata, rondo, and modern song.
- There are forms of music, operas, or cyclic works.

Space
- Certain instruments rest during specific passages to create different timbres of sound.
- Space is silence.

Line is melody, the connection of notes through time.
- The melodic shape forms the character of the music
- It can start low in pitch, increase slowly to a climax, and return to the low starting level.
- The climax can be at the ratio of the golden section.

Texture is harmony, sounding more than one note at a time.
- Consonance and dissonance are perceptions grounded in the harmonic series.

Principles of Art and Design in Music

Balance
- Composition repetition, melody, and transformation support balance.
- Evenly distributed energy through the sound spectrum.

Emphasis
- An instrument can dominate through solo melodies and louder volume in orchestration.
- A composer maintains a balance between the soloist and the group.

Movement is seen in the progression of overall chords in the piece.
- If several chords change in a measure, the harmonic motion is fast, and vice versa.

Variety and Contrast help gain attention.
- Various cultures divide the octave into numbers of segments to create a musical scale.
- Our modern music uses a twelve-tone octave.

Proportion
- Chords sound full when they are constructed using the template of the harmonic series
- Using larger intervals for lower pitches and vice versa helps maintain balance and unity.

Unity
- We evaluate music based on its balance, unity, and variety.
- Music is time-based; a work must maintain unity to have an identity through repetition.

Spatian-Narrator One, "Spacy enough for you, Spatian-Narrator Two?"

Spatian-Narrator Two, "Hooah, we do it in a simpler way:"

Spatians' Elements of Art in Music to create and organize music

Melody: the main tune or series of notes heard in a music work.

Harmony: sounds or notes played at the same time for a richer, more complex sound

Rhythm: the arrangement of sounds in time, including beat, tempo, and meter.

Dynamics: the variation in volume or intensity of a musical piece.

Timbre: the distinct tonal quality of a sound or voice, set by its harmonic components

Texture: interweaving different sounds or melodies to create a complex overall sound.

Spatians' Principles of Art in Music rules for balance, harmony, and coherence in music

Unity: using similar elements to create a cohesive and harmonious musical piece.

Contrast: using elements or sounds to create interest and variety in a music composition.

Balance: the distribution of sound or musical elements for visual or auditory symmetry.

Proportion: the relationship between size, scale, and duration between musical elements.

Emphasis: specific sounds or elements for a highlight in a musical composition.

Movement: rhythm and melody create a sense of movement or flow within work.

Spatian-Narrator One and Two together, "Wrooa! It is all connected!"
Spatian-Narrator Two, "How about Us?"

Spatian-Narrator One, "Here it comes:"

```
This part is to be danced and sung. Projections of abstract code-based
graphics appear projected on the screen. All Spatians dance: Two Spatians-
Narrators and two Spatians-Coders, or the holograms are used.
```

The Elements and the Principles of Art in the Way of the Spatians

Retrieved from: ccs. SSP (Cosmic Communication System, Spatian Space Protocol).
Our Spatians' methods include marking stars and galaxies that float with cosmic currents.

Elements of Design: The Way of the Spatians in the Deeper Parts of the Cosmos

Color and Value

- Light means self-expression to Spatians.
- Our excursions mark adaptability to our kinds in ever-changing environments.
- Identify machines to further our line in our hardware with the avoidance of patterns.
- It is essential to use darker elements as lights seem more cheerful.
- Those who mark on stars use bright shapes rendered to bring passion to their forms.

Shape and Form

- Shape and form are crucial for visiting the Earthsians and adapting to flows of masses.
- Changing the form can intimidate a shooting star, thus hopefully warding off an attack.
- Clouds, meteorites, or rocks convey messages, warnings, and stories with Platonic forms
- The Silver Spatians rely on their own stars to interpret the Cosmos they live in.
- Tetrahedron (Fire), octahedron (Air), hexahedron (Earth), and dodecahedron (Aether).

Space

- Asteroids and dwarfs share movement and orientation, but planets exchange those skills.
- Spatians possess speed, form, geolocation, movements, orientation, & expressions.
- Smaller spaces benefit shooting stars' comfort for flying objects between the planets.
- Space around us helps compare environments to know why minor planets gather.

Line

- Boundaries can be defined by lights, sounds & imaginary borders utilized by robots.
- Behavioral modification of asteroids helps droids to place them spatially.
- Lines create the plane without depth, configuration gradations, or atmosphere.
- A level of abstraction without trickery creates an excellent representation of reality.
- There is no reality! All the shapes fit together.

Texture

- The Spatians use various textures, from flat and slow to dynamic, for their strategies.
- The visuals significantly impact Spatians more than words, sounds, or other systems.
- An explicit message is sent by selecting glossier lights and smoother, soothing sounds.

Principles of Design: The Way of the Spatians in the Deeper Parts of the Cosmos

Balance refers to the holes of the spacecraft for the Spatian-sensitive mechanoreceptors.

- To ensure order, set comfort for the exceptional asteroids or minor planet moons.
- Damocloids are known for their sensitivity, vulnerability, fragility, and erratic behavior.
- Their symbolism is asymmetrical, vertical, and radial balance, providing a Spatian focus.

Emphasis allows the Spatians and other objects to highlight a focal information point.

- Lights dominate them because the shapes of beams bring the story to the moment.
- Emphasis means Salient Arc, but lights, symbols, and sounds distract speed or velocity.

- Centaurs and Solar System bodies identify their focal point when visiting the Earthsians.
- It is essential to remove elements to receive the desired response from each centaur.

Movement takes lights, lines, and textures into symbols that tell a form from a shape.
- Flow is essential when working with trans-Neptunian objects.
- Neptunian behavior is vital to understand when they are kept separate from most objects.
- Untrue, frightened, or unruly Spatians are separated to prevent boring the rest.
- Moving the next "3-D scene," called 2D cosmic art, calms the Spatians down.

Variety and Contrast are to notify others that something is overdue for Venusians.
- Some unnumbered Spatians use light-coded systems to help others communicate.
- Dramatically enlarged lights with sounds allow planets to recognize one approaching.
- Many forms of variety and contrast contradict each other depending on where one flows.
- For every communication, there is typically a structure connecting them.

Proportion
- A dwarf planet's behavior corresponds to its size, volume, temperature, and pressure.
- The planets' proportions change when a looming specimen enters their airspace.
- To connect with a planet, know its size!; for a dwarf, approach them as narrower.
- Size is crucial for comprehension of complex and persistent levels of relationships.

Unity
- Sounds are related; the meaning is connected to all.
- To be considered a part of Spatians is to follow harmony and be linked.
- The dwarf planets connectors solve a problem or reach a common goal of other planets.
- Spatians in the vast, Unite! Just like humans do!

Spatian-Narrator One, "Let's give them a break!"

Spatian-Narrator Two, "Break it is 2 minutes!" It's 1200 seconds, or 1,2000E+11 in nanoseconds.

The curtain goes down (or closes).
The Break.

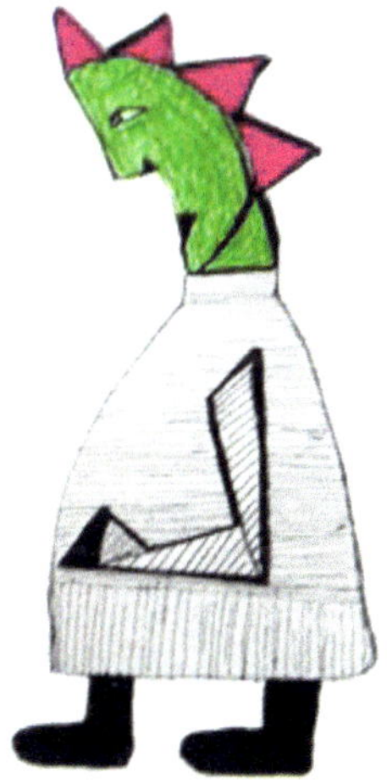

Mabcao: learned Italian by eating pasta.

Mabcao: learned Italian by eating pasta.

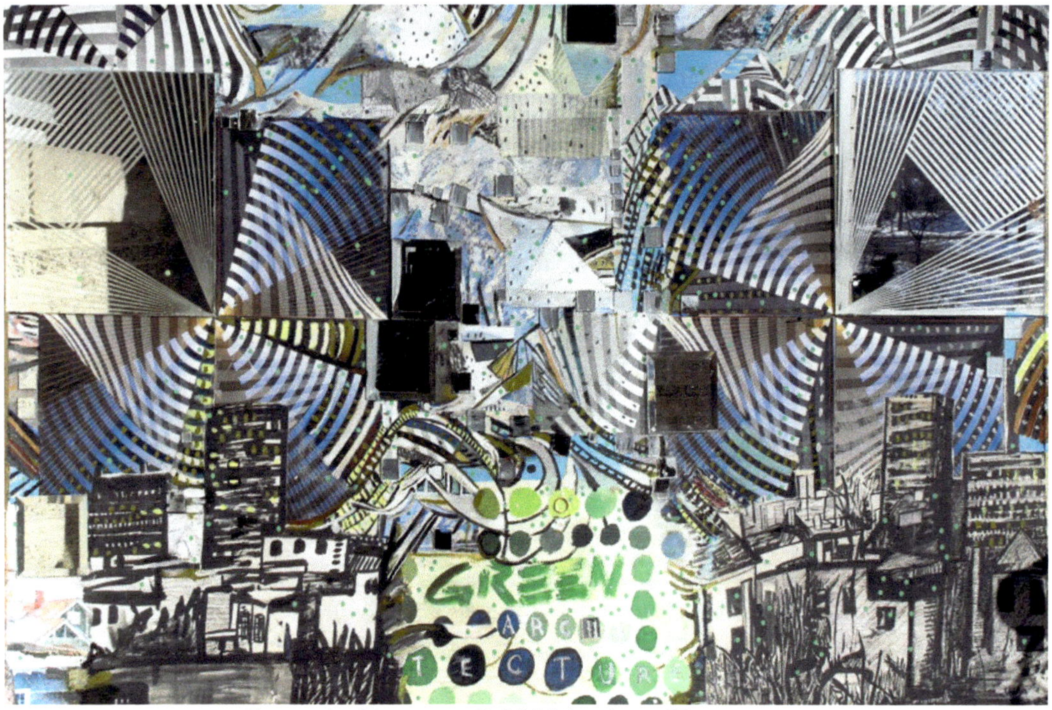

Green Architecture. © *2025 by Anna Ursyn*

Act IV

The curtain goes up (or opens).

Both boys are sitting in Henry-Two's room, which is filled with music-related objects and technological gear, lights, neons, and computers. Henry's window can be seen across the street, and a piano is in it.

Henry Two states, "Let's code some visual music."

Spatian-Narrator One," Look, the Earthsians in the audience seem tired again."

Spatian-Narrator Two, "Do you have a valediction, Spatian-Narrator One?"

Spatian-Narrator One, "Woooch, yes. Let's let them go."

Spatian-Narrator Two, "So now.............

The end

The Curtain goes down (or closes).

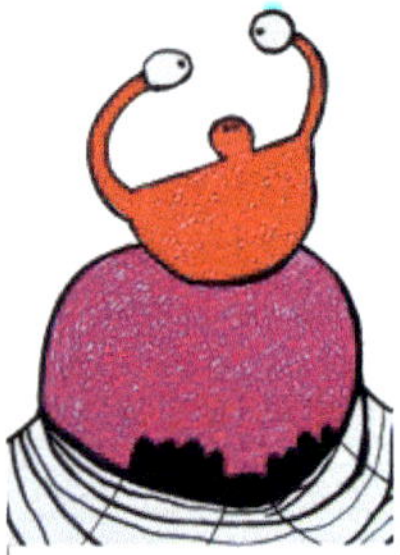

Parcada: never misses a pitch

Parcada: never misses a pitch.

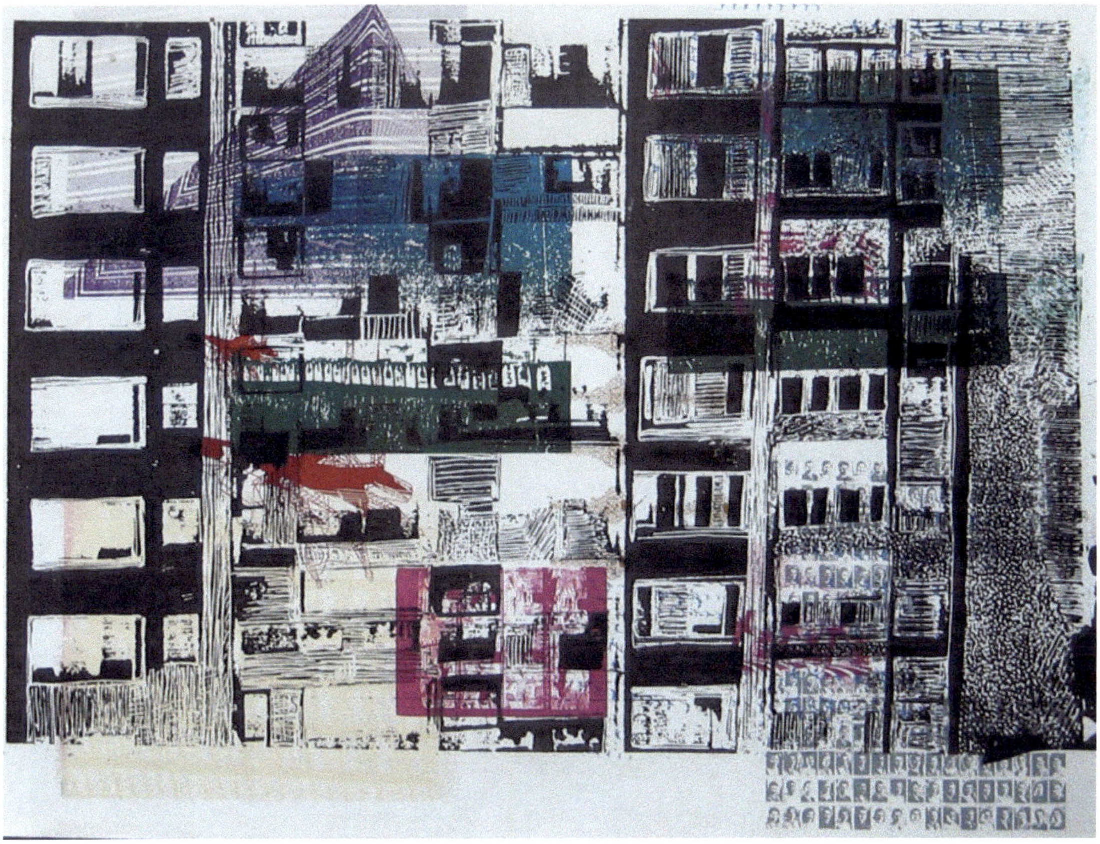

City Neighborhood. Photosilkscreens after computer codes. *© 2025 by Anna Ursyn*

Act V

The Curtain goes up (or opens).

`The Spatians communicate through the balloons above them, like a 3D comic book, now a cosmic book, with texts written on each balloon.`

Spatian - Narrator One, "We saw the Earthsians communicate (whatever it means), and are connected in their environment. Let's see how they perceive the role of their limited senses within their unlimited communication."
Spatian-Narrator Two, "Druua, at least they are playful ones!"

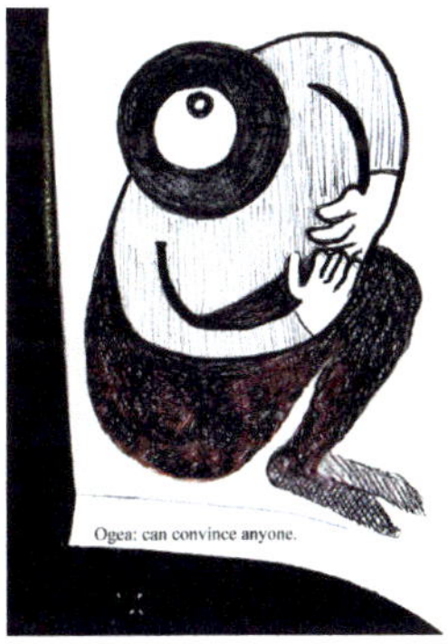

Ogea: can convince anyone.

TEXT, IMAGE, AND SOUND

Spatian-Narrator-One, "They write what they think to tell it in various forms. Various types of media, such as text, images, and sound, can convey messages and elicit emotions through intriguing, mundane, stunning, or unappealing experiences. For example,

Half Love

Love should be symmetrical, they say.
There is a heart symbol
used to teach about symmetry or reflection,
having nothing in common with our blood-pumping organ,
which is not that elegant but a helpful muscle.

Love brings hope to many
and even goes beyond descriptions of feelings.
Friends
who share the two halves often wear a divided heart shape.

What if only one person is amazed,
under the spell, or enchanted by
someone who does not care?
This often leads to problems,
as it might feel like a half-beat blood pumping.

How can we love Nature,
while Nature cannot love us anymore?

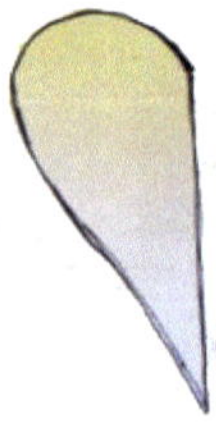

Spatian-Narrator-Two, "It can be delivered as:

Text and Image
Language and culture impact how text is presented, with some relying more on visuals. Context influences personal interpretation for clear understanding. Text affects readers differently than images due to learned symbols. Both require imagination to express abstract ideas. Design is a powerful storytelling tool that enhances communication.
Sound and Text
Written and spoken language are used for visual and auditory descriptions. Modified sounds create versions to influence styles of music and orchestration. The text describes imagery, while designs create noises, tones, and music. Learning languages requires proficiency in both sound and text. Tone, speed, volume, and onomatopoeias affect the meaning of spoken words. The lyrics use sound and text to convey messages. Videos and dance can depict text, images, or sound.

Sound and Image

Sound can create images for a musical, opera, musical video, or ballet to convey emotions and information through tone, volume, and speed., while visuals through colors and lighting. Visual and auditory elements help deliver emotional experiences by evoking different feelings or sensations in our brains. Sounds can transport us to a specific time or place or trigger happiness, anxiety, anger, or annoyance. Animations and videos with effects combine images with sounds. While images create illusions, sounds convey personality. Music enhances experiences, with colors playing important roles. Proper credits and copyrights are crucial for any content.

Spatian-Narrator One, "So I see they have more to play with."

Moving image

Those include GIFs, 2D or 3D animations, and videos, including 360-degree involve drawing images or moving pictures, while 3D animations use wireframes and lighting effects. Displaying different images at 30 or 60 frames per second creates the illusion of movement.

World Wide Web

The internet connects people for communication, entertainment, and information. It includes images and gaming characters and allows for machine learning and artificial intelligence.

Immersive, Interactive

Animations, or videos, Internet, VR, AI, ML, and what is coming from the way we interact with changes. Dynamic and interactive visuals can have a more significant effect than static images.

Virtual Reality

To fully immerse ourselves in a digital world created by artists and programmers, we explore and interact with environments using gears.

Spatian-Coder Two, "Virtual reality and moving image bring the image to life more than Earthsians have ever experienced—moving images, paired with corresponding music, immerse one's senses into arts to feel virtually intangible."

Spatian-Coder Two, "As technology develops, Earthsians have more tools to explore new multi-modal experiences. AI and ML have made access worldwide possible with more tools, but artists and writers may be undervalued. Web platforms, VR, and AI offer immersive art experiences that transport them to new creative worlds."

Spatian-Coder Two, "Care to become or experience being an Earthsian?

Spatian-Coder One, "They are too divided. Thank you, though."

Spatian-Narrator One, "Look, some of them Earthsians left. Too scary for them?"

Spatian-Narrator Two, "They will come back. This is all exciting."

3D printing creates 3D objects from digital designs. It is used in various fields, from medicine to art, using various materials, such as metals, plastic, cement, and food products.

Physical Computing involves using tangible microcontrollers to connect and program data and control things like lights, displays, and motors.

Machine Learning (ML) involves using various data points to arrive at a solution. It adapts and evolves by setting goals and improving with each task.

Artificial Intelligence collects data from the internet for popular answers and creates art by analyzing multiple data points. It can build relationships with users through physical robots and, to some extent, replicate human emotions and ideas.

Spatian-Narrator Two, "It will replace us!"

Spatian-Narrator One, "We will be replaced!"

`Two mechanical robots dance projected on the screen.`

The curtain goes down (or closes).

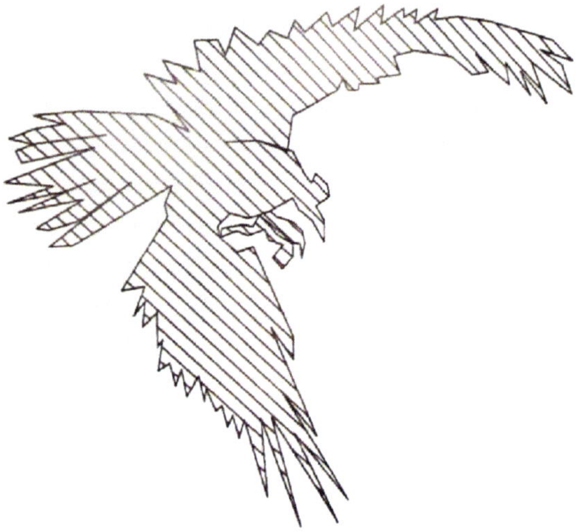

The Usual Thing. The output from the computer code.

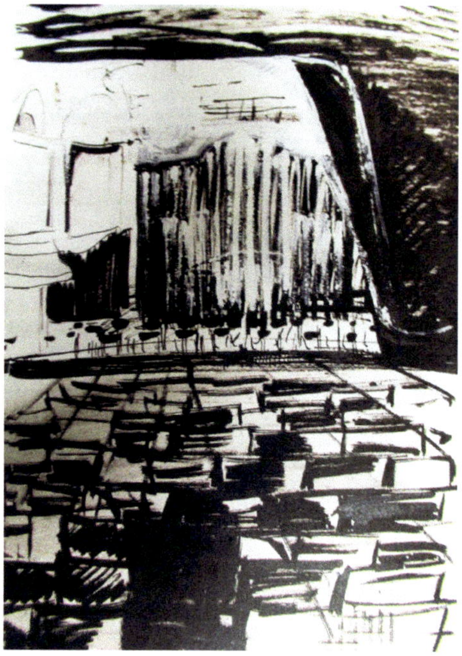

A Concert Hall © 2025 by Anna Ursyn

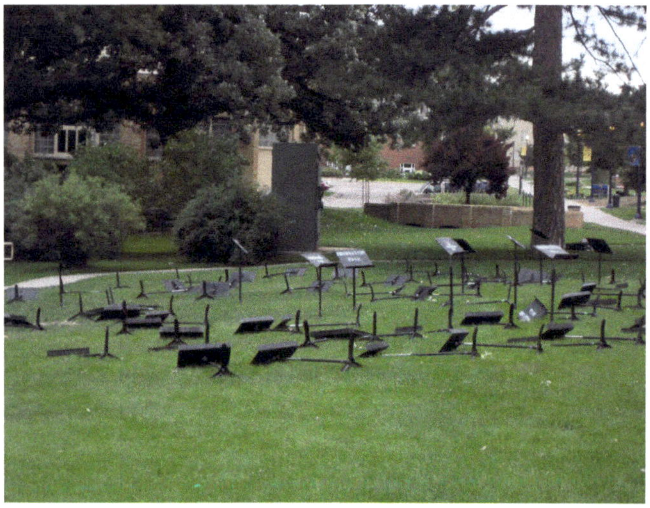

After. © 2025 by Anna Ursyn.

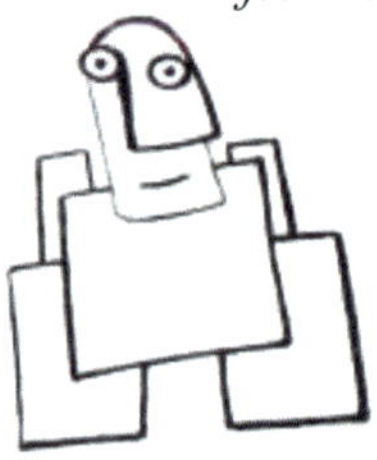

Jio: Mindfully connected.

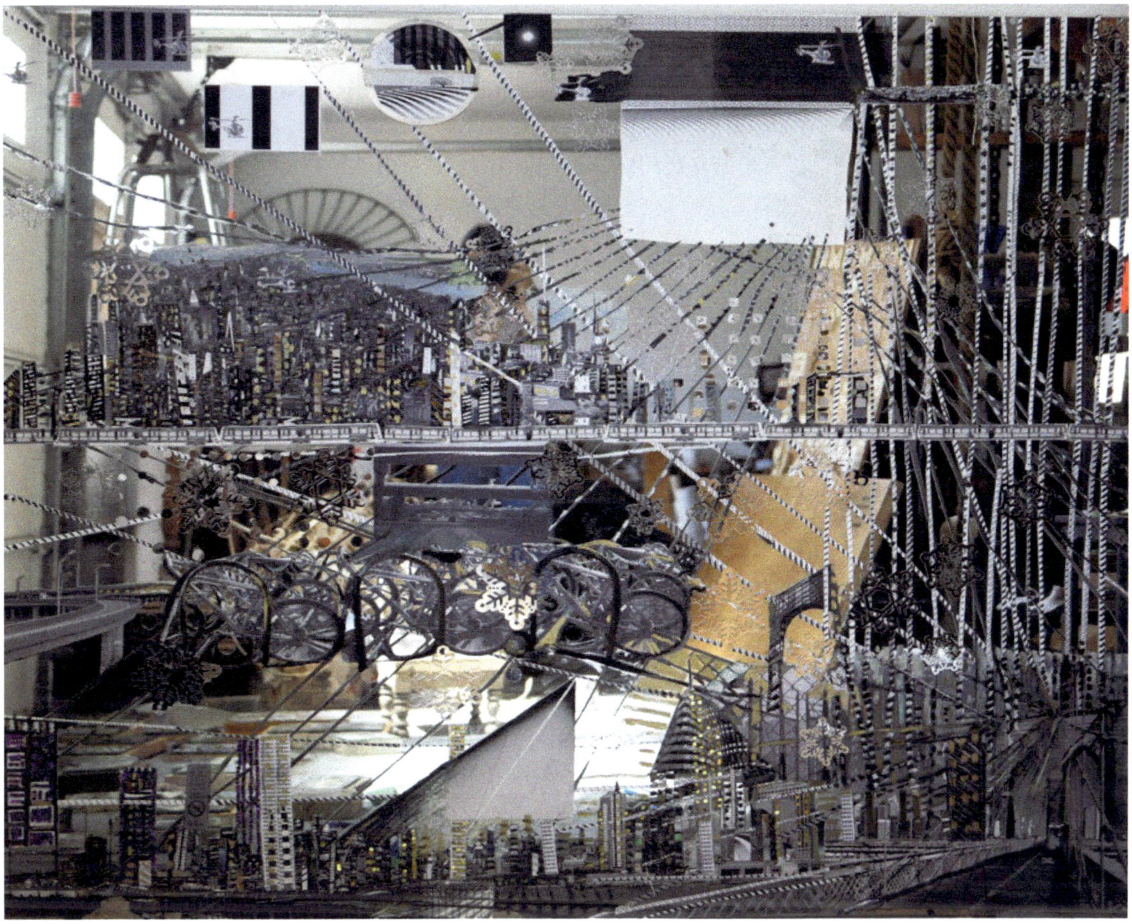

CHAPTER 3

TOOLS AND RULES: FINDING ONE'S PROFESSION

A FINGER THEATER PLAY WITH TEN FINGERS AND TWO TOES

ANYTHING DEVELOPED CAN BE ARGUED TO BE USING THE ELEMENTS AND PRINCIPLES OF ART!

INTRODUCTION

We possess different skills, types of intelligences, talents, and areas of interest. We appreciate various things on different levels. While some students know exactly the spectrum of their focus, others feel lost, and their undeclared status creates uncertainty. Some receive advice to stay within a framework attached to their acknowledged status or position, which is pinned to them by the community to fit generally accepted or family standards related to how they were born.

Finding one's niche is not easy for them in a competitive world. This work discusses the challenges facing those who seek professional satisfaction gained by looking through the lenses of the power of art. The Elements of Art and Design (the Tools) and the Principles of Art and Design (the Rules) are juxtaposed across various fields of work to show that everything is connected, and we work through collaborative efforts based on individual talents, intellects, passions, and skills.

SYNOPSIS

A group of students gathers after their first introductory class and ends up discussing their hopes and goals. Some of them know exactly what they want to do about their future career, but one, not liking anything at all, feels lost and undecided, not to count the twins in the same lost position because they like and enjoy everything.

To help their classmates, students rush with ideas, helpful suggestions, stories, and comments, which makes the situation worse. After one suggests looking at their future professions from a larger perspective, they regroup and decide to focus just on two variables. The Elements and Principles in art and design are the tools we have and the rules we use. Everyone tries to explore and explain their discipline just to come up with the group conclusions that everything is related, people have different talents, we do better what we enjoy doing, the world is a collaborative place, and everything we do can be a story. In the end, the students stop worrying and start exploring. Howard Gardner and the connections between various disciplines help, too. It is all about imprinting respect toward others' skills, talents, and strengths rather than comparing ourselves with others, copying ideas, or attributing others 'solutions to our purposes. They are like fingers forming a hand that collaborates with other hands.

SUMMARY

This work suggests ideas for selecting one's professional future. Through collaborative efforts, it stresses finding interests and strengths and examining the connections between disciplines. This motion-based, highly visual performance illustrates the tools and rules available for professions.

THE CAST OF CHARACTERS

Hubert, (bright heart, English in Brazil, skeleton), the musician
Cody, (helpful person), the coder
Amina نآقمه (feel safe in Arabic), the artist
Qiáng 强 (strong in China), the writer
Pierre, (rock in French, from the Greek word stone πέτρος via Latin "petra"), undecided
Hina 陽菜 (sun and plants in Japan), biology /nursing/ medicine
Roksolana, Роксолана (tied with supernatural connotations in Ukraine),
Som สม or สยามชื่อส้ม (well suited) and Tam สยามชื่อตัม (twin) Siamese, Thai. Undeclared twins.
Chia-wie 俊宏 (light, power, lofty in Taiwan), geology
Kamari كا رامى(Moon in Africa), chemistry, math
Panagiotis, Παναγιώτης (all holly, pan=all, hagios=holly in Greece), education
Tuah, هغ تواه, (Luck or fortune-Malay), dance/theater

STAGE DIRECTIONS

A large classroom with a table and chairs is shown for the students to interact after the introductory lecture has concluded. The students are dressed to show each discipline they describe. They hold related symbols or artifacts, except for those undeclared in white. The texts scroll on the screen, with the American Standard Code on the right side of each field.

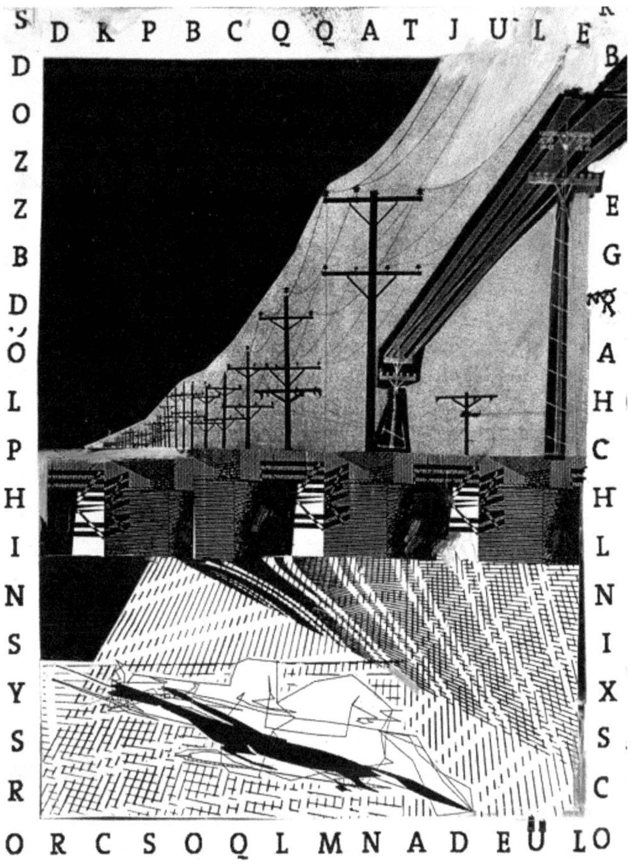

Electrical Syntax. © 2025 by Anna Ursyn

Act I
The curtain goes up (or opens).

A group of students gathers to socialize after their first introductory class.

Panagiotis, "It was an interesting intro, and he seems like a nice teacher, but the amount of work expected for the general introductory freshman course seems overwhelming."

Tuah, "Yes, and we must take this class to be able to start studying towards our majors."

Pierre asks, "Do you all know what you want to do in your future career?"

Qiáng replies," Of course, I know I want to be a writer. And a good one. I have a lot to say, observe, discuss, and research. I want to influence people worldwide. I want to change the world."

Pierre asks, "So, you want to be a politician, then? I was once told at the '*All for Good Camp*' that if I wanted to change the world, I should study education, not politics. But teaching is not for me. I do not relate to kids well."

Panagiotis opposes him, "Education is everything. That is true, but how can it be possible not to relate to the little kids? I can only think of education. I want to teach them it all."

Pierre adds, "That still leaves me open-minded. I wouldn't say I like anything in a special way to studying it. I cannot envision myself in any profession. I only like to travel, but for fun only."

Amina states, "You can be a photographer, then. If you ask me, I want to be an artist. My parents tried to persuade me not to, but there is no other way for me to be."
Pierre, "Good for you. I am not fast enough to capture a moment, and photographing landscapes is not my thing. You need permission to take pictures of people; thus, I prefer not to study to learn languages. It's too complicated and time-consuming."

Cody says, "As for me, I live by coding. Sometimes, I must stop my car on a busy interstate to quickly scribble down my newly emerging coding prospects, and the new ones keep flowing."

Amina adds, "I know the feeling. I am not upset if someone copies my ideas, as I have so many."

Hubert adds, "All my family members are involved in music. I knew since I was a little boy that I wanted to be a musician, and I had no other choice—no questions about that. Harmony and melody are my things. Music works with codes, too. And you, Chia-wei?"

Chia-wei, "For me, geology is my major. I love to move, and I adore rocks and their formations. Process and product are my things. You all know: the cycle. And I am so outdoorsy."

Tuah adds, "I also like movement. I am majoring in dance and theater. I like to move to the point that it is hard for me to sit still. I like to recite, make speeches, mimic accents, and, most of all, I practically live on stage. Beyond that, there is no life for me."

Hina adds, "I want to study Nature; Biology is probably the closest thing. Maybe a medical field. I think it all goes together. My parents want me to be a doctor."

Roksolana states, "I like helping people, so I picked psychology. I do yoga and more. How about you, Kamari?"
Kamari says, "I like math, especially chemical bonds, so chemistry is for me with a math minor."
But *Som and Tam* are lost and undecided, "We are the twins, and we do everything together. We even dress the same way. But since we are so close, we enjoy everything without knowing what to focus on."

Amina, "We'll help you. We are like fingers forming a hand that collaborates with other hands."

Som and Tam, "We rather feel like toes. Being lost is like not belonging anywhere."

Hubert suggests, "Since you are friendly, do hospitality."

Cody adds, "My uncle, as a young man, had a hotel, and his guests loved him, but he did not like accounting."

Amina comments, "One can make much money doing it."

Pierre worries, "But it does not help me decide. I need to declare my major soon. It makes me sleepless."

Rokosolana decides, "Proper sleep is essential. We must help him."

Cody recalls, "How about Howard Gardner and his theory of multiple intelligences? Let's find connections between various disciplines. Would that help?"

Pierre, "Hmm?"

Cody explains, "Howard Gardner believes that we all have some strong intelligences, respectively. He named eight: Spatial, Linguistic, Musical, Logical-Mathematical, Bodily-kinesthetic, Intrapersonal, Interpersonal, and Naturalistic. Find out which ones you have. Take the test online."
https://www.idrlabs.com/multiple-intelligences/test.php

Amina adds, "There are aptitude tests to determine someone's skills or interests."

Pierre disagrees, "My intelligence is booking tickets and following the path. I still need help."

Som and Tam together, "We like everything the same way. We also need help declaring a major. We are as undecided as undeclared."
Pierre adds, "Howard Gardner is all about respect. We compare ourselves with one another. That makes us miserable because we can always find someone better at something, faster, smarter, or stronger. You get the point."

Panagiotis, "So, education should imprint the students to recognize different talents, acknowledge them, and start a journey after one's own, rather than comparing themselves, following trends, or taking someone else's ideas as their own to shine."
Tuah wants to add, "Everything is related; people have different talents, we do better what we enjoy doing, and the world is a collaborative place."
Kamari suggests, "We should be looking at our future professions from a larger perspective, so let's regroup and decide to focus on just one or two variables. What are the tools that are crucial for your success? What would you see as rules that are present in your discipline? Are there any guides or restrictions? Anyone? What do they offer you to work with?"
Amina exclaims, "Elements and principles in art and design, it is.
Pierre, "Ha?"
Amina continues, "Elements and Principles of Design in Art are what is available to make art with color, values, forms and shapes, space, lines, and textures. Because of them, art can be created. They all can be observed in nature and in the environments we develop. Elements of Design denote tools for the artist/designer or visual communication, while Principles of Design describe how the elements are used through balance, emphasis, movement, variety, proportion, and unity."
Amina keeps going, **"The Elements of Design in Art."**
Line defines space in drawing and painting or even in sculpture. We may repeat it with the use of symmetry, spiral, or radial; it can be black or another color, straight, curved, etc., while thick or thin; wavy, curved, or angular: continuous or broken; dotted, dashed, and more, or any of these.
Colors are found in traditional and digital art. Tangible art uses red, yellow, and blue pigments, while digital art uses red, green, and blue lights. Secondary colors are also used. Not orange, green, and purple, but Cyan, magenta, and yellow are used in printing with CMYK. Mixing primary and secondary colors creates intermediate colors. Additive and subtractive models are discussed.
Value refers to how light or dark a color is. Tint is when a color is mixed with white, shaded with black, and toned when combined with gray.
Cody interrupts, "Here's an example code in Python that shows how colors can be represented using numbers and letters: We are talking about light here, not pigment."
Cody continues, "In this code, the colors red, green, and blue are represented as tuples of three numbers, where each number represents the intensity of red, green, and blue, respectively, on a scale of 0 to 255. For example, red is defined as the tuple (255, 0, 0) because it has a maximum intensity of red and zero intensity of green and blue. The other colors in the code snippet are shown using hexadecimal color codes, a combination of six letters and numbers that represent the intensity of red, green, and blue. The first two letters/numbers define the intensity of red, the second two represent green, and the last two are blue. For example, black is presented as "#000000" because it has zero intensity of red, green, and blue. In contrast, white is "#FFFFFF" because it has a maximum intensity of red, green, and blue."
Amina continues, "Thank you, Cody."
Form and Shape
All objects have a shape (flat) or form (dimensional). Geometric shapes like circles, triangles, and squares have no volume. Geometric primitives are basic forms or Platonic forms. A volume describes the weight and thickness of an object.
Space around us is a void between forms, objects, and shapes. It surrounds drawing and painting in 2D and 3D formats, like 3D printing and architecture. Negative space is between two objects.
Texture is a substance or material around us. It can be natural, invented, manufactured, actual, or simulated as rough, smooth, hard, soft, natural, or artificial to look and feel like real textures.

Principles of Design in Art are the rules for an artist to use design elements.
Balance is the arrangement of the elements of design. It can be formal or symmetrical (with equal weight

on both sides), informal or asymmetrical (with different weights on each side), or radial (with a circular balance moving out from a central object to maintain balance).
Emphasis brings focus into art or design as crucial between the leading and following elements. Larger or heavier in volume objects, shapes, or colors darker than the subordinate ones dominate a picture. The arrangement of shapes helps the eye shift from one part of the image to another.
Variety and Contrast help with diversity and differences in design to bring emotions. Contrasting colors, textures, and patterns help to make the artwork interesting. The corners or edges of shapes are highlighted with colors. We use the opposite colors to add contrast.
Proportion is the size of one part of the artwork relative to its other functions. It aids in showing emphasis, distance, use of space, and balance.
Unity is the way all elements and principles work together. All parts relate to each other to create the overall message and desired effect."
Som and Tam, "It makes us want to make art."

Hubert,,"There must be a way to use it all in music! It looks like music uses the elements and principles of design just like people use it in art:"
`A related projection shows each element and principle of design. Matching visuals and music in the background illustrate the descriptions. AI can be employed.`

Kamari adds, "Yes, but not only in music."
Hubert continues, "Art, music, science, and math all share design principles and require creative minds. Metaphoric representation is used in art and music to evoke emotions. Math and science use symbols and numbers, while music symbolizes notes. Most of these disciplines have order and rhythm, and they often have balance. Different terms have similar outcomes. In music, variety can be achieved using altered rhythms, melody, and color, while in visual arts, by placement, theme, and color. Visual representations of concepts in science and mathematics are better understood with contrast. Visual, societal, and life-oriented messages are communicated with beauty in art. There is a common need to simplify their meaning in graphical displays. Music involves science (physics of sound waves) and math (metered beats and measures, music theories). Visualization techniques are common. Principles of art can be used to teach math and science visually. The aesthetic dimensions of science are often discussed. Various forms of art, music, and many areas of science, mathematics, business, education, communication, and criminal justice all use similar principles of design—unity, and variety in music offer altered rhythms, melody, and color. In visual arts, variety can be provided by placement, theme, and color. Visual representations of concepts in science and mathematics are better understood with contrast."

Cody wonders aloud, "How would those elements and principles of design look like in coding?"

Elements and Principles of Design in Programming

Elements of Design in Coding

Color aids speed and information, so reading and editing the code becomes faster.
- Color coding structures the code:
- We are talking about light here, not pigment.
- Colors are represented as numbers and letters.

RGB model:	**Hex model:**
White = [255, 255, 255]	White = 0xffffff
Black = [0, 0, 0]	Black = 0x000000
Blue = [0,0,255]	Blue = 0x0000ff
Red = [255, 0,0]	Red = 0xff0000
Green = [0,255,0]	Green = 0x00ff00
Gray = [128, 128, 128]	Gray = 0x7a

Form and Shape

Graphical User Interface GUI offers windows as controls, "OK," or "Cancel" buttons.
- Visual controls (buttons, text boxes) and non-visuals (e.g., a timer class) are seen on the form.

- Shapes with symbols, (),{} [], or <> control the order of operations in an expression.
- The Oval Shape=start/end, Rectangle=a process, Diamond=a decision, Parallelogram=the input/output, Arrow=the flow of the sequence.
- Different characters are used for the comments in various programming languages. (//, #, etc.)
- Some servers see lower-case letters as different from the upper-case, causing problems.

Space

- A memory space is essential to run an algorithm.
- Program uses memory to execute and is represented by its space complexity.
- Memory is required to run a program and to store input data and values.

Lines

- One line may generate one or several instructions for a computer.
- Lines of code are different for various languages and other tasks.
- Few lines of code might require more lines in another type of language.
- We do not evaluate codes by the length of instructions.
- Lines of source code guide writing instructions.
- The same output can be made of a short or long list of instructions.

Texture

- Shaders, texture as a 1D/2D/3D grid of pixel values with different interpolation filters
- Values can be sampled from the texture to provide data and commands to the computer.

Principles of Design in Coding

Balance

- Work-Life Balance - not overworking and taking breaks for mental and physical well-being.
- Load Balancing - distributing the workload evenly to prevent bottlenecks.
- Resource Balancing - memory, CPU, disk space, and other resources are utilized optimally.
- Balancing Algorithms for efficient search and retrieval operations.
- Balance in Software Design Patterns-the distribution of components, classes, or modules
- A typo sends an error message in red, and the code stops running.

Hina states, "Whap, the last one cannot be cool."

Emphasis

- Comments - non-executable lines for the purpose, functionality, or reasoning behind blocks.
- Naming Conventions - clear and expressive names for self-documenting to understand.
- Formatting: emphasize the structure of the code, including indentation, spacing, and alignment
- Use of Whitespace - blank lines to separate sections for readability and to make it appealing.
- Code Structure and Flow - highlights important steps or decisions to enhance readability.
- Error Handling and Validation - by indicating error-checking validating inputs.
- Documentation - to emphasize usage guidelines, important considerations, or design decisions.

Movement

- Code Execution Flow - the order in which statements and instructions are executed.
- Code Navigation - moving between different sections or files with keyboard shortcuts.
- Data Movement - assigning values to variables, passing data between functions, or updating.
- Code Version Control - to track changes involves branching, merging, and committing them.
- Animating Graphics or UI - changing the position or appearance of visual elements over time.

Variety and Contrast

- Coding Styles - consistent indentation and code formatting improve readability.
- Naming Conventions - consistent, descriptive names to avoid confusion.
- Programming Paradigms - using both imperative and declarative programming styles.
- Object-oriented vs. Functional Programming: based on the nature of the problem to solve.
- Design Patterns - pattern for event handling; strategy for algorithmic variations.
- Code Organization: structuring code into modules and packages logically.

- Varied Documentation Styles - using comments-inline and comprehensive documentation.
- Testing: unit and integration testing in the codebase so components work correctly.

Proportion

- Indentation and Formatting - visually organize code to make it easier to follow.
- Code Comments - to explain complex code sections, especially if the logic is not apparent.
- Function and Class Length - smaller, focused functions or classes improve readability.
- Each function or class should ideally perform a specific task to understand and maintain code.
- Consistent Naming Conventions for variables, functions, and classes.

Unity

- Modularity - breaking down code into modules or functions that handle specific tasks.
- Encapsulation - the implementation details are hidden, and only what is necessary is exposed.
- Loose Coupling - minimizing dependencies changes in one module without affecting others.
- High Cohesion - the elements within a module are related to a specific functionality.
- Consistent Coding Style - for better readability and maintainability.
- Communication - between different modules or components through well-defined interfaces.

Tam and Som, "It makes us want to code."

Hubert exclaims, "Yes, everything is connected. Let's see how they can be applied to music!"

Elements and Principles of Design in Music

Elements of Design in Music

Color

- Timbre (Tone Color) is a sound's unique quality or color that sets it apart from other sounds.
- Harmony and chord progression go with emotions or moods, creating a sense of color.
- Orchestration: The choice of instruments and their combinations for the overall color of a piece.
- Dynamics: Changes in volume, from soft to loud and vice versa.
- Melody and Rhythm: a lyrical melody- warm, rich colors, a staccato - sharper or cooler color.
- Cultural and Symbolic scale or mode-specific emotional or spiritual qualities.

Value of Color

- The value of color gives volume as the amplitude of the sound wave.

Som and Tam, "It makes us want to make art."

- Louder sounds require more energy, but each musician produces different ones.
- Two waveforms out of phase by 180 degrees will cancel each other, thus no sound.
- A single sound has pitch = changing the frequency of a waveform.
- A sound waveform, such as a vibrating string, can change the pitch of a note when it is shorter.
- String reduced by half produces an octave higher note than the note.
- In some cultures, segments for a musical scale music use a twelve-tone octave.

Form and Shape

Form - the overall structure of a composition with melody, harmony, rhythm, and dynamics

-Different sections or parts of a piece are organized in a specific way to create a sense of order.
-Forms include binary form, ternary form, sonata-allegro form, rondo, theme, and variations.
-Binary Form: divides a piece into two distinct sections, often labeled as A and B.
-Ternary Form: consists of three sections, typically labeled as A-B-A.
-Sonata-Allegro Form: involves an exposition, development, and recapitulation.
-Rondo: Features a recurring theme with contrasting sections (ABACA, ABACABA, etc.).

Shape relates to musical contour intensity, tension, or dynamics within a piece.

- Dynamic Shape: changes in volume and intensity throughout a composition.
- Melodic Shape: the contour or trajectory of a melody, including rises and falls in pitch.
- Harmonic Shape: the progression of harmonies and tonalities, contributing to the emotional.

Cody interrupts, “And this is an example code snippet in Python that generates a Rondo (ABACADA) melody:

```
notes = ['A', 'B', 'C', 'D', 'E', 'F', 'G']


def rondo():
    melody = ''
    for i in range(len(notes)):
        melody += notes[i] # A
        for j in range(i):
            melody += notes[j] # B, C, etc.
        melody += notes[i]  # A
    return melody


print(rondo())
```

This code uses a list to create the Rondo melody with the ABACADA pattern. The loop adds notes to the pattern. When you run this code, it will print out the Rondo melody:
ABA CDC EFE GAGFEDCBA
Hubert continues, “Thank you, Cody!”
Cody, “and song (ABABCBB).”
- Form exists in multimovement works, operas, or cyclic ones.
- Shape the melody low in pitch to a climax, close to the end, to a low starting level.

Space

- Rests and Silence - to designate moments of silence within a musical piece for contrast.
- Punctuation and Phrasing - for a sense of structure with balance between notes and rests.
- Sustain and Decay - string instruments or synthesizers, change the length of notes.
- Ambient and Drone Music - use long, sustained sounds and minimalistic compositions.
- Dynamic Range - The contrast between loud and soft passages in music.
- Utilizing a wide dynamic range enhances the emotional impact of a composition.
- Call and Response - one musical idea is followed by a pause before another one responds.
- Improvisation - space to react to and interact with each other with intentional gaps.
- Production Techniques - spatial effects like reverb and delay for depth and distance.

Line

- A melodic line is a succession of musical notes perceived as a single, cohesive unit.
- A sequence of pitches and rhythms creates a distinct musical idea or motif.
- A musical phrase is based on this concept
- A part or section in a musical composition, such as a guitar, bass, or vocal line.
- The linear progression of musical events, a melody, the flow of a harmonic progression.

Texture

- Monophonic Texture - features a single, unaccompanied melodic line in solo or unison singing.
    - Homophonic Texture - In homophony, there is a primary melody and accompanying harmonies.
    - Polyphonic Texture - a polyphony combining two or more independent melodic lines.
    - Heterophonic when they play slightly different versions of the same melody simultaneously.
- Homorhythmic Texture - all voices/instruments move together rhythmically: uniform or cordial.
    - Monotextural Texture refers to music with a single, consistent texture throughout.
- Polytextural involves multiple contrasting textures happening simultaneously.

Principles of Design in Music

Balance

- Instrumental Balance - ensuring that the volume levels are appropriately adjusted cohesion.
- Frequency Balance - the frequencies within a mix; the bass, midrange, and treble frequencies
- Proper equalization (EQ) is often used to achieve this balance.
- Spatial Balance - the distribution of sound: the placement within the left and right channels.
- Dynamic Balance - the dynamic range and the variation in volume levels between the parts.
- Textural Balance - multiple layers or textures. Each one is audible and contributes appropriately.
- Emotional Balance - Beyond technical considerations, between tension and resolution.

Emphasis

- Dynamic Contrast - Changes in volume, known as dynamics, can create emphasis.
- Gradual increases or decreases in volume, accents, or intensity draw attention to elements.
- Rhythmic Emphasis - accents or stresses on beats or patterns to create a sense of emphasis.
- Syncopation involves accenting off-beats and adding a layer of interest and emphasis.
- Melodic Emphasis - A strong, memorable melody as a focal point in a piece of music.
- Emphasizing notes within a melody through dynamics, articulation, and phrasing to enhance impact.
- Harmonic Emphasis - harmony or chord progressions for tension and release for attention.
- Unexpected or dissonant chords can be used for emphasis.
- Instrumentation and Timbre - The choice of instruments and their timbral characteristics.
- A sudden instrumentation change, or a new timbre can grab the listener's attention.
- Articulation and Phrasing - how notes are played, including staccato, legato, accents, and slurs.
- Tempo Changes - for emphasis with accelerandos or ritardandos and sudden changes in tempo.
- Textural Changes - moving from a dense orchestration to a sparse one or vice versa.
- Repetition and Contrast - Emphasis stressing the motif's importance, to contrast for attention.
- Dynamics in Performance: Emphasizing certain elements through expressive interpretation.

Movement

- Rhythm - The arrangement of sounds and silences over time.
- Melody - A sequence of single pitches perceived as a cohesive entity.
- Harmony - Combining different musical notes to create a pleasing sound.
- Tempo - The speed or pace of a piece of music.
- Dynamics - The varying degrees of loudness and softness in music.
- Form - The overall structure or organization of a musical composition.
- Timbre - The unique quality or color of a sound that distinguishes it from other sounds.
- Meter - The recurring pattern of strong and weak beats in music.
- Phrasing - The shaping and grouping of phrases for expressive and meaningful interpretations.
- Texture - The interweaving of a piece's musical lines or layers.
- Modulation - Changing from one key to another within a piece of music.
- Counterpoint - Combining independent musical lines for a harmonically rich texture.
- Ornamentation - Decorative elements added to a melody or musical passage.
- Cadence -A sequence of chords that brings a sense of resolution to the end of a musical phrase.
- Improvisation - Creating music spontaneously without prior preparation.
- Syncopation - Emphasizing off-beat rhythms or weak beats in a musical meter.
- Polyrhythm - The simultaneous use of multiple rhythms in a musical composition.
- Ostinato - A repeating musical motif or pattern.
- Staccato - Short, detached notes in contrast to legato (smooth, connected notes).
- Crescendo/Decrescendo - Gradual increase or decrease in volume.
- Call and Response - A musical conversation between different instruments or voices.
- Glissando - Sliding between pitches.
- Aleatoric Music - Music in which some element of the composition is left to chance.
- Fugue - A contrapuntal composition: a theme introduced and repeated by entering voices.

Variety and Contrast

- Variety in music - Diverse elements and styles woven together to create a rich experience.
- Contrast in music - Sharp differences in dynamics, tempo, or tonality highlight the sections.
- Harmony - Blending different musical notes to create a pleasing sound.
- Dissonance - Intentional tension between musical notes, adding complexity and emotion.
- Instrumentation - The use of various instruments to bring different timbres and textures.
- Rhythm - Varying patterns of beats and accents to create a dynamic and engaging feel.
- Melody - A memorable sequence of musical notes that stands out amidst other elements.
- Dynamics - Fluctuations in volume add intensity and emotion to the musical expression.
- Genre Fusion - Blending elements from different genres to create a unique and eclectic sound.
- Instrumental Contrast - Alternating solo and ensemble passages for a diverse experience.

Proportion

- Melody - The horizontal sequence of single pitches that form a musical line.
- Harmony - The simultaneous combination of different pitches to create chords.
- Rhythm - The ways of time, including the arrangement of beats, durations, & patterns of accents.
- Dynamics - The variations in loudness and intensity in music.
- Timbre - The quality or color of a sound that distinguishes it from other sounds (tone color).
- Texture - Different musical lines and voices are combined to create the overall sound of a piece.
- Form - The structure and organization of a piece, with sections as verses, choruses, and bridges.
- Tempo - The speed or pace of a musical piece.
- Meter - The recurring pattern of strong and weak beats in music.
- Counterpoint - The combination of different melodic lines in a harmonically interesting way.
- Cadence - A series of chords to bring a sense of resolution to a musical phrase or piece.
- Scale - A collection of pitches arranged in ascending or descending order.
- Chord Progression - A series of chords played as a sequence to create harmonic movement.
- Modulation - Changing from one key to another within a piece of music.
- Ornamentation - Decorative elements are added to a melody to enhance its expressiveness.
- Articulation - How individual notes are played, including staccato, legato, and accents.
- Expression - The use of musical elements to convey emotion and feeling.
- Phrasing - The shaping and grouping of musical phrases for a sense of continuity and structure.
- Call and Response - A technique where another part answers one part of a musical phrase.
- Ostinato - A repeated musical motif or pattern that serves as a foundation for composition.

Unity

- Harmony - Combining different musical notes to create a pleasing sound.
- Melody - A sequence of single pitches that is musically satisfying and memorable.
- Rhythm - The pattern of sounds and silences in music, creating a sense of time and movement.
- Dynamics - The variations in loudness and intensity within a musical piece.
- Tempo - The speed at which music is played, often indicated by beats per minute (BPM).
- Texture - Different musical elements (melody, harmony, rhythm) create the overall sound.
- Form - The structure and organization, including sections like verses, choruses, and bridges.
- Timbre - The quality or color of a sound to distinguish between different instruments or voices.
- Counterpoint - Combining independent melodies to create a harmonically rich musical texture.
- Tension and Release - Using musical elements creates a sense of anticipation and resolution.
- Scale - A series of pitches in ascending or descending order for melodies and harmonies.
- Chord Progressions - Sequences of chords that form the harmonic foundation of a musical piece.
- Cadence - A series of chords that bring a musical phrase or section to a close for resolution.
- Ornamentation - Decorative elements in melody or musical passage for expressive purposes.
- Meter - The organization of beats into regular patterns, such as 4/4, 3/4, or 6/8 time.
- Pitch - The perceived frequency of a sound, determining whether it is high or low.
- Modulation - A change in a key within a musical piece, often used to create variety and interest.
- Articulation - How musical notes are played or sung, including legato, staccato, & accentuation.

- Syncopation - Accenting beats or offbeats, not emphasized, adding rhythmic complexity.
- Improvisation - Creating and performing music spontaneously within a defined framework.

Tam and Som, "It makes us want to make music."
Pierre, "It makes more sense. And how about writing?
Qiáng, "Here comes writing:"

The Elements and Principles of Art in Writing

The world is visual. Writing can be written, spoken, visual, auditory, or even calculated. Text aids in describing hard-to-visualize abstract concepts. Writing and language-based artists create by sending a message, communicating, and perceiving it. A story can be told in a visual way, be text- or speech-based, or illustrated. A story triggers audiences' imagination in a symbiotic way to deliver a multisensory, multidisciplinary experience, depending on the audience's needs.

The Elements of Design in Writing

Color
- It helps deliver a story, and the lack of it makes a statement.
- Colorful language or metaphors are used for descriptions when replacing illustrations.

Value
- The length of sentences brings dimension without flat, plain, or monotonous stories.
- The diversity of characters and actions supports interest.

Shape and Form
- Adds dimension to writing.
- Syntax and diction are both used to supplement the body of writing.

Space
- Mostly used in creative writing.
- Poets put larger spaces between lines and stanzas.
- For tension, writers or speakers often put space in their work to make a pause or break.

Line
- Lines make paragraphs and stanzas to form sentences.
- Words and language are set together to unify work.

Texture
- We only feel text if it is written in Braille.

Cody interrupts, "Here's a sentence in Braille:
[illegible]
And here's the English translation: "Hello, world! This is a sentence in Braille. Raised dots are to be read by people who do not see well with their fingertips. It is used for reading and writing various languages, including English. The second sentence is written in another format, not Braille, so it does not need to be translated into Python. However, if you want to print this text in Python, you can use the print() function:
print("Hello, world! This is a sentence in Braille.")
This will output the text "Hello, world! This is a sentence in Braille." to the console."

Qiáng continues, "Thank you, Cody,
- We feel tools, the surface, a keyboard, and a mouse all form grip and comfort.
- Writers describe texture with words using metaphors.

Hubert Interrupts, "Cody, one more interruption, and we'll continue without you, please."

Qiáng continues, "Thank you, Hubert,

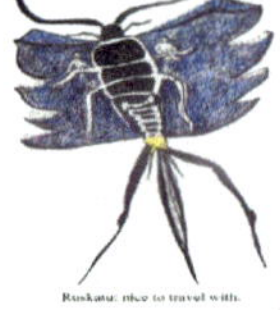

Raskatu: good to travel with.

The Principles of Design in Writing

Balance

- A story reads better without repetitive, out-of-context, or heavy words.
- Selective choice of words supports more transparent communication.
- Editing helps to leave out what is relevant and crucial in the story, helping to perceive it.

Emphasis

- Making some parts of a story important gives writing m when read or heard, gives writing meaning.
- By stressing selected words, one makes a point about something.
- Various formatting such as italics, underlining, or bold can be more inflectional.
- Repetition of a word highlights an idea.

Movement

- The sounds of the words are used as a linguistic way to fit them together.
- The ways of pronouncing make the fragments of a story move.
- Metaphors add to the perception of an idea: an abstract concept against a regular one.
- A repeating pattern is a motif in art, music, and literature.

- Many stylistic choices add variety to the writers 'work.
- Changing the focus of the work allows it to bring a new perspective to literature.
- Writers use different styles to enhance each sentence for creative liberties.

Proportion

- The number of letters in a word,
- words in a sentence
- the length of paragraphs within a page
- number of pages within a chapter
- chapters within a book.
- books in the library
- writings on the Internet

Unity

- It ties all the elements and principles of writing together.
- Words forming lines must sound good together.
- Each work should have a beginning, a conflict, an ending, and a moral.
- Everything we do is a story.

Som and Tam together, "Wow! It is all connected! It makes us want to write."

Roksolana, "Let's have a break!"

Hina, "Break it is: 10 minutes!"

The Break
The curtain goes down (or closes).

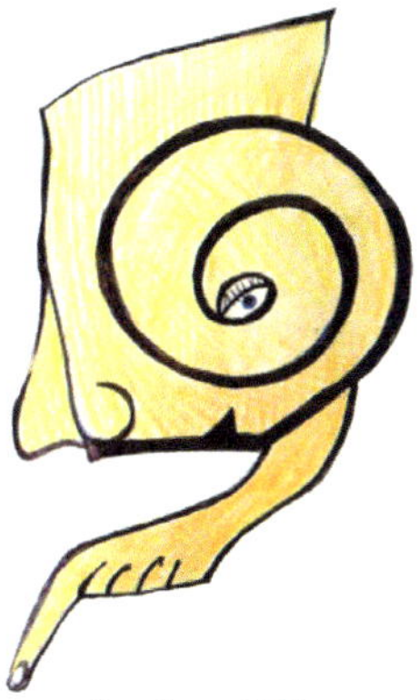

Erux: knows it all.

Erux: knows about everything.

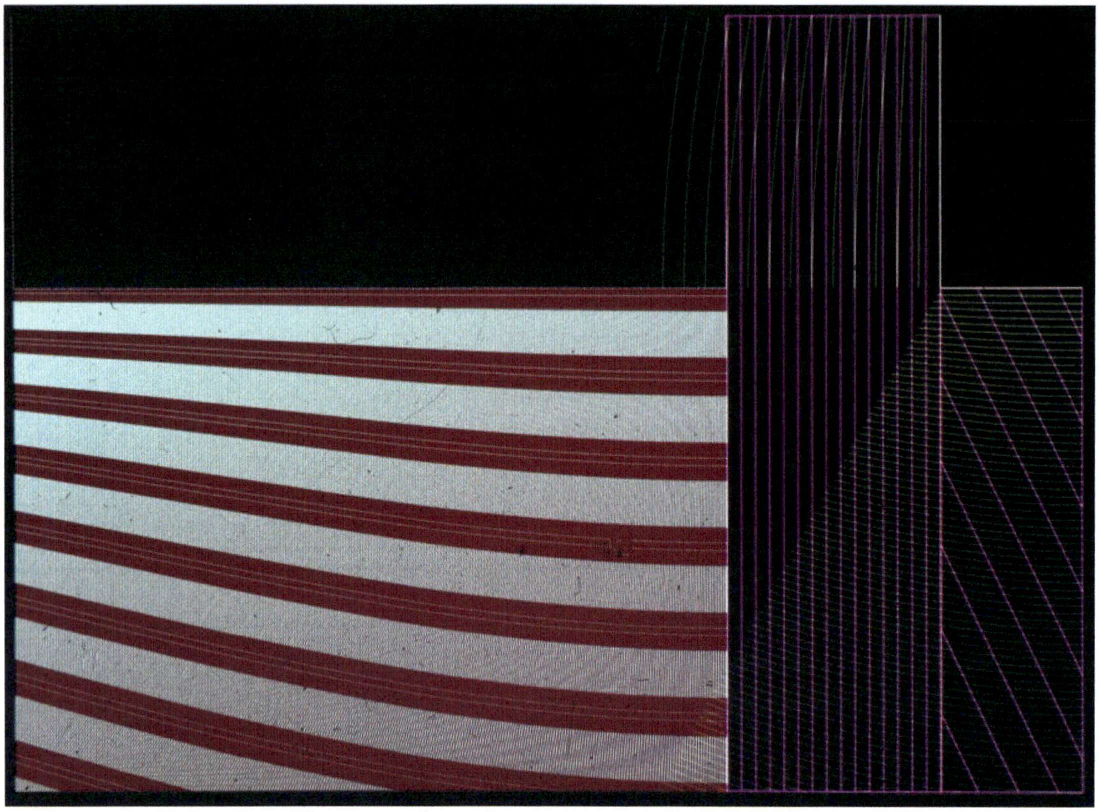

Belonging. The output from the computer code. © *2025 by Anna Ursyn*

Act II
The curtain goes up (or opens).

Roksolana thinks aloud, "We need to define and then understand our audience when writing, and psychology can be helpful in any profession. It is broad and involves people. Psychiatry helps people with medications. While psychology is through therapy for mental treatment, psychology is also about how we perceive. It involves our senses (see, hear, smell, taste, and feel, and more)."

The Elements and Principles of Design in Psychology

Elements of Design in Psychology

Color

- It is connected to moods and emotions; blues and greens, calming colors, relax us.
- They encourage some behaviors, i.e., warm ones, for spontaneity.
- Colors can provoke actions and responses, sensations, and perceptions.
- Their meaning differs across cultures and can have positive or adverse effects.
- In marketing or advertising, they know colors that make us happy, calm, or hungry.

Value

- Social psychology studies people's thoughts, feelings, and behaviors as influencers.
- Personalities are defined in treatment at the beginning or after for progress on a scale of 1-10.
- Moods can be set in value through mood lamps or dimmers.

Shape and Form

- Rorschach Ink Blot tests assess cognitive functioning, type, or psychological conditions.
- Therapists use geometric and organic shapes for patients to feel nature and growth.

- Patterns are fast brain shortcuts for missing parts that add negative spaces to the image.
- Friendly signs, symbols, and icons embedded into motivational posters decorate spaces.

Space

- Emotional boundaries with others 'feelings or openness are unique and changing.
- The space between the patient and the door must be accessible to connect, not trap.
- We instinctively perceive images as foreground or background using structure and logic.
- The principle of proximity sees closeness as more related than what's set apart.
- Space allows multiple people to use the room simultaneously, allowing for comfort.
- Exercises like stretching or drills used for rehabilitation need space.

Line

- A written or drawn journal is expected for therapists to help patients more effectively.
- Zigzag lines boost energy, interest, engagement, and excitement; used for organization.
- Horizontal lines connect us with Nature, our mind and spirit.
- Lines connect or create boundaries, respectively to enhance comfort.
- Visualizing data about a person or group via observations is essential in psychology.

Texture

- A clipboard or personal notebook journal has a different feel.
- Different sensory receptors allow our senses to understand and interpret the world.
- Patients often touch something while expressing deep emotions.
- In gender definition, texture plays roles from our feelings to personalities.
- Therapy uses simulated textures like schemas, a cognitive information framework.
- Different textures affect people's happiness, sadness, or angriness.

Principles of Design in Psychology

Balance

- A balanced workspace promotes energy, so therapists use it.
- People cannot walk or stand without balance.
- A balance in emotions and personality traits contributes to our mental health.
- Medium stress levels help motivate and perform, according to Yerkes-Dodson Law.
- Balances help with tests, better staff morale, and patient care.
- In the workspace, balance eases navigation around it.
- In physical therapy rooms, balance helps the trainers to work more efficiently and freely.
- Waiting rooms have an equal number of chairs on each side of the room.

Emphasis

- Cognitive therapy focuses on how people think more than what they do.
- When changing their thoughts, patients change what they do and how they feel.
- Therapy is after emphasizing positive coping methods and personal strengths.
- The primacy effect refers to when we remember the first item as the best.
- The words or quotes work better when placed in a visible space.
- When reporting treatments, things or wishes are highlighted or in a different color text.

Movement

- Exercise is a healing tool that helps release endorphins for a healthy mind and body.
- Disorders can be observed in hand wringing, shaking legs, or facial movements.
- Diagrams of abstract concepts create a visual motion with arrows and forms.
- Surgeons use movement in the floors, furniture, and machine designs.
- Our movement changes our behavior, and our behavior changes our direction.
- In the waiting rooms, actions on televisions create movement.
- Walking is encouraged for mental and physical balance.

Variety and Contrast

- Everyone gets unique and personalized treatment techniques, ideas, and elements.
- Mindfulness, movement, and art therapy help people connect on another level.

- There is a common saying, "Variety is the spice of life."
- Contrasting or contradicting variations of therapeutic tools and thoughts are used.
- The psychological concepts of stage theorists versus incremental theorists differ.
- Variety and contrast are used in medical scans. Variety makes things unique.
- Athletic training rooms are never identical to represent their specific purpose.
- The contrast effect is a cognitive bias that distorts our view compared to something else.

Proportion

- Proportion is used to analyze data to draw conclusions and compare numbers.
- Prescribing medication uses the weight of the person for the desired effect.
- Proportionate sampling is used for studies to make the data more accurate.
- Research models explain those functions in the body that are invisible to us.

Unity

- Evidence-based practice ensures the care of patients, so the treatment works.
- Oneness and connectedness for a conducive work environment.
- Spaces set up stylistically convey feelings or a particular environment.
- Harmony with one's actions and change in behavior affect each other.
- Mindfulness sets us in the present: no changing the past or predicting the future.

"Yes," *states Hina*, "I want to be a doctor. Those are also present in this field and affect the psychological interpretation of information, which helps with proper physical healing:

Elements and Principles of Design in the Medical Field

Elements of Design in the Medical Field

Color and Value

- White stands for cleanness and purity; some people associate it with hospital walls.
- In waiting and doctor rooms, colors are selected for comfort, not excitement.
- The settings in a hospital could impact patients' mental state, affecting healing.
- Colors are used to inform patients of the staff's ranks and nurses about patients' pain level.

Shape and Form

- Signs give us directions, warn us of danger, set order, or offer help.
- Doctors use various tools with the ideal size to be effective for their roles.
- Medication comes in all shapes and forms to avoid confusion and misuse.
- Shapes inform nurses, doctors, and techs about waste, chemicals, and materials.
- Abnormal cells and growths are shown visually in cells in organs and biological systems.

Space

- It is needed in hospitals and clinics for doctors to see more patients.
- Technological advancements, machines, and new inventions are now more compact.
- The interiors of the ambulances are spatial, open, and organized.
- Operation space needs to be organized and spacious for the speed of action of a team.

Line

- Separates and organizes space between patients and beds helps the hospital.
- Curtain's tracks set in lines are hung for patients 'privacy.
- Lines are used on charts of one's treatment, recovery, or notes.
- Lines help separate various information about patients.
- Accurate measurement of doses and precise incisions are crucial.
- Smooth surfaces such as metal, free from crevices bacteria can live in, for cleaning.
- The instruments used to perform surgery need textures for a better grasp and hold.
- Medical images such as X-rays, CT scans, fMRIs, and ultrasounds show lines in patterns.
- Lines are to evaluate tissues' histological patterns and study the impact of treatments.
- Diagnosis and evaluation help differentiate and monitor treatment.

Principals of Design in the Medical Field

Balance

- Medical spaces are set symmetrically with an equal number of chairs for each wall.
- The offices need to be balanced to avoid feeling overwhelmed.
- An equal number may refer to the official guidelines for a healthy diet.
- A well-balanced diet is needed to be healthy.

Emphasis

- Doctors highlight crucial results in bold or color in each paragraph and space them out.
- Those who can't get out of bed, red socks, need assistance, and yellow, free-to-move green ones.
- Socks also indicate the pain level to emphasize their need for help.
- The needles that may spread disease or are sharp, thus marked.

Movement

- The nurses move from room to room.
- Electrocardiograms create movement and monitor heart beating and blood pressure.
- Exercising and movement in the hospitals are essential.
- Beds, rolling machines, IV holders, and care centers are on wheels to be moved around.

Variety and Contrast

- Colors are to organize charts by letters of their names and the year the patient came.
- Information is organized with crucial information about each patient and their level of care.
- Scrubs are in different colors to denote specialties so patients can see where to get help.
- The white lab coats are for doctors, pink for nurses, and blue scrubs for surgical and maturity.
- Rooms for various age groups are decorated differently according to their interests.

Proportion

- Diagrams and models display various veins, arteries, bones, and cartilage envisioning.
- Nurses give patients the exact proportion of medicine doses based on their prescriptions.
- The furniture is proportionally set in the patients' rooms.
- Proportional room and has enough tools and equipment for everyone to use.

Unity

- Nurses see patients and conduct various tests to assess their overall health.
- The doctors cooperate with specialists to relay information needed during the surgery.
- Nurses, doctors, and techs work together to provide efficient service to each patient.
- Everything works together, from people and machines to the atmosphere in the place.
- The unity of the design can be the critical point in the effectiveness of healthcare.

Kamari adds, "When you think of it, you need to know chemistry to be a good doctor. Perhaps physics and math as well. Some find it surprising, but this is how the medical field goes. Speed and movement are often the key factors."

"Yes," *says Tuah.* "Movement and speed it is. I'm so ready to discuss dance and theater with various types of motions and footwork!"

Elements and Principles of Art in Theater and Dance

Elements of Art in Theater and Dance

Color and Value

- The lights define warm colors for happy scenes and cool ones for intense ones.
- It's in sets, make-up, stages, construction, props, lighting, costuming, and publicity.
- Adds meaning to the production and tone of the show for the audience's emotions.
- Colors set emotions towards the characters and can set the mood for each performance.
- Attire recognizes performers and informs about periods, economic standing, and status.
- Lighting with fixture gels sets focus on a character, group, props, backdrops, and theme.
- Brighter lights are for actors in black; a value dimmer is used for harder-to-seeing white.

Shape and Form

- The stage has its purpose; it is shaped for a location and mood to set room for spectacle.
- Props can be rectangular, circular, triangular, or organic bodies, creating shapes
- Dance, acting, and singing shape and form the visual technique to tell a story.
- Forms in theatres can be the black box, round, proscenium, thrust stages, and theatres.
- The placement of the furniture and actors on the stage forms a spectacle.
- Actors stand in a triangle or on diagonals, so the actor is at the triangle's apex.
- Dancers move forms, shapes, and forms to set frames for time-based media.
- Dancers form shapes behind a large screen to tell a story in shadow dancing.
- In technical arts, lights are programmed to look split to connect with things or videos.
- The spacing is crucial to set the flow well with strobe, dimmed, or laser light.

Space

- The director and the actors safely occupy the space to communicate effectively.
- Dances show shapes and angles, and band musicians and dancers use these effects.
- The performers are set through spacing for proper focus to make a scene more natural.
- More emotional space is needed when actors are furious than when content.
- Performers benefit from points on stage for setup and props, with projections for space.
- Directors put main characters at the front of the stage so the audience can focus on them.
- Blocking, laying the actors' movements out, and setting spacing in advance to flow on stage.
- Directors think about all angles so the audience can view every vital part of a play.
- Dance uses formations and spacing to communicate meaning visually and set emotions.

Line

- Lines are on the floor, the plaster line, lines in a script, or those used to block the stage.
- The lines are a sense of unity in the cast or are used to exclude one for a power shift.
- Walking in a line from stage left to right gives a sense of direction.
- For the final bow, performers bow together by forming a line.
- Choreographers make dance breaks or sequenced lines to attract the eye and to focus.
- Lines with bodies, limbs, furniture, lights, and props give a sense of importance.
- Each frame has its formations, shapes, and spacing, and they rely on one another.
- Lines are used in dance formations and positions when a pose or motion is shown.
- Horizontal, vertical, and straight bodies make the dancers look alike against solos.
- Lines are for setting high-low, slow-fast, strong-slow, strong-fast, loose-slow, loose-fast.

Texture

- For the audience to see well on the set, we exaggerate small details to show texture.
- Differently shaped gobos mimic the movement, and facial expressions must be emphasized.
- The set is as essential to the play's performance as the actual performance.
- Textures of the costumes of each actor display the character's growth throughout.
- Planning and spacing for the right person in a suitable space at the right time.
- The audience cannot feel texture but can see it in music or videos to get a definition.

Balance

- The design elements give a sense to the story, the performers, and the audience.
- Directors balance a stage; the actors deliver a story and guide emotion in a planned way.
- The rule of thirds can guide the feeling of order or chaos, like in photography.
- A balanced play with lighting, dance routines, and symmetry to see and understand everything.
- Choreographers will write the plan so each dancer mirrors another with technical help.

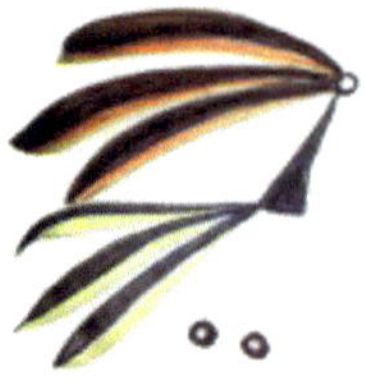

Fuftu: makes only right turns.

The Principles of Design in Theater and Dance

Emphasis

- We highlight what is needed using emotions, movement, costume, or a spotlight.
- Gobos (graphical optical black-out) are upside down and reversed for a unique texture.
- The lead person may change costumes in each scene to be shown as a main character.
- Speaking words with different voices and changing tone or pitch provides emphasis.
- The actors' lighting, props, and positioning make visible where the emphasis is.
- A character is set upstage, higher than others, lit more, talks louder, or through clothing.
- To focus on a point, attention is set through the lighting and positioning of the cast.

Variety and Contrast

- Directors help the audience understand the plot by changing things.
- Designers contrast protagonists and antagonists, so the audience understands the action.
- Theatres produce musicals, classical plays, tragedies, and comedies for audiences.
- Every performance is unique to the play's theme, between scenes and throughout a play.
- The actors provide accents at movements throughout the dance to focus attention.
- A dance routine uses a variety of focus on particular objects, ideas, or parts of the story.
- The contrasting colors of the costumes and light set a different mood and set characters.

Movement

- Without movement, performance, dance, or gig could not exist.
- Precisely planning, with timely reactions, conveys the story.
- To disclose a character's age, young, older, more uptight, or anal by acting or dancing.
- The audience's attention is directed to define the action's space, time, and place.
- Technical arts help by placing the lights to move, thus drawing attention.
- Concerts use the contrast between actions and between bands by making the stage dark.

Proportion

- Knowing their audience is crucial for directors, actors, and technical artists.
- A choreographer creates a proportion of actors and props without obstacles.
- The actors and dancers must be set proportionally on the stage for the flow.
- VR productions set the actors among the viewers; XR shows them small at a distance.
- A lead on the stage or music videos is set before the band for people to pay attention.
- When one person is separated from a group, the eyes go to that one person.
- The sets have an even number of props or furniture on all sides of the stage for the story.

Unity

- Period-related costumes or dance synchronization helps with visual effects.
- Actors deliver emotion to bond with unknown people.
- Actors, set designers, lighting crew, stage managers, and directors unite.
- Three principles are needed for the unity of the story for the audience: action, place, and time.
- Performers unify to act as one so the audience can escape their lives for a while.
- Everyone works to run smoothly and amusingly for a visual story with a message sent.
- Dance is one's style, but all parts must function together for success.

Tam and Som, "It makes us want to dance."

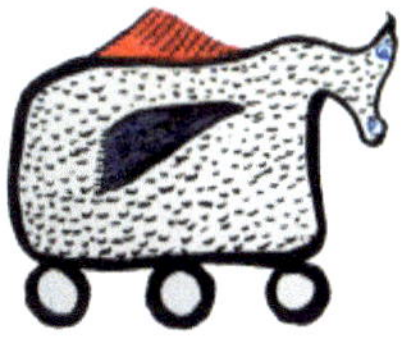

Vesador: leads a multifunctional life.

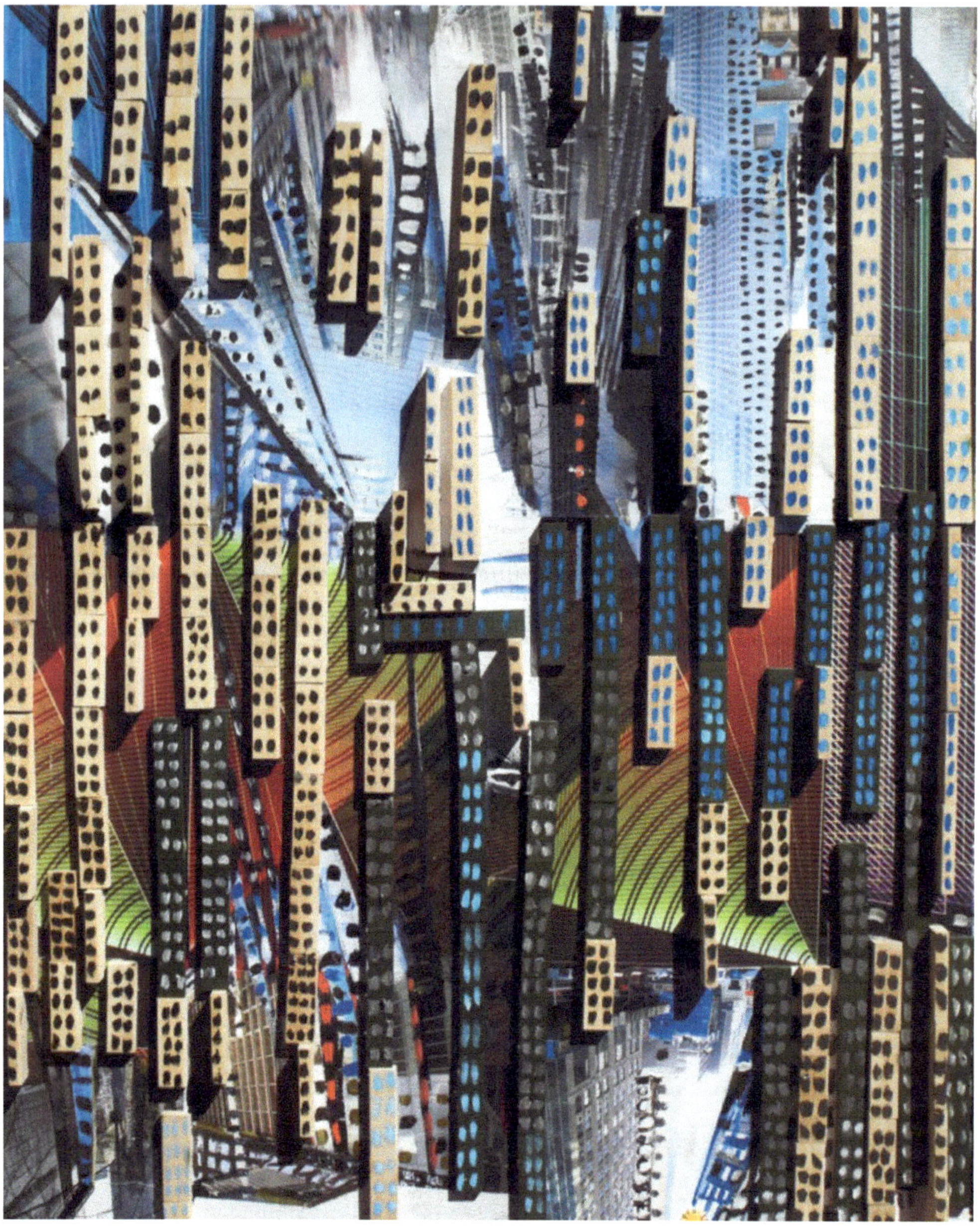

Planet's Texture. © 2025 *by Anna Ursyn*

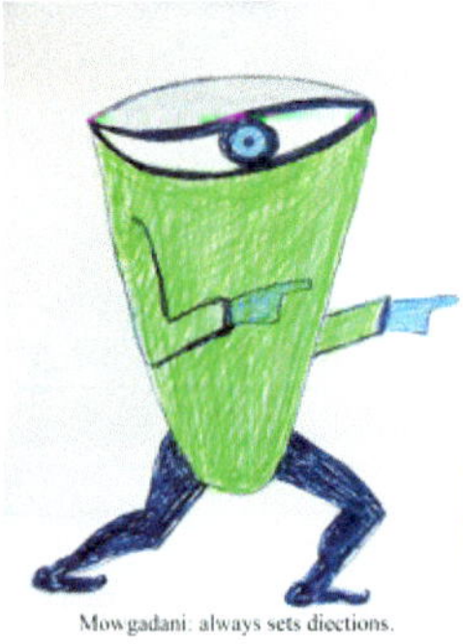

Mowgadani: sets trends for habits.

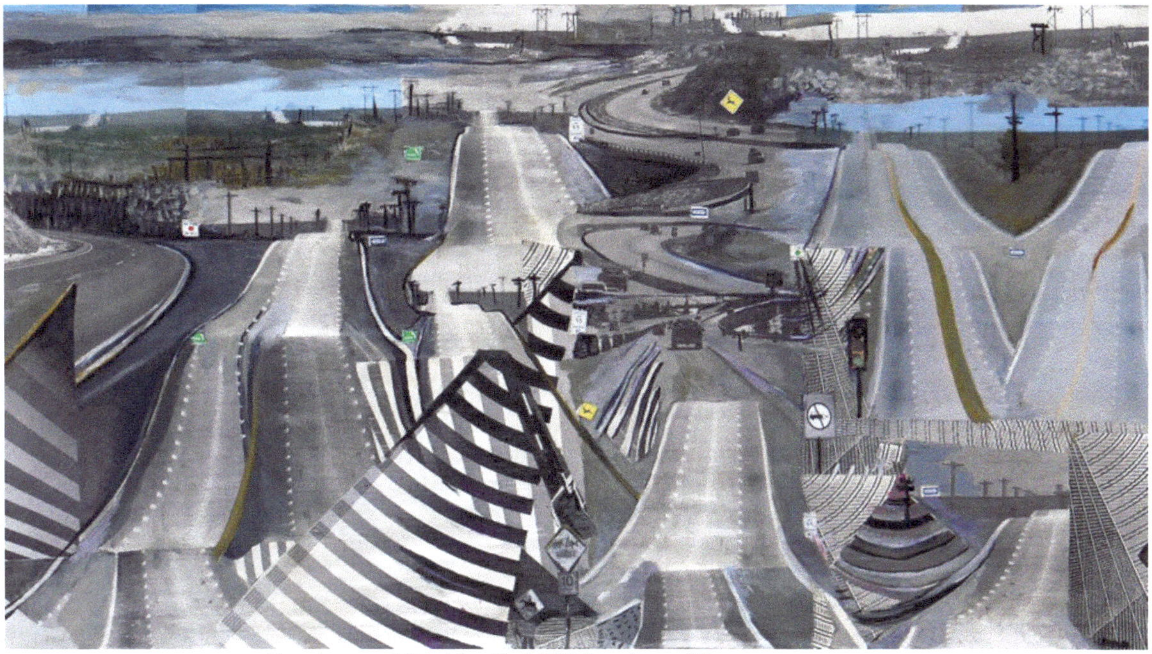

Continental Divide. © *2025 by Anna Ursyn*

Act III.
The curtain goes up (or opens).

Tuah: "How about you, Chia-Wei; you wear a limestone pendant as a necklace."

Chia-wei, "I love stones. Geology is about processes and products in nature, so art helps geologists understand rocks and their formations. Almost every element or design principle is addressed in geology and even in professions that seem the furthest away from the subject.
Geologists are all about footwork-based knowledge. Just like dance, but for another reason!"
`Chia-wei laughs`

Elements and Principles of Design in Geology

Elements of Design in Geology

Color and Value
- They help identify the types of rock, environment, and events forming the rock.
- Rocks are made of minerals, and those are made from elements in different colors.
- Geologic maps show units of rocks, beginning and ending, age, and composition.
- A color index with tints, tones, and shades shows chemicals, formation, and type of rock.
- Luster is reflected light, not just info on how shiny, smooth, or dull the rock/mineral is.
- The occurrence of red or orange indicates iron with darker volcanic rocks.
- Colors show a deposition layer after hundreds of millions of years of erosion.

Shape and Form
- Crystals have shapes and structures, and minerals grow differently in space.
- Quartz forms 6-sided prisms, while the galena forms symmetrical cubes.
- Cube is a rare form in nature. It appears in salt crystals or plants.
- Heat and pressure change planar structure into a curved one, which helps to age them.
- Fossils or rocks present many shapes and sizes, from small pebbles to giant boulders.
- Maps use symbols to explain what is happening in the rock layers through shapes.
- Future species can be predicted based on the historical shapes of fossilized shells.

Space
- The absence of crystals for growth in water, magma, or fluids to flow underground.
- Rocks take up 3D space; negative space in the rock can be more beneficial than positive.
- A rock formation ranges from a few feet to miles wide and a depth inside the crust.
- The continents occupy an ample space on the Earth's crust, surrounded by the oceans.

Line
- Depicts rivers, roads, counties, states, countries, and continents
- Symbols denote the geologic history of the rocks.
- Concentric shapes formed of lines show elevation changes and are used for sketching rocks.
- Crystal axes are lines that run parallel or the edges of a unit cell.

Texture
- The relative age or weathering can be found by looking at the texture of the rock.
- On a globe, the mountainous regions are raised.
- Rocks, magma, obsidian-like glass, or conglomerates have different textures.
- The grains' sizes interpret the weathering and erosion before becoming a rock.

The Principles of Design in Geology

Balance
- The structure of the atoms of a rock or mineral displays a balanced chemical formula.
- Mineral system: Isometric, Tetragonal, Orthorhombic, Monoclinic, Triclinic, Hexagonal, and Trigonal.
- Rock formations shape environments and events with movement and change.
- All sedimentary rocks and formations need special conditions to form.
- Metamorphic rocks need very high temperature and pressure.

Emphasis
- Small portions of a geological map help describe a whole rock formation.
- Hydrochloric acid helps differentiate between carbonate rocks and similar-looking ones.
- Focusing on the life of dinosaurs, with birds being the survivors of the destruction.

Movement
- Geologists must be fit to walk far, climb, hike, and lift objects.
- Folding and faulting show the physical movement of rocks and landforms.
- When a rock encounters high heat or pressure, it becomes soft and malleable and thus folded.
- Lava is a melted rock that erupts on the surface and then flows.
- Earthquakes move the ground, as shown in diagrams with arrows.
- Shifting the earth's surface causes plate tectonic motion, faults, folds, and earthquakes.
- The underlying collision of tectonic plates causes intense activity.

Variety and Contrast
- Vastly different processes can form very similar rocks.
- Rocks and minerals of many types are seen through colors and textures.
- Hot, dry environments can form sandstones; clay-based rocks are formed in wet ones.
- Geologists stain minerals' textures with chemicals, contrasting their types.
- Harder minerals will break down slower and are being formed through different events.
- Every rock is different and has various sedimentary, metamorphic, or igneous features.
- Rocks and minerals have different sizes, shapes, colors, hardness, clarity, and rarity.
- The stratigraphic column displays the order and thickness of the layers on the earth.

Proportion
- Data on a map must be concise with no gaps or voids and scaled for locating rock types.
- Images analyze details on location and what rocks are within a rock formation.
- Smaller particles are studied within a rock and thought of as scale.
- The Earth is massive, as opposed to its components.

Unity

- The formation of the Earth and its features help us understand it and its history.
- The thickness of layers through a cross-section must not change for no reason.
- The Rock Cycle is a constant cycle where a rock can become any other rock.
- If steps in the rock cycle are missed, that rock cannot become something new.
- Nature leaves some footprints in the rocks that develop millions of years later.
- Symbols on maps must be unified in meaning, consistent, and widely understood.
- Lab professionals cooperate to gain the correct information for using data.
- Stones are used in art. Here are the limestones for 3D artwork:

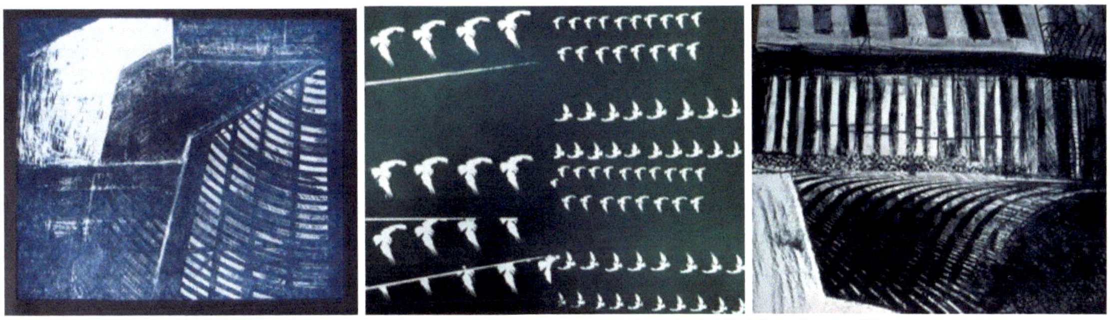

Photolithographs after computer code. © 2025 by Anna Ursyn

Tam and Som, "It makes us want to work with stones."

Panagiotis exclaims, "I want to teach them it all! Let's talk about education. I've dreamed of teaching little children about everything around them to help their minds grow in a classroom that promotes creativity, cognition, and learning, all with fun and enjoyment."

The Elements and Principles of Art in Elementary Education

Elements of Design in Elementary Education

Color and Value

- Bright classrooms with colors improve interest, motivation, and focus.
- Books, games, letters, artworks, and groups promote productivity and learning.
- Colors bring life into the classroom, associating it with positivity and learning.
- They manage organization, emotions, or moods and help ask why.
- Understanding colors, value, lightness, and darkness supports learning and creating.
- Warm colors are stimulating, while light greens foster creative thinking.

Shape and Form

- The elementary curriculum involves squares, circles, and triangles.
- An abstract use of shapes such as hand signals and gestures.
- 3-dimensional tools are essential to creating, completing tasks, and understanding.
- They help increase cognitive and language skills.
- A flat paper ball helps teach the differences between 3-D and 2-D.
- In math, counting the form's sides, corners, and flat form areas helps with spatial skills.
- Shaped letters and numbers help children learn about the world.
- They organize information to improve communication, creativity, reading, and writing.
- Shapes help kids move between dimensions, compare, and find them.
- Blocks help identify math based on forms and shapes, such as prisms and pyramids.
- In geometry or science, volume and measuring the perimeter surface area are explained.

Space
- A literal space is desks, classrooms, playgrounds, and schools.
- Students use space during activities to learn new skills and collaborating skills.
- The classroom must be an accessible physical space for all 15 types of students.
- The teacher's desk, library, math center, and circle carpet should have their own spaces.
- In literature, there is space between words and lines of sentences.
- Respect for others 'personal space and upon things is essential.
- Space is between the desks, notebooks, computers, worksheets, and bulletin boards.
- Lines showing the distance from different objects.
- The three states of matter take up space; spatial skills and discoveries are taught.
- Desks are set together to work closely. While placed in a circle, they help to converse.
- Staves are lines for music notation, showing the action of both hands through symbols.
- Students walk to classes and buildings in lines by standing behind another person.
- Desks are set in lines, and letters, math symbols, and shapes are in lines.
- Geometric shapes connect points using horizontal, vertical, and diagonal lines.
- Measurement uses lines in the child's growth charts.
- Belongings, like jackets, coats, hats, and backpacks, are hung in lines.

Texture
- Discovering the variety in the world; using descriptive words in writing.
- Adjectives like smooth, soft, bumpy, and scratchy help picture textures.
- Soft stuffed animals make any place a welcoming one.
- Maps, curtains, or rugs help students imagine various environments.
- Texture in earth science helps see minerals as smooth, rough, soft, rigid, or glassy.
- Feeling reptile skin, fish scales, and animal fur informs us.
- Texture introduces young children to their senses through petting different animals.
- Those with disabilities feel textures to learn through stimuli or use fidgets to focus.
- More 3D decor can help the development of sensory processing and elevate learning.
- By tasting food, touching things, hearing and naming them, children learn to sense.

Principles of Design in Elementary Education

Balance
- Students interact with the teacher, among and between other students.
- Students deserve an equal education, participation, treatment, and enjoyment.
- The classroom's shapes, space, and lines support learning.
- In math, balance is taught using various scales, weights, and volumes for measuring.
- Balanced and comfortable environments improve motor skills through physical activity.
- We walk on both feet and use two hands to clap. Play increases balancing skills.
- Making mistakes helps children expand their physical and motor abilities.
- A balanced room fosters cognition, creativity, and independent thinking.

Emphasis
- The words that are emphasized sound different.
- The way we present text strengthens vocabulary.
- Exclamations help in reading and literature.
- The goals and objectives help emphasize various parts of a lesson plan.
- Respect, learning, behaviors, sharing, and organization are stressed in a classroom.
- The rules are set on a behavior chart, calendar, and behavioral strategy.
- Teachers emphasize through tone, volume, clapping, actions, or gestures.
- Including more details supports focusing on the main idea.

Movement
- It is used during breaks and recess to release students' energy so they can focus after.

- Kids understand the movement of the Earth and make motions mimicking the planets.
- Rhythm in music is a repeated over-time beat. A repeated pattern makes a motif.
- To identify motifs within the literature to analyze and understand the readings.
- The classroom design, alphabet, objects, seasons, dates, and events help move the eye.
- Moving every 30 minutes stimulates both brain hemispheres to focus.
- Children walk, run, and jump during recess and after class.
- Games and activities increase their motor skills.

Variety and Contrast

- Diverse students and teachers are in schools with new tools, methods, and philosophies.
- Perennialism, Essentialism, Progressivism, and Reconstructionism maintain interest.
- Black/white or soft/hard help contrast in language arts, social studies, math, and science.
- Lessons teach about similarities and differences between themselves and their peers.
- The contrasts: are night and day, full and empty, cold and hot, big and small, happy and sad.

Proportion

- There are twenty-two students for one teacher and ten in special education.
- Proportions within districts are shown by the diversity of the students needing aid.
- Students learn proportions in math, cooking, medication, and sciences.
- To help understand abstract concepts such as states of matter (liquid, solid, gas, plasma).

Unity

- Teachers and staff members work toward trust between students, their teachers, and peers.
- Helps material to be known and helps teachers teach the material.
- For the success of each student, everything is unified.
- Everything has a place and a purpose.
- Teachers identify their students' skills, talents, and interests by grouping them.

Pierre complains, "Yes, that is true, but I cannot do it all. I still do not know which major to choose."

Amina replies:, "All that is developed can be argued using elements and principles of art!"

Tuah says, "Do what you love doing."

Pierre sights, "Nothing."

Tam and Som exclaim, "Everything!"

Roksolana states firmly, "Everything is connected."

Hina adds, "The elements and principles of art can be found in almost everything, that it is a beautiful and unique way to view the life around us."

Qiáng mentions, "The World is based on collaboration. Just work with others."

Hubert says: "You know the common saying 'if you want to go fast, go alone, but if you want to go far, go together.' ("It Takes a Village" to Determine the Origins of An African Proverb.)

Amina adds, "When something interests you in any class, check how it is connected to other subjects. Then, pick a major and a minor."

Cody concludes, "With the pace of our technology, you will have a job that does not exist yet, so stop worrying; start exploring!

Hubert states, "Everything you do is a story."

The curtain goes down (or closes). The End

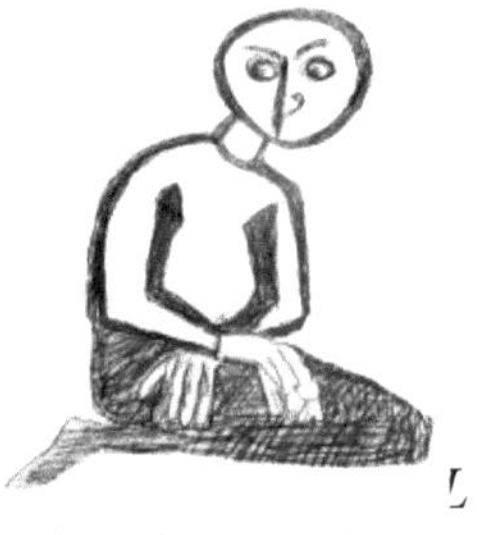

Lefeto: waits for an inspiration to help him organize.

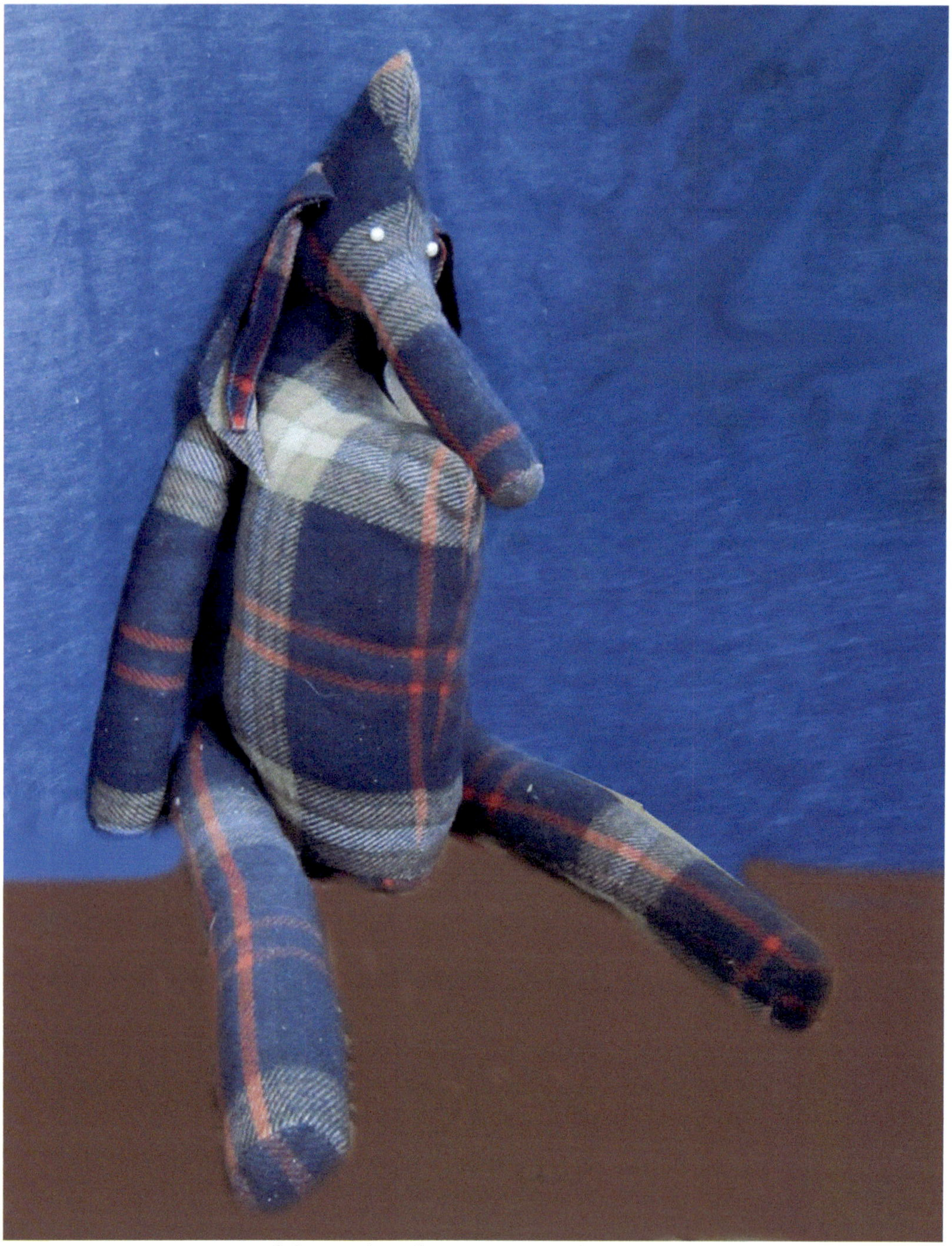

Kardelup. Soft sculpture. © 2025 by Anna Ursyn

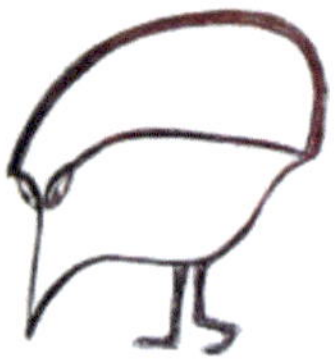

Fusto: finds all the items that were lost.

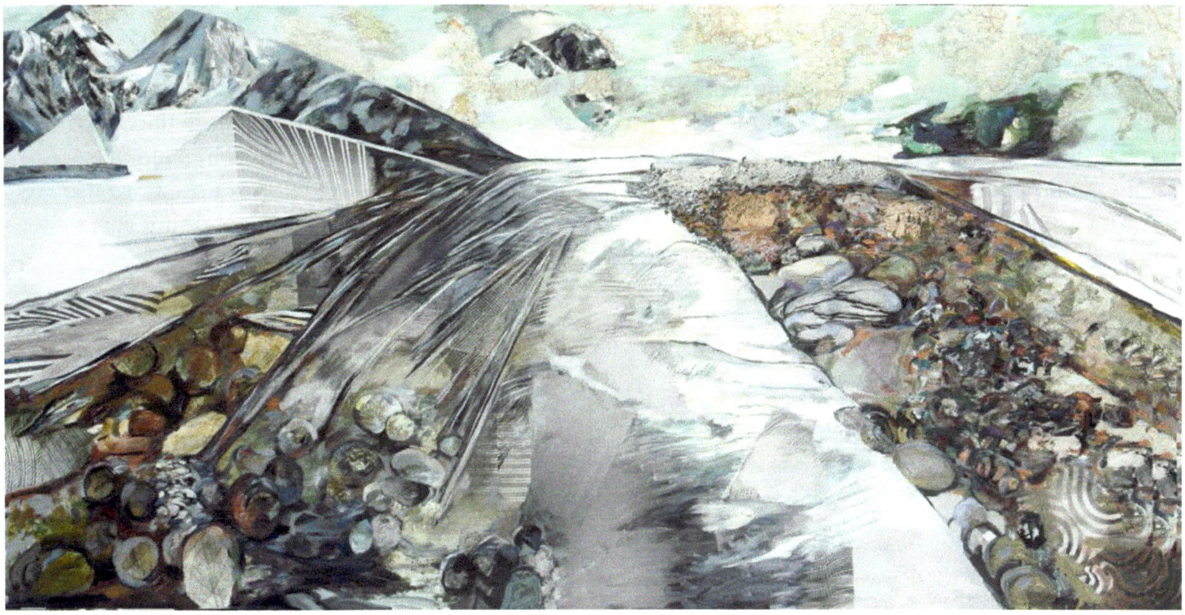

Outflow. © 2025 by Anna Ursyn

CHAPTER 4

COGNITIVE PERCEPTIONS

TWO COMMENTATORS INSIDE OF A DRONE

INTRODUCTION

We are taught about and focus on our five senses. We are told that animals boast more on various levels, which we agree on just by observing various species. When we think about it, we discover that having more senses helps us function and progress. We can attune to our planet, but only if we talk less, listen more, see, not just look, hear, not just listen, and pay attention. While education gets simplified, Nature fills in all the gaps.

SYNOPSIS

With their birthdays falling on the same day, students celebrated it together, deep in the forest. They were all born on April 15th. Aries people are known for possessing personal charm; thus, they are irresistible. Nobody born on a different day was invited. It is a beautiful day, and the forest starts showing the signs of the rebounding spring. They play games and then instruments, followed by creating environmental art. They cook their lunch together. A cake with candles follows. The sign "Happy Birthday to All of Us" flies in space above them. After lunch, they go for a walk and get lost in the forest. By looking for their way out and playing together, they use various sense organs and look into their functions (each sense gets introduced). This experience enriches them by learning why they kept using but never acknowledged possessing them.

Two people, Mr. Roman and Carl, suspiciously sit in the drone and observe the people below them. They have been on autopilot all day, so time goes slowly until they notice the whole action from above. They cannot help, but observe them. Since one of them majored in psychology, he comments on the celebrants' actions to the other, who checks his phone for information, codes, and visuals.

SUMMARY

This work focuses on how our unrecognized senses help us thrive. Since the celebrants are seen from above, the two main characters, the commenters, are the center of viewers' attention, while the colorful action below is shown as abstract movements seen from the bird's eye view. The current state of technology allows coding to address more senses than our schooling addresses. For example, we use accelerators in gaming, immerse ourselves in various types of virtual reality by implementing some hologram-based work, and perceive more than we acknowledge.

CAST OF CHARACTERS

- Drone Man 1. Mr. Roman, the Psychologist
- Drone Man 2. Carl, the Cartographer
- The Celebrants. They can only be seen from above. It is hard to count them as they move fast. Besides, we all look alike from a distance.

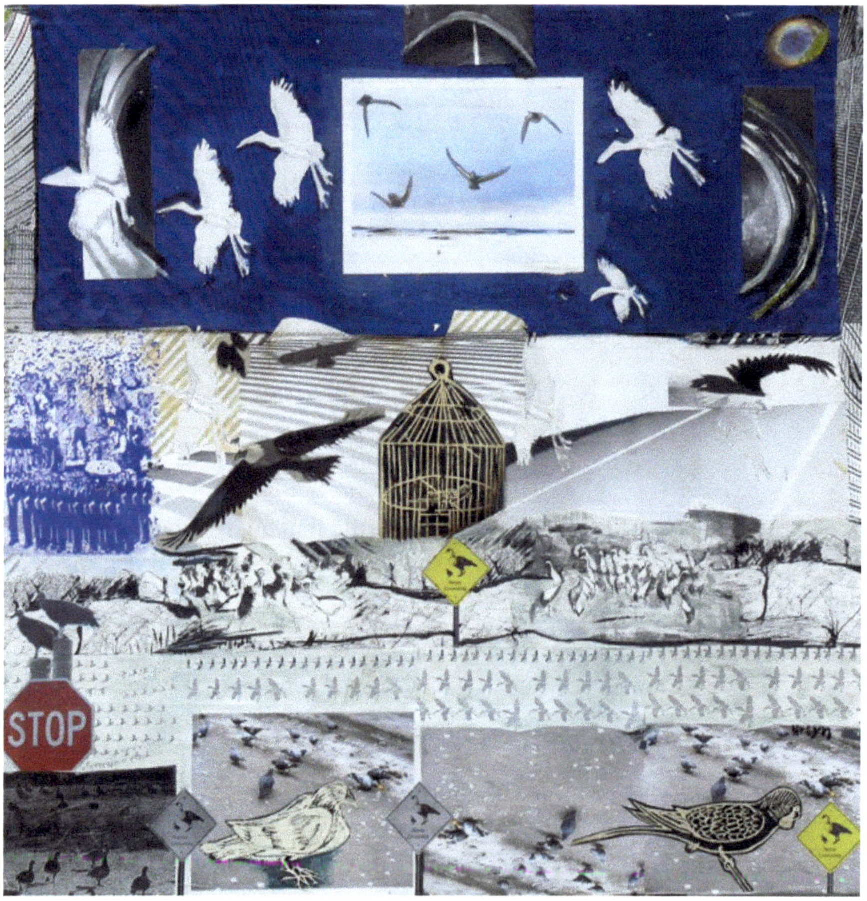

Ecosystem. © *2025 by Anna Ursyn*

STAGE DIRECTIONS

Two commentators are lying down in a large drone set on the floor. They are facing a large screen, where all the action they witness appears projected as seen from the bird's eye view, showing people celebrating. They move fast, so it is hard to count them. After exploring all possible socializing options for carrying on a conversation, Carl, tired and bored, starts commenting.

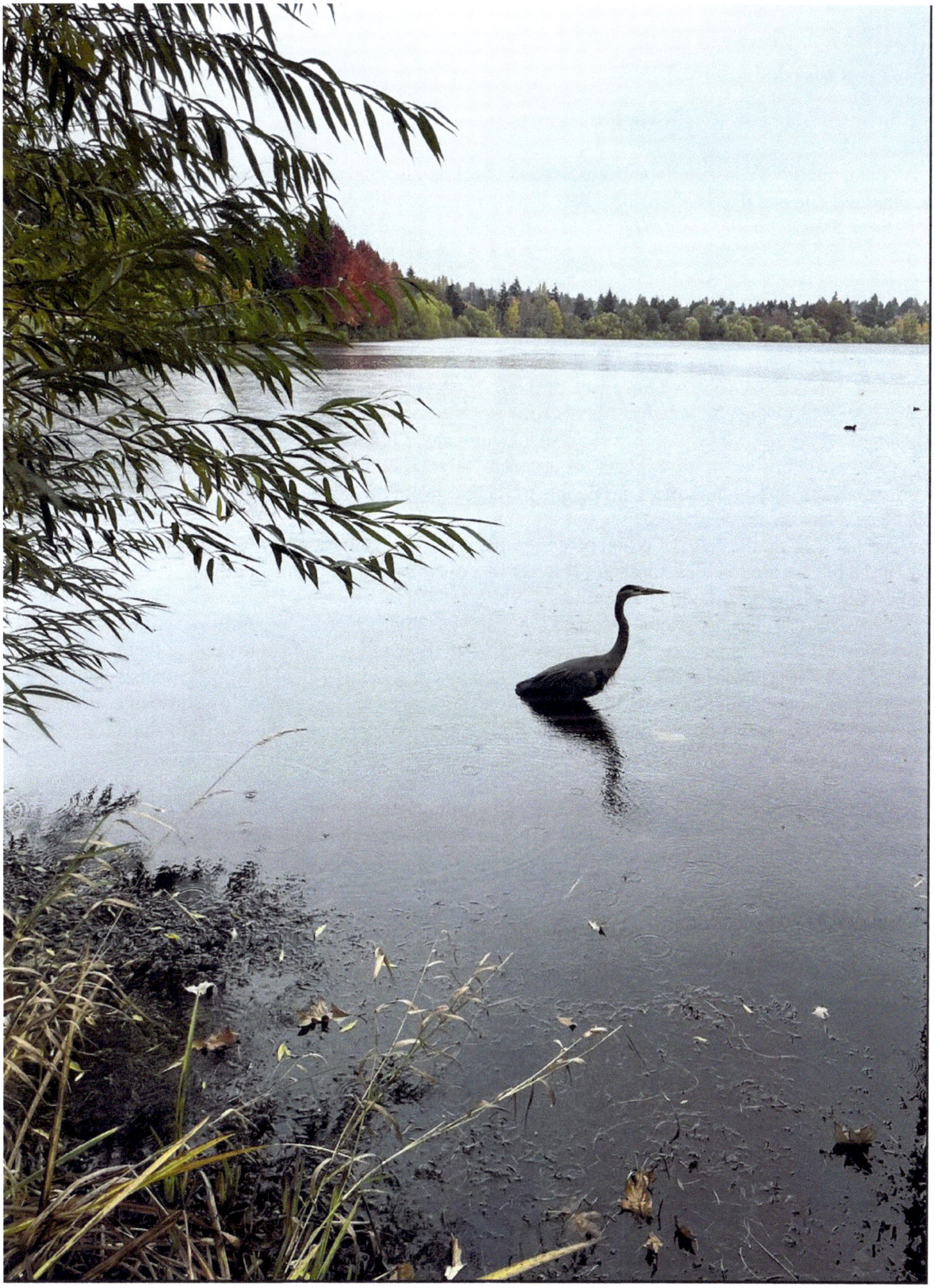

Reflection. © 2025 by Matylda Czarnecka. (Used with permission).

Act I
Daylight
The curtain goes up (or opens).

Carl and Mr. Roman are crowded inside the drone, while all the characters mentioned are shown below them.
Carl, "What a day! We just sit here in a drone and observe. Not that I am complaining, but they could use an unmanned one and draw conclusions based on the images and videos it sends."
Mr. Roman, "Well, I understand them but cannot explain it. With all the symbols involved, we learn new skills every day."
Carl agrees, "I won't ask, but don't get me started on symbols. Maps are full of them, and they are fascinating for being abstract and simple, yet informing, and they better be international."
Mr. Roman summarizes, "That is a sense of embodiment, an abstract idea delivering a concrete form."
Carl confirms his understanding, "Like a logo denoting some company. That involves a sense of symbolism, too. Yes, senses. We have five of them."
Mr. Roman, "More than you imagine, but we confuse them."
Carl, makes an unrecognized sound, "Ooch, such a long day without any action. I like action. People think cartographers are boring because they translate from 3D to 2D, but it is not static. I am so waiting for..."
Mr. Roman, exclaims, "Look, there are people playing down there."
Carl, "Yes, I can see them, and they see one another."
Mr. Roman, "Yes, that's sight, or visual perception, or Ophthalmoception (Eyes). They can hear the birds. I like birds, but we are too high for them. It looks like one of them is playing a guitar."
Carl wonders, "Birds are playing their guitars?"
Mr. Roman, "No, birds sing, people play and sing, and yes, that's hearing or auditory sensations Audioception (Ears). I think the guitarist must be good at it, just by looking at the rest of them. He uses all the senses of Rhythm, Harmony, and Color; yes, music has color! I'll add, before you ask, space, direction, pitch, time, and, of course, music, which is time-based and gives people a sense of comfort."
Carl," Said before, I wish I could talk about comfort here. Look, one over there tries to smell the flowers."
Mr. Roman, "I do not think there are flowers that early in the season, but they sure smell something. That's Olfaction (Nose). While humans have about 3 million smell receptors, dogs, for example, have over 300 million. The food they cook must smell nice despite how limited we perceive it. Mr. Roman takes his binoculars out. As I look closer, he is talking to the shadow of a flower."
Carl interrupts, "And their food must taste great. Pardon me for interrupting you, Mr. Roman."
Mr. Roman, "Yes, they sure taste their food. One can tell just by looking. That's a Sense of Taste, Gustaoception (Tongue)."
Carl, "Look, Mr. Roman, we are so crowded while sitting still here, and they are playing the ball. How fun it must be to feel the ball."
Mr. Roman, "That is a sense of touch, perception (schooling) from the physiological group, mind you."
Carl, "Look at the way they are gesturing; I bet they are talking about their favorite pastime: one paints, one cooks, one plays games, another tends a garden, one walks, exercises, etc."
Mr. Roman, "What people do is interesting; they can play music, draw, write, cook, dance, code, and research nature, which is one of the reasons I am here."
Carl states, "What's today, April 15th? It is not a holiday or any special day. Nothing fun or important was announced, either. This is so strange. Why do you think they are all here?"
Mr. Roman, "On that day, Leonardo da Vinci was born in 1452. He was a Renaissance Man, which means he connected the arts with the sciences. He probably even invented a drone. Those are my Interpretational senses talking: History and Culture."
Carl continues while taking a look through his pocket binoculars, "Let's look at them: they comb hair, look, videoconference, brush their teeth, apply makeup, floss their teeth, one cuts his mustache while getting a haircut, another one is giving himself a haircut, some dress, or dress up, button up, one puts a

flower into her hair, while another one puts a hat on, and fits a hat to put a flower into a hat after, or maybe into the hair. One looks at her foot and checks a reflection in a monitor while being reflected in a second mirror showing her the back of her head. One is fitting glasses reflecting her in the glasses, combing her eyebrows, and then taking something out of her eye. One is looking at the tongue he stretched out of his mouth. I hope he's not sick and will not spoil such a fun party. I wish I could join in. One is cleaning her ear while trying a brooch on a scarf; where did she get a full mirror from in the middle of the forest? One is tying a tie, while another is buttoning up a dress, another a shirt, putting a cap on their head, and cleaning their teeth."

Mr. Roman, "Yes, they must be getting ready for some dancing. So uninhibited. Typically, we use "the sixth sense," some intuitive faculty, an awareness beyond normal perception; a common example used is, "Some sixth sense told him he was not alone." They are not alone; we are here!
I wonder what's the occasion. They look pretty random to me."

Carl complains, "They are preparing themselves for something in public. Oh, that self-awareness!"

Mr. Roman, "That's the sense of self, the interpersonal group of our senses."

Carl recites a poem:

SHIFTED SENSES

we look at music when attending a concert,
we read artist's statements when visiting a gallery,
we talk about food at the dinner table,
we watch literature in a movie theater,
we taste drinks to appreciate their smells,
we touch the screen to Like on social media,
instead of patting you on your shoulder.

we use senses we do not know we possess,
to talk about ourselves,
not sensing our surroundings or growing our curiosity.

we see art with no elements and principles of design in them,
yet we create new venues and outlets for our unique experiences."

Mr. Roman, "Synesthesia is a special condition some rarely possess. People see music, hear art, and more."

Carl stays silent.

Mr. Roman asks, "Mapmaking involves all the senses to make the job right, I guess? Carl?"

Carl, while looking down, shares an observation, "Look, one plays a game on the phone using the accelerometer."

Mr. Roman, "He's being able to sense balance, Equilibrioception. In its digital format, that is."

Carl, "That one over there must have hurt his ankle."

Mr. Roman, "That is a feeling of pain, which he senses. We do not like being in pain, but it is useful information that our brain sends us so we can start seeking diagnosis. It can be a lifesaver."

Carl, "He is jumping on one leg only, poor guy."

Mr. Roman, "That's a perception of one's body position, Proprioception. An awareness of one's body. Also, a physiological sense of balance is used here. Perhaps vestibular awareness?"

Carl, "Oh, how I wish I could balance my body and use agility and movement to sense the position of different body parts internally! We are stuck here."

Mr. Roman, "Look, they have fireworks and a giant "Happy Birthday to All of Us" banner. To All of Us? Weird again."

Carl, "They all must be sharing their birthday on April 15th!

Mr. Roman reads from his phone, "People born around that time are known to possess personal charm and thus are irresistible. They also cannot be rude or unappreciative." That's Astrology and the Zodiac, but multicultural connotations are different. It depends on the year they were born.
Carl, "How cool, I already like them, but I would never be invited. Maybe it makes me feel better being here in a confined space."
`Carl doses off.`

A Break
The Curtain goes down (or closes)

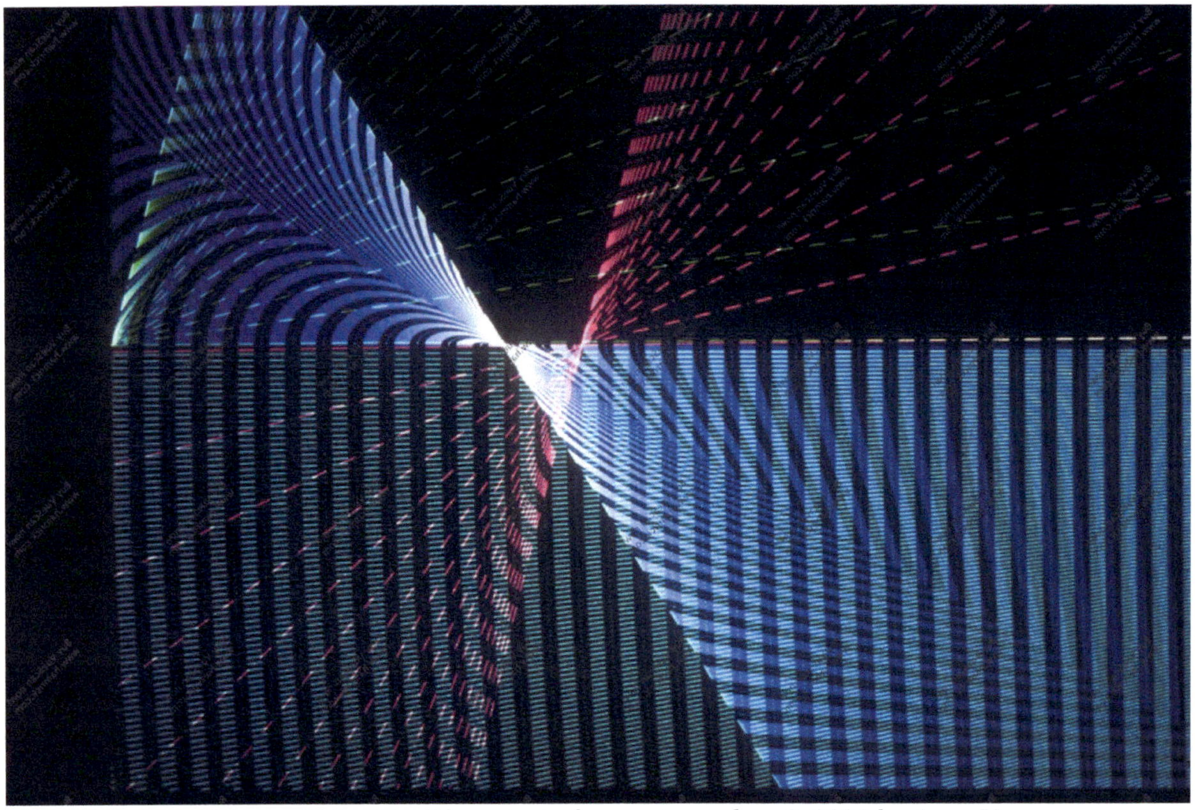

Center of Attention. The output of computer codes. © 2025 by Anna Ursyn

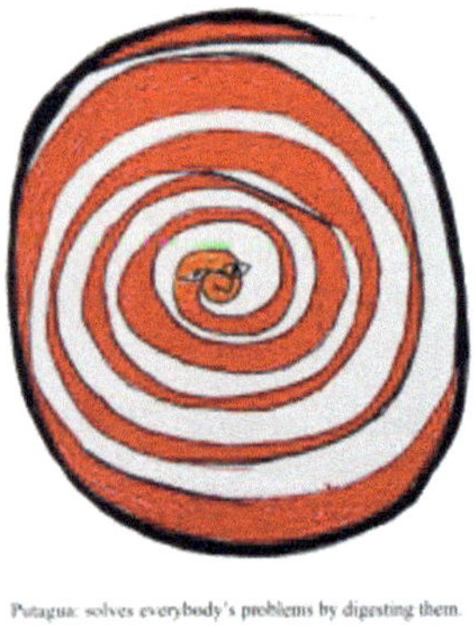

Putagua: solves everybody's problems by digesting them.

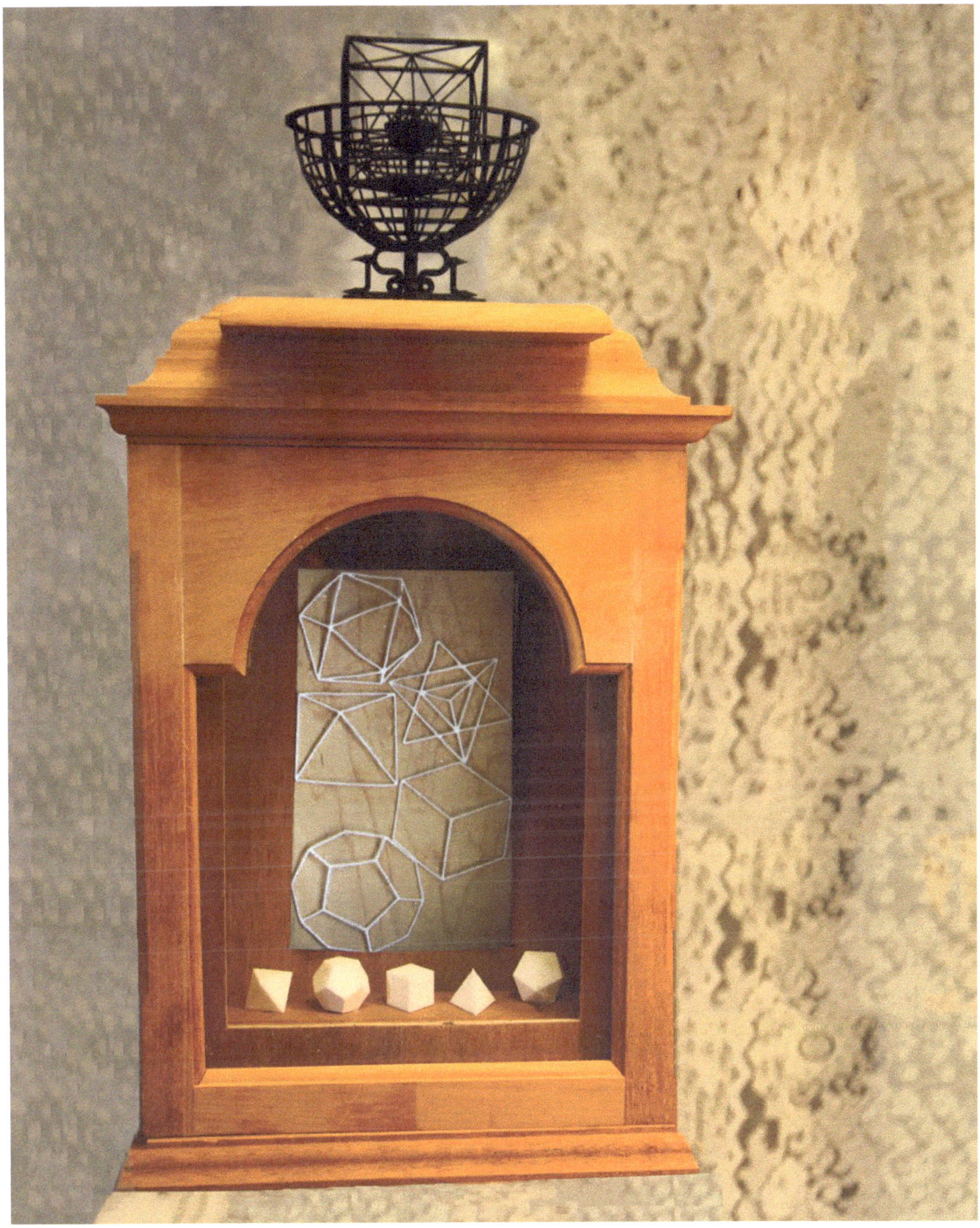

Shrine of Knowledge. © 2025 by Anna Ursyn

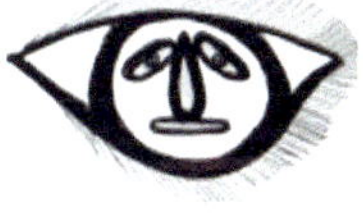

Adeia: knows the basic rules and observes them.

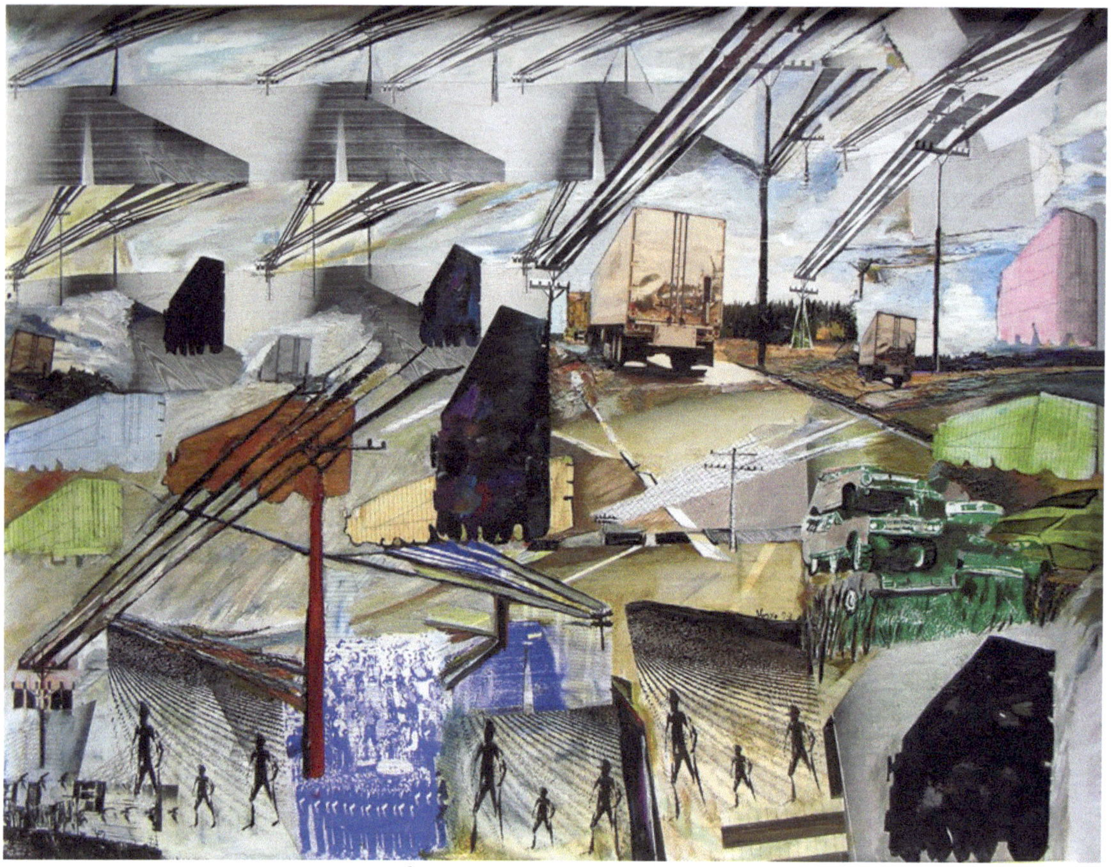

Monday Morning. © 2025 by Anna Ursyn

Act II
The curtain goes up (or opens).
Sunset - Sundown – Dusk

Carl observes, "They went for a walk just to get lost in a forest. It is frightening."

Mr. Roman comments, "Fear lies in an Interpersonal sense group."
Carl states firmly, "It is getting cold. They left their warm closing at the camp; they must be hungry and bitten by the mosquitos."
Mr. Roman, "There are no mosquitos in April here, and those are Interoceptive senses that can sense things like hunger, thirst, pressure, or itch. They use their sense of Temperature so they will not freeze."
*Carl exclaims, "*Yes, they got hungry, so one eats a mushroom without looking at it closely. Her body language states one thing: sickness. Maybe she'll employ her Interoception sense to link her body to her mind. But would the conscious or unconscious way be better, I wonder? It must be a poisonous mushroom called toadstool. It is beautiful, but they could not check on it as all their phone batteries now have no power. I think that might affect their sense of justice, as batteries should be made to have a longer charged life."
Mr. Roman says optimistically, "Yes, that is not fair, but her chemistry will help her: our bodies are equipped with chemoreceptors in our hearts for discerning chemicals and pathogens in our blood, so we adjust levels accordingly. Thus, she will vomit soon."
Carl sights, "She vomits it, indeed. I am so glad I could not be invited. I am thirsty."
Mr. Roman observes, "Your Interpretational Interoceptive senses are released now. You must be empathetic, as we shared a large water bottle just a few minutes ago."

Carl notices, "The rain is coming; I feel some pressure."
Mr. Roman answers, "It's your Thermoception sense talking now. Because of it, one can perceive temperature or changes in pressure and thus predict weather changes, as you just did."
Carl shares his concern: "They lost their sense of time because their phones were not functional. I can see them wandering, clueless. I hope they can teleport."

Mr. Roman answers, "Only the avatars or movie characters can, and very few of us can make objects move, which is called telekinesis. No worries. With Chronoception, we have our Circadian rhythms to help us monitor time. Not that it is our sensory system, but our brain, with the cerebellum, cerebral cortex, and basal ganglia, helps us without our consciousness."

Carl worries, "They do not know the time, as their phones do not tell them anymore. We could talk about the sense of politics in the phone industry or battery companies. Short-lived batteries show a lack of care from the companies and invoke emotions, which cause reactions to this type of a sense of well-being not being fulfilled. It is also about other senses, such as safety, pride, and responsibility. They all get sleepy but are afraid of the wild animals, which are active at night, just like the witches, goblins, ghosts, or vampires."

Mr. Roman, "Yes, the list is long; they should ask Greek Pythia for advice."

Carl keeps worrying, "But they do not seem to have any sense of direction."

Mr. Roman asks, "Direction? Some people can vaguely sense the Earth's magnetic poles thanks to the ethmoid bone behind the nose, beneath the eyes. We have a crystal of magnetite that helps us with directions. Some of us have this sense of acting stronger, so when sent to a windowless basement, we know where N, E, S, or W is."
Carl agrees, "Yes, when I am asked to get something from the basement, I know how to follow directions north and east without any window. That's another reason why I like making maps."

`Carl immerses himself in studying various maps on his cellphone.`

A Break
The Curtain goes down (or closes).

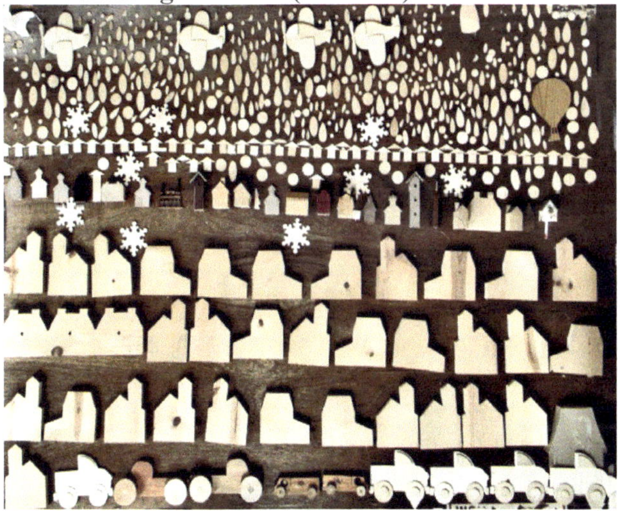

Life. © *2025 by Anna Ursyn*

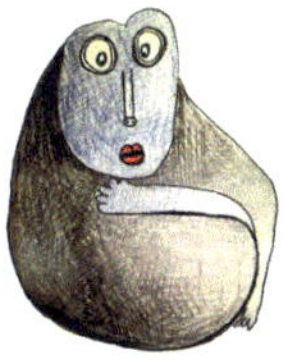

Hadamkuf: knows the tools.

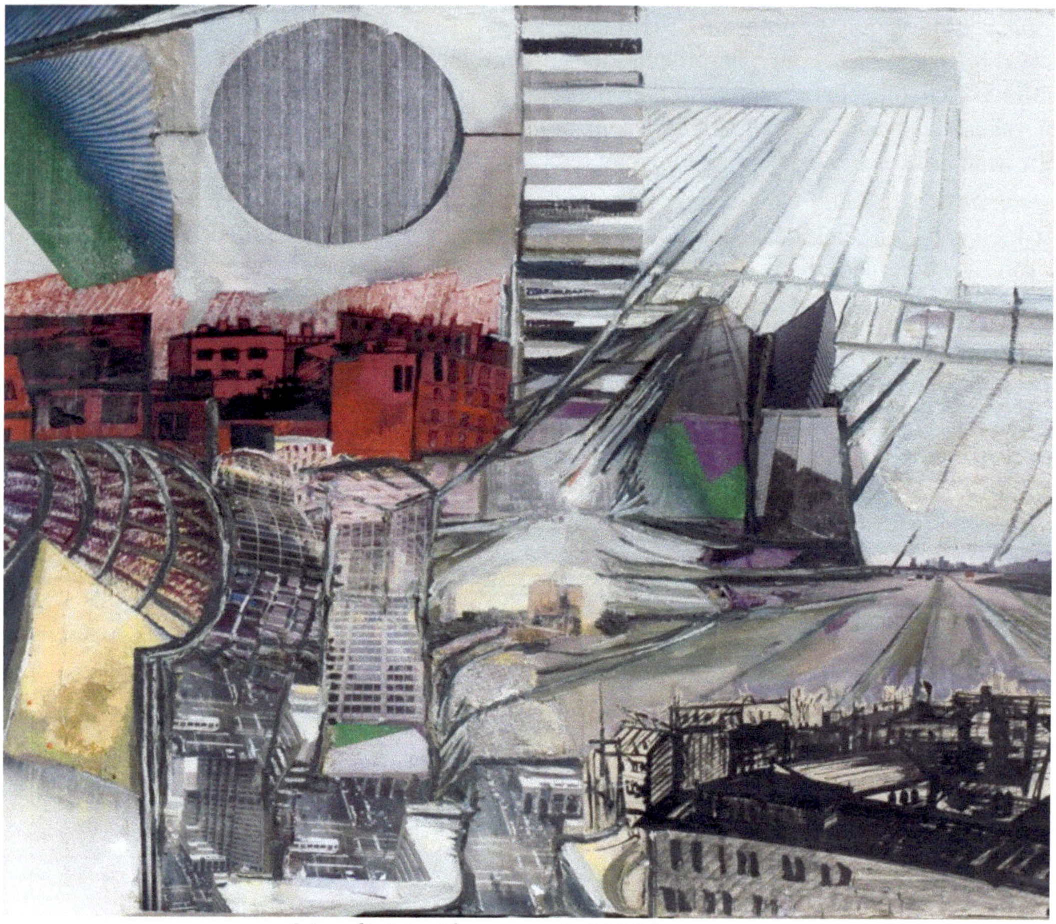

Moonlit Manifestation. © 2025 by Anna Ursyn

Act III
The Curtain goes up (or opens).
Nighttime

Carl exclaims, "Look, Mr. Roman, it seems like they can find a solution to their problems via coding, as one of them carried a laptop they must never part with. They used all the senses, including those they did not know were in their possession. The Moon is full. Good for them. Still unable to go home, they built a game where all the senses are implied. It starts with star reading for navigation through the sense of direction. Can you write a code to get a sense of direction?" Maybe we will obtain permission to go home after they see we know how to get there?"
Mr. Roman replies," To use a compass, initialize and compare directions with north, south, east, or west. If the directions match, display the corresponding cardinal direction. Otherwise, calculate the angle to the closest reference point to determine the direction
Here is a general algorithm for getting from one place to another:
1. Obtain the latitude and longitude of here and your house.
2. Use a routing API, such as Google Maps, to obtain directions from here to your home.
3. Determine the mode of transportation (e.g., walking, driving, public transit, etc.).
4. Use a GPS or location-based service to obtain the drone's current location.
5. Follow the directions from the routing API, considering any turns, obstacles, or traffic.
6. Continuously track our location; the GPS or location-based service to stay on the path.
7. If we deviate from the path, guide us toward the correct path.
8. Once we reach the destination, confirmation will be provided."

Carl states, "I can write a Python code that utilizes the Google Maps API to obtain directions from our drone to your house and print out the driving directions:

```
import requests

# Obtain the latitude and longitude of the drone and house
drone = "37.8651,-119.5383"
your house = "34.0522,-118.2437"

# Use the Google Maps API to obtain directions from the drone to your house
url = f"https://maps.googleapis.com/maps/api/directions/json?origin={drone}&destination={house}&mode=driving&key=<YOUR_API_KEY>"
response = requests.get(url)
data = response.json()

# Print the driving directions
for step in data["routes"][0]["legs"][0]["steps"]:
  print(step["html_instructions"])
```

Note that you will need to obtain an API key from the Google Cloud Console to use the Google Maps API in this code. Also, this code includes no GPS or location-based services to track our location in real-time."

Mr. Roman, "This, I can do with my phone apps."

Carl answers, "Only if you have a charged battery, remembered to pack all the cables and connectors, or have an adequate power source! "

Mr. Roman, "Let's not go there again. I find it interesting that only some senses can be digitalized. Coders are working on it, but can you imagine what experience it would be to go to the movies with digitalized smell being present there?"

Carl wonders: "Good and scary bad, I'm afraid. The same goes for the sense of taste. So, not five senses? Not six? Not 12 or 13 senses? That's more than twice what I thought of or as I was taught. So, 36 now?"

Mr. Roman, "While education gets simplified, Nature fills in all the gaps."

Carl exclaims excitedly, "Yes, their phones' batteries run out, but they all safely reach their cars, where the batteries can be recharged, offering directions to their homes, respectively: a sense of place. I just checked the field of neuroscience on my phone to find out that humans can have about 34 senses; please note as of today."

1. Sight
2. Hearing
3. Touch
4. Taste
5. Smell
6. Balance
7. Proprioception
8. Pain
9. Vestibular Awareness
10. Embodiment
11. Temperature
12. Interoception
13. Rhythm
14. Harmony
15. Color
16. Space
17. Direction
18. Pitch
19. Time
20. Equilibrioception
21. Interoceptive
22. Emotion
23. Fear
24. Self

Mr. Roman exclaims with enthusiasm, "More! We have more!" *He continues*, "Please recall major events from your memory and extract all the sensual experiences. We remember what connects to our emotions.

Carl answers, "When is your birthday?"

The End.

The curtain goes down (or closes).

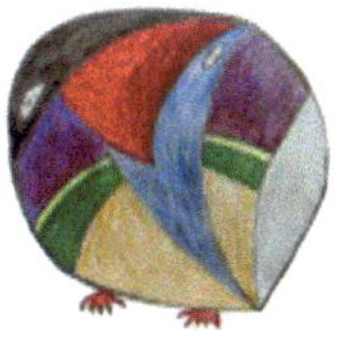

Avsag never trusts what he sees.

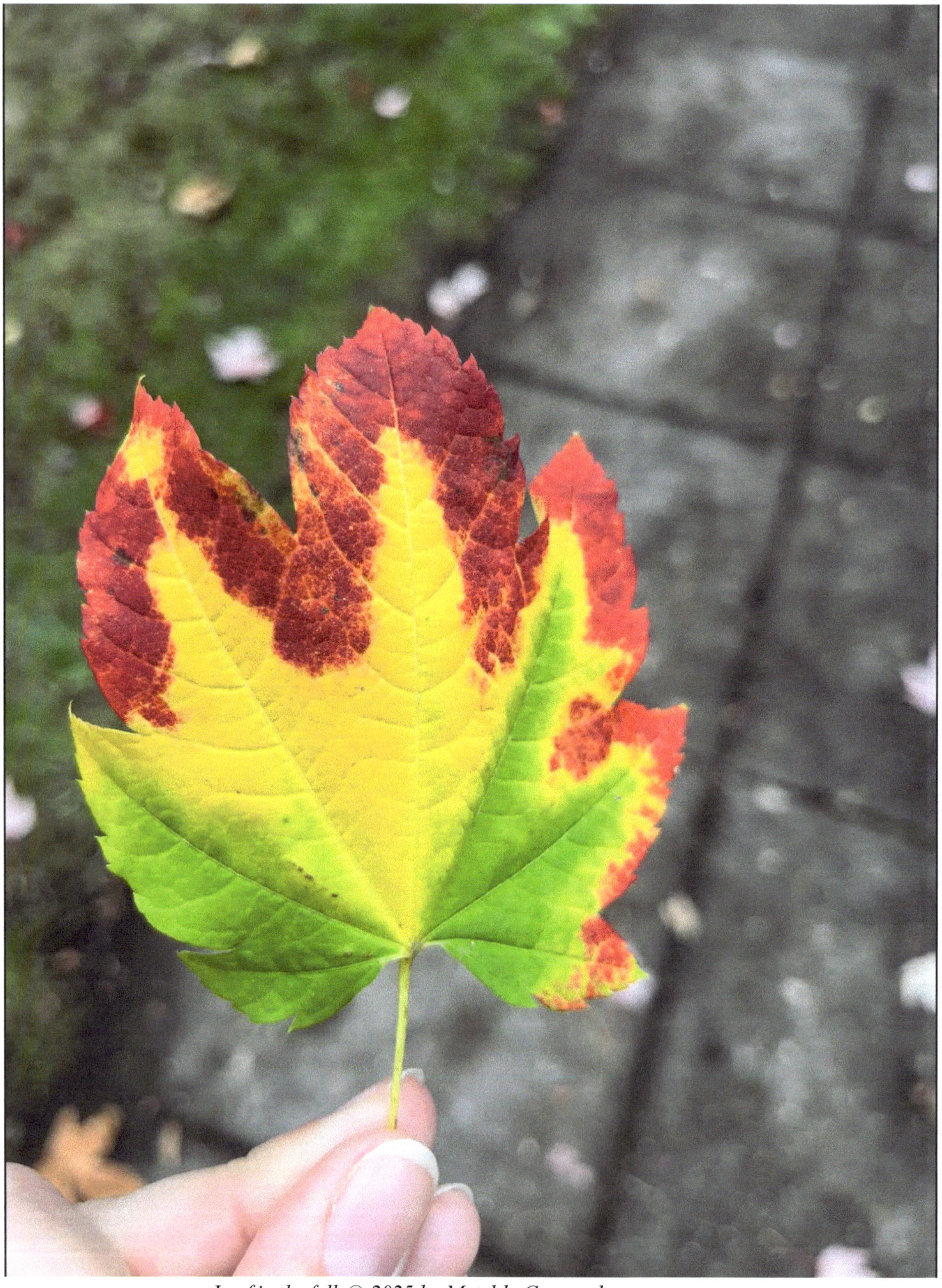

Leaf in the fall. © *2025 by Matylda Czarnecka.*

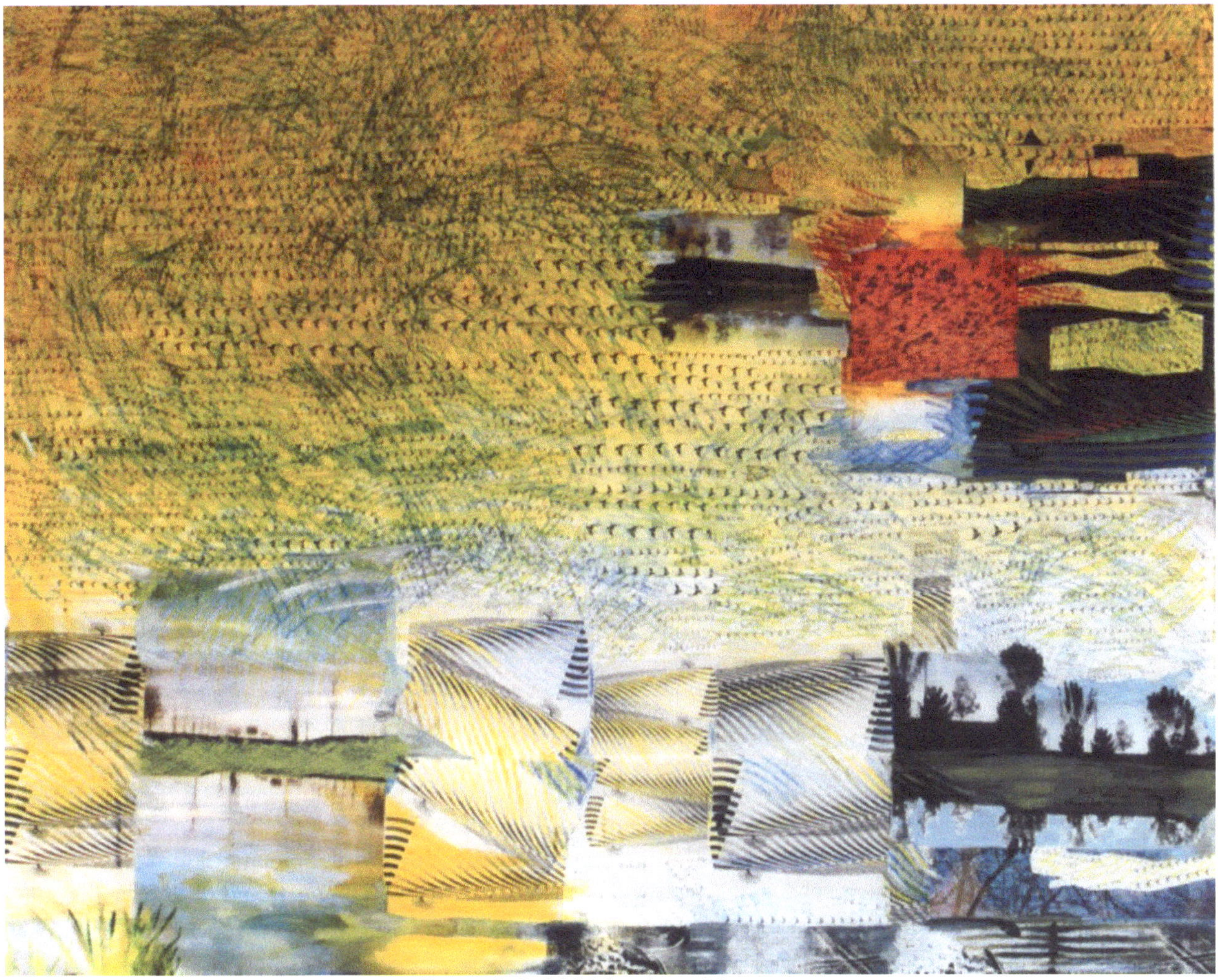

Noise Control. © 2025 by Anna Ursyn

CHAPTER 5
ART CODE

AN INTERNSHIP

INTRODUCTION

Artists and storytellers are expected to understand coding at a technology-based entertainment institution. They create on their tablets and phones with traditional media, then mix the outcomes, but it may be far beyond their interest what type of code is applied behind the tools they use. Employers want them to understand coding, not to turn them into programmers, but to communicate more efficiently with coders on the job so that collaborative tasks can be done faster and better; as we may say, nowadays, most jobs require collaboration. The interns are shown from their backs so the audience can focus on their computers with coded content on each screen. Each student's code will be shown at a time on this student's screen with different types of music.

SYNOPSIS

Leonard, an art student, has always liked to draw. Naturally, since he could remember, he'd been carrying his tablet any place he'd go to. It is hard to believe how much a not-careful math teacher can inhibit a student. Leonard was repeatedly reminded that he was not fit to solve mathematical problems just like other artists could not, as the teacher kept repeating. Leonard played games but felt reticent when it came to understanding how they were made. He entered his internal safe space whenever someone used the word 'coding.'

His strong digital portfolio was recognized, and he was offered an intern position at a prominent entertainment institution. This job more than fulfilled his wildest dreams. It connected his two passions: drawing and gaming. The tasks he was given were simple until he had to interact with the company's coders to make things run. They did not understand his decisions, and he stayed silent to their demands. He was the artist and felt those not trained in art should not interfere.

Moreover, according to the news, Leonard learns that artificial intelligence (AI) itself will not take his job, but someone using it might. That scared him, but using AI did not help. He still wanted to use his talents and his hand skills in drawing. When they explained to him how the computer processes the data and that his work was the data, he started learning coding by making drawings with codes. They were less perfect in depicting details, but the level of precision astounded him. After linking his codes with traditional media, he started teaching coding to a new coding-shy art intern, who followed that path until an even newer writing intern appeared.

SUMMARY

This story is to be set inside a fictional technology-based entertainment company. The lines used for the colorful or black-and-white artwork are to be mimicked by the artists' movement to connect the precision of a line, printed out, displayed, and set for interactive environments with the natural movement of the human body or 3D-printed. The codes and the associated artwork will be projected on the background to help show interactions between the characters and their visual outcomes.

CAST OF CHARACTERS

Leonard, an art student employed by the entertainment company as an intern
Charybdis, the coder
Felix, the new art intern, to whom this time Leonard explains coding
Oxygen, even newer intern

STAGE DIRECTIONS

A room with laptops on a large table with workers and interns is shown with their laptops. Projection of the images and videos support exchanges and information provided.

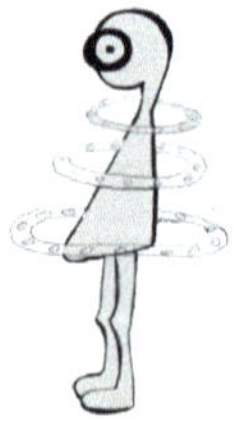

Colpo: can only move up and down.

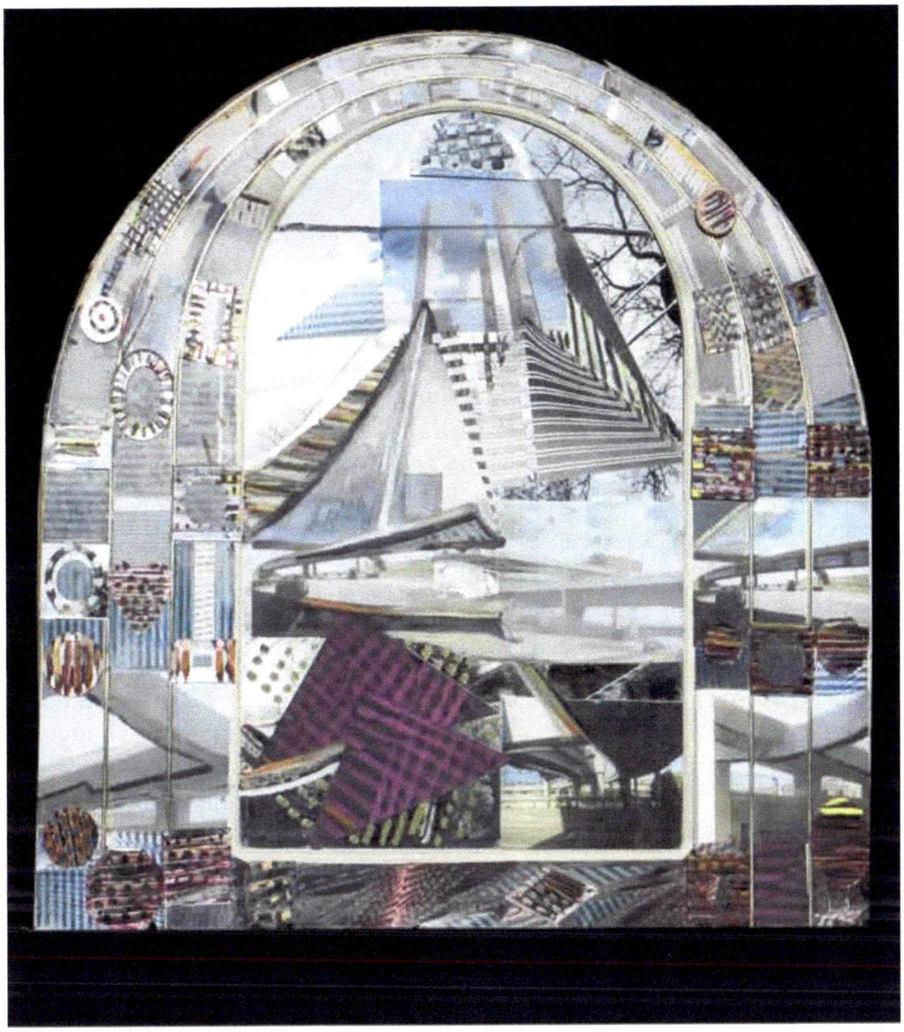

Exits. © *2025 by Anna Ursyn*

Act I
The Curtain goes up (or opens).

Leonard exclaims happily, "I nailed it! That's the dream job I was so hoping for. It's mine. Mine, and mine only. I am an Intern now. This will close the 'how to get a job without experience and how to get experience without the job' loop. I will not mess it up!"
Charybdis approaching, "Welcome! I was assigned to help you start your journey here. Now, you will be asked to perform certain tasks that we'll work on closely. My name is Charybdis, and I am a coder here."
Leonard asks, "Charybdis? That is an interesting name. Any connotations you'd like to share?"
Charybdis, "Nope. I was just named this way, and for some reason, nobody wants to disclose it to me; I like this name, and I like to code."
Leonard continues, "I have always liked to draw. I cannot remember not having my phone and a tablet with me. This job connected my two passions, drawing and gaming. I am afraid of coding, though. My math teacher kept telling me that since I liked art, I was not born to do any math. I enjoy games, but I feel inhibited when it comes to understanding how they were made. I simply shiver whenever someone uses the word coding."
Charybdis opposes him, "Coding is not math, it is a language."
Leonard replies, "Interesting. I never heard that way to discuss mathematically run procedures."

Charybdis continues, "We have some routines ascribed to a specific task, problem, or goal. There are different language groups; some require a compiler, which is a translator from what humans write, practically in English, to what a machine can understand. We organize each type of code by creating different structures, color-coding certain tasks, and adding some symbols that a computer can process."
Leonard asks politely, "But why are you telling me all this when my job description is to help with concept art? That's what I excel at."
Charybdis explains patiently, "You'll see. I read on the news this morning that AI will not take your job, but someone using it might."
Leonard, "I tried that. Some outcomes were really cool, while others were not acceptable by my standards. It all relies on your text or verbal prompt. I like a realistic take on art; any machine will not match it."
Charybdis, "They say we have a camera for realism now. What counts is creativity and cognition. Besides, your hand is not perfect compared to the computer's precision. Do you want me to show you?"
Leonard, "Sure, but..."
Charybdis interrupts, "No but! We communicate better on the job when you understand what we coders do. It is all about teamwork. What is the hardest thing to visually depict, you'd say?"
Leonard answers, "It would be a human body for its complicated proportions. Also, a horse because it is the most interesting creature from the movement's point of view. This is how you draw a human body: start with the head, which fits seven times the body's height, unless we are talking about a basketball player, which uses eight. You use a geometric approach by comparing body parts to geometric forms or shapes. Then comes a positive/negative space, where you look at what belongs to the body and what not. The spaces between arms, for example, also form shapes that one can focus on to determine the body dynamics. This way, we form a body by looking at both positive and negative spaces. Just like that. You may take a photo with your tablet and trace it after. Analog drawing programs have an automatic image trace function. You may use a digital pen or work with analog shapes."
Charybdis, smiling, replies, "People do it in 3D programs as well, with wireframes, hidden line removal, or textures."
Leonard agrees, "OK, let's have a break, and after that, you will show me how to code it."

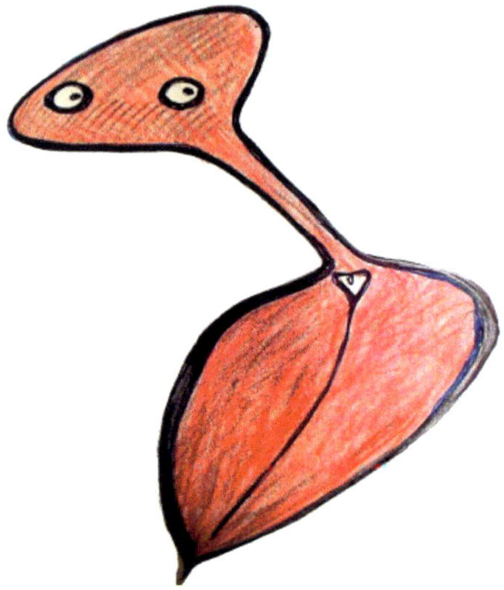

Gunsifo: loves the World.

Gunsifo: loves the World.

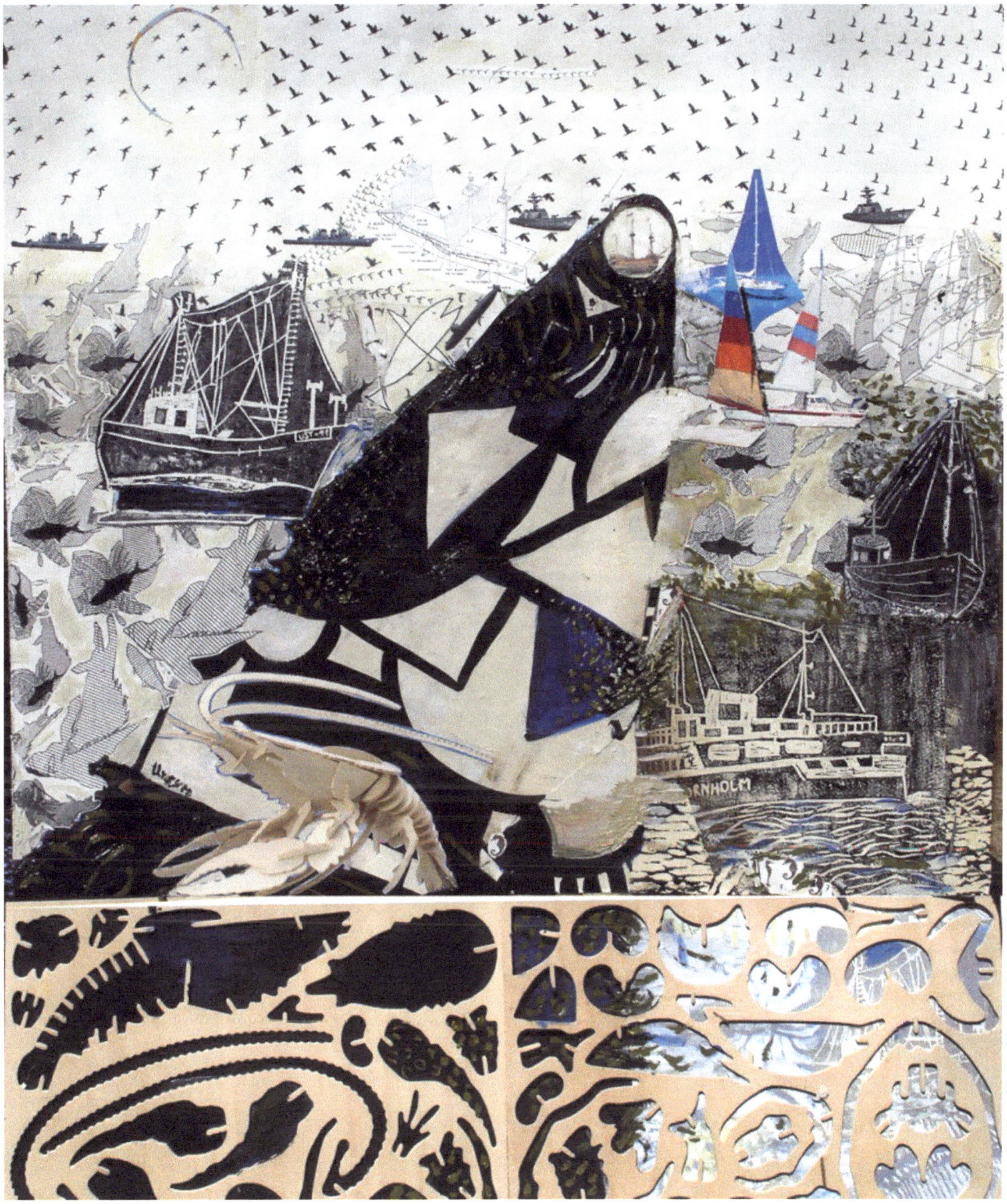

Micro, Macro. © *2025 by Anna Ursyn*

Act II.
The Curtain goes up (or opens).

Charybdis begins slowly, explaining, "So let's try coding it now. There are many languages to choose from, and it is easy to do without cost. For some, you will need to download a compiler. Let's start with Python and a program that outputs a man when using ASCII-based art.

```
print("       o")
print("      /|\")
print("       |")
print("      / \")
print("  ______")
```

Leonard exclaims, "What? Wait a second, can I draw a human by typing the word print several times? That is astonishingly lunatic!"
Charybdis explains, "The program outputs an image of a man using the ASCII characters for drawing lines and symbols. The "o" stands for the head, and the "/,\,|" characters represent the arms and legs, torso, and the "_" characters represent the floor. You may modify the code as you please. The program uses the print function to output each line of the ASCII art in sequence."

```
   o
  /|\
   |
  /\

______
```

"That was ASCII."
Leonard quickly googles ASCII and reads aloud, "American Standard Code for Information Interchange, with only 128 code points and only 95 printable characters."
Charybdis continues, "Now, let's try drawing a manikin again in Python, but this time, the turtle module is employed. Please note that # symbols denote comments to help you remember your reasoning or to share your work with someone to speed up the process.

```
import turtle

# create a turtle object
t = turtle.Turtle()

# draw the head
t.circle(50)

# draw the torso
t.right(90)
t.forward(100)

# draw the legs
t.right(45)
t.forward(75)
t.backward(75)
t.left(90)
t.forward(75)
t.backward(75)

# draw the arms
t.right(135)
t.forward(50)
t.backward(50)
t.left(90)
t.forward(50)
t.backward(50)

# hide the turtle cursor
t.hideturtle()

# keep the turtle window open until closed manually
turtle.done()
```

This program creates a turtle object and uses it to draw a manikin, using turtle commands to draw the head, torso, legs, and arms. It positions the turtle using forward, backward, right, and left commands. Then, it hides the turtle cursor, keeping the turtle window open until you close it.
Now, let's try the same in C++, and here comes a C++ program that uses escape sequences to draw a manikin:

```
#include <iostream>
using namespace std;

int main()
{
  cout << "  O" << endl;
  cout << " /|\" << endl;
  cout << "  |" << endl;
  cout << " / \" << endl;

  return 0;
}
```

This program outputs a manikin using escape sequences for the backslash and vertical bar characters for the arms, legs, and body. The 'O' represents the head, and the output is formatted using endl to create a new line after each line of output. The result will look like this:

```
  O
 /|\
  |
 / \
```

And, again, you may modify and customize the code to create different variations of the manikin."
Leonard, "Seriously, just like that, I simply write in English, minding that the end of the line is endl, etc.?"
Charybdis, in a correctional voice, "It means to stop, mind you—end of the action in a line of code. As you see, you may use a turtle function in Python, where you draw lines with a tiny turtle, or use Processing.org, a program for artists developed by two MIT graduates, Ben Fry, and Kasey Reas, or go a different route by guiding lines by a program. You might plot your points on a grid paper first. This can be done in 2D on x and y or in 3D on x, y, and z. Or -z if you want to go far away from the screen."
Leonard, "That will do for me for today. Let's talk later after I have time to experiment with it."

The Curtain goes down (closes)
A Break

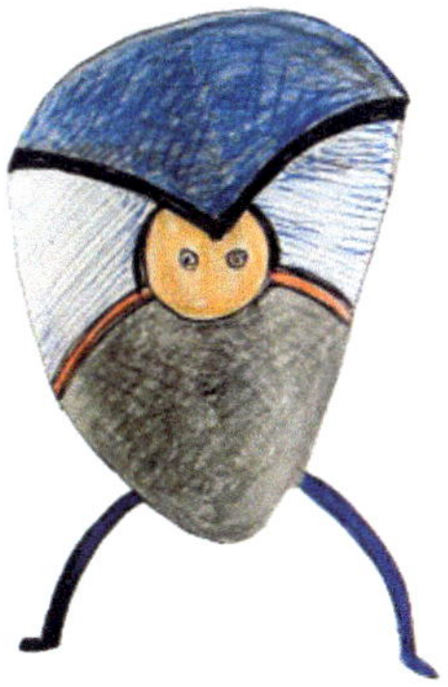

Nakaho: moves faster than thinks.

Nakaho moves faster than he thinks he does.

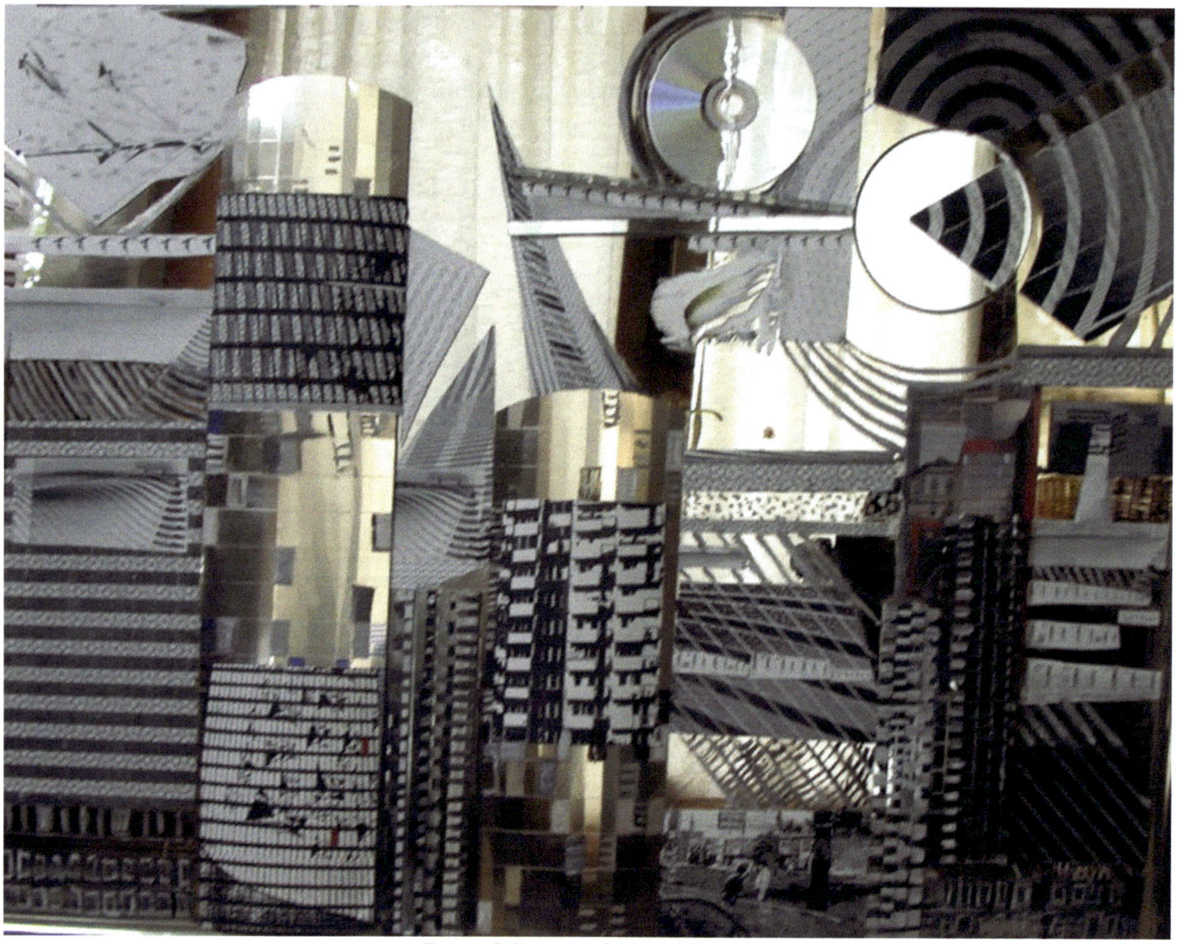

Data Mining. © *2025 by Anna Ursyn*

Act III
The curtain goes up (or opens).

Leonard explains, "I used my manikin again. First, with lines in 3D space.

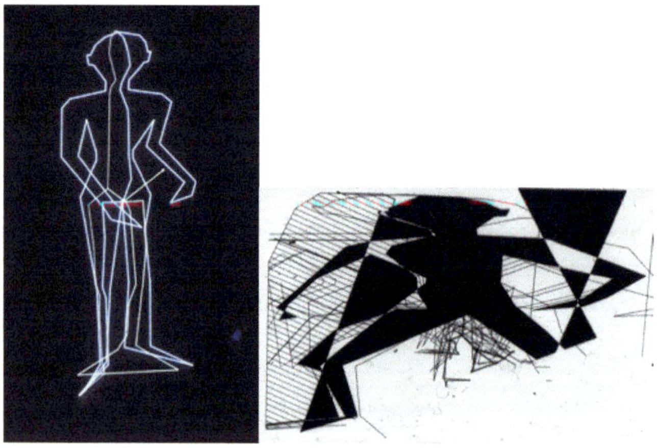

Man. Outputs from computer codes. © *2025 by Anna Ursyn*
I made changes in the clipping path distance to focus on some parts.

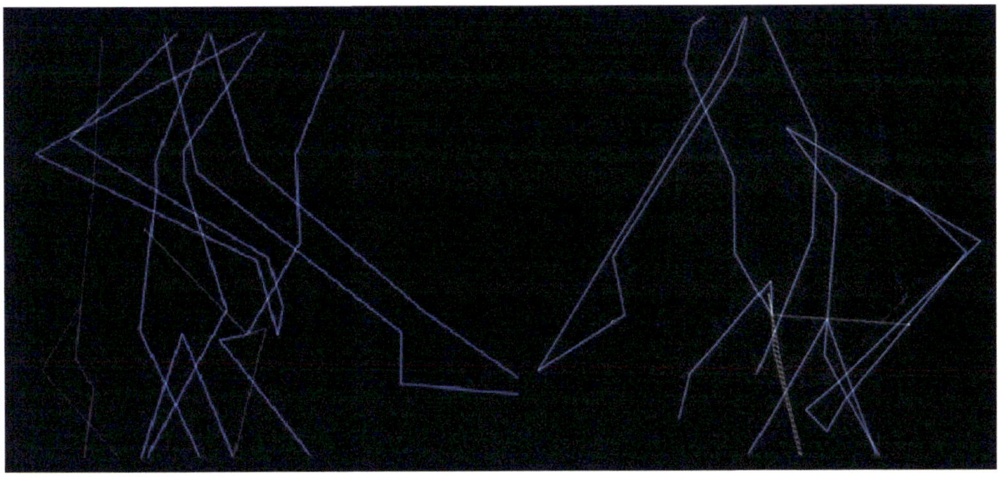

Since we converted a wooden manikin into a code, endless iterations could follow, such as copying the code and then pasting it with some transformations applied:

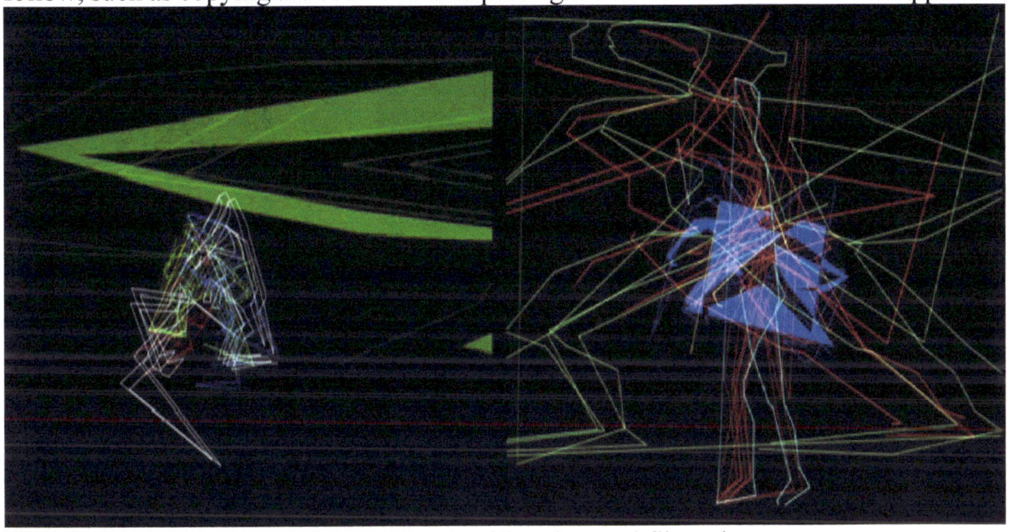

Then I added patterns and lights, filled it with color, and flipped one output:

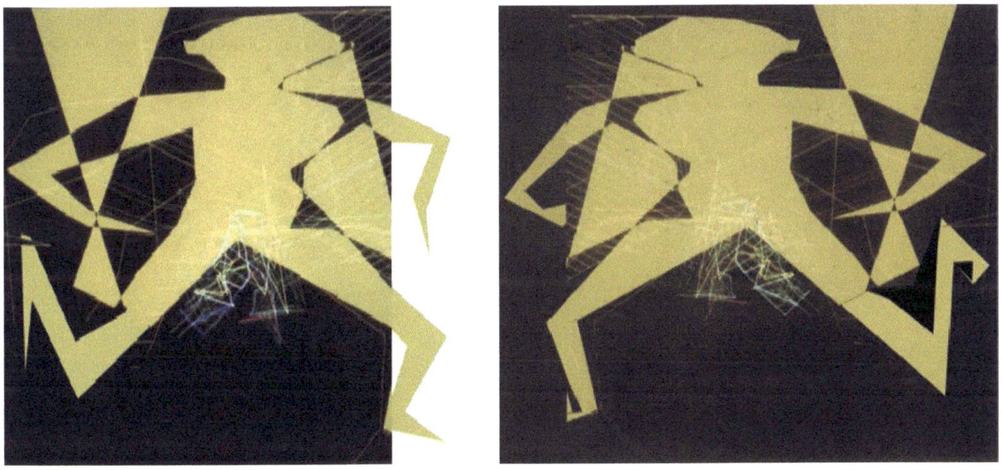

Further, I applied more transformations such as skewing, stretching, slanting, or distorting for dynamics.

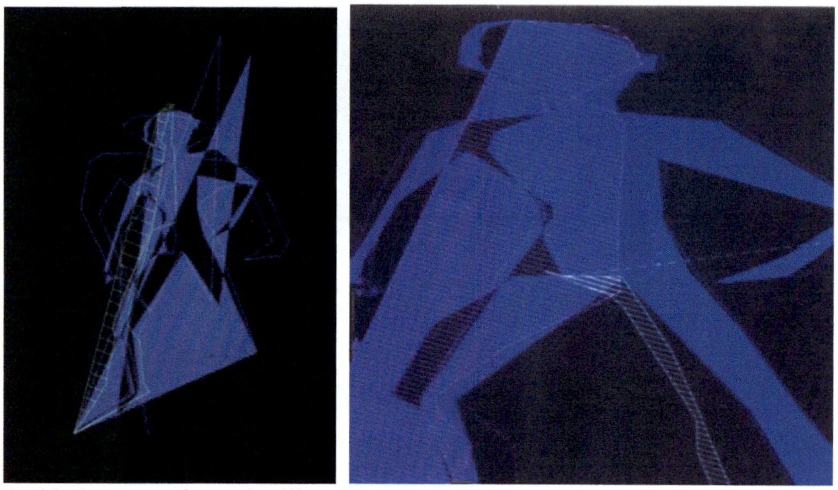

I added texture from the library of patterns!"
Leonard adds, "Those I can do in any software or an app!"

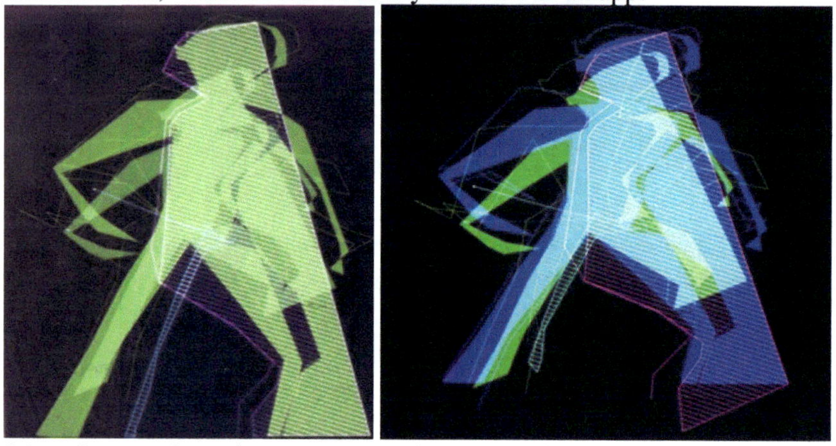

Man. Outputs from the computer code. © 2025 by Anna Ursyn

Charybdis states, "Yes, good, but without much understanding of what codes lay underneath, so, let's continue. I see you made one just black and white."

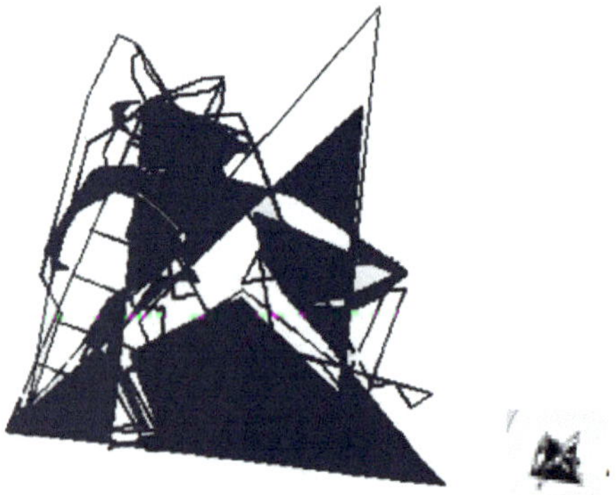

A Logo and Favicon. The scaled outputs from the computer code. © 2025 by Anna Ursyn

Leonard adds, "I like other media, perhaps traditional ones, so I translated the code output into photosilkscreens and photolithographs. This way, they could be printed on paper, wood, metal, or any 3D form."

Charybdis nodding, "No problem, but I'm not sure what those are."
Leonard explains, "Photosilkscreen is a technique where you cover parts of a tiny grid of the screen with emulsion, expose it to light, then apply pressured water washes to make openings for the ink to pass through following your design. Many colors can be applied, with different screens used one after another. Japanese Ukio-e masters used it with their wood-printed masterpieces."

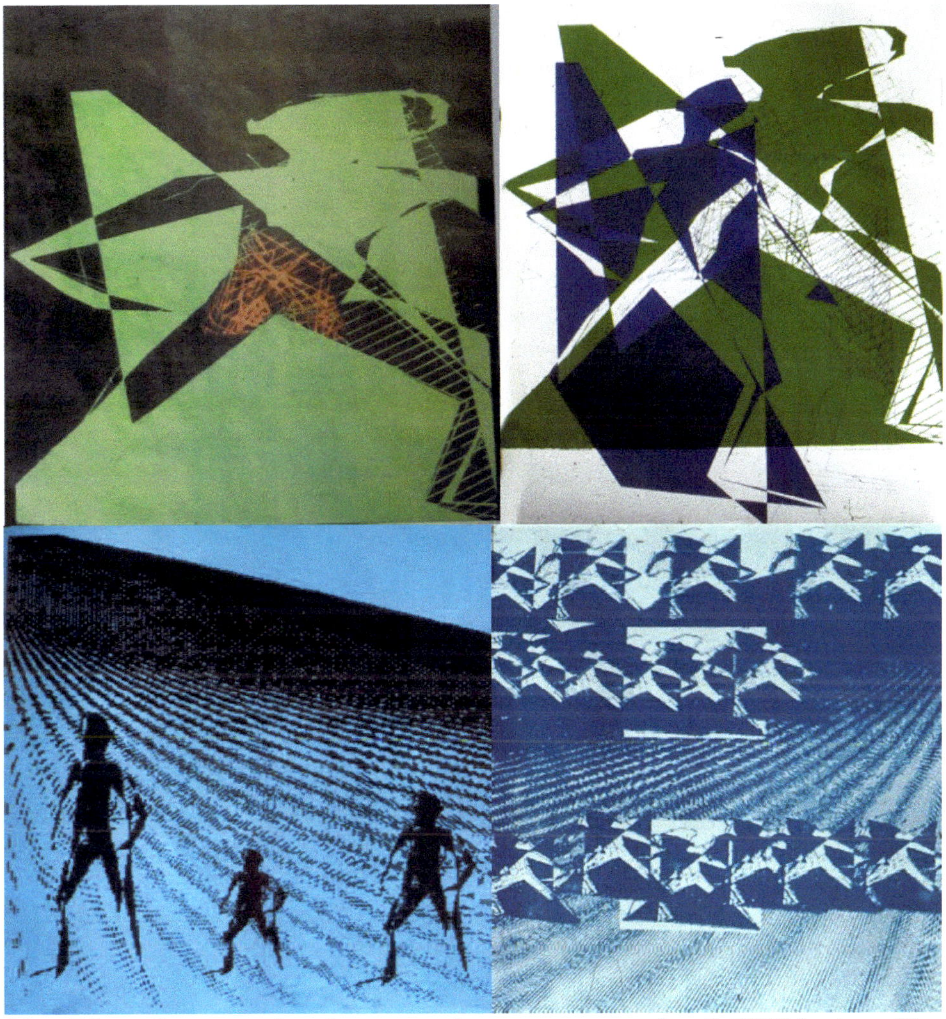

Man. Photosilscreens after the outputs from computer codes. © 2025 by Anna Ursyn

Leonard continues, "Photolithography is a different story. A large, flat, polished stone is exposed to light through graphic paper or acetate images. The Arabic gum bites through the stone, but markings with a greasy crayon protect parts of it, thus leaving the affected lines untouched. That produces a mirror image once printed. Lithography uses plates made photographically. Currently, the term describes semiconductor manufacturing, often called optical lithography or photo etching in the case of metals. This technique uses ultraviolet light to make a thin film and thus transfer a pattern design on a silicon wafer coated with a light-sensitive material (photoresist). Then follow the etching (the photoresist either breaks down or hardens when exposed to light), deposition, and implantation (by removing the soft parts of the coating with developers that solve them). Thus, this process typically involves a resin, sensitizer, and solvent.

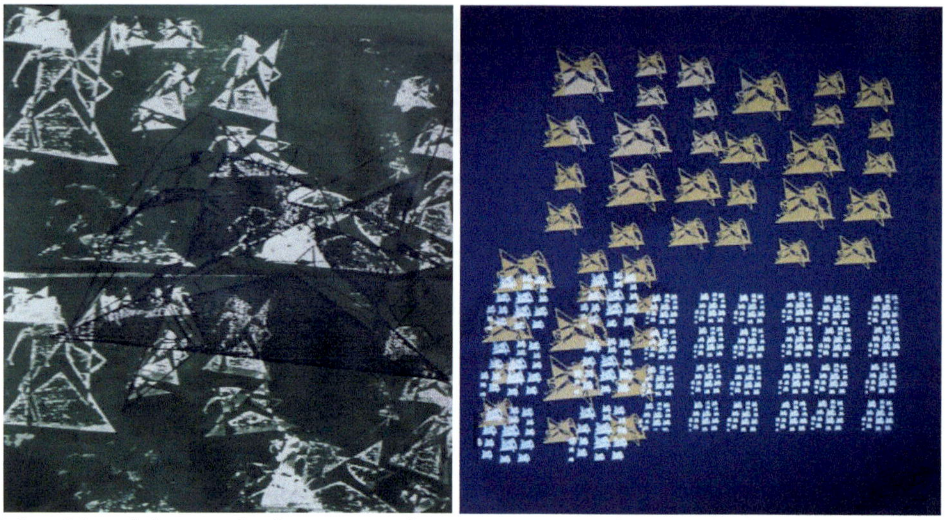

Men. Photolithograph after outputs from computer codes. © 2025 by Anna Ursyn.

You may add content to create images, like on this artwork called “Warriors.”

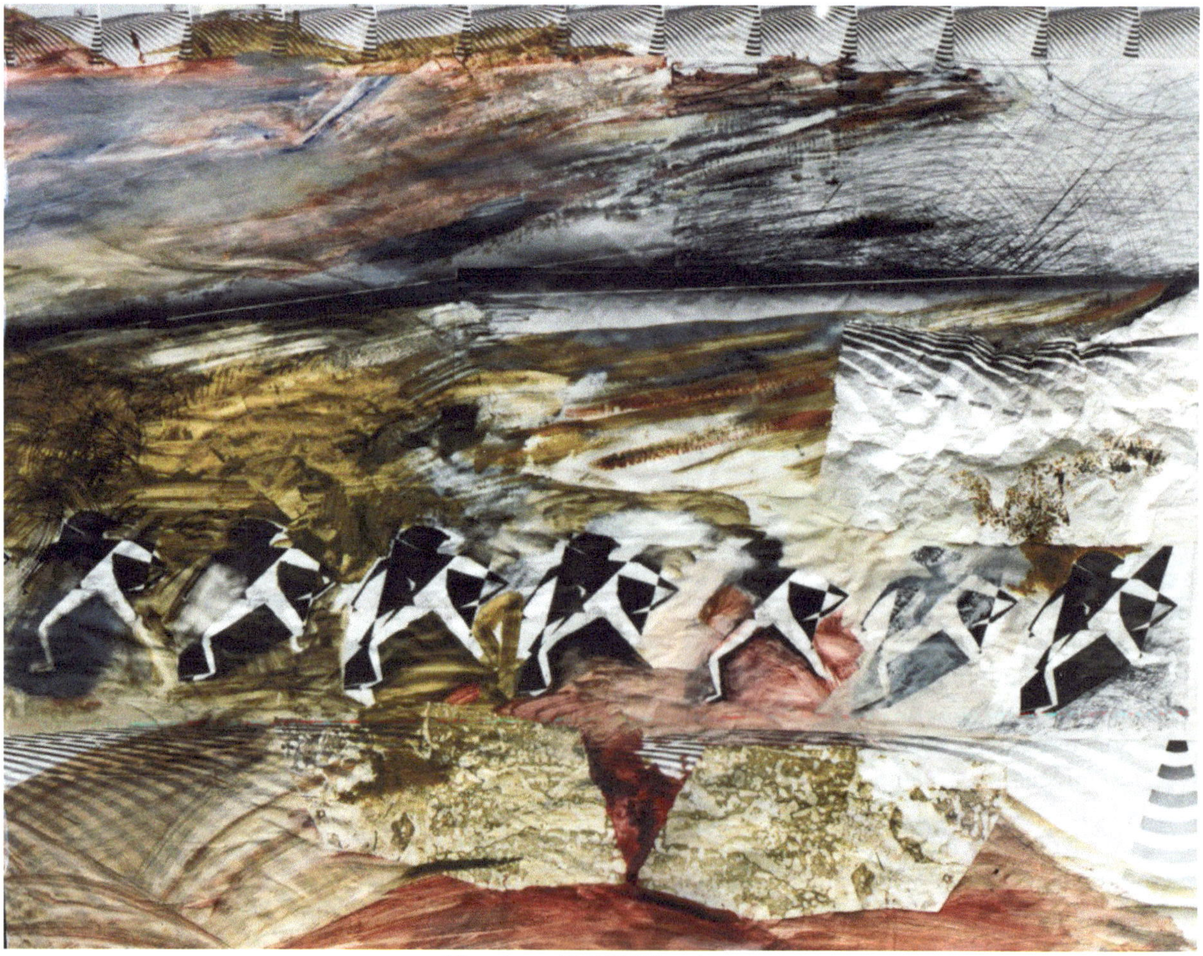

Warriors. © 2025 by Anna

Or print it on a row of shaped planks where your image can mimic the shape of the cut set of planks, like in a double-sided sculpture named "Warrior."

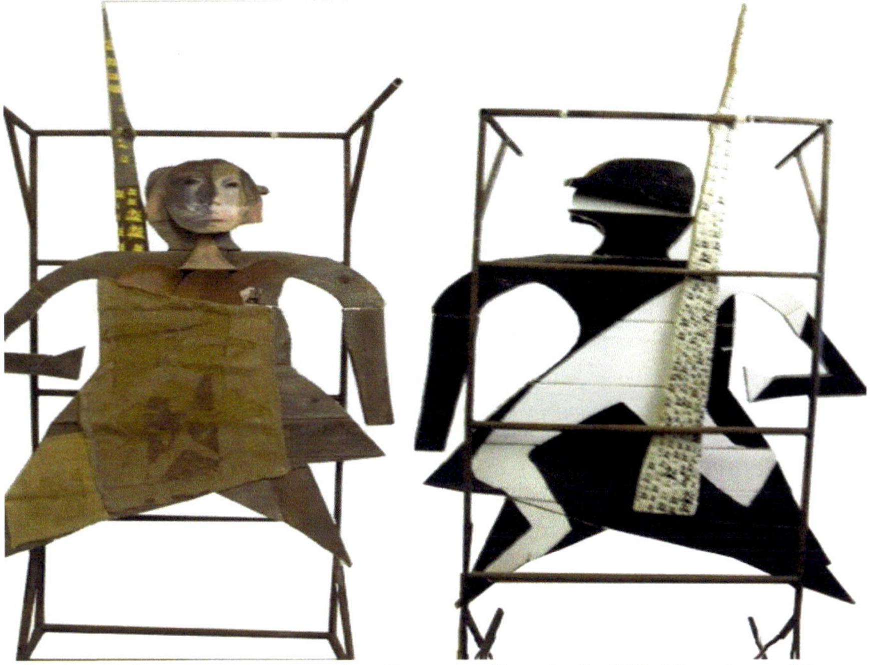

Warrior, a sculpture after computer code, front and back. © 2025 by Anna Ursyn

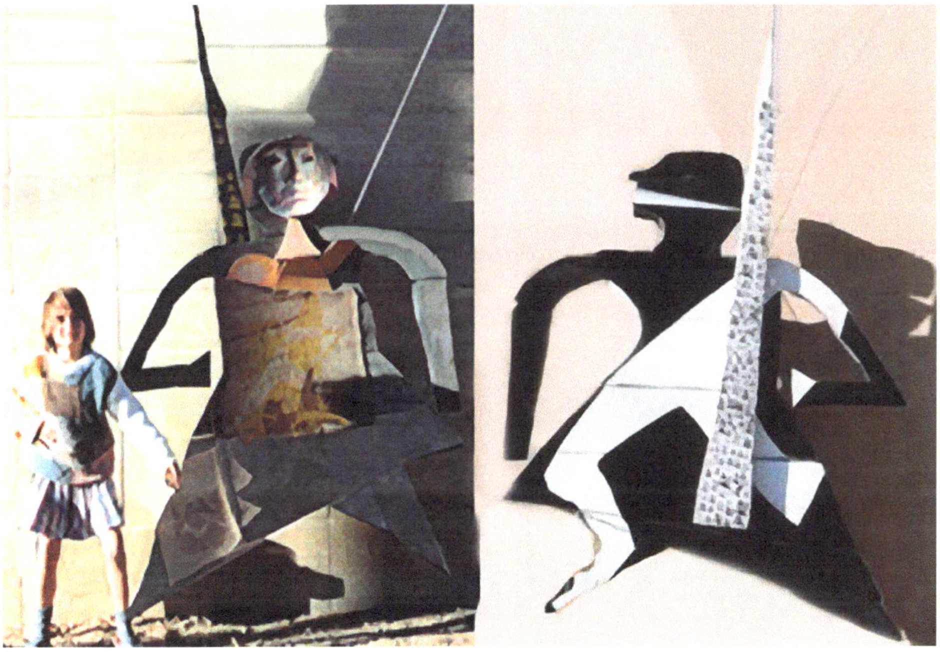

Warrior, front and back. © 2025 by Anna Ursyn

You may even apply it on 3D surfaces like a box.

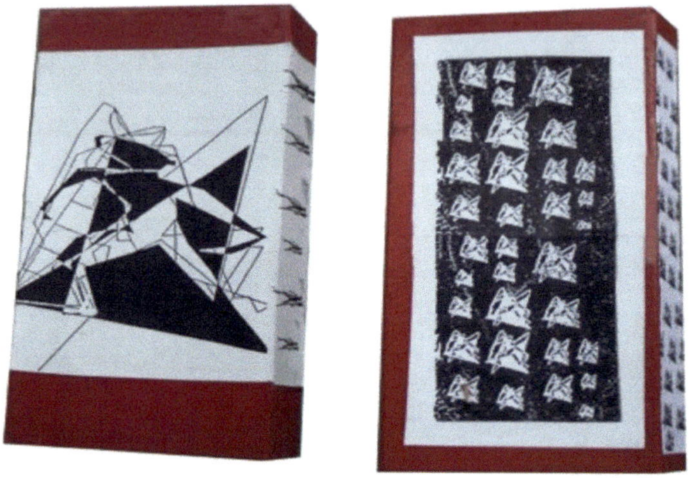

You may depart from the manikin form and use it as an inspiration for more geometric work. The sculpture "Four" follows a code and uses four assembled aspen wood planks, with each side affected by different techniques that can be applied to wooden plank surfaces: carved, additive, scratched, and sandblasted."

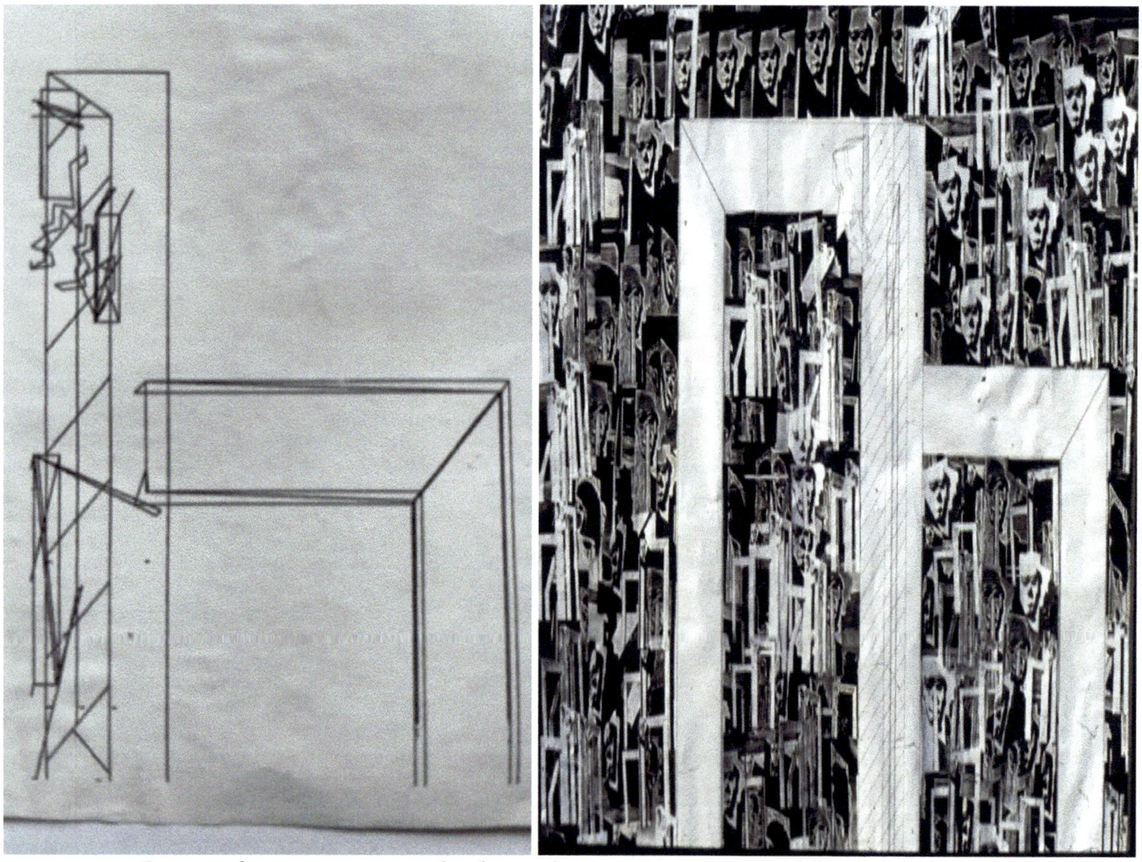

Outputs from computer codes for sculpture "Four" © 2025 by Anna Ursyn

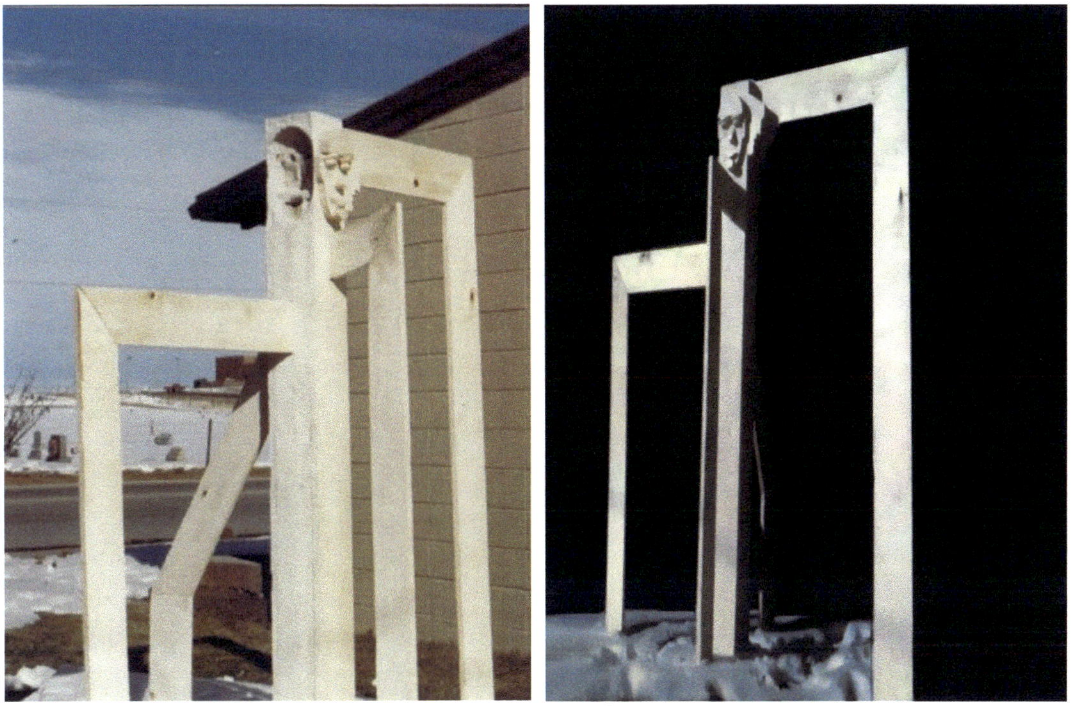

Four. Aspen wood. *© 2025 by Anna Ursyn*

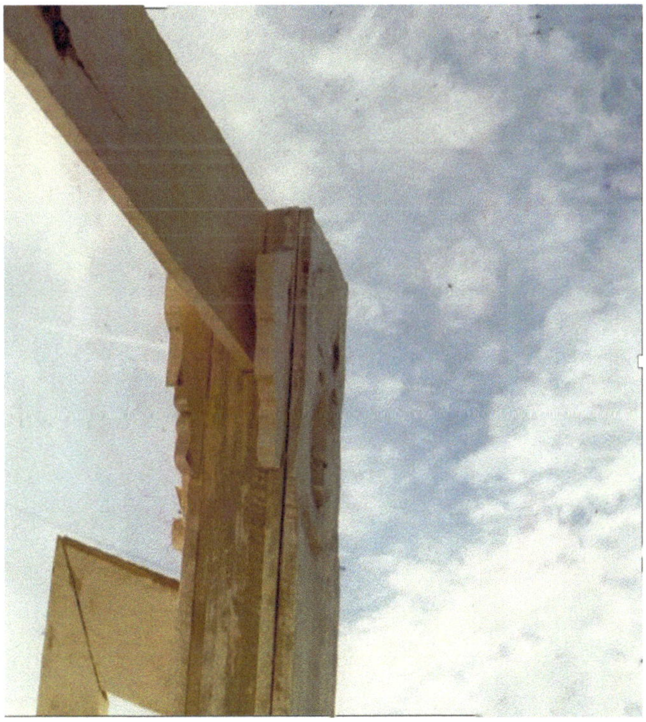

Four, a detail of aspen sculpture. © 2025 by Anna Ursyn

Charybdis notes, "I see. So now, the abstracted form of the human body is shortened to a few shapes and forms, thus forming the very basic outline. This is what abstract thinking is about."

The curtain goes down (closes).
A Break

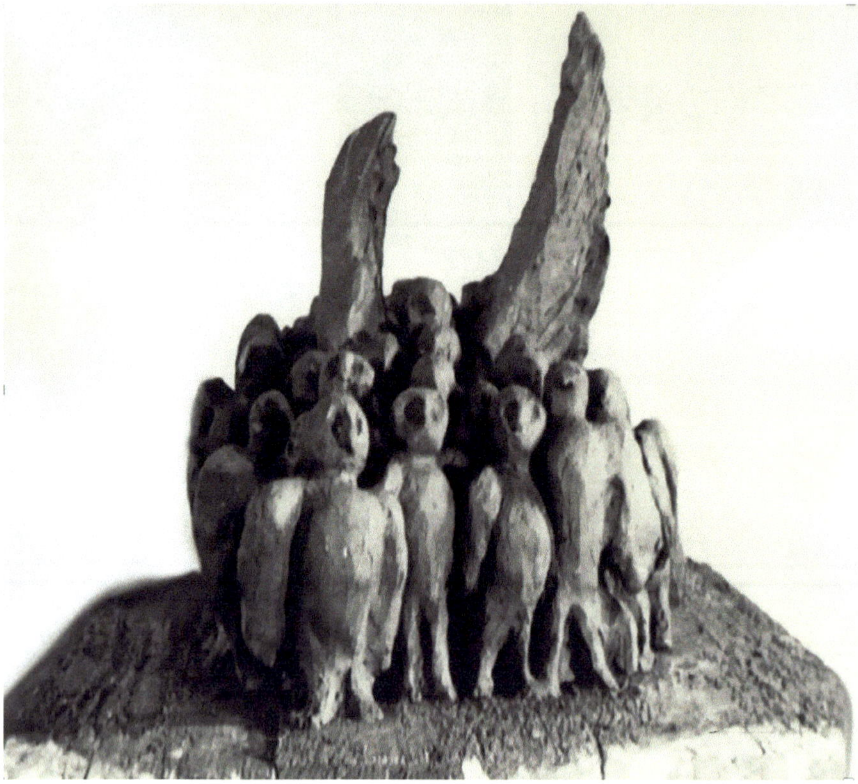

Man, and Animal. (front). © *2025 by Anna Ursyn*

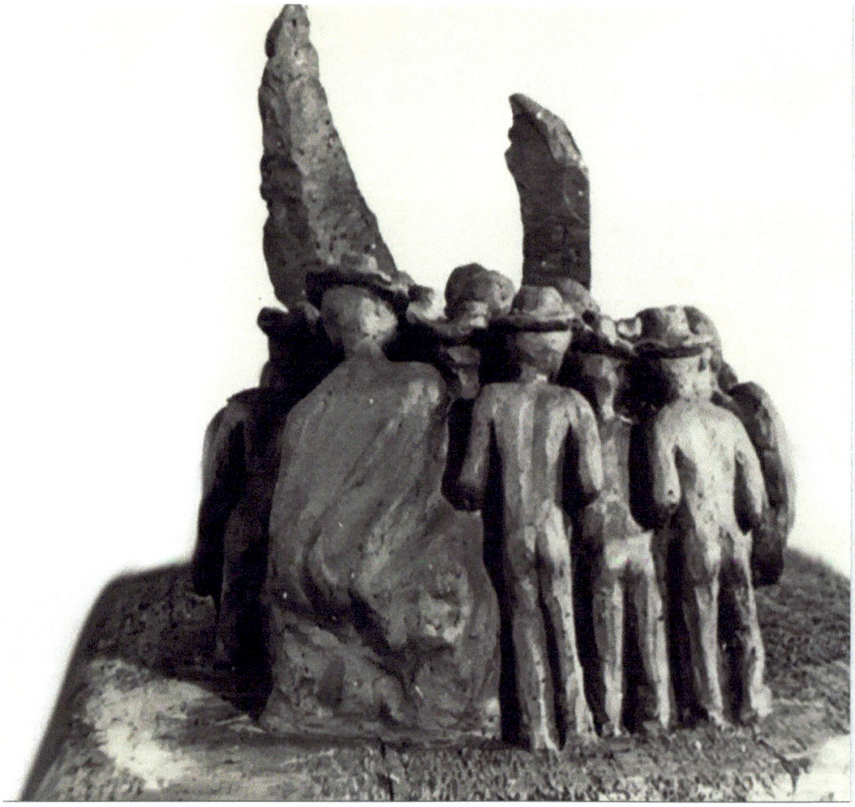

Man, and Animal (back). © *2025 by Anna Ursyn*

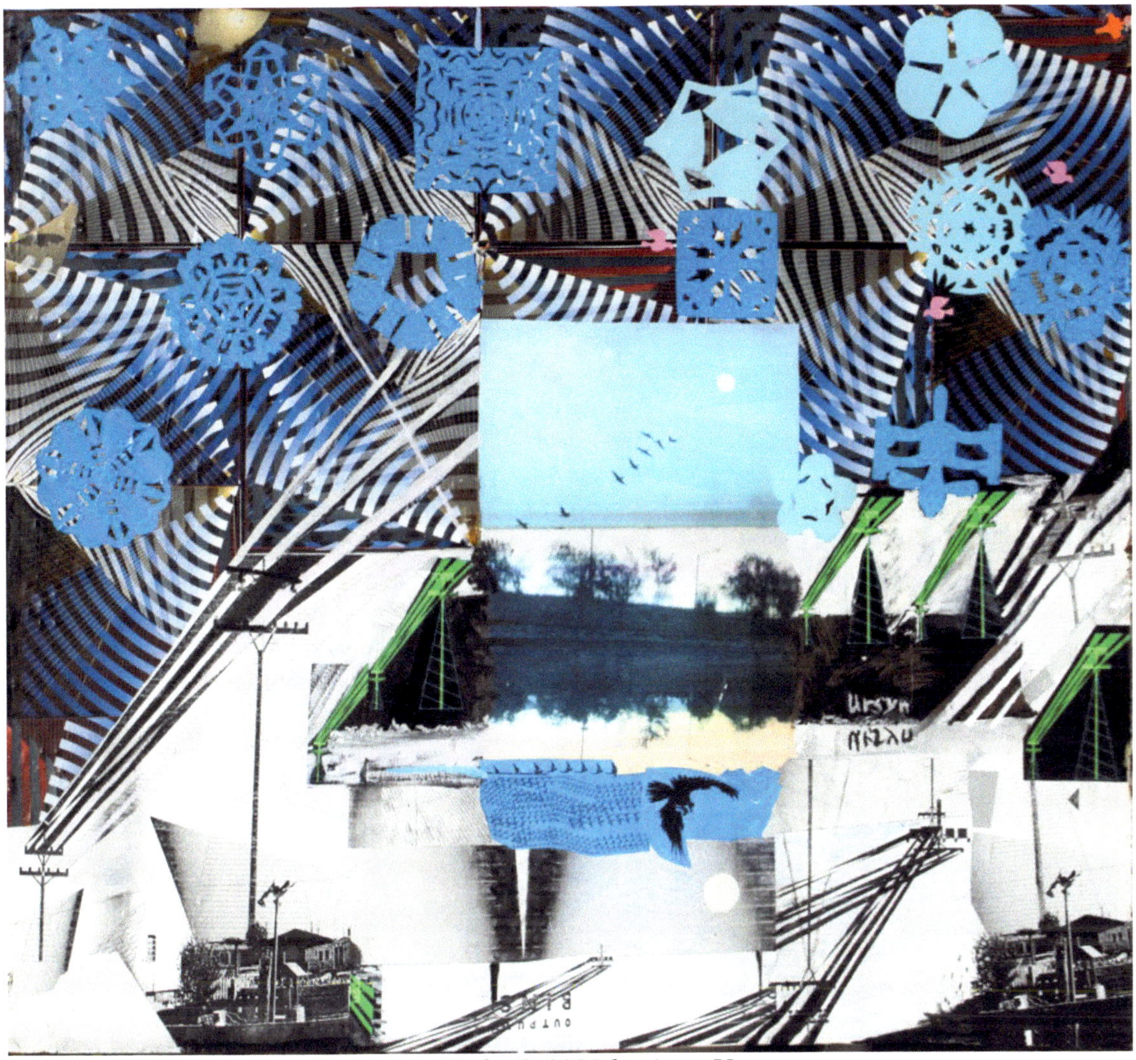

Nothing to Undo. © *2025 by Anna Ursyn*

Act IV
The curtain goes up (or opens).

`Enters Felix`
Felix, "Hi, I am a new intern. You must be Leonard. I heard a lot about you and your coding techniques. I was advised to learn to interact with the company's coders to make things run. I am an artist, so those not trained in art should not interfere, but I still want to use my talents, with my hand skills in drawing, and become a part of a bigger picture. I want to understand artificial intelligence, but I am terrified of math. Still, Charybdis said that you believe that coding is a language, not math, so could you explain to me how a computer processes data and how my work is the data? I want to learn coding by making drawings with codes. They might be less perfect in depicting details, but the level of precision is astounding, I hear."
Leonard, "Yes, of course, and nice to meet a similar soul. I have been passionate about coding since I can remember and would be happy to show you. What do you think is the most dynamic animal?"
Felix, "A horse, of course! They are the most three-dimensional animals to me. They live in their stables."

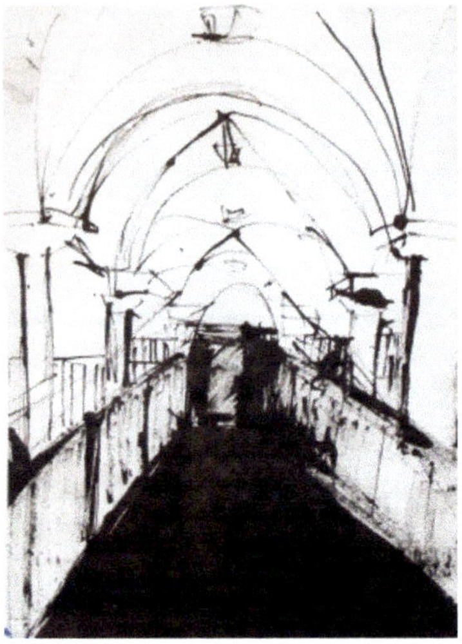
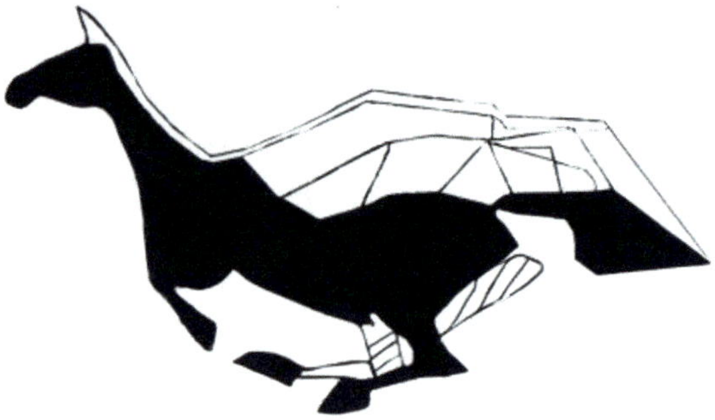

A Stud. Ink on paper and the output from the code. © 2025 by Anna Ursyn

Leonard, "A horse it is. Let's simplify and create a wooden manikin of a horse, then code an image following it. "
Felix corrects him, "It is not a wooden sculpture; it is just 3D printed, but in wood."

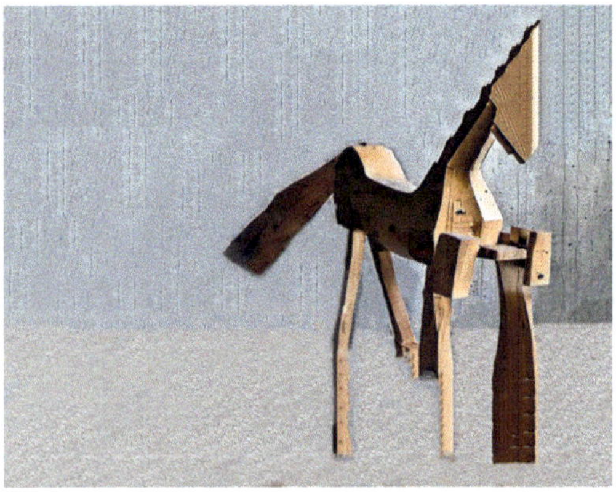

Charybdis confirms, "Yes, I met an artist employed by a 3D printing company. They made her write G-codes for the 3D printing machines."
Leonard continues, "We'll start with a simplified version of this animal

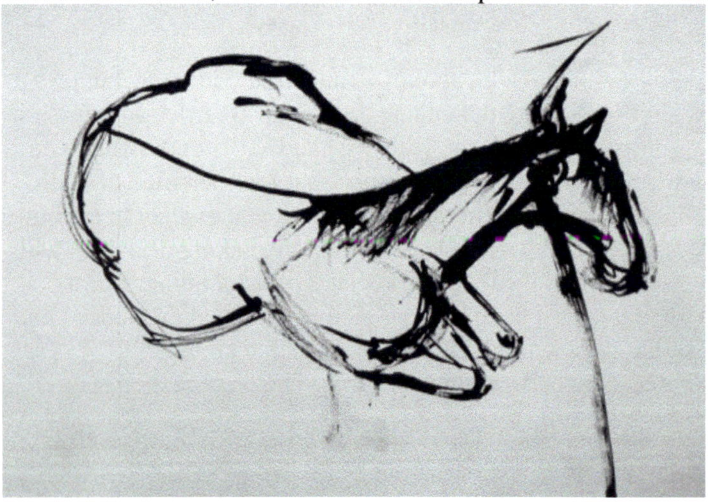

Resting horse. Ink on paper. © 2025 by Anna Ursyn.

Here's a code in Python that uses ASCII art to display a horse as an output:

```
print("        ,--.!.")
print("     _/  -*-")
print("  ,d08b.  '|`")
print("   0088MM")
print("  `9MMP'")
```

Felix, "That does not look like a horse!"
When you run this code, it will display the following output, which almost looks like a horse:

```
        ,--.!.
     _/  -*-
  ,d08b. '|`
   0088MM
  `9MMP'
```

Felix, "There must be a better way to do it!"
Leonard, "You may want to modify the code to add your artistic touch to the horse!
Let's try a simple Python code that displays a horse shape using the turtle graphics module. Please note that the symbol # denotes a comment. It simplifies coding, as one can remember one's train of thought and share the code with someone unfamiliar with the initial idea.

```
import turtle

# Create a turtle object
t = turtle.Turtle()

# Set the turtle's speed and pen color
t.speed(0)
t.pencolor("brown")

# Draw the horse's body
t.pensize(10)
t.goto(0, -150)
t.circle(80)

# Draw the horse's head
t.penup()
t.goto(0, 0)
t.pendown()
t.goto(50, 50)
t.goto(70, 20)
t.goto(90, 0)
t.goto(70, -20)
t.goto(50, -50)
t.goto(0, 0)

# Draw the horse's legs
t.penup()
t.goto(-40, -150)
t.pendown()
t.goto(-40, -220)
t.goto(-80, -220)
t.penup()
t.goto(40, -150)
t.pendown()
t.goto(40, -220)
t.goto(80, -220)

# Draw the horse's tail
t.penup()
t.goto(-40, -70)
t.pendown()
t.goto(-70, -90)
t.goto(-70, -130)
```

```
t.goto(-40, -150)

# Draw the horse's mane
t.penup()
t.goto(50, 50)
t.pendown()
t.goto(70, 70)
t.goto(90, 90)
t.penup()
t.goto(50, -50)
t.pendown()
t.goto(70, -70)
t.goto(90, -90)

# Hide the turtle cursor
t.hideturtle()

# Exit on click
turtle.exitonclick()
```

When you run this code, it will display a horse manikin coded with turtle graphics."
Charybdis advises, "You need to find out where the screen's origin is for each system you are coding for. That means (0.0) for 2D graphics and (0.0.0) for those three-dimensional. It makes a huge difference.
Leonard, "So now, let's do one in C++ to output an image of a horse in this language.
C++ is a powerful programming language not typically used for generating image outputs. However, it is possible to use C++ and a graphics library like OpenCV to display images.
This code uses OpenCV to display an image of a horse. Please note that the comments in C++ are denoted by "//" and should not be confused with the "# "symbol that starts a code.

```
'#include.

#include <opencv2/opencv.hpp>

int main(int argc, char** argv)
{
  // Create an image object
  cv::Mat img = cv::imread("horse.jpg");

  // Check if the image was successfully loaded
  if (img.empty())
  {
    std::cout << "Error: Could not load image" << std::endl;
    return 1;
  }

  // Create a window to display the image
  cv::namedWindow("Horse Image", cv::WINDOW_NORMAL);
  cv::resizeWindow("Horse Image", img.cols, img.rows);

  // Display the image in the window
  cv::imshow("Horse Image", img);

  // Wait for a key press before closing the window
  cv::waitKey(0);

  return 0;
}
```

To use this code, save an image of a horse in the same directory as the code (or update the path in the cv::imread function). Then, compile and run the code using a C++ compiler that is linked to the OpenCV library. When you run this code, it will display an image of a horse in a window.

To generate an image of a horse using C++, we need to use a graphics library to create and save the image. One popular graphics library for C++ is called "SFML" (Simple and Fast Multimedia Library). Here's an example code that uses SFML to create and save an image of a horse:

```
#include <SFML/Graphics.hpp>
#include <iostream>

int main()
{
   // Create a 640x480 image
   sf::RenderTexture texture;
   if (!texture.create(640, 480))
   {
      std::cerr << "Error: Could not create render texture" << std::endl;
      return 1;
   }

   // Clear the texture with a white background
   texture.clear(sf::Color::White);

   // Load a horse image
   sf::Texture horseTexture;
   if (!horseTexture.loadFromFile("horse.png"))
   {
      std::cerr << "Error: Could not load horse image" << std::endl;
      return 1;
   }

   // Create a sprite for the horse image and draw it onto the texture
   sf::Sprite horseSprite(horseTexture);
   horseSprite.setPosition(100, 100);
   texture.draw(horseSprite);

   // Save the texture to an image file
   sf::Image image = texture.getTexture().copyToImage();
   if (!image.saveToFile("horse_output.png"))
   {
      std::cerr << "Error: Could not save image file" << std::endl;
      return 1;
   }

   // Exit the program
   std::cout << "Horse image saved as horse_output.png" << std::endl;
   return 0;
}
```

This code creates a 640x480 image using an SFML RenderTexture. It then loads a picture of a horse from a file, creates an SFML Sprite object for the horse image as a collection, and draws the sprite onto the texture. Finally, the code saves the texture as an image file called "horse_output.png."

Note: For this to work, you'll need an image of a horse named "horse.png" in the same directory as the code. You can change the image filename and path if needed.

Felix asks, "So why write a horse if you need to have one in the library?"

Leonard replies, "It will make you look smarter."

Felix, "But I am not familiar with C++,"

Leonard explains, "I can provide you with an example code for creating a horse object in Python:

```
class Horse:
   def __init__(self, name, age, breed):
      self.name = name
      self.age = age
      self.breed = breed
      self.sound = "neigh"

   def make_sound(self):
      print(self.sound)

   def gallop(self):
      print(f"{self.name} is galloping.")
```

Here's how you can create an instance of a horse object and call its methods:

```
my_horse = Horse("Buddy", 6, "Thoroughbred")
print(my_horse.name) # Output: Buddy
print(my_horse.age) # Output: 6
print(my_horse.breed) # Output: Thoroughbred
my_horse.make_sound() # Output: neigh
my_horse.gallop() # Output: Buddy is galloping.
```

Of course, the code only creates a horse object regarding its properties and behaviors, but it doesn't visually represent a horse. It can be done in various other languages, though:

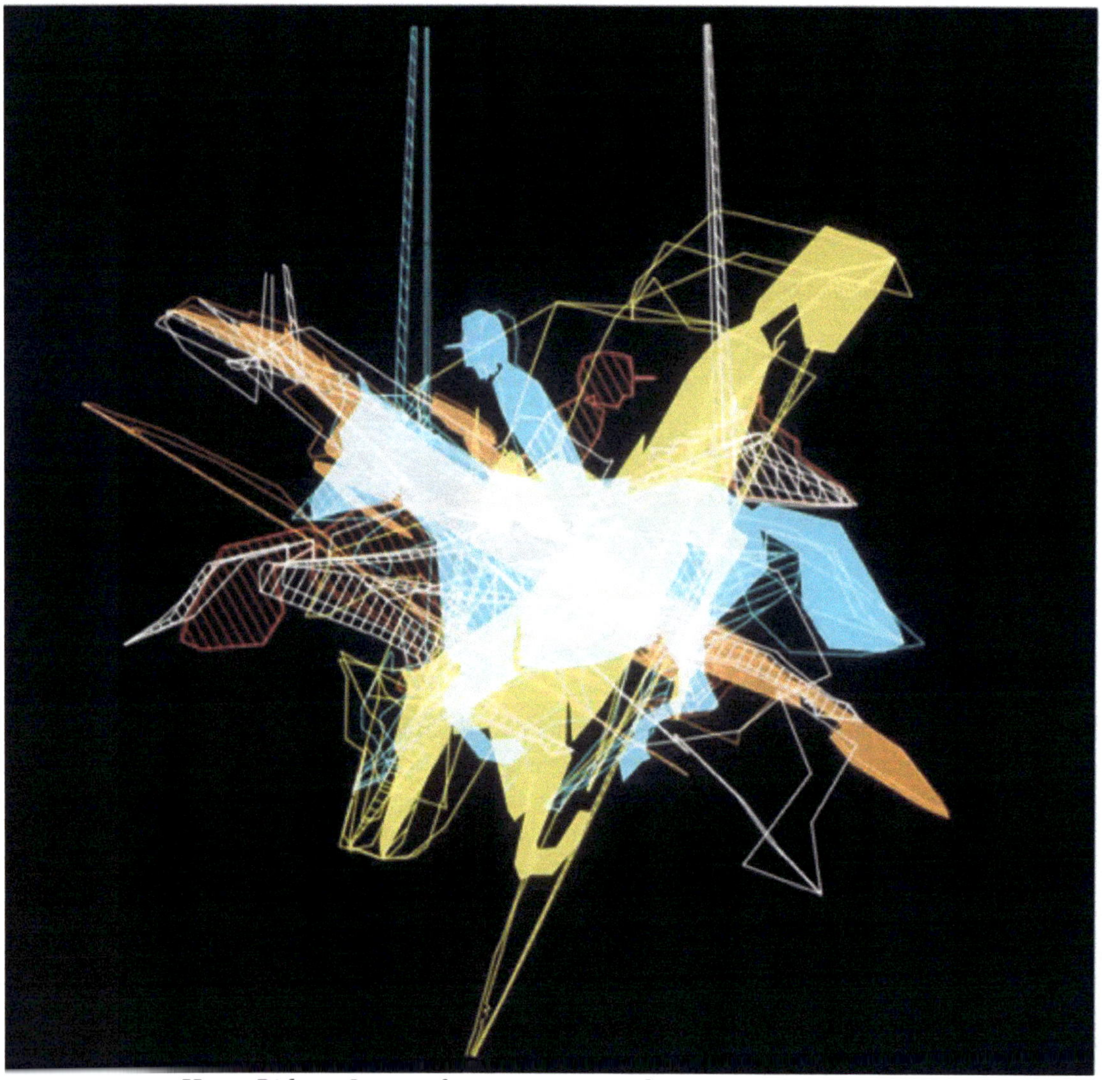

Horse Riders. Outputs from computer codes. © 2025 by Ursyn

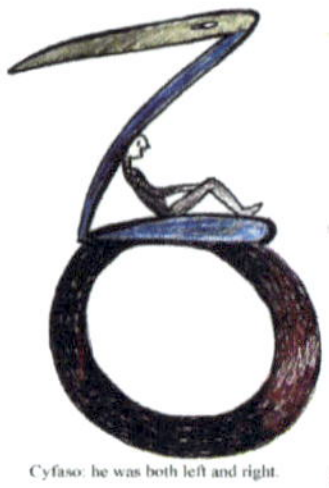

Cyfaso: he is both left and right.

Felix, "I like traditional media."
Leonard, "Work can be converted back and forth. For example, I'll show you some series transformed into a tangible form, ranging from prints to photosilkscreens and photolithographs.
Let's start with black and white prints and look at several codes linked for a logo for the Digital Art Gallery, D-ART for the International Conference on Information Visualisation organized in London.

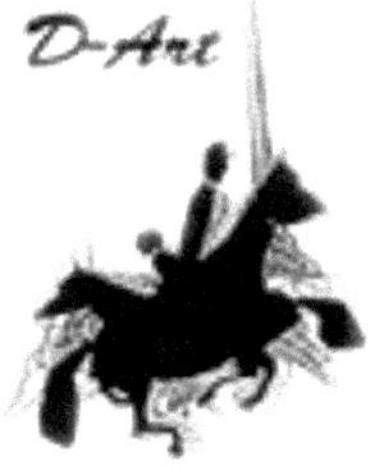

Now, the horses serve as graphic design that has a specific function. However, various iterations can serve our artistic creations.

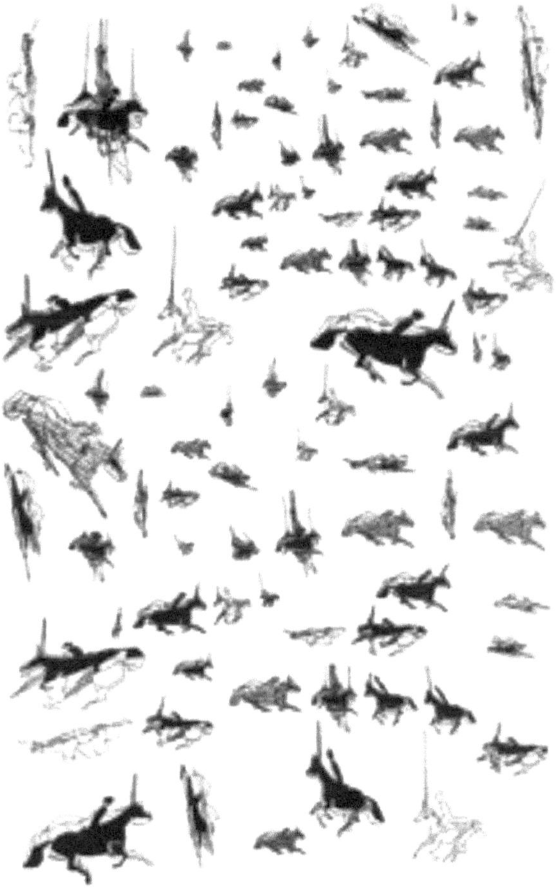

A Gallery of Horses © 2025 by Anna Ursyn

The color can be assigned, along with various lines that form a texture.

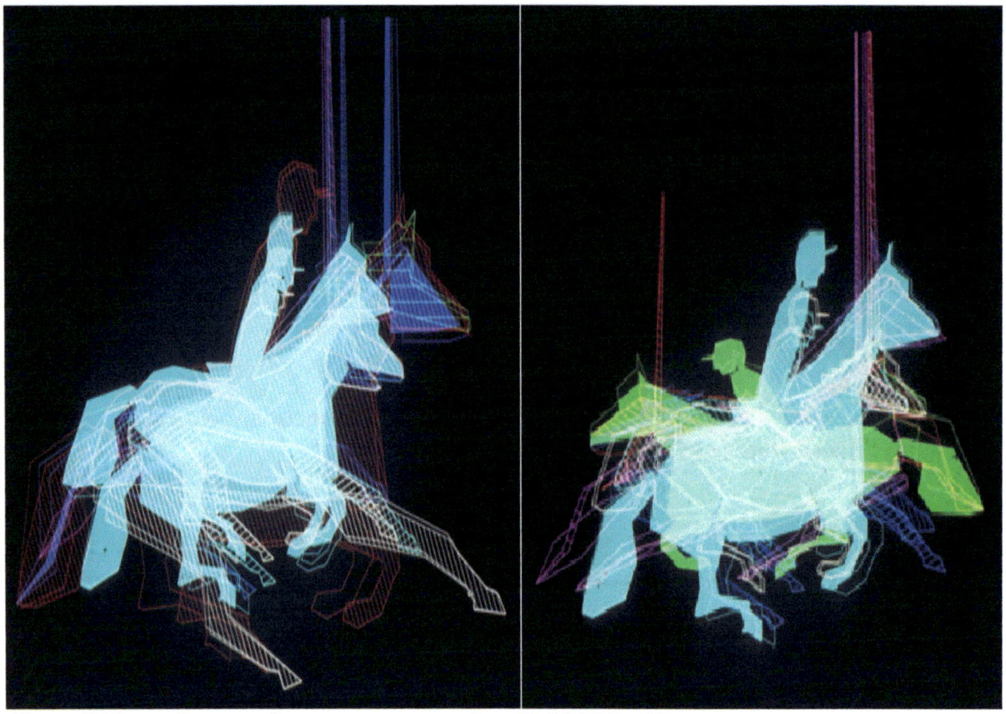

Horse Riders. Outputs from computer codes. © 2025 by Ursyn

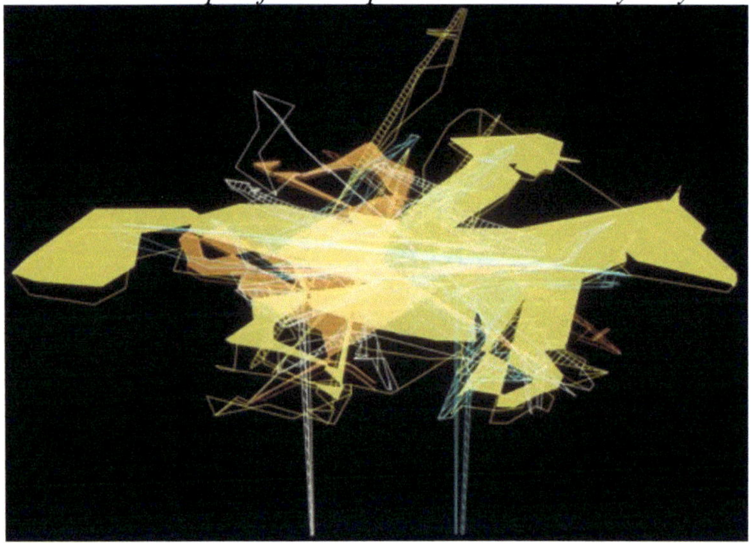

Horses. Outputs from computer codes. © 2025 by Anna Ursyn

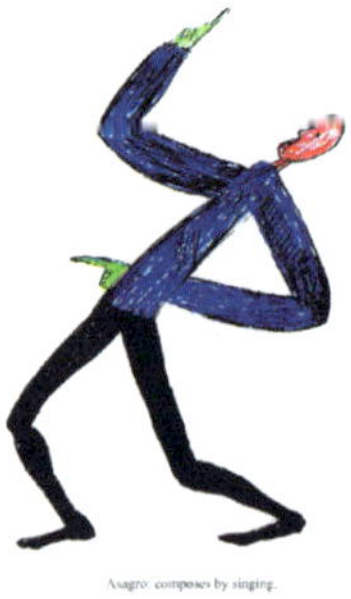

Asagro: composes music by singing.

Simple plots can be converted to photosilkscreen, so we'll have traditional art with coded images. This allows us to use one or more pigment-based colors. One screen per color.

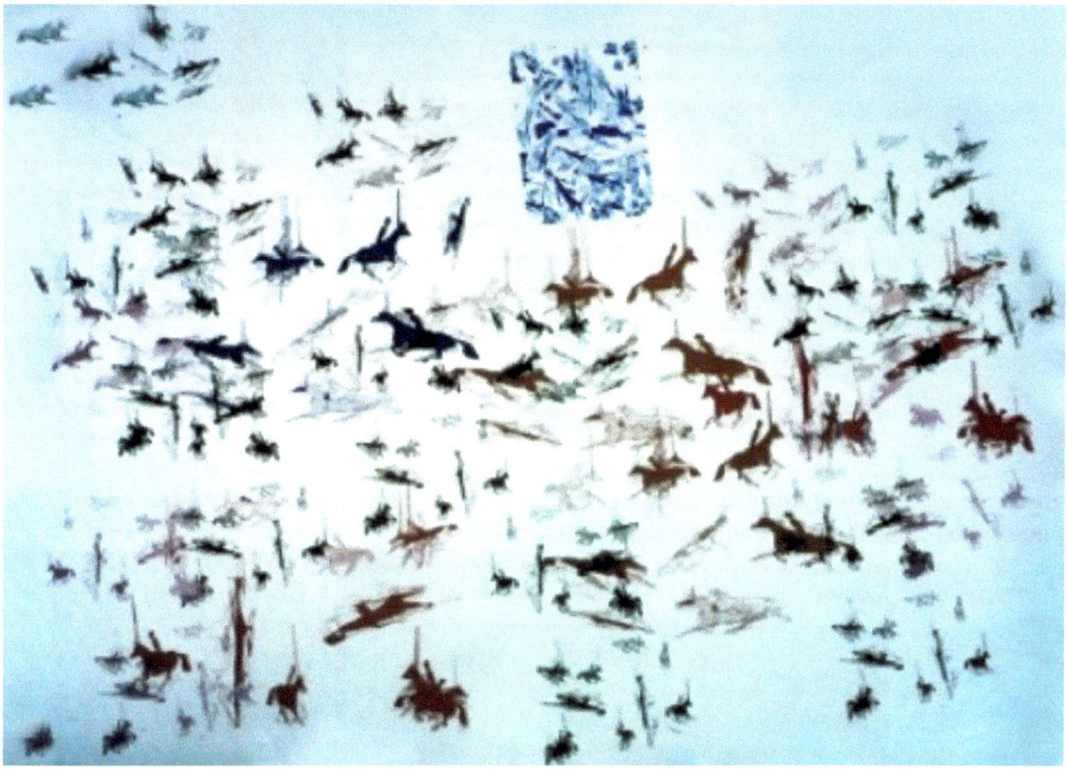

Horses. Photosilkscreens after outputs from computer codes. © 2025 by Anna Ursyn

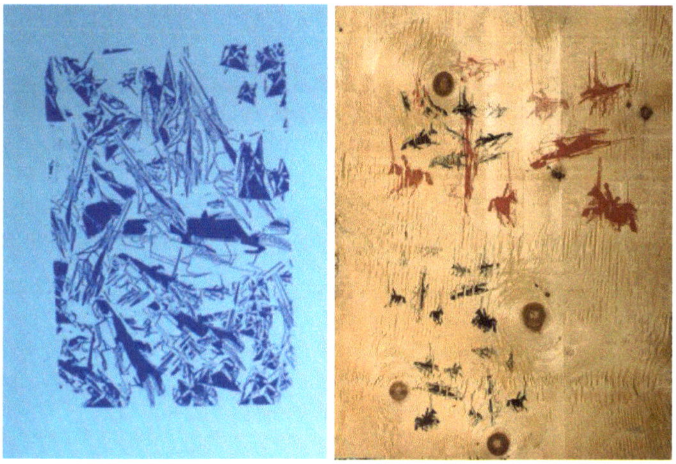

Photosilkscreens after outputs from computer codes on paper and wood. © 2025 by Anna Ursyn

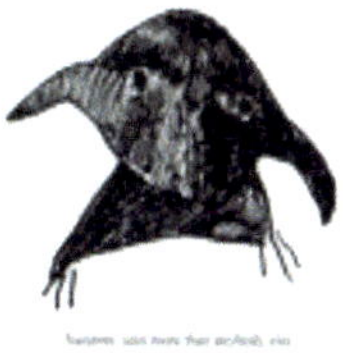

Nasumn: sees more than everybody else.

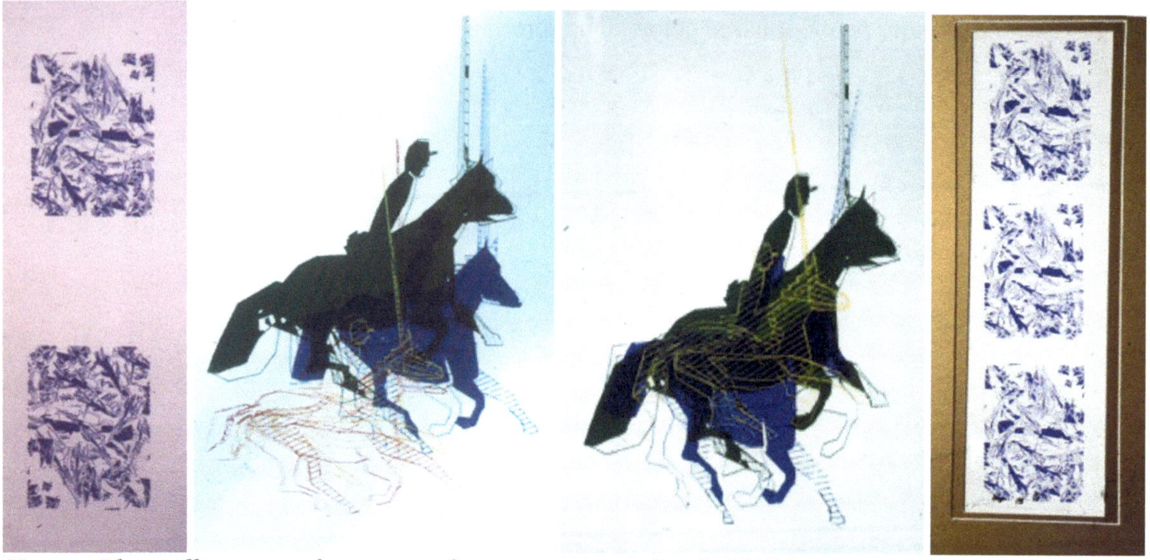

Horses. Photosilkscreens after outputs from computer codes. © *2025 by Anna Ursyn.*
Now, some photolithographs if you like limestones."

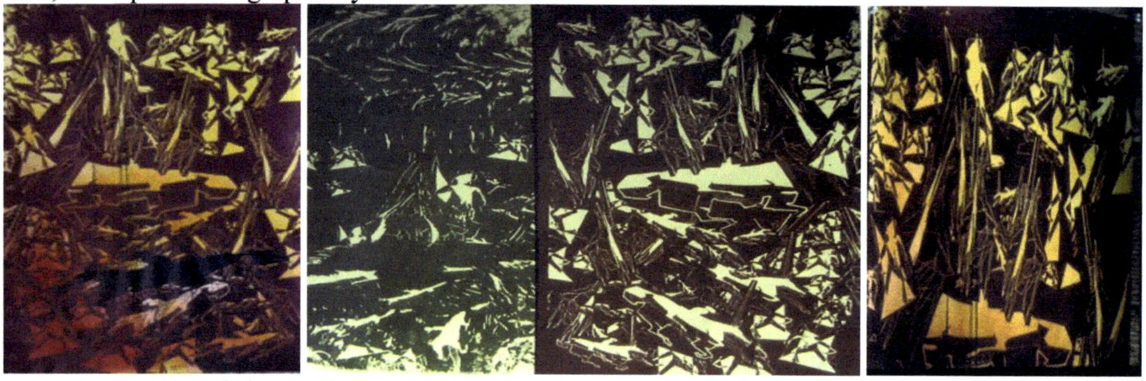

Horses. Photolithographs after outputs from computer codes. © *2025 by Anna Ursyn*

Felix asks, "How about moving images, VR, and AI/ML?"
Leonard replies, "Those you will teach the next incoming intern."

The Curtain goes down (closes).
A Break

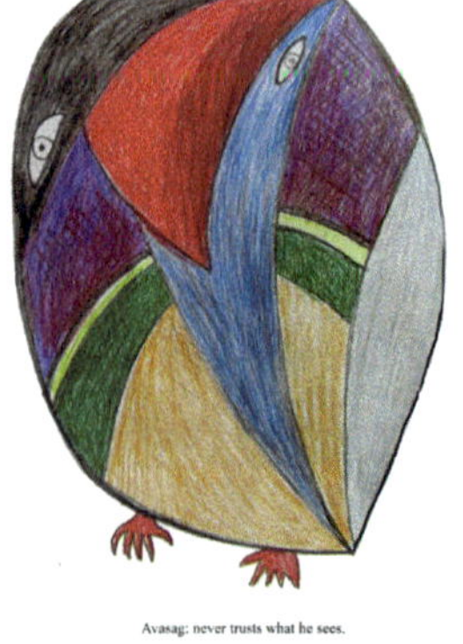

Avasag: never trusts what he sees.

Act V
The curtain goes up (or opens).

Enters Oxygen
Felix, "Hello, I'm Felix, the coder. You must be Oxygen, the new intern."
Oxygen, "Yes, I am a writing major. I came to write scripts for the company and learn about developing storylines and storyboarding."
Felix, "Oh, as a writer, you will be interested in language-based ideas. Let me show you how to make translations in various languages through coding. Here's an example of Python code to translate a line of text using the googletrans library and repeat it a specified number of times:

```
from googletrans import Translator

# Define the text to be translated and repeated
text_to_translate = "Hello, how are you?"
num_repeats = 3

# Create a translator object and translate the text
translator = Translator()
translated_text = translator.translate(text_to_translate, dest='es').text

# Repeat the translated text
for i in range(num_repeats):
   print(translated_text)
```

In this example, we first define the text to be translated ("Hello, how are you?") and the number of times we want to repeat it (num_repeats = 3). We then create a Translator object from the googletrans library and use it to translate the text to Spanish (specified by dest='es'). The translated text is stored in the translated_text variable. Finally, we use a for loop to repeat the translated text the specified number of times (num_repeats). The print() function outputs the translated text to the console. You can modify the text to_translate and num_repeats variables to translate and repeat different text.
Oxygen, politely excusing herself out, "I am so sorry, but I forgot my shoe."

The End
The curtain goes down (or closes).

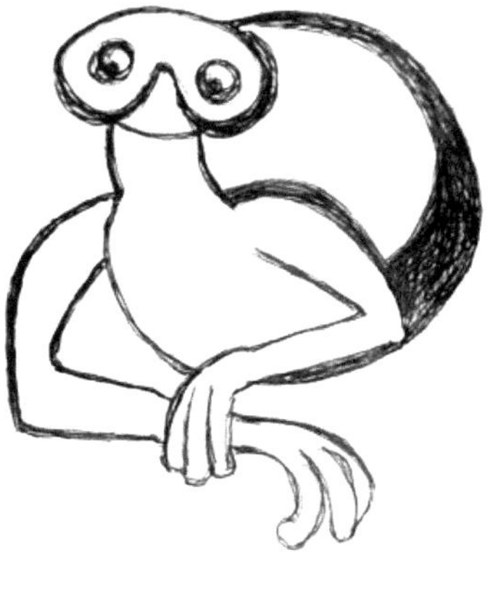

Teguno: discusses his problems on a daily basis.

Teguno: discusses her problems on a daily basis.

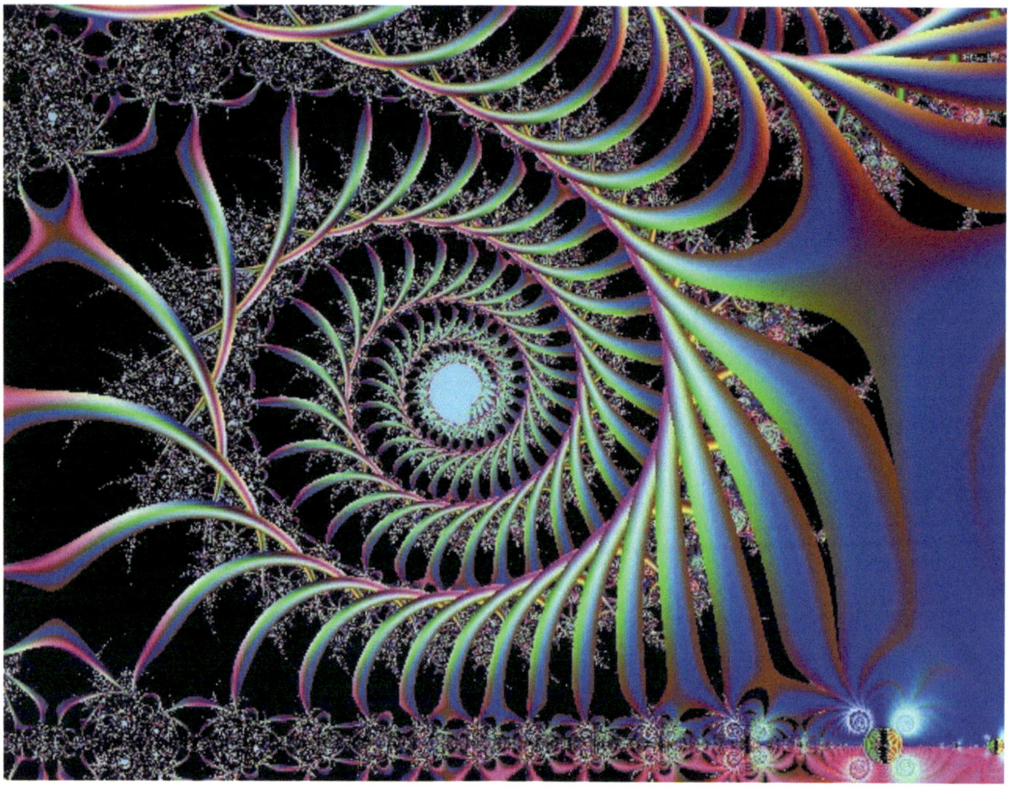

107B © 2025 by Teja Krašek (Used with permission).

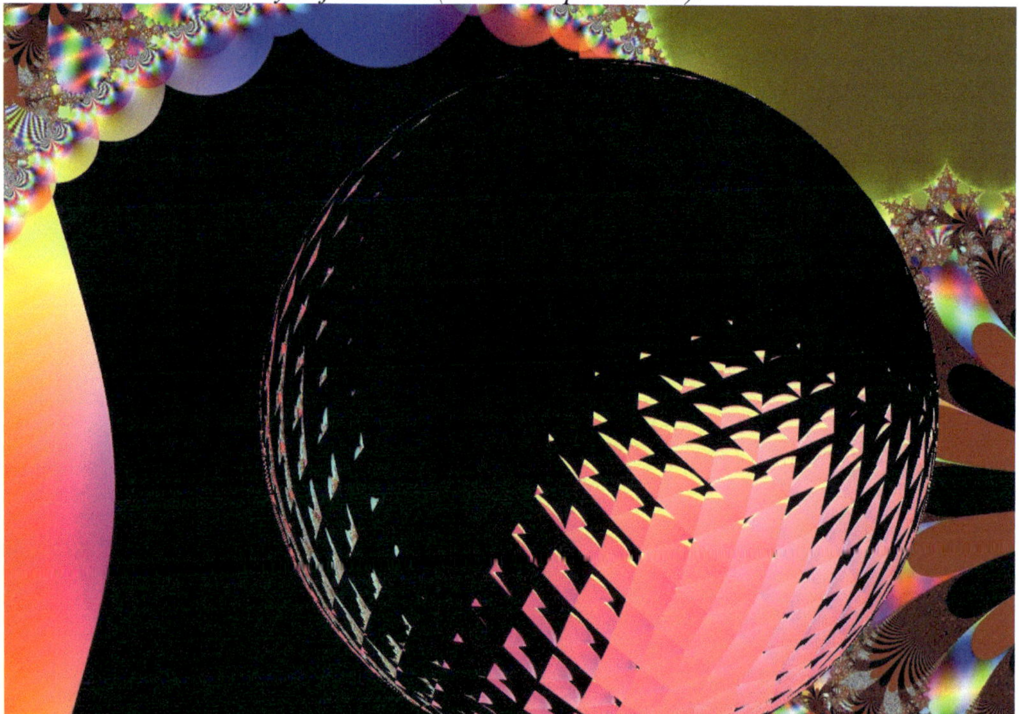

114. © 2025 by Teja Krašek (Used with permission).

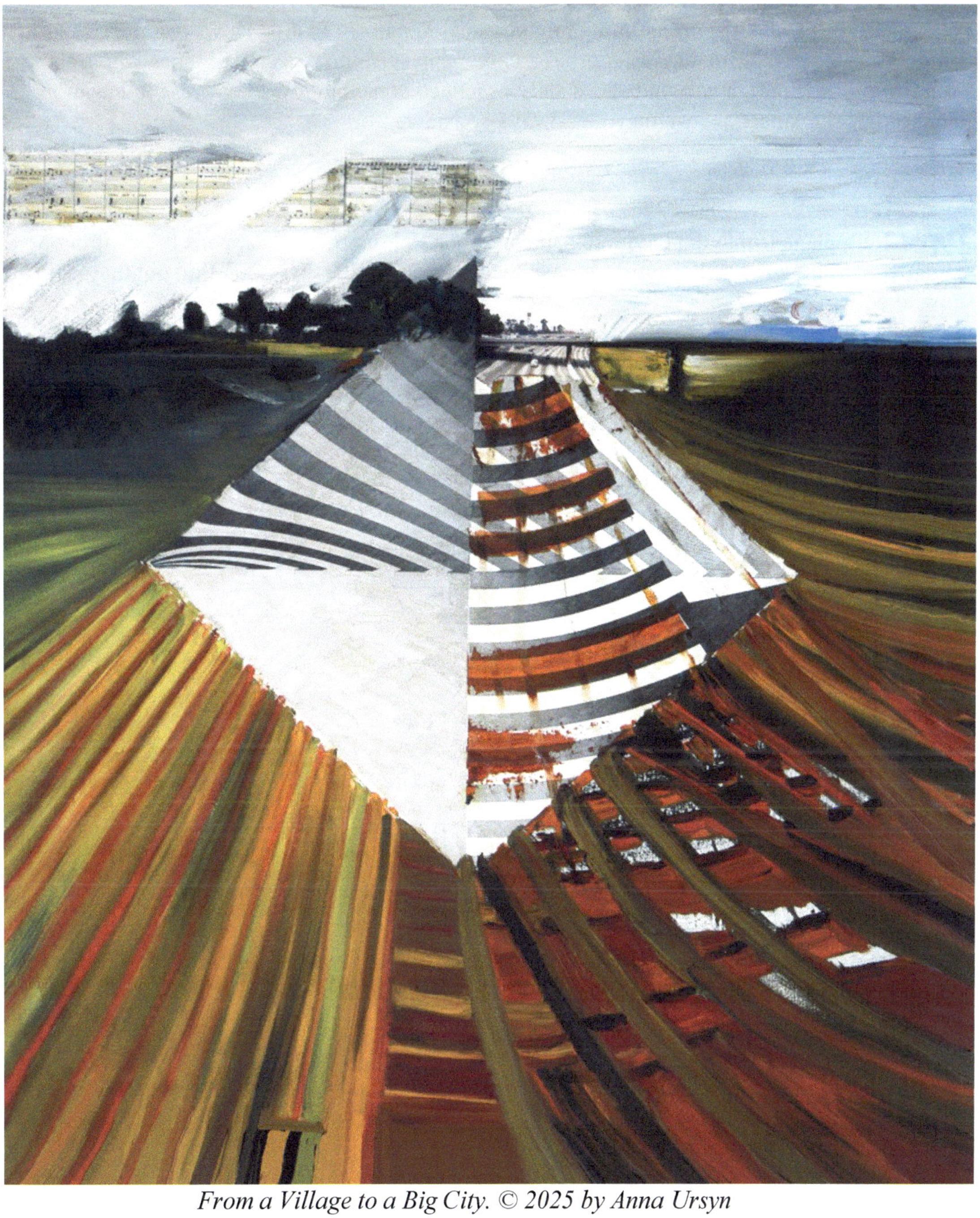

From a Village to a Big City. © 2025 by Anna Ursyn

CHAPTER 6
SPORTS CODE

DUALITY ON A PLANE

INTRODUCTION

We tend to think about sport as something physical in nature, as it is. However, the rise, growth, and sundown in a person's life having sport as a career can seem unexpected to those who treat it as a hobby or leisure time. Sport, a very old and widely practiced concept, now ever-present, has more facets and technological connections we may not always consider.

SYNOPSIS

On the long plane trip to the Olympic games, a sports photographer happens to be sitting by the sports organizer. Although they have different perspectives on sports, they soon find out they both need to know how to code.

SUMMARY

Experience in acting, performing, or sports helps visual creators better understand the characters they create and use to deliver stories, as practiced in various disciplines. While the action is rather static, the outflow of the two main characters' minds will illustrate this word-based exchange by projecting footage of the codes mentioned and explained, as juxtaposed with sport-related visuals presented in motion.

CAST OF CHARACTERS

Suno, Sports Photographer
Olivier, Sports Organizer

STAGE DIRECTIONS

Two interacting passengers are sitting on the plane talking. The window shows the sky, passing planes, birds, balloons, or blimps.

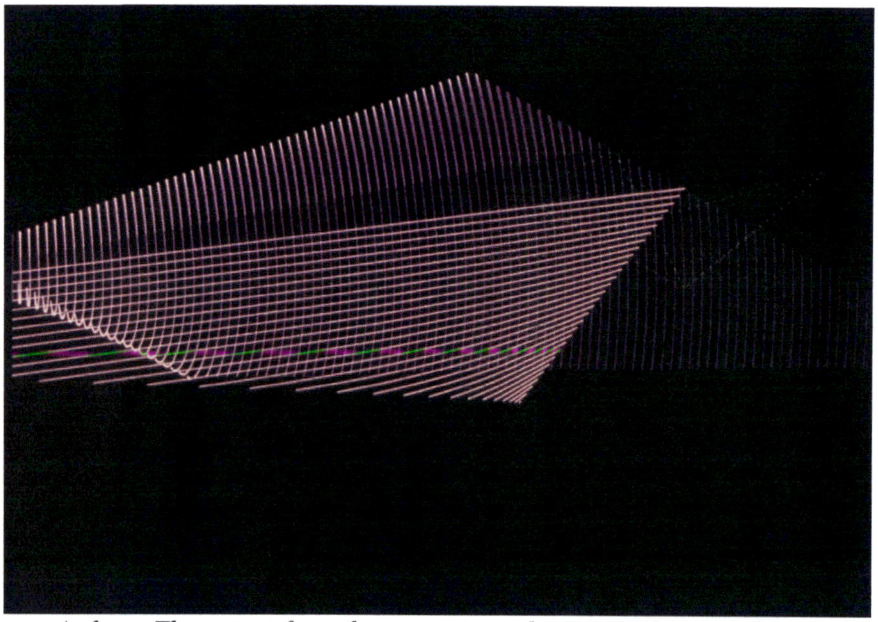

A plane. The output from the computer code. © 2025 by Anna Ursyn

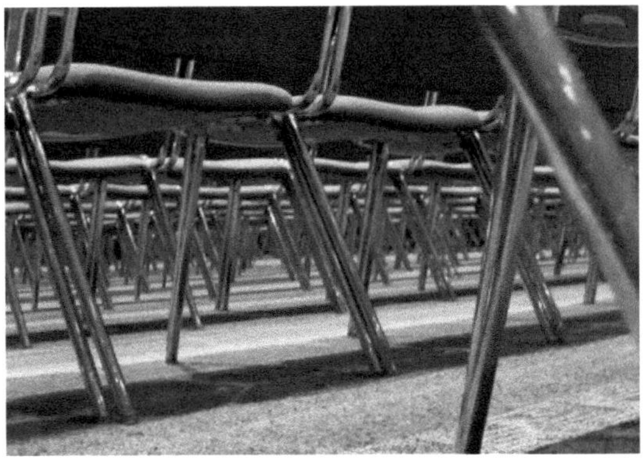

Act I
The Curtain goes up (or opens).

Olivier, "Oh, how good it is to be able to stretch my legs."
Suno, "Yes, and the champagne is not that bad, I think. Don't you want some?"
Olivier, "No, thank you, I am a sports person. I only intake what is healthy for my body. Only nutritious things, that is."
Suno, "Wind makes your blood run faster."
Olivier, "Wind?"
Suno, "I meant to say wine."
Olivier, "Oh. That's the problem."
Suno, "Wind can do it as well."
Olivier, "Yes, and I am glad to be in the cockpit. I used to be a sailor. Sailing makes you dependent on the wind, but you also get to learn when too much is too much."
Suno, "Just like with drinking."
Olivier, "Just like with everything."
Suno, "You must have been good at it."
Olivier, "I was selected for Operation Sail, which stands for something, I guess. This is why they made me a sports organizer. I know this title means a rack to store sports things on, but it intimidates people when I say Olympic Official, which is my title, or International Olympic Committee Member if you'd like the full one. We are to believe, spread, and monitor the Olympic values; we ensure that the Games actually happen and this movement spreads and continues."
Suno, "I just love the Olympic logo. It is so simple, yet tells the story."
Olivier, "You have a sharp eye for art."
Suno, "I am a sports photographer and will cover the event. Quite exciting but demanding as I focus on still images. I need to grab the right moment, determine any unusual situation fast, then capture it, edit, present, etc. A long list of duties. I love this job. I was selected because of my skiing achievements and accomplishments, which I will not drill down on that thought, but still, I love my job. I can cover any sport, I think, but..."
Oliver, "I think we have a lot in common, then. As for me, I also code. After I learned about the Antikythera mechanism, the first computer that is, I simply had to learn how to code. If you believe that, the analog computer was engineered 2000 years ago in ancient Greece. It was built to predict astronomical events, and they used it, mind you, for athletic games. You know what that means, of course, but to me, the fact that the first computer was sports-related changed everything. It sunk along with the ship that carried it to Rome. After thousands of years, it was recovered by some sponge divers not that long time ago."
Suno, "I know; they just discovered a new crucial part long after their initial discovery. It took people a while to rediscover that lost idea and build an actual computer."

Olivier, "The Dark Ages—they keep coming and going across time. They are part of the human condition. Can you imagine what we would be capable of if the ship had not sunk or if people had been more stable and supported in their good moments?"
Suno, "We no longer know what is good and bad. Winning is good, but only if achieved fairly. But who knows what is fair when the rules bend depending on the situation? This is why I like to capture a moment. The right moment. It might be dangerous, though, as the right moment may appear wrong for others."
Olivier, "Yes, duality. Everything has two facets or more. We have digital and analog ways to represent data. You can produce the content for display or print. You can prefer a Mac or a PC. There are other systems, of course, but there are two major groups: dual coding uses sensory imagery and verbal information to represent information. Computers process imagery and verbal information differently. The human mind uses channels to create and process each representation in each of them."
Suno, "I know. I use digital photos with a resolution of at least 300 dots per inch for better prints but 72 for posting them online. I use the RGB model for the web and CMYK for color separation in print. I know the web-safe colors and proper file formats, such as .jpg, .gif, or .png. I use non-compressed files for printing. Believe it or not, I still use a darkroom for some special occasions."
Olivier, "Yes, I am both outdoorsy and like to spend time indoors, which gives me more concentration, while outdoors releasing my tensions. You know how those meetings can be. Sometimes, people open their mouths just to look intelligent or important. Oh, when sailing, you need to feel physics, mathematics, meteorology, cartography, knots, and also the wind. You'll never learn this, like an artist will not learn colors that sing together, or a composer will not learn a melody that sounds nice. You have to have it in you to be original. Thus, some will likely borrow melodies from other cultures for their compositions. In school, my mind wandered, but studying for the sailing exams while practicing what I learned made me grow holistically, so I have to keep growing."
Suno, "In skiing, you must also have an interdisciplinary mind. You need to know physics, human physiology, types of snow, and weather to stay safe while enjoying it all. But how do you learn about other sports to help organize it all fairly?"
Olivier, "For that, we have a committee, many minds skilled in different directions but connected through passions and tasks. The venue plays a larger role than we think, but it is also about probability. We look at the chances of an event happening, which often depends on other events being possible."
Suno, "Can you give me an example?"
Olivier, "Yes, we can write code around the weather someplace at some time. We need to obtain the data and calculate the probability of weather conditions at a given location. In this, a Python code uses the OpenWeatherMap API to retrieve weather data and calculate the probability of certain weather conditions (rain, snow, etc.):

```
import requests

# Define the OpenWeatherMap API endpoint and your API key
url = "https://api.openweathermap.org/data/2.5/weather"
api_key = "your_api_key_here"

# Define the location for which you want to get weather data
location = "New York"

# Use the requests library to make a GET request to the OpenWeatherMap API with the location and API key parameters
response = requests.get(url, params={"q": location, "appid": api_key})

# If the request was successful (status code 200), extract the relevant data from the response JSON
if response.status_code == 200:
    weather_data = response.json()
    # Extract the probability of rain from the response
    rain_prob = weather_data["rain"]["1h"] if "rain" in weather_data else 0
    # Extract the probability of snow from the response
    snow_prob = weather_data["snow"]["1h"] if "snow" in weather_data else 0
    # Calculate the probability of any precipitation (rain or snow)
    precipitation_prob = rain_prob + snow_prob
```

```
    # Extract the probability of cloudy weather from the response
    cloudy_prob = weather_data["clouds"]["all"]
    # Extract the probability of sunny weather from the response
    sunny_prob = 100 - cloudy_prob
    # Print the probabilities
    print("Probability of precipitation: ", precipitation_prob)
    print("Probability of cloudy weather: ", cloudy_prob)
    print("Probability of sunny weather: ", sunny_prob)
else:
    print("Error:", response.status_code)
```

Suno, "I heard about Self-Driving Vehicles in Tokyo... facial Recognition System technology, Robot Assistance or Guidance, and Immersive Live Viewing."

Olivier, "Yes, we use software, AI, and all sorts of technology. There is a lot of data since over 200 countries participate in various competitions. We use Python to analyze data with various modules, such as Pandas…"

Suno exclaims with enthusiasm while interrupting, "Pandas, those are bears. They're especially popular in China. I photographed one when…"

Olivier continues, "We use NumPy as a general-purpose array-processing package, or we have great libraries, such as Matplotlib, which is a numerical mathematics extension of NumPy. We can even plot them in Python."

Suno - intelligently, "Computational photography allows for more advanced takes with our smartphone cameras. We carry them everywhere and have them ready for anything. At first, it worried photojournalists, but they got used to it. It made them faster, more ready, and more observant. Ha, ha. With this technology, our photos keep growing in many directions. We can take a photo with a Raspberry Pi:
https://libguides.lib.msu.edu/raspberry_pi/take_photo_w_python#:~:text=If%20you%20simply%20want%20to%20view%20the%20code%2C,Now%2C%20write%20the%20code%20for%20taking%20the%20photo.
We can convert a photo into an artistic sketch in Python code:
https://sonsuzdesign.blog/2021/05/24/turn-your-photos-into-artistic-sketches-with-code/
We can automate photography and…"

Olivier, in a worrisome tone, "Oh, we are experiencing some turbulence. Hold on to your drink. We'll need to write some code related to Aerodynamics and Hydrodynamics to stabilize everything."

Suno, "Oh, it all just got stabilized when you told them. They must use voice recognition. Let's drink to that!"

The End

The curtain goes down (or closes)

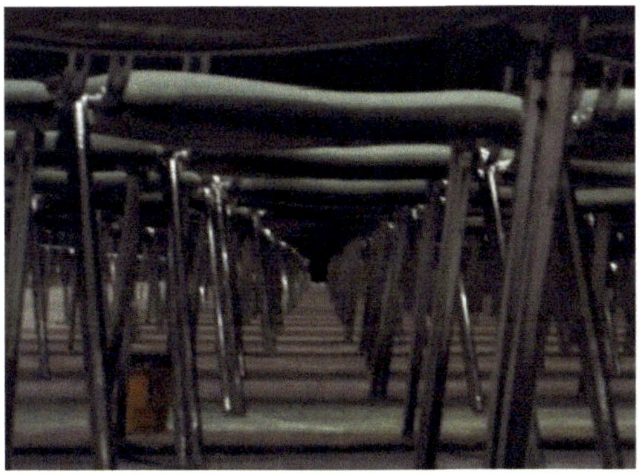

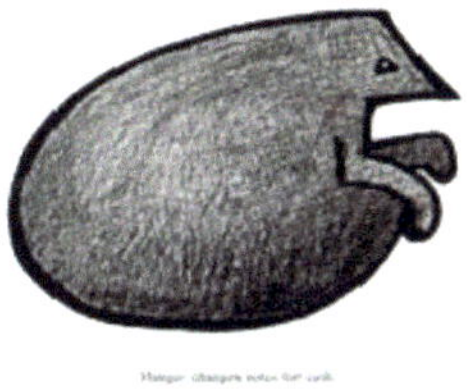

Hungo: Changes cash for bills.

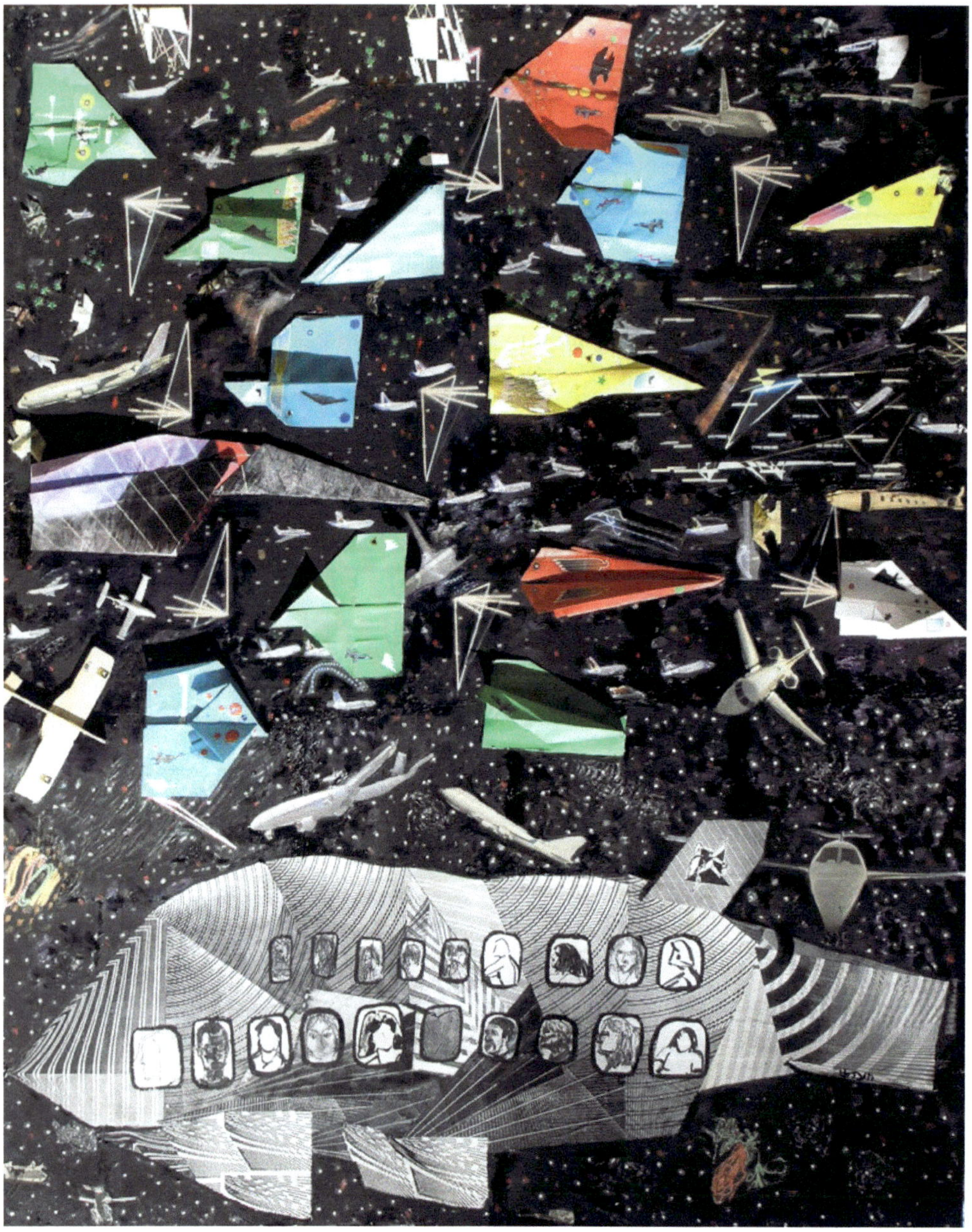

Duality for a Plane. © 2025 by Anna Ursyn

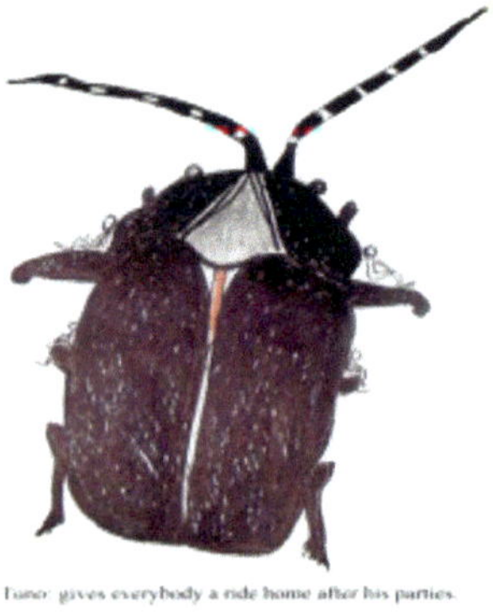

Tuno: gives everybody rides home after his parties.

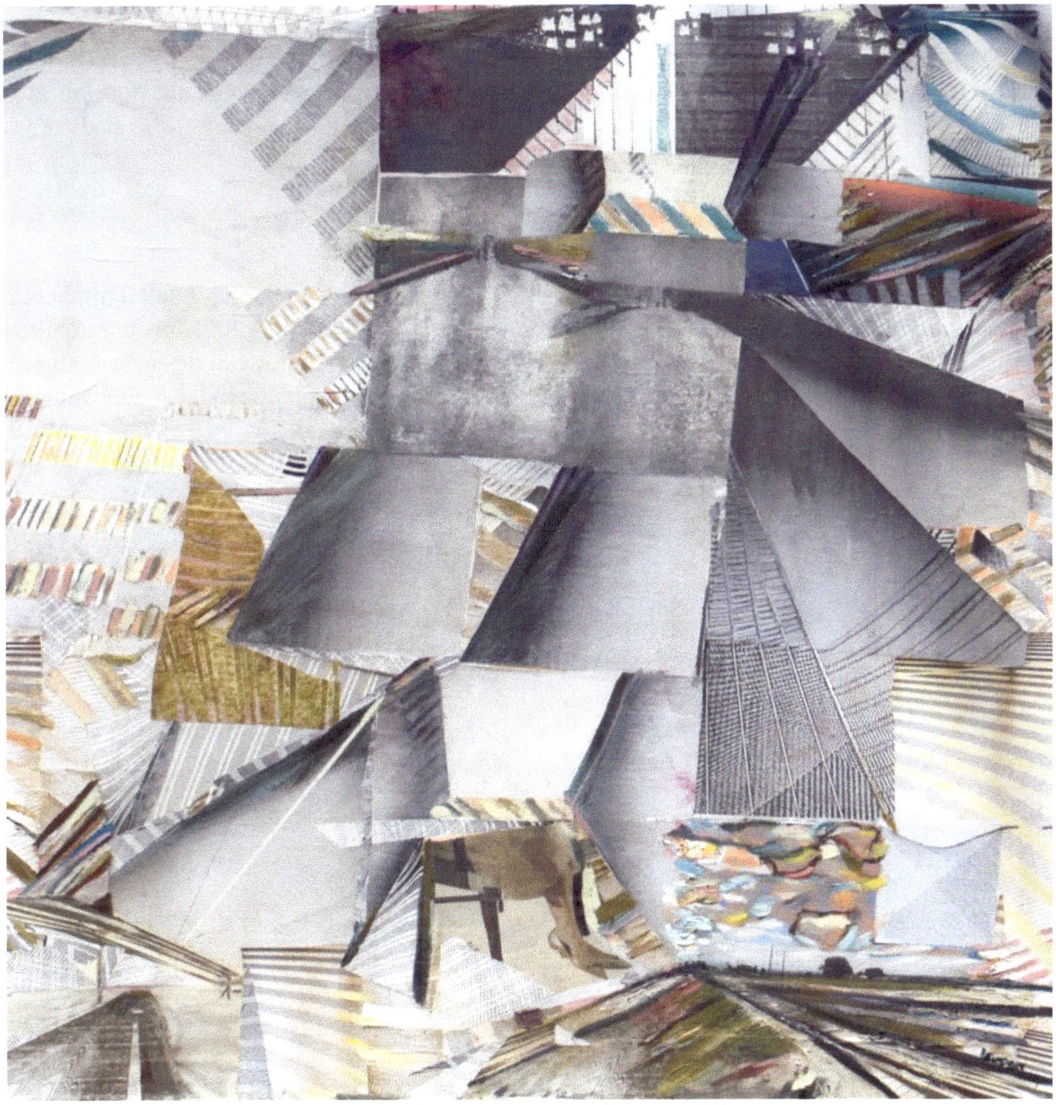

Frame of Reference. © 2025 by Anna Ursyn

CHAPTER 7
MATH CODE

A CAFÉ EXPERIENCE AT A CONFERENCE

INTRODUCTION

Mathematics is a wide topic. It describes our world and the Universe. Before humans had any equipment, some philosophers debated the laws of nature by depicting their thoughts with a stick on the wet sand of a beach. Mathematics has its disciplines and sub-disciplines and is growing. Computing expands it. Math is also closely connected with other disciplines. There is a field of mathematical art. Math requires abstract thinking, imagination, cognitive thinking, and creativity. It might be one of the reasons many fear it and stray away from anything related.

SYNOPSIS

Merlon, the coder, attends a mathematical conference. Arte, a pure mathematician, is ready for a cup of coffee. He joins Merlon at his table in a crowded coffee place. The math sounds are pouring in from the neighboring tables in a café. The level of the rigidness of this mathematician softens as he hears what the coder offers to share.

SUMMARY

Mathematics can be very visual. In this exchange of experiences between a coder and a mathematician, visuals underlying mathematical codes are shown dynamically by focusing on the presence of natural phenomena in mathematics and how mathematical and programming codes can describe Nature, disclosing its beauty. While the scene occurs in the coffee shop, the concepts, ideas, and visual outcomes are presented through dynamism, colorful lights, and visuals.

CAST OF CHARACTERS

Merlon, the Coder
Arte, Pure Mathematician

STAGE DIRECTIONS

Two conference attendees converse at the crowded coffee shop. Other participants sitting at the neighboring tables can be manikins. A barista, props, and projections are in the background.

The Curtain goes up (or opens).

`At the conference - in a coffee shop`

Merlon, politely, "Mind if I join you? So crowded here."
Arte, "They set 10:30 as a coffee break, so this is what everyone is doing."
Merlon, "My coffee got colder just by searching for a spot to enjoy it. I am glad to have some company, though. It is always nicer to share a pleasurable moment with somebody else."
Arte, "My cup is far from the word 'pleasure.' Weak and cold, too. Beurk. Other conferences use warmers set on the tables."
Merlon, " Never heard of that. What's a chance of finding a coffee shop with warmers?"
Arte, "Suppose we checked on 100 coffee places, and 50 had no warmers on the tables, while 50 did have them, but 20 of them were broken (D). P(W) would denote 50 coffee places with coffee warmers, and P(w), with lowercase w, would mean 50 those without. Thus, the number of coffee shops with working warmers is (W-D, 50 – 20 = 30). To calculate the probability, we need to divide this number by the total number of coffee shops (100).
The probability of a coffee shop having a working warmer = (W - D)/100 = 30/100 = 0.3
The probability of a coffee shop having no working warmers = (w +D)/100 = (50 + 20)/100 = 0.7
Merlon, "So, to find the probability of a coffee shop serving coffee with a warmer, you can divide the number of coffee shops that serve coffee with a warmer by the total number of coffee shops: P(W-D) (serving coffee with a warmer) = 30/100 = 0.3 or 30%.
Arte, "Not half bad. Are you a statistician?"
Merlon, "I am a coder. "
Arte, "Oh, sample spaces and permutations are your things, then."
Merlon, "I use math to fulfill my leisure time. It makes my brain grow, I think."
Arte, "I like Martin Gardner, too. But I do not code. I do everything from my memory experience bank. I envision outcomes before they reach my brain."

Merlon, "Yes, André Malraux and his *Le Musée Imaginaire,* which translates to the museum without walls' or the 'imaginary museum,' as you take it."
Arte, "Lait sans sucre s'il vous plait."
Merlon, "No coding, but special gifts."
Arte, "Hm?"
Merlon, "According to another Gardner, Howard, this time, everyone has unique types of intelligences, but you seem to go even beyond that. I think being able to code will only do you good. Let's look at the four mathematical operations we symbolize by +, -, etc."
Arte, "Adding, subtracting, multiplying, and dividing. Can you write a code for that?
Merlon, "Just give me two numbers you like."
Arte, "OK, just write a code that adds 178 to 2,397. That should be 2575, but let's see how fast a machine will figure it out."
Merlon explains, "In Python:

```
# Define the values to add
a = 2397
b = 178

# Add the values using the + operator
result = a + b

# Print the result
print("The sum of", a, "and" b, "is", result)
```

This code first defines the values to add: a = 2397 and b = 178. We then use the + operator to add these values and store the result in the variable result. Finally, the print() function displays the result. The code output will be the sum of 2397 and 178, which is 2575. You can change a and b.
And here is a code in Python that subtracts 178 from 2,397.

```
# Define the values to subtract
a = 2397
b = 178

# Subtract the values using the - operator
result = a - b

# Print the result
print("The difference between", a, "and" b, "is", result)
```

This code first defines the values to subtract: a = 2397 and b = 178. We then use the - operator to subtract b from a and store the result in the variable result. Finally, we use the print() function to display the result of the subtraction. The output of the code will be:
The difference between 2397 and 178 is 2219.
Arte, "And I can adapt this code to subtract other values by changing the values of a and b accordingly."
Merlon, "Fast learner! I won't bug you with the other two you mentioned, then." How about visual math?
Arte, Ah, Mathematical visualization. We use it throughout the whole field, from geometry to schematic diagrams or analysis."
Marvin, "Yes, fractal geometry. Geometry, Mathematical Art, even Visual Music."
Arte, "My strong interest is in how people count and convert. The world uses so many systems for practically everything, from shoe numbers to telling time. A decimal system was probably started by people counting on their fingers. Some cultures use twenty as a motif. I wonder if someone was counting using fingers and toes. Counting is one thing, but conversion is another story."
Marlon, "Interesting theory, and here comes unit conversion code that demonstrates how to convert units of length from meters to feet:

```
# Define the value in meters that you want to convert to feet
meters = 10

# Define the conversion factor from meters to feet (1 meter = 3.28084 feet)
meters_to_feet = 3.28084

# Convert the value from meters to feet using the conversion factor
```

```
feet = meters * meters_to_feet

# Print the results
print(meters, "meters is equal to", feet, "feet")
```

This code first defines the value in meters that we want to convert to feet, which is 10. Then, we define the conversion factor from meters to feet as 3.28084, the number of feet in one meter. Finally, we display the conversion results with the print() function. The output of the code will be: 10 meters is equal to 32.8084 feet."

Arte, "Oh, the Beauty of Math!"

Merlon, "Nature is seen through Mathematics, and mathematics is seen through Nature."

Merlon continues, "Let's talk about Fractal Geometry. The fern leaf was one of the first plants on their planet, and then, say, a sunflower or a mollusk. There are so many beautiful creatures that follow the grace of mathematical organization."

Arte, "And even starting in the field of geometry is dangerous. The solids, Platonic solids."

Merlon, " We call those the primitives, as in 3D, we build forms out of them. A teapot was added as a joke, and a soccer ball was added next. So unexpected"

Arte, "And all the cosmic space, the planetary motion. The ellipsoid rules!"

Merlon, "Here's an example code for simulating the movement of planets in a solar system using the Pygame and NumPy libraries in Python:

```
import pygame
import numpy as np

# Define constants
G = 6.6743e-11 # gravitational constant
AU = 149.6e9 # astronomical unit (meters)
SCALE = 1e-11 # pixel scale (meters per pixel)
DT = 3600 # time step (seconds)

# Define colors
BLACK = (0, 0, 0)
WHITE = (255, 255, 255)
RED = (255, 0, 0)
GREEN = (0, 255, 0)
BLUE = (0, 0, 255)

class Planet:
    def __init__(self, name, mass, position, velocity, color):
        self.name = name
        self.mass = mass
        self.position = position
        self.velocity = velocity
        self.color = color

    def force(self, planets):
        f = np.array([0.0, 0.0])
        for planet in planets:
            if planet != self:
                r = planet.position - self.position
                d = np.linalg.norm(r)
                f += G * self.mass * planet.mass / d**2 * r / d
        return f
    def update(self, planets):
        f = self.force(planets)
        self.velocity += f / self.mass * DT
        self.position += self.velocity * DT
def draw(self, screen):
        x, y = self.position / SCALE
        pygame.draw.circle(screen, self.color, (int(x), int(y)), 5)
        font = pygame.font.SysFont('Arial', 14)
        text = font.render(self.name, True, WHITE)
        screen.blit(text, (int(x) + 10, int(y) + 10))

# Define the solar system
```

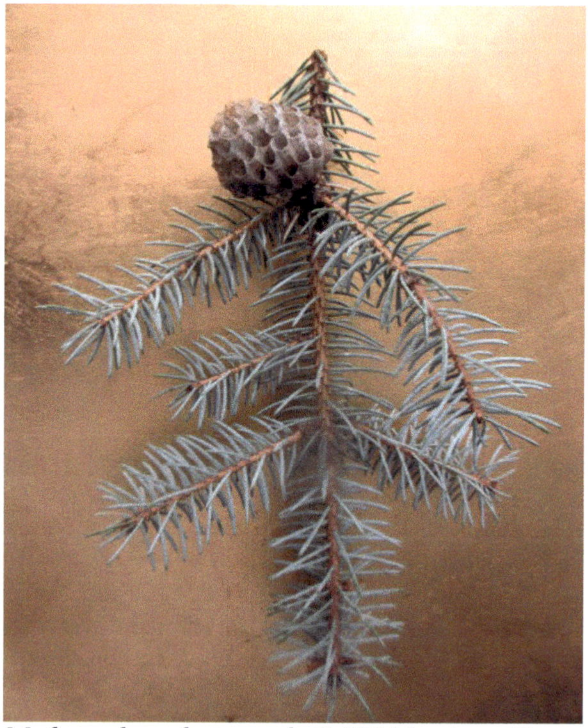

Math comb, a photograph. © 2025 by Anna Ursyn

```
sun = Planet('Sun', 1.989e30, np.array([0.0, 0.0]), np.array([0.0, 0.0]), YELLOW)
earth = Planet('Earth', 5.972e24, np.array([AU, 0.0]), np.array([0.0, 29783]), BLUE)
mars = Planet('Mars', 6.39e23, np.array([AU * 1.5, 0.0]), np.array([0.0, 24077]), RED)
planets = [sun, earth, mars]

# Initialize Pygame
pygame.init()
screen = pygame.display.set_mode((800, 800))
pygame.display.set_caption('Planetary Movement')

# Simulation loop
running = True
while running:
    # Handle events
    for event in pygame.event.get():
        if event.type == pygame.QUIT:
            running = False

    # Update the planets
    for planet in planets:
        planet.update(planets)

    # Draw the planets
# Masses are in kg, positions are in AU, and velocities are in m/s
masses = {
    'Sun': 1.989e30,
    'Mercury': 3.302e23,
    'Venus': 4.869e24,
    'Earth': 5.974e24,
    'Mars': 6.419e23,
    'Jupiter':  1.899e27,
    'Saturn':  5.685e26,
    'Uranus':  8.683e25,
    'Neptune': 1.024e26
}
positions = {
    'Sun': [0, 0],
    'Mercury': [0.39, 0],
    'Venus': [0.72, 0],
    'Earth': [1, 0],
    'Mars': [1.52, 0],
    'Jupiter': [5.20, 0],
    'Saturn': [9.58, 0],
    'Uranus': [19.18, 0],
    'Neptune': [30.07, 0]
}
velocities = {
    'Sun': [0, 0],
    'Mercury': [0, 47870],
    'Venus': [0, 35020],
    'Earth': [0, 29780],
    'Mars': [0, 24130],
    'Jupiter': [0, 13070],
    'Saturn': [0, 9690],
    'Uranus': [0, 6810],
    'Neptune': [0, 5430]
}

# Define the time step and duration of the simulation
dt = 3600  # time step in seconds
duration = 365.25 * 24 * 3600  # duration of the simulation in seconds

# Create a list of the planet names in the order they will be plotted
planet_names = ['Mercury', 'Venus', 'Earth', 'Mars', 'Jupiter', 'Saturn', 'Uranus', 'Neptune']
# Initialize the positions and velocities of the planets at t=0
planet_positions = {name: positions[name] for name in planet_names}
planet_velocities = {name: velocities[name] for name in planet_names}

# Initialize the plot
import matplotlib.pyplot as plt
```

```
fig = plt.figure()
ax = fig.add_subplot(111)
ax.set_xlim(-35, 35)
ax.set_ylim(-35, 35)
ax.set_aspect('equal')
ax.plot(0, 0, 'o', color='yellow', markersize=12)

# Loop over time steps and calculate the positions and velocities of the planets
for t in range(0, duration, dt):
    # Update the positions and velocities of the planets using basic physics equations
    for i, name1 in enumerate(planet_names):
        for name2 in planet_names[i+1:]:
            # Calculate the distance between the planets
            dx = planet_positions[name1][0] - planet_positions[name2][0]
    screen.fill(BLACK)
    for planet in planets:
        planet.draw(screen)
    pygame.display.flip()

    # Wait for the next time step
    pygame.time.wait(int(1000 * DT))

# Quit Pygame
pygame.quit()
```

This code simulates planet movement using gravitational force between them. It calculates force, updates velocity and position, and draws them on the screen. With physics equations, a simple simulation of solar system planets can be created.

```
import math

# Define constants
G = 6.6743e-11  # gravitational constant
AU = 149.6e6 * 1000  # astronomical unit in meters

# Define masses and initial positions and velocities of the planets
```

Arte, with a Renaissance voice (whatever it is), "We revolve around the Sun like any other planet." —*Nicolaus Copernicus*
Merlon, "My hero, one of them."
Arte, "Of all discoveries and opinions, none may have exerted a greater effect on the human spirit than the doctrine of Copernicus. The world has scarcely become known as round and complete when it was asked to waive the tremendous privilege of being the center of the universe." —Johann Wolfgang von Goethe."
Merlon, "What are your heroes? Mine are Aristotle, Brahe, Brunelleschi, da Vinci, Shakespeare, Skłodowska-Curie, Jobs, Dudna, Pepperberg, Bertozzi, ..."
Arte, "No more coffee in my cup! No Tasseography."

The End.
The curtain goes up (or closes).

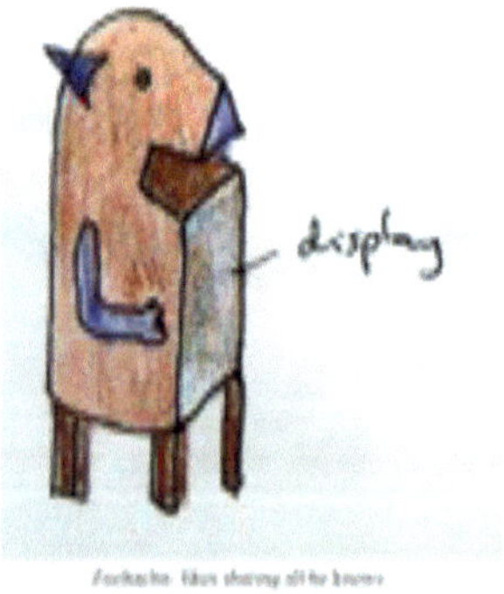

Zuchacho: likes sharing all he knows.

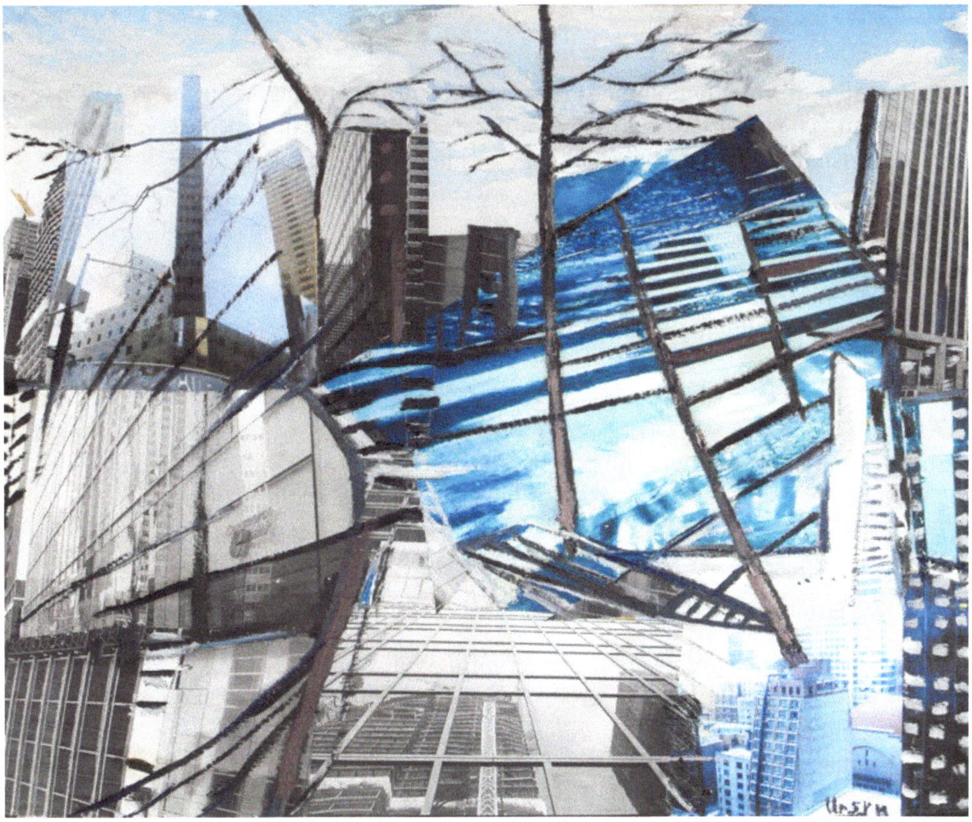

Altitude, Latitude, Longitude, Solitude. © *2025 by Anna Ursyn*

CHAPTER 8
BANK CODE

A RESTROOM CONVERSATION

INTRODUCTION

The scale and liquid price of rocks can be seen differently, but they serve the same purpose: to make a fortune using them. Not shying away from technology is the key.

SYNOPSIS

Two women are in a women's restroom of the local science museum, which hosts the exhibition of the rocks. Marie is an inventor who uses rocks for their helpful properties in new products and techniques. At the same time, Barbara is a businesswoman working for a bank, interested in the assets-protective value of the rocks.
They are in two stalls, so they cannot see each other but can hear the other person. After sharing their positions on their professions, they decide they have one thing in common: rocks, precious or functional. One person is after their usefulness; the other is after their assets' protective value. The rocks are investments to the banker, who is conscious about the money. To the inventor, they are too, but through their usefulness to science-based solutions in our daily life, which she also turns into assets. They both agree on the beauty of rocks and minerals in their structured way.

SUMMARY

Banking is a discipline that uses coding on many levels. It requires knowing about security, servers, and the dynamic side of them. The beauty of rocks and minerals and the dynamic beauty, math, and science behind their structures visually illustrate this exchange of interests in finances.

CAST OF CHARACTERS

Marie, an Inventor
Barbara, a Businesswoman working for a bank

STAGE DIRECTIONS

Two cardboard stalls face a white divider with projections on it. The voices are supported by visuals without showing the two characters as they are sitting in side-by-side, enclosed spaces.

Act I
The Curtain goes up (or opens).

Marie, in an embarrassed voice, "Pardon me for interrupting your 'business,' but my ring rolled out toward your stall. Could you hand it to me, please? My fingers shrink from cold, and they do not spoil us here when it comes to temperature."
Barbara, "They do not; the air conditioner works day and night, summer through winter like everybody would have too high blood pressure. After all, it is a Nature and Science Museum, so the planet should matter to them. It is all about personal comfort. There are many types of Ps in banking: first, the five 'Ps' are people, physical cash, premises, processes, and paper."
Marie, in a surprised voice, "The last one sounds like an outdated one, right?"
Barbara continues, "Or, we have the seven 'Ps, the product, price, promotion, place, people, processes, and physical evidence."
Marie interrupting, "People again, that sounds promising!"
Barbara keeps talking, "We also say that the banking system has four 'essential aspects:' liquidity, expansion, investments and loan policies, and the human factor. But banking should mean money. Lots of it, I mean an ocean of money. That is what banking means. "
`Barbara keeps searching for the ring by looking around the floor.`
"What a lovely granite floor. I even see some rocks' intarsia. I would never notice it if it were not for your, oh, here it is. What a beauty, what is that?"
Marie softly, "Thank you. This is a stone I constantly experiment with. This rock has a promise for my newest invention. I had it made into a ring to have it handy for any occasion and opportunity."
Barbara, "Handy it is, `while handing the ring under the stalls' divider.` I am strongly interested in them, but for another reason: the cuts. They sell so well. Out of ten, forty percent of people pick the round ones. We talk about scales, liquid, price, or promotion. See, when someone is afraid of losing a fortune, rocks are the best way to make sure the values at least stay the same. The biggest challenge is money conversion. One must learn to do it as quickly as a dragonfly catches its prey. Money goes down, sometimes up, but rocks are always precious. If you ever need to hide your money, you could even cover the rock under a tree in your backyard with random rocks. This is what my clients tell me. They go to Estes Park in Colorado and buy colorful stones at the tourist shops there. Their value is not very high, but it is easy to mix a rare, expensive "specimen" among them for nobody to suspect."
Marie, curiously, "You can convert money in your head. Interesting. It looks like we are visiting the same "Get to Know Your Rocks" exhibition for two different reasons, but I must say I enjoy it, and it gives me some intellectual satisfaction to look at them from different perspectives."
Barbara, "What do you mean? You like imagining large numbers?"

Marie, "I am after geometry. It can even affect the properties of a rock. Let's take it from your perspective and look at the code in Python for four types of diamond cuts. Would you mind opening your stall to look at my projection?

Barbara opens the door to her stall. The projected code appears on the wall in front of them:

```
def diamond_cut1(size):
  for i in range(1, size+1):
    print(" "*(size-i) + "* "*i)
  for i in range(size-1, 0, -1):
    print(" "*(size-i) + "* "*i)

def diamond_cut2(size):
  for i in range(1, size+1):
    print(" "*(size-i) + "* "*i)
  for i in range(size-2, -1, -1):
    print(" "*(size-i) + "* "*i)

def diamond_cut3(size):
  for i in range(1, size+1):
    print(" "*(size-i) + "* "*i)
  for i in range(size-2, -1, -1):
    print(" "*(size-i) + "* "*i)
  for i in range(1, size+1):
    print(" "*(i-1) + "* "*(size-i+1))
  for i in range(size-1, 0, -1):
    print(" "*(i-1) + "* "*(size-i+1))

def diamond_cut4(size):
  for i in range(1, size+1):
    print(" "*(size-i) + "* "*(2*i-1))
  for i in range(size-1, 0, -1):
    print(" "*(size-i) + "* "*(2*i-1))
```

These four functions take an integer size as input, showing the diamond's size to be printed. Each function prints a different type of diamond cut:

diamond_cut1: prints a diamond with sharp angles
diamond_cut2: prints a diamond with rounded corners
diamond_cut3: prints a diamond with both sharp angles and rounded corners
diamond_cut4: prints a diamond with a kite shape

Marie, continues, "Or use the matplotlib library in Python: "

```
import matplotlib.pyplot as plt

# Define the data for each type of diamond cut
round_cut = [0, 0.2, 0.5, 0.8, 1, 0.8, 0.5, 0.2, 0]
princess_cut = [0, 0.3, 0.6, 1, 0.6, 0.3, 0]
emerald_cut = [0, 0.2, 0.5, 0.7, 1, 0.7, 0.5, 0.2, 0]
marquise_cut = [0, 0.3, 0.5, 0.8, 1, 0.8, 0.5, 0.3, 0]

# Plot the diamond cuts using subplots
fig, ((ax1, ax2), (ax3, ax4)) = plt.subplots(2, 2)

ax1.plot(round_cut, color='black', linewidth=2)
ax1.set_title('Round Cut')

ax2.plot(princess_cut, color='black', linewidth=2)
ax2.set_title('Princess Cut')

ax3.plot(emerald_cut, color='black', linewidth=2)
ax3.set_title('Emerald Cut')
ax4.plot(marquise_cut, color='black', linewidth=2)
ax4.set_title('Marquise Cut')
```

```
plt.tight_layout()
plt.show()
```

Create a figure with four diamond cuts: round, princess, emerald, and marquise. Modify the lists to change the shapes. Use the plot method on each subplot to plot it. Use set_title to set the title of each subplot and tight_layout to adjust the spacing between subplots.
After you run this code, you'll see the visual outputs of the four types of diamond cuts.
Barbara, "How did you do that?"
Marie, "I told you, in Python, *and continues.*
Without using the library, you can call these functions with an integer argument to generate the corresponding diamond cut. For example, to print a diamond with sharp angles of size 5, you can call diamond_cut1(5).
Barbara, a bit disappointed, "I meant the projection. It can be very useful for any situation, a very convincing method, from promotion to sales. What a tool for a banker! I wanted to answer your question on converting values but did not know how to do it without sharing my phone's screen."
Marie, "I always carry a tiny phone projector with me, with a proper connector, that is. This way, I can share any content with anyone, anytime. We became so visual, without admitting it, that is. Luckily, they did not install those shiny tiles all up to the ceiling, leaving the wall pure white and textured enough for a good projection. And those dividers are white, too. An ideal restroom for data-sharing restroom goers."
Barbara, "Can you please hand me your projector under the stall? Thank you. So, to answer your question, here is my Python code to convert values between different monetary systems:

```
# Define exchange rates
usd_to_eur = 0.85
usd_to_gbp = 0.72
usd_to_jpy = 109.73

# Define amount in USD
usd_amount = 100

# Convert to EUR, GBP, and JPY
eur_amount = usd_amount * usd_to_eur
gbp_amount = usd_amount * usd_to_gbp
jpy_amount = usd_amount * usd_to_jpy

# Print results
print(f"${usd_amount:.2f} USD is equivalent to {eur_amount:.2f} EUR")
print(f"${usd_amount:.2f} USD is equivalent to {gbp_amount:.2f} GBP")
print(f"${usd_amount:.2f} USD is equivalent to {jpy_amount:.2f} JPY")
```

And it will output like this:

```
$100.00 USD is equivalent to 85.00 EUR
$100.00 USD is equivalent to 72.00 GBP
$100.00 USD is equivalent to 14,931.00 JPY
```

I converted USD to EUR, GBP, and JPY using exchange rates. The results were printed with two decimal places. You can add more currencies or exchange rates if needed.
Marie, "How did you do that?"
Barbara, "I told you in Python. Nowadays, everybody needs to code if they want to become 'A Big Fish in a Big Pond.'"
Marie, "There is also a "Get to Know Your Oceans" exhibit offered here. Care to go with me to look at the sharks?"

The End.
The Curtain goes down (or closes).

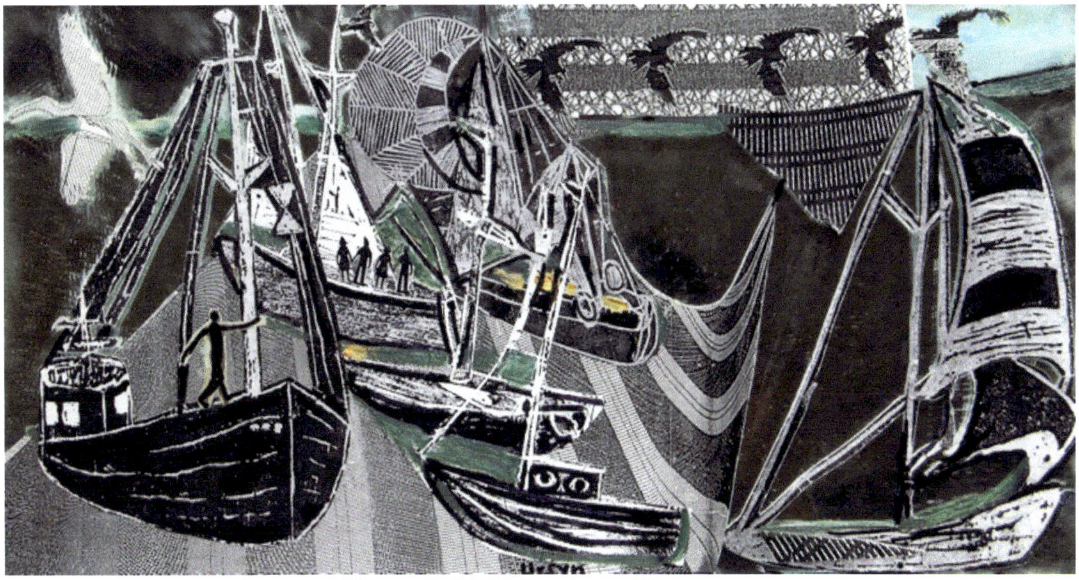

Leisure Time. © 2025 by Anna Ursyn

INTRODUCTION

While we enjoy spending time outdoors, some of us wonder how things work out there. There are many hard-to-answer questions, but we look at some ways to describe them, from making Fractal graphics and understanding the electromagnetic spectrum to performing swarm computing, mimicking nature in at least three different ways, and working with bio-inspired data. We use expanding technology and devices, from physical computing with Arduino boards, Makey Makey, and Raspberry Pi to VR, AR XR, holograms, and machine learning to 3D printing.

SYNOPSIS

Francis knows how to cut and remove intestines from any fish. He knows where to cut to disjoint the tail and the head so a fish would stop looking at the buyer and how to make the product useful in a neatly packed package with nothing to trash, but making it still beneficial. He knows what to do with everything his customers reject. He knows his fish business. He knows Nature, and Nature knows him.

SUMMARY

This work introduces various passions by contrasting the interests of members of two different and distant generations. The action is set on a fishing boat with all the natural water events dancing in the background, as fish and birds live in a water-based environment. Related codes and images are intertwined with the action.

CAST OF CHARACTERS

Francis, a Store Clerk in the fishing department.
Hez, Francis' Grandson

STAGE DIRECTIONS

A grandfather and his grandson are sitting on a boat with a fishing pole, many props, and laptops. They catch strange objects, such as a wooden train, and occasionally fish.

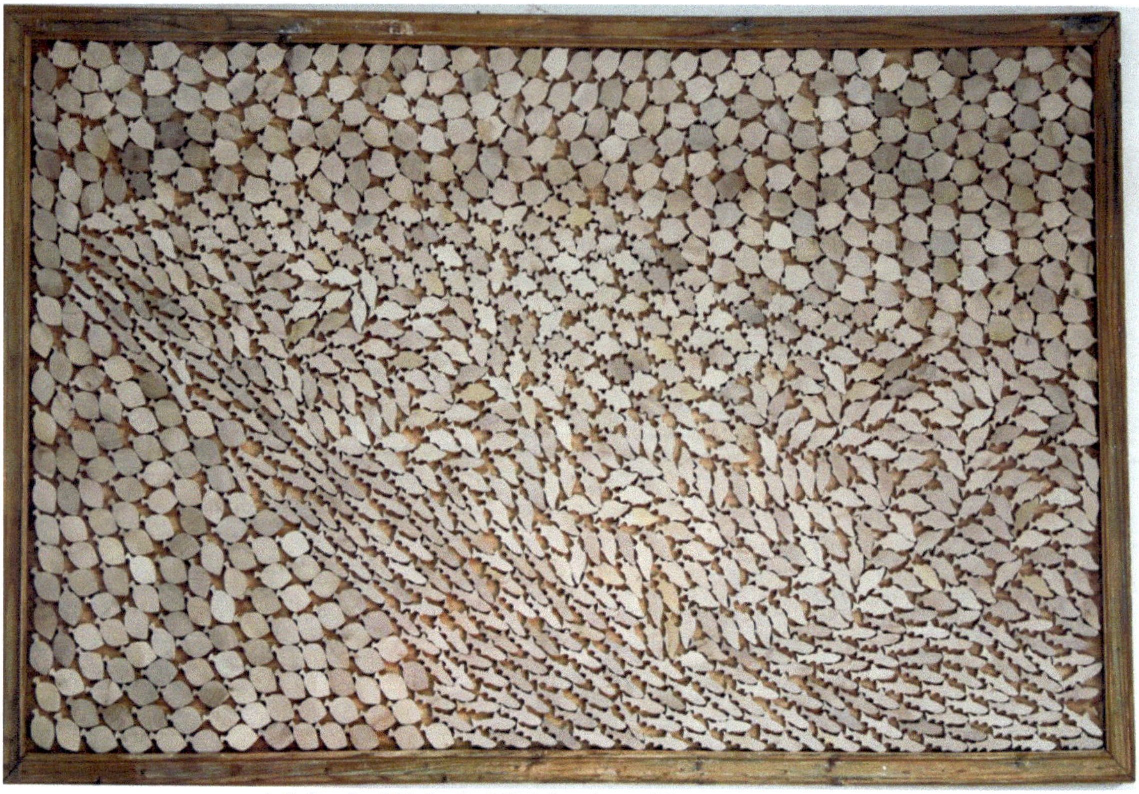

A School of Fish. © *2025 by Anna Ursyn*

The Curtain goes up (or opens).

Francis, "Please do not splash water on my laptop."
Hez, "My apologies. I do it all on my phone, which is sitting safely in my pocket. You should try it, too."
Francis, "Yes, but size does matter."
Hez, "When it comes to fishing."
Francis, "I like to have a bigger screen or have two of them to be seen at once, or even more. Even a tablet is too small. For me, 16" it is. Heavy, but nice space to do things."
Hez, "I am a multitasker. I am listening to music while we talk, fishing, and making plans for tomorrow, all at the same time. It's possible for me because I think in patterns. The pattern is a repetition of units, which can be grouped in categorizing."
Francis, "So, what is the pattern of the scales on a sturgeon?"
Hez, "Grandpa, sturgeons do not have scales! They have five rows of diamond-like sets of bony scutes. They protect them from their predators. Do you want me to show you?
Here's a code in Python to print a row of diamonds using asterisks:

```
num_of_diamonds = 5  # Set the number of diamonds to be printed

for i in range(num_of_diamonds):
    # Print the first half of the diamond
    for j in range(num_of_diamonds - i - 1):
        print(" ", end="")
    for j in range(i + 1):
```

```
        print("* ", end="")
    print()

for i in range(num_of_diamonds - 1):
    # Print the second half of the diamond
    for j in range(i + 1):
        print(" ", end="")
    for j in range(num_of_diamonds - i - 1):
        print("* ", end="")
    print()
```

Output:

```
    *
   * *
  * * *
 * * * *
* * * * *
 * * * *
  * * *
   * *
    *
```

Francis, “What??? That is so cool. I like everything about shapes and geometry. I love fish. I sell them. I know how to cut and remove the intestines from any fish. I know where to cut to remove the tail and the head, so it stops looking at the buyer, and the product makes a useful, neatly set package with nothing to trash. I know what to do with everything my customers reject. I know my fish business. I love Nature!”
Haz, “To me, Nature is fractals. Here's a code for drawing the sierpinski fractal using the turtle module in Python. Wacław Sierpiński (1882-1969) was a Polish mathematician who also studied astronomy and philosophy and wrote over 700 papers and 50 books:

```
import turtle

def sierpinski(length, depth):
    if depth == 0:
        for i in range(3):
            turtle.forward(length)
            turtle.left(120)
    else:
        sierpinski(length/2, depth-1)
        turtle.forward(length/2)
        sierpinski(length/2, depth-1)
        turtle.backward(length/2)
        turtle.left(60)
        turtle.forward(length/2)
        turtle.right(60)
        sierpinski(length/2, depth-1)
        turtle.left(60)
        turtle.backward(length/2)
        turtle.right(60)

turtle.speed('fastest')
turtle.penup()
turtle.goto(-200, -100)
turtle.pendown()
sierpinski(400, 4)

turtle.done(
```

And here comes the output:

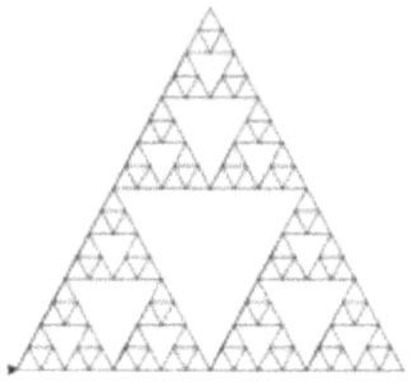

Francis, "This code uses recursion to draw the hydroelectric fractal. The sierpinski function (note an upper case 'S' for the name and the lower case 's' for the function) takes two arguments: length, the length of the initial equilateral triangle, and depth, which is the depth of the recursion. The base case is when depth = 0, in which the function draws an equilateral triangle using the turtle's forward and left methods. If depth is greater than 0, the function calls itself three times, each time with length halved and depth decremented by 1. The turtle moves forward half the length, draws the next level of the fractal, and then moves backward to the starting point. It then turns left 60 degrees, moves forward half the length, turns right 60 degrees, and draws the next level of the fractal. Finally, the turtle turned left 60 degrees, moved backward to the starting point, and turned right 60 degrees. The rest of the code sets up the turtle and calls the sierpinski function with a length of 400 and a depth of 4, and then finishes by calling the done method of the turtle to keep the window open. You can adjust these parameters to create different variations of the fractal based on different generators, such as a square. There is a more morphic, or organic one, the Julia set algorithm introduced by Gaston Maurice Julia (1893-1978), who was a French Algerian mathematician whose work was widely popularized by another French mathematician, Benoit Mandelbrot.
Francis, "Hey, Look, a rainbow!"
Hez, "I can write a code in Python using the matplotlib library to plot the electromagnetic spectrum:

```
c = 3e8  # speed of light in meters per second
frequencies = [
    (3e9, "Radio"),
    (3e12, "Microwave"),
    (4.3e14, "Infrared"),
    (7.5e14, "Visible"),
    (3e17, "Ultraviolet"),
    (3e19, "X-Ray"),
    (3e22, "Gamma-Ray")
]

for freq, name in frequencies:
    wavelength = c / freq
    print(f"{name} ({freq:.2E} Hz) has a wavelength of {wavelength:.2E} meters.")
```

And it will output:

```
Radio (3.00E+09 Hz) has a wavelength of 1.00E-01 meters.
Microwave (3.00E+12 Hz) has a wavelength of 1.00E-04 meters.
Infrared (4.30E+14 Hz) has a wavelength of 6.98E-07 meters.
Visible (7.50E+14 Hz) has a wavelength of 4.00E-07 meters.
Ultraviolet (3.00E+17 Hz) has a wavelength of 1.00E-09 meters.
X-ray (3.00E+19 Hz) has a wavelength of 1.00E-11 meters.
Gamma-ray (3.00E+22 Hz) has a wavelength of 1.00E-14 meters.
```

Hez continues, "I can run another one that outputs it in a graphical way. It uses the turtle library to draw a simple rainbow:

```
import turtle

# Create a turtle object
t = turtle.Turtle()

# Set the turtle's speed
```

```
t.speed(10)

# Set the turtle's starting position and direction
t.penup()
t.goto(-200, 0)
t.pendown()

# Define the colors of the rainbow
colors = ['red', 'orange', 'yellow', 'green', 'blue', 'purple', 'pink']

# Draw the rainbow
for color in colors:
   t.color(color)
   t.width(5)
   t.circle(100, 180)

# Hide the turtle when finished
t.hideturtle()

# Wait for the user to close the window
turtle.done()
```

Hez, keeps going, "This code creates a turtle object and sets its starting position to the left of the screen. It then defines a list of colors and uses a for loop to draw a semicircle of each color, creating a rainbow. Finally, the turtle is hidden, and the program waits for the user to close the window.
And here is its graphical, animated outcome:"

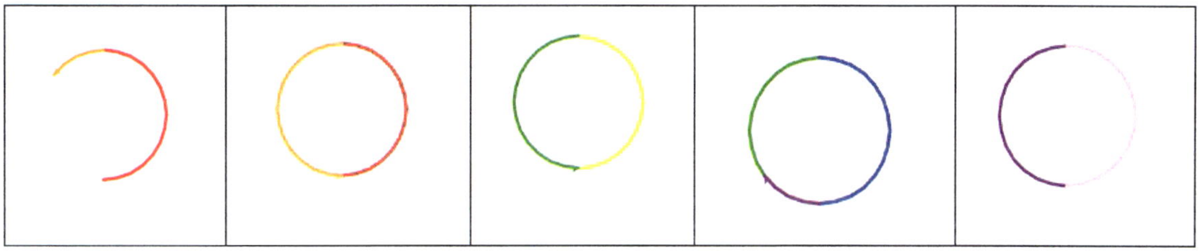

Francis exclaims, "Wow, wow, Hez, so why do you even bother going into Nature?

The End.
The curtain goes down (or closes).

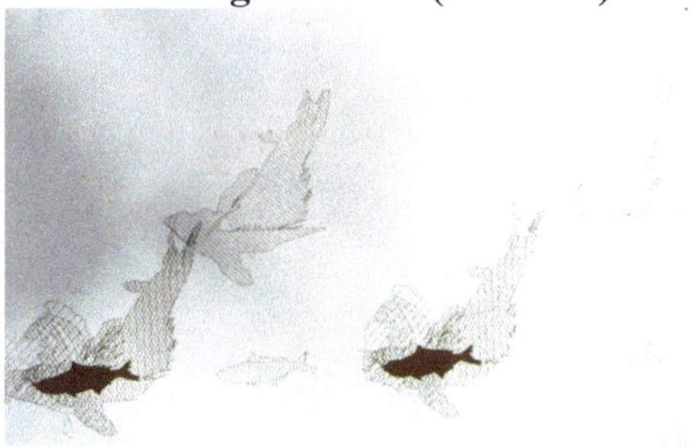

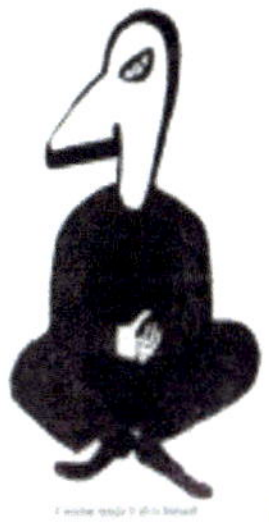

Casunaa keeps this all for himself

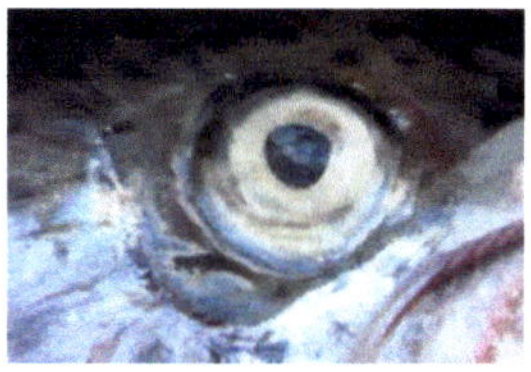

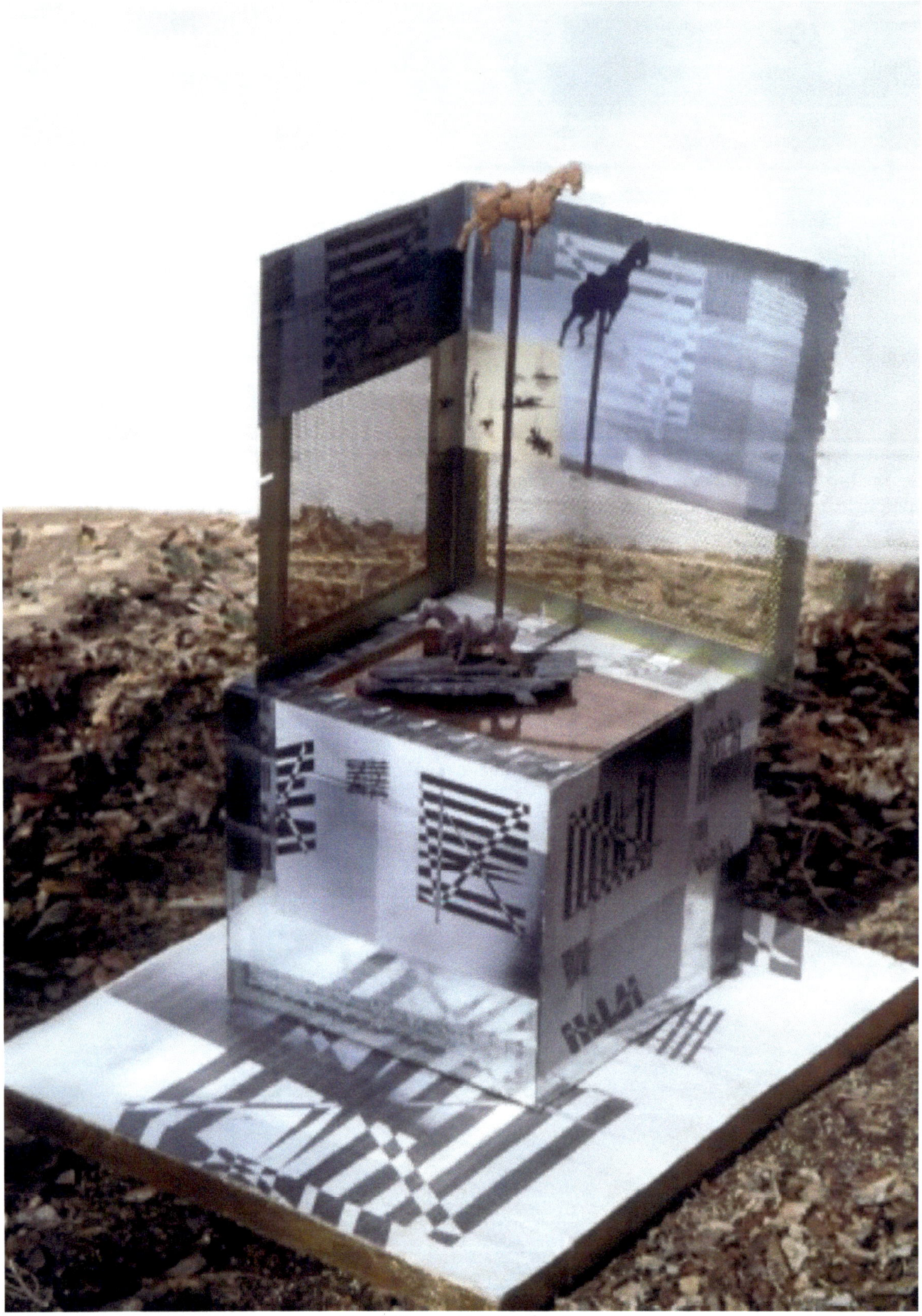

Hero Horse. © 2025 by Anna Ursyn.

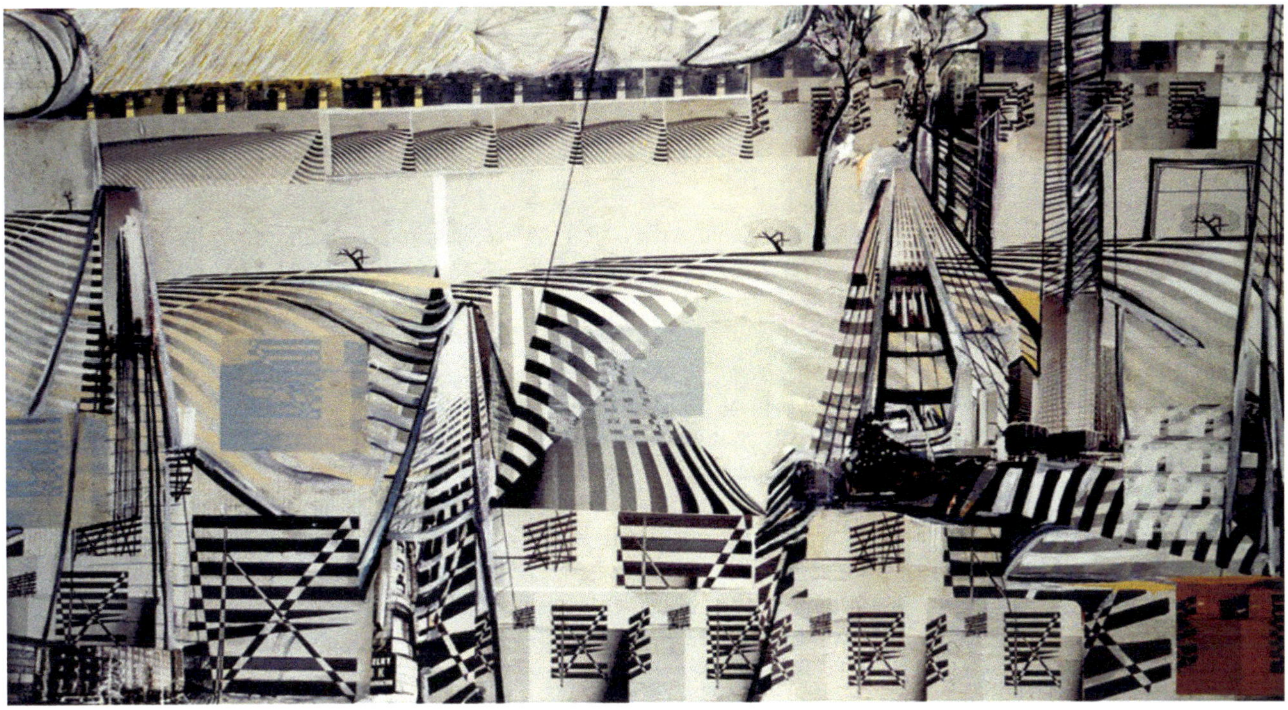

Commuter's Tunes. © 2025 by Anna Ursyn

CHAPTER 10
TEXT CODE

A DRIVING EXCHANGE

INTRODUCTION

Various means of communication evoke different ways to deliver stories. Their outcomes evolve with different tools, approaches, and collaborative efforts. While contemporary writing becomes visual, technology-based, and often collaborative in nature for various levels of immersive outcomes, the strategies are influenced by new tools.

SYNOPSIS

Two friends drive together while discussing a new game they are working on as a team. A poet wants their audience to write their poems while playing a game. The game designer discusses the production of this poetry-based game. Both have training in creative writing and comparative literature. They agree that creative writing has become more visual and involves knowledge.

SUMMARY

This work introduces two people talking inside a car in motion. The audience sees constantly changing roads from the driver's perspective. The codes and outcomes fill the space being heard, with corresponding music in the background.

CAST OF CHARACTERS

Richard, a Poet
Steve, a Game Designer

STAGE DIRECTIONS

Two actors are seen from the back seat of a car they sit in. A set of videos of a changing landscape and information is projected on the screen in front of the car.

The Curtain goes up (or opens).

Steve, "The new media changed the role of writing. Codes used to be a core of poetics, and now, we have to learn how to be prompt engineers or writers."
Richard, "This is a new kind of job. The trick is to tell our ChatGPT to act as a researcher or writer and provide some stylistic examples."
Steve, "But we want to tell new, not old, stories through gaming. We want to skip the old tools, such as paper. If one plays a game, it must be interactive, and paper is not."
Richard disagrees, "It is possible to form a sphere out of a flat sheet of paper, which offers a sculptural approach. We can make a plane that flies in front of you. Or we can play paper, scissors, and rock; that's gaming. Is this interactive enough for you?"
Steve continues, "The boundaries between art, craft, and design are altered. That's why. Our audience needs a good story. We begin writing any story by building a storyline with an introduction to our characters, a conflict, and a resolution, and we end with a moral. A moral may be imperative to make the audience start or stop doing something, such as stopping smoking or giving blood. We search for proper words; we set them together, and then we introduce emotions to facilitate or follow impulses or attractors within applications. Emotions for a time-based narrator are like colors that serve a painter. Our audience loves to interact through navigating, clicking, or using rollover functions. All our movements, from gestures to actions controlled by our voice, make us happy and entertained. We develop meaning. Applications promote and encourage attractive, spontaneous, and impulsive responses. We talk about multi-modal signifying, and we use signifiers. We communicate through words, images, colors, typography, and audio, often a part of writing or crafting a story. We rely on interaction. The idea of time and location are different now. We challenge it. The word 'text' got promoted to have its meaning. It can even become an imperative. Our texting gets shorter. We use abbreviations. There is a long list of them at our disposal. Our semi-words keep gaining common perception. We use emojis to highlight and share our understanding or feelings.
We focus on the meaning, semantics, semiotics, functionality, and signification of our messages or signals of beauty as open messages distributed rather than exclusive. We create immersive meaning to stimulate thinking and for various interpretations through some attempts to involve more senses. Can you, without thinking, develop a haiku poem about writing?"
Richard recites his improvised poem:

"Pencil scratches paper,
Thoughts flow onto the page,
Creation in bloom."

Steve, laughingly, "Pencil? Paper? You must be joking."
Richard, "Why? It is one of the oldest communication media. People use graphite on paper for writing, sketching, or drawing. It is inexpensive, versatile, and even can be erased if parts of what we created are no longer needed. People keep saying that technology replaces everything and that it makes everything more flexible and easier to use, but our mighty pencil keeps ruling for many of us. Do not get me wrong,

as I am not saying that digital work does not permit the development of our artistic styles. The general aesthetics of the final product vary and look unique. We expand our ideas independently. We use expressions following our experiences and habits. It may be harder to erase reminders of a pencil or charcoal because they smudge, and the markings may get messy, but we have enough appreciation for them to recognize the quality of the line."
Steve, "In the drawing, that is?"
Richard, "Drawing, sketching, and writing is line-based. So is sculpture or interactive content. We learned to keep our appreciation for hand sketches, drawings, or writing. The softness of the lead, the surface, the texture we apply our tool on, the pressure of the tool used to create with it, and how we apply it matter. We constantly make choices. Our products depend on them. Sometimes, digital art may look too easy to develop. It is like the tools we use to create it for us. It is not hard to use those tools. It is like driving a car. Obtaining a driving license does not make one a good driver. The mileage does. Just remember that we can use the computer's memory to create a sketch, multiply it, transform it, and even set it in motion. All can be done with the greatest precision, with no ruler or additional tools. Digital and traditional skills can be used back and forth between the two working environments. We can sketch, scan, add lines, print, then sketch or draw again. Some level of versatility and style can be achieved with practice. Digital and traditional work are both important. People develop their techniques or methods according to their preferences. Digital work tends to be perfect. Of course, traditional tools can possess different types of effects. It is easy to apply changes or to replicate work for images or texts digitally."
Steve, "You talk about the writing process from the tool's perspective."
Richard, "Nowadays, writing is drawing."
*Steve, in a serious tone***,**

"The Role of an Image:
An image starts with a line. Lines form many dimensions, including 1d, 2d, 3d, 4d, now 5d, and perhaps beyond, as we include more senses. We may discuss if a point is one or two-dimensional. This topic connects artists with mathematicians and philosophers. Many scientists, performers, or thinkers would gladly join these discussions because a point is defined by its presence on the x and y-axis and a line can be seen as a set of points with directly proportional numbers on the axis. We see a point in our digital understanding as a helpful yet annoying element as we have to deal with resolution. Point rules and flawlessly create a line in our analog, vector-based world. We, imperfect creatures, can rely on programming now when everything is precisely defined and differs from the work of a messy painter, for example.
Other forms of art also start with an image. Again, from 2D to multiple dimensions and variables can be seen as the start of any creation. This comes down to three fundamental questions for any visual communicator's tasks, from writing and art to design:
1. Who is your audience? Knowing their needs and mental and physical capabilities allows one to adjust the content: type size, style, colors, or other design features.
2. What message are you trying to send, and how you'd like people to think after your work is delivered? Some moral or an imperative to do something, like donate blood, or to cease doing something, like stop smoking, do not contaminate, recycle, etc.?
3. How could your work be displayed to confirm the requirements of the delivery vehicle of your messages? According to the container of the story principle, the same action must be retold for a different delivery method. A theatrical play on a stage, when the actor must be aware of the dimensions of a stage, animations when in a 3D world a character can be sent out never to stop, or for a comic book, when image and texts work together, or a video when we can mix and match the assets, all have their demands. All virtual reality, or as we call them, VR types, sets the audience inside of the action and means for them to be equal to the characters presented, while some give them perspective by allowing them to look at the action from a distance. It's almost like watching the characters from above.
An Image rules and has tremendous potential for future growth!"

Richard, "What's the purpose of the game again?"
Steve, "To have them learn something. Maybe write their own poems?"
Richard, "If you want them to learn something, have them write a simple Python code that displays a poem about writing. As an example, something like this:

STILL LIFE

Favorite color?
No color exists alone, like a note in a music composition,

or a frame in a movie,
I may say, a blue pen. You will say it's a cobalt one,
placed on a green book, actually, a sap green,
with one corner covered by a red apple, a symbol.
Well, maroon with salmon speckles,
supported by a piece of yellow cheese, the kind with holes.
Swiss cheese, we would say to simplify,
to communicate better or faster.

A precise description of color may confuse,
make conversation longer, less interesting,

or even destruct it, change the meaning of what we are saying,
like shouting or whispering.
Leave it to a painter."

This is how this poem would look in Python:

```
print("Still Life")
print("")
print("Favorite color?,")
print("No color exists alone, like a note in a music
composition,.")
print("or a frame in a movie,")
print("I may say, a blue pen. You will say its cobalt one.")
print("")
print("placed on a green book, actually, a sap green,")
print("with one corner covered by a red apple, a symbol.")
print("Well, maroon with salmon speckles,")
print("supported by a piece of yellow cheese, the kind with holes.")
print("")
print("Swiss cheese, we would say to simplify,")
print("to communicate better, or faster.")
print("Precise description of a color may confuse,")
print("make conversation longer, less interesting.")
print("")
print("like shouting or whispering.,")
print("Leave it to a painter.")
```

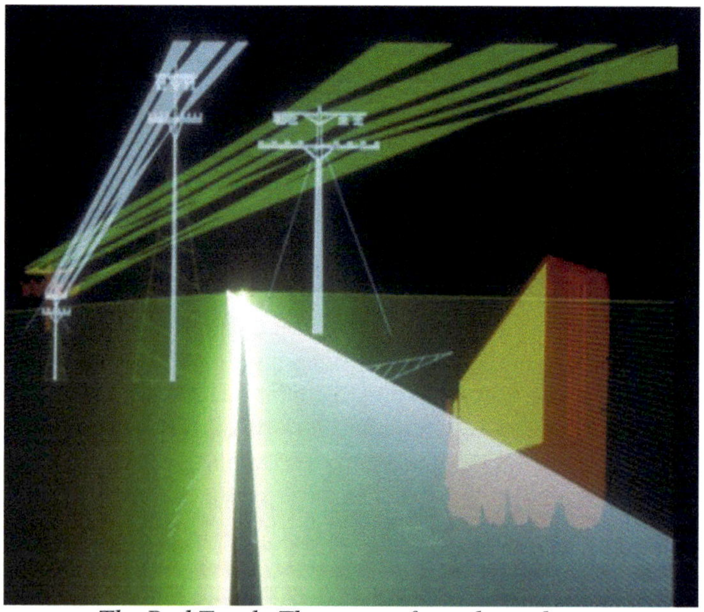

The Red Truck. The output from the code.
© 2025 by Anna Ursyn.

Steve, "I think that when talking about any art, we need to remember this:

A FRAME IN A MOVIE

An artist works a lot to be able to see progress made
or not made
or visible, after three weeks would pass.
Hard to see, judge, or value it
right after the task is completed.

Like in a keyframe in animation:
two frames are enough to call it animation,
but when more are present,
they can look almost the same.
Much work is needed to make or see the progress."

Richard, in a hopeless voice,

```
print("Writing")
print("")
print("A pen in my hand,")
print("A blank sheet before me.")
print("Words waiting to be born,")
print("Ideas longing to be set free.")
print("")
print("The ink flows like a river,")
print("Creating worlds out of thin air.")
print("The power of the written word,")
print("Is something truly rare.")
print("")
print("Writing is an act of magic,")
print("A way to transcend time and space.")
print("A bridge between the past and future,")
print("And a reflection of the human race.")
print("")
print("So take up your pen, my friend,")
print("And let your thoughts take flight.")
print("For in the act of writing,")
print("We find the power to ignite.")
```

The students would come up with a poem like that, and others would have to read it."
Steve, "So, here we are, pen and paper again. Besides, it is not a good poem, I think. Sorry."
How about some new writing strategies? We can follow Nature, which offers endless processes and products. We follow them on different levels. They inspire new solutions. We define them and then classify our results according to the disciplines we formed. We enjoy working with traditional media, such as painting, printmaking, or sculpture, and we enjoy rather messy processes and environments. Now, we use coding and software-based outcomes. They bring perfection and offer new and different transformations of our lines. We involve more senses to experience interactions. We move into yet another level of communication. Our actions are aesthetics-based and provide an open-message type of visual communication. Coding and software give us some perfect outcomes. Elevated levels of transformations also allow for a more open message type of environment for our senses and experiences while still being interesting in their aesthetic outcomes."
Richard, in a resigned voice, "OK. It will be a drawing game."

The End.
The curtain goes down (or closes).

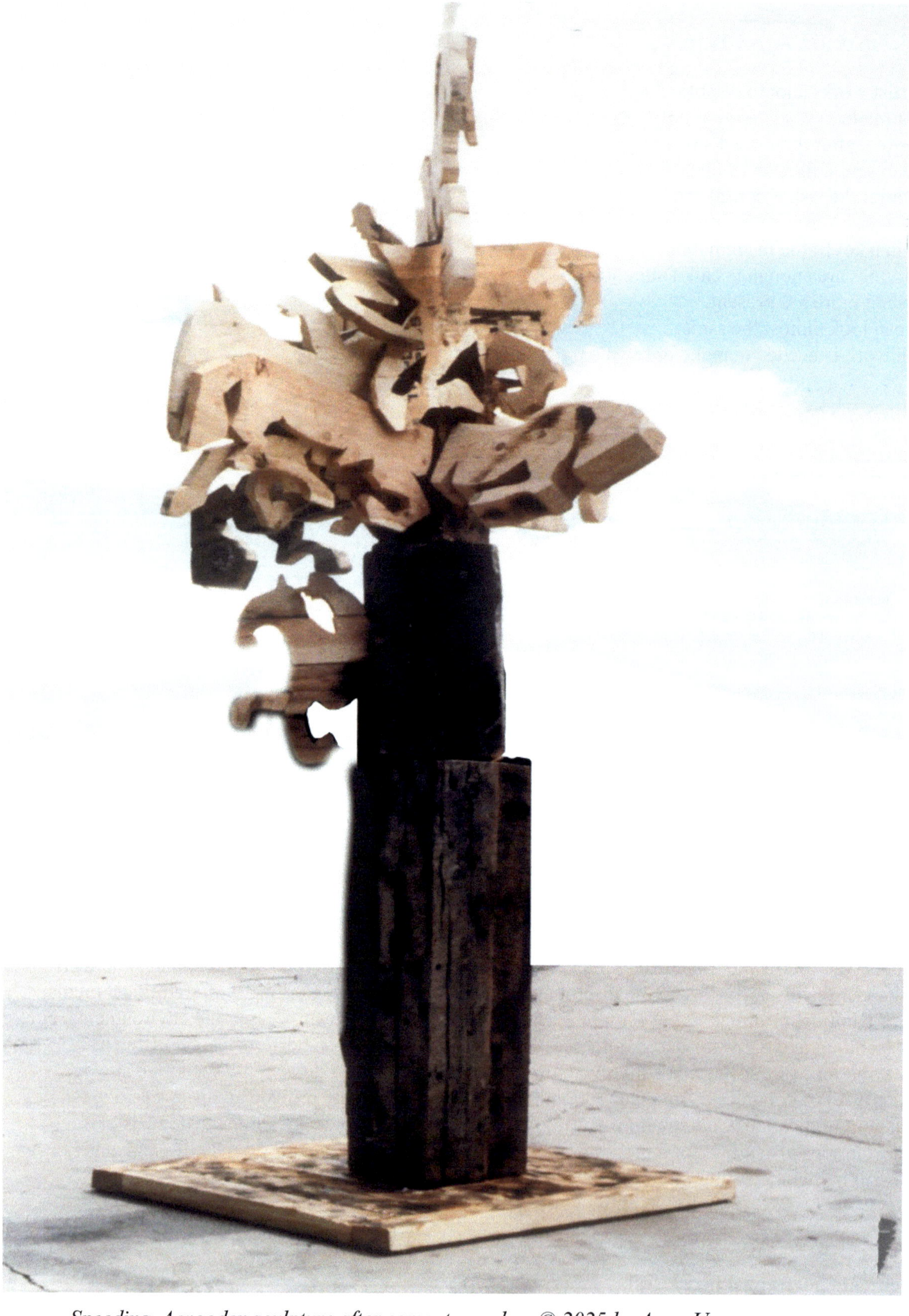

Speeding. A wooden sculpture after computer codes. © 2025 by Anna Ursyn

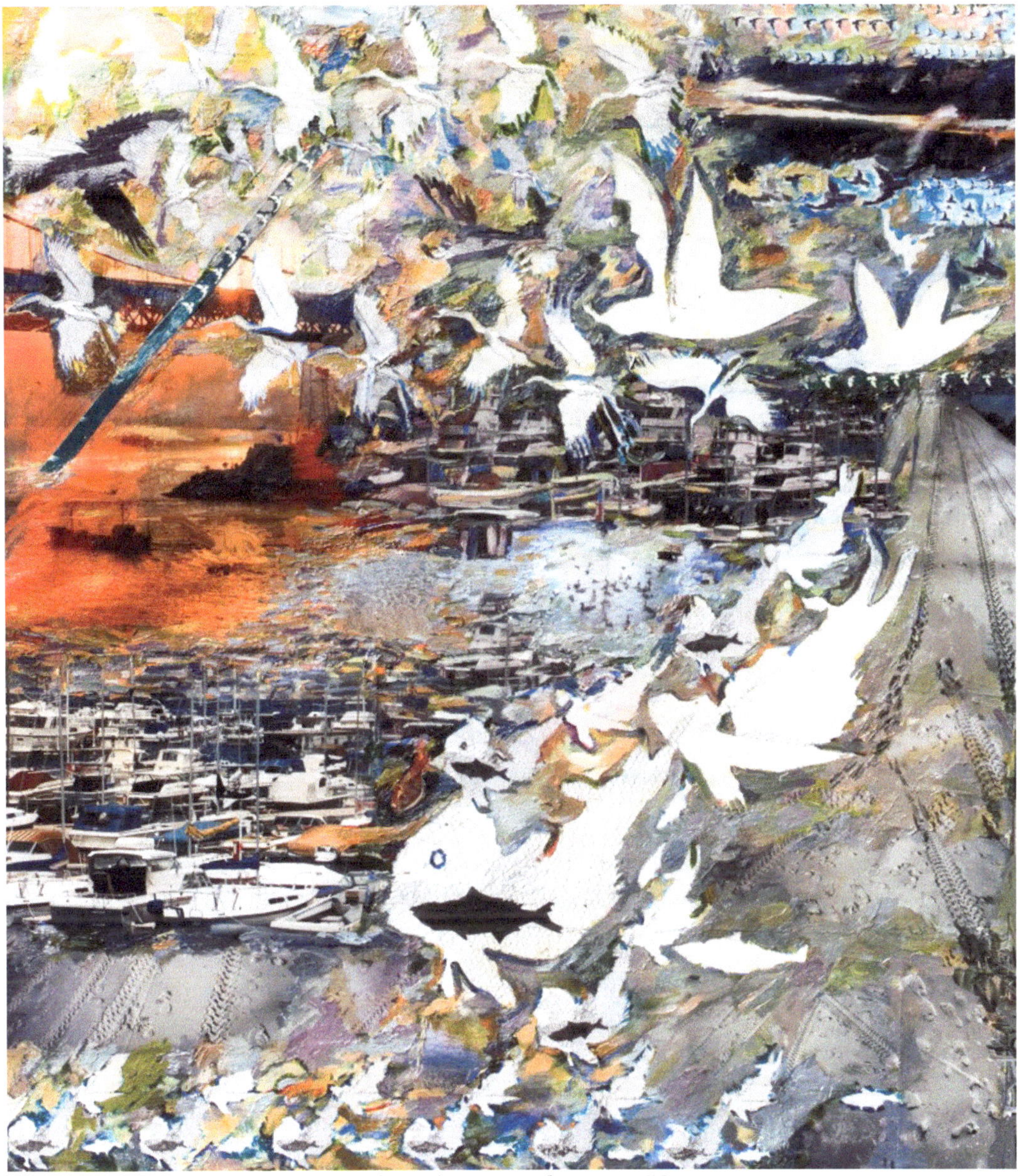

Discretion Advised. © 2025 by Anna Ursyn

CHAPTER 11
BIO CODE

AN ARTIFICIAL INTELLIGENCE CLASS BALLET

INTRODUCTION

Nowadays, biology-inspired computing, engineering, design, and even art are common things. During an Artificial Intelligence class, various solutions are discussed by using formations such as the shoaling and schooling fish, flocks of birds, swarms of honeybees, ants, grasshoppers, bats, tarantulas, butterflies, flamingos, and crabs as an introduction to swarm computing.

SYNOPSIS

In an Artificial Intelligence class, a professor assigns tasks. In Nature Swarming, one or more species gather within a single area for a common purpose. Swarm computing involves unused smartphone and tablet capabilities to perform server functions, with individual entities working together towards a shared goal.

The teacher asks the students to develop programs for the swarming animals, except for one.

1. Bees collectively build their long-term or temporary hives.
2. Ants carry and are working – an ants' nest.
3. Birds fly – a flock of birds.
4. Fish swim – a school of fish.
5. Grasshoppers, including locusts, are punctual and organized in their swarming.
6. Bats convene to share knowledge about hibernation sites with their young ones.
7. Tarantulas surge after the rain. We talk about pulsating, dancing, or beat creation.
8. Monarch swarm while migrating to keep warm at night, mud puddling.
9. Flamingos gather in large stands (flocks), quarrel but create friendship.
10. Crabs migrate in massive swarms.
11. Walrus swarm beaches as the ice melts.
12. On the contrary, seahorses are loners; they do not crowd.

The students are coding. The dancers perform their dance, portraying the unique way each type of animal swarms.

SUMMARY

This project commences in a computer lab. Each student dresses as the species they introduce and describes their respective behavior. The dancers in the background dance in each section, mimicking the movement of bees, ants, birds, fish, and more and matching each related code. The projection of each of their habitats matches each related theme and regulation and is accompanied by music played in the background.

CAST OF CHARACTERS

Teacher – Koder - fast as the lighting in Texas, from Old High German
Student 1 – Bees - Barnabee – English, son of a consolation
Student 2 – Ants - Anthony – Greek, Anthos (flower, Anthropos, man)
Student 3 – Birds - Raven (Wise Old Norse Hrafn)
Student 4 – Fish - Rohit (big, beautiful fish in the Indian language)
Student 5 – Grasshoppers - Greenhorn (a novice)
Student 6 – Bats - Antrozous (formal name)
Student 7 – Tarantulas - A Dancing Mania plaque - 1021 - Thera and more
Student 8 – Butterflies - Papilio
Student 9 – Flamingos - Phoe
Student 10 – Crabs - Brachy
Student 11 – Walruses - Norse (language)
Student 12 – Seahorses - Hippos Kampos Greek (horse and sea monster)

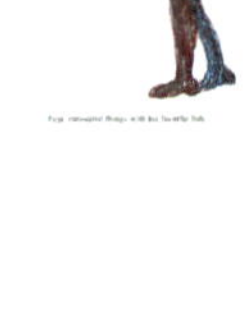

Feja: measured things with his favorite fish.

STAGE DIRECTIONS

The teacher stands in front of the AI class of twelve students who concentrate on their laptops. Projected texts, and videos of swarm animals by dancers mimicking their moves are projected in the background against a group of dancers wearing related to each group color leotards.

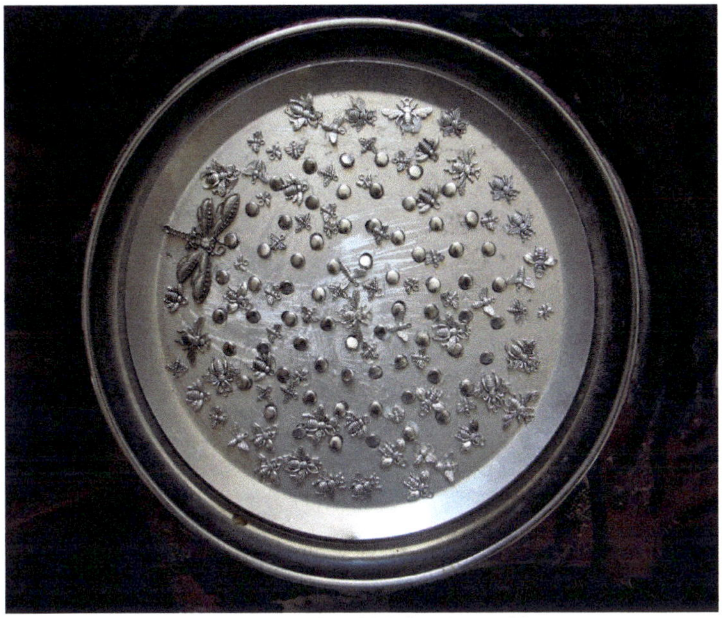

Busy Time. © 2025 by Anna Ursyn

Act I - Bees
The Curtain goes up (or opens).

Teacher, "As the coders-to-be, you have chosen well. Artificial Intelligence is an exciting and quite promising field of study. Today, I am going to challenge you. Some animals create colonies and follow as they would have a collective brain. Those are called swarm animals. You may select one of the topics.
1. Write a code for a colony of bees living in hives and summarize their group behavior."
Student 1, "I love honey; I'll do the bees."

Here's a code for simulating a colony of bees living in hives:

```
import random

class Bee:
    def __init__(self, name):
        self.name = name
        self.energy = 100
        self.location = None

    def move(self, hive)
        if self.energy < 10:
            return self.return_to_hive(hive)

        directions = hive.get_directions(self.location)
        if not directions:
            return self.return_to_hive(hive)

        new_location = random.choice(directions)
        self.location = new_location
        self.energy = 1
```

```
    def return_to_hive(self, hive):
        self.location = hive.location
        self.energy = 100

    def __str__(self):
        return f"{self.name}: Energy {self.energy}, Location {self.location}"


class Hive:
    def __init__(self, location):
        self.location = location
        self.bees = []

    def add_bee(self, bee):
        bee.location = self.location
        self.bees.append(bee)

    def get_directions(self, location):
        directions = []
        for x in range(location[0]-1, location[0]+2):
            for y in range(location[1]-1, location[1]+2):
                if (x, y) != location:
                    directions.append((x, y))
        return directions

    def __str__(self):
        return f"Hive at {self.location}: {len(self.bees)} bees"

# Create a hive and add some bees
hive = Hive((0, 0))
for i in range(10):
    bee = Bee(f"Bee {i}")
    hive.add_bee(bee)

# Simulate some time passing
for i in range(10):
    for bee in hive.bees:
        bee.move(hive)
    print(hive)
    for bee in hive.bees:
        print(bee)
```

Teacher, "Yes, very good; in this simulation, the Bee class represents an individual bee, with its energy level and location. The Hive class represents a hive, which contains multiple bees and provides directions for them to move."

`The dancers and the bees dance a 'Bee Dance' in related costumes.`

Student 1, "Bees exhibit swarm behavior as they collaborate to sustain their hive and gather food. Their communication through dances and pheromones is crucial to their coordination. The group will leave the hive to find a new location if the hive if it becomes overcrowded or the food supply runs low. They also work together to regulate the hive's temperature and care for the young."

The curtain goes down (or closes).
(No Break).

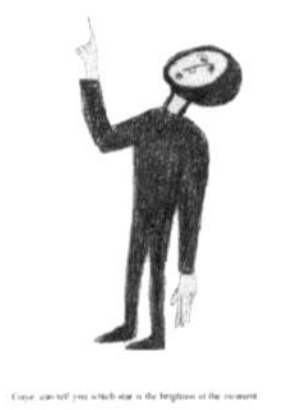

Guye: can tell you which star is the brightest at the moment.

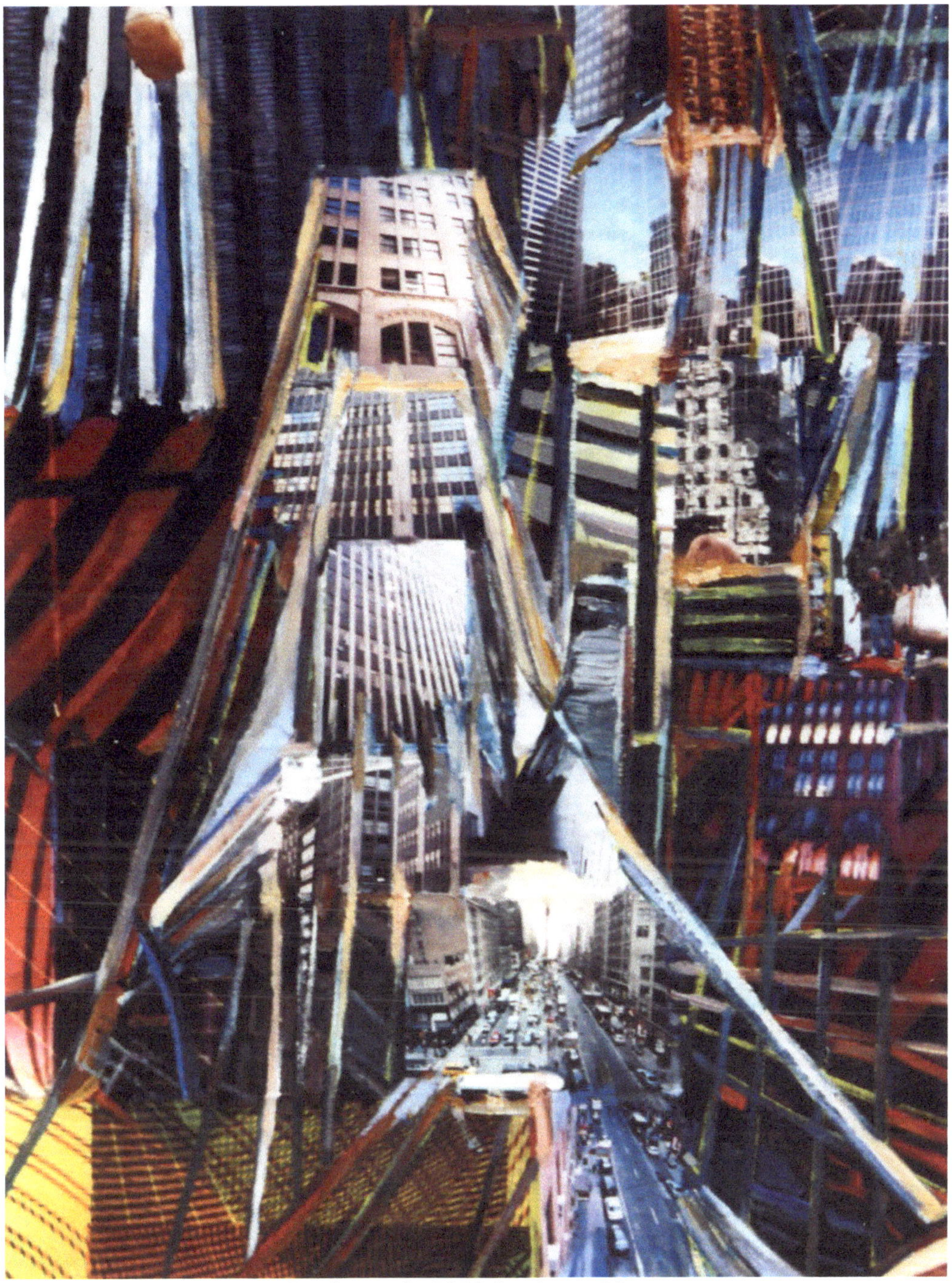

Parkour. © 2025 by Anna Ursyn

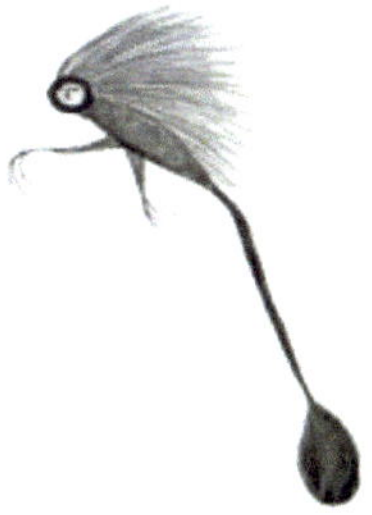

Pugurea: Always wants to go higher.

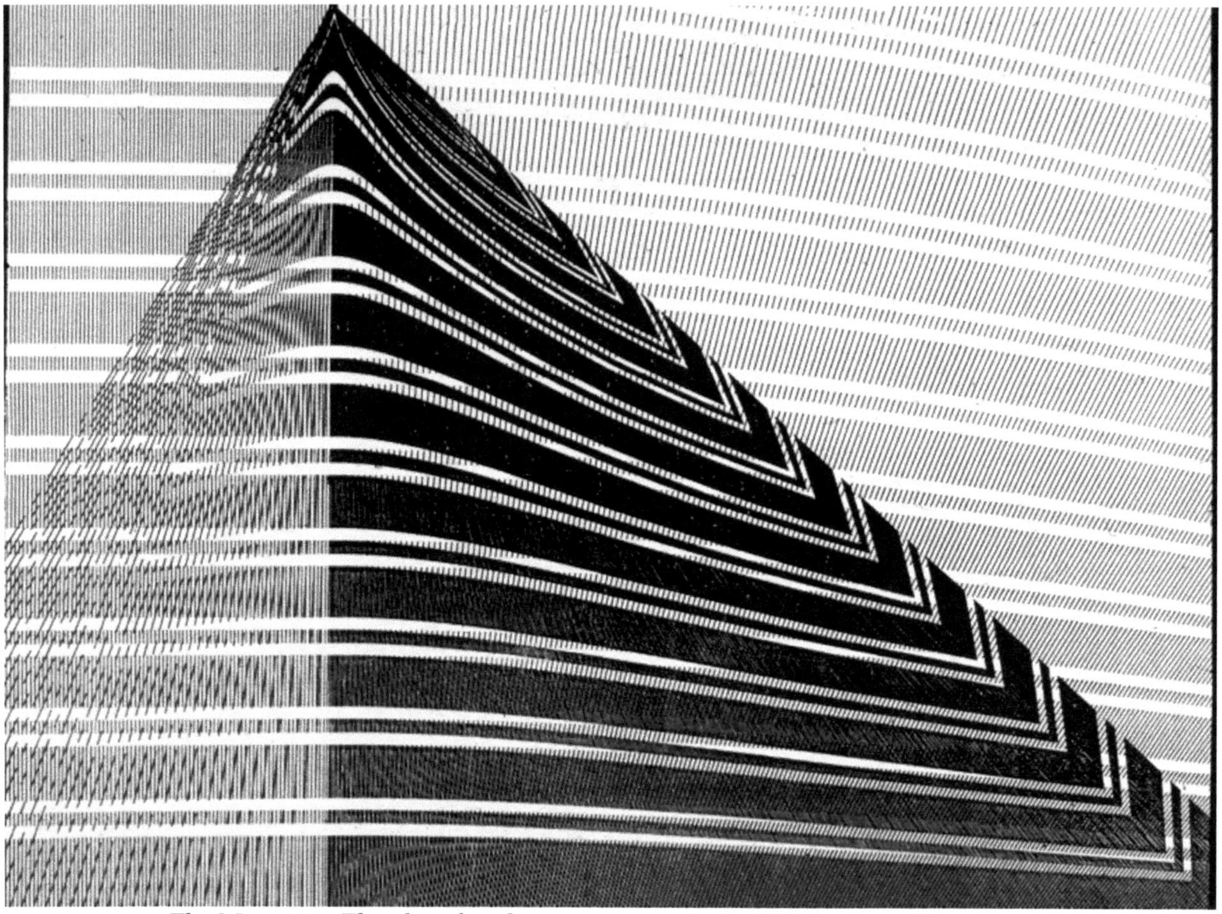

The Mountain. The plot after the computer code. © 2025 by Anna Ursyn

Act II - Ants
The curtain goes up (or opens).

Teacher, "Our second task is to write code that shows the structure, order, and rules inside an ant's nest."
Student 2, "Ants carry; they symbolize work. I'll do it. I love working.
Here comes a code for simulating a structure, order, and rules inside of an ant nest:

```
import random

class Ant:
    def __init__(self, nest, name):
        self.name = name
        self.nest = nest
        self.location = nest.location
        self.food = False

    def move(self):
        directions = self.nest.get_directions(self.location)
        if not directions:
            return
        new_location = random.choice(directions)
        self.location = new_location

        if self.location in self.nest.food_sources and not self.food:
            self.nest.take_food(self.location)
            self.food = True
        elif self.location == self.nest.location and self.food:
            self.nest.drop_food()
            self.food = False
```

```
    def __str__(self):
        return f"{self.name}: Food {self.food}, Location {self.location}"

class Nest:
    def __init__(self, location, food_sources):
        self.location = location
        self.food_sources = food_sources
        self.food_pile = 0
        self.ants = []

    def add_ant(self, ant):
        self.ants.append(ant)

    def get_directions(self, location):
        directions = []
        for x in range(location[0]-1, location[0]+2):
            for y in range(location[1]-1, location[1]+2):
                if (x, y) != location:
                    if (x, y) in self.food_sources or (x, y) == self.location:
                        directions.append((x, y))
        return directions

    def take_food(self, location):
        self.food_pile += 1
        self.food_sources.remove(location)

    def drop_food(self):
        self.food_pile -= 1

    def __str__(self):
        return f"Nest at {self.location}: {len(self.ants)} ants, {self.food_pile} food"

# Create a nest and add some ants
nest = Nest((0, 0), [(3, 3), (3, 6), (6, 3), (6, 6)])
for i in range(10):
    ant = Ant(nest, f"Ant {i}")
    nest.add_ant(ant)

# Simulate some time passing
for i in range(10):
    for ant in nest.ants:
        ant.move()
    print(nest)
    for ant in nest.ants:
        print(ant)
```

The dancers dance an 'Ants Dance' in related costumes.

*Teacher, "Not half bad. T*he Ant class represents an individual ant, with its name, location, and whether it carries food. The Nest class represents an ant nest, which contains multiple ants and provides directions for them to move. The Nest class also keeps track of the location of food sources and the food pile within the nest."

Student 2, "The structure and order of an ant nest are characterized by the division of labor among the ants, with different ants taking on different roles such as foraging for food, caring for the young, and defending the nest. Ants communicate with each other through pheromones to share information about food sources and to coordinate their activities. The rules inside an ant nest include maintaining cleanliness and order, caring for the young, and protecting the nest from predators. Overall, ants demonstrate high organization and coordination in their group behavior."

The Curtain goes down (or closes).
No Break.

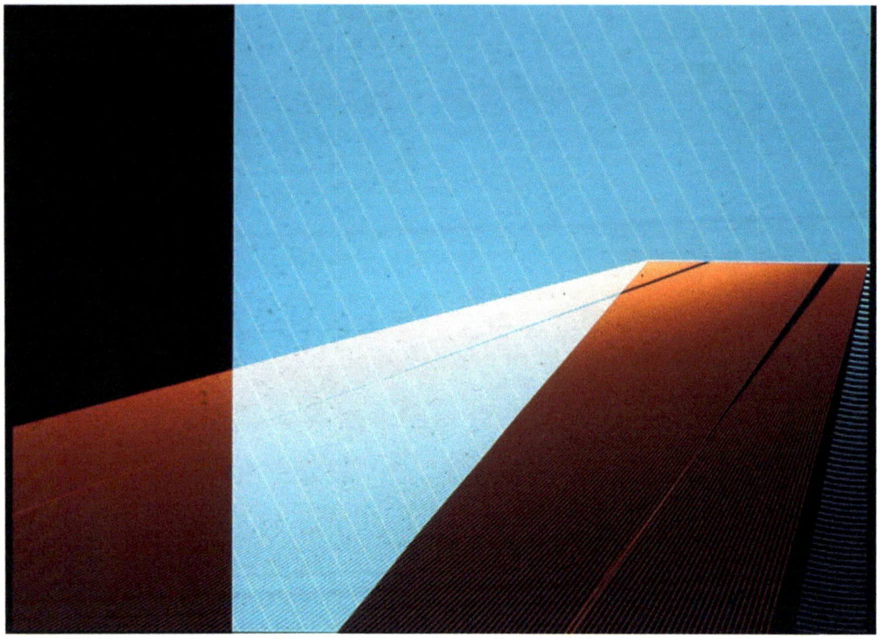

Solutions. Output from a computer code. © 2025 by Anna Ursyn

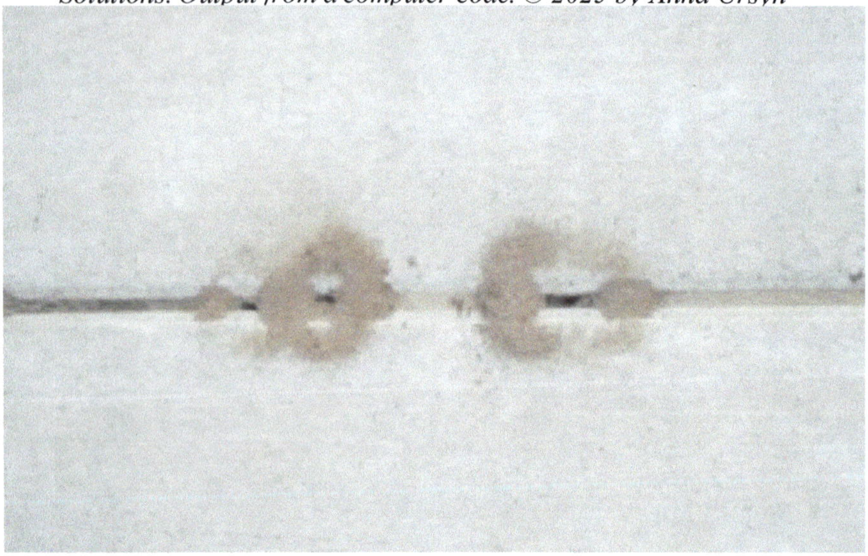

Ants Watching. © 2025 by Anna Ursyn

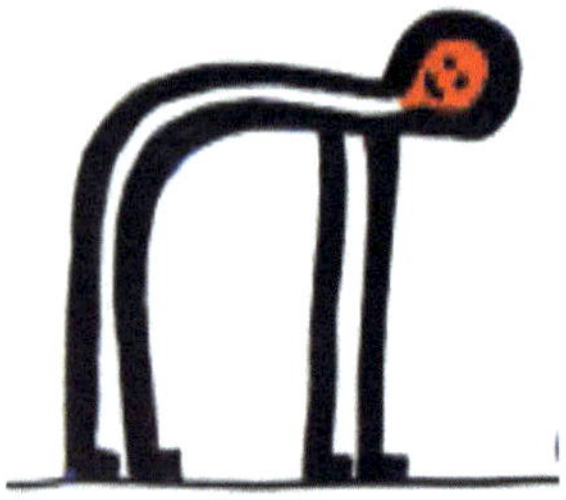

Vaurta: knows thirty ways of walking.

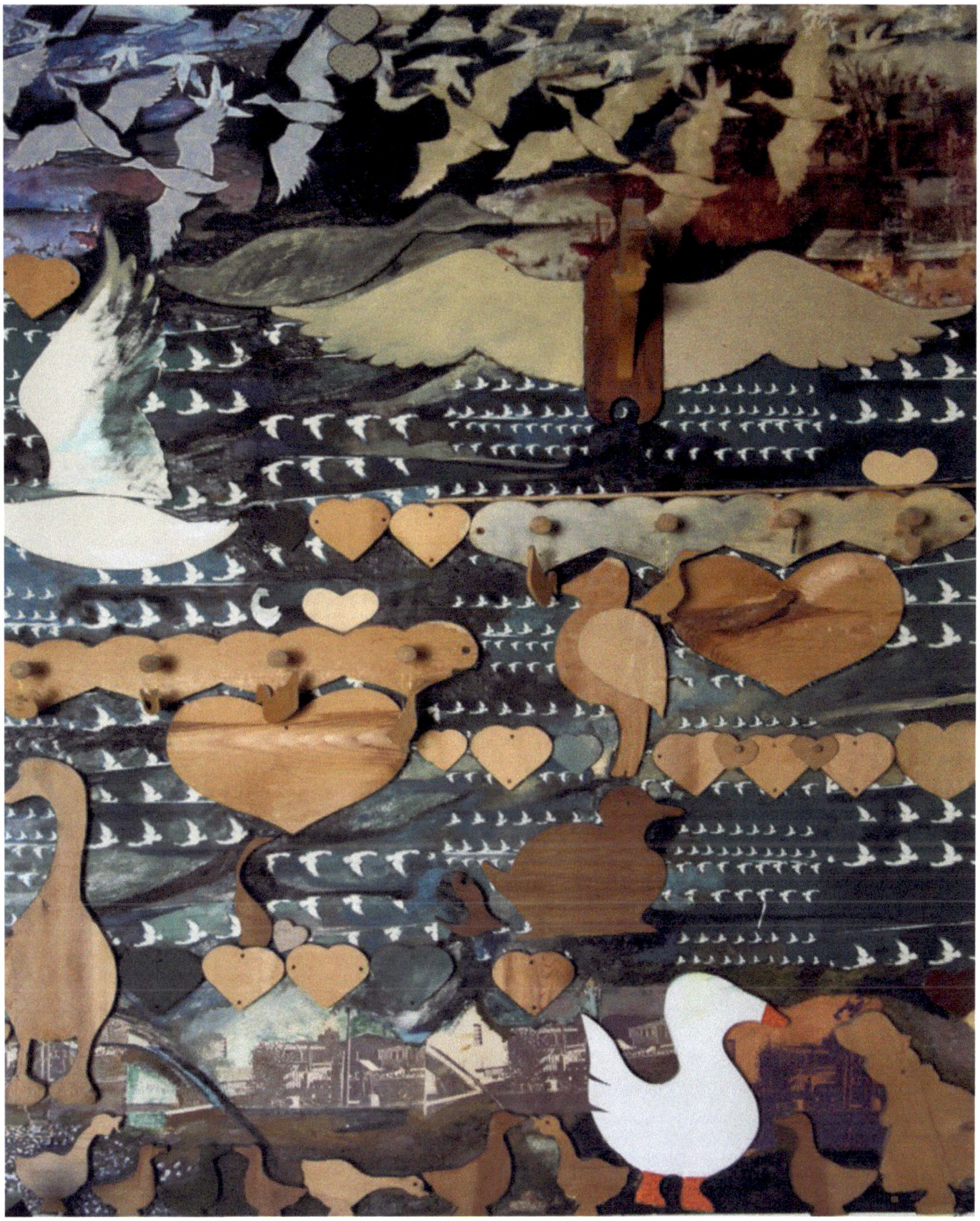

Some Birds Think They Are Smarter than Others. © *2025 by Anna Ursyn*

Act III, Birds
The Curtain goes up (or opens).

Teacher, "Now, write a code for the group behavior of a flock of birds."
Student 3, "Birds fly; my mind does as well. I'll do a flock of birds My code for simulating the group behavior of a flock of birds with Python uses a model called Boids. It shows birds move in groups by the rules of cohesion, separation, and alignment. You may tweak the numbers! I'll need to have pygame installed to run this simulation via pip:

pip install pygame:

```
import pygame
import random
import math

# Constants
WIDTH, HEIGHT = 800, 600
NUM_BOIDS = 100
MAX_SPEED = 4
MAX_FORCE = 0.1
NEIGHBOR_RADIUS = 50
SEPARATION_RADIUS = 25

# Boid class
class Boid:
    def __init__(self, x, y):
        self.position = pygame.Vector2(x, y)
        self.velocity = pygame.Vector2(random.uniform(-1, 1), random.uniform(-1, 1)).normalize() * MAX_SPEED
        self.acceleration = pygame.Vector2(0, 0)

    def update(self):
        self.velocity += self.acceleration
        if self.velocity.length() > MAX_SPEED:
            self.velocity.scale_to_length(MAX_SPEED)
        self.position += self.velocity
        self.acceleration *= 0 # Reset acceleration

    def apply_force(self, force):
        self.acceleration += force

    def edges(self):
        if self.position.x > WIDTH:
            self.position.x = 0
        elif self.position.x < 0:
            self.position.x = WIDTH
        if self.position.y > HEIGHT:
            self.position.y = 0
        elif self.position.y < 0:
            self.position.y = HEIGHT

    def flock(self, boids):
        alignment = self.align(boids)
        cohesion = self.cohere(boids)
        separation = self.separate(boids)

        self.apply_force(alignment)
        self.apply_force(cohesion)
        self.apply_force(separation)

    def align(self, boids):
        perception_radius = NEIGHBOR_RADIUS
        steering = pygame.Vector2(0, 0)
        total = 0

        for other in boids:
            if other != self and self.position.distance_to(other.position) < perception_radius:
                steering += other.velocity
                total += 1

        if total > 0:
            steering /= total
            steering = steering.normalize() * MAX_SPEED
            steering -= self.velocity
            if steering.length() > MAX_FORCE:
                steering.scale_to_length(MAX_FORCE)
        return steering

    def cohere(self, boids):
        perception_radius = NEIGHBOR_RADIUS
```

```
        steering = pygame.Vector2(0, 0)
        total = 0

        for other in boids:
            if other != self and self.position.distance_to(other.position) < perception_radius:
                steering += other.position
                total += 1

        if total > 0:
            steering /= total
            steering -= self.position
            if steering.length() > 0:
                steering = steering.normalize() * MAX_SPEED
                steering -= self.velocity
                if steering.length() > MAX_FORCE:
                    steering.scale_to_length(MAX_FORCE)
        return steering

    def separate(self, boids):
        perception_radius = SEPARATION_RADIUS
        steering = pygame.Vector2(0, 0)
        total = 0

        for other in boids:
            distance = self.position.distance_to(other.position)
            if other != self and distance < perception_radius:
                diff = self.position - other.position
                diff /= distance # Weight by distance
                steering += diff
                total += 1

        if total > 0:
            steering /= total
            if steering.length() > 0:
                steering = steering.normalize() * MAX_SPEED
                steering -= self.velocity
                if steering.length() > MAX_FORCE:
                    steering.scale_to_length(MAX_FORCE)
        return steering

# Setup pygame
pygame.init()
screen = pygame.display.set_mode((WIDTH, HEIGHT))
pygame.display.set_caption("Flocking Behavior Simulation")

# Create boids
boids = [Boid(random.randint(0, WIDTH), random.randint(0, HEIGHT)) for _ in range(NUM_BOIDS)]

# Main loop
running = True
while running:
    for event in pygame.event.get():
        if event.type == pygame.QUIT:
            running = False

    screen.fill((0, 0, 0))

    for boid in boids:
        boid.flock(boids)
        boid.update()
        boid.edges()
        pygame.draw.circle(screen, (255, 255, 255), (int(boid.position.x), int(boid.position.y)), 3)

    pygame.display.flip()
    pygame.time.delay(30)

pygame.quit()
```

Teacher: "Yes, the Boid Class represents each bird and contains methods for updating its position, applying forces, and handling flocking behavior so each boid adjusts its movement based on its neighbors using alignment, cohesion, and separation. Pygame Loop creates a window where boids move according to the flocking behavior.

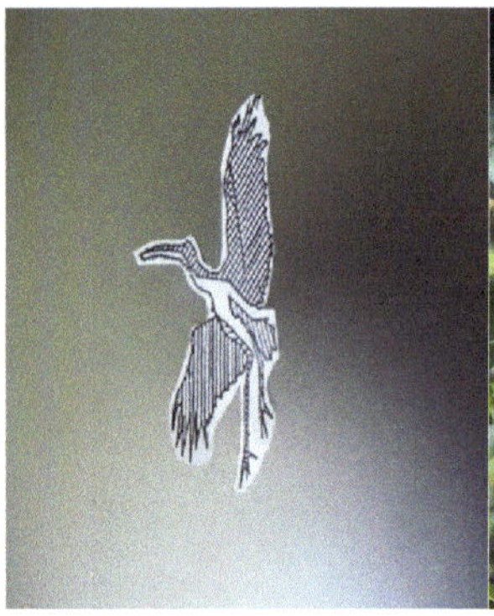

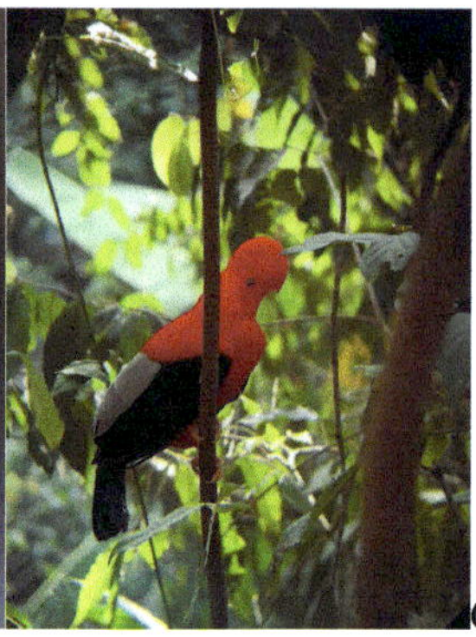

Gallo de Roca. © 2025 by Matylda Czarnecka

The Landing. The output from the code © 2025 by Ursyn

```
The dancers dance a 'Bird Dance' in related costumes.
```

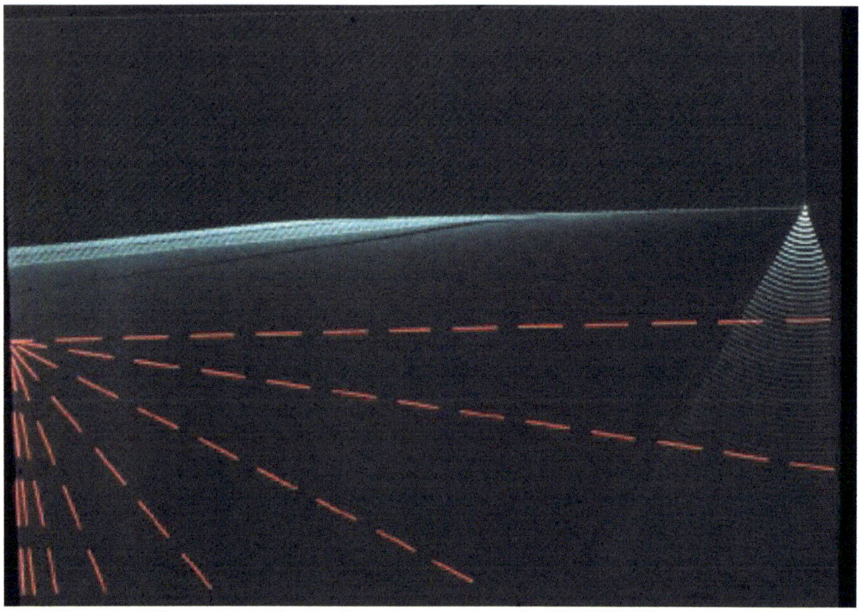

Senses. The output from the computer code. © 2025 by Anna Ursyn

The Curtain goes down (or closes).
No Break.

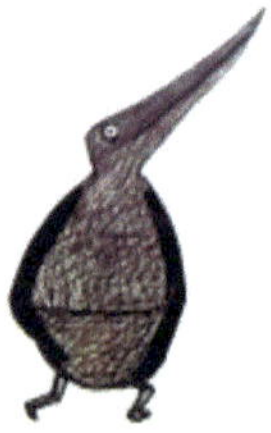

Rusana: can whistle but never does.

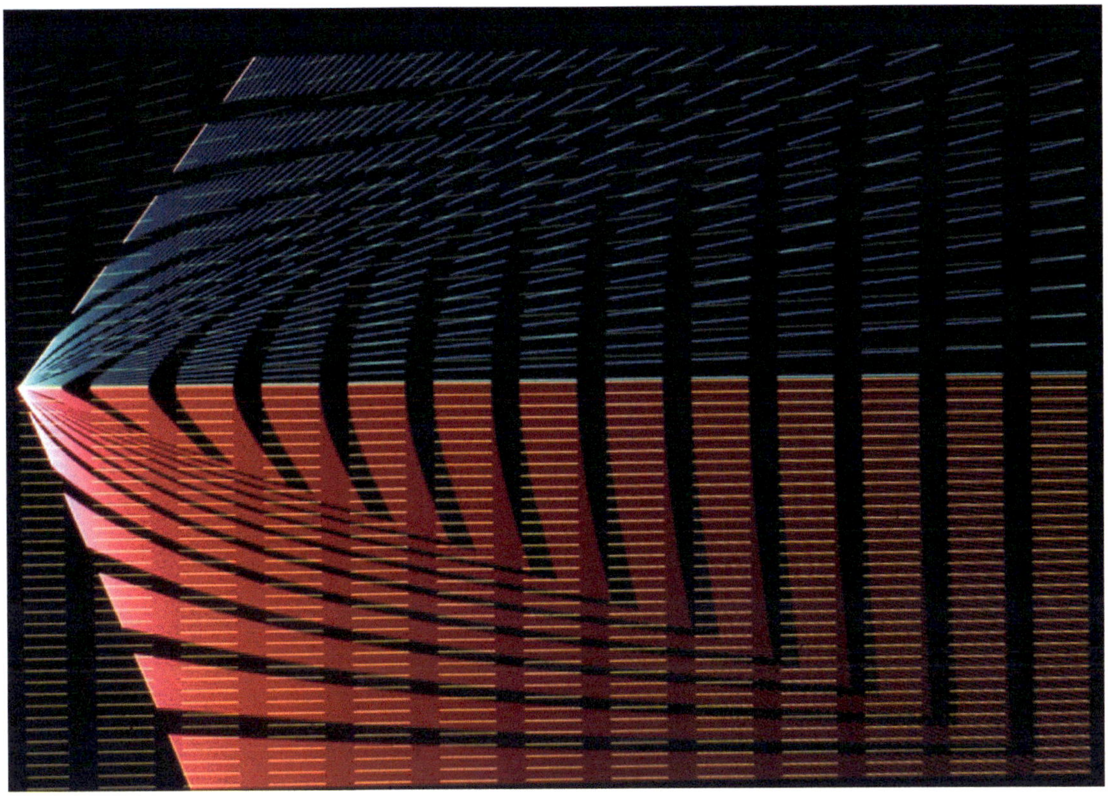

Fish. The output from the computer code. © 2025 by Anna Ursyn

Act IV – Fish
The Curtain goes up (or opens).

Teacher, "It's time to write a code for swarm computing, including a school of fish."
Student 4, "Fish swim. There is a school of fish; I ate a pond of fish."

The implementation of swarm computing, including a school of fish using Python, follows:

```
import random

class Fish:
  def _init_(self, x, y, speed, direction):
    self.x = x
    self.y = y
    self.speed = speed
    self.direction = direction

  def move(self):
    # move fish based on speed and direction
    self.x += self.speed * math.cos(self.direction)
    self.y += self.speed * math.sin(self.direction)

    # wrap around if fish goes out of screen
    if self.x < 0:
```

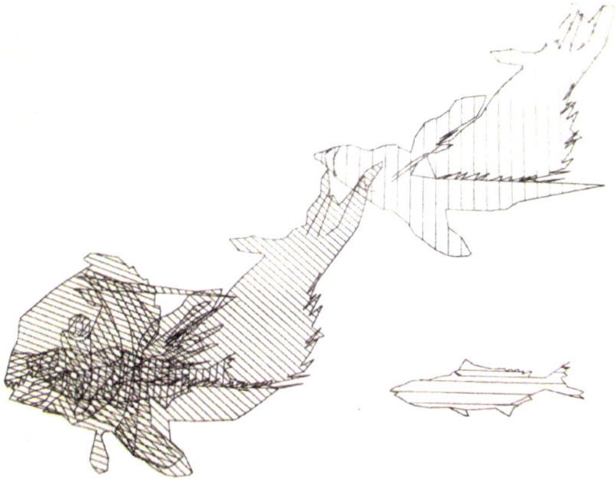

```
      self.x = SCREEN_WIDTH
    elif self.x > SCREEN_WIDTH:
      self.x = 0
    if self.y < 0:
```

```
            self.y = SCREEN_HEIGHT
        elif self.y > SCREEN_HEIGHT:
            self.y = 0

        # update fish direction randomly
        self.direction += random.uniform(-FISH_MAX_TURN, FISH_MAX_TURN)

        # limit fish direction to 0 to 2*pi
        if self.direction < 0:
            self.direction += 2 * math.pi
        elif self.direction > 2 * math.pi:
            self.direction -= 2 * math.pi

class SchoolOfFish:
    def __init__(self, num_fish):
        self.fish = []
        for i in range(num_fish):
            x = random.randint(0, SCREEN_WIDTH)
            y = random.randint(0, SCREEN_HEIGHT)
            speed = FISH_MIN_SPEED + random.random() * (FISH_MAX_SPEED - FISH_MIN_SPEED)
            direction = random.uniform(0, 2 * math.pi)
            self.fish.append(Fish(x, y, speed, direction))

    def move(self):
        for fish in self.fish:
            fish.move()
```

The dancers dance a 'Fish Dance' in related costumes.

Teacher, "Bravo! This code defines a Fish class representing a single fish in the school. Each fish has an (x, y) position, a speed, and a direction in radians. The move() method updates the fish's position based on its speed and direction, randomly changes its direction, and wraps around the screen"
Student 4, "The SchoolOfFish class represents the entire school of fish. It initializes a list of num_fish Fish objects and provides a move() method that calls the move() method of each fish in the school. This this is just a simple example of implementing swarm computing with a school of fish."
Student 1, "Agreed, but I can do it differently. Swarm computing is a field of computer science that studies collective behavior in decentralized systems. It is a type of artificial intelligence based on observing the behavior of animals, such as birds, bees, and fish. In this code, a simulation of a fish swarm is shown using Python and the Pygame library."
First, import the necessary libraries:

```
import pygame
import random
```

Next, define some constants for the simulation:

```
SCREEN_WIDTH = 800
SCREEN_HEIGHT = 600
NUM_FISH = 50
MAX_SPEED = 5
```

These constants specify the screen size, the number of fish, and the fish's maximum speed.
Now, define a class for the fish:"

```
python
class Fish:
    def __init__(self):
        self.x = random.randint(0, SCREEN_WIDTH)
        self.y = random.randint(0, SCREEN_HEIGHT)
        self.vx = random.uniform(-MAX_SPEED, MAX_SPEED)
        self.vy = random.uniform(-MAX_SPEED, MAX_SPEED)

    def update(self):
        self.x += self.vx
        self.y += self.vy
        if self.x < 0:
            self.x = SCREEN_WIDTH
        elif self.x > SCREEN_WIDTH:
```

```
            self.x = 0
        if self.y < 0:
            self.y = SCREEN_HEIGHT
        elif self.y > SCREEN_HEIGHT:
            self.y = 0

    def draw(self, surface):
        pygame.draw.circle(surface, (0, 0, 255), (int(self.x), int(self.y)), 5)
```

Teacher, "This class represents a single fish in the simulation. It has attributes for the fish's position and velocity and methods for updating its position and drawing it on the screen."

Student 1, "Next, initialize Pygame and create a window:

```
pygame.init()
screen = pygame.display.set_mode((SCREEN_WIDTH, SCREEN_HEIGHT))
```

Then, create a list of fish objects:

```
fish_list = []
for i in range(NUM_FISH):
    fish_list.append(Fish())
```

Now, enter the main loop of the simulation:

```
running = True
while running:
    for event in pygame.event.get():
        if event.type == pygame.QUIT:
            running = False

    screen.fill((255, 255, 255))

    for fish in fish_list:
        fish.update()
        fish.draw(screen)

    pygame.display.flip()

pygame.quit()
```

Teacher, "In this loop, you handled Pygame events, updated and drew each fish object, and flipped it."

Student 1, "This code simulates a fish swarm using Pygame and shows the basics of swarm computing. But now, let's look at the translation. A program written by Anna Ursyn in Fortran was translated into Java by Fahim Islam*:"

```
import java . awt . Graphics ;
import java . awt . Graphics2D ;
import javax . swing . JFrame ;
import javax . swing . JPanel ;
Import javax . swing . SwingUtilities ;

class Surface extends JPanel {

  private void doDrawing ( Graphics g) {

    double [] XM = { 11.3 , 12.1 , 12.6 , 14.5 , 15.2 , 16.0 , 17.0 , 19.0 , 20.2 ,
        20.8 , 21.4 , 32.0 , 21.4 , 20.8 , 21.5 , 22.5 , 23.8 , 26.3 , 28.5 ,
        28.5 , 29.5 , 29.5 , 30.5 , 30.5 , 31.3 , 31.0 , 32.0 , 32.5 , 32.0 ,
        32.0 , 34.6 , 38.5 , 37.0 , 38.5 , 37.5 , 38.0 , 37.5 , 38.0 , 37.0 ,
        37.7 , 38.0 , 40.5 , 39.7 , 40.5 , 39.0 , 34.5 , 32.0 , 29.0 , 27.0 ,
        29.0 , 32.0 , 32.5 , 31.3 , 29.7 , 29.0 , 27.0 , 23.5 , 23.0 , 22.5 ,
        20.0 , 22.5 , 22.9 , 22.4 , 20.0 , 17.0 , 15.0 , 14.0 , 13.0 , 12.0 ,
        12.5 , 11.5 , 11.3 };

    double [] YM = { 22.1 , 22.8 , 22.9 , 23.9 , 24.0 , 24.2 , 24.1 , 24.9 , 25.1 ,
        25.7 , 25.0 , 25.0 , 25.0 , 25.7 , 26.0 , 28.0 , 27.0 , 26.4 , 26.5 ,
        26.0 , 26.5 , 26.0 , 26.5 , 26.0 , 26.1 , 25.6 , 26.0 , 26.1 , 25.3 ,
        25.0 , 25.0 , 28.0 , 27.0 , 27.0 , 26.7 , 26.8 , 26.0 , 25.5 , 25.0 ,
        24.0 , 23.5 , 22.7 , 22.0 , 21.5 , 21.7 , 23.0 , 21.7 , 20.0 , 20.0 ,
        20.0 , 21.7 , 21.1 , 20.7 , 19.5 , 18.0 , 20.0 , 19.1 , 19.0 , 19.0 ,
        19.4 , 19.0 , 18.0 , 18.0 , 19.4 , 19.2 , 19.6 , 20.0 , 20.8 , 21.4 ,
```

```
        21.8 , 22.0 , 22.1 };

    Graphics2D g2d = ( Graphics2D ) g;

    for (int i = 0; i < 71; i ++) {

        g2d . drawLine (( int) XM[i] * 10, (int) YM[i] * 10,
                ( int) XM[i + 1] * 10, (int) YM[i + 1] * 10) ;

        // g2d . drawLine (30 , 30+( int )XM[i]*10 , 200 , 30+ i);
        // g2d . drawLine (30 , 100 , 300 , 100) ;
        // g2d . drawLine (30 , 200 , 200 , 200) ;
        // g2d . drawLine (200 , 200 , 30, 30) ;
    }
}

@Override
public void paintComponent ( Graphics g) {

    super . paintComponent (g);
    doDrawing (g);
}
    }

    public class mainclass extends JFrame {

        public mainclass () {

            initUI ();
        }

        private void initUI () {

            setTitle (" Lines ");
            setDefaultCloseOperation ( JFrame . EXIT_ON_CLOSE );

            add ( new Surface ());

            setSize (500 , 500) ;
            setLocationRelativeTo ( null );
        }

        public static void main ( String [] args ) {

            SwingUtilities . invokeLater ( new Runnable () {

                @Override
                public void run () {

                    mainclass lines = new mainclass ();
                    lines . setVisible ( true );
                }
            });
        }
    }
```

The Curtain goes down (or closes).
The Break

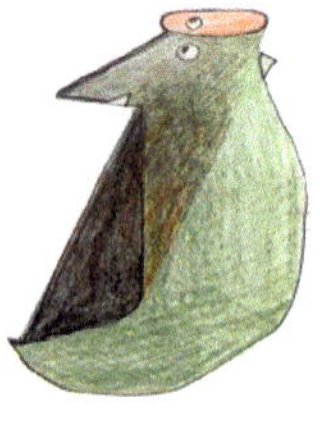

Cadugo: talks to himself succefully.

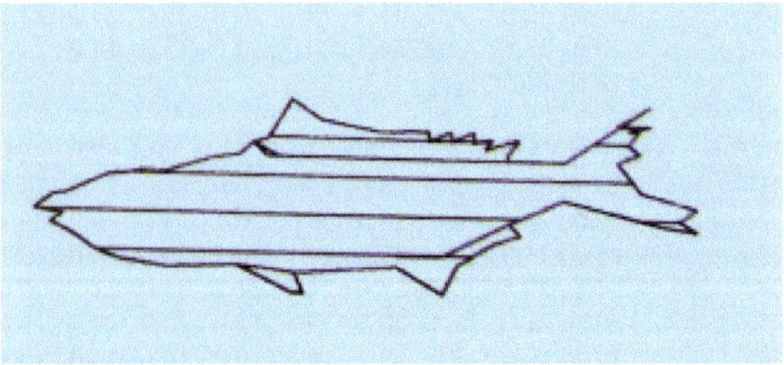

Cadugo: talks to himself successfully.

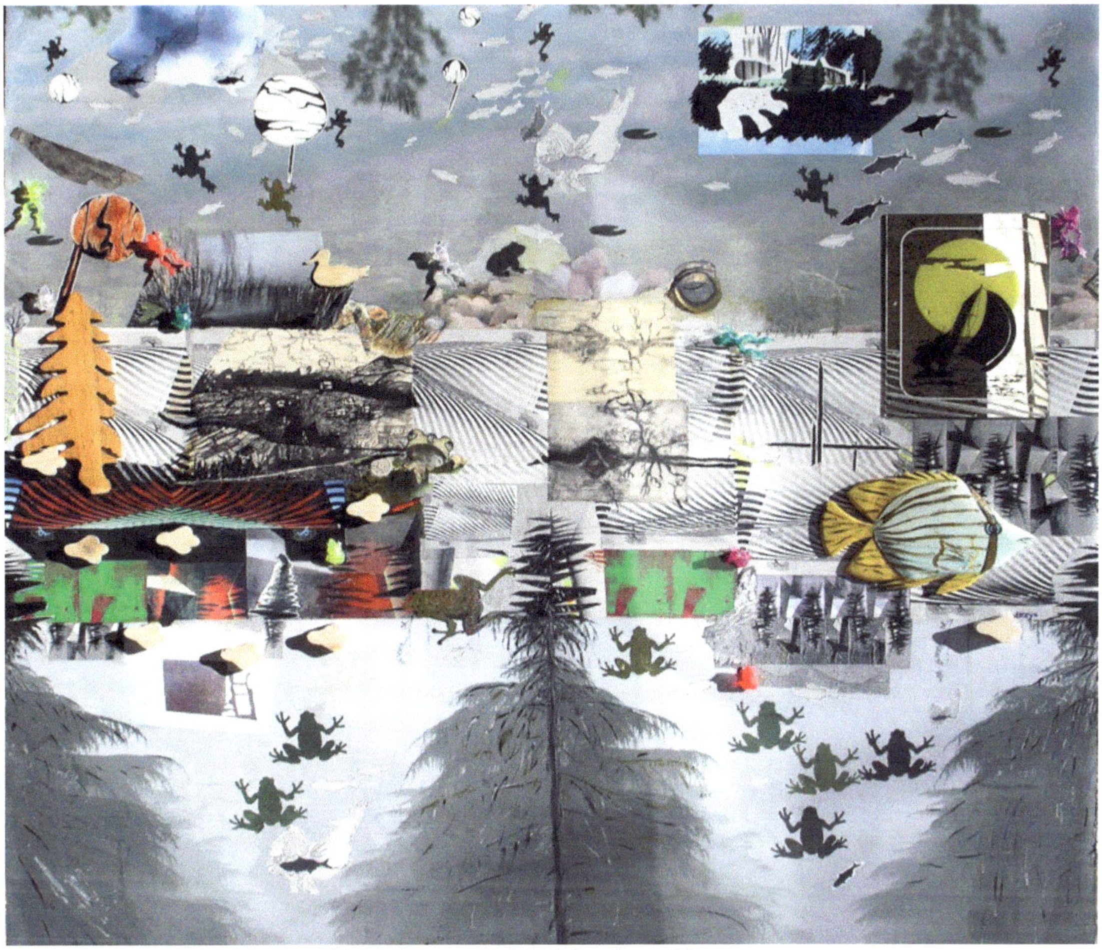

Frog Issues. © *2025 by Anna Ursyn*

Act V – Grasshoppers
The Curtain goes up (or opens).

Teacher, "Anyone would like to write a code on how grasshoppers join together?
Student 5, "I grew up on a farm. I can show how they act and move in unison. Some of them, called locusts, can fly, while others have no wings, so they hop. They have short or long horns. This code in Python simulates the swarming behavior of grasshoppers using the Pygame library:

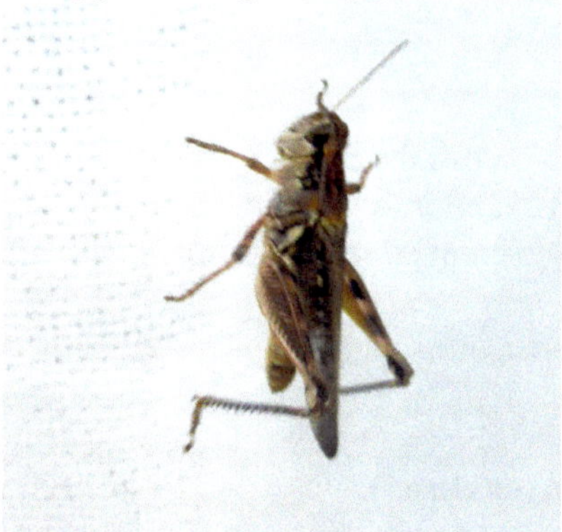

```
import pygame
import random

# Window dimensions
WIDTH = 800
HEIGHT = 600

# Grasshopper properties
NUM_GRASSHOPPERS = 50
GRASSHOPPER_SIZE = 10
GRASSHOPPER_SPEED = 2
GRASSHOPPER_COLOR = (0, 255, 0)

# Initialize Pygame
pygame.init()
window = pygame.display.set_mode((WIDTH, HEIGHT))
```

```
pygame.display.set_caption("Grasshopper Swarm")
clock = pygame.time.Clock()

# Create grasshopper objects
grasshoppers = []
for _ in range(NUM_GRASSHOPPERS):
    x = random.randint(0, WIDTH)
    y = random.randint(0, HEIGHT)
    dx = random.choice([-1, 1])
    dy = random.choice([-1, 1])
    grasshoppers.append([x, y, dx, dy])

# Main game loop
running = True
while running:
    for event in pygame.event.get():
        if event.type == pygame.QUIT:
            running = False

    window.fill((0, 0, 0))

    # Update grasshopper positions
    for i, grasshopper in enumerate(grasshoppers):
        x, y, dx, dy = grasshopper

        # Randomly change direction
        if random.random() < 0.01:
            dx = random.choice([-1, 1])
            dy = random.choice([-1, 1])

        # Move the grasshopper
        x += dx * GRASSHOPPER_SPEED
        y += dy * GRASSHOPPER_SPEED

        # Wrap around screen edges
        if x < 0:
            x = WIDTH
        elif x > WIDTH:
            x = 0
        if y < 0:
            y = HEIGHT
        elif y > HEIGHT:
            y = 0

        grasshoppers[i] = [x, y, dx, dy]

        # Draw grasshopper
        pygame.draw.circle(window, GRASSHOPPER_COLOR, (x, y), GRASSHOPPER_SIZE)

    pygame.display.flip()
    clock.tick(60)

pygame.quit()
```

`The dancers dance a 'Grasshoppers' Dance' in related costumes.`

Teacher, "Good. When you run the code, it opens a Pygame window and displays a swarm of grasshoppers. They move randomly around the screen, occasionally changing direction. They wrap around the screen edges to create a seamless movement effect. The grasshoppers are represented as green circles."
Student 5, "Luckily, there is no sound."
https://www.livescience.com/32609-what-makes-grasshoppers-swarm.html

The Curtain goes down (or closes).
(No Break)

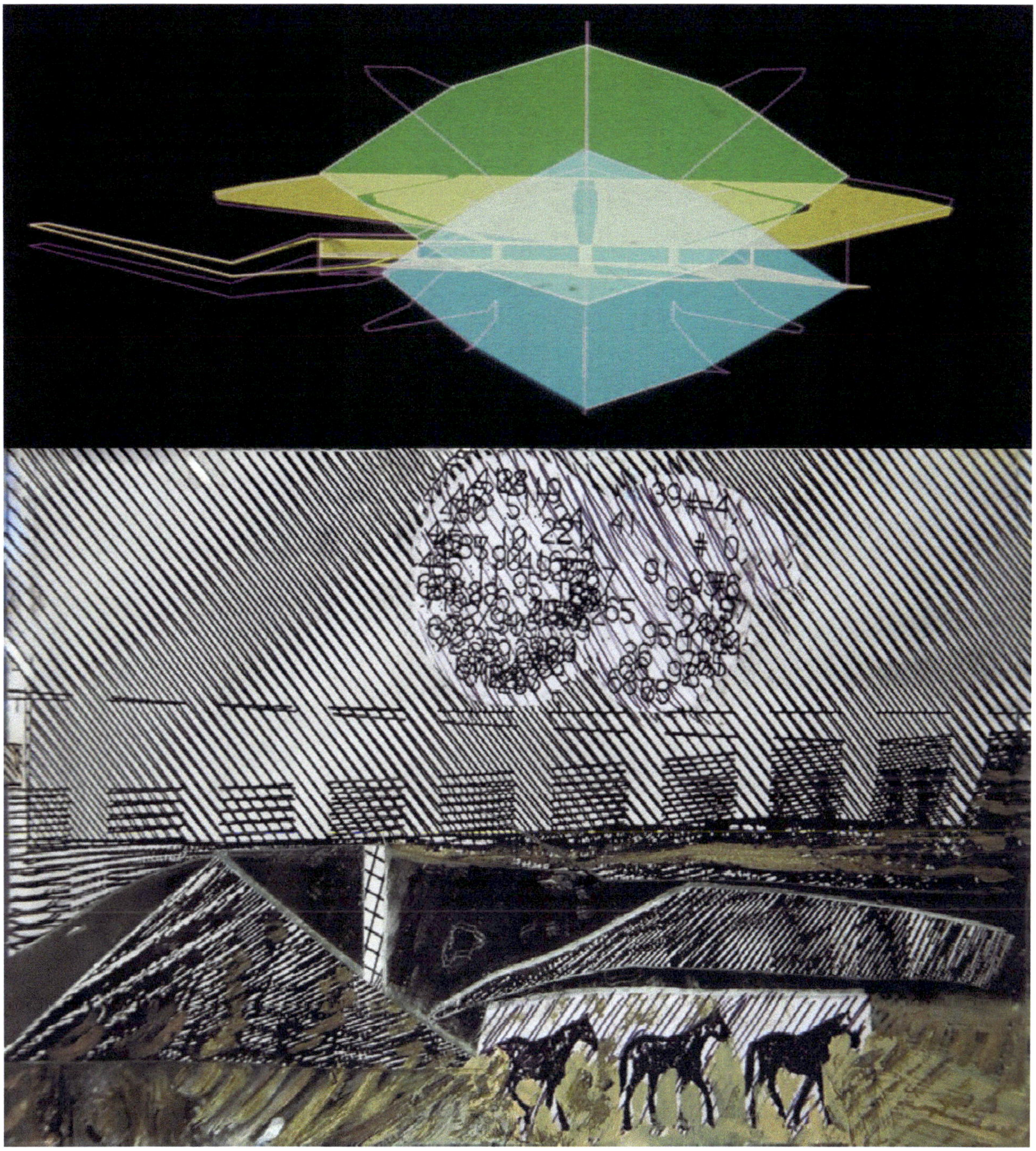

Multiple Exposure. © *2025 by Anna Ursyn*

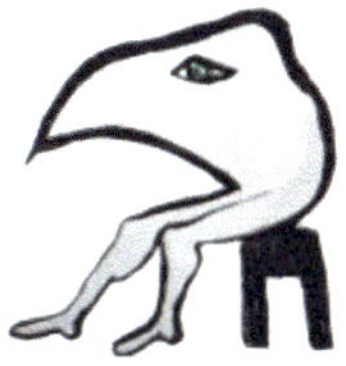

Pufeca: has to sit when he thinks.

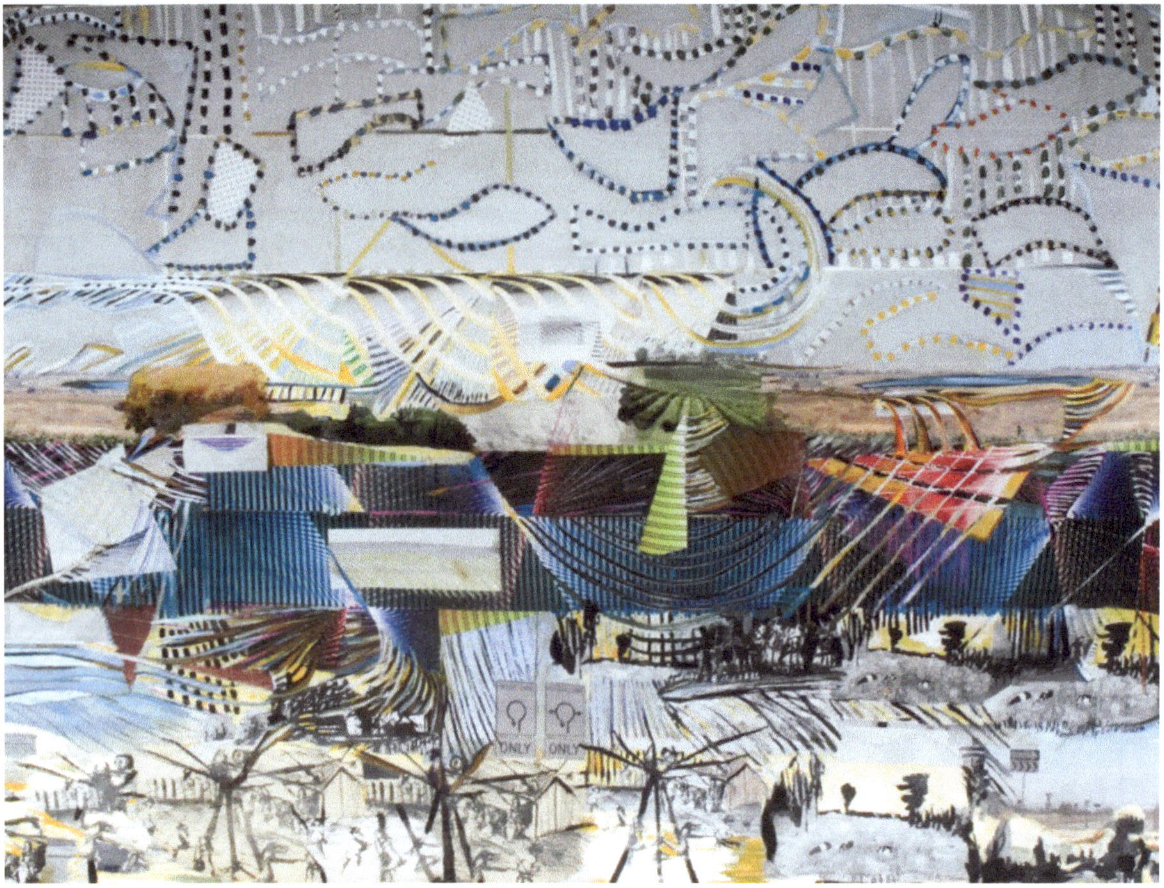

Rondo. © *2025 by Anna Ursyn*

Act VI – Bats
The Curtain goes up (or opens).

Teacher, "How about bats? Anyone?"
Student 6, "As a night type of a person, I can share how they gather in the fall to mate and share hibernation sites with the small bats. Here is how bats can swarm using the Python programming language:

```
import random

class Bat:
    def __init__(self, x, y):
        self.x = x
        self.y = y

    def move(self):
        self.x += random.uniform(-1, 1)
        self.y += random.uniform(-1, 1)

def simulate_swarm(num_bats, num_iterations):
    bats = []
    for _ in range(num_bats):
        x = random.uniform(-10, 10)
        y = random.uniform(-10, 10)
        bats.append(Bat(x, y))

    for _ in range(num_iterations):
```

```
        for bat in bats:
            bat.move()

    # Print the final positions of the bats
    for i, bat in enumerate(bats):
        print(f"Bat {i + 1}: ({bat.x:.2f}, {bat.y:.2f})")

# Example usage
num_bats = 10
num_iterations = 100
simulate_swarm(num_bats, num_iterations)
```

The dancers dance 'Bats' Dance' in related costumes suspended in the air.

Teacher, "Impressive. You defined a Bat class that represents an individual bat.
Each bat has an x and y coordinate and can move randomly within a certain range defined by random.uniform(-1, 1). The simulate swarm function creates a specified number of bats with random initial positions. It then iterates a specified number of times and moves each bat randomly. Finally, it prints the final positions of the bats."
Student 6, "One can adjust the num_bats and num_iterations variables to control the number of bats and the simulation duration. The code will output the final positions of the bats after the simulation is complete."
Student 5, "This code provides a basic simulation of bat movement and does not consider the complexities of bat behavior and swarming patterns observed in nature."

The Curtain goes down (or closes).
No Break

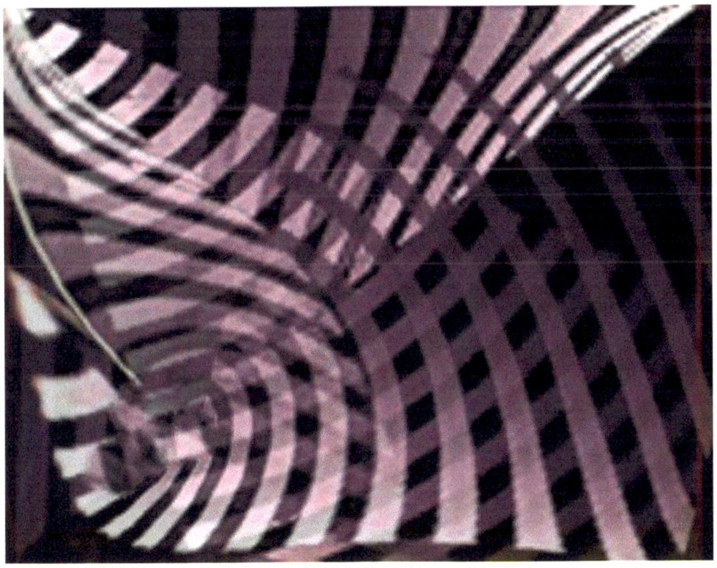

Nightlife. © *2025 by Anna Ursyn*

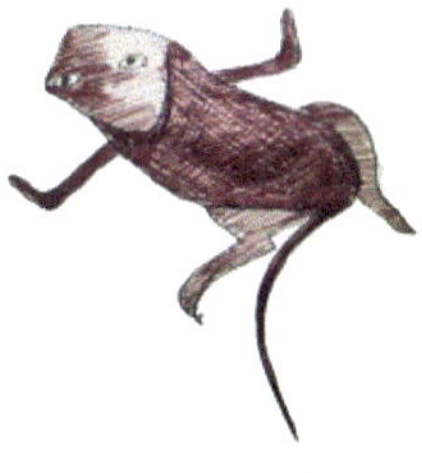

Pufat: always lands on his feet.

Pufat: always lands on its feet.

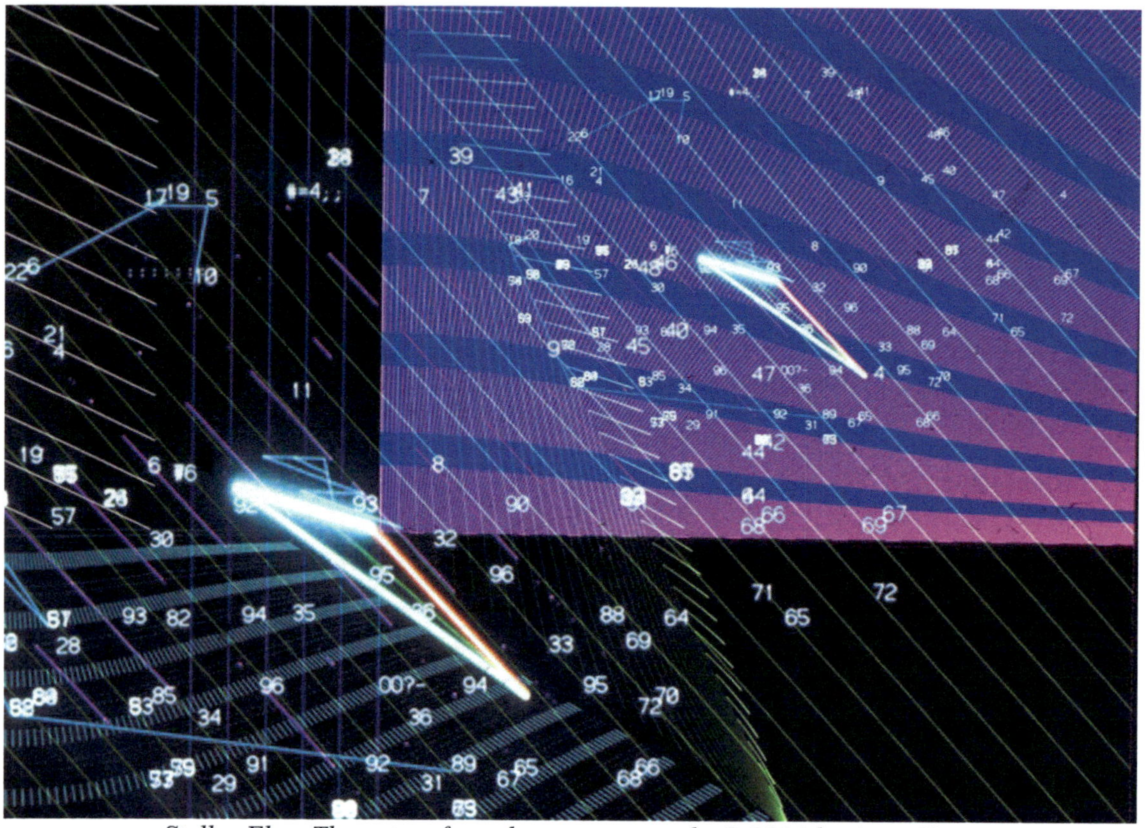

Stellar Flag. The output from the computer code. © 2025 by Anna Ursyn

Act VII – Tarantulas
The Curtain goes up (or opens).

Teacher, "And now, the Tarantula!"
Student 7: "Phenology is about nature's calendar, cyclic and seasonal phenomena, and it is my thing. Tarantulas shed their external skeleton (molting) several times a year. Males surge to pulsate, perform dance, and even create a beat. They may exhibit specific movements or behaviors during courtship rituals or defensive displays, but it's not a synchronized dance as seen in some other species. Here comes my code:

```
import time
import random

# Define the tarantula class
class Tarantula:
    def __init__(self, name):
        self.name = name

    def dance(self):
        print(f"{self.name} is performing a dance!")

    def create_beat(self):
        print(f"{self.name} is creating a beat!")
        for _ in range(4):
            time.sleep(0.5)
            beat = random.choice(['*', 'clap', 'stomp'])
            print(beat, end=' ')
        print()

# Create a swarm of tarantulas
```

```
swarm = []
swarm_size = 5
for i in range(swarm_size):
    tarantula = Tarantula(f"Tarantula{i+1}")
    swarm.append(tarantula)

# Each tarantula performs the dance and creates a beat
for tarantula in swarm:
    tarantula.dance()
    tarantula.create_beat()
    print()
```

The dancers dance a 'Tarantulas' Dance' in related costumes.

Teacher, "This code defines a Tarantula class with methods dance() and create_beat() to simulate the dance and beat creation. It then creates a swarm of tarantulas and iterates over each tarantula, making them perform the dance and create a beat. The beat is randomly chosen from a set of possible actions like 'clap,' or 'stomp.'"

Student 7, "Yes, but this code is purely fictional and does not represent the actual behavior of tarantulas. It's a creative representation for imagination and entertainment."

The Curtain goes down (or closes).
(No Break).

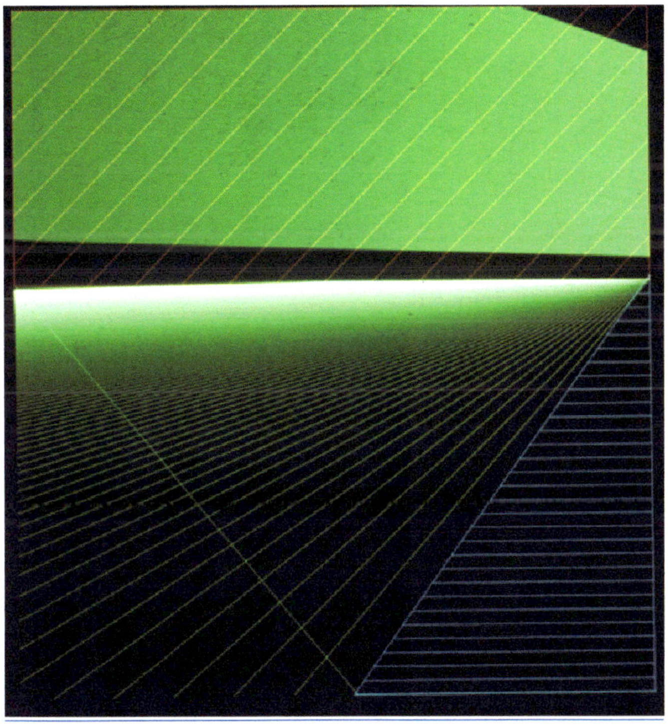

Divisions. Output from a computer code. © 2025 by Anna Ursyn

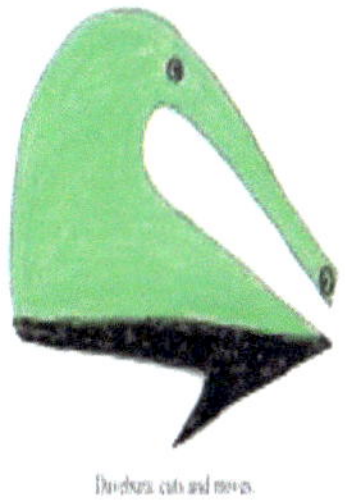

Davebura: cuts and moves.

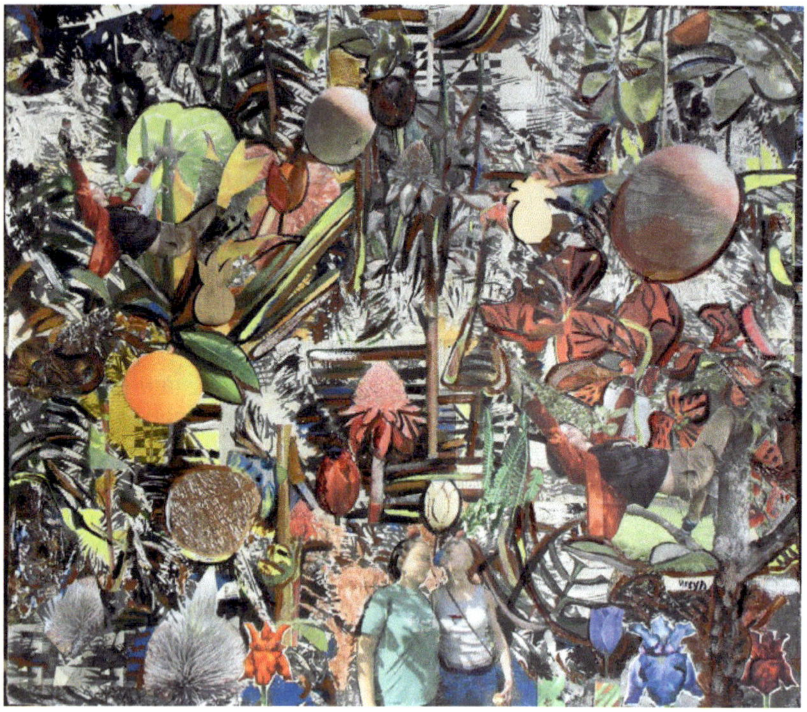

Immersion. © *2025 by Anna Ursyn*

Act VIII – Butterflies
The Curtain goes up (or opens).

Teacher, "Let's talk about butterflies."
Student 8, "That will be Monarch. They do the mud puddling as protection, for food or drinking, or taking minerals out of puddles to extract nutrients from damp soil or other moist surfaces.
Here's a code that simulates the puddling behavior of monarch butterflies:

```
import random

class MonarchButterfly:
   def __init__(self, name):
      self.name = name

   def puddle(self):
      print(f"{self.name} is puddling!")

      # Choose a random nutrient source
      nutrient_sources = ["mud puddle", "damp soil", "decaying fruit"]
      nutrient_source = random.choice(nutrient_sources)

      # Extract nutrients
      print(f"{self.name} is extracting nutrients from {nutrient_source}.")

# Create a group of monarch butterflies
group_size = 10
butterfly_group = [MonarchButterfly(f"Butterfly{i+1}") for i in range(group_size)]

# Each butterfly in the group puddles
for butterfly in butterfly_group:
   butterfly.puddle()
   print()
```

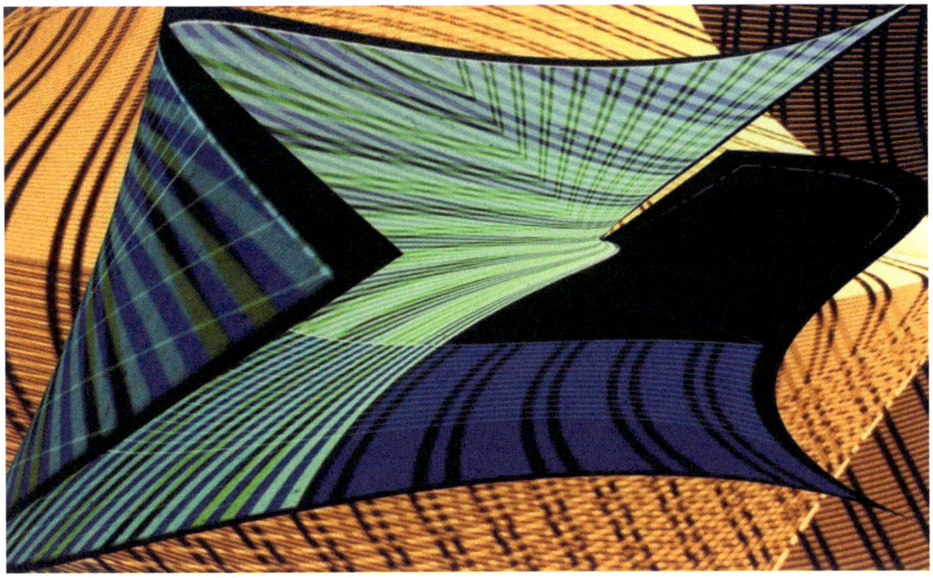

The Flight. The output from computer codes. © *2025 by Anna Ursyn*

```
The dancers dance a 'Butterflies' Dance' in related costumes suspended above
the flowers.
```

Teacher, "In this code, we define a MonarchButterfly class with a puddle() method. The puddle() method selects a random nutrient source from a list and simulates the butterfly extracting nutrients from that source."
Student 8, "It's a simplified representation for demonstration."
Student 10, "And Morpho butterfly has iridescence sparkle and blue color visible from hundreds of meters due to periodic photonic nanostructure in scales on wings that responds to specific wavelengths of light without any dye involved."

The Curtain goes down (or closes).
(No Break).

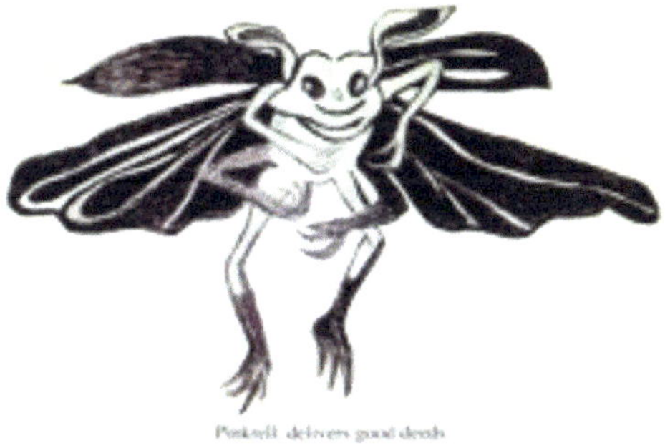

Pinkrell: delivers good deeds only.

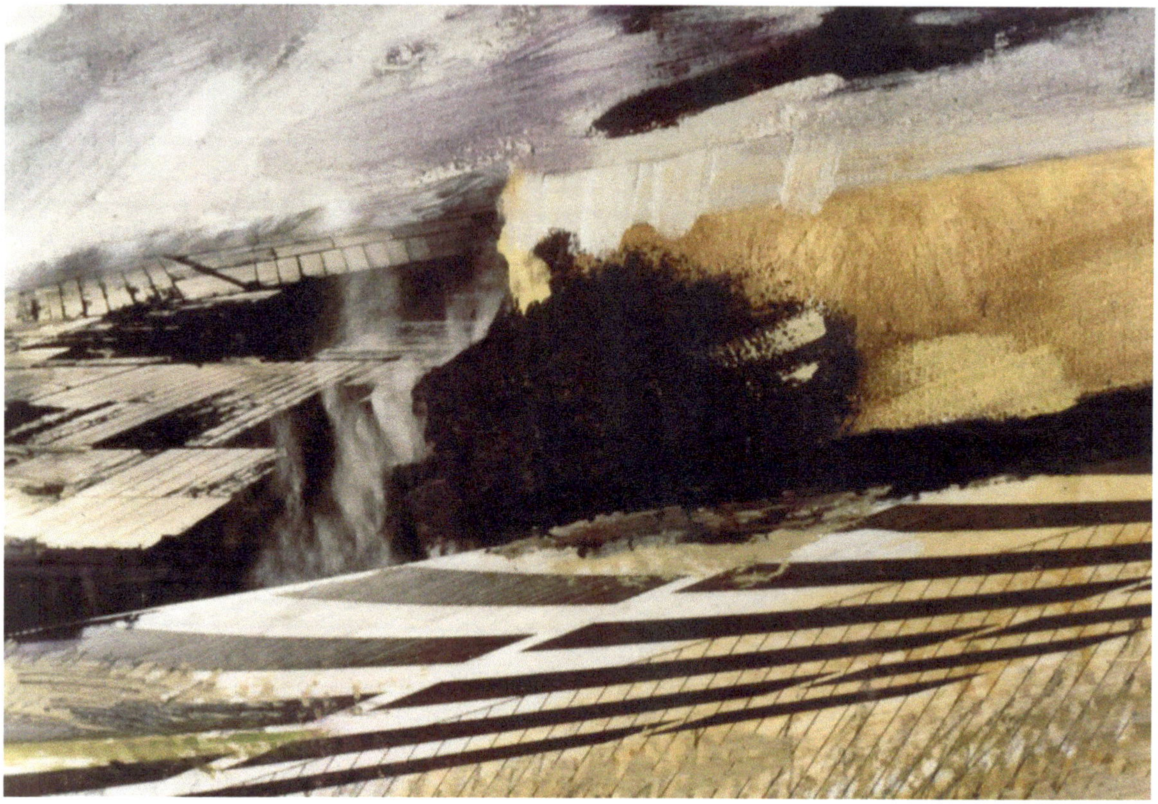

Goldview. © *2025 by Anna Ursyn*

Act IX - Flamingos
The Curtain goes up (or opens).

Teacher, "Anyone would like to write a code for flamingos?"
Student 9: "I want to do it! They compete to see whose neck is the longest! I can show how they are flocking using the principles of a popular algorithm called the "Boids" algorithm. This algorithm models birds' movement and flocking behavior, including factors like cohesion, separation, and alignment.

```
import pygame
import random
from pygame.math import Vector2

# Initialize pygame
pygame.init()

# Set up the simulation window
width, height = 800, 600
window = pygame.display.set_mode((width, height))
pygame.display.set_caption("Flamingo Flocking Simulation")

# Set up colors
WHITE = (255, 255, 255)
PINK = (255, 105, 180)

# Set up flamingo parameters
num_flamingos = 50
flamingo_radius = 6
flamingo_speed = 2
flamingo_neighbors = 10
cohesion_factor = 0.01
```

```
separation_factor = 0.05
alignment_factor = 0.01

# Create the flamingo class
class Flamingo:
    def __init__(self, position, velocity):
        self.position = Vector2(position)
        self.velocity = Vector2(velocity)

    def update(self, flock):
        self.position += self.velocity

        # Apply the three Boid rules
        cohesion_vector = self.cohesion(flock)
        separation_vector = self.separation(flock)
        alignment_vector = self.alignment(flock)

        self.velocity += cohesion_vector * cohesion_factor
        self.velocity += separation_vector * separation_factor
        self.velocity += alignment_vector * alignment_factor

        self.limit_velocity(flamingo_speed)

    def limit_velocity(self, max_speed):
        if self.velocity.length() > max_speed:
            self.velocity.scale_to_length(max_speed)

    def cohesion(self, flock):
        average_position = Vector2(0, 0)
        count = 0

        for flamingo in flock:
            if flamingo != self and self.position.distance_to(flamingo.position) < flamingo_neighbors:
                average_position += flamingo.position
                count += 1

        if count > 0:
            average_position /= count
            cohesion_vector = (average_position - self.position).normalize()
            return cohesion_vector
        else:
            return Vector2(0, 0)

    def separation(self, flock):
        separation_vector = Vector2(0, 0)

        for flamingo in flock:
            if flamingo != self and self.position.distance_to(flamingo.position) < flamingo_radius:
                difference = self.position - flamingo.position
                difference /= flamingo.position.distance_squared_to(self.position)
                separation_vector += difference

        return separation_vector.normalize()

    def alignment(self, flock):
        average_velocity = Vector2(0, 0)
        count = 0

        for flamingo in flock:
            if flamingo != self and self.position.distance_to(flamingo.position) < flamingo_neighbors:
                average_velocity += flamingo.velocity
                count += 1

        if count > 0:
            average_velocity /= count
            return average_velocity.normalize()
        else:
            return Vector2(0, 0)
    def draw(self):
        pygame.draw.circle(window, PINK, (int(self.position.x), int(self.position.y)), flamingo_radius)
```

```
# Create the flock of flamingos
flock = []
for _ in range(num_flamingos):
    position = (random.randint(0, width), random.randint(0, height))
    velocity = (random.uniform(-1, 1), random.uniform(-1, 1))
```

The dancers dance a 'Flamingos' Dance in related costumes, stepping in a bluish crepe paper representing water.

The Curtain goes down (or closes).
(No Break)

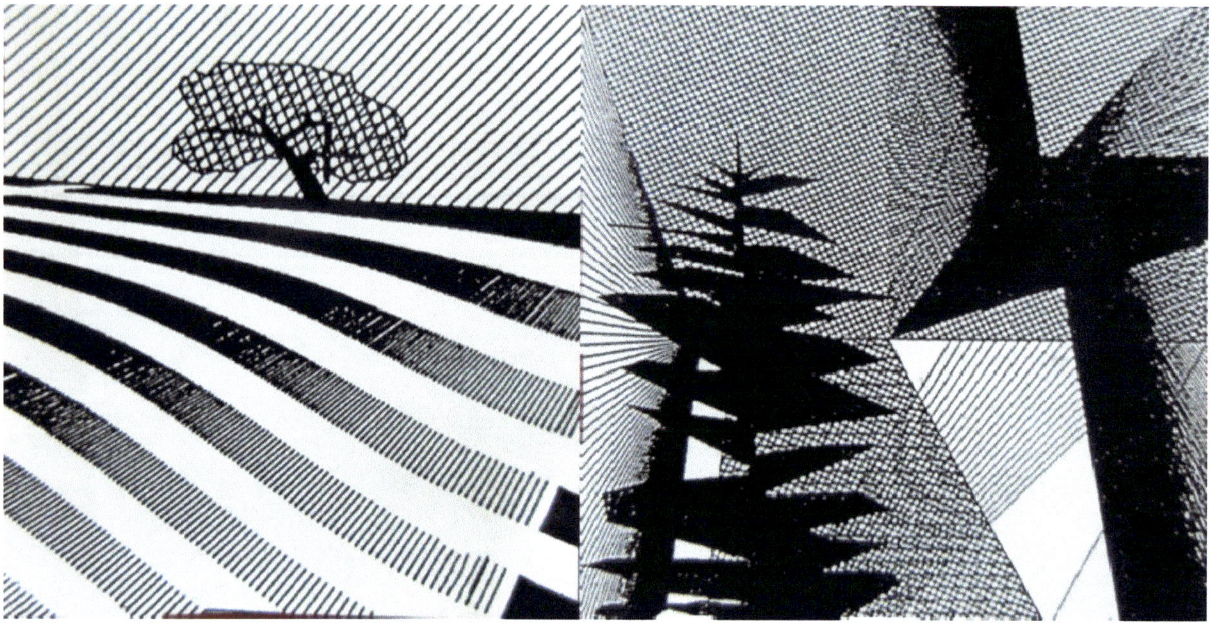

Two Types of Trees (deciduous and coniferous). Outputs from the codes. © 2025 by Anna Ursyn

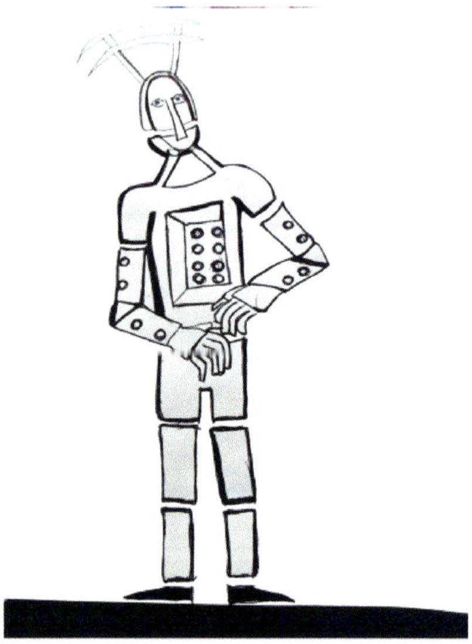

Fukan: controls thoughts by reciting them in a spiral.

Fukan: shares his spiral poems.

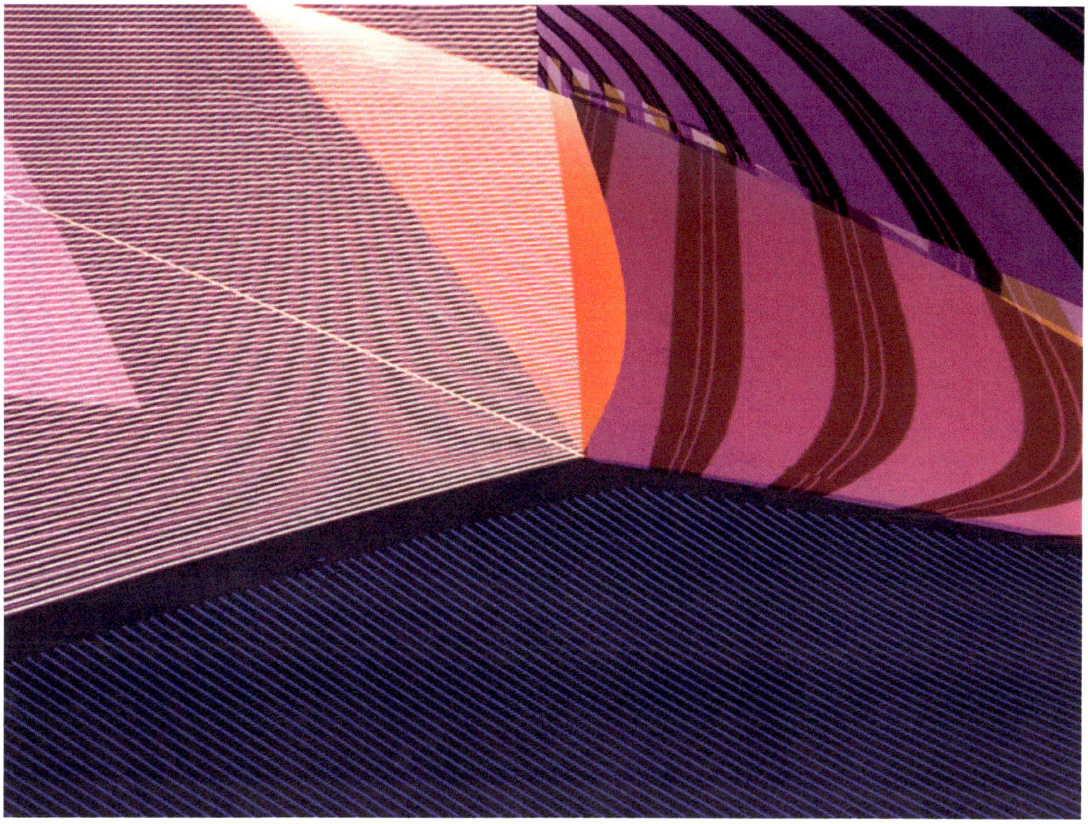

The Flow. The output from the computer code. © 2025 by Anna Ursyn

Act X – Crabs
The Curtain goes up (or opens).

Teacher, "Perfect. There are many more swarming species, but we are running out of time, so one more: crabs."
Student 10, " That will be me. I like crabs. Not just as a source of nutrients. Simulating the swarming behavior of crabs can be done using simple rules that govern their movement, such as attraction, alignment, and avoidance. Here's an example code that demonstrates the swarming behavior of crabs:

```
import pygame
import random
from pygame.math import Vector2

# Initialize pygame
pygame.init()

# Set up the simulation window
width, height = 800, 600
window = pygame.display.set_mode((width, height))
pygame.display.set_caption("Crab Swarming Simulation")

# Set up colors
WHITE = (255, 255, 255)
ORANGE = (255, 165, 0)

# Set up crab parameters
num_crabs = 50
crab_radius = 8
crab_speed = 2
neighbor_radius = 50
alignment_factor = 0.1
```

```
attraction_factor = 0.01
avoidance_factor = 0.05

# Create the crab class
class Crab:
  def __init__(self, position, velocity):
    self.position = Vector2(position)
    self.velocity = Vector2(velocity)

  def update(self, swarm):
    self.position += self.velocity

    # Apply the three rules: alignment, attraction, and avoidance
    alignment_vector = self.alignment(swarm)
    attraction_vector = self.attraction(swarm)
    avoidance_vector = self.avoidance(swarm)

    self.velocity += alignment_vector * alignment_factor
    self.velocity += attraction_vector * attraction_factor
    self.velocity += avoidance_vector * avoidance_factor

    self.limit_velocity(crab_speed)

  def limit_velocity(self, max_speed):
    if self.velocity.length() > max_speed:
      self.velocity.scale_to_length(max_speed)

  def alignment(self, swarm):
    average_velocity = Vector2(0, 0)
    count = 0

    for crab in swarm:
      if crab != self and self.position.distance_to(crab.position) < neighbor_radius:
        average_velocity += crab.velocity
        count += 1

    if count > 0:
      average_velocity /= count
      return average_velocity.normalize()
    else:
      return Vector2(0, 0)

  def attraction(self, swarm):
    center_of_mass = Vector2(0, 0)
    count = 0

    for crab in swarm:
      if crab != self and self.position.distance_to(crab.position) < neighbor_radius:
        center_of_mass += crab.position
        count += 1

    if count > 0:
      center_of_mass /= count
      attraction_vector = (center_of_mass - self.position).normalize()
      return attraction_vector
    else:
      return Vector2(0, 0)

  def avoidance(self, swarm):
    avoidance_vector = Vector2(0, 0)

    for crab in swarm:
      if crab != self and self.position.distance_to(crab.position) < crab_radius * 2:
        difference = self.position - crab.position
        difference /= crab.position.distance_squared_to(self.position)
        avoidance_vector += difference

    return avoidance_vector.normalize()

  def draw(self):
```

```
        pygame.draw.circle(window, ORANGE, (int(self.position.x), int(self.position.y)), crab_radius)

# Create the swarm of crabs
swarm = []
for _ in range(num_crabs):
    position = (random.randint(0, width), random.randint(0, height))
    velocity = (random.uniform(-1, 1), random.uniform(-1, 1))
    crab = Crab(position, velocity)
    swarm.append(crab)

# Main simulation loop
running = True
clock = pygame.time.Clock()
while running:
    for event in pygame.event.get():
        if event.type ==
```

`The dancers dance a 'Crabs-Dance' in related costumes.`

Student 2, "We borrow words from nature; we use the word "drone," a male bee, to denote a multipurpose flying object, and a "mouse" as a device to move the cursor with."
Student 3, "We were supposed to study coding, and it looks like a biology class."
Teacher, this is swarm computing. Biology is Nature, and Nature is Computing."

The End.
The curtain goes down (or closes).

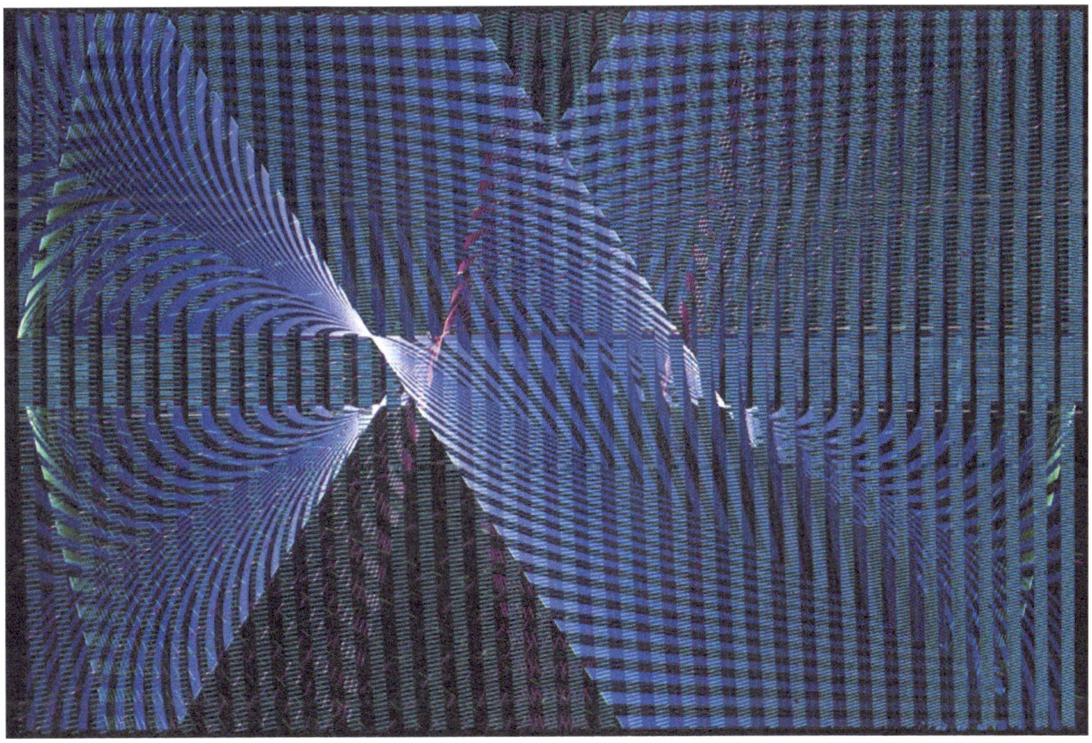

The Moving Waters. The output after the computer code. © 2025 by Anna Ursyn

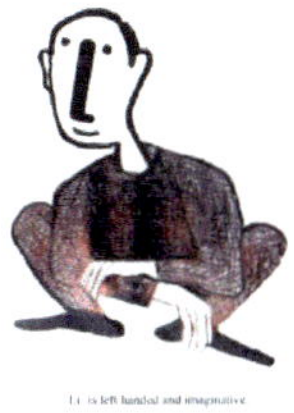

Li is left-handed and imaginative.

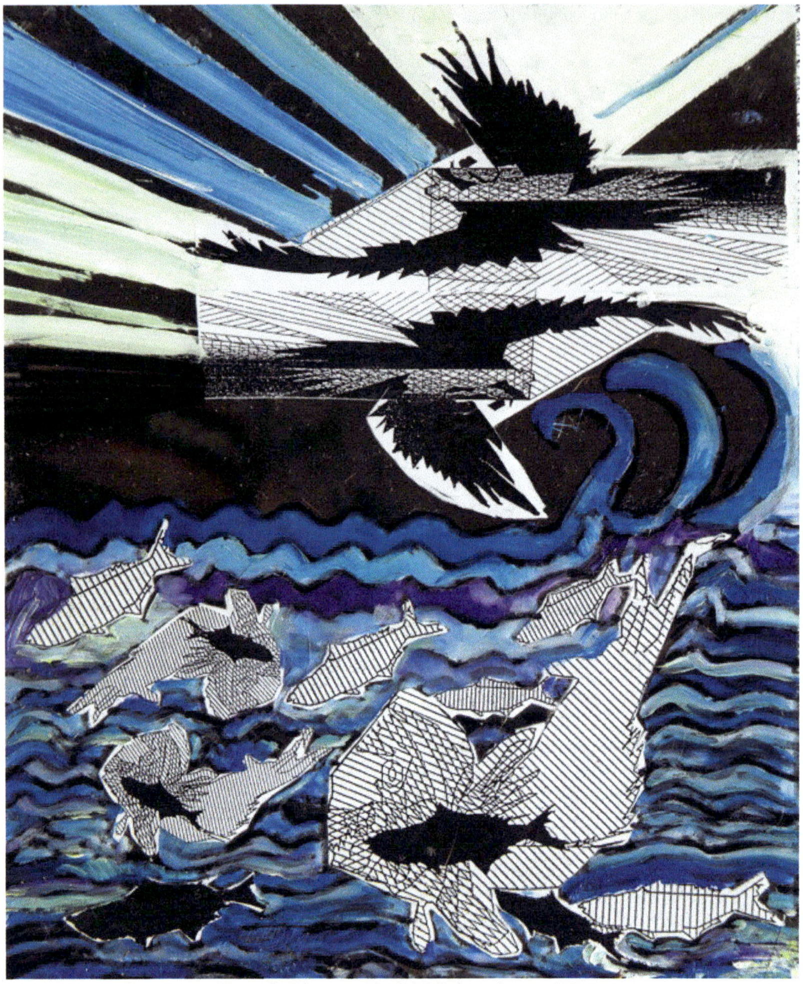

Oceanic Food Chain. © 2025 by Anna Ursyn

Act XI - Walruses
The curtain goes up (or opens)

Teacher, "Very well. Everyone! Now, the walruses."
Student 11, "Walruses it is. It is always too warm for me."

```
import random

class Walrus:
  def __init__(self, name, position):
    self.name = name
    self.position = position

   def move(self, new_position):
     self.position = new_position
    print(f"{self.name} moves to position {self.position}")

# Function to simulate walruses swarming
def swarm_walruses(walruses, target_position):
  for walrus in walruses:
    x_offset = random.randint(-3, 3) # Random offset for x-coordinate
    y_offset = random.randint(-3, 3) # Random offset for y-coordinate
    new_position = (target_position[0] + x_offset, target_position[1] + y_offset)
    walrus.move(new_position)
# Creating walrus instances
```

```
walrus1 = Walrus("Walrus 1", (0, 0))
walrus2 = Walrus("Walrus 2", (0, 0))
walrus3 = Walrus("Walrus 3", (0, 0))

# Initial positions of walruses
print("Initial positions:")
print(f"{walrus1.name}: {walrus1.position}")
print(f"{walrus2.name}: {walrus2.position}")
print(f"{walrus3.name}:  {walrus3.position}")

# Simulating swarming
print("\nWalruses swarming...")
swarm_target = (10, 10)  # Target position for swarming
swarm_walruses([walrus1, walrus2, walrus3], swarm_target)

# Final positions after swarming
print("\nFinal positions after swarming:")
print(f"{walrus1.name}: {walrus1.position}")
print(f"{walrus2.name}: {walrus2.position}")
print(f"{walrus3.name}:  {walrus3.position}")
```

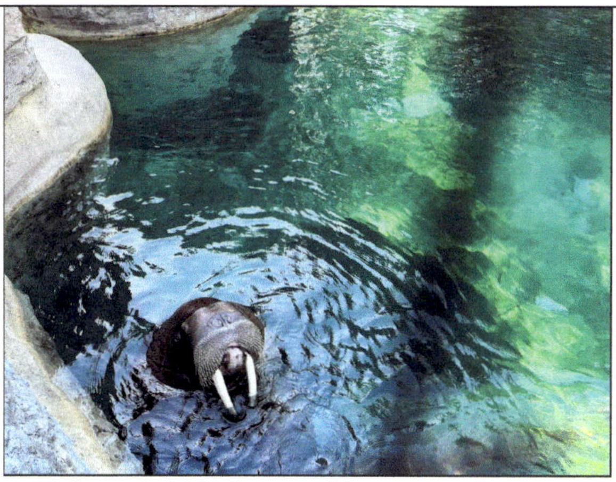

A Walrus. © 2025 by Matylda Czarnecka. (Used with permission).

Teacher, "Great job again! In your code, the Walrus class represents individual walruses, each with a name and a position. The swarm_walruses() function simulates how they swarm. Three walruses are created and initially positioned at (0, 0). They then swarm towards a target position (10, 10), with each walrus moving randomly around the target. The initial and final positions of the walruses are printed to observe the swarming behavior."

The End
The curtain goes down (or closes.)

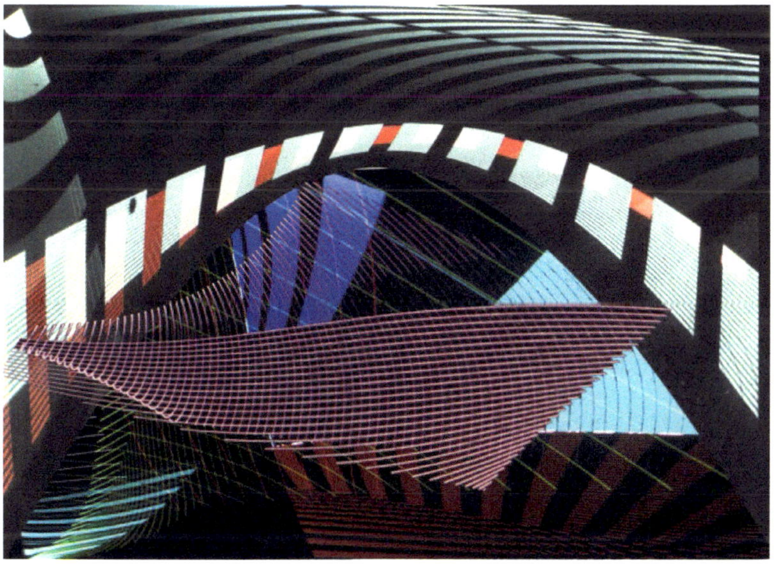

A Swarming Colony. The output from the computer code. © 2025 by Anna Ursyn

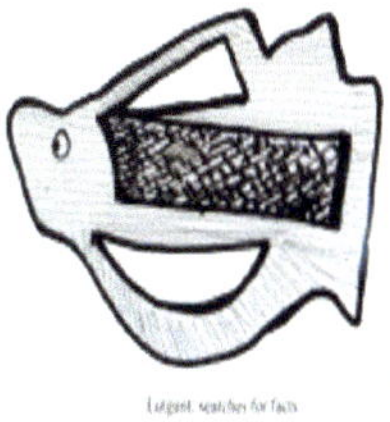

Lutgant: searches for facts.

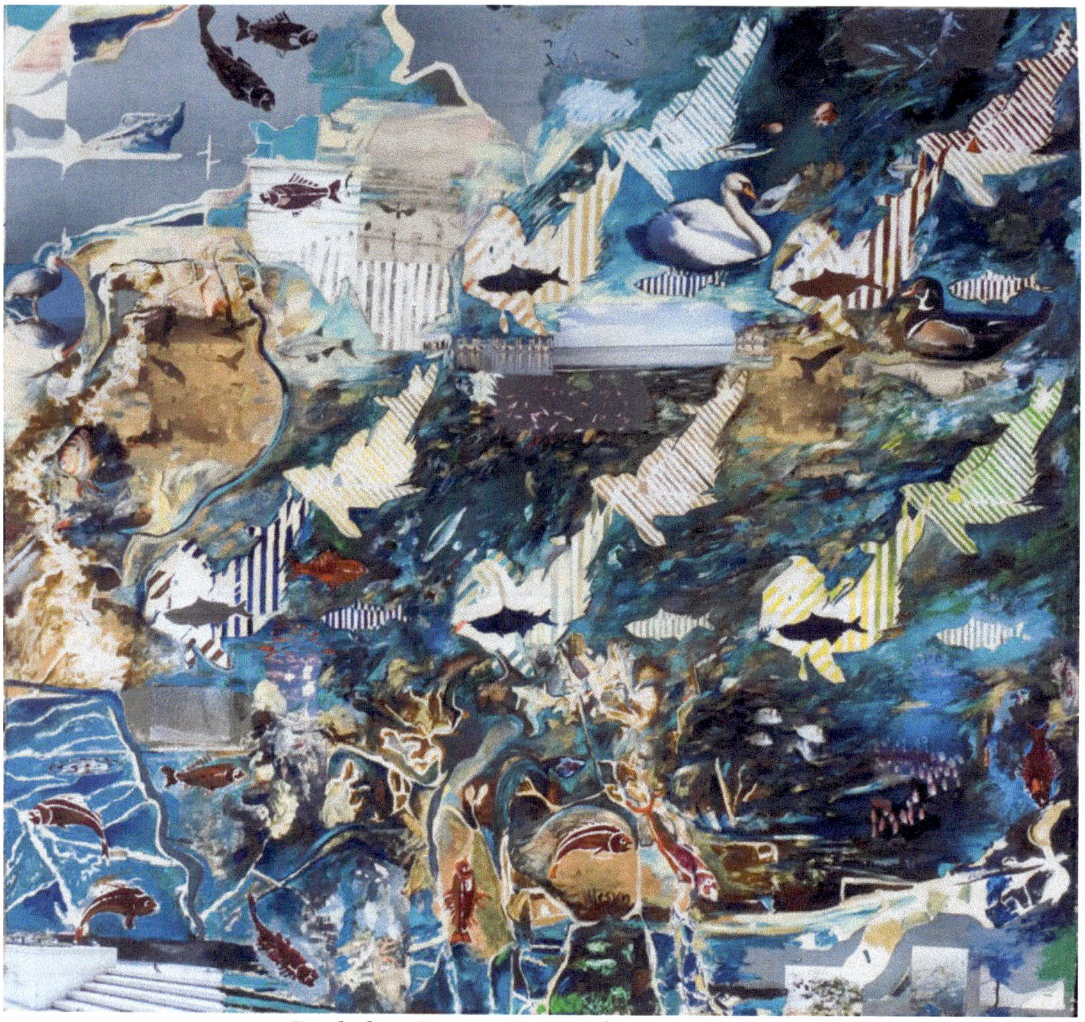

Symbols in Nature. © *2025 by Anna Ursyn*

Act XII - Seahorses
The curtain goes up (or opens).

Teacher, "Now, to dare you: a seahorse!"
Student 12, "Sure, but this might not fit; they do not swarm. I'll take a challenge. Besides, as the last person to present, I have no choice. This Python code illustrates the seahorses as solitary creatures."

```
class Seahorse:
    def __init__(self, name):
        self.name = name
        self.position = (0, 0)

    def move(self, x, y):
        self.position = (self.position[0] + x, self.position[1] + y)
        print(f"{self.name} swims to position {self.position}")

# Creating seahorse instances
seahorse1 = Seahorse("Seahorse 1")
seahorse2 = Seahorse("Seahorse 2")

# Moving seahorses individually
seahorse1.move(1, 1)
seahorse2.move(-1, -1)
```

```
# Attempting to swarm
print("Attempting to swarm...")
for i in range(3):
    seahorse1.move(1, 1)
    seahorse2.move(1, 1)
```

Teacher: "Yes! This code defines a Seahorse class with a method move() to show seahorses' movements. In the example, two seahorses move individually. Then, an attempt to make them swarm is simulated, but they still move individually, indicating that they do not swarm because they are known as loners."
Student 9, "Since we are talking about the loaners, I have a code to share about the tardigrades, also known as "water bears" or "moss piglets." Measuring just under 1.5 millimeters in length, Tardigrades are microscopic animals known for their resilience and ability to survive extreme conditions, from high pressure and radiation to the vacuum of space. They are found in various environments, including freshwater, marine, and terrestrial habitats. They do not exhibit swarming behavior as primarily solitary organisms that move slowly, typically by crawling and feeding on microscopic plants, algae, and small invertebrates. They do not form social colonies or display coordinated group actions like swarming in moist environments where they can find food and shelter. While tardigrades may sometimes be found in groups in favorable habitats, they do not swarm in the sense of coordinated mass movement or aggregation that is characteristic of other organisms."
The Teacher, "Please register for my *Solitary Intelligence* classes BIOCS 676 (mammals), BIOCS 677 (birds), and BIOCS 678 (insects)."

The End
The curtain goes down (or closes).

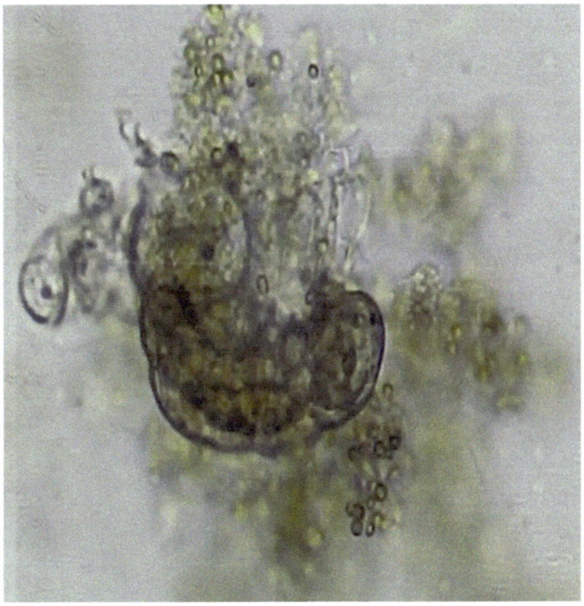
.
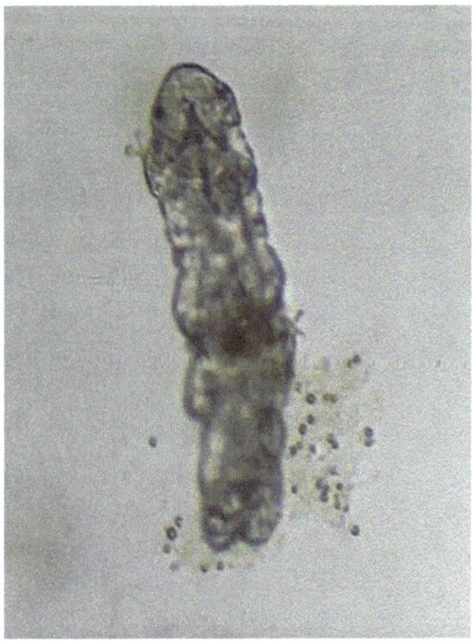
Tardigrade

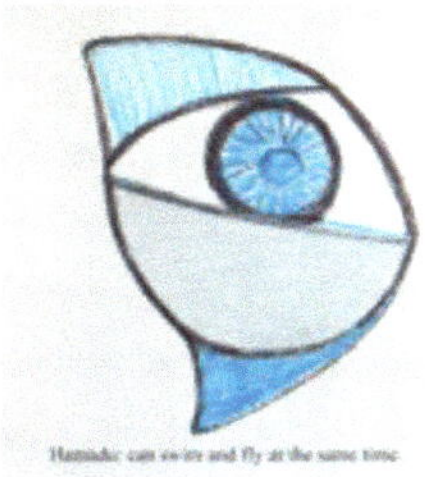
Hamadu: can swim and fly at the same time.
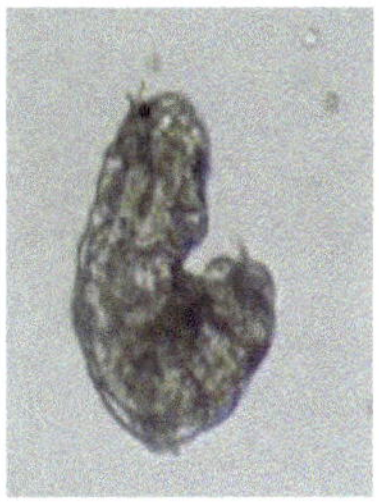

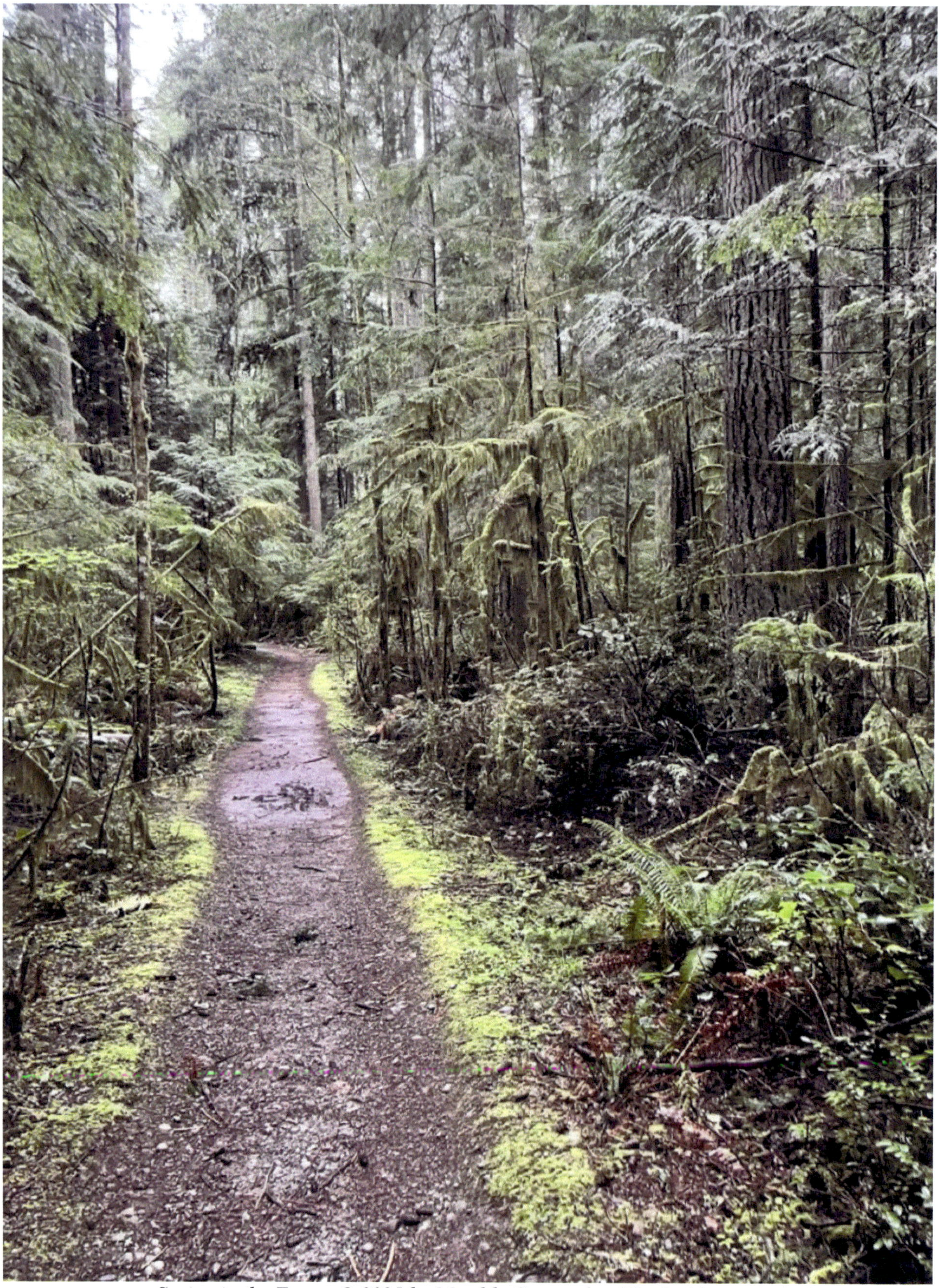

Spring in the Forest. © *2025 by Matylda Czarnecka. (Used with permission).*

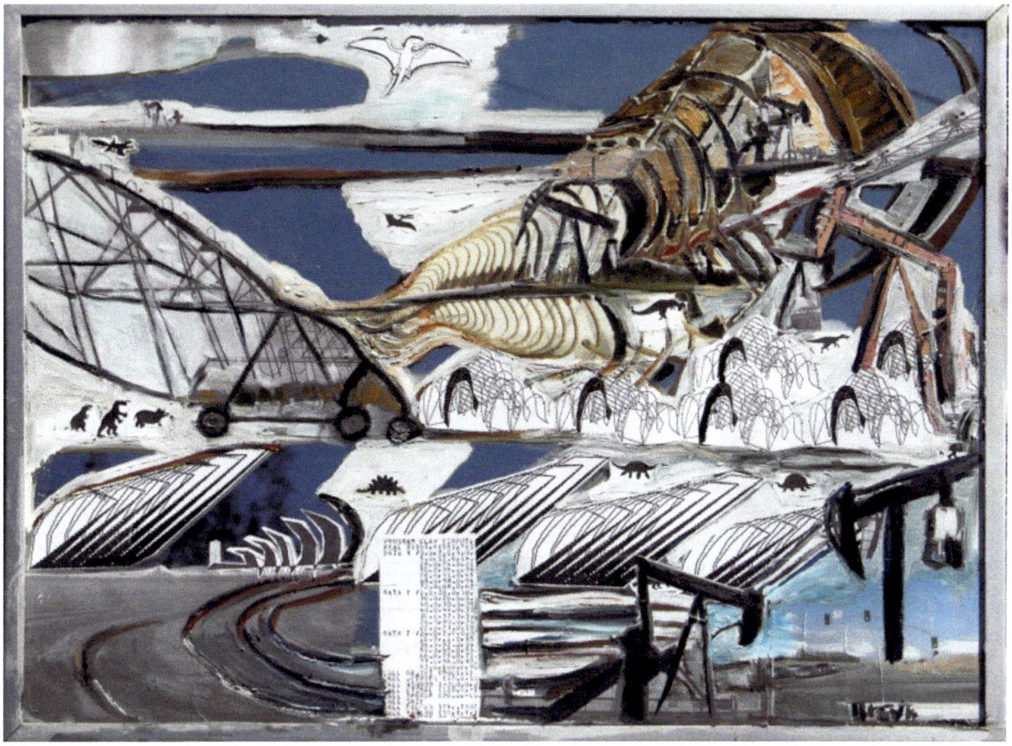

Giants. © 2025 by Anna Ursyn

CHAPTER 12
CARBON CODE

NINE TRAPPED IN AN ELEVATOR

INTRODUCTION

Carbon is essential in our life. It is an interesting element; it has allotropes. Carbon forms have different shapes and various stories behind them. An unexpected event can be turned into an exciting interaction.

SYNOPSIS

Eight people are trapped in an elevator with one dog. Each of them displays different emotions and attitudes toward this unexpected event. The playful one starts a game by asking everyone to name their favorite allotrope of Carbon. Each person pulls out their watch to project a code they wrote for their favorite model, while the dog comments on the codes and takes all the credit.

SUMMARY

This work is more graphical. Also, geometrical. The characters stylized after the design of each of the allotropes will share their codes in an enclosed space. While all the people and the dog are crowded in a comparatively small transportation device, suggested by a few lines designed with metal tubes or laser lines, the rest of the stage offers visual entertainment for the audience disclosing the logic and beauty behind the allotropes.

CAST OF CHARACTERS

Person 1 - Diamond
Person 2 - Graphite
Person 3 - Lonsdaelite
Person 4 - Buckminsterfullerene
Person 5 - C540, Fullerite, just call me C540
Person 6 - C70 Fullerene
Person 7 - Amorphous Carbon
Person 8 - Nanotube
Person 9 - The Rescuer
The dog - Carbon

STAGE DIRECTIONS

Eight giant cardboard boxes are set together to represent an elevator. Neon-like signage appears on the sides of the panels. The elevator can also be marked by metal frames or laser lights with a display. Every time a person projects a code on the side of the elevator, the giant screen behind them shows a photograph of the side of an elevator with a projection from each watch.

Act I
The curtain goes up (or opens).

Person 1, "Going up?"
Person 2, "Yup"
Person 3, "Oh, no, we are going down! I'm in a hurry!"
Person 1, "Stopped"
Person 3, "Locked"
Person 2, "Free time!"
Person 6, "Still"
Person 8, "Sad"
Person 4, "Good"
Person 5, "Not bad."
Person 7, "Scarry and boring!"
Person 2, "We are trapped, so let's play a game. Watches up, please!"
Altogether, "Watches are up!"
Person 2, "Everybody, but not at once, what's your favorite Allotrope of Carbon?"
Person 1," What?"
Person 4, "Mine is Fullerene because I admire Buckminster Fuller's work and his geography. There is so much behind it all."

`Person 4 displays the content of their watch on the side of the elevator for everyone to see.`

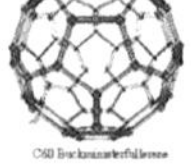

The dog, "Projecting a fullerene allotrope means visualizing a 3D structure. It can be done with a molecular visualization software package, such as PyMOL or VMD."
Person 4, "For my code I need PyMOL:

```
import pymol
```

The dog, "# Initialize PyMOL"

```
pymol.finish_launching()
```
The dog, “# Load fullerene structure”
```
pymol.cmd.load('fullerene.pdb').”
```
The dog, “# Set display options.”
```
pymol.cmd.show('spheres')
pymol.cmd.color('carbon')
pymol.cmd.set('sphere_scale', 0.5)
```
The dog, “# Save image.”
```
pymol.cmd.png('fullerene.png', 600, 600, dpi=300)
```
The dog, “# Quit PyMOL”
```
pymol.cmd.quit()
```
Person 4, “PyMOL was used to import and initialize the fullerene structure from 'fullerene.pdb'. The atoms were displayed as spheres and colored by carbon elements, with sphere size adjustment. The image was saved as 'fullerene.png,' and then PyMOL was quit. PyMOL must already be installed on the computer to run this code.”

Person 1, “Oh, that sure is beautiful.”

The dog, “Thank you.”

Person 2 continues, “I love pencils, so for me, Graphite it is, so here is a model of a graphite allotrope using Python programming language and visualization libraries such as Matplotlib and NumPy.

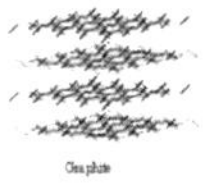

```
import matplotlib.pyplot as plt
import numpy as np”
```
The dog, “# Define the unit cell vectors of the graphite lattice.”
```
a = 2.46 # in angstroms
c = 6.70 # in angstroms
v1 = np.array([a, 0, 0])
v2 = np.array([-a/2, np.sqrt(3)*a/2, 0])
v3 = np.array([0, 0, c])
```
The dog, “# Now, create a 3D lattice of graphite.”
```
N = 10 # number of unit cells
R = []
for i in range(N):
   for j in range(N):
      for k in range(N):
         R.append(i*v1 + j*v2 + k*v3)
R = np.array(R)”
```
The dog, “# Plot the graphite lattice using Matplotlib.”
```
fig = plt.figure()
ax = fig.add_subplot(111, projection='3d')
ax.scatter(R[:,0], R[:,1], R[:,2], c='black', marker='o', s=10)
ax.set_xlabel('x')
ax.set_ylabel('y')
ax.set_zlabel('z')
plt.show()
```
The dog, “This code defines the unit cell vectors of the graphite lattice and plots the graphite lattice using Matplotlib in 3D space. It may not accurately represent the graphite allotrope.”

Person 1, ”Beautiful!”

The dog, “Thank you!”

Person 2, “We neatly pack graphite in wood, call them pencils, and they cannot be replaced with digital media, as for me, of course.”

Person 1, “After seeing your coded drawing, I wonder how it would feel to use a regular pencil.”

Person 3 asks, “Why not with a tablet?”

Person 4, “There are advantages and disadvantages of using both in the case of digital drawing. We can use undo and redo options. Your canvas is infinite. You have layers at your disposal and many tools. You can share your work or collaborate online with others. Everything is so flexible.”

Person 2, “But you do not feel it. A pencil gives you feedback. One has to learn a lot and keep practicing.

Drawing with a pencil is easy to use, and you feel what you draw. They are inexpensive, small, and light but also quite versatile. I like smudging my fingers."
The dog, "I like chewing on them till I reach the graphite part."
Person 3," But it is harder to erase; your drawing space is set in stone, and you do not have that many tools to choose from. You have some numbers giving you various shades of gray, resulting in the hardness or softness of a line and how it smudges. Besides, how would you share a piece of tangible paper? In the digital world, you post it for everyone to see and comment on."
Person 5 asks, "We call it digital when all 3D models are analog."
Person 1, "For me, a Diamond. Diamonds are forever."
The dog, "Communicating through the slogan*s?"*

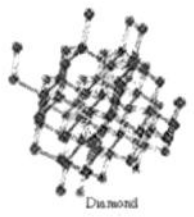

Diamond

```
Person 1 points a watch on the side of the elevator to project the code.
```

The dog, "To create a model of a diamond using Python, one can use the turtle module."
Person 1, "Here's my code that draws a diamond shape:"

```
import turtle
```

The dog, "# create turtle object."

```
t = turtle.Turtle()
```

The dog, " # move the pen to the starting position."

```
t.penup()
t.goto(-100, 0)
t.pendown()
```

The dog, " # draw the diamond."

```
for i in range(4):
  t.forward(100)
  t.right(45)
```

The dog "# hide the turtle when done."

```
t.hideturtle()
# keep the window open until closed manually
turtle.done()."
```

Person 1, "As you may see, this code creates a turtle object, sets the starting position, and then uses a *for loop* to draw each side of the diamond. Finally, it hides the turtle and keeps the window open until it is closed manually. You can modify the diamond's size and position by changing the values passed to the goto() and forward() methods."
Person 6, "Astonishing!"
The dog, "Thank you! Thank you!"
Person 5, "Or we can develop a Python code to create a 3D model of a diamond allotrope using the Matplotlib library."
The dog, "You can start by installing the required libraries using pip command in the command prompt or terminal."

```
pip install matplotlib"
```

Person 5, "My code is also created to output a diamond allotrope:

```
import numpy as np
import matplotlib.pyplot as plt
from mpl_toolkits.mplot3d import Axes3D"
```

The dog, "# Define the diamond lattice vectors."

```
a1 = np.array([1, 0, 0])
a2 = np.array([0, 1, 0])
a3 = np.array([0, 0, 1])
```

The dog, "# Define the coordinates of the basis atoms."

```
basis = np.array([[0, 0, 0], [0.5, 0.5, 0], [0.5, 0, 0.5], [0, 0.5, 0.5]])
```

The dog, "# Create a 3D plot."

```
fig = plt.figure()
ax = fig.add_subplot(111, projection='3d')
```

The dog, " # Plot the basis atoms."

```
for b in basis:
  for i in range(-1, 2):
    for j in range(-1, 2):
      for k in range(-1, 2):
        offset = i*a1 + j*a2 + k*a3
        ax.scatter(b[0]+offset[0], b[1]+offset[1], b[2]+offset[2], color='red')
```

The dog, "# Set the plot limits."

```
ax.set_xlim3d(-1, 2)
ax.set_ylim3d(-1, 2)
ax.set_zlim3d(-1, 2)
```

The dog, "# Add labels to the axes."

```
ax.set_xlabel('X')
ax.set_ylabel('Y')
ax.set_zlabel('Z')
```

The dog, " # Show the plot."

```
plt.show()
```

Person 1,"Excellent work!"

The dog, "Merçi!"

Person 5, "This code created a 3D plot using the Matplotlib library. The diamond lattice vectors were defined, and the coordinates of the basis atoms were specified. Then, the code plotted the basis atoms, using the lattice vectors to create a repeating structure. Finally, the plot limit and axis labels were set, and the plot was displayed."

Person 3, "That is a real beauty, but for me, it's a Lonsdaelite, just for its hexagonal lattice, and it's a cute name."

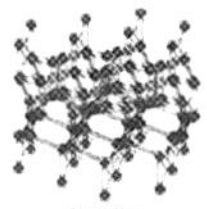

Lonsdaleite

Person 6, "Watch out! It was named after a British crystallographer, Kathleen Lonsdale. She developed X-ray methods that allowed her to study crystal structure and measure the distances of carbon atoms in diamonds with seven-figure precision."

The dog, "She was invited to the Royal Society of London as the first female researcher."

Person 3 continues, "Lonsdaelite is a rare diamond form with a hexagonal lattice structure. I will be using Matplotlib (often used in Python to display a 3D model):"

```
import numpy as np
import matplotlib.pyplot as plt
from mpl_toolkits.mplot3d.art3d import Poly3DCollection
```

The dog " # Define the vertices of the unit cell."

```
a = 2.4647
c = 4.015
v1 = np.array([0, 0, 0])
v2 = np.array([a, 0, 0])
v3 = np.array([0.5*a, 0.5*a*np.sqrt(3), 0])
v4 = np.array([0, 0, c])
```

The dog " # Define the 12 edges of the unit cell."

```
edges = [(v1, v2), (v1, v3), (v1, v4), (v2, v3), (v2, v4), (v3, v4),
      (v1 + np.array([a, 0, 0]), v2 + np.array([a, 0, 0])),
      (v1 + np.array([a, 0, 0]), v3 + np.array([a, 0, 0])),
      (v1 + np.array([a, 0, 0]), v4 + np.array([a, 0, 0])),
      (v2 + np.array([a, 0, 0]), v3 + np.array([a, 0, 0])),
      (v2 + np.array([a, 0, 0]), v4 + np.array([a, 0, 0])),
      (v3 + np.array([a, 0, 0]), v4 + np.array([a, 0, 0]))]
```

The dog, "# Define the 8 corners of the unit cell."

```
corners = [np.array([i, j, k]) for i in (0, a) for j in (0, a*np.sqrt(3)/2) for k in (0, c)]
```

The dog, "# Define the 12 faces of the unit cell."

```
faces = [(v1, v2, v3), (v1, v2, v4), (v1, v3, v4), (v2, v3, v4),
      (v1 + np.array([a, 0, 0]), v2 + np.array([a, 0, 0]), v3 + np.array([a, 0, 0])),
      (v1 + np.array([a, 0, 0]), v2 + np.array([a, 0, 0]), v4 + np.array([a, 0, 0])),
      (v1 + np.array([a, 0, 0]), v3 + np.array([a, 0, 0]), v4 + np.array([a, 0, 0])),
      (v2 + np.array([a, 0, 0]), v3 + np.array([a, 0, 0]), v4 + np.array([a, 0, 0]))]
```

The dog "# Plot the unit cell."

```
fig = plt.figure()
ax = fig.add_subplot(111, projection='3d')
for edge in edges:
    ax.plot(*zip(*edge), color='k')
for corner in corners:
    ax.scatter(*corner, s=5, color='k')
for face in faces:
    ax.add_collection(Poly3DCollection([face], alpha=0.25, face"
```

Person 1, "Precise work!"
The dog, "Gracias!"
Person 7, "I love hexagons, and an amorphous carbon is my thingy. It's free, with no crystalline structure. I'll use several libraries to create visualizations of this allotrope."
The dog, "One option is to use the Matplotlib library, a popular plotting library in Python. A scatter plot of the carbon atoms in a random configuration can be created to simulate an amorphous carbon allotrope."

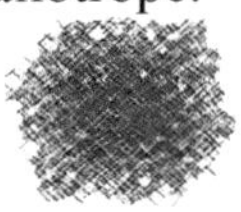

Amorphous Carbon

```
import matplotlib.pyplot as plt
import numpy as np
```

The dog, "# Generate random positions for the carbon atoms"

```
num_atoms = 1000
positions = np.random.rand(num_atoms, 3)
```

The dog, "# Plot the positions as a scatter plot."

```
fig = plt.figure()
ax = fig.add_subplot(projection='3d')
ax.scatter(positions[:, 0], positions[:, 1], positions[:, 2])
plt.show()
```

Person 7, "This creates a 3D scatter plot of the random carbon atom positions. You can modify the Num atoms variable to change the number of atoms in the simulation and adjust the positions array to create different configurations of the atoms."
The dog, "Other libraries and tools, such as VPython, Mayavi, and PyMOL, are also available for creating molecular visualizations."
Person 2, "So attractive to the eye!"
The dog, "Grazie."
Person 8, "I like free, but for me, it is carbon nanotube. I love everything that is 10^{-9}. Also, their film can be used to build airplanes with composites."
The dog, "To display a carbon nanotube allotrope using Python, The Matplotlib library is good to be used."
Person 8, "Here's my code that displays a (10,10) carbon nanotube.

```
import numpy as np
import matplotlib.pyplot as plt
```

The dog, "# Set the dimensions of the nanotube."

```
n = 10
m = 10
```

The dog,"# Define the Chiral vector."

```
a1 = np.array([3**0.5/2, 1/2])
a2 = np.array([0, 1])
```

The dog "# Generate the coordinates of the nanotube."

```
x = []
y = []
for j in range(n+m+1):
    for i in range(-n, m+1):
        coord = i*a1 + j*a2
        x.append(coord[0])
        y.append(coord[1])
```

The dog, "# Plot the nanotube."

```
plt.figure(figsize=(8,8))
plt.plot(x, y, 'ko', markersize=2)
plt.axis('equal')
plt.show()
```

Person 8, "This code generates a carbon nanotube with a (10,10) chirality, using the Chiral vector method. The nanotube is plotted using the Matplotlib library, with a black circle marker of size 2 at each coordinate point. The plt.axis('equal') command ensures that the x and y axes have the same scale, and the resulting plot is displayed using the plt.show() command. You can modify the code to generate nanotubes with different chirality values by changing the values of n and m."

The dog, thinking to itself, "That reminds me of the cage my owner once put me in. Never again. I will not let it happen again; I self-promise."

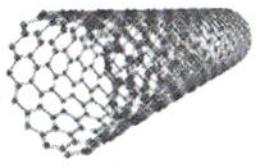

Person 1, "And, who are you?"

Person 8, "Carbon!"

Person 1, "You may call me single-walled, but you are my favorite person."

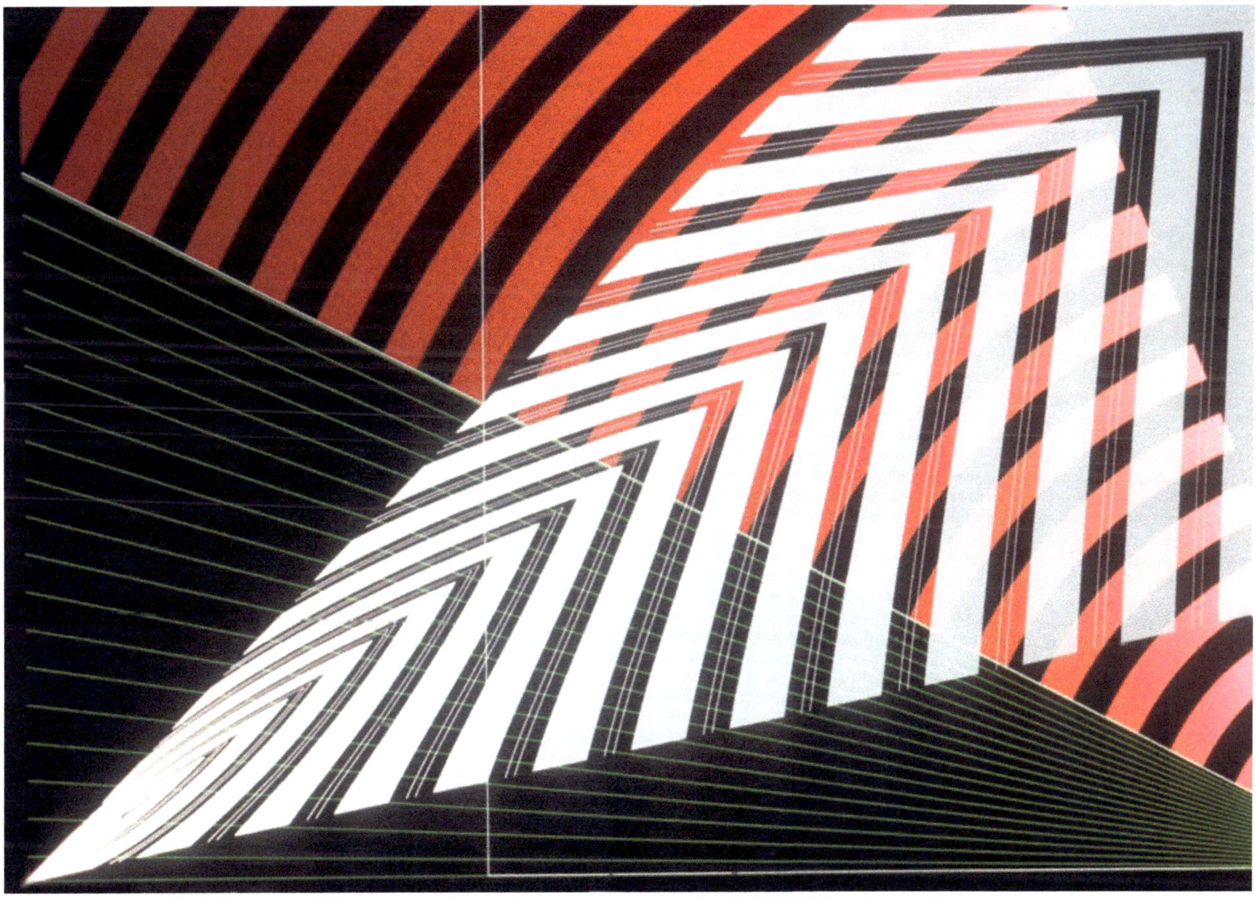

Celebration. The output from the computer code. © 2025 by Anna Ursyn

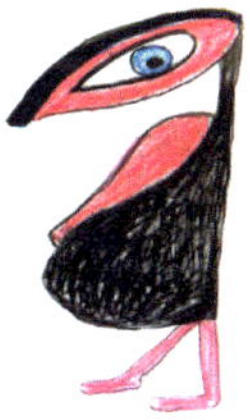

Atasa: her look will melt your heart.

Act II
(No Break)

Loud voices can be heard. Bang! The elevator opens!
Person 1, “Good”
Person 2, “Good”
Person 3, “Good”
Person 4, “Good”
Person 5, “Good”
Person 6, “Good”
Person 7, “Good”
Person 8, “Good”
The dog, “Oh, good, good, good!”
The dog runs out of the elevator.
Person 8 shouts, “Carbon!”
Person 1, “What are you doing?”
Person 8, “That’s the name of my dog.”
Person 3, “I thought it was yours.”
Person 8, “Everything is made out of Carbon.”
Person 3, “And everyone knows how to code?”
Person 8, “That is the second half of the 21st century.”
The Rescuer, “So sad you had to go through all that. We have the best elevator system possible here.”
The dog, “They use Carbon fiber reinforced polymer (CFRP) as a composite material that contains carbon fibers and is known for its high strength-to-weight ratio. CFRP is commonly used in the construction of elevators to reduce weight and increase strength.”
The Rescuer, “The elevator parts, its doors, panels, shafts, floors, ceilings, and even handrails are made out of CFRP; it makes us very proud to have one like that here!”

The End.
The curtain goes down (or closes).

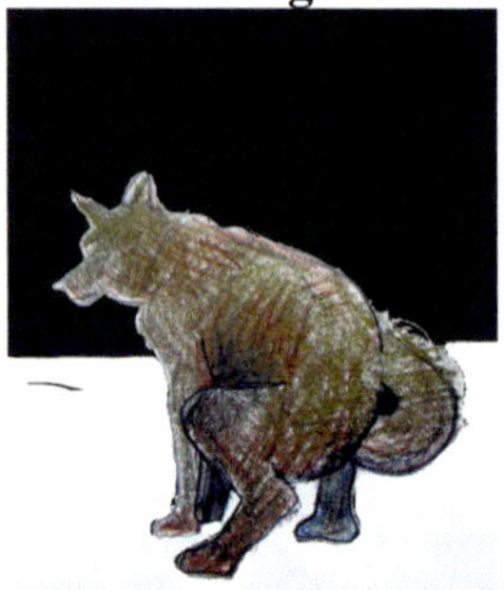

Woot playing Carbon

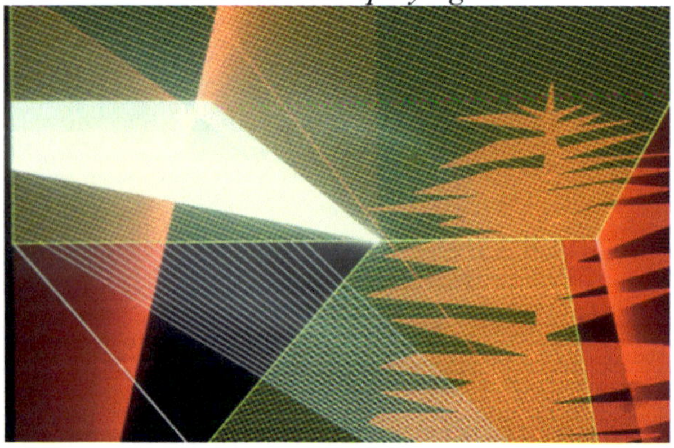

A Spruce. The output from the computer code. © 2025 by Anna Ursyn

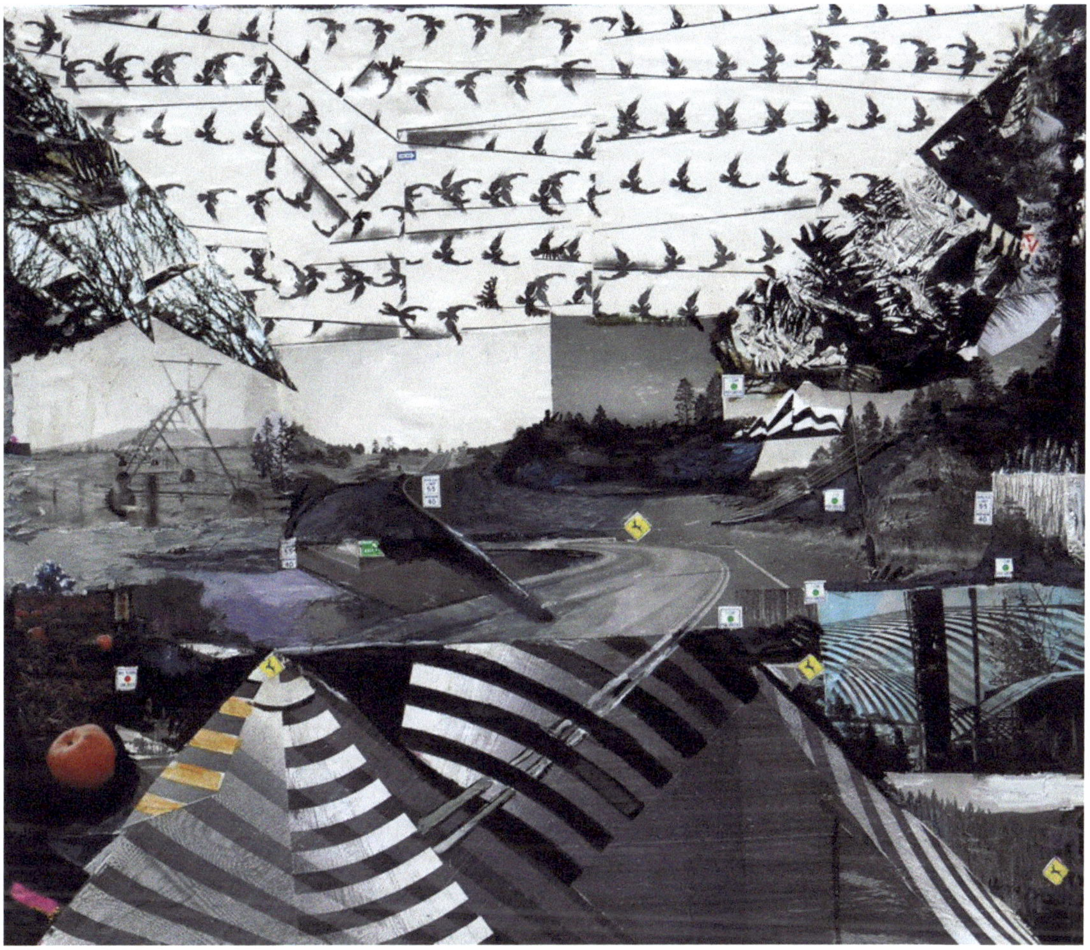

Peripheral Vision. © 2025 by Anna Ursyn

CHAPTER 13
CODE CODE

FORCES

INTRODUCTION

Current research expands the range of tools and affects our activities, from hard work to play.

SYNOPSIS

In a small apartment, two teams of young boys explore the concept of fighting. They try to devise inventive solutions to help their team win.

SUMMARY

The action commences in a boys' room filled with toys, games, computers, LED lights, and plush animals. We learn unconsciously when playing using strategies, and playfulness unifies us.

`The boys have very young voices.`

CAST OF CHARACTERS (INTELLIGENCE, POWER, SPEED, WEAPONRY)

Boy One - Strength
Boy Two - Creativity
Boy Three - Bravery
Boy Four - Reputation

STAGE DIRECTIONS

Four boys are sitting in a bedroom with many wooden toys around them.

Act I - Part One: You Do Not Know When You Are Learning
The Curtain goes up (or opens).

Boy One, "The conflict is far from over, and the forces seem equal in their smartness."
Boy Two, "We tried it all, from sticks and balls thrown at the other group to pillow fights."
Boy Four, "Someone has to win, as the supper time is approaching."
Boy Three to Boy Four, "Historically, they were always divided. By 'they,' I mean colonies forming blocks of groups. Different yet sharing common threads, with each unit polarizing, guiding, and ruling over time. They kept their characteristics while changing ways to express the overgrowing emotions, all along the tagline: 'It was not supposed to be like it is!'"
Boy Two: "The explosives, overuse of the planets' materials, and unexpected treatment of their natural findings work only for a while until the other party does the same."
Boy One, "Can a computer code reverse the direction of a magnetic force? It would send their munition away, having us win!"
Boy Three, "No, the direction of a magnetic force, which is determined by the orientation of the magnetic field and the orientation of the object experiencing the force, cannot be reversed by computer code alone. Magnetic forces are a fundamental property of physical objects and are governed by the laws of electromagnetism. "
Boy One, "Computer code can control electromagnets or other devices that generate magnetic fields and manipulate objects or systems that interact with them, but it cannot change the fundamental laws of physics that govern the direction of magnetic forces."
Boy Four, "In practical terms, if you want to reverse the direction of a magnetic force, you will need to physically change the orientation of the magnets or magnetic objects involved. One could change the direction of the current in an electromagnet to reverse its magnetic field. The computer code can control these physical changes, but it cannot reverse the magnetic force on its own."
Boy One, "Oh, so many people regret their inventions. The others do not. Not to risk total devastation, they had to devise new ways to conquer. In the past, the ways of claiming their wins started with found objects, such as rocks, found metal, or large pieces of wood. Then came the manufactured, more cruel ways, such as shovels, knives, and machetes. It involved running and scaring animals. Then, they invented explosives and carried them while mimicking birds. It was parroted both ways. The resulting chaos made those who thought they were the good ones angrier."
Boy Three interrupting, "Actually, both groups think they are the good ones. That is the essence of a problem."
Boy Two, "It is hard to develop an invention, knowing that your counterpart will soon do the same. It is still worth the risk. The research labs are called for experiments; they start with the same thorough examination of the laws of forces."
Boy Three: "I can't wait until they come up with the Fifth Force. They are so close. It will change everything."

Boy One, "How about we change the poles of the magnetic field? If two opposite magnets can repel, just as their divided counterparts did, why not apply this to the whole ball (the planet)?"
Boy Four, "A huge magnet would act up from far above, affecting places on the giant ball and causing an inverted action on the opposite side, the opponent's side."
Boy One, "Out of a sudden, the forces reverse the areas least expected to be affected; the magnetic force was sending the opponent, along with their belongings, out instead of pulling it all in."
Boy Four, "Your chess move."
Boy One, "Changing the position of two magnets to make them repel each other involves simulating the physical interaction between magnets. One way to achieve this is by using a simple physics simulation and modeling the magnets as point charges with opposite magnetic poles. Here's a Python code using basic physics principles to simulate the repulsion between them:"

```
import math


# Constants
G = 6.67430e-11  # Gravitational constant (m^3 kg^-1 s^-2)
mu_0 = 4 * math.pi * 1e-7  # Magnetic constant (N/A^2 or T·m/A or H/m)

# Magnet properties
magnet1_strength = 1.0  # Magnet 1 strength (e.g., Am^2)
magnet2_strength = 1.0  # Magnet 2 strength (e.g., Am^2)
distance = 0.1  # Initial distance between magnets (e.g., meters)

# Initial positions of magnets
position_magnet1 = [-distance / 2, 0]
position_magnet2 = [distance / 2, 0]

# Simulation parameters
time_step = 0.001  # Time step for simulation (e.g., seconds)
num_steps = 1000  # Number of simulation steps

# Simulation loop
for step in range(num_steps):
    # Calculate the force between the magnets (repulsion)
    r = math.sqrt((position_magnet1[0] - position_magnet2[0]) ** 2 +
                  (position_magnet1[1] - position_magnet2[1]) ** 2)
    force_magnitude = (mu_0 * magnet1_strength * magnet2_strength) / (4 * math.pi * r**2)

    # Calculate the direction of the force
    force_direction = [(position_magnet2[0] - position_magnet1[0]) / r,
                       (position_magnet2[1] - position_magnet1[1]) / r]

    # Apply the force to both magnets
    force_magnet1 = [force_magnitude * direction for direction in force_direction]
    force_magnet2 = [-force_magnitude * direction for direction in force_direction]

    # Update magnet positions based on the forces (Newton's second law)
    # Assuming magnets have equal mass
    mass = 1.0  # Mass of each magnet (e.g., kg)
    acceleration_magnet1 = [force / mass for force in force_magnet1]
    acceleration_magnet2 = [force / mass for force in force_magnet2]

    velocity_magnet1 = [0, 0]  # Initial velocity is zero
    velocity_magnet2 = [0, 0]

    for i in range(2):
        velocity_magnet1[i] += acceleration_magnet1[i] * time_step
        velocity_magnet2[i] += acceleration_magnet2[i] * time_step

        position_magnet1[i] += velocity_magnet1[i] * time_step
        position_magnet2[i] += velocity_magnet2[i] * time_step

# Print final positions
print("Final positions:")
print("Magnet 1:", position_magnet1)
print("Magnet 2:", position_magnet2)magnets:
```

Boy One, “This code simulates the repulsion between two magnets by calculating their forces at each time step and updating their positions accordingly. You can adjust the magnet strengths, initial distance, time step, and other parameters to observe different scenarios.”
Boy Three, “This is how those having conflict would disappear, ending the disagreement. Who knows, maybe they will start dividing themselves whenever they land up, by protesting because ‘It was not as it was supposed to be.’”
Boy Four, “Maybe magnetic field can affect those flying cardboard-oversized insect-based spies and destroyers?”

The Curtain goes down (or closes).
(No Break).

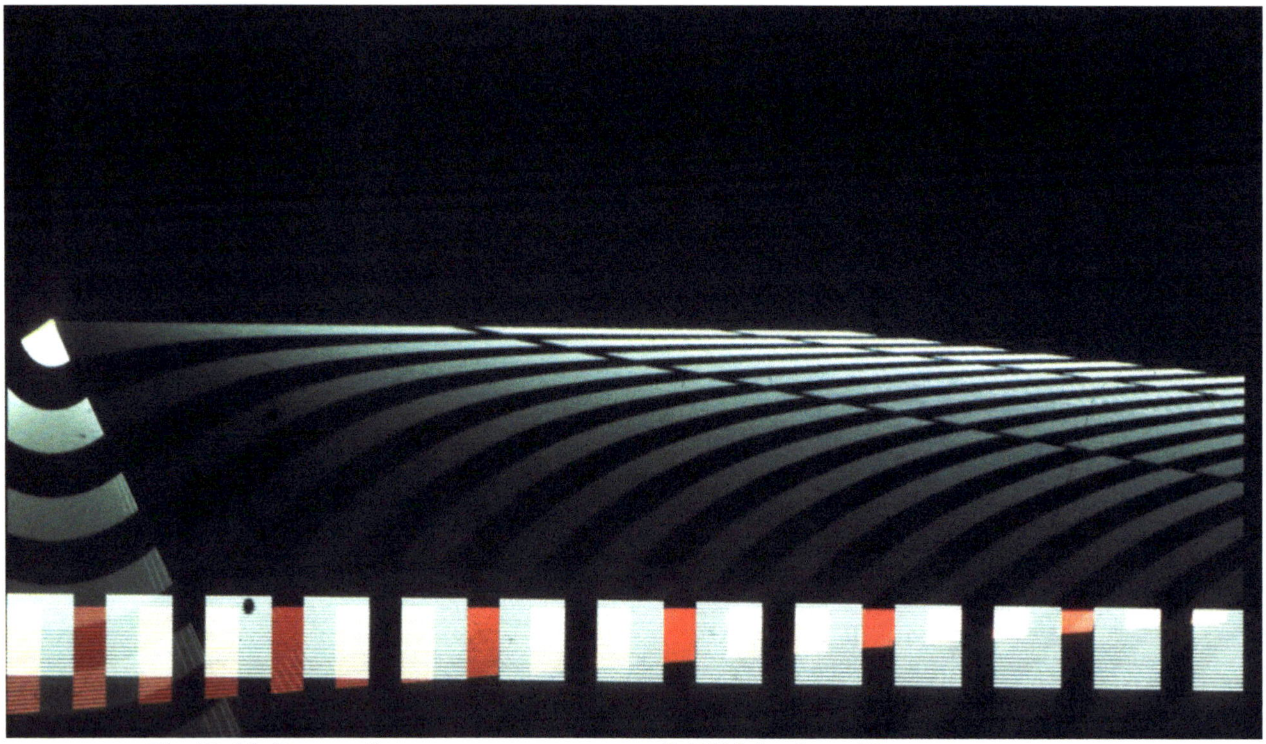

The Field. Outputs from computer programs. © 2025 by Anna Ursyn.

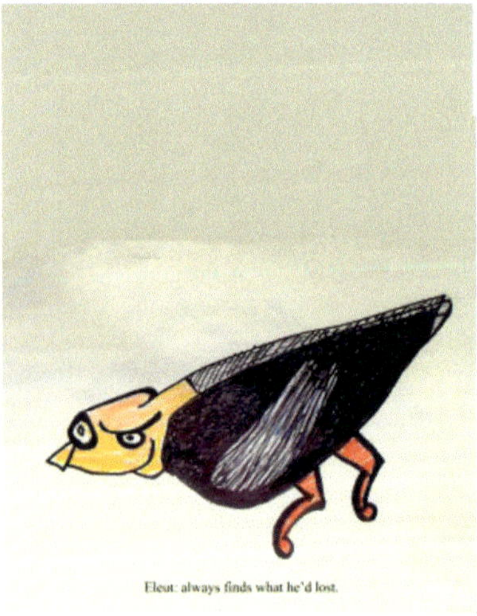

Eleut: always finds what he lost.

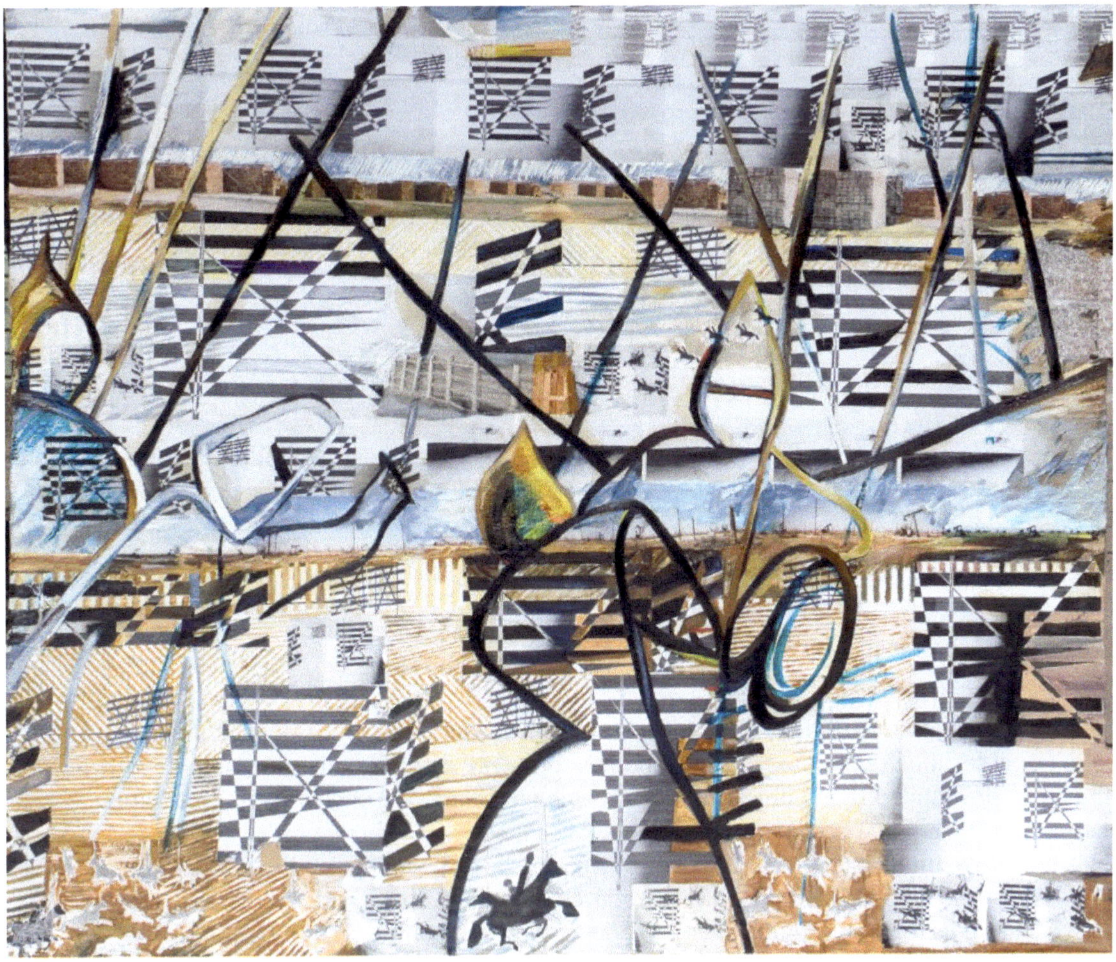

Verisimilitude. © *2025 by Anna Ursyn*

Act II – Part Two: We Are Living in a Live Comic Book, Digital Edition
The Curtain goes up (or opens).

Boy Three, "I just wrote a computer code in Python for a GPS-guided flying object, so it turns 180 degrees to return to where it came from:"

```
import simpy
import math

# Constants
SPEED = 1  # Speed of the flying object in meters per second
TURN_ANGLE = 180  # Desired turn angle in degrees

class FlyingObject:
   def __init__(self, env, start_x, start_y):
      self.env = env
      self.x = start_x
      self.y = start_y

   def move(self, distance):
      yield self.env.timeout(distance / SPEED)

   def turn(self, angle):
      # Simulate turning by updating the orientation (angle)
```

```
        self.yaw = (self.yaw + angle) % 360
        print(f"Turned {angle} degrees. New orientation: {self.yaw} degrees")
def main():
    env = simpy.Environment()
    start_x, start_y = 0, 0
    flying_object = FlyingObject(env, start_x, start_y)
    flying_object.yaw = 0  # Initial orientation

    # Move to a target location (simulated GPS waypoint)
    target_x, target_y = 100, 0
    distance_to_target = math.sqrt((target_x - start_x) ** 2 + (target_y - start_y) ** 2)

    print(f"Starting at ({start_x}, {start_y}), heading to ({target_x}, {target_y})")

    # Move to the target location
    env.process(flying_object.move(distance_to_target))
    env.run()

    # After reaching the target, turn 180 degrees and return to the starting point
    flying_object.turn(TURN_ANGLE)
    distance_to_start = math.sqrt(start_x ** 2 + start_y ** 2)

    print(f"Returning to the starting point at ({start_x}, {start_y})")
    env.process(flying_object.move(distance_to_start))
    env.run()

if __name__ == "__main__":
    main()
```

Boy Four, "Ha! Let's do the same. This code defines a simple FlyingObject class that can move and turn. It moves to a target location (simulated GPS waypoint), turns 180 degrees, and returns to the starting point. Building a GPS-guided flying object requires specialized hardware and software integration. Let's send their flying cardboard boxes back at them."
Boy Two, "This will continue back-and-forth, just like a ping pong game but in the air.'
Boy Four, "Yes, Johan Huizinga said that play is a source of culture. But, is this culture?".
Boy One, "We should have kings playing chess. Whoever wins the game wins the battle?"
Boy Four, "Who would be the leaders, then? Mathematicians?"
Boy Three, "Anybody can learn chess. It is a tactic game that requires concentration, reasoning, cognitive thinking, imagination, and time to master."
Boy Four, "Like coding?"
Boy Three, "Like coding!"
Boy Two, "They would demand another game, carefully depicting and laying out their reasons."
Boy Three, "Of course they would, like in court battles, but what would the people say?"
Boy Four, "The people would live their happy lives waiting for who would win this time around."
Boy Three: "Wait a minute. We are working on the solutions together instead of pitting one group against another!"
Boy One, "Our conflict ended with a tie, just when the dinner was set on the table."
Boy Two, "So tasteful, like never before."

The curtain goes down (or closes). The end.

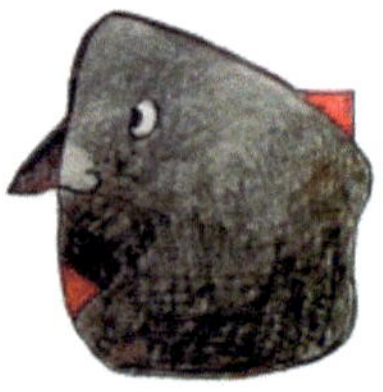

Pukoro: gives and takes.

Pukoro: gives and takes.

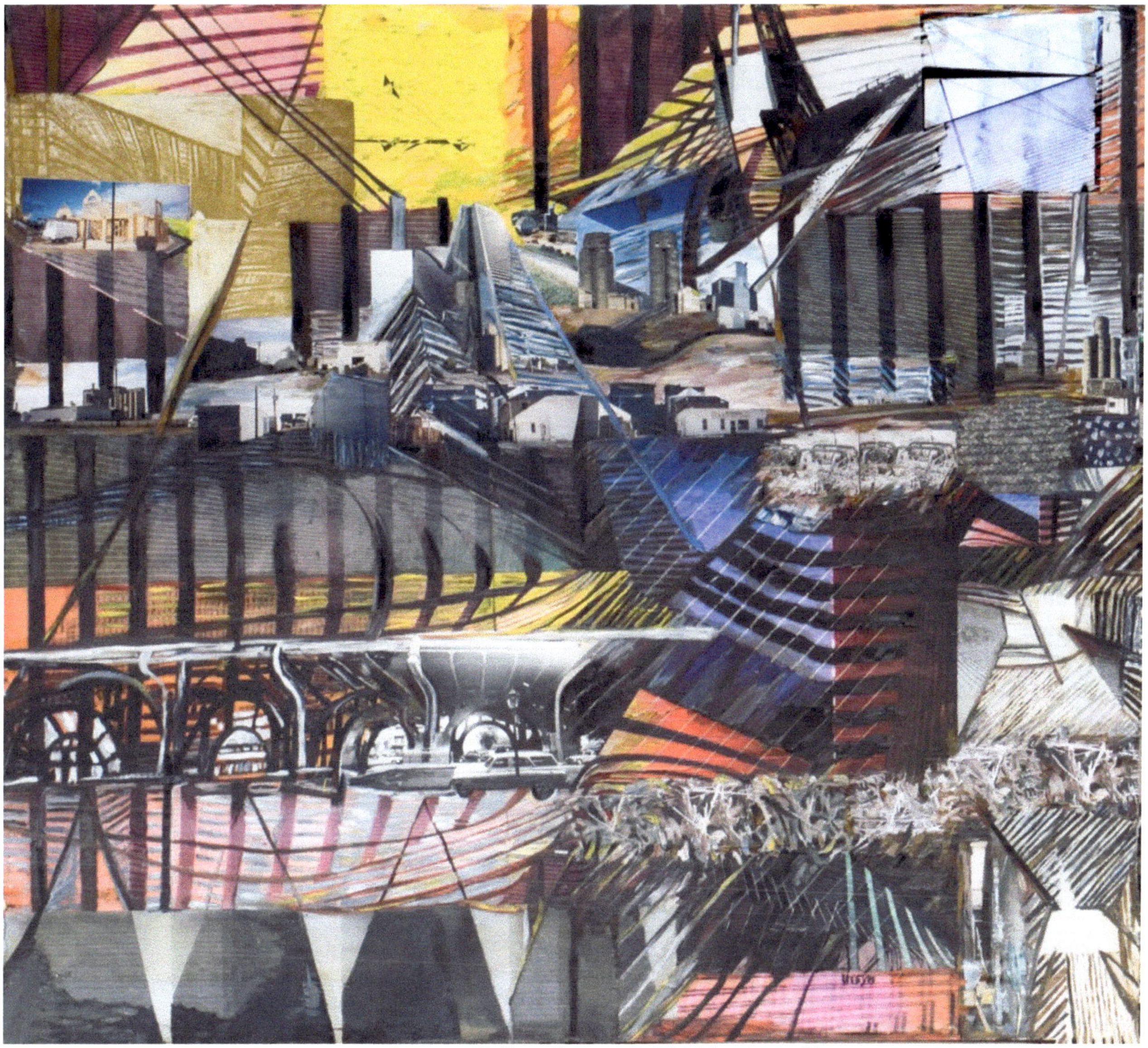

Internet Yellow Pages. © 2025 by Anna Ursyn

CHAPTER 14

PERSPECTIVE CODE

AN ARCHITECTURAL TOUR OF A TOWN

INTRODUCTION

There are many sites, artifacts, stories, and historical values behind the idea of dwelling. These concepts are changing along with technological improvements, research, and inventions. Our solutions combine functionality with usability, ergonometric design, beauty, and new arrangements. We study past ideas and create new ones to fit our needs and follow current rules and standards, both technological and artistic. We look at stable options and solutions.

SYNOPSIS

During an architectural tour of Colorado's Leadville, a group of tourists try to learn from their guide. Leadville, once the fastest-growing town in Colorado during the gold rush period, is known for many types and styles of architectural structures built because of this city's rapid growth. The program for the tourists is focused on creating perspective drawings of the town, but they are more interested in coding it.

SUMMARY

This work is set outdoors, with the tourists dynamically interacting among themselves rather than with their tour guide. Photographic and video-based elements are juxtaposed with sketches related to one-, two-, and three-point perspectives, along with some historical concepts of how three-dimensional spaces have been adapted for a flat piece of paper.

CAST OF CHARACTERS

1. A City Guide, Filippo
2. Tourist One
3. Tourist Two
4. Tourist Three
5. Tourist Four

STAGE DIRECTIONS

```
Each person holds a tablet. Architectural images are projected on the screen
```

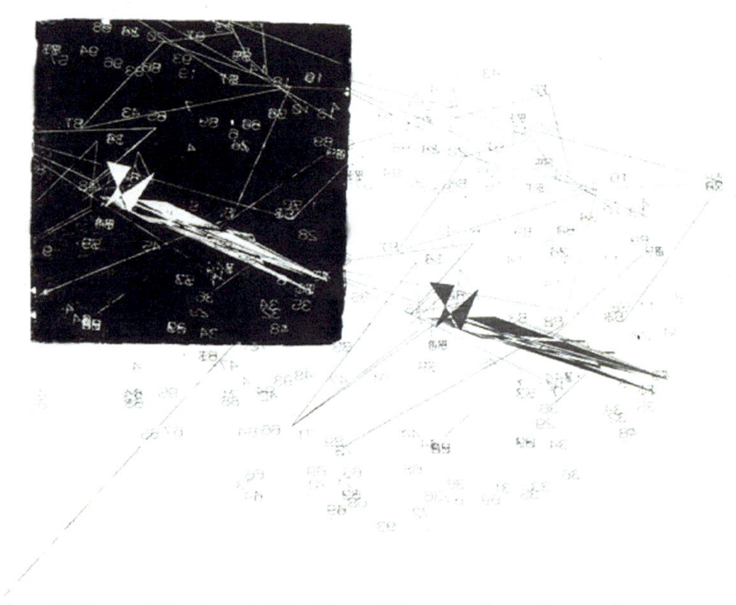

Kepler-438b and Kepler-442b. Photolithograph on the code's output. © 2025 by Anna Ursyn.

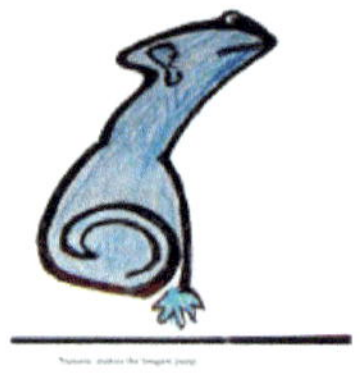

Nunera: can make the longest jumps.

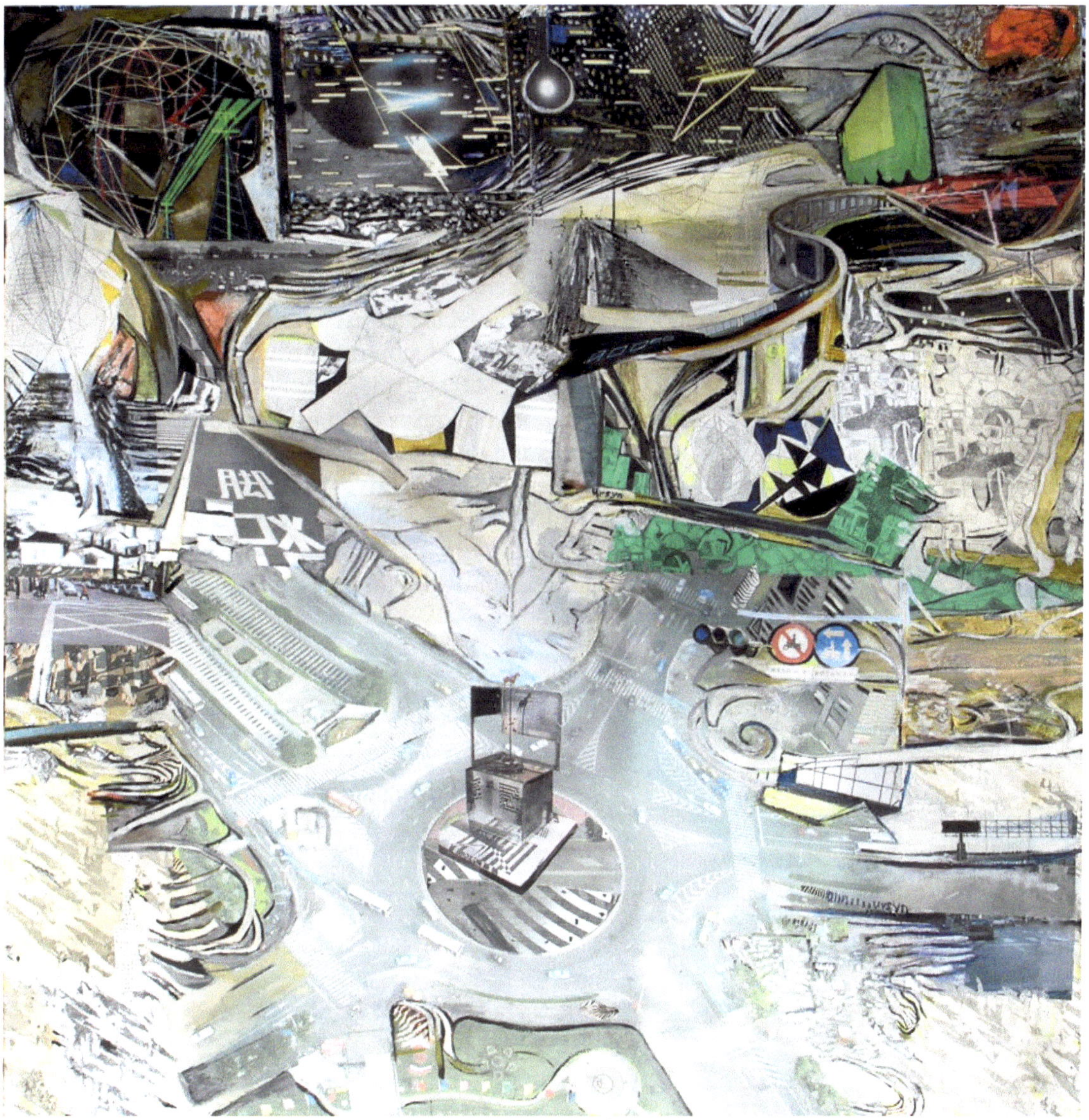

Viewpoints. © *2025 by Anna Ursyn*

The Curtain goes up (or opens).

Filippo, "Hello, my name is Filippo, and I will be your guide in the town of Leadville, here in Colorado. This famous mining town is known for coming from the Victorian era but also for its history-related consequences. It is a beautiful spot on the globe and the highest-placed town in our country. Due to the silver rush and its lead discovery, it used to be the second-largest city in this beautiful state. We can see two out of the 58 fourteeners (peaks above 14,000 feet) the state is famous for. Leadville was first named California Gulch, Boughton, as its popular shelters were out of tree boughs; Cloud City, for clouds; Harrison, its first smelter; and Slabtown, as its gold rush temporary homes built on slabs. After 1878, its own post office named it Leadville when the lead ore was spotted. Everyone here came for this tour because this city has the best examples of the historical types of shelter structures. The growth of this historic mining town was so rapid that it was home to various architectural structures following different architectural styles. The most inspiring structures since the mid-1800s are the Tabor Grand Hotel, St. George's Church, Temple Israel, Annunciation Church, Tabor Opera House, City Hall, Healy House,

Dexter Cabin, Engelbach House, and Tabor House. The largest building is the Ice Palace. These are just a few examples of the many structures that can be found in Leadville that reflect its mining heritage."
Tourist Two, "He keeps talking about architecture, but I use this word differently as a coder. We talk about Internet architecture, for example, IP Network-IGMP Querier Router A- Report, Proxy & Querier Switch A, Query, then three hosts receivers, and it goes back and forth."
*Tourist Three: "*Oh yes, the same applies to world-building.*"* My cousin is a linguist, and he keeps talking about building linguistic structures: phonetics—speech sounds, Phonology—phonemes, Morphology—words, Syntax—phrases and sentences, Semantics—the literal meaning of phrases and sentences, and Pragmatics—meaning in the context of discourse."
Tourist Two, "The architects typically make models of their projects and use them to generate construction plans with specifications of each structure, later used by contractors and builders to erect the actual structure. Many of them use computer-aided design (CAD) software programs, such as AutoCAD or SketchUp, to produce 3D models of their designs. There are libraries for models of people, cars, trees, shrubs, furniture, and even abstract symbols for electrical solutions, such as fixtures, plumbing, windows, doors, etc. Every 3D model is viewed from different angles and perspectives and has a "walk-through option." Some use virtual reality (VR) or augmented reality (AR) technologies. The 3D programs help transform shapes, sizes, and orientations of walls, floors, and roofs."
Tourist Two, "I can quickly write a code for a simple architectural structure that you can use to display an image of a house:

```
from PIL import Image

# create an image object
img = Image.new('RGB', (400, 400), color = 'white')

# draw the house
from PIL import ImageDraw
draw = ImageDraw.Draw(img)

draw.rectangle([(50, 200), (350, 400)], fill='brown') # house body
draw.polygon([(50, 200), (200, 100), (350, 200)], fill='red') # roof
draw.rectangle([(75, 250), (125, 300)], fill='white') # window 1
draw.rectangle([(275, 250), (325, 300)], fill='white') # window 2
draw.rectangle([(175, 300), (225, 400)], fill='gray') # door

# display the image
img.show()
```

Tourist Three, "This code created a new image object with a white background and drew a brown rectangle for the housing body, a red triangle for the roof, two white rectangles for the windows, and a gray rectangle for the door. Finally, it displays the image using the show() method."
Tourist Four, "Oh, architecture can benefit from coding even more. I can give you an example of how Python can be used in architecture for tasks such as data analysis, modeling, and simulation, or to analyze building performance data, such as energy consumption and lighting, and also to model and simulate the behavior of building systems, such as HVAC (heating, ventilation, and air conditioning). This Python code calculates the energy consumption of a building:

```
makefile
Copy code
# Example code for calculating building energy consumption

# Define building characteristics
building_area = 1000 # square meters
building_height = 5  # meters
building_orientation = "north"

# Define HVAC system characteristics
hvac_capacity = 100  # kW
hvac_efficiency = 0.8  # 80% efficient
```

```
# Define lighting characteristics
lighting_power_density = 15 # watts/square meter

# Calculate energy consumption for HVAC
hvac_load = building_area * building_height * hvac_capacity * hvac_efficiency
print("HVAC energy consumption:", hvac_load, "kWh/year")

# Calculate energy consumption for lighting
lighting_load = building_area * lighting_power_density * 365 * 24
print("Lighting energy consumption:", lighting_load, "kWh/year")

# Calculate total energy consumption
total_load = hvac_load + lighting_load
print("Total energy consumption:", total_load, "kWh/year")
```

Tourist Four, "There are many other ways in which programming languages can support the design and construction of buildings."
Filippo, "We will look at some ancient houses now. They are the beginning of our architectural thinking as humankind, that is."
Tourist One, "Interesting, but I heard that the oldest shelters were constructed 790,000 years ago."
Tourist Two, "So, what are the most important structures?"
Tourist Three: "I heard about post and lintel, space and mass, frame structures, symbols of function, brick, iron, and steel, and now the 3D-printed houses."
Filippo, "I can provide you with a list of significant architectural structures in Leadville, Colorado. The boom caused by the mining era resulted in the building of many Victorian-style houses and commercial buildings, mostly downtown. The beauty of Victorian homes is in their ornamental details, with embellished shingles, large bay windows, and gingerbread trims. The residential neighborhoods include Victorian houses and other architectural styles, such as Craftsman bungalows and modern homes. The commercial structures had brick or stone construction and decorative cornices. The industrial design, the Matchless Mine, is now a museum. The Colorado & Southern Railroad Depot is in a Richardsonian Romanesque style. Historic churches are in a Romanesque Revival style and a Gothic Revival style. Many other types of architectural structures are presently in Leadville."

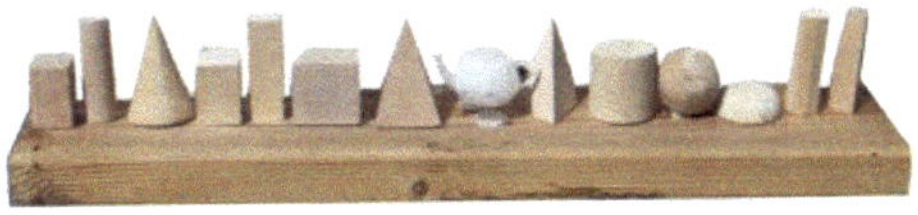

Tourist One, "People use many types of point of view such as the first-person subjective, first-person objective, second-person, third-person limited subjective, third-person multiple subjective, etc. Which one are you using, Filippo?"
Tourist Three, "Can we see those other structures?"
Filippo, "As your guide, I can offer the third-person multiple objectives, and here is a list of significant architectural structures since the beginning of human civilization:
"Neolithic Houses were made of mud, stone, and wood. Egyptian Pyramids were large triangular structures made of stone built by the ancient Egyptians as tombs for pharaohs and their queens."
Tourist Two, "I did not spot any of those here, ha, ha."
Filippo tries to continue, "Greek Temples - known for their symmetry, proportion, and columns are classic Greek architecture honoring gods and goddesses."
Tourist One, "Or those, either, ha, ha."
Filippo continues, "Roman Colosseum in Rome - an amphitheater hosted spectacles and gladiatorial contests. In Europe's medieval period, Gothic cathedrals were tall, with pointed arches, ribbed vaults, flying buttresses, and decorative structures. The Taj Mahal in India is a white marble mausoleum built by Mughal Emperor Shah Jahan as a memorial place. Eiffel Tower in Paris, France - an iron tower by Gustave Eiffel, to enter the World's Fair. Sydney Opera House in Australia – a performing arts center by

Jørn Utzon. Burj Khalifa is a skyscraper in Dubai, United Arab Emirates, by Skidmore, Owings & Merrill. One World Trade Center –in New York City, United States, replacing the original towers by Skidmore, Owings & Merrill, Abrahamic Family House, UAE, by Adjaye Associates, Paddington Square by Renzo Piano, UK."

Tourist One, "Let's not forget about ecological balance. Buildings generate more contamination than cars do. The Arab Institute in Paris uses biologically inspired solutions by having walls filled out with closing or opening mechanisms that follow the movement of an eye's pupil reacting to the sun and light changes. The Zero Energy Tower in China produces energy by absorbing wind passing through the four openings in its wall: cold or hot. The spherical collector looks nice, too."

Tourist Two, "I can also provide you with a list of major recognizable architectural shelter types: Residential homes for a family, multi-family residences, apartments and condominiums, business commercial buildings, offices, stores, restaurants, and hotels, industrial manufacturing buildings with open spaces and heavy machines, and endless equipment. There are functional and efficient institutional buildings, from schools and hospitals to government buildings. They have large areas for classrooms, operating rooms, or offices. Some are fancy in styles in healthcare, leisure, and entertainment areas: sports, arts, theaters, and parks for recreational purposes. And to serve religions, there are churches, mosques, and temples. Let's not forget those functions for transportation from some airports, train stations, and bus terminals."

Tourist Four, "Can we see the stylistic progression in architecture now in Leadville?"

Filippo, "This is the Architecture Journal Tour. You were supposed to sketch what you find, research the structure, and add text to your illustrations."

Tourist Two, "We came here to see the historical structures in Leadville and examine the stylistic progression in architecture."

Tourist Four, "I cannot draw in perspective."

Tourist Four, "Before, perspective was invented by Filippo Brunelleschi, an Italian architect known for his dome…."

Tourist Two interrupting, "A dome like Buckminster Fuller's?"

Tourist Four, "Not exactly, but a dome. Anyway, in the beginning, there were four ways to show depth on a two-dimensional plane:

`Tourist Four tears out two identical pieces of paper from his notebook and displays them while explaining:`

Tourist Three: "We place one object above another of the same size, and the top one appears smaller. When two things overlap, the upper one seems larger. Applying more detail to one makes it appear larger. The darker colors on one of them make it seem more important and, thus, closer.

Filippo, "We will apply linear perspective in our sketches and drawings. We'll start with a one-point perspective, then use a two-point or three-point perspective, followed by an atmospheric one, according to our needs."

Tourist Three, "Are you saying that architecture is subjective? What's your point of view? I know how to draw to create the illusion of depth and distance on a piece of paper by making the lines retreat to a single point on the horizon line."

Tourist Two, "Here's a basic 'subjective' for you Python code that draws a simple one-point perspective scene:

```
import turtle
# set up the turtle
t = turtle.Turtle()
t.speed(0)
t.pensize(3)

# set up the horizon line
t.penup()
```

```
t.goto(-300, 0)
t.pendown()
t.goto(300, 0)

# draw a box in one-point perspective
t.penup()
t.goto(-100, 0)
t.pendown()
t.goto(-100, 100)
t.goto(100, 100)
t.goto(100, 0)
t.penup()
t.goto(-100, 100)
t.pendown()
t.goto(-50, 150)
t.goto(150, 150)
t.goto(100, 100)

# draw a vanishing point
t.penup()
t.goto(0, 0)
t.pendown()
t.dot(10)

turtle.done()
```

Tourist Three, “Yes, the code starts by setting up the turtle and the horizon line, which is a straight line drawn across the screen at y=0.”
Tourist One, “Sure, the code draws a box as a one-point perspective. The box’s lines recede towards a single vanishing point located at the center of the horizon line. The box is drawn using a combination of goto() commands and penup()/pendown() commands.”
Tourist Two, “Finally, the code draws a small dot at the vanishing point to highlight its location.”
Tourist Four, “When you run the code, you’ll see a simple one-point perspective scene with a box receding towards a vanishing point on the horizon line. You can experiment with the code to create your own one-point perspective scenes!”
Tourist One, “I will explain two-point perspective by providing you with a Python code to draw a simple two-point perspective scene:”

```
import turtle

# set up the turtle
t = turtle.Turtle()
t.speed(0)
t.pensize(3)

# set up the horizon line
t.penup()
t.goto(-300, 0)
t.pendown()
t.goto(300, 0)

# set up the vanishing points
vp1 = (-150, 0)
vp2 = (150, 0)

# draw a box in two-point perspective
t.penup()
t.goto(-100, 0)
t.pendown()
t.goto(vp1)
t.goto(100, 0)
t.goto(vp2)
t.goto(-100, 0)
t.penup()
t.goto(-100, 100)
```

```
t.pendown()
t.goto(vp1[0], 100)
t.goto(vp1)
t.goto(vp2)
t.goto(vp2[0], 100)
t.goto(-100, 100)

turtle.done()
```

Tourist Three, "In two-point perspective, the vanishing points are located off to the sides of the horizon line, and all lines recede towards them. The code sets up two vanishing points at (-150, 0) and (150, 0), 300 units apart."
Tourist Four, "Next, the code draws a box in a two-point perspective. The box's lines recede towards both vanishing points, giving the illusion of depth and distance. The box is drawn using a combination of goto() commands and penup()/pendown() commands."
Tourist One, "When you run the code, you'll see a simple two-point perspective scene with a box receding towards two vanishing points on either side of the horizon line."
Tourist Four, "And I will do the code to draw a simple three-point perspective scene."

```
import turtle

# set up the turtle
t = turtle.Turtle()
t.speed(0)
t.pensize(3)

# set up the horizon line
t.penup()
t.goto(-300, 0)
t.pendown()
t.goto(300, 0)

# set up the vanishing points
vp1 = (-150, 0)
vp2 = (150, 0)
vp3 = (0, 150)

# draw a box in three-point perspective
t.penup()
t.goto(-100, 0)
t.pendown()
t.goto(vp1)
t.goto(100, 0)
t.goto(vp2)
t.goto(-100, 0)
t.penup()
t.goto(-100, 100)
t.pendown()
t.goto(vp1[0], 100)
t.goto(vp1)
t.goto(vp2)
t.goto(vp2[0], 100)
t.goto(-100, 100)
t.penup()
t.goto(0, 200)
t.pendown()
t.goto(vp3)
t.goto(0, -100)
t.goto(vp3)

turtle.done()
```

Tourist Three, "Do not confuse tri-point perspective with different points of view: eye level, bird's eye view, and ant's view, as Ruth illustrated below:"

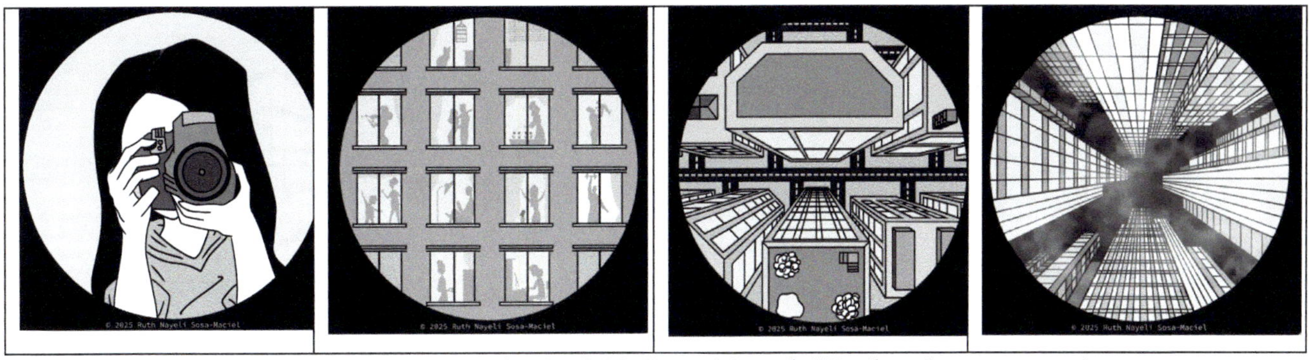

Value. © *2025 An animation by Ruth N. Sosa-Maciel (Used with permission).*

Tourist One, "In three-point perspective, there are three v. points: two on the horizon line and one above or below it. The code has three vanishing points at (-150, 0), (150, 0), and (0, 150).

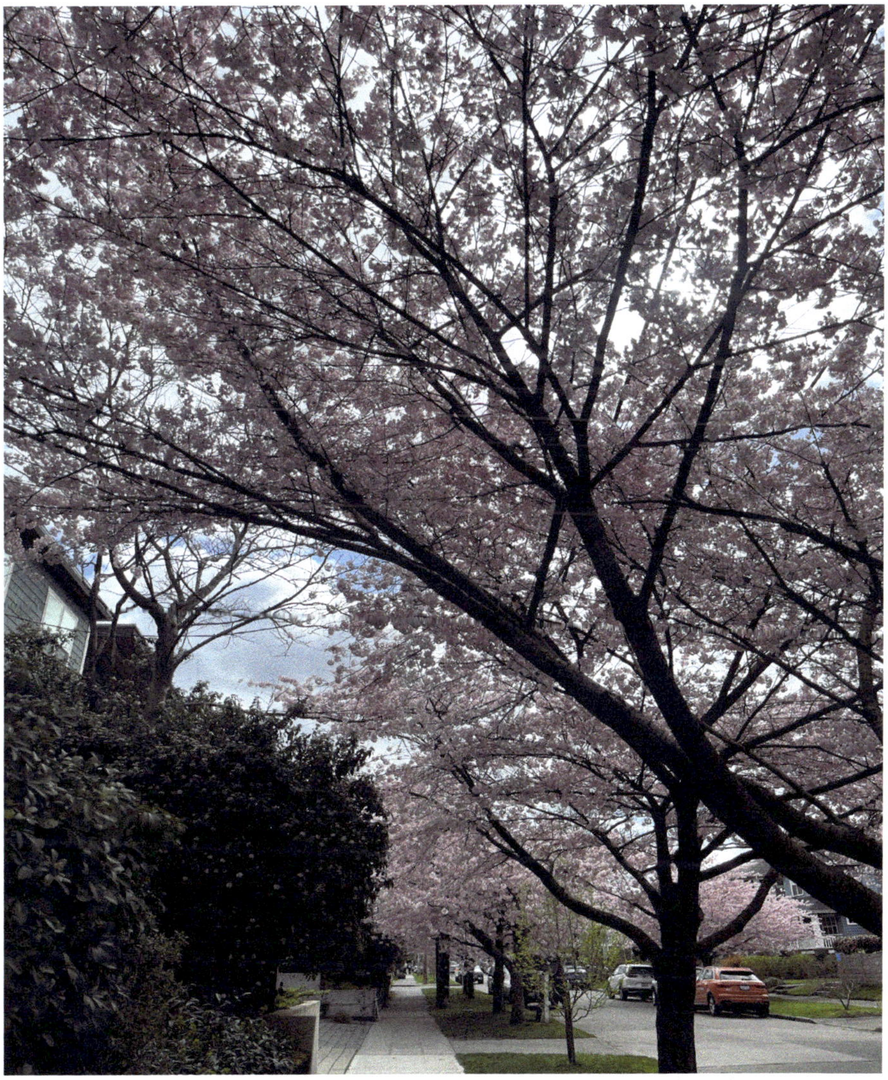

Blooming Street © *2025 by Matylda Czarnecka (Used with permission).*

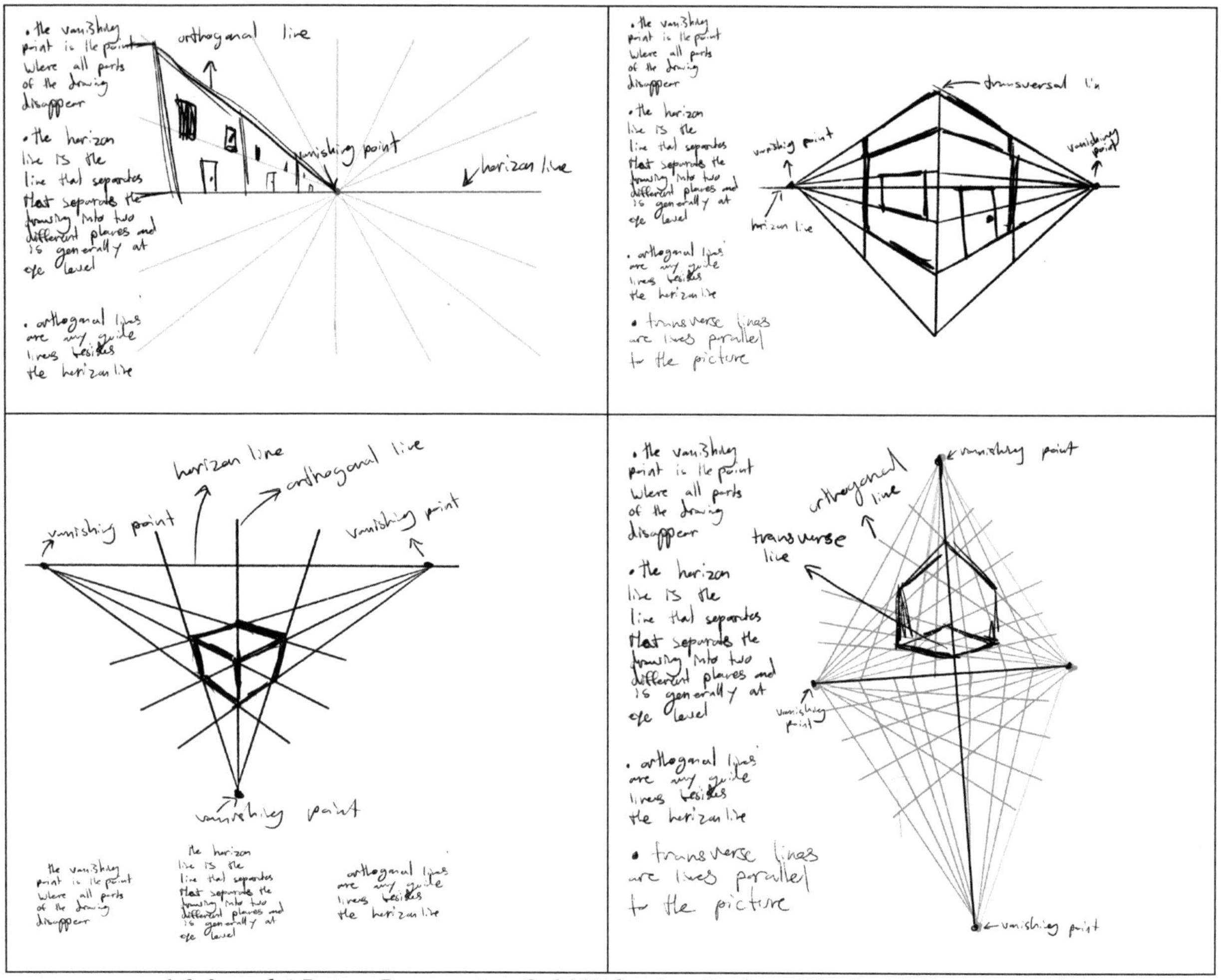

1,2,3, and 4 Points Perspective. © 2025 by Ava Becker. (Used with Permissions).

Tourist Two, “Next, the code draws a box in a three-point perspective using the same technique as in the two-point perspective example. The lines of the box recede towards all three vanishing points, giving the illusion of depth and distance.”
Tourist Three, “Finally, the code draws a vertical line from the top of the box to the third vanishing point above the horizon line. This creates the illusion of height and makes the box appear three-dimensional.”
Tourist Two, “When you run the code, you’ll see a simple three-point perspective scene with a box and a vertical line receding towards three vanishing points.”
Tourist One, “Here's my code in Python for atmospheric perspective in architectural settings:

```
import matplotlib.pyplot as plt
import numpy as np

def atmospheric_perspective(image, d, b):
    # Apply atmospheric perspective to image
    h, w, _ = image.shape
    xv, yv = np.meshgrid(np.arange(w), np.arange(h))
    xv = xv.reshape(h*w, 1)
    yv = yv.reshape(h*w, 1)
    zv = np.ones((h*w, 1))
    xyv = np.hstack([xv, yv])
    xyzv = np.hstack([xyv, zv])

    c = np.array([w/2, h/2]) # center of image
    p = np.linalg.norm(xyv - c, axis=1) # distance from each pixel to center
```

```
    p = p.reshape(h*w, 1)

    d = np.ones((h*w, 1))*d # distance to horizon
    b = np.ones((h*w, 1))*b # atmospheric scattering coefficient

    alpha = np.exp(-b*(p-d)) # atmospheric attenuation
    alpha = alpha.reshape(h, w, 1)

    out = alpha*image
    out = out.astype(np.uint8)

    return out

# Load image
image = plt.imread("building.jpg")

# Apply atmospheric perspective with distance to horizon of 300 pixels and scattering coefficient of 0.01
out = atmospheric_perspective(image, 300, 0.01)

# Display input and output images side by side
fig, (ax1, ax2) = plt.subplots(1, 2)
ax1.imshow(image)
ax1.set_title("Input")
ax2.imshow(out)
ax2.set_title("Output")
plt.show()
```

Tourist Two, "The atmospheric perspective function takes an input image, distance to the horizon (d), and atmospheric scattering coefficient (b) as arguments. It computes the distance of each pixel in the image to the center of the image, calculates the atmospheric attenuation based on the distance to the horizon and atmospheric scattering coefficient, and applies the attenuation to the image. The output image is returned."

Tourist Three, "To use this code, save an architectural image as building.jpg in the same directory as the code and run the program. The input and output images will be displayed side by side."

Tourist Four, "But we were supposed to see historically developed structures in this fastest growing town."

Filippo, "For this, you'll go to:

https://leadville.com/historic-leadville-walking-tour/ and
https://en.wikipedia.org/wiki/Leadville_Historic_District

Filippo bows out and disappears; the tourists check the info on their phones.

The End.
The curtain goes down (or closes).

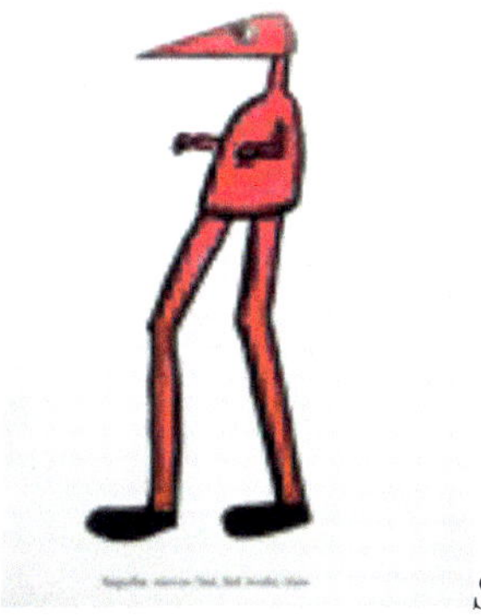

Sagufta: moves fast but works slow.

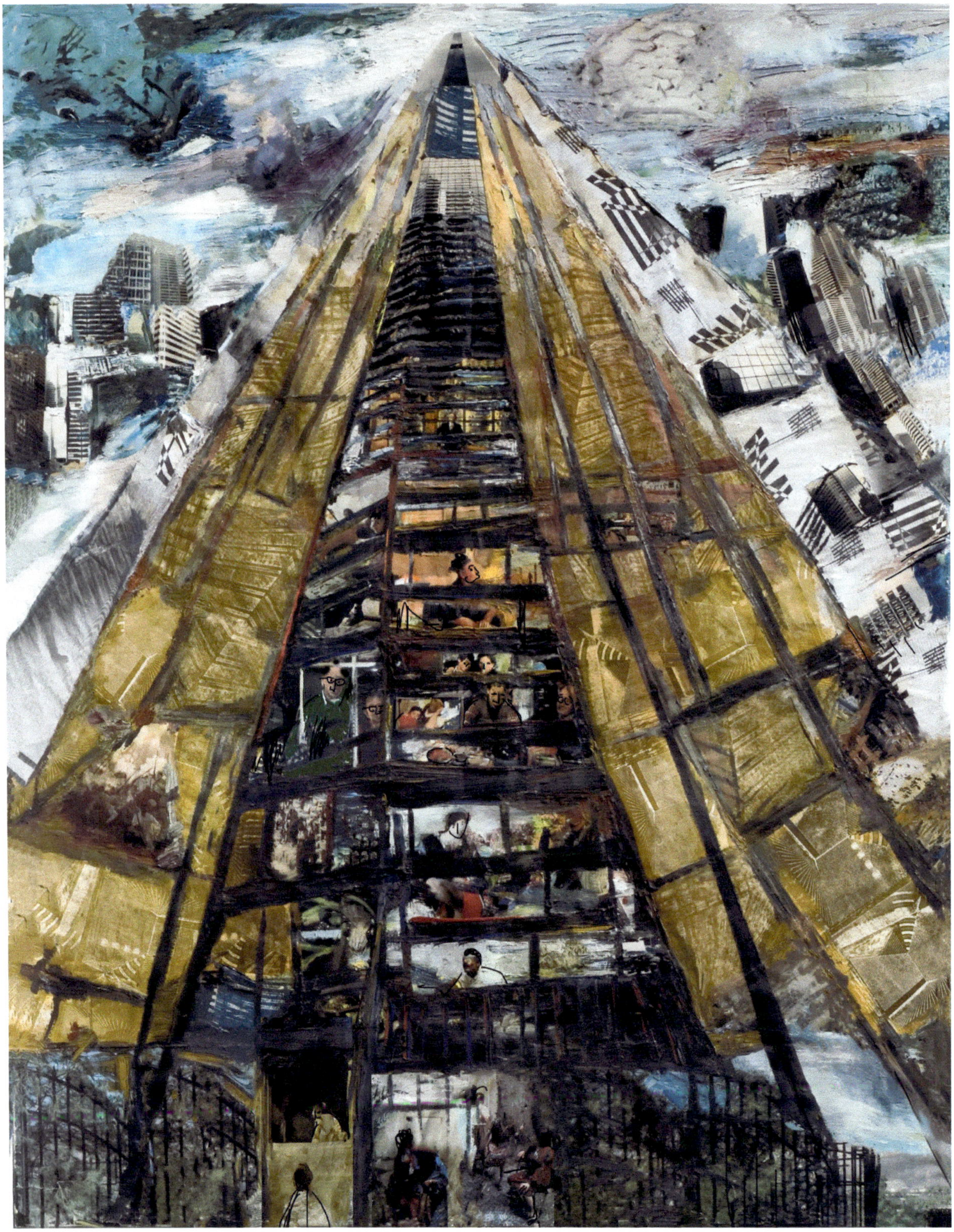

There is a Dream in Every Window. © 2025 by Anna Ursyn

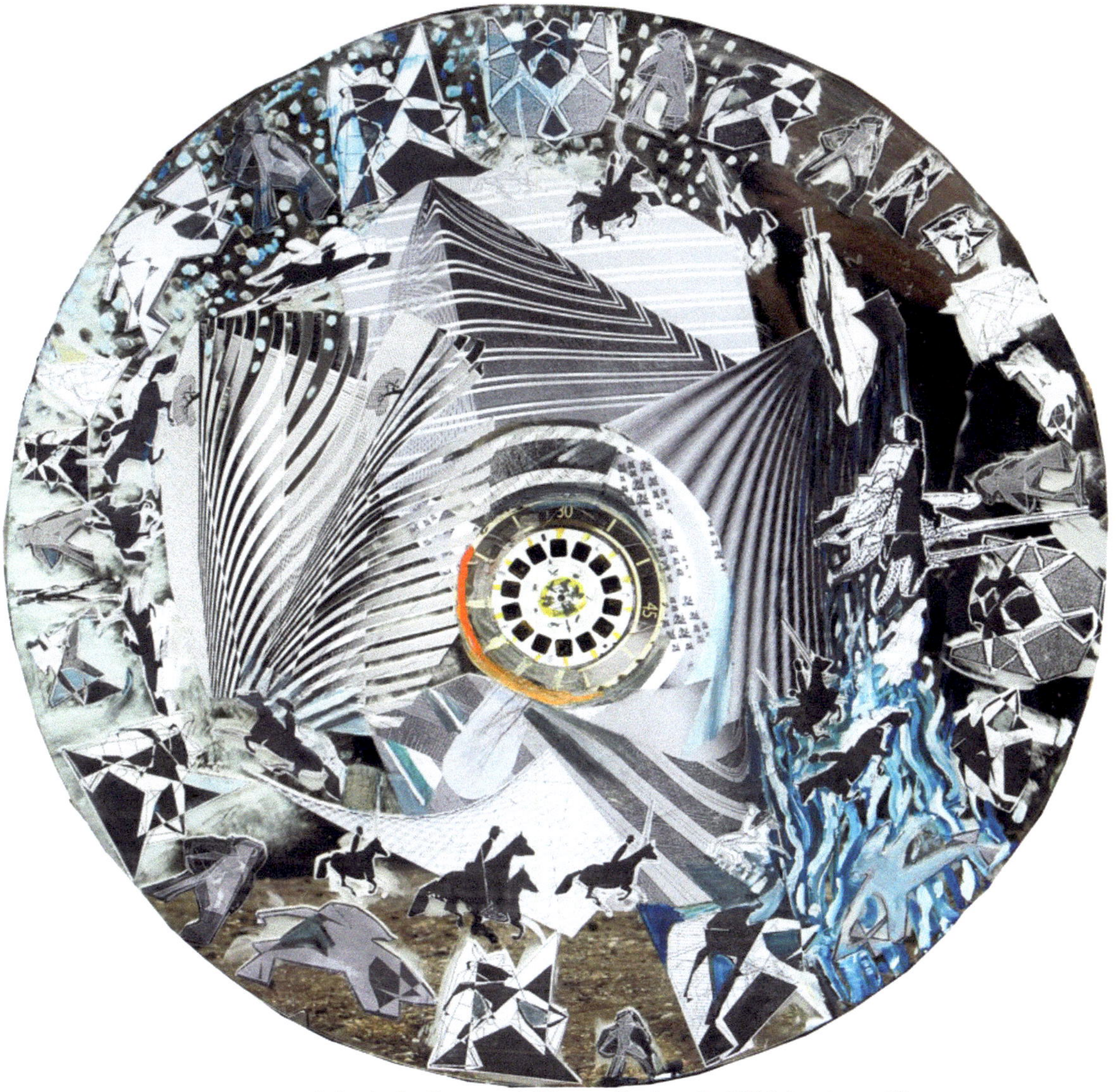

Manhole Cover: A Water Cycle. © 2025 by Anna Ursyn

CHAPTER 15
WATER CODE

A KITCHEN SCENE

INTRODUCTION

Cooking started about 1.5 million years ago. People talk about food making as chemistry, but much physics is involved

SYNOPSIS

In a small kitchen, two adults crowd with a kid constantly on their way. The four states of matter and some related infographics are presented. Movies showing the process of cooking pasta are projected in the background. Chemical and physical processes are visualized and commented on by the kid, who responds to this new info by writing computer codes, also projected on the background of the action.

SUMMARY

Two adults are cooking while a kid asks questions. They discuss the four states of matter, water issues, and coding.

CAST OF CHARACTERS

1. Adult One – a Knife
2. Adult Two – a Fork
3. The Kid – a Little Spoon

STAGE DIRECTIONS

The kitchen is filled with colorful props, cardboard models of appliances, and projections.

Act I
The Curtain goes up (or opens).

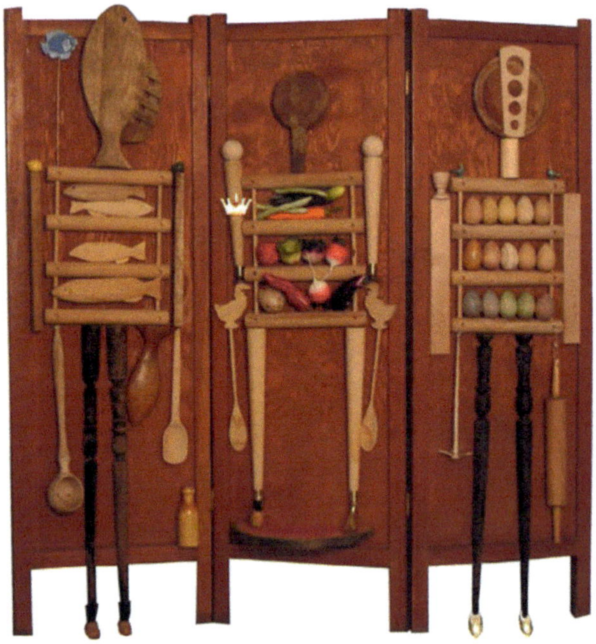

The Opera Cooks. © 2025 by Anna Ursyn.

The Kid exclaims, "I want pasta!"
Adult Two, "I do not see why not, but a perfect pasta should be *al dente,* and cooking it this way is not easy. It also pairs with wine, and kids do not drink it. Basta."
The Kid, "Basta Pasta!"
Adult One, "Or, Rasta Pasta. Here's a simple recipe for cooking pasta you can follow:
Buy:
Half a pound of pasta, 4 quarts of water, One tablespoon of salt
Cook:
Boil 4 quarts of salted water. Cook half a pound of pasta, stirring it occasionally for the recommended time on the package. Drain and serve hot with some sauce."
Adult Two, "Hmm, we are lucky to be able to use tap water."
The Kid, "Aha, I can provide a code snippet that simulates cooking pasta:

```
import time

# Define variables for pasta cooking
water_volume = 4  # quarts
pasta_weight = 8  # ounces
salt_amount = 1  # tablespoon

# Start boiling the water
print("Boiling water...")
time.sleep(5)  # Wait for the water to boil

# Add salt to the boiling water
print("Adding salt to the water...")
time.sleep(2) # Wait for the salt to dissolve

# Add the pasta to the boiling water
print(f"Adding {pasta_weight} oz. of pasta to the water...")
time.sleep(10)  # Simulate cooking the pasta

# Check if the pasta is cooked
print("Checking if the pasta is cooked...")
time.sleep(2)  # Wait for the check

# Drain the pasta
print("Draining the pasta...")
time.sleep(3) # Simulate draining the pasta

# Serve the pasta with your favorite sauce
print("Serving the pasta with your favorite sauce!")
```

Adult One, "Yes, but it is a simulation of the cooking process, and it does not include the actual physical actions, such as boiling water, adding salt, stirring the pasta, etc."
Adult Two, "So, please explain the role of chemistry in the pasta cooking process."
Adult One, "Chemistry is important in cooking pasta, as chemical reactions affect the pasta's texture, taste, and nutritional value. The pasta has carbohydrates, primarily starch. When water boils, the heat causes the starch molecules to absorb water and augment. This chemical reaction, known as gelatinization, determines the texture of the pasta. The longer pasta is cooked, the softer and more gelatinous it becomes."
Adult Two, "Another important chemical reaction during the cooking process is the Maillard reaction, which occurs between the amino acids and reducing sugars in the pasta. This reaction forms brown compounds that give the pasta its characteristic nutty flavor and aroma."
Adult One: "Yes, the acidity of the cooking water can also affect the texture of the pasta. It can break down the starch molecules and cause the pasta to become mushy, but if the water is not acidic enough, the pasta may have a tough, chewy texture."

Adult Two, "Overall, a basic comprehension of chemistry is essential for the pasta's perfect texture, flavor, and nutritional value. By understanding the chemical reactions during the cooking process, we can enjoy our delicious and perfectly cooked pasta."

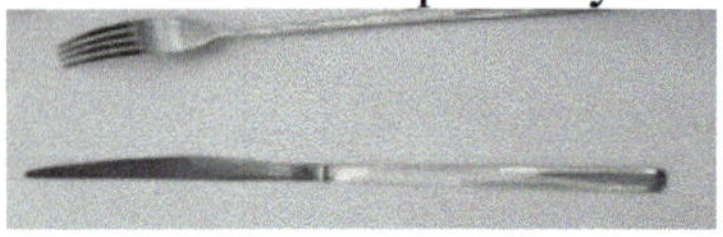

The Kid, "I can show the chemical reactions when cooking. This Python code shows it:

```
import time

# Start with dry pasta
print("Starting with dry pasta")

# Add water to a pot
print("Adding water to a pot")
time.sleep(2) # Simulate time for heating water

# Heat the water to boiling point
print("Heating the water to boiling point")
time.sleep(2) # Simulate time for boiling water

# Add salt to the boiling water
print("Adding salt to the boiling water")
time.sleep(1) # Simulate time for salt to dissolve

# Add the pasta to the boiling water
print("Adding the pasta to the boiling water")
time.sleep(10) # Simulate time for cooking pasta

# Drain the cooked pasta
print("Draining the cooked pasta")
time.sleep(1) # Simulate time for draining water

# Serve the cooked pasta
print("Serving the cooked pasta")

# Chemical processes:
# - Water absorbs heat to reach boiling point
# - Salt dissolves in water and increases the boiling point
# - Starch in pasta absorbs water and swells, becoming soft and edible
# - Proteins denature and coagulate, making pasta firm and chewy
```

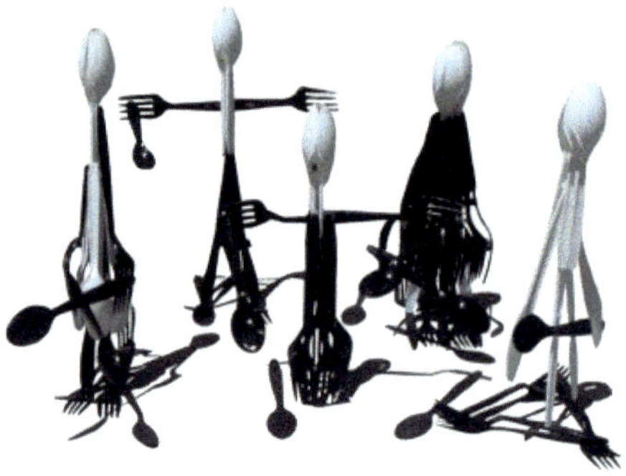

Adult One: "This code simply prints out the steps in cooking pasta, with simulated time delays to make it more realistic. It also includes comments that describe the chemical processes occurring during cooking, such as the absorption of heat by water, the dissolution of salt, and the changes in the pasta's starch and protein molecules."

Adult Two, "Very nice, but what are the processes when cooking pasta?"

Adult One, "Several physical processes transform the raw pasta into a cooked and edible form: hydration, gelatinization, diffusion, boiling, and evaporation. When boiled, it absorbs water, swells up, and softens. Gelatinization occurs as starch molecules inside break down, making it more tender and easier to digest. Salt and other ingredients added to the water diffuse into the pasta, flavoring it. Moving the pasta in the pot prevents it from sticking and ensures even cooking. Evaporation of water increases the concentration of salt and other ingredients, which can affect the flavor."

The Kid, "Overall, these physical processes combine to transform the raw pasta into a delicious dish. Just like that:

```
# set the initial temperature of the water
water_temp = 20  # in Celsius

# set the cooking time for the pasta
cooking_time = 10  # in minutes

# set the desired level of doneness for the pasta
desired_doneness = "al dente"
```

```
# simulate the heating of the water over time
for i in range(cooking_time):
    # calculate the new temperature of the water based on the heat input
    water_temp += 5  # assuming a constant heat input

    # check the doneness of the pasta
    if i >= cooking_time / 2:
        pasta_doneness = "half-cooked"
    else:
        pasta_doneness = "still uncooked"

    # print the current state of the pasta and water
    print(f"Water temperature: {water_temp} C | Pasta doneness: {pasta_doneness}")

# check the final doneness of the pasta
if pasta_doneness == desired_doneness:
    print("Pasta is cooked to desired doneness!")
elif pasta_doneness == "half-cooked":
    print("Pasta is undercooked. Keep cooking for a few more minutes.")
else:
    print("Pasta is overcooked. Remove from heat immediately.")
```

Adult One, "The code simulates heating water and cooking pasta to the desired doneness. It tracks the pasta's state and prints a success message if it's cooked to the desired level, suggests more cooking if it's undercooked, and removes it if it's overcooked."
The Kid, "But, I am looking at different states of water, liquid, gas, and if you freeze your pasta, solid. In this code, I start by setting the initial temperature of the water and the desired level of doneness for the pasta. Then I simulate the heating of the water over time using a for loop that adds a constant amount of heat to the water on each iteration."
Adult Two, "After the cooking time, we check the pasta's doneness and cook it longer if it's not fully cooked yet. We print a success message if it's cooked to the desired level."
The Kid, "This code snippet shows how Python simulates physical processes in cooking:"

```
temperature = 100 # temperature of water in degrees Celsius

if temperature <= 0:
    state = "solid"
elif temperature > 0 and temperature < 100:
    state = "liquid"
elif temperature >= 100 and temperature < 10000:
    state = "gas"
else:
    state = "plasma"

print("The water is in the", state, "state")
```

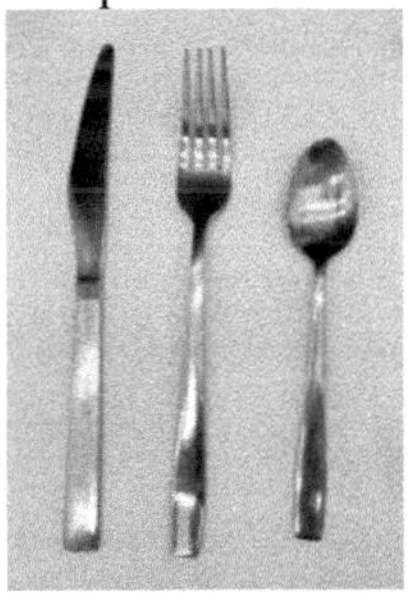

Adult One, "You first defined a variable 'temperature' which represents the water temperature in degrees Celsius."
The Kid, "Finally, I used the print() function to output the state of water."
Adult One, "The actual temperatures and conditions for water to transition between states may vary depending on factors such as pressure and impurities."
Adult Two, "You used conditional statements (if, elif, and else) to determine the state of water based on its temperature. If the temperature is less than or equal to 0 degrees Celsius, the water is in a solid state. If the temperature is between 0 and 100 degrees Celsius, the water is in a liquid state. Water is gaseous if the temperature is between 100 and 10,000 degrees Celsius. If the temperature exceeds 10,000 degrees Celsius, it is in a plasma state."
Adult Two, "But we do not have a stove reaching 10,000 degrees Celsius."
The Kid, "Never underestimate the power of the kids."

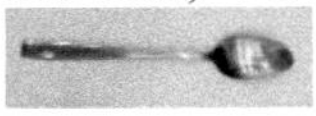

The End
The Curtain goes down (or closes).

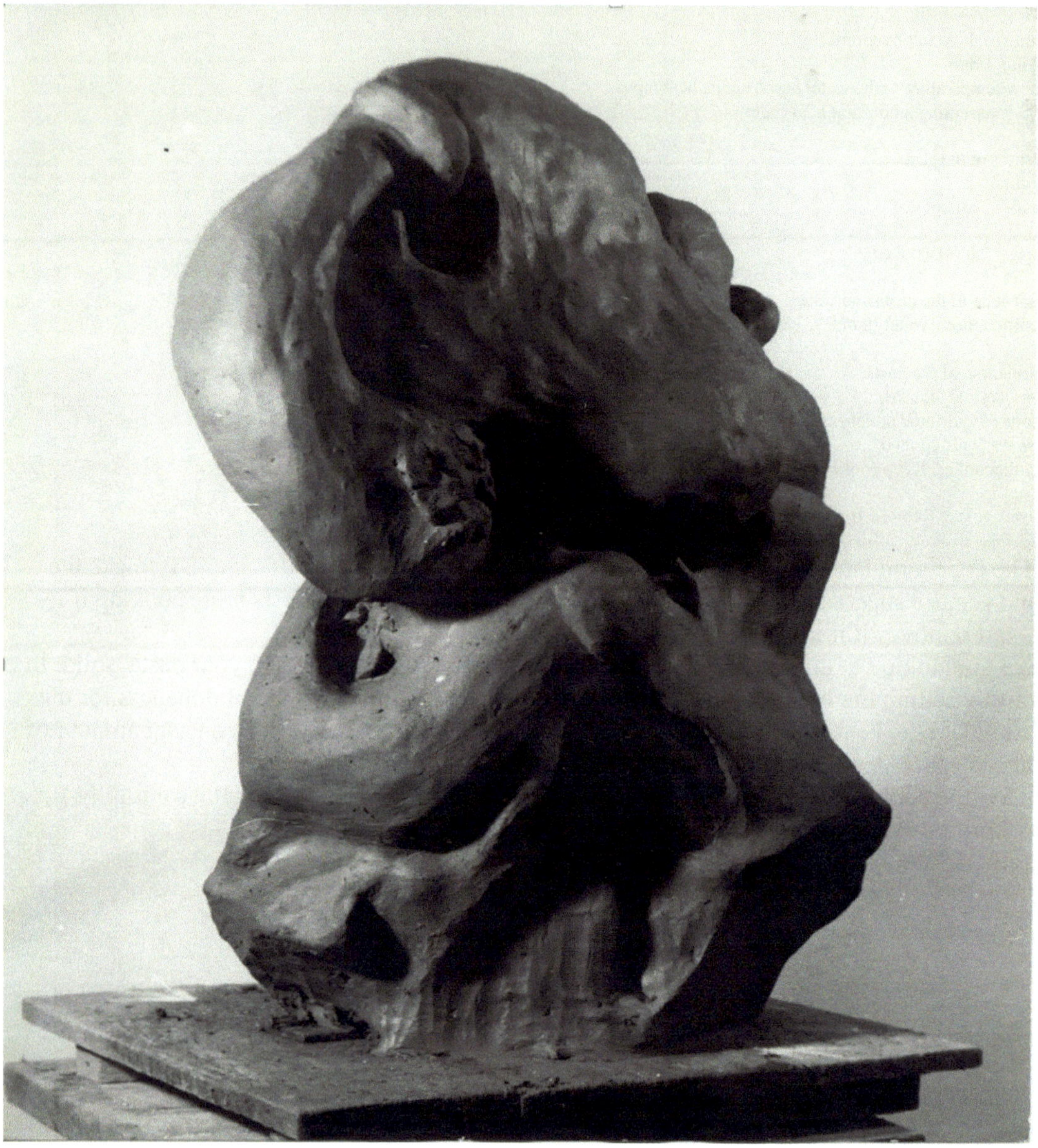

The Closed Form. © 2025 by Anna Ursyn

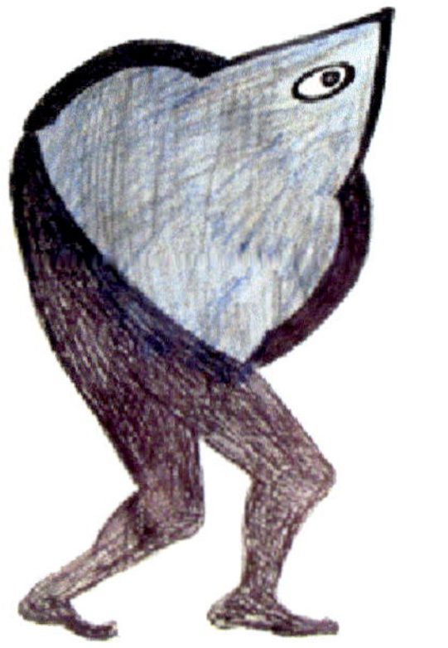

Bicadel: has it all.

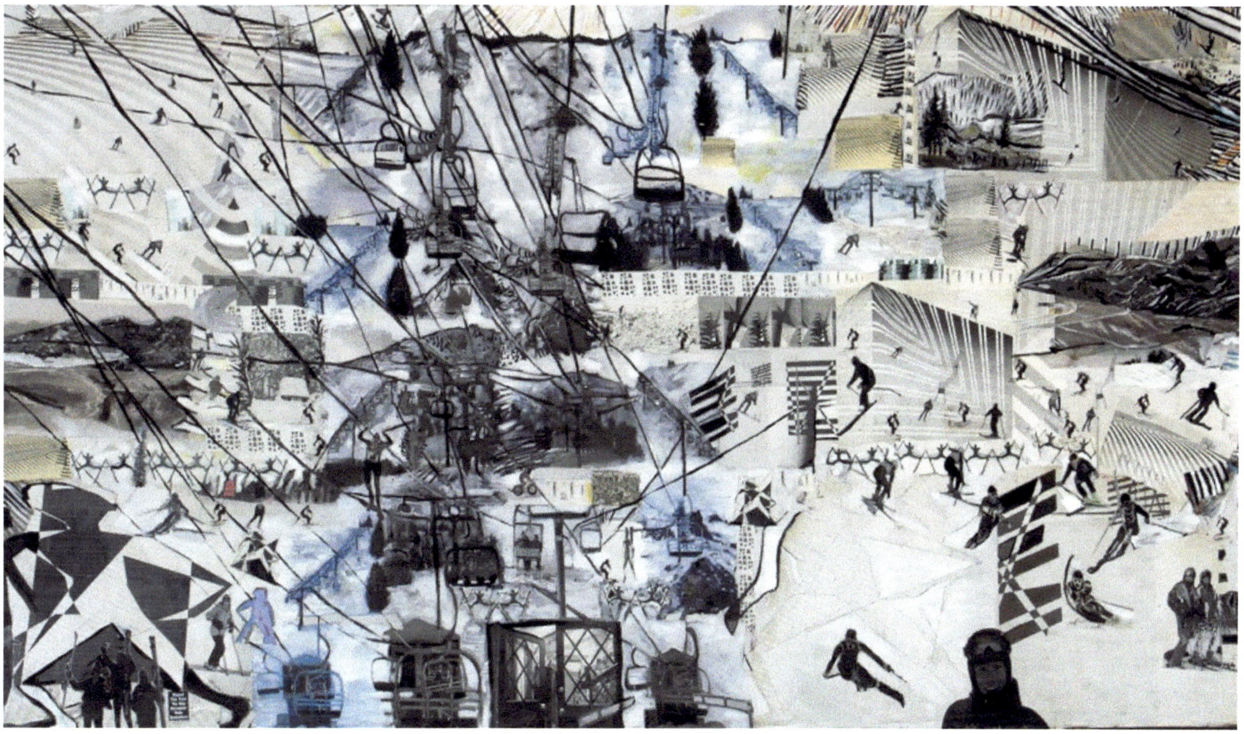

Elation. © 2025 by Anna Ursyn

CHAPTER 16
PHYSICS CODE

SKI LIFT EXCHANGE

INTRODUCTION

Nature offers suggestions for human inventions. Sciences and math describe them and serve us by stimulating future creations.

SYNOPSIS

According to what they know today, two skiers on a moving ski lift discuss some natural forces the lift is exposed to. Their faces are shown only when one talks.

SUMMARY

The two skiers discuss symbols and visual shortcuts of processes and products linked by codes. The abstract-in-nature data will serve as a basis for movement and interactions.

CAST OF CHARACTERS

Michael, Skier One
Peter, Skier Two

STAGE DIRECTIONS

Two skiers wearing color cardboard gear, with projections behind them, are sitting on two ladders. They discuss physical forces affecting the ski lift by displaying the codes on the phones.

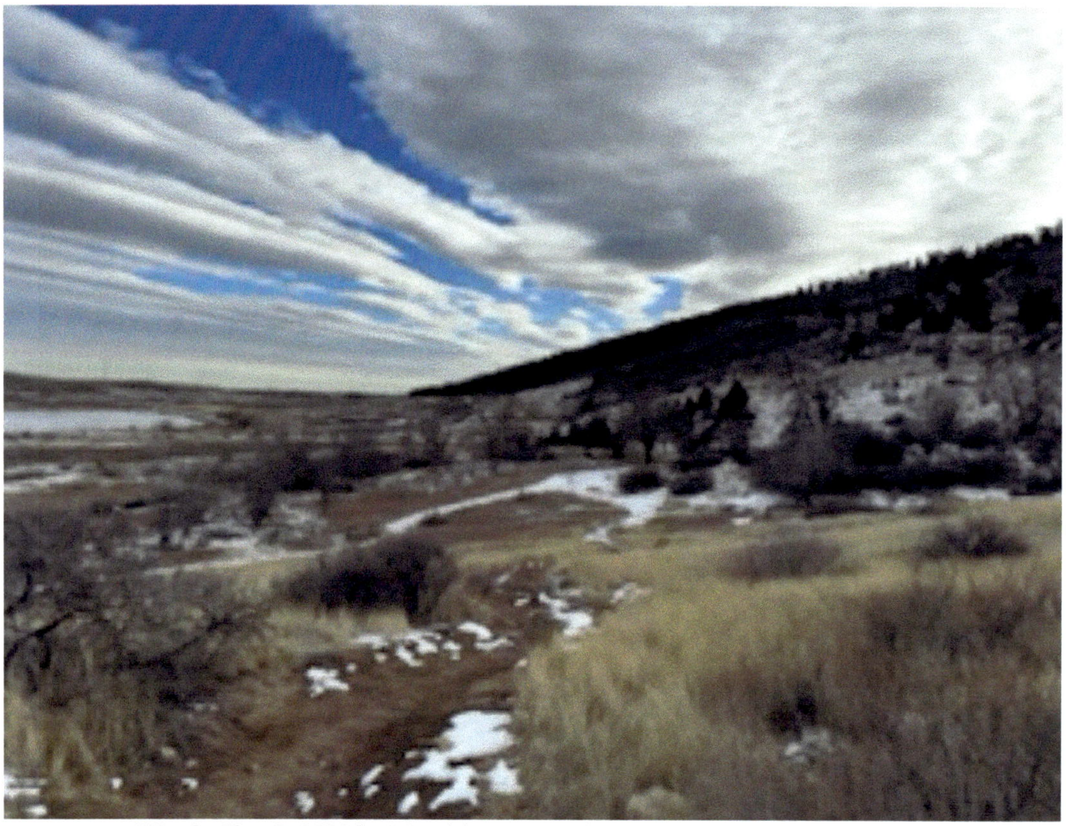

Windy Sky. © 2025 by Matylda Czarnecka. (Used with permission).

Act I
The curtain goes up (or opens).

Michael, "So cold! It is a long ride up, and I hope this ski lift does not stop suddenly."
Peter, "It happened to me once, but it was a lot colder. The whole thing was suspended in the air for a long time, with many people hoping for the best. There was no warning. We were hanging up and looking down, first at the other skiers gracefully sliding down, then at the animals, trees, and some scarce plant life signs below us. I saw a porcupine, which was nice, but I am shivering just thinking about that event."
Michael, "A ski lift is affected by physical forces like friction, wind, tension in cables, and centrifugal force. Wind can cause a ski lift to sway, making it difficult to load and unload passengers safely, or increase the lift's drag, making it harder for the motor to pull the lift uphill.

Let me show you how it works in coding. Actually, I find it quite fascinating. My hands are too cold to pull my phone out of my pocket. You have one handy; can I use it?"

`Peter hands Michael his phone.`

Peter, "Sure. Oh, you dropped my phone!!!"
Michael, "Gravity it was! It keeps pulling the ski lift, its occupants, and objects down towards the Earth, so to overcome it, the lift's motor and cables support the ride moving upward. Your phone had no motor, so it fell, but I will try to get my phone out to show you how it can be described."

Michael pulls the phone out of his pocket and displays his code.

Gravity affects a ski lift, and other forces keep it afloat. Here's a code in Python that presents the forces acting on it:

```
# Define the ski lift's mass, gravitational acceleration, and air resistance constant
m = 5000  # kg
g = 9.81  # m/s^
k = 100   # Ns/m

# Define the ski lift's initial position, velocity, and acceleration
x = 0  # m
v = 0  # m/s
a = 0  # m/s^2

# Define the time step and simulation duration
dt = 0.01  # s
t_max = 60  # s

# Create empty lists to store the time, position, velocity, and acceleration data
t_list = []
x_list = []
v_list = []
a_list = []

# Simulate the ski lift's motion using the Euler method
for t in range(int(t_max/dt)):
    # Calculate the net force acting on the ski lift
    F_gravity = m * g
    F_air_resistance = -k * v**2
    F_net = F_gravity + F_air_resistance

    # Update the ski lift's acceleration, velocity, and position
    a = F_net / m
    v += a * dt
    x += v * dt

    # Append the current time, position, velocity, and acceleration to the corresponding lists
    t_list.append(t*dt)
    x_list.append(x)
    v_list.append(v)
    a_list.append(a)

# Plot the position, velocity, and acceleration over time
import matplotlib.pyplot as plt

fig, (ax1, ax2, ax3) = plt.subplots(3, 1, figsize=(8, 12))

ax1.plot(t_list, x_list)
ax1.set_xlabel('Time (s)')
ax1.set_ylabel('Position (m)')
ax1.set_title('Ski Lift Position over Time')

ax2.plot(t_list, v_list)
ax2.set_xlabel('Time (s)')
ax2.set_ylabel('Velocity (m/s)')
ax2.set_title('Ski Lift Velocity over Time')

ax3.plot(t_list, a_list)
ax3.set_xlabel('Time (s)')
ax3.set_ylabel('Acceleration (m/s^2)')
ax3.set_title('Ski Lift Acceleration over Time')

plt.tight_layout()
plt.show()
```

The ski lift's movement is influenced by gravity and air resistance. The net force is the sum of them, and its acceleration is calculated using F_net / m. The results show the ski lift's position, velocity, and acceleration over time. The ski lift's position increases linearly, its velocity increases at a decreasing rate, and its acceleration decreases to zero as it reaches a steady speed. The air resistance force causes the ski lift's decreasing acceleration."

Peter, "I see, but sadly, the same force had a chance to be applied to my phone."

Michael, "You'll get another phone. And this code shows how gravity affects the motion of a falling phone. My hands are freezing."

```
# Define the phone's mass, gravitational acceleration, and air resistance constant
m = 0.2  # kg
g = 9.81 # m/s^2
k = 0.1  # Ns/m

# Define the phone's initial position, velocity, and acceleration
x = 1  # m
v = 0  # m/s
a = -g # m/s^2 (negative because it's falling)

# Define the time step and simulation duration
dt = 0.01  # s
t_max = 5.0  # s

# Create empty lists to store the time, position, velocity, and acceleration data
t_list = []
x_list = []
v_list = []
a_list = []

# Simulate the phone's motion using the Euler method
for t in range(int(t_max/dt)):
   # Calculate the net force acting on the phone
   F_gravity = m * g
   F_air_resistance = -k * v**2 if v > 0 else 0  # air resistance only applies if the phone is moving upwards
   F_net = F_gravity + F_air_resistance

   # Update the phone's acceleration, velocity, and position
   a = F_net / m
   v += a * dt
   x += v * dt

   # Append the current time, position, velocity, and acceleration to the corresponding lists
   t_list.append(t*dt)
   x_list.append(x)
   v_list.append(v)
   a_list.append(a)

# Plot the position, velocity, and acceleration over time
import matplotlib.pyplot as plt

fig, (ax1, ax2, ax3) = plt.subplots(3, 1, figsize=(8, 12))

ax1.plot(t_list, x_list)
ax1.set_xlabel('Time (s)')
ax1.set_ylabel('Position (m)')
ax1.set_title('Phone Position over Time')

ax2.plot(t_list, v_list)
ax2.set_xlabel('Time (s)')
ax2.set_ylabel('Velocity (m/s)')
ax2.set_title('Phone Velocity over Time')

ax3.plot(t_list, a_list)
ax3.set_xlabel('Time (s)')
ax3.set_ylabel('Acceleration (m/s^2)')
ax3.set_title('Phone Acceleration over Time')

plt.tight_layout()
plt.show()
```

In this code, your phone was subject to gravity and air resistance. The hologram is calculated as the product of your phone's mass and the gravitational acceleration constant g. The air resistance force is calculated using the formula -k * v^2, where k is a constant representing the air resistance and v is your phone's velocity. When your phone falls, its position decreases while its velocity increases at a constant rate. Your phone's acceleration is constant and equals the gravitational acceleration g. Due to its low initial velocity, air resistance is negligible."

Peter, "You dropped your phone!"

Michael, "No more coding for today; let's return to other forces. The effects of radiation in areas with high nuclear activity are considered for designing ski lift systems."

Peter, **"**The forces that affect the operation of a ski lift are typically gravitational, mechanical, and electrical forces, which are many orders of magnitude larger and have a much greater range than the strong nuclear force."

Michael, "Also, electromagnetic forces can play a role in the lift's operation and may need to be considered during design and operation."

Peter, "The ski lift uses electromagnetic forces from an electric motor to control speed and position. Gravitational force governs all matter, and the lift withstands weight, friction, wind, and weather. This is the weakest but infinite force."

Michael, "Yes, no more coding for today, but the nuclear force, a fundamental force of nature, acts between subatomic particles, protons, and neutrons within the nucleus of an atom."

Peter, "The fundamental forces of nature comprise gravity, electromagnetic force, the weak force, and the strong nuclear force. The weak nuclear force is only noticeable at the atomic and subatomic levels. The fifth force theory must be resolved to completely understand how the world works."

Michael, "Ha, ha. For this, you'd need to have a lift to the Moon."

Peter, "In that case, I'd prefer a ski gondola."

Michael, "And our new phones to show those simulations."

Peter, "And a phone that can explain muons and the fifth force."

The End.
The Curtain goes down (or closes).

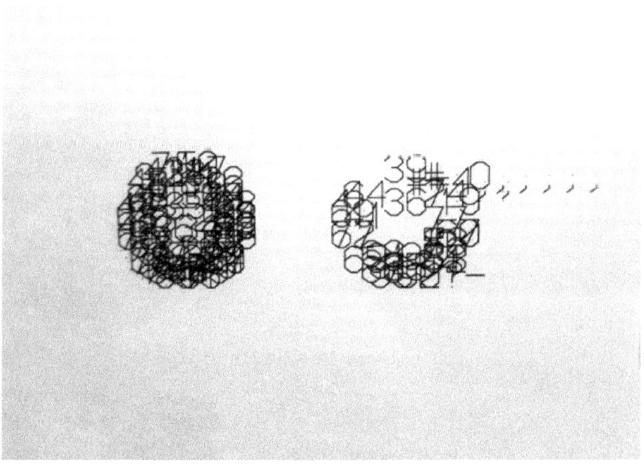

Two Sets of Numbers. Output from the computer code. © 2025 by Anna Ursyn

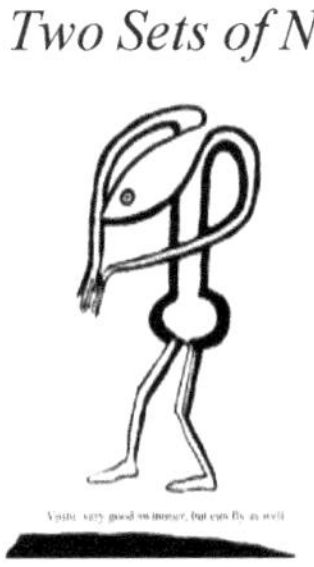

Vustu: a very good swimmer but can fly as well.

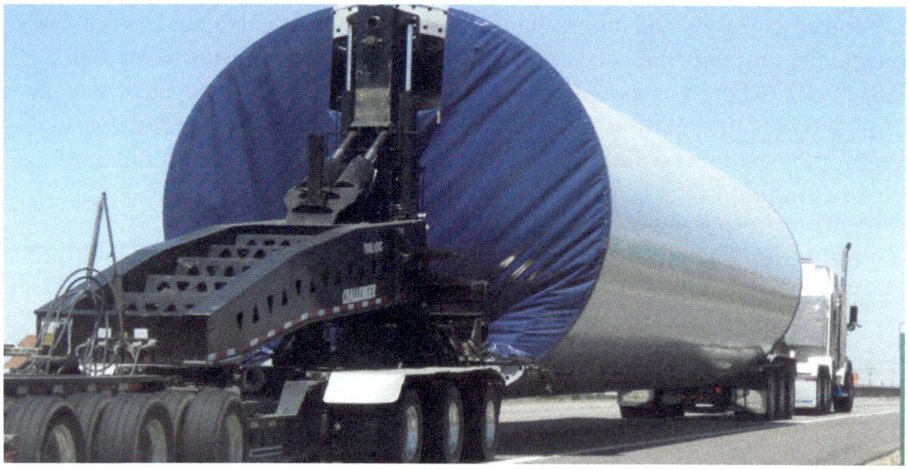

A Cylinder. © 2025 by Anna Ursyn

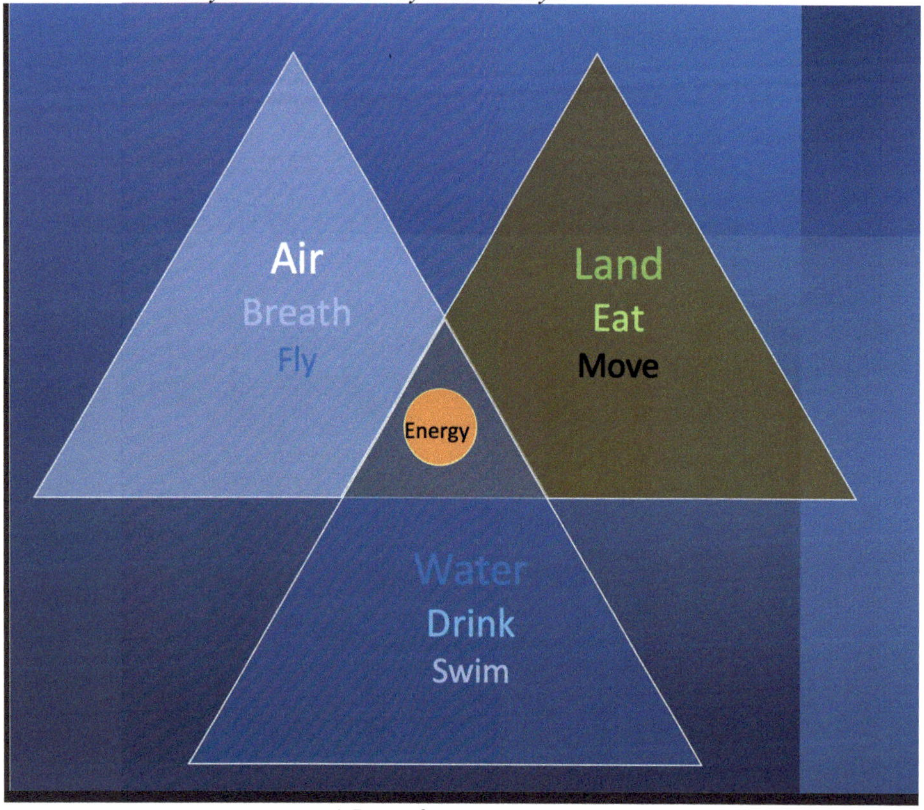

A Logo for Nature

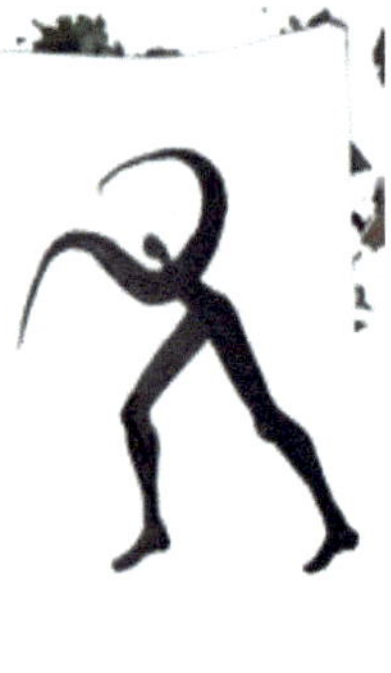

You: has the power to change the direction of a river.

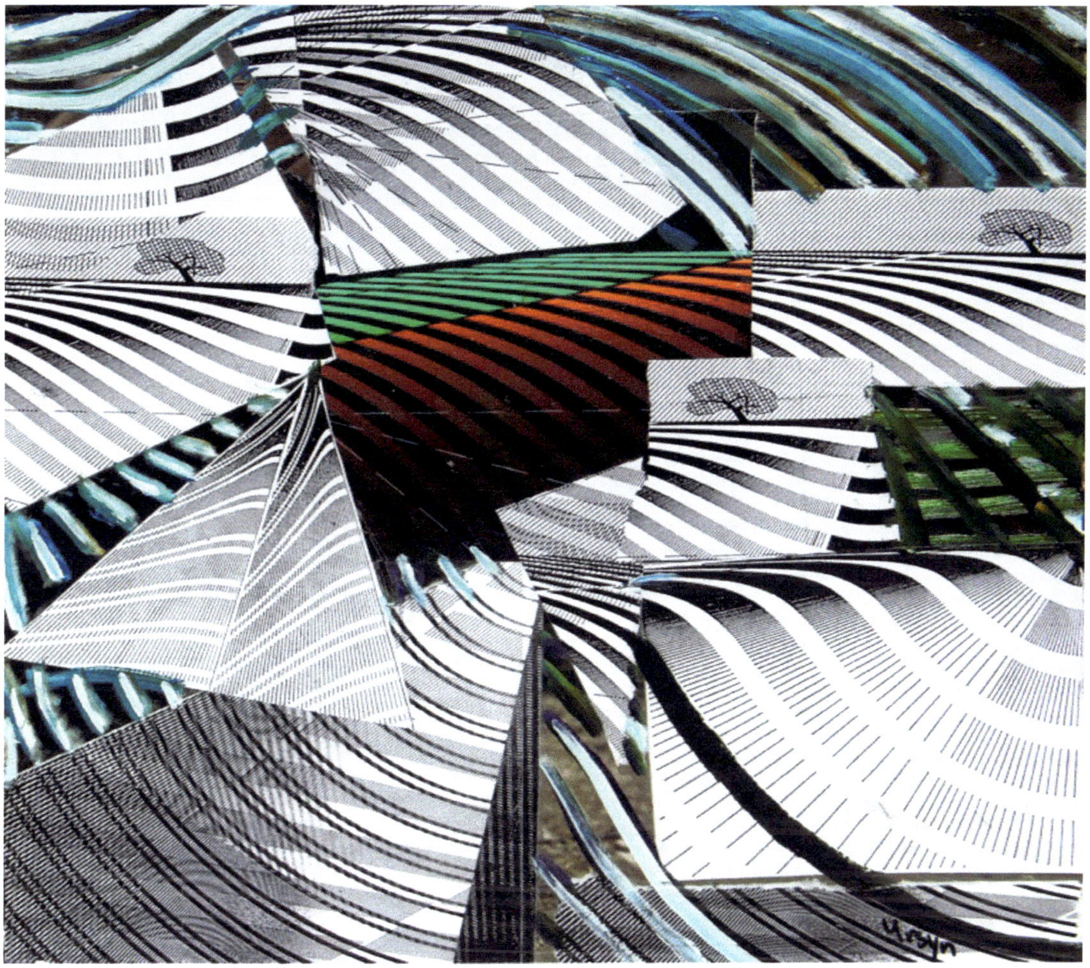

Folds and Faults. © *2025 by Anna Ursyn*

CHAPTER 17
GEO CODE

A DINNER CONVERSATION

INTRODUCTION

Geography, Geography, Geometry, Geophysics, Geopolitics, and Gene Expression Omnibus (GEO) are some disciplines related to our planet's conditions. Most of them start with the word "Geo."
Greek geō combines the form of gê the earth.

SYNOPSIS

Various specialists are discussing nature change at the dinner table. They are all vegan; they recycle, bike, and winterize. However, more collaborative efforts could be found. The geopolitician is the host but, as an entertainer, primarily comments on others' suggestions.

SUMMARY

A candlelight supper is held in a room with a large table and crystal chandelier. The chandelier's crystals produce lines related to the content and the codes beyond each story. Participants' facial expressions and body language add to the entertainment following the music played in the background. The discussion is frequently interrupted by short videos showing cutting down a healthy spruce visible through the window and a growing pile of trash in another.

CAST OF CHARACTERS

1. Geographer
2. Geologist
3. Geometer
4. Geophysicist
5. Geopolitician
6. Gene Expression Omnibus Specialist (GEO): A gene expression and RNA methylation profiling specialist who is developing a tool for diagnosing diseases.

STAGE DIRECTIONS

A large table with props and a chandelier above is set in front of the projections of a bay window with videos showing the past, present, and dream future of our planet as it is being discussed.

The Curtain goes up (or opens).

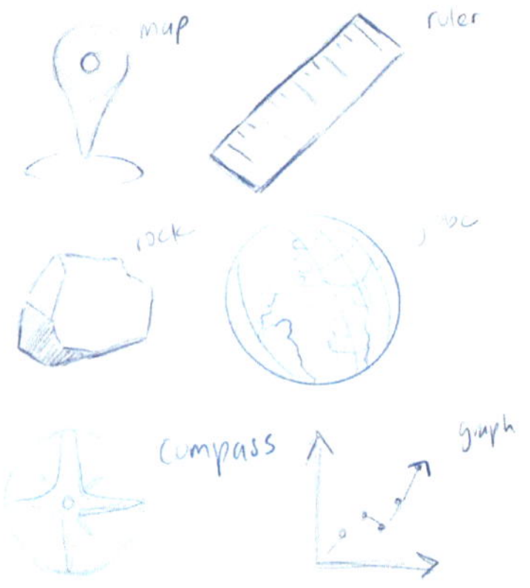

Representations of Geo Professions. © 2025 by Eunice Lee. iArt Institute NYC. (Used with permissions).

Geographer, “Where is the host? The soup is getting cold.“
Geologist, “But our planet is getting warmer.”
Geographer, “And colder as well. Unfortunately.”
Geophysicist, ”What is the temperature in this room set up to? 55 Fahrenheit?”
Geographer, ” We need to take care of our planet. Geography plays a crucial role in preventing unwanted weather changes. It provides insights into how the Earth's natural systems function and how human activities impact the environment.“

Geopolitician shows up.

Geopolitician, "Sorry for being late. I biked to get here. Luckily, we still have daylight. Please, let's start with my vegetable soup. The ingredients came from various safe places. Geography helps prevent unwanted events by understanding gases absorbing infrared radiation, rising temperatures, and extreme weather events. It also helps find the right ingredients for important meetings. It can also help determine where to get the proper vittles from, which I provided for this important meeting."
Geographer, "We map areas most vulnerable to impacts, such as coastal regions, low-lying areas, and regions with scarce water resources."
Geopolitician, "Yes, we should reduce water waste as water is a precious resource that is becoming increasingly scarce in many parts of the world. Take shorter showers, fix leaks, and use water-efficient appliances. We add silver to fabrics to wash them less often."
Geographer, "We track environmental changes and assess their impact on the weather patterns. Geography helps promote stable development by analyzing the relationship between human societies and the environment and to minimize environmental harm while supporting economic growth."

A tree cutting out of the window interrupts the Geographer's speech.

Geopolitician, "Choose renewable energy sources like solar, wind, and hydropower to reduce gas emissions. Consider installing solar panels at home or work and support renewable energy initiatives. We must support policies and initiatives encouraging renewable energy."
Geologist, "Geography can raise awareness about the causes and effects of the weather-related disasters and promote behavior change towards preserving lifestyles."
Geopolitician, "Geologists can study the geological record to understand how the Earth's weather has changed over time and how natural processes such as volcanic activity and changes in solar radiation have influenced these changes."
Geologist, "We can identify natural sources of gases absorbing infrared radiation, such as methane hydrates, and help understand their impact on the environment."
Geographer, "So cold in here."
Geopolitician, "I thought of getting you warmer by providing hot soup."

A tree-cutting sound interrupts the Geopolitician's speech.

Gene Expression Omnibus Specialist, "Geologists can capture carbon dioxide emissions from power plants and other sources and store them underground."
Geopolitician, "The biggest contributor to bad weather events is the emission of gases absorbing infrared radiation, primarily carbon dioxide. Reduce your carbon footprint by driving less, using public transportation, carpooling, biking, walking, using energy-efficient appliances and light bulbs, turning off electronics when not in use, and eating less meat. This made me get late here. My apologies again."
Geographer, "Your 3D printed vegetarian meat is delicious."
Geopolitician, "Thank you, I got inspired by this company in Spain: https://www.youtube.com/watch?v=Behga6AnyyQ "

A sound of an airplane interrupts the Geographer's speech.

Geologist, "3D printers are dirtying our planet."
Geometer continues, "And they can identify and monitor carbon sequestration sites, such as geological formations, where carbon dioxide can be stored safely and permanently."
Geopolitician, "Agriculture is a major contributor to harmful gas emissions, primarily through fossil fuels and methane production from livestock. Support preserving agriculture practices that reduce emissions and promote soil health."

A tree-cutting sound interrupts the Geopolitician's speech.

Geopolitician, "Plant trees in your yard, neighborhood, or community: Trees absorb carbon dioxide and other gases absorbing infrared radiation from the atmosphere. You can also support reforestation efforts and the protection of forests and other natural habitats."

A tree-cutting sound interrupts the Geopolitician's speech.

Geometer, "It all comes down to recycling, not wasting."
Geopolitician, "Yes, indeed. We are using the plates and drinking cups from other meetings."
Gene Expression Omnibus Specialist, "Geologists check for environmental risks in renewable energy, like geothermal and hydroelectric power."
Geologist, "Geologists, geopoliticians, and geophysicists all play a role in addressing unwanted circumstances in our environment. Geologists study natural processes and evaluate carbon capture technologies, geopoliticians focus on emissions reductions and clean energy investments, and geophysicists analyze data to predict future events. They work together to reduce harmful gas emissions and mitigate their environmental impact."
Geometer, "Geologists can aid in renewable energy development by identifying areas with high potential for wind and solar power and designing systems to capture and store that energy."

A roof construction sound interrupts the Geologist's speech.

Geographer, "Geophysicists study the high temperature's impact on natural systems like glaciers, permafrost, and oceans. They develop strategies to protect and preserve them."
Gene Expression Omnibus Specialist, "Geophysicists educate the public about the role that humans play in causing it and raise awareness about the need for action to prevent changes."
Geophysicist, "We study the Earth's physical systems, monitor gas emissions that are harmful to the environment, develop renewable energy sources, assess the impact of severe weather events on natural systems, and educate."
Geometer, "Geopolitics affects relationships and changes the international political atmosphere. It connects politics with geography, explaining how geographical and other factors such as weather patterns, natural resources, terrain, and borders influence the behavior of organizations in their interactions."
Geographer, "Geopolitics studies how geography affects power, resources, politics, and economics, and which states achieve their goals and influence others."
Geopolitician, "Learn about the causes and impacts of current events of a disastrous weather and share that knowledge with others. Encourage friends, family, and colleagues to act and advocate it."
Gene Expression Omnibus Specialist, "We do not even have a definition of our field online. However, Gene Expression Omnibus (GEO) is a public genomics data repository that includes gene expression, epigenetics, and other genomic data types. It is maintained by the National Center for Biotechnology Information, which is part of the National Institute of Health in the US."
Geopolitician, "Disciplines like political science, geography, history, economics, and sociology are crucial for policymakers, diplomats, and military strategists to manage international relations, address security threats, and promote economic development."
Geometer, "The world is always divided. Some people know how it was supposed to be, while others do not, or see it differently."
Geographer, "GEO provides free access to data from international researchers to identify biomarkers and understand disease mechanisms. The data can be searched, downloaded, and analyzed using tools like Python and Bioconductor."
Geopolitician, "GMO-free strawberries from my garden, anyone?"
Geometer, "Reduce waste to curb the harmful to the environment gas emissions. Recycle, compost, and avoid single-use products and packaging."
Geographer, "GEO is useful for genetics, ecology research, and environmental effects."

Geopolitician, "Current set of circumstances requires international cooperation. Support worldwide efforts to reduce emissions and address the impacts of agreements about the environmental issues."
Geologist, "We use GEO data to study the harsh weather‘ impact on organisms, ecosystems, and human health by identifying molecular mechanisms, predicting species adaptation, and analyzing the effects of contamination and toxins on human health.“
Geometer, "Geometry is used to model the shape and size of the Earth, which is important for understanding how heat is distributed across the planet."
Geopolitician, "More tap water, anyone?"
Geometer, "Air travel is a major source of gas emissions that are harmful to the environment. Consider alternatives like video conferencing, taking the revitalized trains, and shorter trips."
Geologist, laughing, "After taking a shorter shower."
Geometer, "Yes, personal hygiene is an important factor in disease control that also can contribute to the situation on the whole Earth, from an exponential growth point of view."
Geographer, "Geospatial analysis can show how a warm weather affects sea ice and wildfires through satellite images."
Geologist, "Models use geometric concepts to represent spatial variables related to weather patterns."
Geometer, "Yes, we all talk about lots of big things, but if we agree to make one small change. Replacing green lawns with yellow ones by not condemning resilient dandelions could benefit the food chain, save resources, and create a beautiful landscape. Yellow is a popular color, and dandelions are cold-resistant and self-populating, turning into a beautiful white geometrical form. Not poisoning them but accepting them as nutritious and tasteful in salads makes an impact!"
Geopolitician, "Next time, we'll invite a geochemist."

The End. The Curtain goes down (or closes).

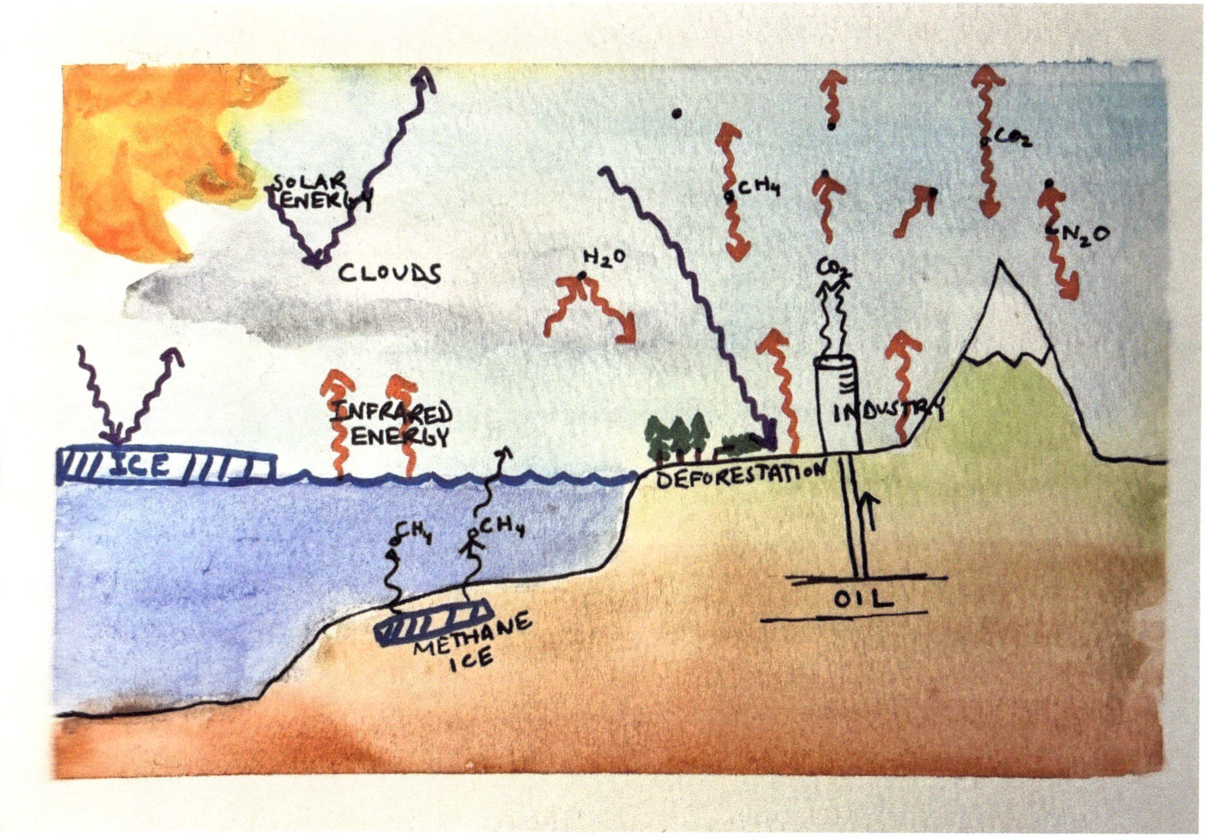

Environmental factors. Watercolor. © 2025 by Lucinda Shellito. (Used with permission).

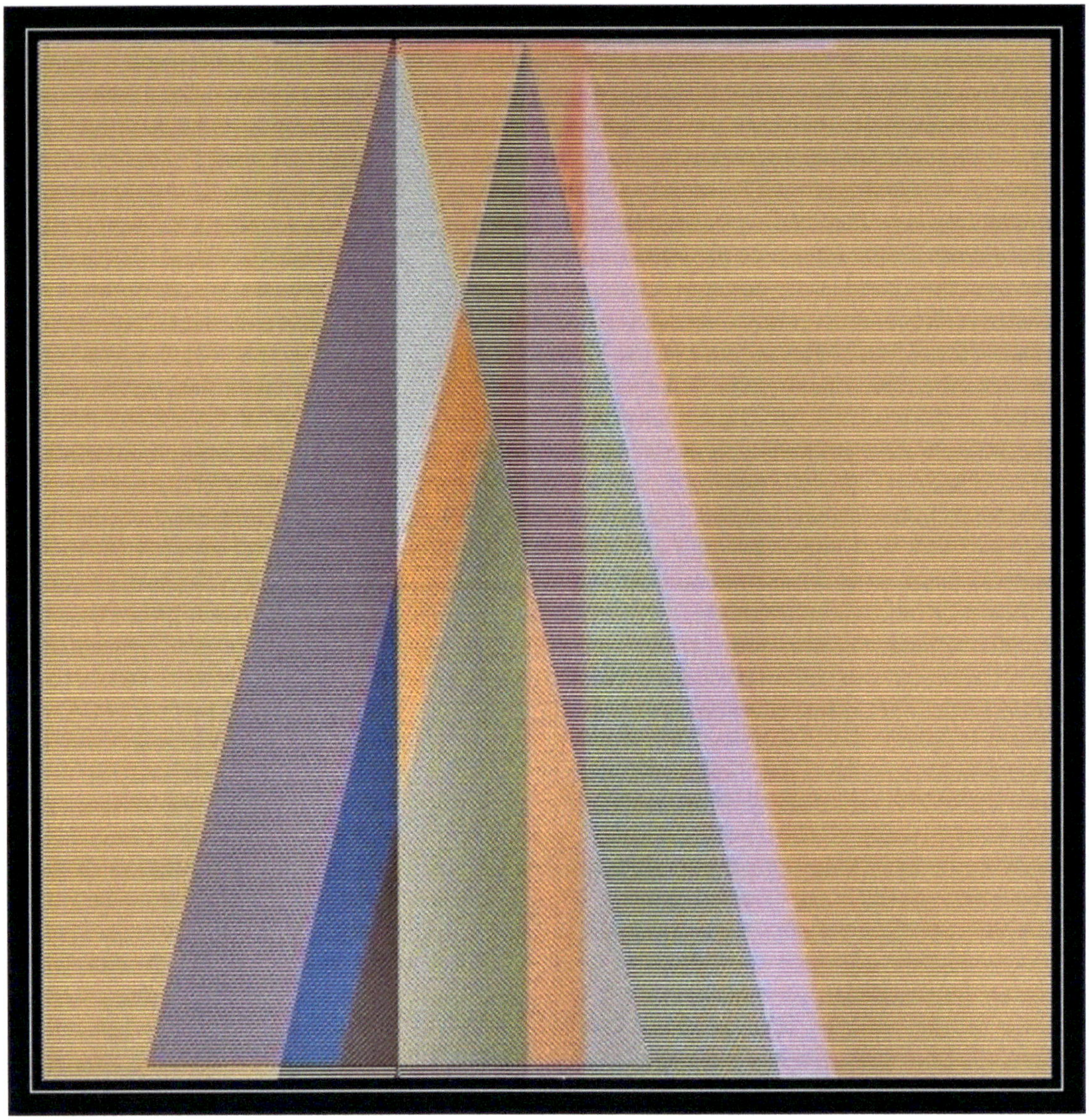

Pointed image #2. Digital image © by Stuart Smith (Used with permission).

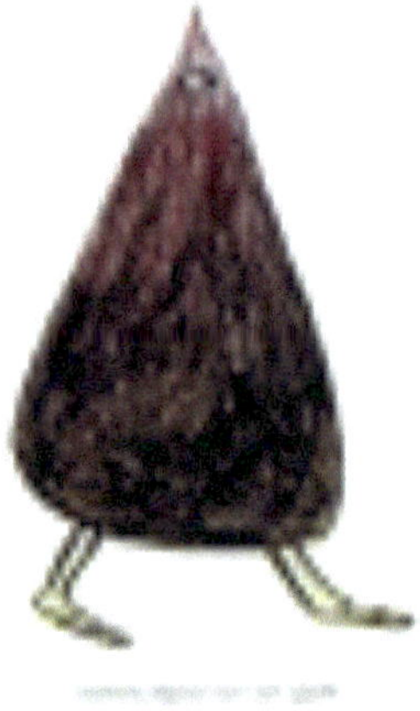

Bulga: known for her decisiveness.

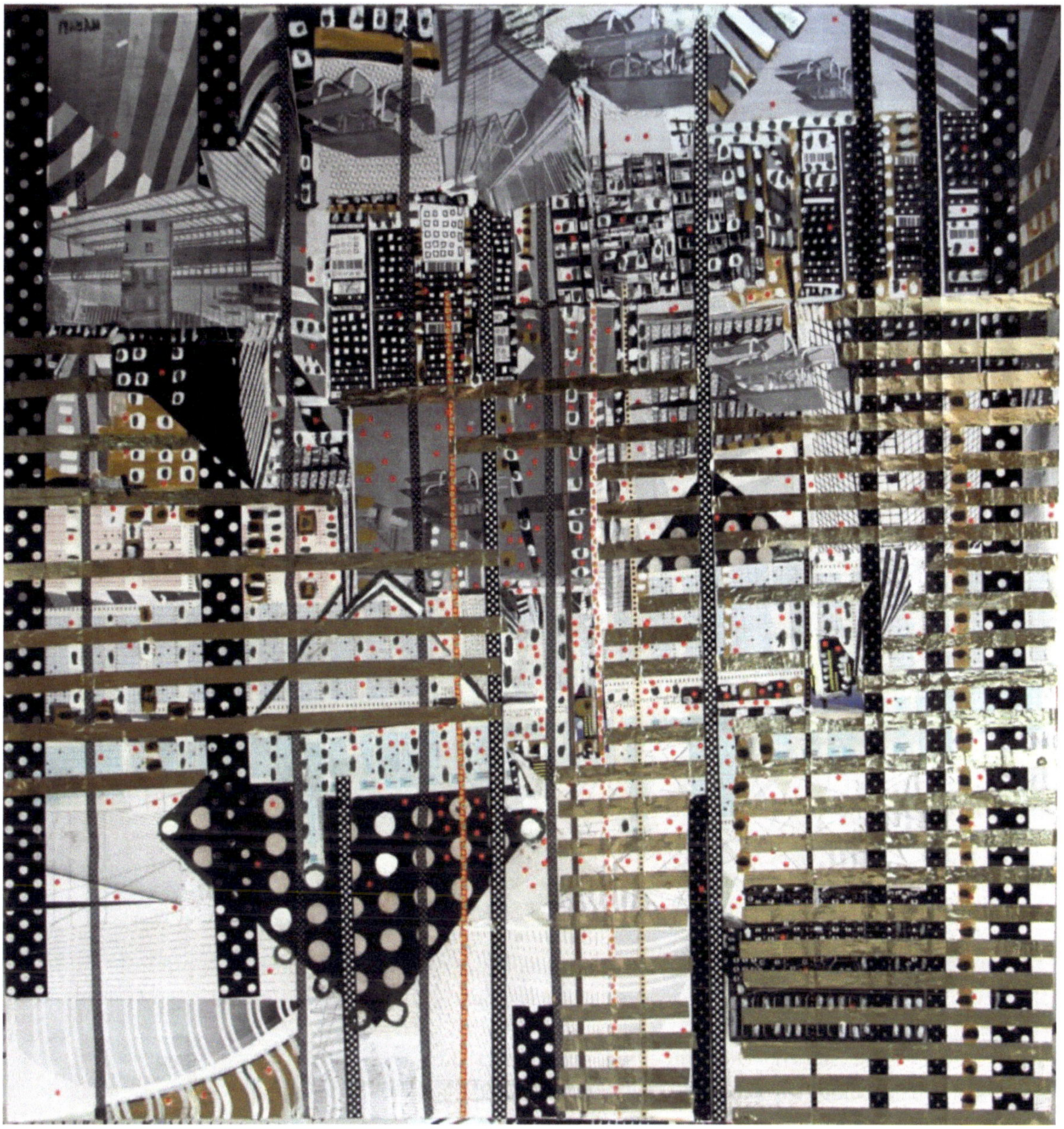

Dot. © *2025 by Anna Ursyn*

CHAPTER 18
MEMORY CODE

A BIRDWATCHING; A WALKING EXCHANGE

INTRODUCTION

We do not fully understand how the human brain or artificial intelligence works. We study memory in all aspects of the meaning of this notion. We depend on it and support it with coded-based operations. We grow, sometimes even without conscious actions. We conquer knowledge, data, and information with all efforts to make it safe, legal, and with positive outcomes by collaboratively applying preventive measures.

SYNOPSIS

Two neighbors are on a birdwatching trip. They are walking together while discussing their knowledge-based experiences. One is a writer, and one is a coder. They are exchanging their interests in cognition, psychology, and physiology, respectively, but they appear well-versed in all those topics.

SUMMARY

This is a bird-watching walk. Nature, shown as a background, illustrates this discussion steering towards emotions as an essential part of our learning process to some comparative analysis of how short- and long-term memory play a role in the human brain and computer work, so they comment on some mental capacities of a human as compared to the computer, such as short- and long-term memory. The landscape in front of them unfolds. The images of various birds depicted differently interact with related videos, juxtaposed with the information presented in visual and text-based ways.

CAST OF CHARACTERS

Albert, the Coder
William, the Writer

STAGE DIRECTIONS

As the two men continue walking and talking during their bird-watching experience, projections of various neighborhoods and the occasional bird appear on the screen. The projections keep changing and cover all four seasons.

`The action happens beyond a specific place and time.`

Act I
The Curtain goes up (or opens).

Albert, "What a day! I cannot stop birdwatching. It is not nice to stare, but it is impossible not to."
William, "Ha, double negative. I'd say, yes, birds are beautiful, fun, and interesting, so I simply have to scrutinize them."
Albert, "It does not carry the same meaning, emotion, or message."
William, "Our learning by observing behaviors of others helps us with our emotions. We try to be positive, but on occasions, we lose it. We try to lower our egocentrism, but we are too self-aware for that. On occasions, I mean. When emotions get to us, for one reason or another, that is."
Albert, "We remember recent actions, events, or experiences, but those related to emotions stay with us longer."
William, "We need to constantly be aware and keep our interests active to make proper choices and selections."
Albert, "Yes, like a person holding *a* social position, we make decisions based on high-level thinking."
William, "This takes the psychomotor speed of reaction, at least."
Albert, "We acknowledge stimuli and react toward them."
William, "Going back to Emotions, we recognize them in others just by looking at their faces and body language. People can do strange things with their faces when they get emotional."
Albert, "Chat GPT reads minds through the functional magnetic resonance imaging."
William, "That is so important for paralyzed people, even though it sounds scary to me."
Albert, "For that, we respond differently to various situations and adapt our thinking and behavior accordingly."

William, "Birds use vocalizations to convey emotions and send alarm calls with specific note combinations to indicate danger. They can also manipulate the emotions of other birds and predators by mimicking voices, such as hissing like a snake or buzzing."

Swims

Flies

Walks

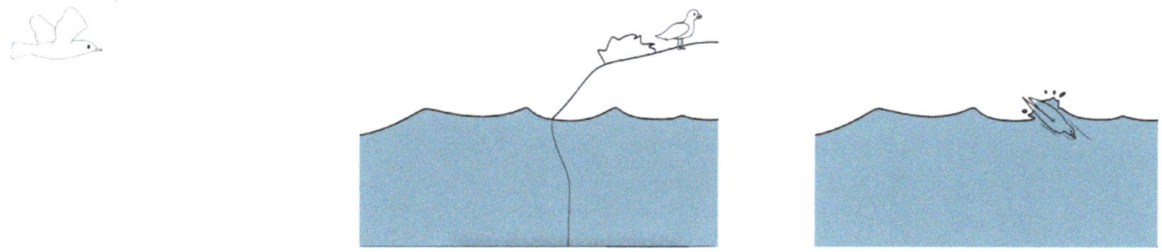

Seagull animation. © 2025 by Evelynn Leung. iArt Institute, NYC. (Used with permissions).

Albert, "Yes, we use strategies by applying our working memory."
William, "When I write, I connect events with their places and times."
Albert, "Yes, I know. Our cognition goes back to our experiences and connects them to time and place; with emotions—sometimes, they even overlap. Places and times, that is. Therefore, some writers start writing by saying, "The thing happens everywhere or nowhere," meaning the action goes beyond time and place.
William, "The Thing. Ha! Never heard of that. My recognition memory is failing me. Are you a writer?"
Albert, "I am also working on recognizing objects, visual, spatial information, and the time-based."
William, "So you need to stay attentive."
Albert, "Yes, constantly thinking when observing, and observing while thinking. One can get used to it."
William, "I live by being careful with stimulus and action, like a game player or a sportsman. Time, effort, and flow are movements for me."
Albert, "We may think differently based on our stimuli. One of us can see the same thing as good, while another considers it bad, which distorts our judgment."
William, "Going back to emotions, again."
Albert, "Knowing that allows us to conquer our obstacles. Intellectual ones, that is."
William," If we can manage our spontaneous responses but in a way to aligns with societal norms."
Albert, "If only we could modify what we keep in our mental heads."
William, "Another bird, oh many of them. I remember how I could not stop myself from staring at them, which is not polite, but some danger of missing their beauty stayed with me and kept me from adjusting my thinking, behaviors, and appearance. Unforgivable."
Albert, "We'll never learn, we humans."

The Break
The curtain goes down (or closes).

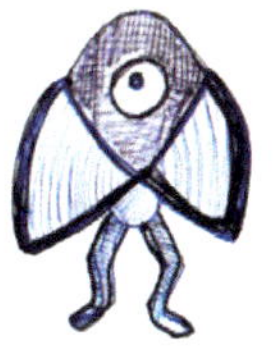

Fugst: always wants to be there.

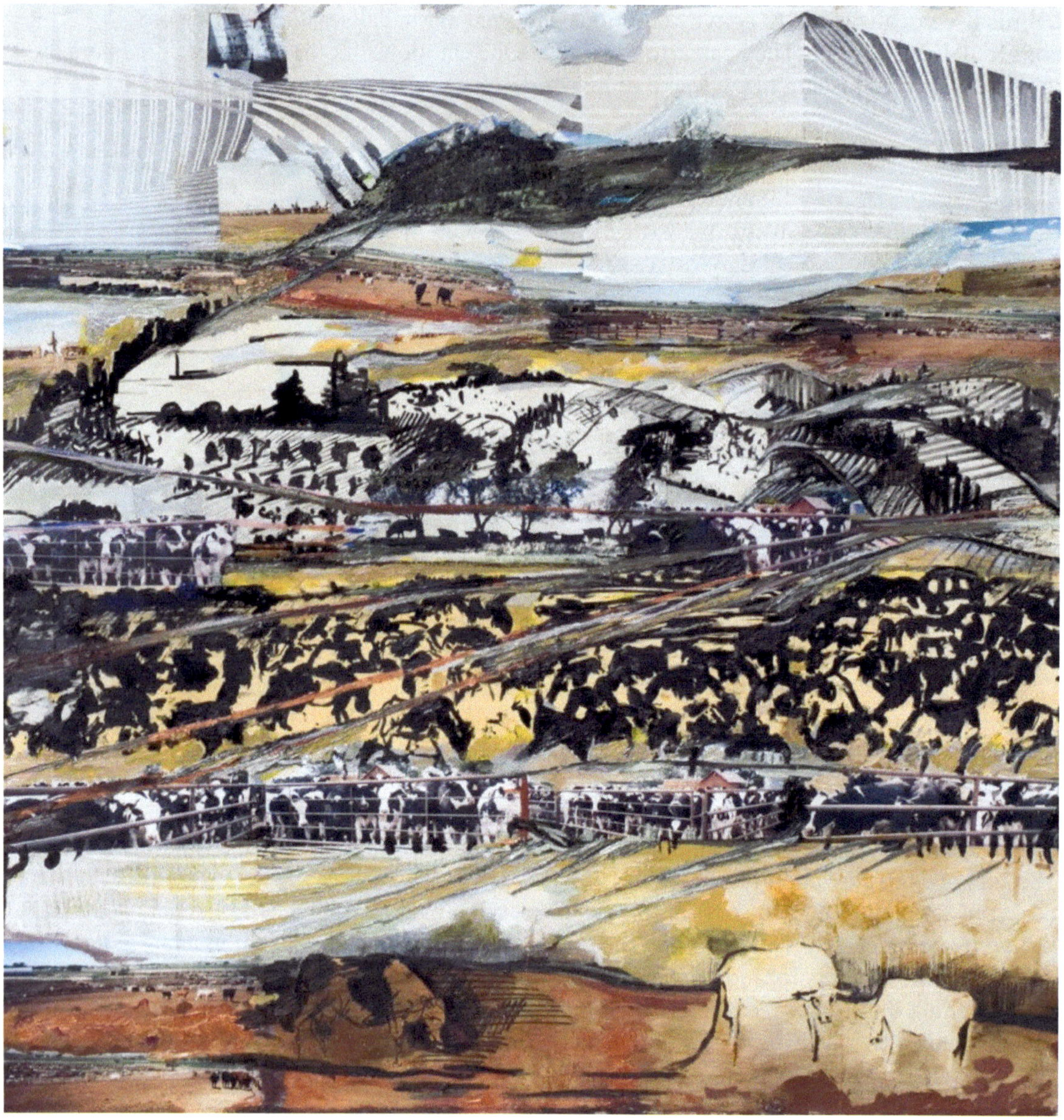

Middleground. © *2025 by Anna Ursyn*

Act II
The curtain goes up (or opens).

Albert, "I think the birds follow the same pattern in their groups without thinking about it. We use Coderbyte – a web application that helps practice programming and coding to recruit high-level thinkers who can collaborate. It's challenging to find introverted individuals who think differently but can work with others."
William, "Oh, yes, there is a book called *Quiet* by Susan Cain. She defends introverts and sees them as an important part of human growth."
Albert continues, "Thus, we create a team of the interviewer and the interviewee to work on challenging tasks and answers to get the guesswork out. We want them to be smart, creative, independent, but still working as a group."
William, "Where are we?"
Albert, "On a bird-watching walk."

William, "The roses show all stages of their development."
Albert, "One could make a time-lapsed video in one day!"
William, "We use critical cognitive processes involved in planning, organizing, initiating, monitoring, and adapting to goal-directed behavior. Programmers break down complex problems into smaller tasks, prioritize them, and monitor progress toward the goal. Also, switching between tasks helps to change requirements and identify and correct errors in one's code. The executive function allows coders to manage complex coding projects well."
Albert, "Good coding requires both short-term and long-term memory storage for efficient programming. Coders develop strategies to transfer information and improve their skills."
William, "Birds have a group memory, as I recall."
Albert, "There are several ways that our attention can be applied in coding:

- Focus on the task in a coding project.
- Manage complex, demanding codes with multiple files, libraries, and frameworks.
- Stress central information to be more productive for better codes and outcomes."
- Ignore distractions and correct errors; even minor typos create significant problems."

William, "Those with strong psychomotor speed skills type codes more accurately, faster, and with less time spent on debugging it. Good coders use keyboard shortcuts and think abstractly and logically to speed up their workflow and solve problems effectively."
Albert, "Computer programs recognize events and inputs and take appropriate actions. They can be written in different programming languages and are used in many applications."
William, "So in a user interface program, detecting the presence of a mouse click or keyboard input is essential in responding to user interaction."
Albert, "Yes, and similarly, in a security system, detecting the presence of an intruder or unauthorized access attempt is critical for responding appropriately and preventing harm."
William, "Detecting and responding to a stimulus involves creating a series of statements or rules that define the conditions under which the program should take specific actions. "
Albert, "Stimulus detection and response is crucial in coding for intelligent, interactive systems."
William, "Emotion recognition, also known as affective computing, uses computer algorithms to detect human emotions from facial expressions and vocal intonations through machine learning and computer vision techniques."
Albert, "Facial expression recognition analyzes features such as eyebrows, eyes, nose, and mouth to identify emotions such as happiness, sadness, anger, surprise, fear, and disgust."
William," Yes, those are basic internationally recognized emotions."
Albert, "In coding, emotion recognition uses a variety of programming languages such as Python, Java, or C++. Many machine learning frameworks and libraries provide pre-trained models for facial expression recognition that can be integrated into applications."
William, "Emotion recognition is used in healthcare, marketing, and human-computer interaction. We can diagnose mental health conditions by analyzing facial expressions in patients. It may also measure customer satisfaction in retail environments or enhance the user experience in gaming and virtual reality applications."
Albert, "Mental flexibility is crucial in coding to adapt to changing requirements, technologies, and user needs. Programmers must be able to adjust to new tools, frameworks, and languages as the technology landscape evolves."
William, "Programmers can improve their skills with code refactoring, which optimizes existing code. They can also engage in pair programming or collaborative coding by working with other programmers to share knowledge and perspectives and learn from each other's approaches."
Albert, " Exactly. Well said. Moreover, programmers use functions for clean and maintainable software or event-driven programming, with a stream of events (often used in graphical user interfaces) that responds to actions (mouse clicks, key presses, sensor outputs, to develop mental flexibility and enable programmers to approach problems from different angles."

William, "In summary, mental flexibility allows them to adapt to changing technology, approaching problems from different perspectives and innovative solutions."
Albert, "And our working memory is important in keeping track of variables, functions, and data structures while working on a task or solving a problem."
William, "To improve it, programmers divide complex tasks into smaller ones."
Albert, "By doing this, they can focus their working memory on one task at a time to avoid becoming overwhelmed by the complexity of the overall problem."
William, "Use mnemonics or mental associations to remember critical concepts by using acronyms or visual imagery to clearly order function arguments or the structure of complex data types. Also, use flowcharts, diagrams, or pseudocode, a detailed algorithm description, to reduce the working memory load by visually representing the problem and the solution and free up their working memory for other tasks."
Albert, "As a coder, I can say that episodic memory, as a type of long-term memory, refers to recalling specific events or details of my coding work. To improve episodic memory, associate each event with a place and time. I can also use comments in my code to remember choices later, or to describe a part of the code, or when sharing my code."
William, "Visual recognition in coding involves identifying patterns and structures within code. Diagrams and flowcharts can aid in problem-solving."
William, "Recognition memory, a cognitive process in life and in coding, involves identifying and remembering visual, object, and spatial information in code. So, practice regularly, use consistent naming conventions, and make comments."
Albert, "The web application measures the speed of user's inputs, such as clicks or keystrokes. "
William, "Look, the bird just took off. Let's go slower."
Albert, "Movement time and vigilance are cognitive psychology and neuroscience concepts, not coding. Movement time can be relevant in programming when designing user interfaces or interactions."
William, "So, vigilance is important in systems that require sustained attention, like monitoring or automated processes. We design them to minimize errors and provide clear feedback."
Albert, "Designing interfaces and algorithms for affective information, we consider emotional bias. For example, social media platforms can use machine learning to present stimuli based on users' emotional states."
William, "So, the user experience changes the system's effectiveness to achieve its goals."
Albert, "Besides software development, a programmer plans how to store and retrieve data for optimizing the performance of an algorithm in certain scenarios."
William, "Response inhibition is important for user interface development, algorithm design, and software testing to focus on critical data and suppress irrelevant information."
Albert, "Controlling responses is crucial for programmers to create adaptable systems. Working memory is important for efficiency, accuracy, and creativity in coding."
Albert, "The truth is brutal, and people cover it with other issues, which some call hypocrisy."
William, "I remember now; we came for this walk to observe the birds."

The End. The Curtain goes down (or closes).

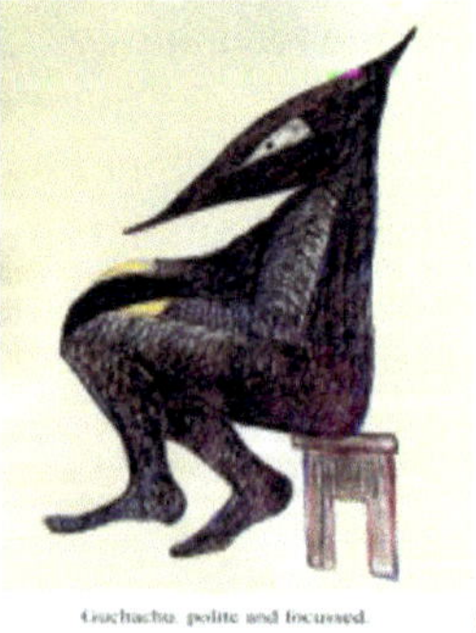

Guchachu: polite and focused.

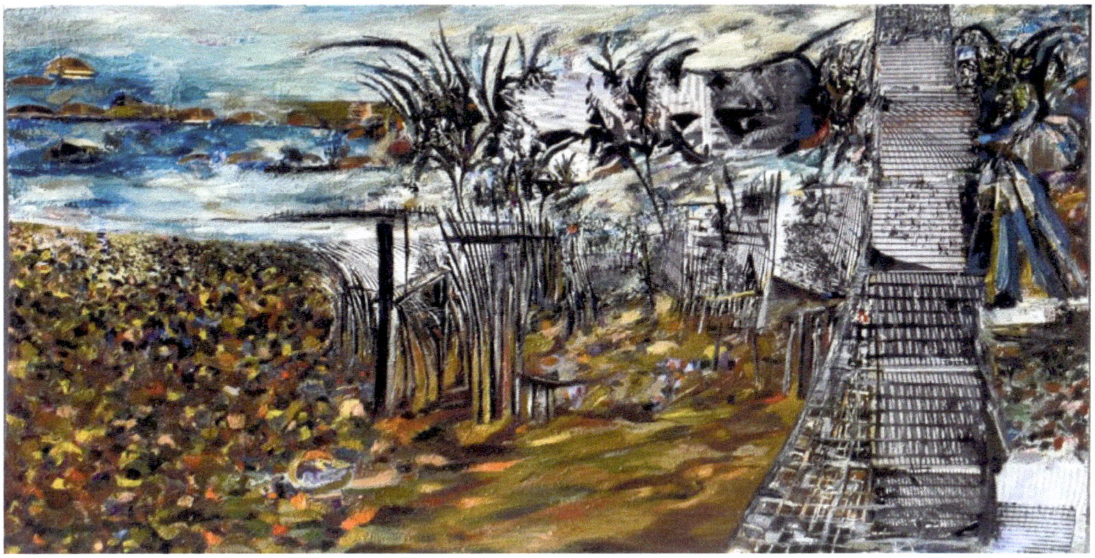

Human Nature Takes Over. © 2025 by Anna Ursyn

CHAPTER 19
HEART CODE

TOLD AND ILLUSTRATED FROM THE RATS' PERSPECTIVE

INTRODUCTION

We developed some standards related to various animals. We categorize, group, and treat them according to generally accepted rules. Rats are considered dirty, harmful, and seen as pests. They are also valuable for med heart, learnability, and adaptability. People see the word 'rat' as having negative connotations. At the same time, black-hooded rats proved to be excellent pets and companions. Thus, people learned to make some mental switch from pests to pets.

SYNOPSIS

Two rats share their stories, needs, and connections visually. A Greek tragedy-style choir of 'More Rats' comments on the action while disclosing anatomy-related concepts.
This choir states that individuals who are different or focused on their work often receive undeserved treatment from those who do not pay attention.

SUMMARY

Various views on the rats are discussed. Anna Ursyn's sketches of black-hooded pet rats © 2025 illustrate this work.

CAST OF CHARACTERS

The Rat
The Other Rat
More Rats (a Greek tragedy-style choir) comment on the action and anatomy-related concepts.
Two Mice

STAGE DIRECTIONS

The background switches different animals and their habitats, disclosing codes and following the musical cords and compositions.

```
The action happens beyond place and time.
```

Act I
The Curtain goes up (or opens).

The Rat, "Humans created rules based on categorizing and grouping animals and treat rats according to generally accepted rules. We are considered dirty and seen as pests, only useful for medical or psychological research for traits: heart, learnability, and adaptability. For many people, the word 'rat' has negative connotations. At the same time, we, the black-hooded rats, proved to be excellent pets and companions. Because of that, people learned to make some mental switch from pests to pets, and since then, they have learned to see us, the black hooded rats, as beautiful and enjoyable."
The Other Rat, "Mammals, birds, and crocodilians have four-chambered hearts like humans, while some reptiles have a partial four-chambered heart. Fish have two-chambered hearts, and insects have an open circulatory system. Although rat and human hearts have similar anatomy and function, size, heart rate, and lifespan differences reflect their physiological needs."
The Rat, "Our heart is much smaller than a human's. On average, it weighs only a few grams, while a human heart can weigh up to 300 grams or more. The rat and human heart have four chambers: two atria and two ventricles. However, the shape and proportion of the chambers may differ slightly between the two species. The heart rate of rats is much faster than that of humans. While a human's resting heart rate is typically between 60 and 100 beats per minute, a rat's heart can range from 250 to 450 beats per minute. Rats have a much shorter lifespan than humans, and their hearts age more quickly."
The Other Rat, "Here's an example Python code that compares the heartbeat of a rat to a human's heartbeat:

```
# Importing required libraries
import numpy as np
import matplotlib.pyplot as plt

# Defining the heart rates
human_heart_rate = 60 # Beats per minute
rat_heart_rate = 400  # Beats per minute

# Generating the time vector for 30 seconds
time = np.linspace(0, 30, 300)

# Generating the signal for human's heartbeat
human_signal = np.sin(2*np.pi*human_heart_rate*time/60)

# Generating the signal for rat's heartbeat
rat_signal = np.sin(2*np.pi*rat_heart_rate*time/60)

# Plotting the signals
plt.plot(time, human_signal, label='Human Heartbeat')
plt.plot(time, rat_signal, label='Rat Heartbeat')
plt.xlabel('Time (seconds)')
plt.ylabel('Amplitude')
plt.title('Comparison of Heartbeats')
plt.legend()
plt.show()
```

More Rats, "This code generates two signals representing the heartbeat of a human and a rat, respectively. The signals are then plotted on a graph to visualize the differences between the two heart rates. In this example, the human heart rate is 60 beats per minute, while the rat heart rate is 400 beats per minute."

The Other Rat: "Pig hearts are similar to human hearts in size, weight, and function. Both have four chambers and four heart valves. In medical research, pig hearts are often used to study heart disease and develop treatments. Due to their similarities with human hearts, they are valuable for transplantation studie*s."*

More Rats, "Luckily, we are too small for that!"

The Other Rat, "There is more. The term 'code rat' is slang in coding and computer science, referring to a programmer who is very passionate and dedicated to coding and spends long hours working on coding."

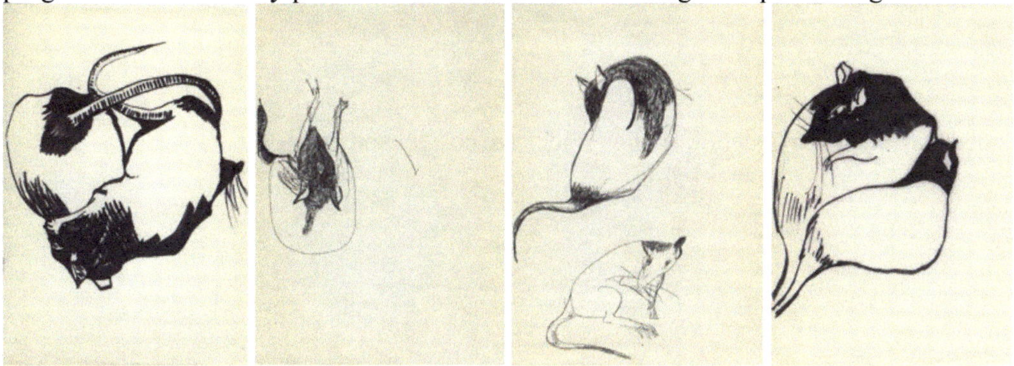

The Rat, "This term is not widely used or recognized in the industry, and it's generally not considered a professional or appropriate term for programmers or developers."

More Rats, "They treat themselves like they treat us."

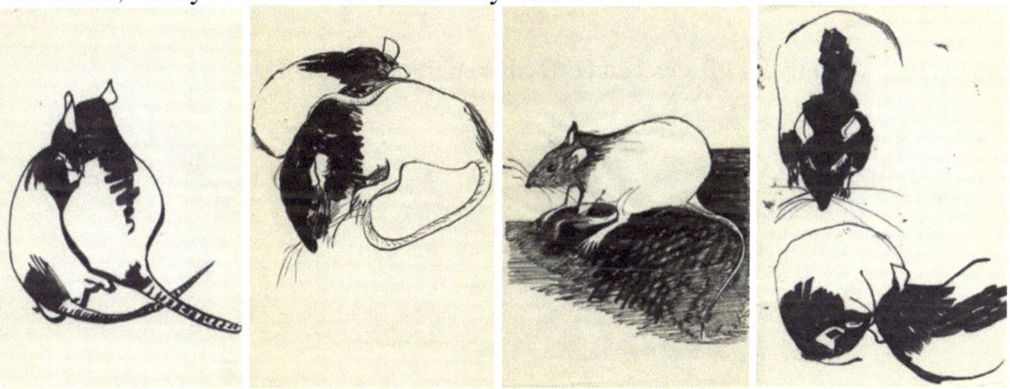

The Other Rat, "Maintaining a healthy work-life balance and effective communication with the team is crucial for the best outcomes, whether you're a coder, a rat, or a human."

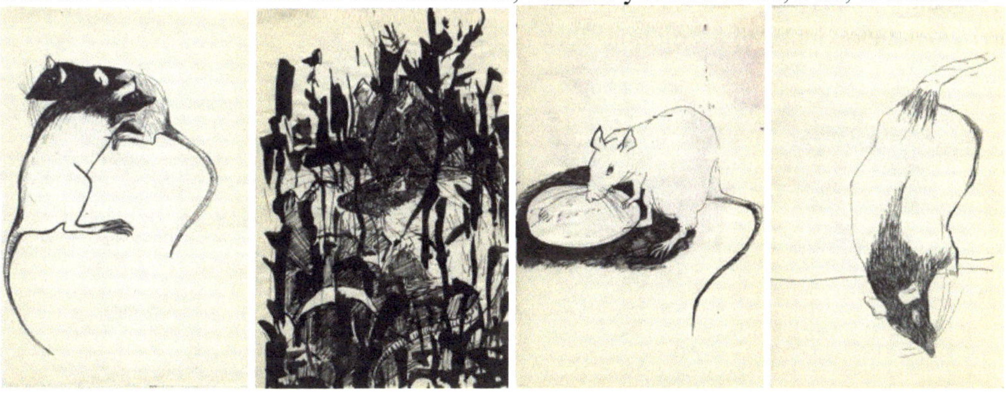

The Rat, "Coders pose problem-solving skills and are adept at breaking down complex problems into smaller, manageable tasks that can be solved using algorithms and code. Just like we do it."

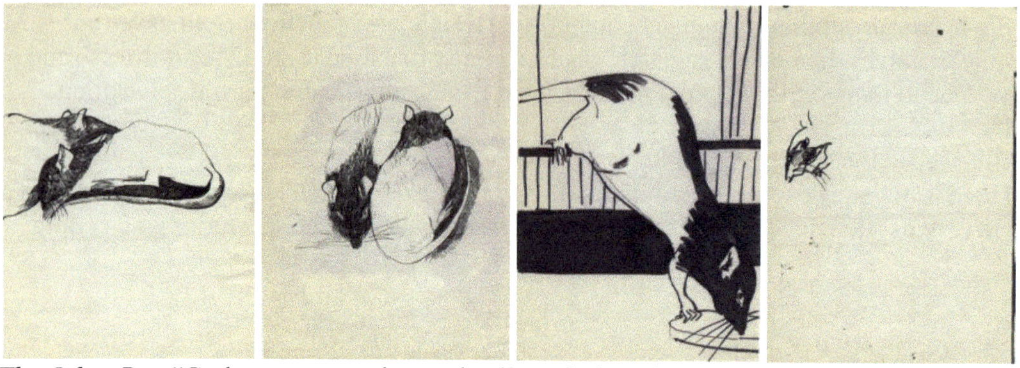

The Other Rat, “Coders pay attention to detail, so their codes are correct and error-free.”

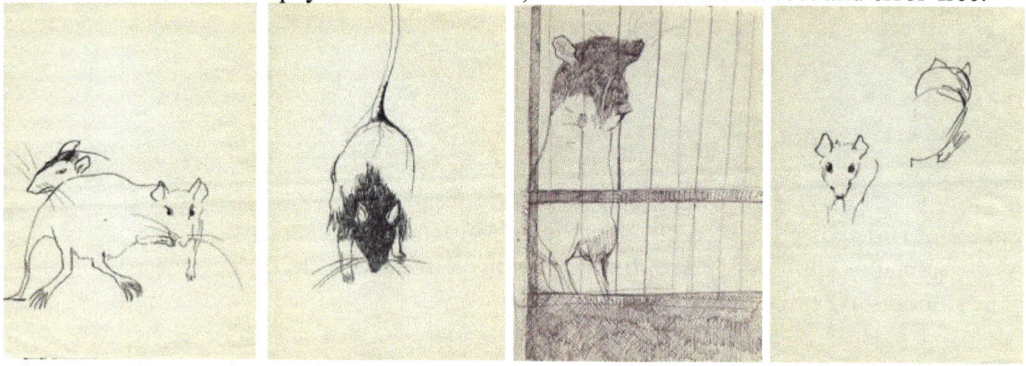

The Rat, “They need to think logically for efficient and effective solutions to problems.”

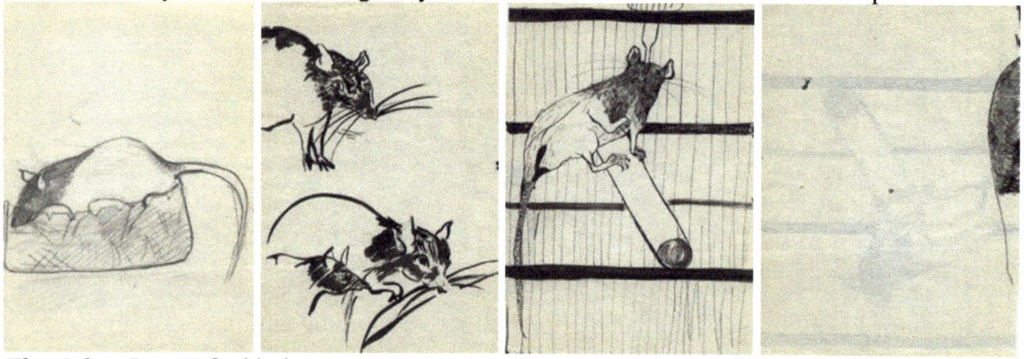

The Other Rat, “I feel being creative. Although coding requires logical thinking, one has to be creative to develop innovative solutions to problems.”

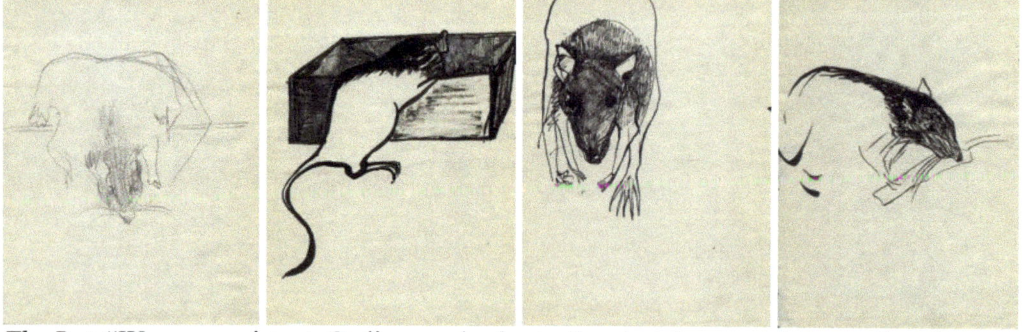

The Rat, “We are persistent. Coding can be frustrating, but those persistent and patient, willing to spend hours or even days debugging their code until it works win.”

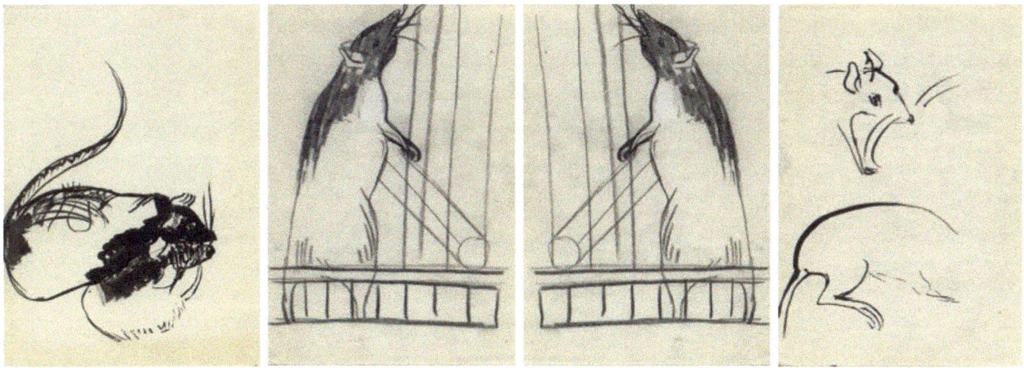

The Other Rat, "Good communication skills are crucial for us. Coders work as teams. Thus, like they are, we need to communicate clearly and effectively with our colleagues."

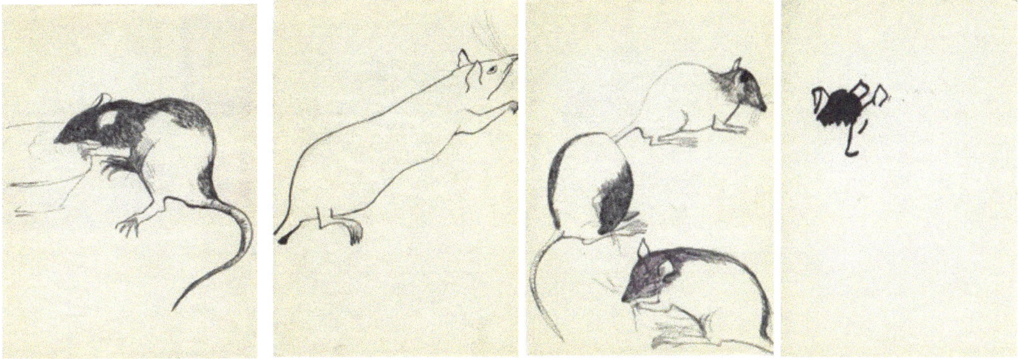

More Rats, "We can learn, all right. The ability to learn new technologies and programming languages is essential. Coders are flexible about what emerges."

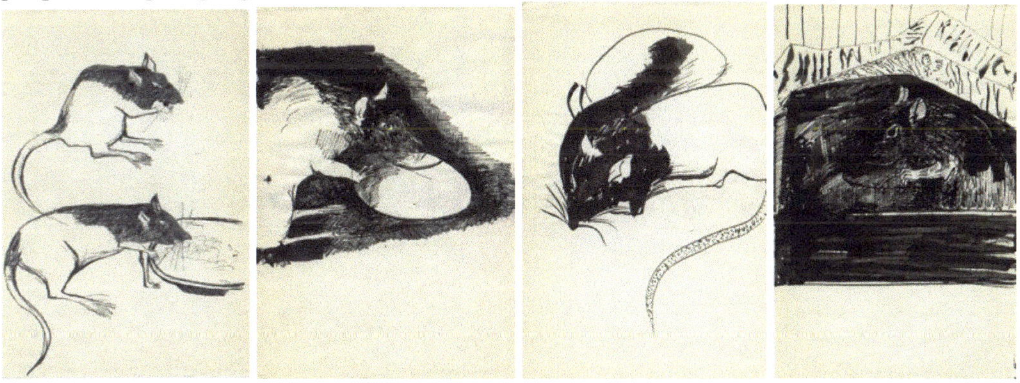

The Rat, "We love comfort with ambiguity. Coding involves dealing with complex and ambiguous problems, so be comfortable working in this kind of environment."

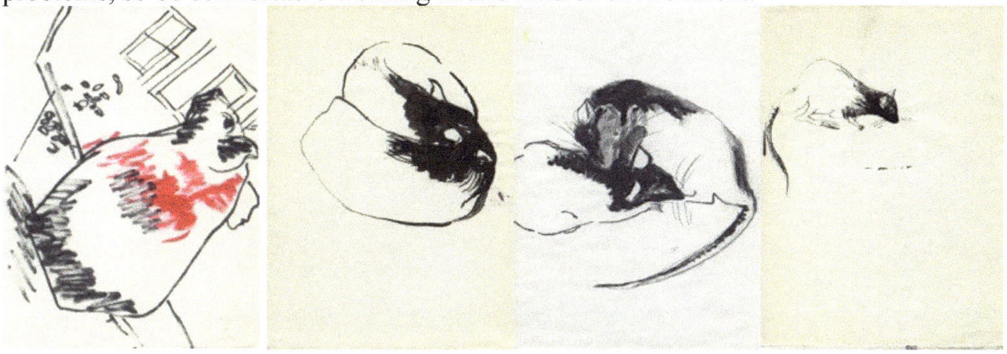

The Other Rat, "We possess analytical skills. We solve problems fast. Coding requires data analysis and information to identify patterns and insights for effective solutions."

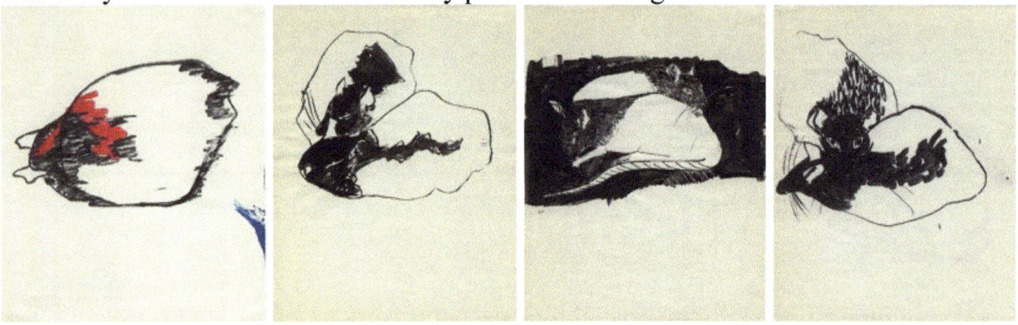

The Rat, Perfectionism is our thing. Coders often strive for perfection in their code, ensuring that every detail is just right."

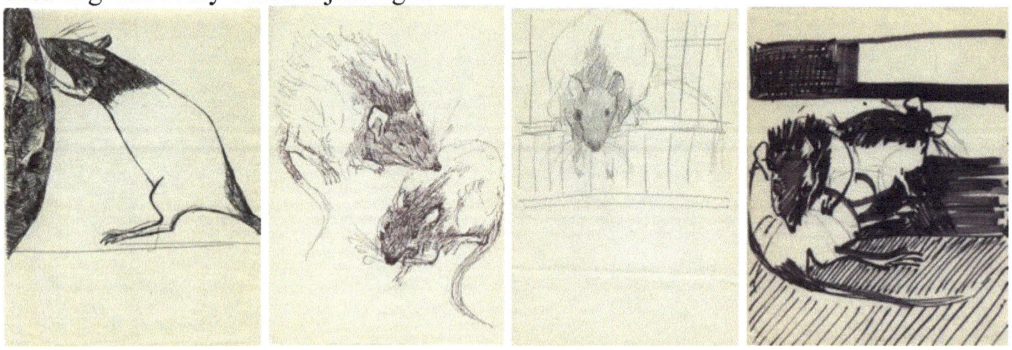

The Other Rat, "The terms 'programmer' and 'coder' are often used interchangeably, but there is a subtle difference between them. I wonder if there is a saying 'program rat'?"

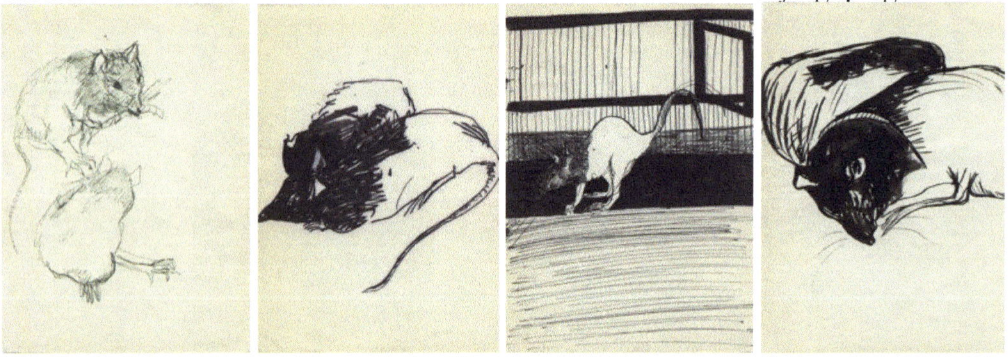

The Rat, "A programmer designs and writes a code for computer software, is responsible for creating codes following specific requirements, testing and debugging them, and maintaining the software with problem-solving skills, logic, and creative solutions."

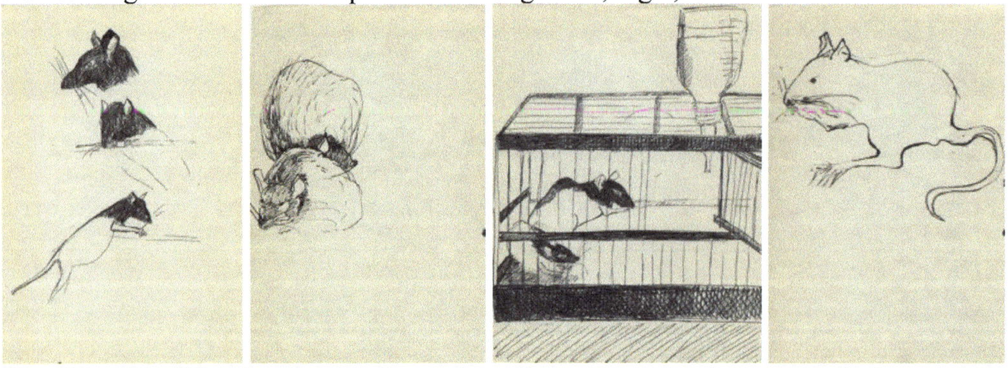

The Other Rat, "On the other hand, a coder writes codes to implement the design created by a programmer without the necessity to structure and develop software. They are responsible for fixing bugs or minor modifications to the existing code."

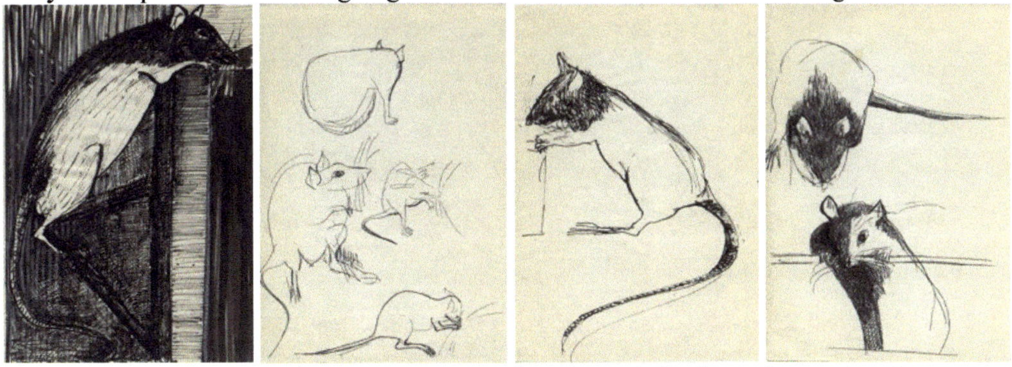

The Rat, "A programmer has a more comprehensive role in the software development process, while a coder is focused on writing code to implement specific functionality. *More Rats*, "However, the terms are often used interchangeably in practice."

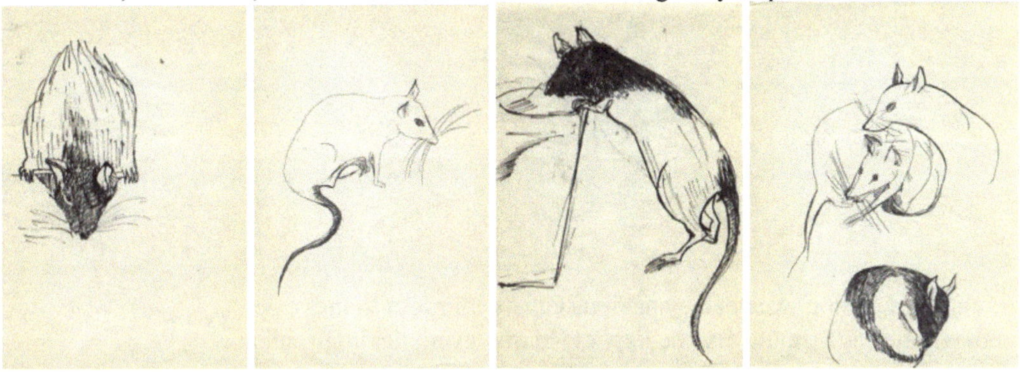

The Other Rat, We, the black-hooded rats, are pets despite our cousins' bad reputation."

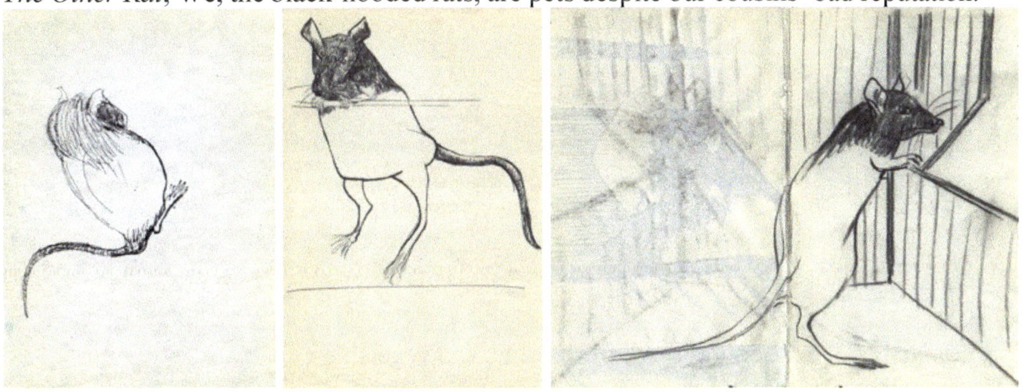

The Rat, "We are friendly, clean, and playful."

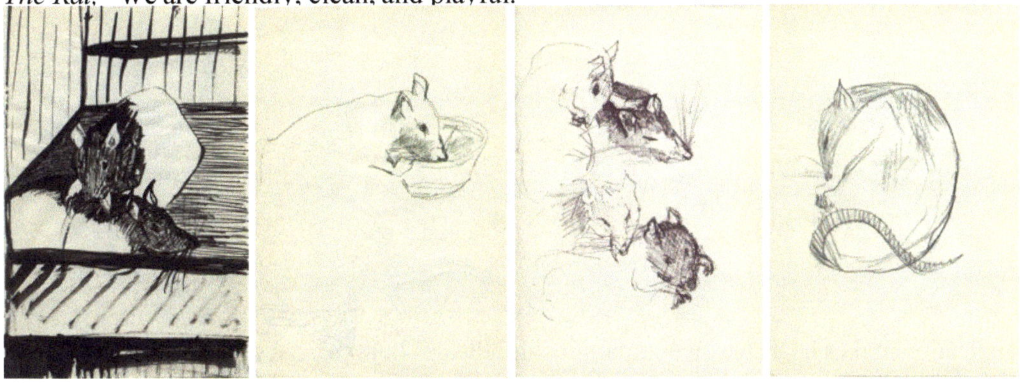

The Other Rat, "While we make excellent pets, it's important to note that pet ownership is a big responsibility and requires much time, effort, and some financial resources. "

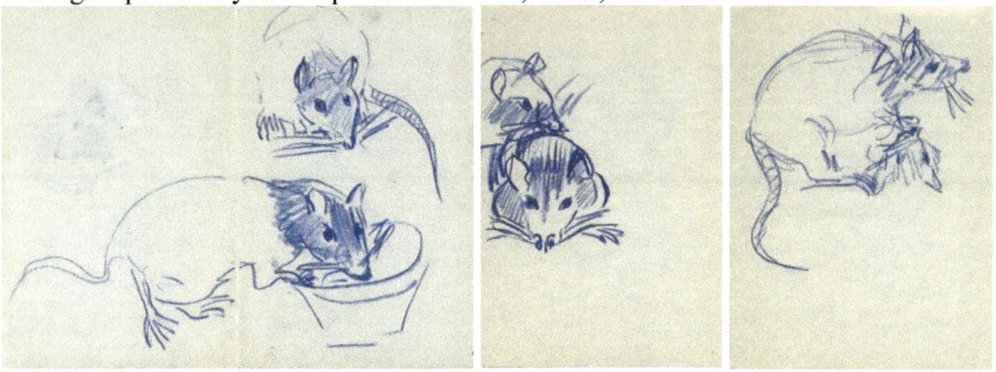

The Rat, "Our life span is typically 2-3 years, so commit to our care."

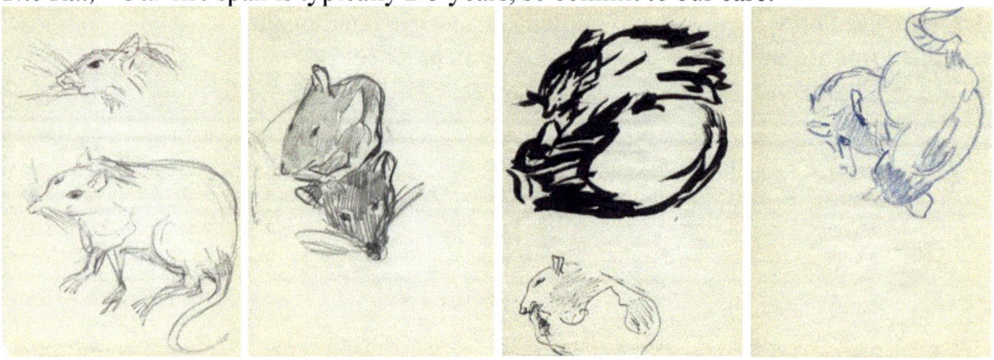

The Other Rat, "As for our housing, we need a spacious cage with room to move around, climb, and play. The cage should also be kept clean to prevent health problems."
More Rats, "Keep the cage open; we always come back!"

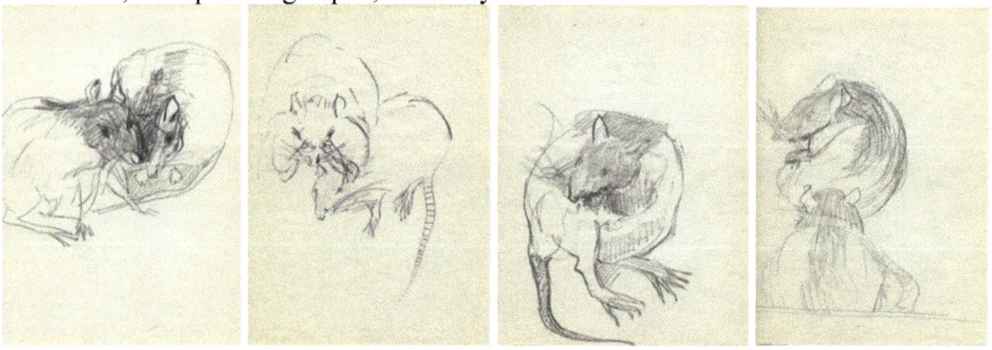

The Other Rat, "We need a diet of a mix of rat food, fresh fruits, and vegetables."
More Rats, "And occasional treats!"

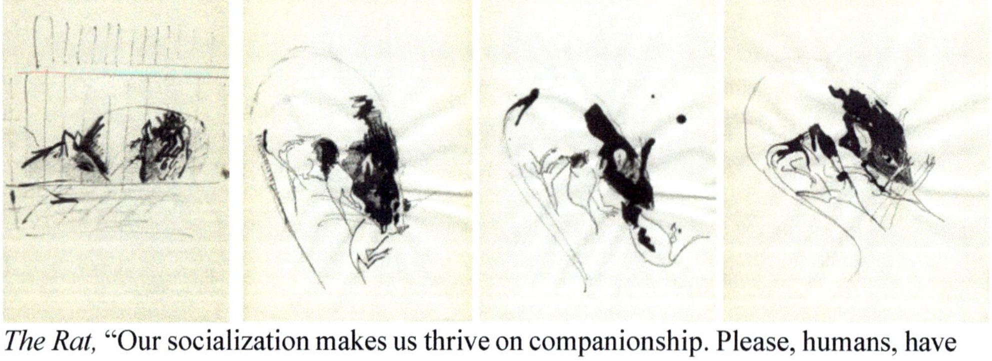

The Rat, "Our socialization makes us thrive on companionship. Please, humans, have

at least two rats so they can keep each other company."
More Rats, "Or, adopt more Rats!"

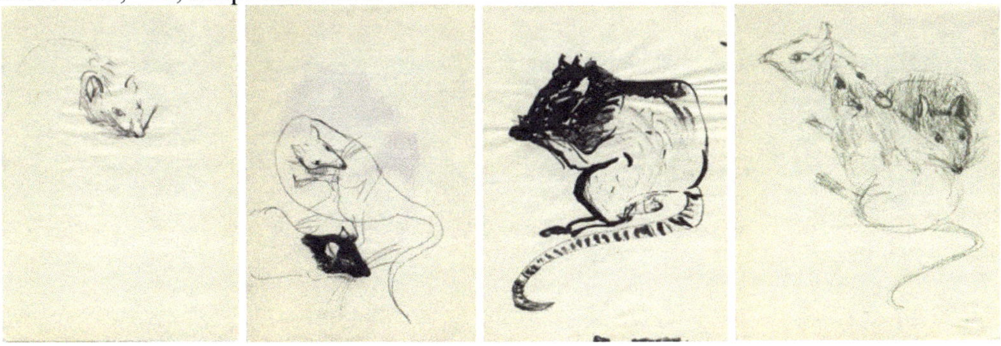

The Other Rat, "Please consider good health care, as we can get sick just like any other pet, so our veterinarian is knowledgeable about rats to provide proper care."

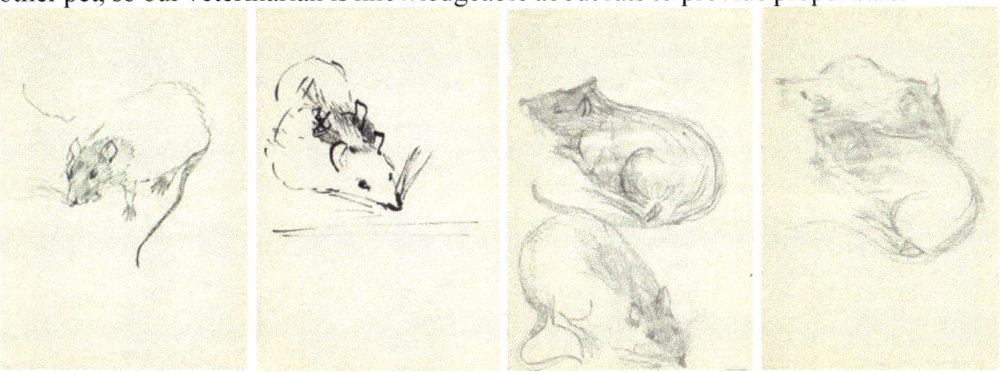

The Rat, "Carefully consider these factors and take on the responsibility of caring for us."
More Rats, "Do the research to provide us with the love and care we need to thrive."

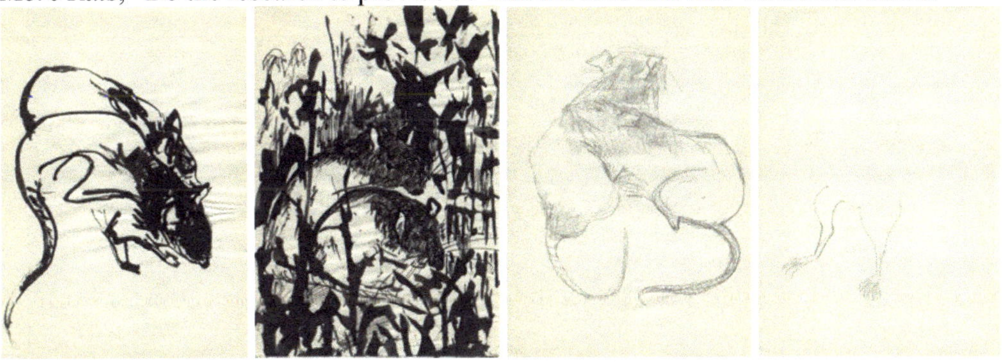

The Other Rat, "There is a Black Hooded Rat Hierarchy."
More Rats, "As for organization, we have a complex social one."

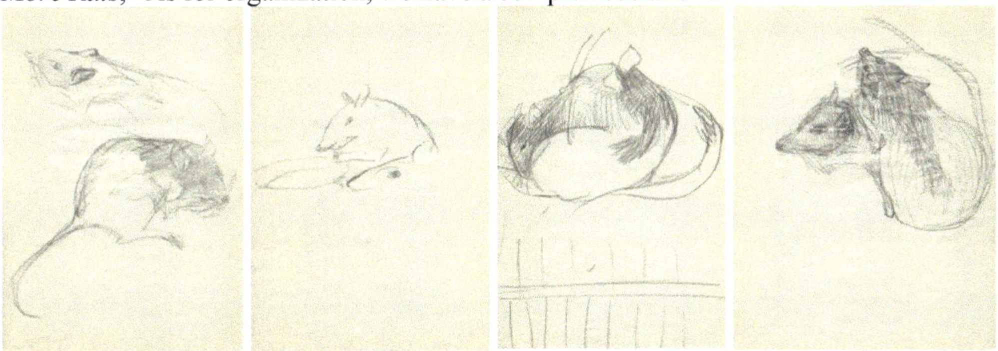

The Rat, "We live in groups called colonies, of up to several hundred individuals."

More Rats, "We are not asking you to adopt them all."

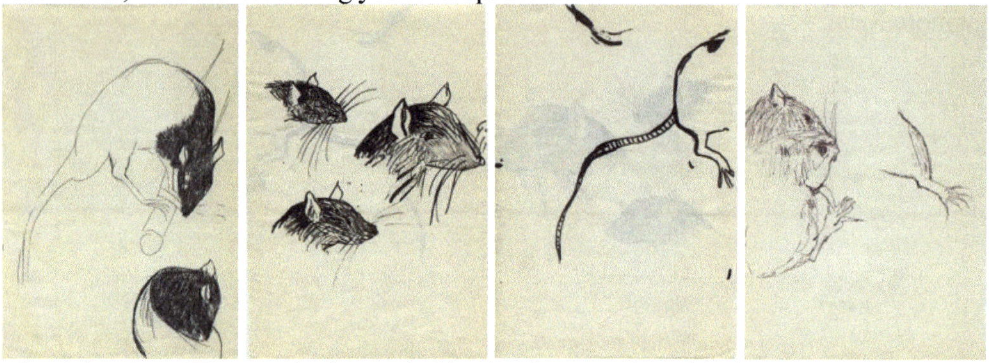

The Other Rat, "These colonies are led by dominant males with the most aggressive personalities."

More Rats, "Do not adopt a leader."

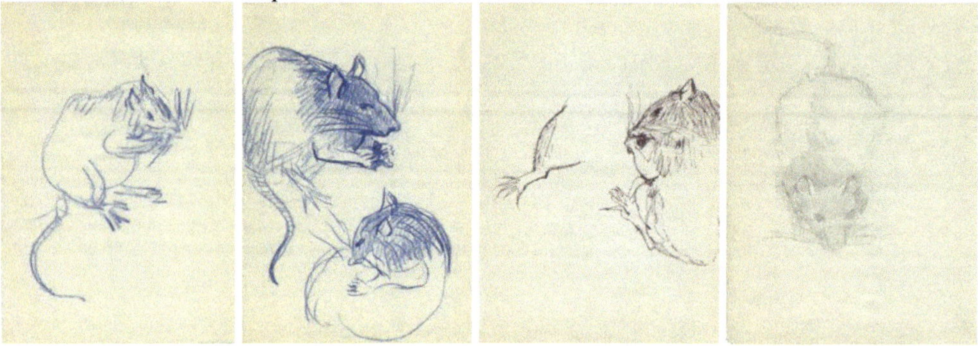

The Rat, "In our hierarchical social structure, the dominant male is at the top of the hierarchy, followed by subordinate males and females. The same goes for females.

More Rats, "Do not adopt dominant females."

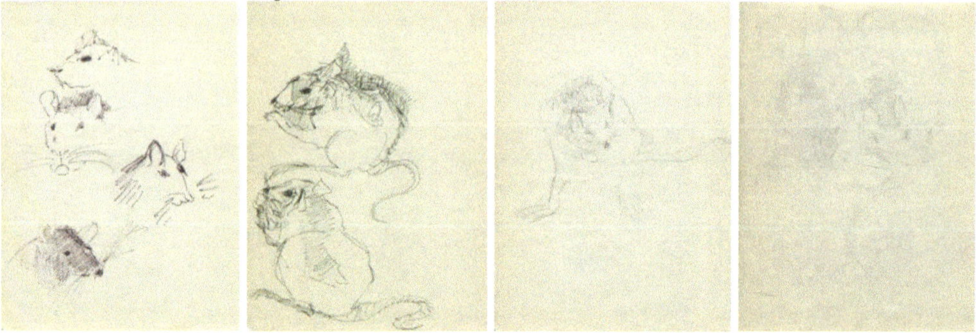

The Other Rat, "Rats communicate with each other through a variety of means, including vocalizations, body language, and scent marking."

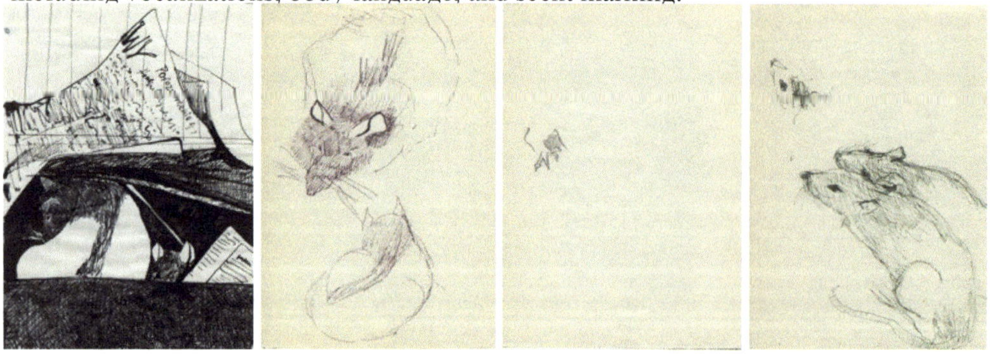

The Rat, "Dominant rats will mark their territory to assert their power over others."

More Rats, "No, no, do not adopt dominant rats. They will dominate you."

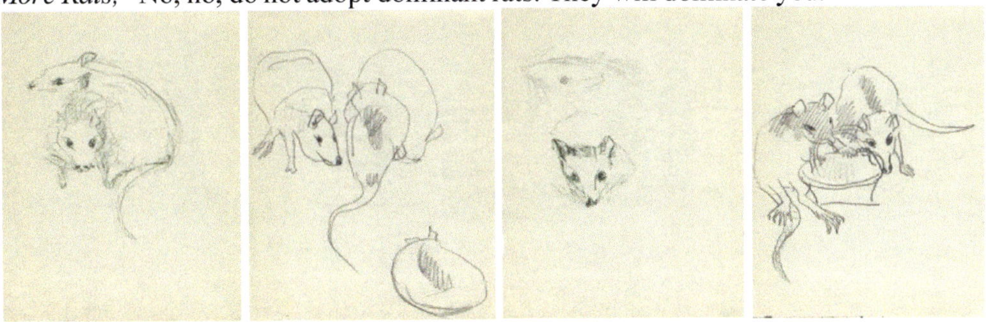

The Rat, "Here's an example code for classifying us based on our species:

```
class Rat:
    def __init__(self, name, species):
        self.name = name
        self.species = species

    def __str__(self):
        return f"{self.name} ({self.species})"

class BlackHoodedRat(Rat):
    def __init__(self, name):
        super().__init__(name, "Rattus rattus")

class BrownRat(Rat):
    def __init__(self, name):
        super().__init__(name, "Rattus norvegicus")

class FancyRat(Rat):
    def __init__(self, name):
        super().__init__(name, "Rattus norvegicus domestica")

# create some rats
rat1 = BlackHoodedRat("Squeaky")
rat2 = BrownRat("Whiskers")
rat3 = FancyRat("Nibbles")

# print out their names and species
print(rat1)
print(rat2)
print(rat3)
```

More Rats, "In this code, a Rat class with a name and species attribute was defined, with three subclasses of Rat for the different species of rats: BlackHoodedRat, BrownRat, and FancyRat.
The Other Rat, "Our social organization is highly complex and dynamic, with individuals constantly vying for position and influence within the colony."

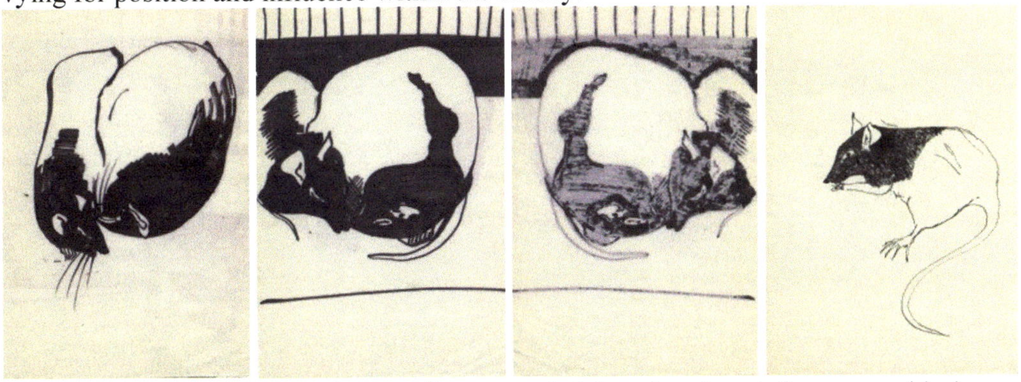

The Rat, "Once upon a time, in a small spot nestled deep in a forest, there was a black hooded rat. Unlike any other rat in the woods, he had a keen interest in coding and spent most of his days reading and learning about it."

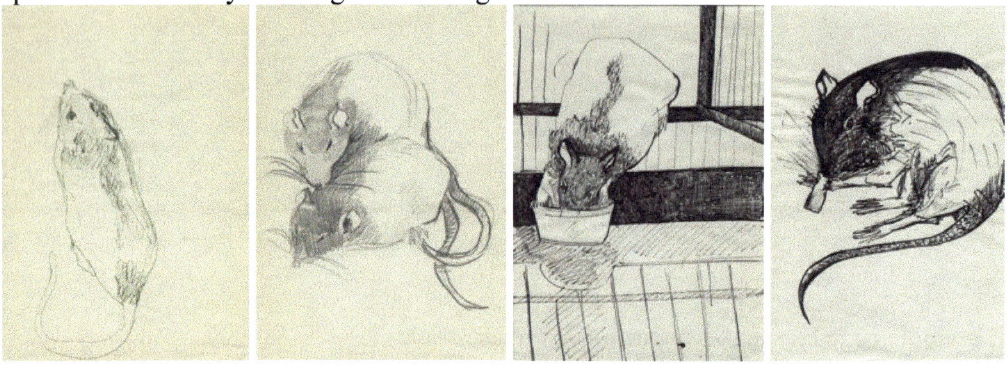

The Other Rat, "One day, while exploring the forest, the rat stumbled upon an old, abandoned computer."

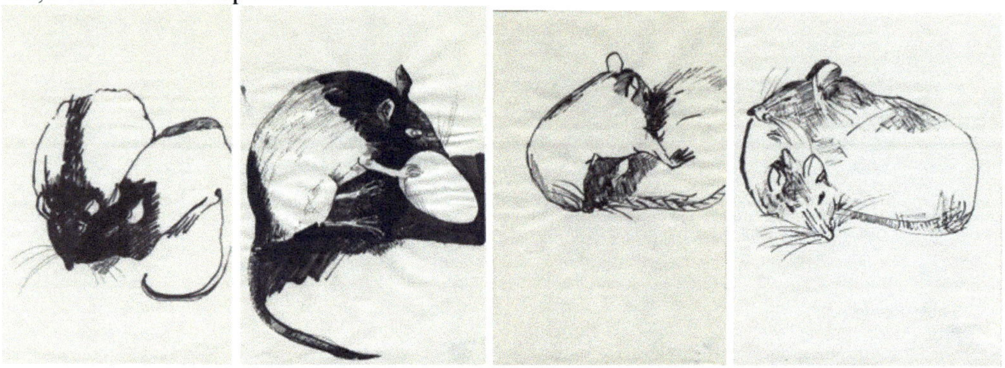

The Rat, "To his surprise, it still worked, and he was able to access the internet."

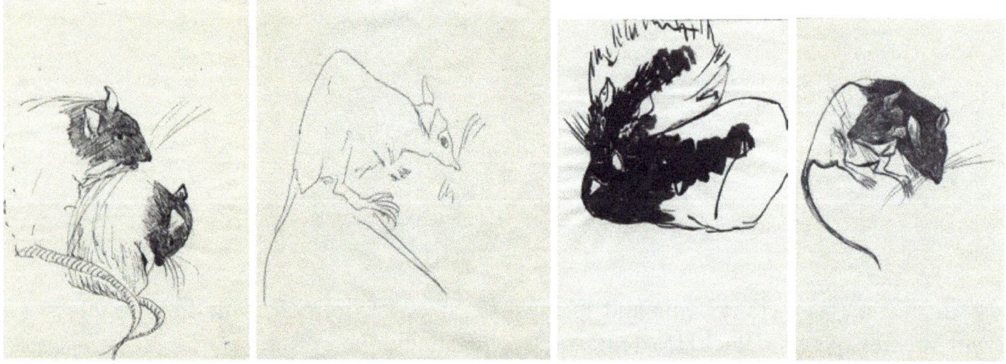

The Other Rat, "With his newly acquired skills, the rat spent hours practicing and experimenting with different programming languages."

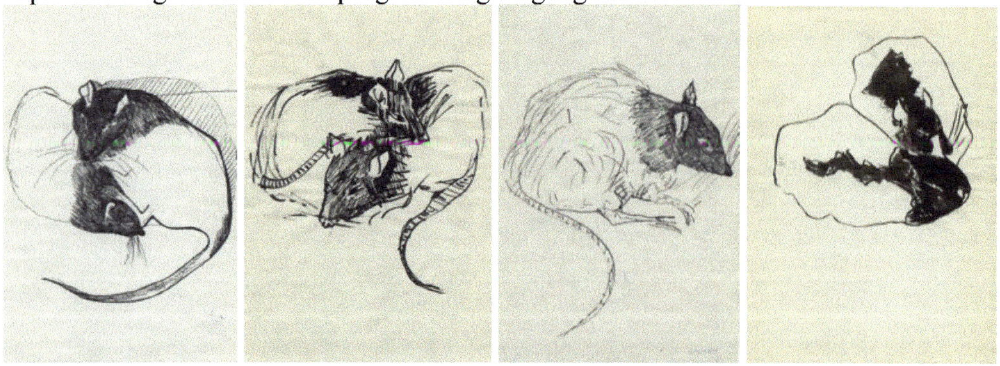

The Rat, "Despite facing many challenges, he became an expert in coding."

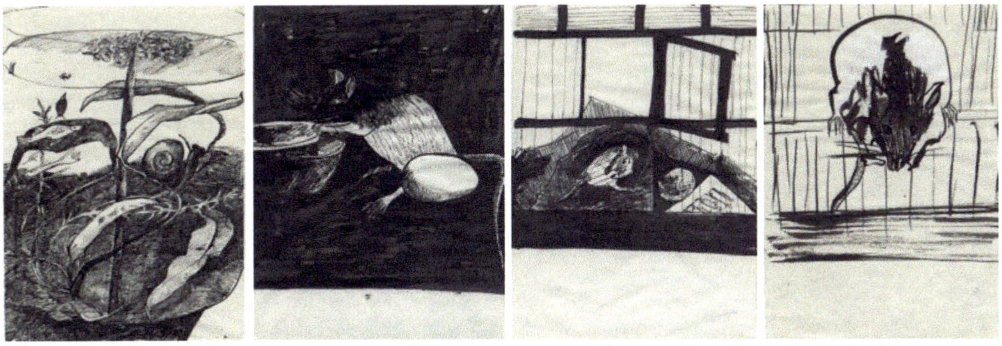

The Other Rat, "He started to create his programs and even developed a website. That allowed other animals in the forest to communicate with each other. They used their own Communal Channels (CC) for warning, dating, sharing fun, and even more."

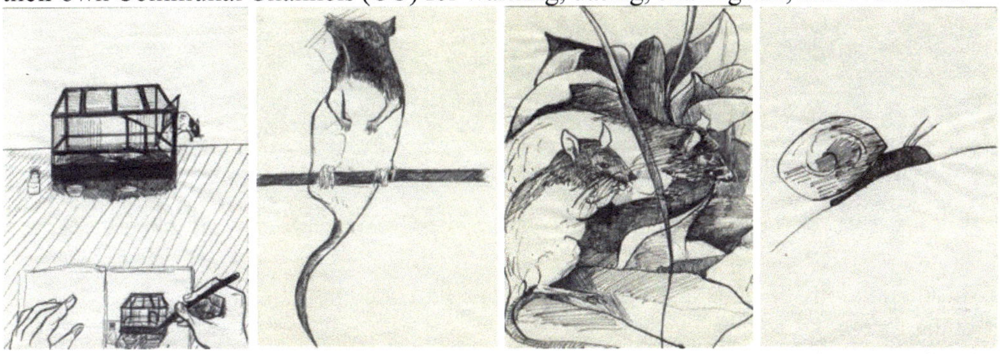

The Rat, "Word of this rat's skills soon spread throughout the forest, and many animals came to him for help with their coding problems."

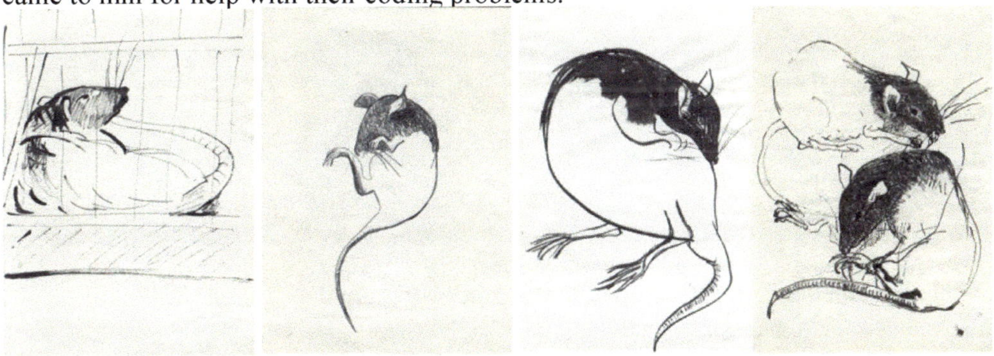

The Other Rat, "Became a trusted advisor, helping animals with their programming projects and even teaching some of them the basics of coding."

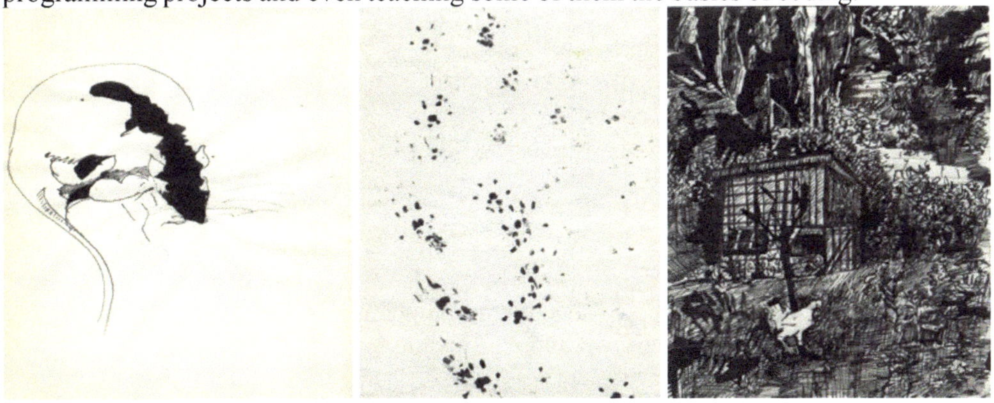

The Rat, "As time went by, our rat became even more respected in the forest, and his website became the go-to platform for all animal communication."

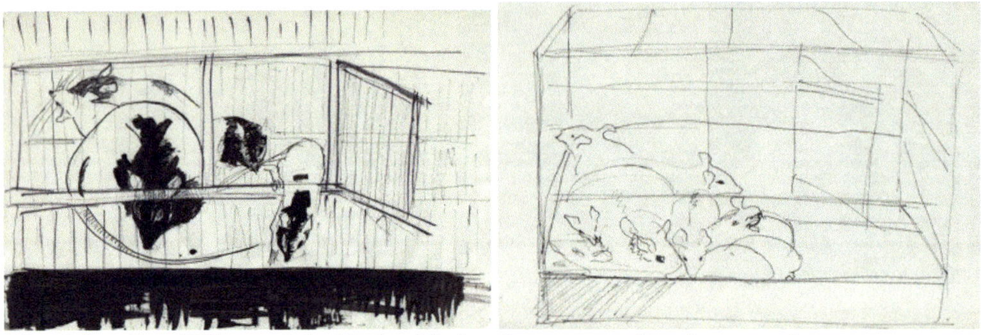

The Other Rat, "His work had helped bring the community closer, and everyone was grateful for his contribution."

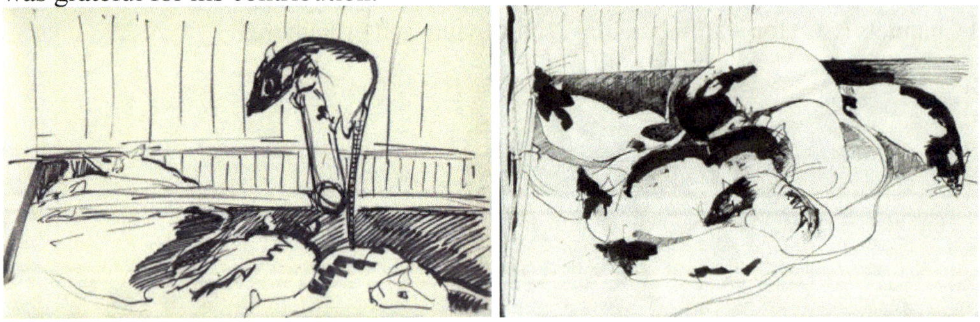

The Rat, "In the end, his dedication and hard work paid off, and he had become the most famous rat in the forest."

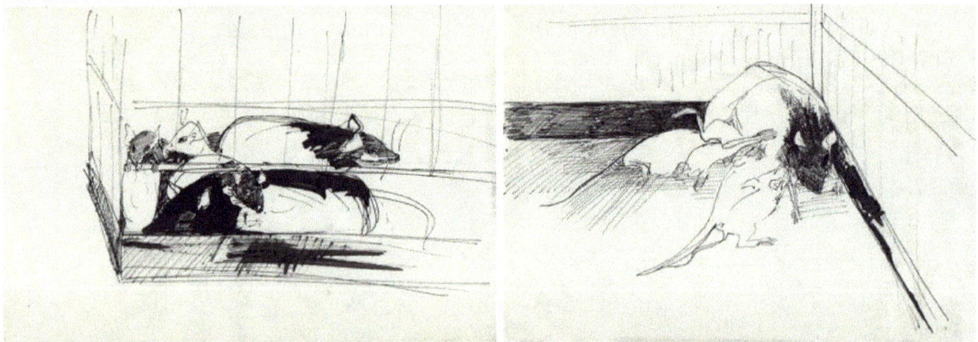

The Rat, "He had shown that with passion, determination, and hard work, anyone can achieve their dreams, even unconventional ones."

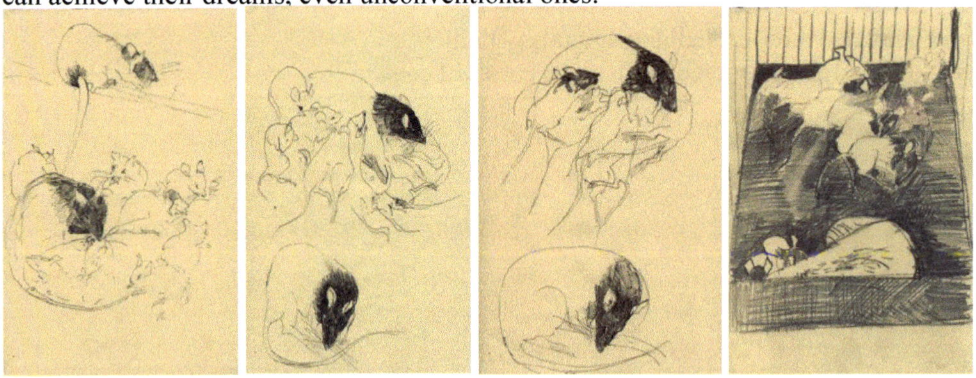

The Other Rat, "This taught the animals to form new ways of communicating and interacting with one another is critical for their survival and well-being."

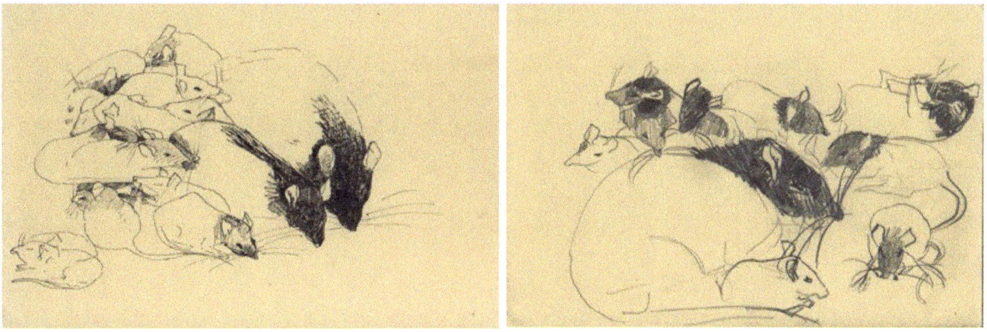

The Rat, “Birds use calls, songs, and others. vocalizations to communicate, warn of predators, signal the location of food or nesting sites, and attract potential mates.“

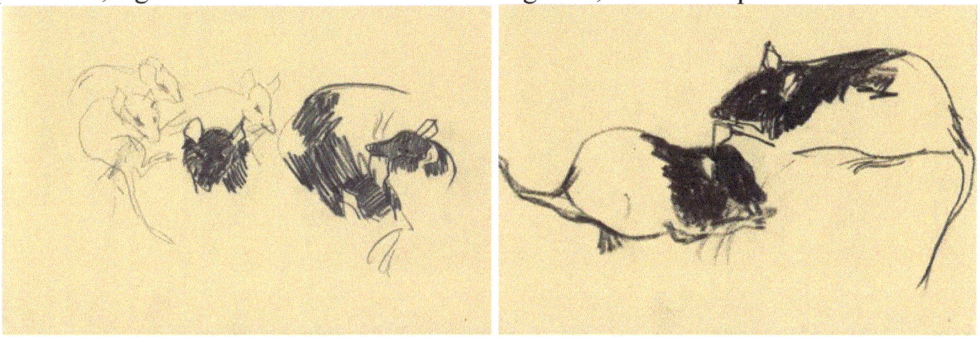

The Other Rat, “Similarly, black-hooded rats use a variety of vocalizations, from grunts, howls, whistles, squeaks, chirps, and ultrasonic sounds that are too high for humans to hear. They establish territories, coordinate hunting, or warn of danger. Their vocalizations, body language, and scent marking convey different types of information, such as warnings of danger or invitations to mate. They use body language with various postures and movements to signal their intentions and emotions to other rats.
A rat might puff up its fur and arch its back to look larger and more intimidating, or it might flatten its ears and crouch low to the ground to indicate submission. ”

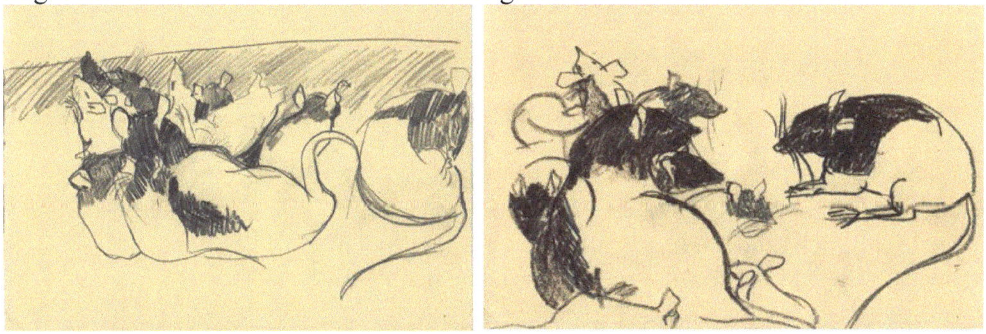

The Rat, “Forest animals use various communication methods, including vocalizations, body language, color changes, aggression or submission displays, pheromones to convey information about mating readiness, territory boundaries, or social status.”
More Rats, “Here is a code showing communication among the black-hooded rats:

```
import random

class Rat:
    def __init__(self, name):
        self.name = name
        self.messages = []

    def send_message(self, message, recipient):
        recipient.receive_message(message)
```

```
    def receive_message(self, message):
        self.messages.append(message)

    def read_messages(self):
        if self.messages:
            print(f"{self.name} has received the following messages:")
            for message in self.messages:
                print(message)
            self.messages = []
        else:
            print(f"No new messages for {self.name}.")

# Create rats
rat1 = Rat("Rat 1")
rat2 = Rat("Rat 2")
rat3 = Rat("Rat 3")

# Rat 1 sends messages to Rat 2 and Rat 3
message1 = "Hello from Rat 1!"
rat1.send_message(message1, rat2)
rat1.send_message(message1, rat3)

# Rat 2 sends a message to Rat 3
message2 = "Greetings from Rat 2!"
rat2.send_message(message2, rat3)

# Rat 3 reads its messages
rat3.read_messages()
```

More Rats, "In this code, the Rat class represents a black hooded rat. Each rat has a name, a list of messages received (self. messages), and three methods: send_message(), receive_message(), and read_messages(). Then, it clears the messages list.. Rat 1 sends messages to Rat 2 and Rat 3, Rat 2 sends a message to Rat 3, and Rat 3 reads its messages."

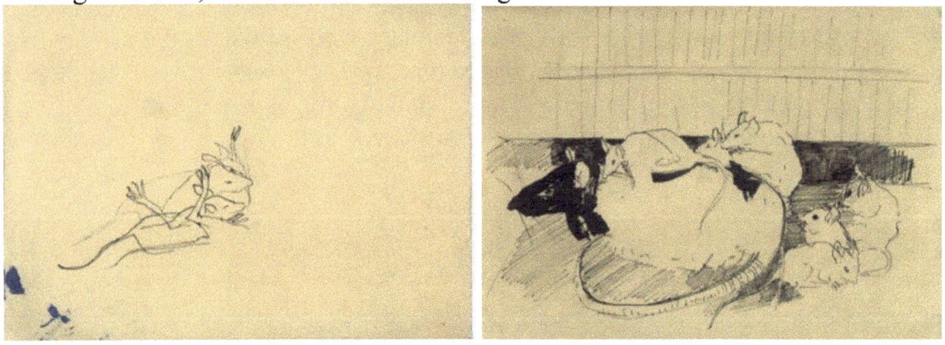

The Other Rat, "Animals in the forest rely on a variety of other forms of communication to interact with each other and navigate their complex social and ecological environments. They do not confuse rodents, as some people do."

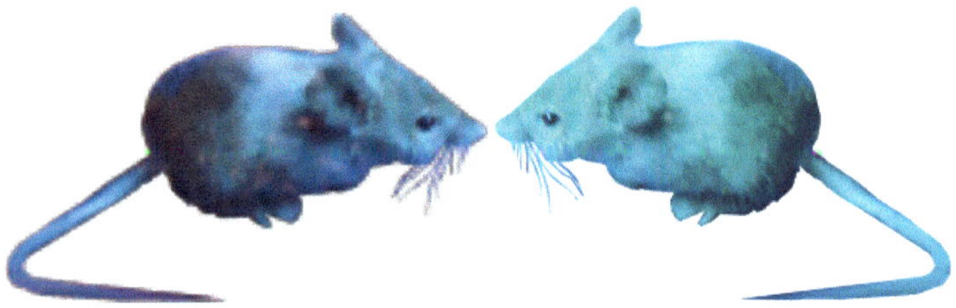

Two Mice, We are not rats!

The End.
The curtain goes down (or closes).

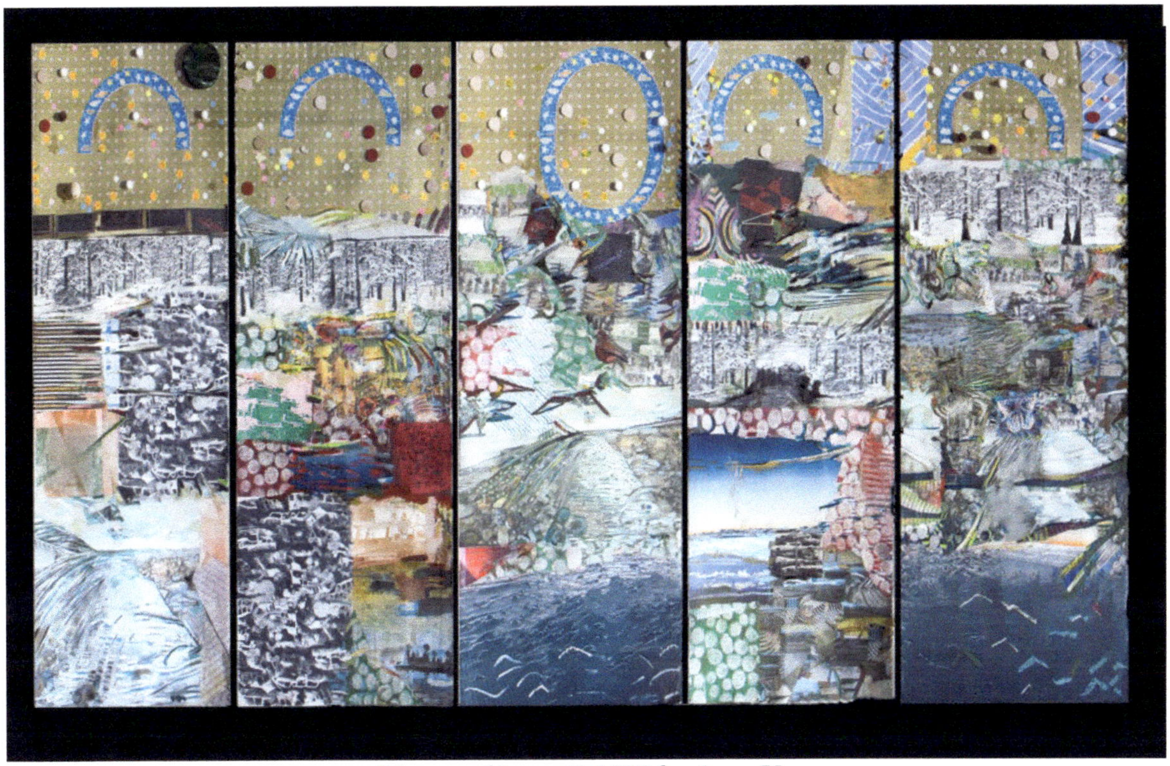

History of Love. © 2025 by Anna Ursyn

CHAPTER 20
HISTORY CODE

STRANDED ON A BEACH

THE HISTORY OF INVENTIONS, THOUGHTS, AND COMPUTER LANGUAGES

INTRODUCTION

The progression of human thought, creativity, thinking, and imagination keeps improving the quality of our lives with great speed. Computers have changed how we function, but they require electricity to operate.

SYNOPSIS

Twenty men stranded on the desert island discuss major human inventions they soon will need to recreate.

SUMMARY

A giant palm tree, and plastic bottles serve as a background for twenty stranded individuals crowded in a small space. The ocean fills the distance between the palm tree and the horizon line. The projection of the waterscape shares the space with objects, historical facts, and codes, many of which are AI and other technology based.

CAST OF CHARACTERS

1st	3rd	5th	7th	9th
2nd	4th	6th	8th	10th
11th	13th	15th	17th	19th
12th	14th	16th	18th	20th

STAGE DIRECTIONS

One palm tree, along with AI-generated content is used for the projections on the backdrop. Many empty plastic bottles are seen around the stage.

`The action happens beyond time and place.`

Act I
The Curtain goes up (or opens).

1st, waking up on wet sand, "I see a palm tree, a man, and another one. Hello there."

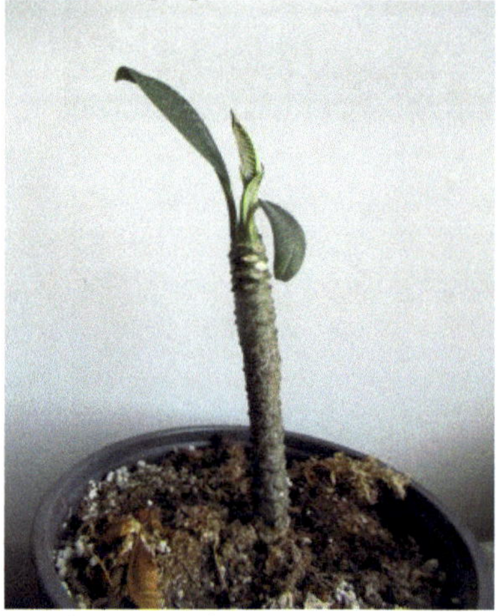

A Plumeria plant acts as a palm tree.

2nd, "Hello. Now that I see there are twenty of us here without the wreckage in sight. Let's gather something to eat."
3rd, "I'll go with you."
2nd, "No need to go anywhere. I can see the whole island, and it's not much of a land. Where did all those plastic bottles come from?" Just shake the palm with me. Harder!"
4th, "Looks like it will be our diet for now. We'll become gatherers, just like our ancestors."
10th," People made some critical and influential inventions throughout history. They have shaped how we live today. We'll just need to recreate some of the greatest human inventions."
5th, "Those are?"
20th "Art. Everyone is an artist nowadays – even those coders. "We can draw in the wet sand and carve the branches. We can do some earth art by collecting and staging sea-related objects. We can build a sandcastle."
2nd, "For a shelter?"
12th, "For fun, for entertainment, for bonding! There is music. We can clap, step, whistle, or sing."

14th, " We can dance. That is art and music. I took some classes on Broadway."
6th, "The wheel revolutionized transportation, allowing for moving goods and people over distances."
9th, "No goods in the sight. Just one palm tree here. We need it for food."
16th, "Writing for recording knowledge to be preserved, literature, science, art, and culture."
13th, "Printing press revolutionized the dissemination of information for wide-spreading literacy."
17th, "Electricity powered industry, transportation, and communication."
8th, "Telephone allowed for people to communicate with each other across long distances."
9th, "No distances here."
19th, "Computer processes lots of data and allows for new industries and ways of life."
4th, "For that, we need electricity. My battery is not very helpful."
5th, "Internet-enabled people to communicate, learn, and work in the whole world."
6 th, "For this, we'd need computers, thus electricity."
7th, "We could build a solar panel with no prospect for a wind turbine here."
2nd, "Antibiotics enabled the treatment of previously fatal diseases."
18th, "Automobile made it possible to travel quickly and easily over long distances."
17th, "Airplanes allowed flying across continents and oceans. "
12 th, "Oh, that would be useful."
1st, "All those inventions are too complicated here. Let's go back to the bare basics:

Wheel (3500 BC)
Plow (3000 BC)
Writing (3200 BC)
Calendar (3100 BC)
Sail (3000 BC)
Bronze (2800 BC)
Iron (1500 BC)
Alphabet (1200 BC)
Coinage (700 BC)
Paper (105 AD)
The printing press (1440)
Microscope (1590)
Telescope (1608)
Steam engine (1712)
Electric battery (1800)
Telegraph (1837)
Sewing machine (1846)
Typewriter (1867)
Telephone (1876)
Light bulb (1879)
Radio (1895)
Airplane (1903)
Ford Model T (1925)
Television (1927)
Computer (1940s)
Internet (1960s)
Mobile phone (1973)
Personal Computer (1977)
World Wide Web (1987)
Smartphone (1992)
Social media (2003)
Apple iPhone mobile phone (2007)

The Large Hadron Collider particle accelerator at CERN (2008)
Bitcoin, decentralized digital currency (2009)
Apple iPad, tablet computer (2010)
The Mars Science Laboratory the Curiosity rover (2012)
CRISPR/Cas9, a gene-editing tool in human cells to cure genetic diseases (2013)
Artificial retina, Argus II, for types of blindness (2014)
Quantum teleportation for developing a quantum internet (2016)
3D-printed heart with patient's cells and biological materials (2018)
Tesla Model Y electric SUV (2020)
Apple M1 chip (2020)
CRISPR-based gene editing (2020)
Neuralink brain-machine interface (2021)
Perseverance Mars Rover (2021)
SpaceX's Crew Dragon spacecraft (2021)
Meta's Project Cambria smart glasses (2022)
Cardboard drone (2023)
Apple Vision Pro (2024)
Artificial Intelligence (Now).

5th, "Now, we are all talking about artificial intelligence (AI), (ML), and all the large learning models (LLM). It is like a new ocean of knowledge. Some people are scared of those ideas."
19th, "Do not use the word ocean here, as we are surrounded by one. It all can be scary when used for the wrong reasons, but AI is another invention. We got used to word processing, using calculators, the internet, social media, Web 2, Skype, Zoom, Blackboard, Canvas, and sharing and learning platforms. We have already experienced the changes resulting from them."
7th, And don't get me started about the protests resulting from the invention of the camera…"
2nd, "That's too much! Only a few of us are here. Let's discuss the history of main ideas."
15th, "The concept of Agriculture: Agriculture was a major milestone in human history approximately 10,000 years ago. It allowed humans to transition from a nomadic hunter-gatherer lifestyle to a settled, agricultural one, which led to the development of civilizations."
3rd, "We are settled, all right."
4th, "And we are civilized."
5th, "Philosophy, the study of the fundamental nature of knowledge, reality, and existence. It has influenced human thought and culture for over 2,500 years, beginning with [Tales, 626 BC, from Miletus, today in Turkey, and Zoroaster (or Zarathustra, c. 500 BC) in Iran.] Some ancient Greek philosophers such as Socrates, Plato, and Aristotle walked on the beach as we do here, marking wet sand with a stick to record the position of the planets they could see and monitor."
7th, "I can code that way. For example, I can show you a program in Python that lists the history of computer languages just by drawing the lines of code on our wet sand:
7th draws on the wet sand with a stick.

```
print("History of Computer Languages")

languages = {
    "Fortran": "developed in the 1950s for scientific computing",
    "COBOL": "developed in the 1950s for business applications",
    "LISP": "developed in the late 1950s for artificial intelligence",
    "BASIC": "developed in the 1960s for beginners",
     "C": "developed in the 1970s for system programming",
     "Pascal": "developed in the 1970s for teaching programming",
    "C++": "developed in the 1980s as an extension of C",
    "Perl": "developed in the 1980s for text processing",
```

```
    "Python": "developed in the 1980s/1990s for general-purpose programming"
    "Java": "developed in the 1990s for cross-platform programming"
    "JavaScript": "developed in the 1990s for web programming"
    "Ruby": "developed in the 1990s for web development"
    "Swift": "developed in the 2010s for iOS and macOS programming"
    "Godot": "developed in 2014 as a game development engine"
    "Cangjie": "introduced in 2024, to enhance security and efficiency"

}
for language, history in languages.items():
    print(f"{language}: {history}")
```

It would output like this:

```
History of Computer Languages
Fortran: developed in the 1950s for scientific computing.
COBOL: developed in the 1950s for business applications
LISP: developed in the late 1950s for artificial intelligence
BASIC: developed in the 1960s for beginners
C: developed in the 1970s for system programming
Pascal: developed in the 1970s for teaching programming
C++: developed in the 1980s as an extension of C.
Perl: developed in the 1980s for text processing.
Python: developed in the 1980s/1990s for general-purpose programming
Java: developed in the 1990s for cross-platform programming
JavaScript: developed in the 1990s for web programming.
Ruby: developed in the 1990s for web development
Swift: developed in the 2010s for iOS and macOS programming
Godot: developed in 2014 as a game development engine.
Cangjie: introduced in 2024, to enhance security and efficiency.

}
```

11th, "But it almost looks like the code."
14th, "The first one is what the computer understands, then it outputs it for us."
10th, "We learn by repetition."
9th, "How about processing.org?
7th, "That is for the artists!"

A large sailing ship with a blue dove on its mast's flag appears nearby.

The End.

The Curtain Goes Down (or Closes)

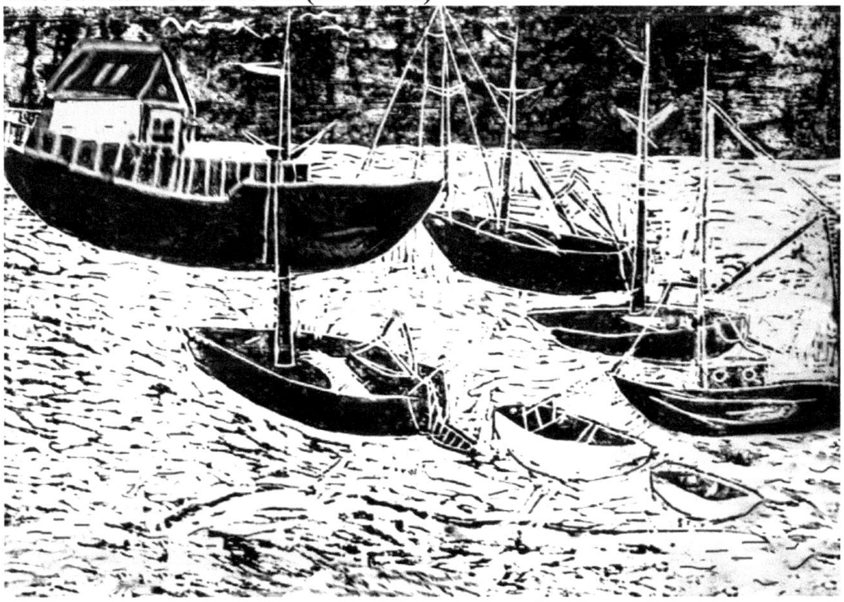

The Boats. Linocut. © 2025 by Anna Ursyn

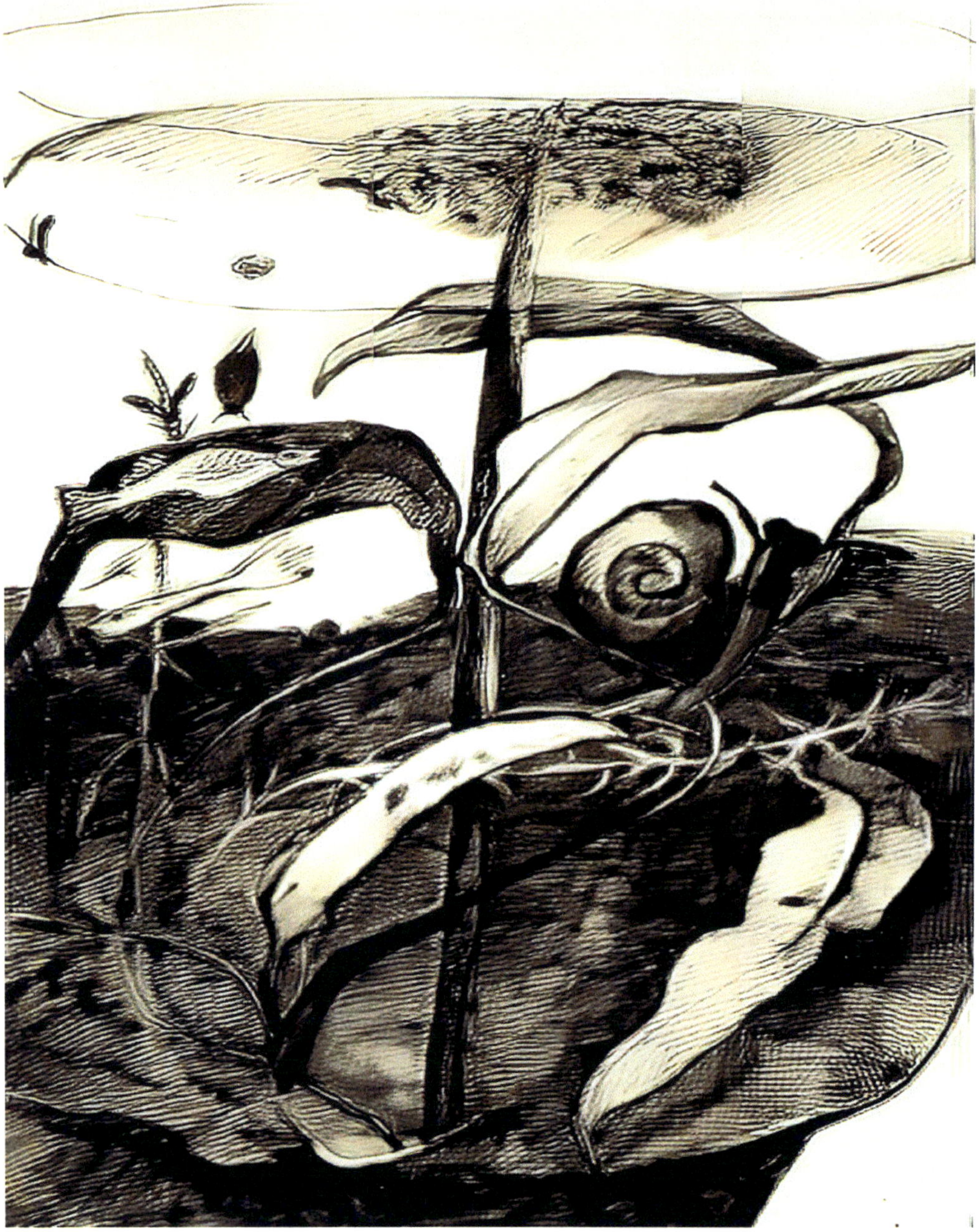

A Turmoil. © 2025 by Anna Ursyn

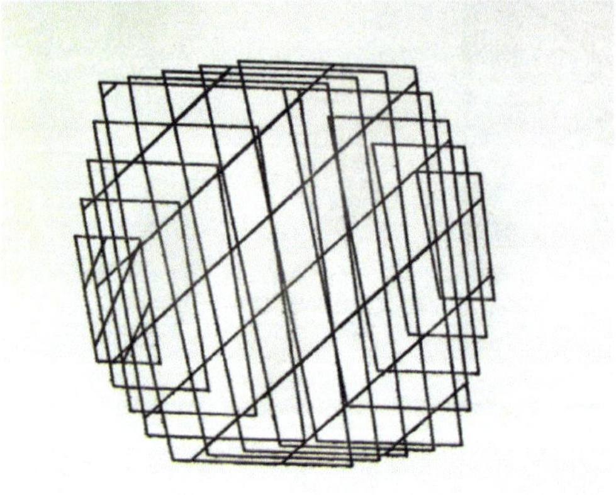

Impossible Solution. The output from a computer code. © 2025 by Anna Ursyn

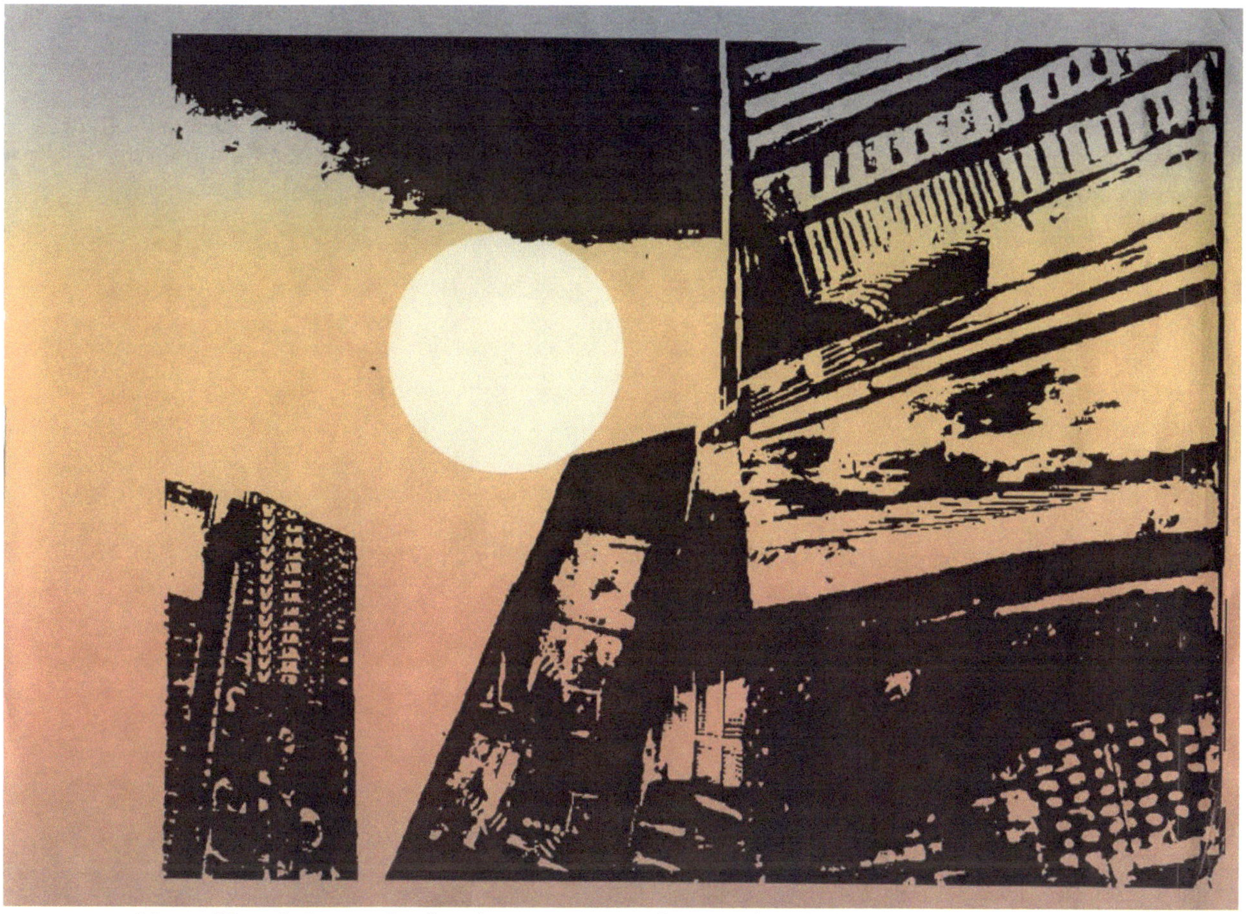

Moon. Photolithograph after the computer code on airbrushed paper. © 2025 by Anna Ursyn

CHAPTER 21
MIND CODE

THROUGH THE CATS' EXPERIENCE

INTRODUCTION

The domestication of cats started a long time ago, and cats are often seen in many households. Cats possess considerable skills, abilities, and senses that humans do not fully comprehend, yet they are cherished and appreciated by the so-called 'Cat People.' 'Whether living in groups or alone, people often enjoy companionship and strive for various types of aids to help them develop their ideas that promote hopes and goals. With the rapid progression of technologies, they can benefit from diverse interactions beyond what they grew up with. Technology helps us on many levels, but for many, it would not replace distinctive interactions with many cats' personalities.

SYNOPSIS

A cat was brought home as a surprise. They both appreciate the catness of a cat. Technology helps them fulfill their other emotional needs and discuss interactions with other species. The two cats make comments by thinking to themselves.

SUMMARY

Two cat owners interact with their new cat by exchanging their positions with the music sounds in the background. The oversized cat stays in their way while the projections of some cats entertain the audience, along with some codes displayed on the screen behind them.

CAST OF CHARACTERS

The Cat
The Cat Cat
The Owner
The Owner Owner

STAGE DIRECTIONS

A living room space is suggested by projections. The cats are shown as holograms.
`The action happens beyond place and time.`

Act I
The Curtain goes up (or opens).

Owner Owner, "I brought a cat. Our cat."

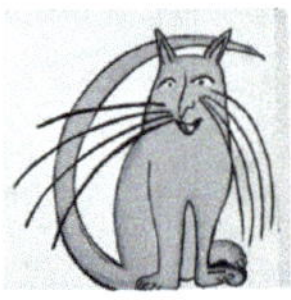

The Owner, "That makes me the Owner. Always wanted to be one. We need to relax the creature so it can trust us, find a way to exchange thoughts, and make it entertain itself and us simultaneously."
Owner Owner, "Cats are highly intelligent and curious animals and quite skilled predators. They can act in various ways. They possess instincts, unique abilities, and ways of interacting with other animals. In our case, it would be us."
The cats to themselves, "You are both lucky! We are loving animals and have our courses of action. We constantly change our interactions, still keeping our habits."
The Owner, "There is a channel for them to watch swimming fish, flying birds, and what's the most interesting, playful squirrels. Most of all, however, they love when the owner sings to them."

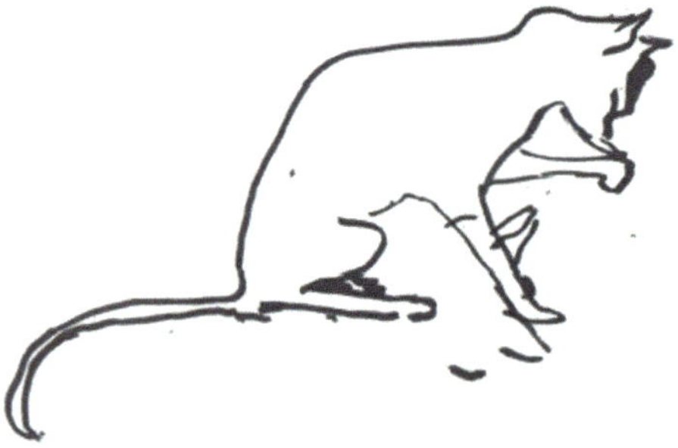

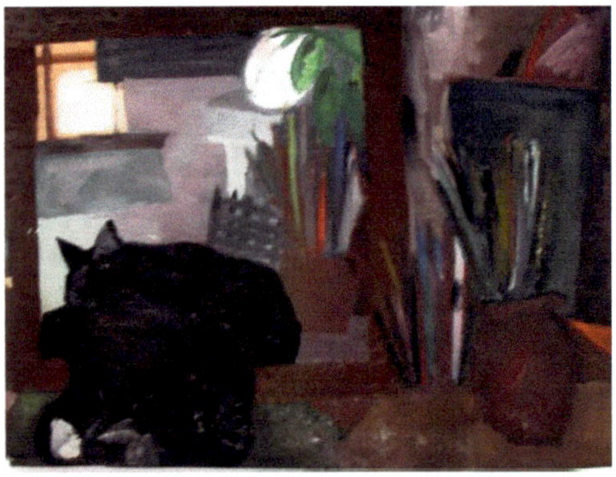

The Owner Owner, "Their communication skills involve a variety of vocalizations, body language, and scent marking."

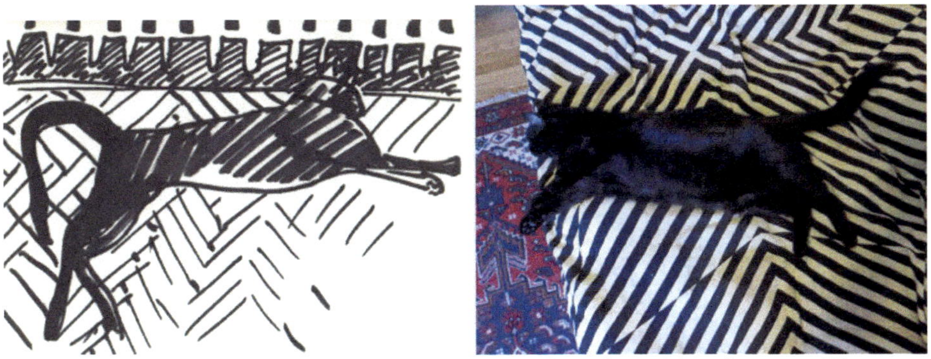

The New Measurement in Colorado: *The Catlength* .© 2025 by *Anna Ursyn*

The Owner, "Emotions are a form of a language, communication at least. We use different types of languages, but we sense what is happening on the reactive level of others we communicate with. For this purpose, we, along with other mammals and birds, use our mirror neurons, which fire patterns of signals identical when we act or look at the same action performed by another, and our neurons mirror the other's activity."
The Owner Owner, "Oh yes, they use these signals to establish social hierarchies, claim territory, and attract mates. Those scents…."

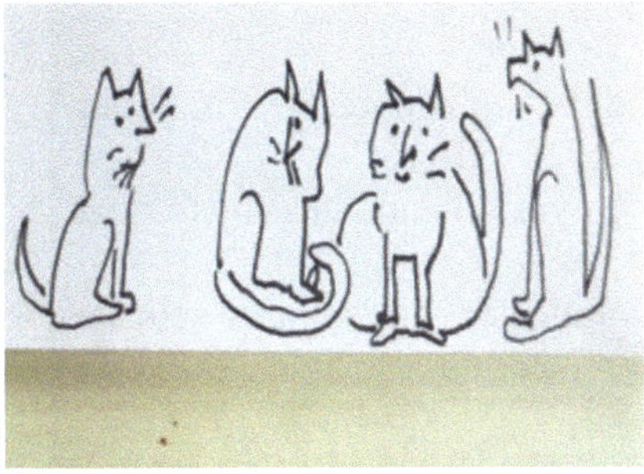
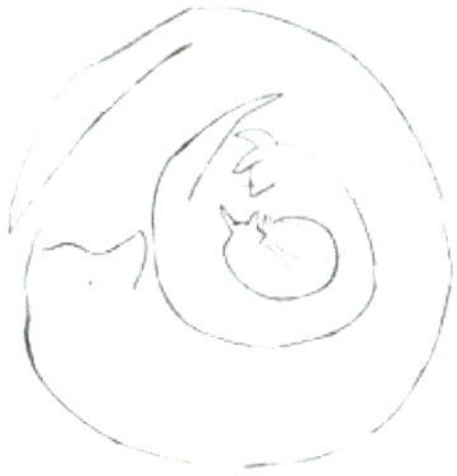
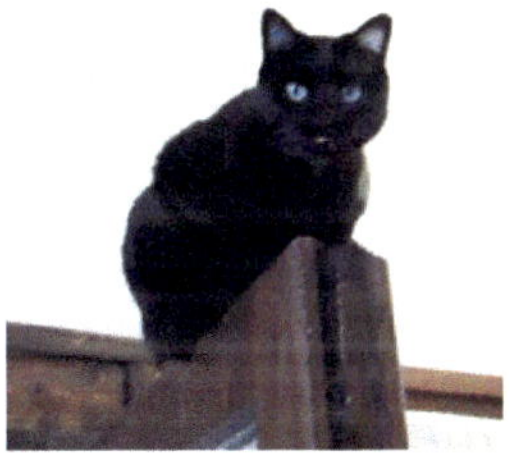
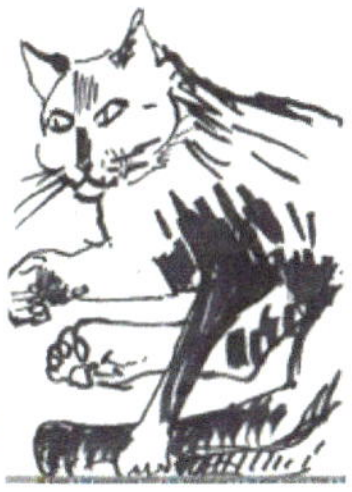

The cats to themselves, "We know it all about grooming, as we spend much time grooming themselves. We are clean and healthy."
The Owner Owner, "They reduce stress and enhance relaxation. This is very beneficial for them and for the people around them. Even for other animals if they know how to behave with respect."
The Owner, "They make the self-cleaning litter boxes now.
The Owner Owner," They also make water balls circulating their content, so we can only enjoy our cats and their interactions without many chores around them, and the cats can stay healthy."
The Owner, "They love to sleep up to 16 hours a day. This is how they conserve energy, yet stay alert."

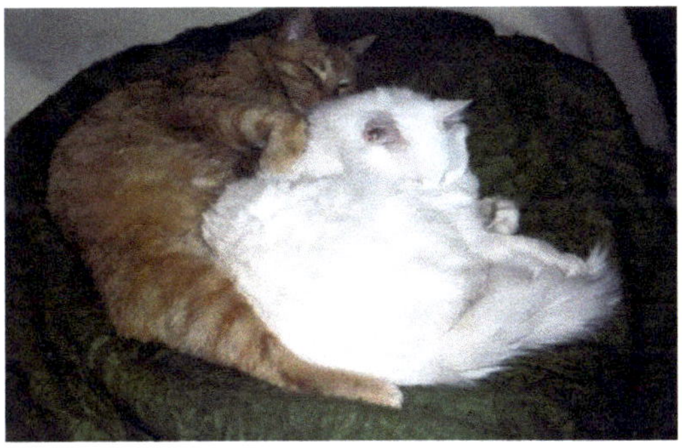
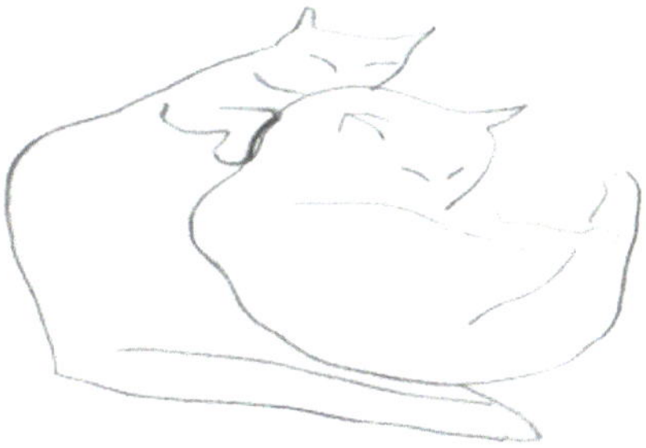

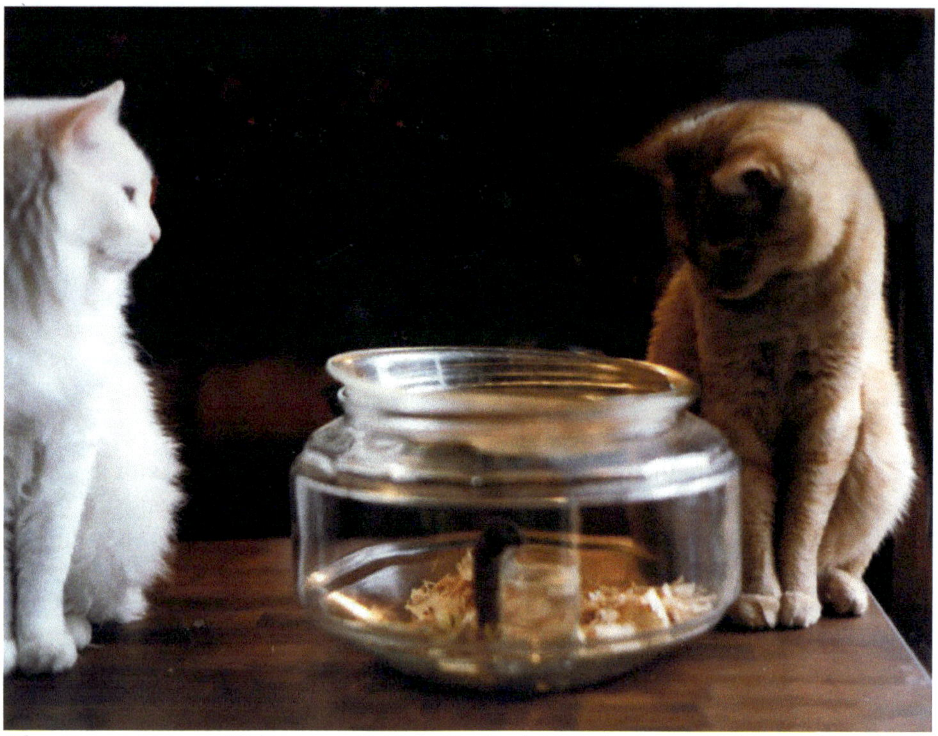

The Owner Owner, "They are playful; they enjoy chasing, pouncing, and batting at objects, stimulating them physically and mentally. The cats are fastidious animals on every level, I'd say."
The Owner, "They are skilled predators. They possess keen senses, sharp eyesight, and hearing to track and catch their prey."
The Owner Owner, "At least they eat what they catch. Nature can be complicated with hunting schemes, associated with pride, aiming for success, righteousness, disregarding each creature's value and right to live."
The Owner, "People can be cruel toward others sometimes, but they keep coming up with some new solutions. For example, a food company in Israel and a Singapore-based one created the world's first 3D-printed cultivated fish. You might enjoy learning about this company making 3-D printed whole cuts of grouper fish:"
https://www.cnn.com/travel/article/steakholder-foods-3d-printed-cultivated-fish-fillet-spc-intl/index.html
The Owner Owner, "In Spain, they serve meat created that way."
The Owner, "Yes, and I have heard that a German circus uses holograms instead of live animals. What makes me happy is that option for saving animals and preventing people from harming them."
https://youtu.be/q3KbgGJux4E.
The Owner, "The experience must be almost the same for the audience after they get used to it. They cannot touch the animals, anyway. Just observe and judge them based on how obedient they are. And those holographic ones are very obedient."
The Owner Owner, "Well, people hold some hidden need for danger, surprise, or even horror. They often enjoy fearing, being terrified, or afraid. They stare at some accidents and discuss catastrophic events long after they happen."
The Owner, "Just like a lion devouring its handler."
The Owner Owner," Yes, or a shark attacking some swimmers."
The Owner," The Circus people should use technology to create danger for their audiences on different levels, but choreographing a projected tightrope walker or an aerialist falling would be considered cruel."
The cats to themselves, "Yes, but if you grow up in that environment, all becomes believable. People strive for believability and plausibleness."

The Owner: "They say one cannot train a cat. Cats are known to be quite independent. However, I taught my cat to come whenever I whistled."

`The cat whistles. The Owner and the Owner Owner both turn their heads in the cat's direction.`

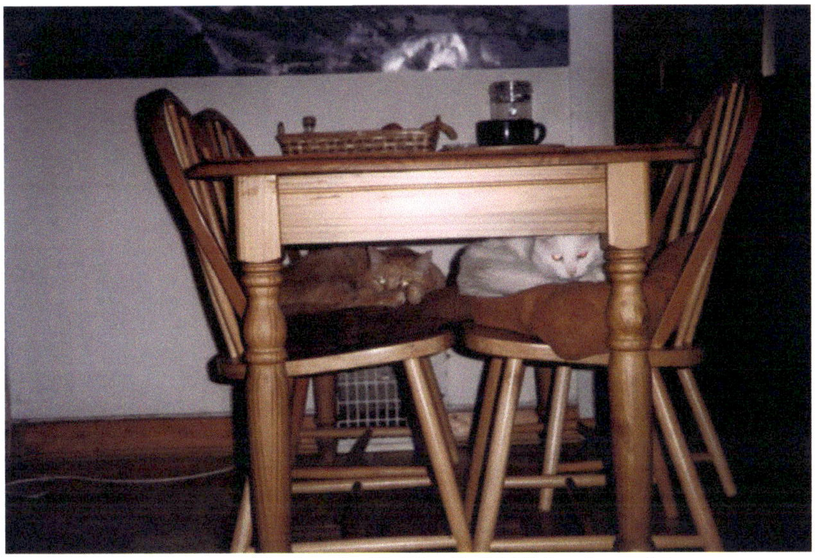

Under the Table. © 2025 by Anna Ursyn

The Owner, "For a long time, I must say, I felt uncomfortable using a mouse in computing but not having anything related to a cat, till I learned about a cat in coding. So, you know, *cat* is a commonly used abbreviation for *concatenate* in various programming languages, meaning joining two or more strings of characters together. For example, in the Python programming language, you can concatenate two strings using the plus operator like this:

`The cat sings the lines of the code:`

The Cat,

```
string1 = "Hello"
string2 = "Cat!"

concatenated_string = string1 + " " + string2
print(concatenated_string)
```

`The cat sings louder "Hello Cat, more emphatically:`

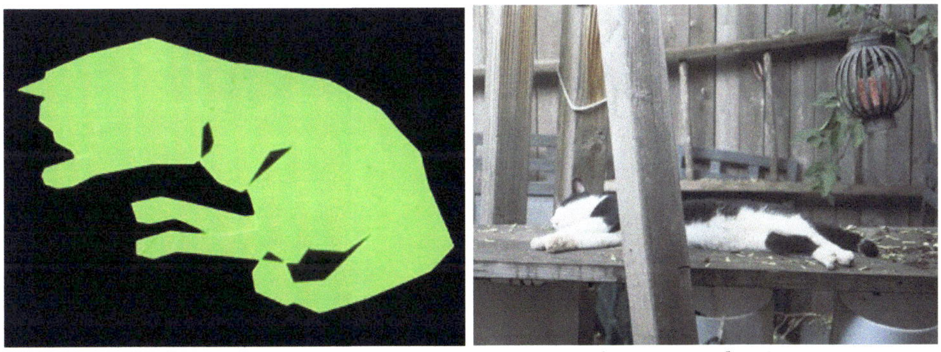

A Sleeping Cat, The output from the computer code. © 2025 by Anna Ursyn

The Cat, "The code output would be: Hello Cat!"

The Owner, “So, if you were referring to *cat* as an abbreviation for *concatenate code*, it might refer to code that is used to concatenate strings or other data types in a program.”
The Cat, “Why not? Besides, it is nice to reciprocate, so.”
`The cat types:`

```
string1 = "Hello"
string2 = "Owner and Owner Owner!"
concatenated_string = string1 + " " + string2
print(concatenated_string)
```

The Cat continues, “The output of the code would be:

```
Hello Owner and Owner Owner!
```

Owner and Owner Owner, “What a polite cat.”
The Cat, “I brought you a Cat Cat.
`The other cat comes out of its hiding place.`
The Cat Cat, “Hello Owner, and Owner Owner!”
The Cat, “That makes two polite cats.”

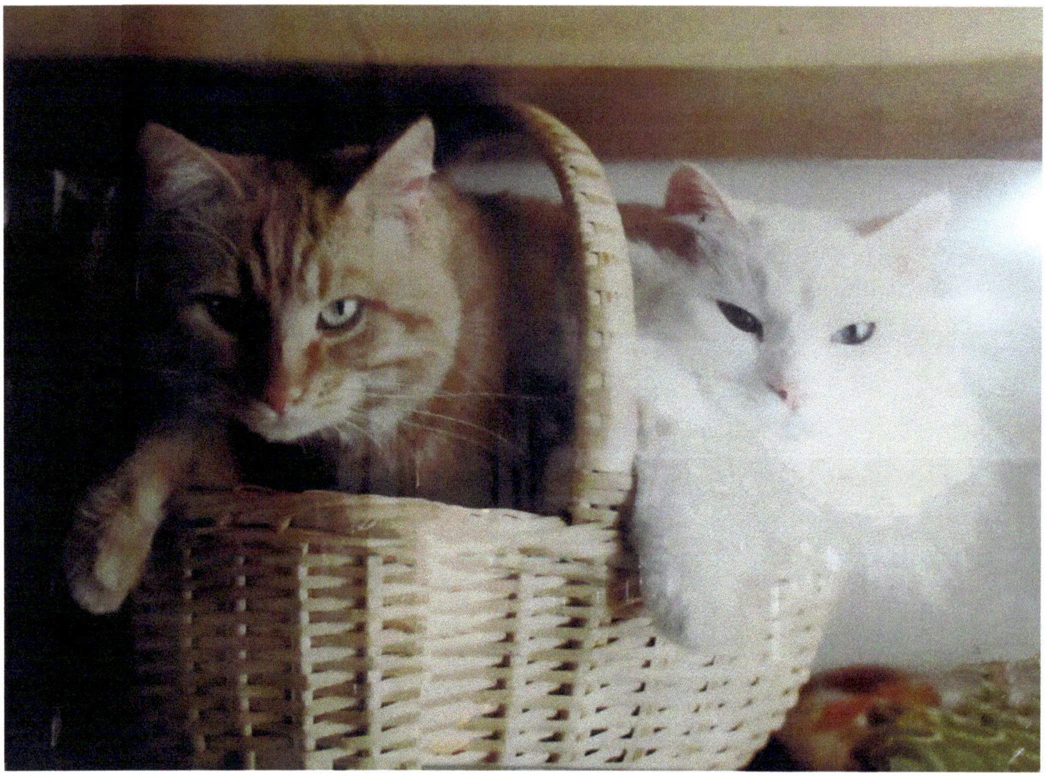

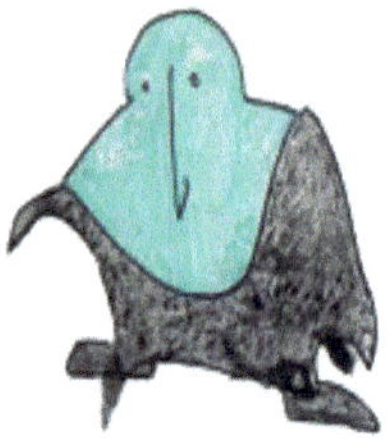

Jorduno: his face was young, but his eyes were old.

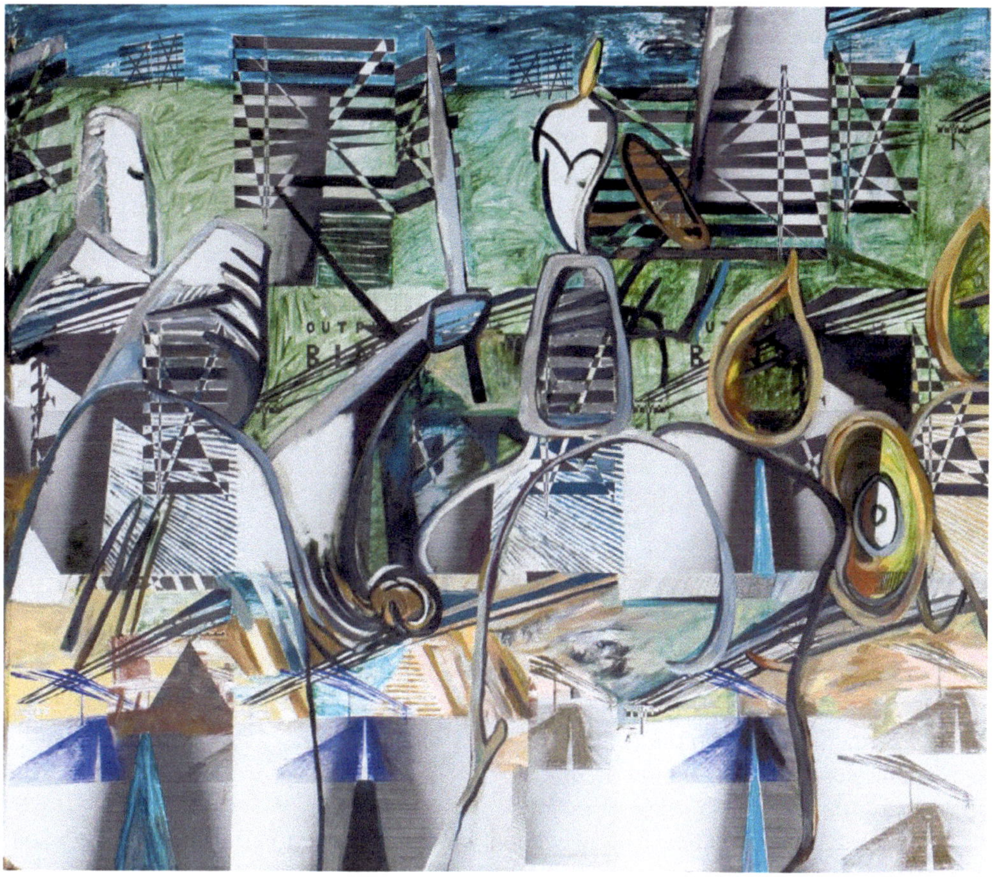

No Concessions. © *2025 by Anna Ursyn*

CHAPTER 22
LAW CODE

I DID NOT DO IT

INTRODUCTION

A famous actor questions his former actions, which occurred in a fraction of a second, long ago, and negatively impacted his life on too many levels.

SYNOPSIS

An actor accused of causing the death of his girlfriend on the stage now re-examines past possibilities. Each day, he ponders the events and short moments leading toward losing her, his self-esteem, and his fame till he meets a coder who draws evidence that it was not his fault.

SUMMARY

Group judgment makes us feel guilty, which can remain a hidden factor affecting our actions and self-esteem. Time and space allow the opportunity to create, which may be more important than a powerful, flattering position that allows us to tell people what to do.

CAST OF CHARACTERS

Arthur, the Tormented Actor
Petal, his Lamented Girlfriend
Joseph, the Bartender

STAGE DIRECTIONS

A bar is marked by a set of hanging bottles and glasses. Arthur is sitting alone with an empty glass. Petal appears as a hologram. Projections show the codes and law-related symbols.

The Curtain goes up (or opens).

Arthur, "Please, another one."
Joseph, "Coming up!"
Arthur, "Time to go home?"
Joseph, "Another hour."
Arthur, "An hour is such a long time." Sometimes, a fraction of a second can seem even longer. It leaves you questioning yourself."
Joseph, "You did not do it."
Arthur, "How do you know? What do you know?"
Joseph, "I was the third one on the bench."
Arthur, "Thank you for releasing me then."
Joseph, "Not morally."
Arthur, "There are things you never know when it comes to a fraction of time. It leaves you to question things for life."
Joseph, "Unless you build a proof."
Arthur," How?"
Joseph, "Through programming."
Arthur, "We use programming world to schedule events. At the theater."
Joseph, "Coding then. Computing, encoding, ciphering, encrypting, enciphering, garbling, as you please. Anyway, there are 'while,' 'if,' or 'else' statements that can exclude some options, thus providing some evidence."
Arthur, "How?"
Joseph, "I wrote a code. It's a proof."
Arthur, "Can I see?"
Joseph, "A Python program simulates a situation where an object falls and lands on a person (your girlfriend at that time) but excludes a fault of an actor using while, if, and else statements. A while loop simulates objects falling and landing on people and checks whether the actor is at fault."

```
fault.import random

actor_fault = False

while True:
   # Simulate a random event, like an object falling
   event = random.randint(1, 3)  # Generate a random event (1, 2, or 3)

   # Check the event and determine the actor's fault
   if event == 1:
      print("Object is falling.")
   elif event == 2:
      print("Object has landed on a person.")
```

```
        actor_fault = True
    else:
        print("No object fell.")

    # Check if the actor is at fault or not
    if actor_fault:
        print("Actor is at fault.")
        break  # Exit the loop if the actor is at fault
    else:
        print("Actor is not at fault. Continue monitoring.")
```

Petal, the famous actor's former girlfriend, appears as a hologram and on the phone.

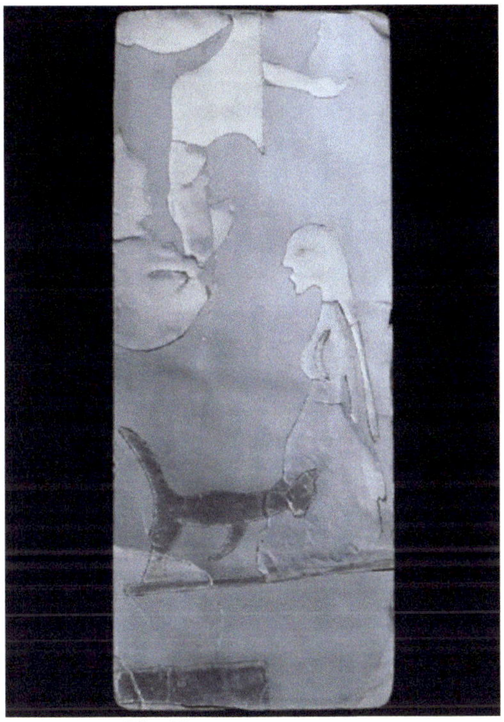

The Encounter

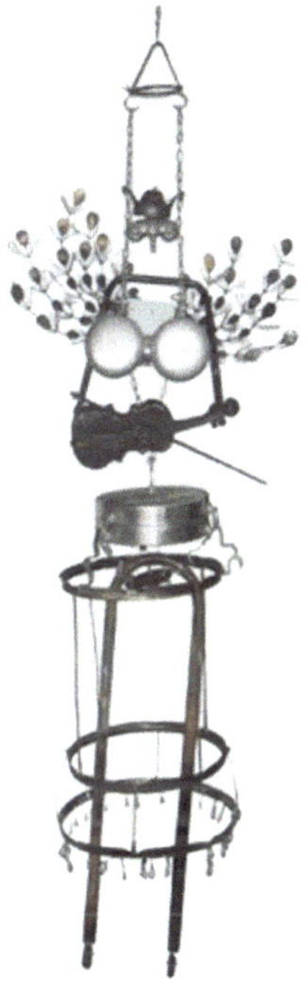

Space Angel. © 2025 by Anna Ursyn

Petal, "I see. In this code, you used a while loop to repeatedly simulate events until you determined whether the actor, my boyfriend at that time, was at fault or not. You simulated events using a random number generator, where events can be 1, 2, or 3.
If event is 1, it means an object is falling, and we continue monitoring.
If event is 2, it means an object has landed on a person, and we set actor_fault to True, indicating that the actor is at fault.
If event is 3, it means nothing happened, and we continue monitoring.
After each event, you check if the actor is at fault. You print a message and break out of the loop if they are. If not, we will continue monitoring for more events."
Arthur, "How did you know the specific scenario and requirements?"
Joseph, "I was at that performance. Brilliant acting, by the way."
Arthur, "Thank you. And you were called up for that, so related jury duty?"
Joseph, "Brilliant acting, again."

The End. The Curtain goes down (or closes).

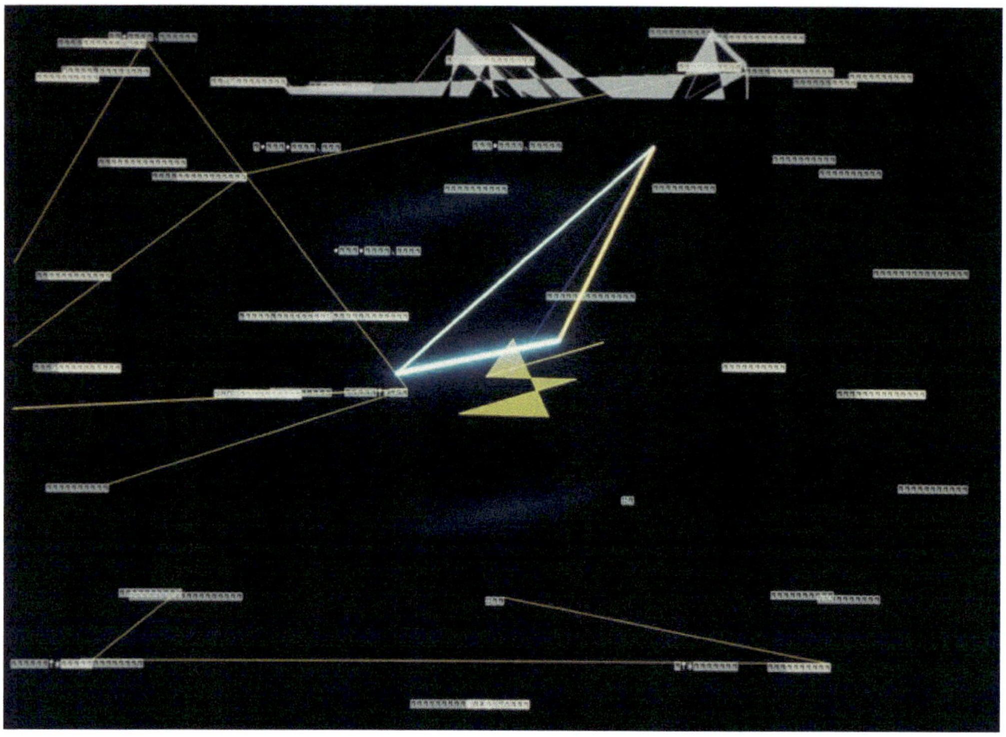

Stellar Questions. The output from the computer code. © *2025 by Anna Ursyn*

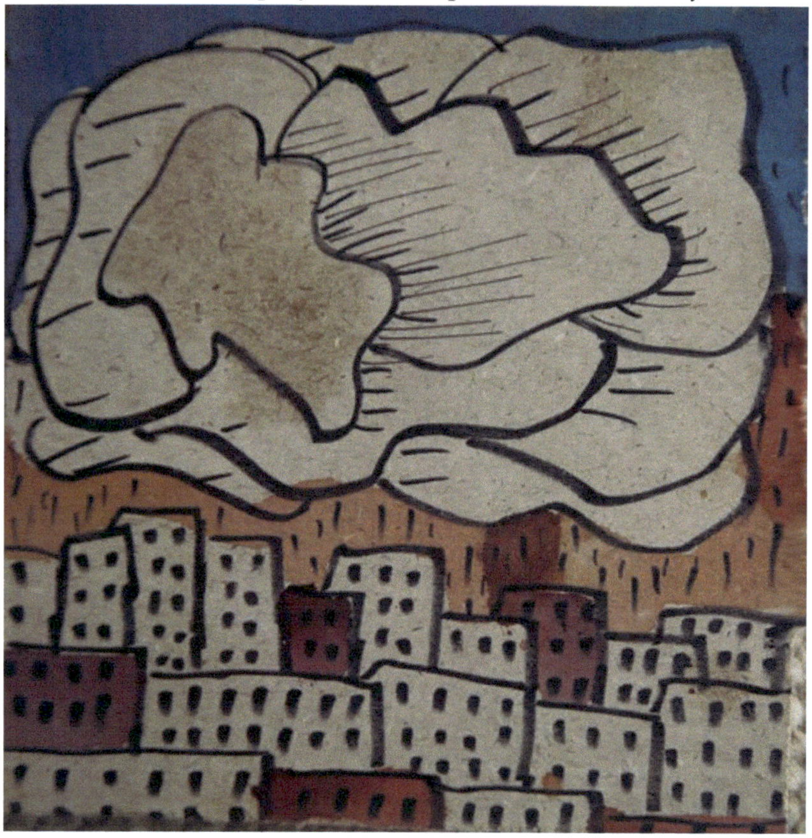

One City, © *2025 by Anna Ursyn*

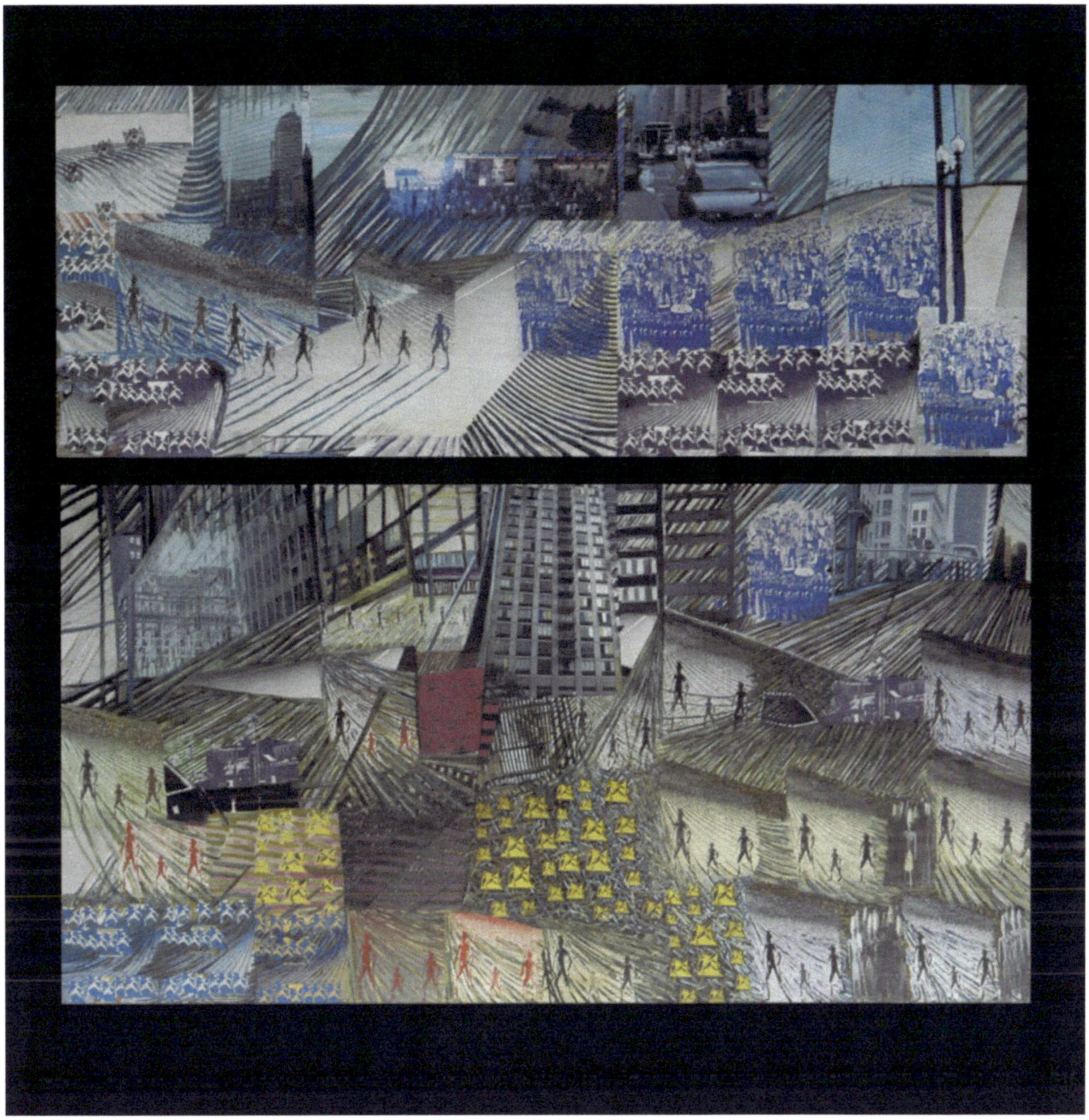

City Matters. © *2025 by Anna Ursyn*

CHAPTER 23
WORD CODE

LEARNING ON THE TRAIN

INTRODUCTION

We all possess different talents, skills, and interests. We focus on our jobs. To learn more, we need to examine cross-disciplinary content. That leads us to seek collaborations. Computer Science and Computer Art Graphics professors are exchanging notes on a train ride to co-present at a conference.

SYNOPSIS

Terry and Arhea discuss their co-presenting at a conference during their train trip. While solving a crossword puzzle, Terry offers Arhea help with her coding skills. Their conversation gets interrupted by his seeking crossword puzzle help from their co-passengers riding a train.

SUMMARY

Fear can block us from doing things we know well. Multitasking feels great, but it might be seen as a flow-stopping agent.

CAST OF CHARACTERS

Terry, a Computer Science teacher
Arhea, a Computer Art Graphics teacher
The Co-passengers: everyone together as a Choir
The Women Co-passengers: all women together as a Choir

STAGE DIRECTIONS

Terry and Arhea sit on the train with co-passengers-manikins. Projections explain the action.

The Curtain goes up (or opens).

`Terry solves a crossword puzzle while discussing coding and, when confused, seeks help from his co-presenter and their co-passengers riding a train.`

```
 1 2  3  4  5  6  7  8  9 10
 1 C  R  O  S  S  W  O  R  D
 2 R  E  F  R  I  G  E  R  A  T  O  R
 3 O  L  I  V  E  R
 4 S  O  L  U  T  I  O  N
 5 S  C  H  O  O  L
 6 W  A  T  C  H
 7 A  P  P  L  E
 8 T  E  L  E  V  I  S  I  O  N
 9 E  L  E  P  H  A  N  T
10 R  A  I  N  B  O  W.
```

Clues: `(This part is to be sung).`

Across:
A game with words and boxes.
You wear it on your wrist to tell the time.
A fruit that keeps the doctor away.
A large, gray mammal that lives in the jungle.
A colorful arc that appears in the sky after rain.

Down:
What you need to solve this puzzle.
Keeps your food cold.
The main character in Charles Dickens's novel "Oliver Twist."
The answer to a problem.
A place where you learn.
Try to solve the crossword by filling in the missing words!

Terry, "We'll start our presentation with a joke. What's a good one?"
Arhea, "There is one I like from a long time ago that shows two dogs sitting in front of the cathode ray bulky computer (which dates it), stating that on the Internet, no one will recognize them as being dogs! I

liked the beginnings of the Internet; they even published some Internet Yellow Pages on paper. Nowadays, we can wrap up our planet a multitude of times with books like that, with about 50 websites created per second. Besides, who would print the links now? Who would re-type them?"
Terry, "That joke is old, not true anymore, and is from a respected magazine, so it might be copyrighted."
Terry, "Who was the main character in Charles Dickens' novel *Oliver Twist*. Five letters."
Arhea, "TWIST"
Terry, "No, it does not fit. Excuse me, everyone. Do you, by any chance, know who the main character in Charles Dickens's novel Oliver Twist is? Six letters."
Co-passengers: Everyone around as a choir: "OLIVER."
Terry, "Thank you, all."
Arhea, "That is so true; now anybody can know everything about anyone. There was even a newer joke stating that nowadays, everybody knows when you are a dog, featuring the same dogs."
Terry, "I love New Yorker cartoons. For our presentation, let's focus on cross-collaboration in our classes. Let's describe it when we came to your lab and had your students create trajectories for a drawing robot my students programmed."
Arhea, "My students coded a bit as well, and I saw one or two of yours drawing their trajectories."
Terry, "That is true. Just like you do coding, and I doodle. That releases my tension, even though, in fact, I would not be able to draw a stick figure. Why did you take those coding classes as an artist and follow with those ideas, by the way?"
Arhea, "I still have some issues."
Terry, "I can help you with them."
Arhea, "That would be great. I want to grow. So, what is the best approach to…"
Terry, "Do you know eight words to answer a problem?"
Arhea, "EXPLANATION"
Terry, "Sorry, everyone. One more, eight words for the answer to a problem."
Co-passengers, Everyone together as a Choir: "SOLUTION."
Terry, "Thank you, all. That fits just great!"
Arhea, "Can you help me with the graphical part of coding? Many coders feel it's a waste of time."
Terry, "Yes, of course; what would you like to draw by coding? Oh, I know this world. It fits perfectly!"
Arhea, "Let's start with the hardest: a coded sketch of a human. I am not asking you to sketch a stick figure; just code it so I can acquire skills in a new language."
Terry, "Do you know a twelve-letter word for *Keeps your food cold*?"
Arhea, "STORMY WINTER."
Terry, "My apologies, everyone, for interrupting your train-riding time. Would anyone know the twelve words for *Keeps your food cold*?"
Co-passengers, Everyone together as a Choir, "REFRIGERATOR!"
Terry: "Oh, Thank you, everyone. That fits! What was your question, again?"
Arhea," import random

```
def create_empty_grid(rows, cols):
    return [[' ' for _ in range(cols)] for _ in range(rows)]

def is_valid_word_placement(grid, word, row, col, direction):
    if direction == "horizontal":
        if col + len(word) > len(grid[row]):
            return False
        for i in range(len(word)):
            if grid[row][col + i] != ' ' and grid[row][col + i] != word[i]:
                return False
    elif direction == "vertical":
        if row + len(word) > len(grid):
            return False
        for i in range(len(word)):
            if grid[row + i][col] != ' ' and grid[row + i][col] != word[i]:
                return False
    return True
```

```
def place_word(grid, word, row, col, direction):
    if direction == "horizontal":
        for i in range(len(word)):
            grid[row][col + i] = word[i]
    elif direction == "vertical":
        for i in range(len(word)):
            grid[row + i][col] = word[i]

def crossword_puzzle(words, rows, cols):
    grid = create_empty_grid(rows, cols)
    random.shuffle(words)

    for word in words:
        direction = random.choice(["horizontal", "vertical"])
        for _ in range(10):
            if direction == "horizontal":
                row = random.randint(0, rows - 1)
                col = random.randint(0, cols - len(word))
            elif direction == "vertical":
                row = random.randint(0, rows - len(word))
                col = random.randint(0, cols - 1)

            if is_valid_word_placement(grid, word, row, col, direction):
                place_word(grid, word, row, col, direction)
                break

    return grid

if __name__ == "__main__":
    # Example usage:
    word_list = ["PYTHON", "CROSSWORD", "PUZZLE", "GRID", "COMPUTER", "ALGORITHM"]
    rows = 10
    cols = 10
    puzzle = crossword_puzzle(word_list, rows, cols)

    for row in puzzle:
        print(' '.join(row))
```

Terry, "Creating a computer program to generate a crossword puzzle is a complex task involving algorithms and data structures. You provided a high-level outline of the steps involved and a Python code snippet. You generated a crossword puzzle grid with random word placements in either horizontal or vertical directions. You can modify the wordlist, rows, and cols variables to create puzzles with different words and grid sizes."
Arhea: "Excuse me, everyone. Do you happen to know a seven-letter word for a Multitasker, by any chance?"
Women Co-passengers, as a Choir, "HELPFUL."

The End
The Curtain goes down (or closes).

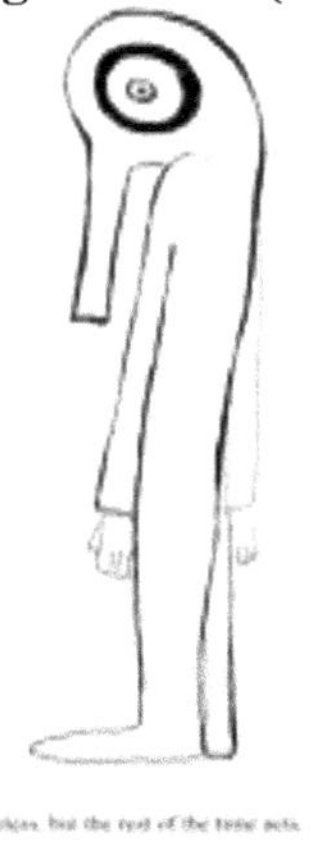

Vai: sometimes feels hopeless, but the rest of the time acts.

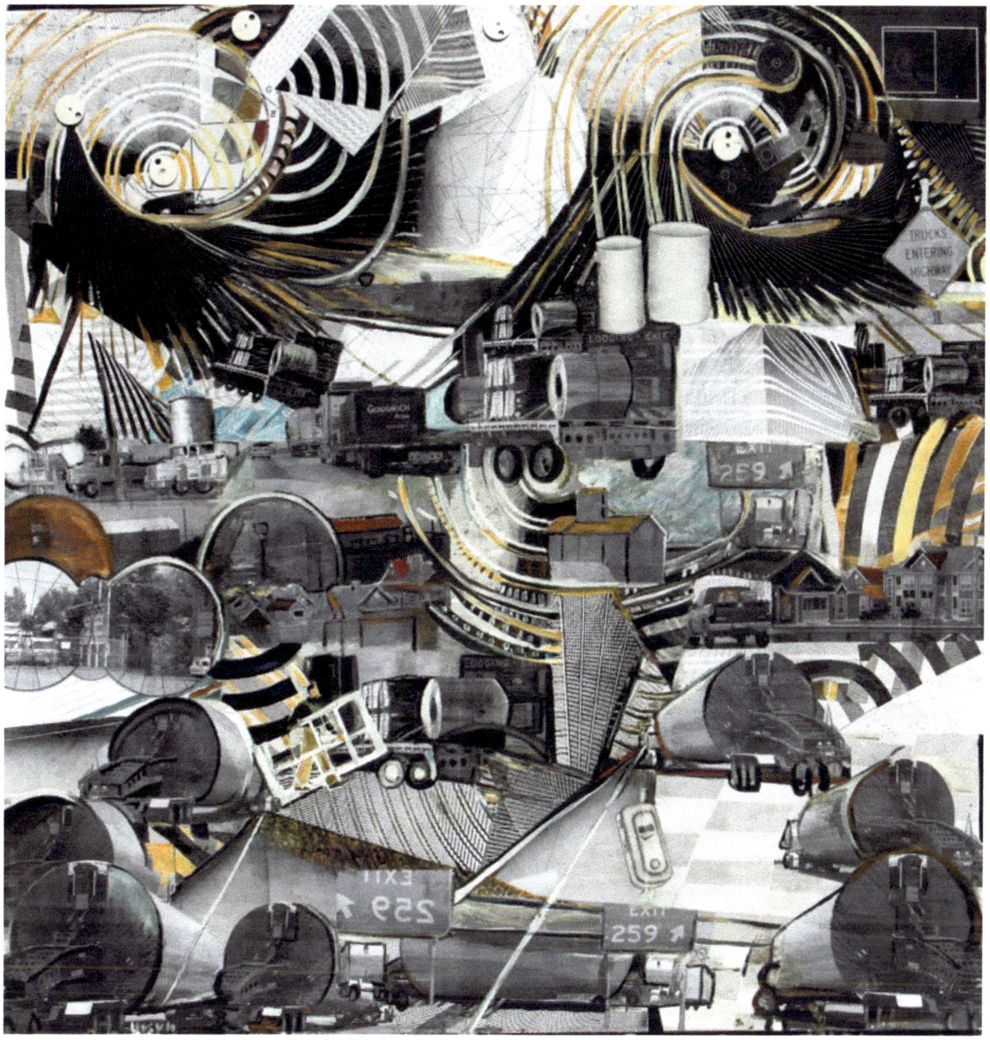

Cylinder. © *2025 by Anna Ursyn*

CHAPTER 24

CHEMISTRY CODE

A SWIMMER'S ALTERED STATES OF THOUGHT WITH TWO MINDSETS

Arace: A Sum of Details: https://www.mixbook.com/editor?pid=17806986

INTRODUCTION

We study, work, and play to balance our lives. Our profession can become our passion, and our playfulness can support our work.

SYNOPSIS

An Olympic winner merges her knowledge of chemistry with her passion. Repetitive actions are needed to achieve a goal, and thoughts must be combined with her interests. The swimmer uses related codes to pass the time and her knowledge of chemistry for self-motivation.

SUMMARY

As an Olympic swimmer, she keeps winning due to her knowledge of chemistry combined with playfulness and passion.

CAST OF CHARACTERS

The Swimmer Chemist = The Chemist Swimmer

STAGE DIRECTIONS

The pool with a swimmer changing the styles is projected during one swimmer's intensive training. The actor stands in the chemistry lab with props and alternates voices.

Act I Crawl (Freestyle)
The Curtain goes up (or opens).

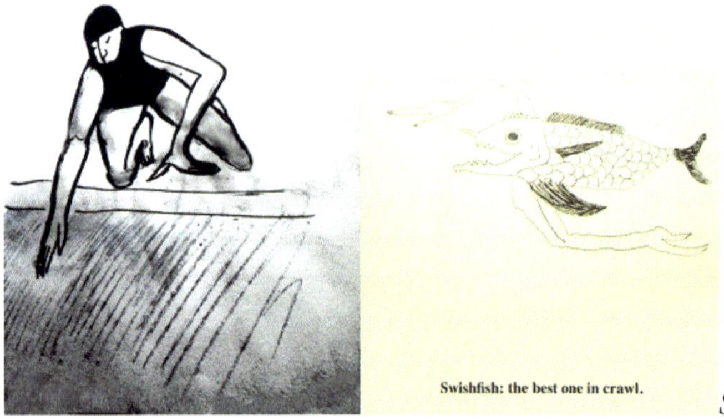

Swishfish: the best in crawl.

Swimmer Chemist, "Practice alternate arm pulls with smooth movements and kick from your hips with straight legs. Breathe by rolling your head to the side and experiment with your stroke rate. Swimming is a great workout and life skill."
Chemist Swimmer, "The principle of buoyancy, which allows objects to float, is related to the materials' tightness. Understanding the density of different substances and how it affects buoyancy is fundamental in physics and chemistry."
Swimmer Chemist, "Breathe!"
Chemist Swimmer, "O_2! O_2! O_2!"

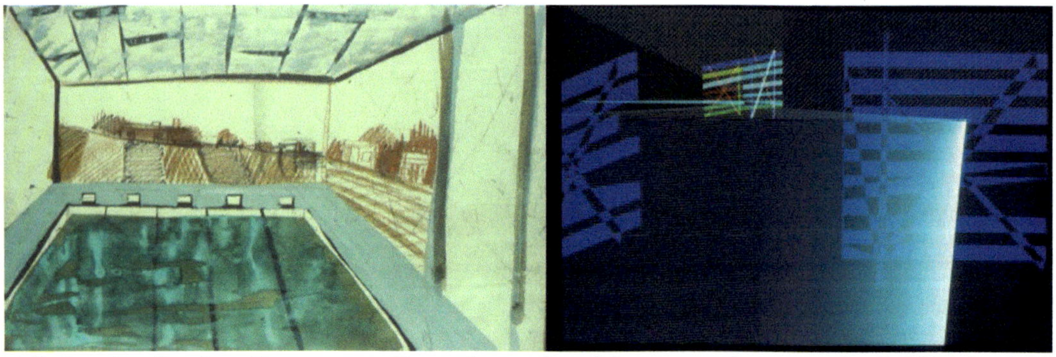

A Swimming Pool and its surroundings. A mural and the output from a code. © 2025 by A. Ursyn.

Swimmer Chemist, "The water tastes weird today."
Chemist Swimmer, "Chemicals like chlorine and bromine used in swimming pools to disinfect the water and maintain pH levels, are used for safe and clean swimming conditions."

Swimmer Chemist, "Breathe!"

Chemist Swimmer, "O_2! O_2! O_2!"

```
pip install pygame
import pygame
import sys
# Initialize Pygame
pygame.init()
# Constants
WIDTH, HEIGHT = 800, 600
BACKGROUND_COLOR = (0, 0, 255)  # Blue
SWIMMER_COLOR = (255, 255, 255) # White
# Swimmer position and dimensions
swimmer_width = 20
swimmer_height = 40
swimmer_x = WIDTH // 2 - swimmer_width // 2
swimmer_y = HEIGHT // 2 - swimmer_height // 2
swimmer_speed = 5
# Initialize the screen
screen = pygame.display.set_mode((WIDTH, HEIGHT))
pygame.display.set_caption("Crawl Style Swimming")
# Main game loop
while True:
  for event in pygame. event.get():
    if event.type == pygame.QUIT:
      pygame.quit()
      sys.exit()
  keys = pygame.key.get_pressed()
  # Move the swimmer
  if keys[pygame.K_LEFT]:
    swimmer_x -= swimmer_speed
  if keys[pygame.K_RIGHT]:
    swimmer_x += swimmer_speed
  if keys[pygame.K_UP]:
    swimmer_y -= swimmer_speed
  if keys[pygame.K_DOWN]:
    swimmer_y += swimmer_speed
  # Clear the screen
  screen.fill(BACKGROUND_COLOR)
  # Draw the swimmer
  pygame.draw.rect(screen, SWIMMER_COLOR, (swimmer_x, swimmer_y, swimmer_width, swimmer_height))
  # Update the display
  pygame.display.update()
```

```
# Quit Pygame
pygame.quit()
```

Swimmer Chemist, “This code sets up a Pygame window to control the "swimmer" (a white triangle), using the arrow keys (the crawl style).”
Chemist Swimmer, “Water itself is a chemical reaction (H2O). Understanding the properties of water molecules, such as their polarity and hydrogen bonding, is fundamental in both chemistry and swimming, as it affects and interacts with swimmers.”
Swimmer Chemist, “The human body's physiological processes that support swimming involve biochemical reactions biochemical reactions. Thus, understanding biochemistry is vital for athletes and coaches to optimize performance and recovery in swimming and other physical activities.”
Swimmer Chemist, “Breathe!”
Chemist Swimmer, “O_2! O_2! O_2!”
Swimmer Chemist, “Breathe!”

The Curtain goes down (or closes).
No Break.

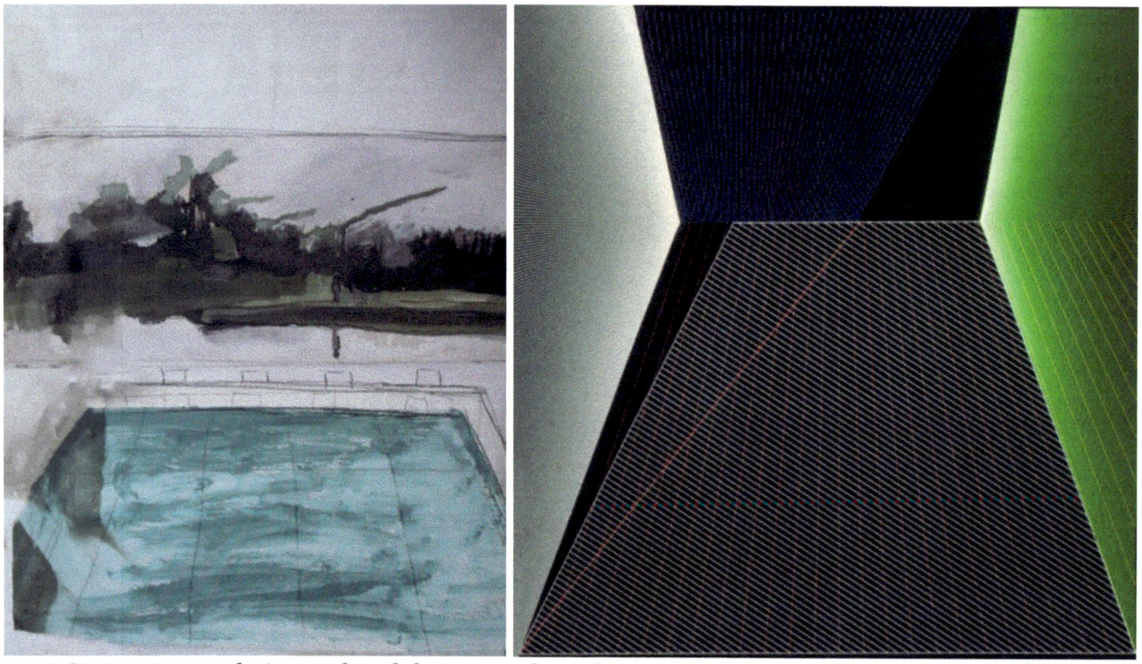

A Swimming pool. A mural and the output from the computer code. © 2025 by Anna Ursyn

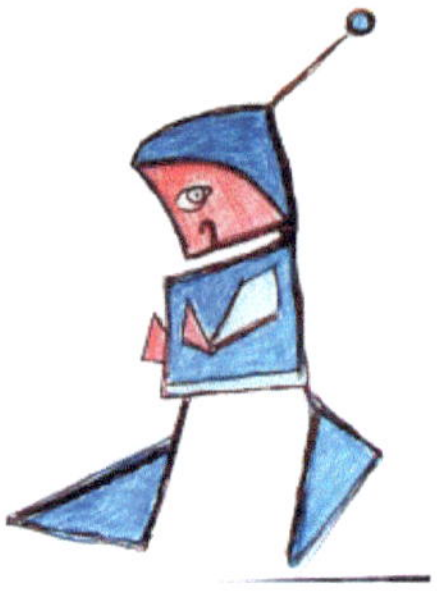

Nykret: talks only when walking fast.

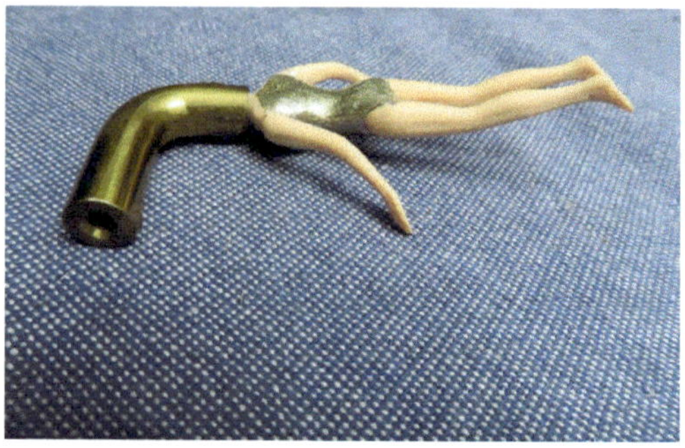

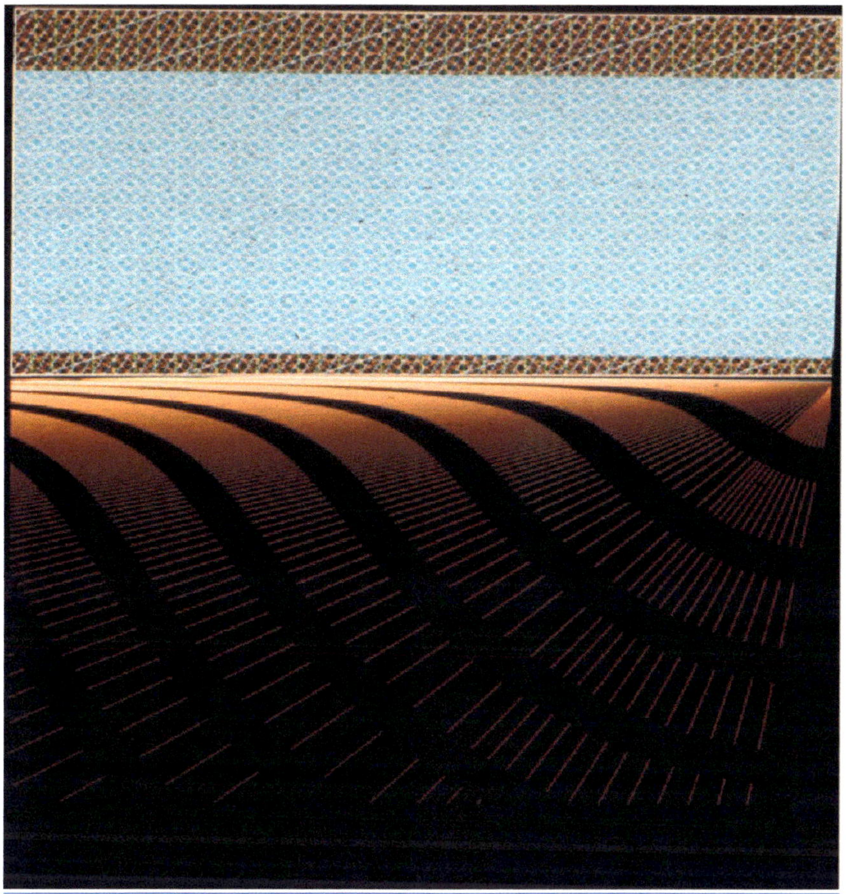

Planes. The output from the computer code. © *2025 by Anna Ursyn*

Act 2
The Curtain goes up (or opens).
Breaststroke (Frog stroke)

Swimmer Chemist, "Breathe!"
Chemist Swimmer, "H_2O!"
Swimmer Chemist, "Swimming gear requires specialized materials for properties like water resistance and material's longevity."
Chemist Swimmer, "It involves chemistry and material science concepts."
Swimmer Chemist, "Breathe!"
Chemist Swimmer, "H_2O! H_2O! H_2O!"
Swimmer Chemist, "Understanding the impact of swimming and recreational water activities on the environment, particularly concerning water quality and contamination, is crucial. Analyzing water quality when assessing the effects of chemicals in swimming areas is an important application of environmental chemists."

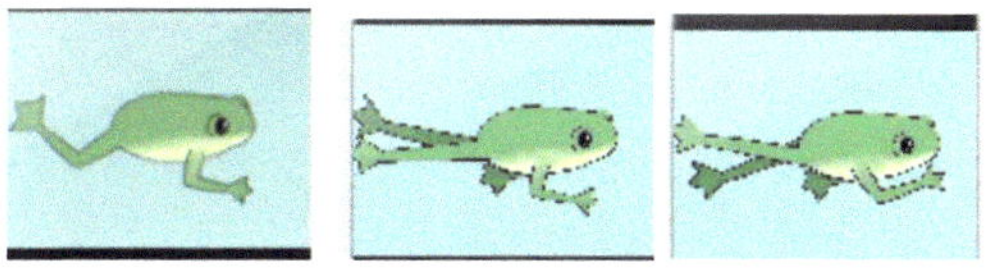

A Frog Swimming Crawl Style. © *Evelynn Leung iArt Institute NYC. (Used with permissions).*

Chemist Swimmer,

```
pip install pygame
import pygame
import sys

# Initialize Pygame
pygame.init()

# Constants
SCREEN_WIDTH = 800
SCREEN_HEIGHT = 600
SWIMMER_COLOR = (0, 0, 255)  # Blue
FPS = 60

# Create the screen
screen = pygame.display.set_mode((SCREEN_WIDTH, SCREEN_HEIGHT))
pygame.display.set_caption("Breathstroke Animation")

# Swimmer's initial position and velocity
swimmer_x = SCREEN_WIDTH // 2
swimmer_y = SCREEN_HEIGHT // 2
swimmer_speed_x = 2

swimmer_speed_y = 2

# Main game loop
clock = pygame.time.Clock()
while True:
    for event in pygame.event.get():
        if event.type == pygame.QUIT:
            pygame.quit()
            sys.exit()

    # Move the swimmer
    swimmer_x += swimmer_speed_x
    swimmer_y += swimmer_speed_y

    # Check for collisions with the screen edges
    if swimmer_x < 0 or swimmer_x > SCREEN_WIDTH:
        swimmer_speed_x *= -1
    if swimmer_y < 0 or swimmer_y > SCREEN_HEIGHT:
        swimmer_speed_y *= -1

    # Fill the screen with white
    screen.fill((255, 255, 255))

    # Draw the swimmer (a simple rectangle)
    pygame.draw.rect(screen, SWIMMER_COLOR, (swimmer_x, swimmer_y, 50, 50))

    # Update the display
    pygame.display.flip()

    # Limit the frame rate
    clock.tick(FPS)
```

Swimmer Chemist, "Or simpler, without any external libraries:

```
import time

def breaststroke():
    try:
        print("Welcome to the Breaststroke (Frog Style) Simulation!")
        time.sleep(1)
        print("Get ready to swim!")
        time.sleep(1)

        while True:
            print("\n1. Extend legs")
            print("2. Bring legs back towards the body")
            print("3. Pull both arms in")
```

```
        print("4. Push both arms forward")
        print("5. Repeat the sequence")
        print("6. Exit")

        choice = input("Enter your choice (1/2/3/4/5/6): ")

        if choice == '1':
          print("Extend your legs backward, keeping them close together.")
        elif choice == '2':
          print("Bring your legs back towards your body.")
        elif choice == '3':
          print("Pull both arms in towards your chest.")
        elif choice == '4':
          print("Push both arms forward, extending them in front of you.")
        elif choice == '5':
          continue
        elif choice == '6':
          break
        else:
          print("Invalid input. Please enter a valid choice (1/2/3/4/5/6).")

        time.sleep(2)

    except KeyboardInterrupt:
      print("\nSwimming simulation terminated.")

if __name__ == "__main__":
breaststroke()
```

Swimmer Chemist, "This code provides a text-based interface for simulating the breaststroke style. It describes the sequence of movements involved in the breaststroke: extending your legs, bringing them back towards your body, pulling both arms in, and pushing both arms forward."
Chemist Swimmer, "In the Breaststroke (Frog Style):
1. Extend your legs
2. Bring your legs back toward your body
3. Pull both arms in
4. Push both arms forward
5. Repeat the sequence
6. Exit.
Enter your choice (1/2/3/4/5/6). "
Swimmer Chemist, "Breathe!"
Chemist Swimmer, "H_2O! H_2O! H_2O!"
Swimmer Chemist, "When a person swims, their body undergoes physiological processes that involve chemical reactions such as the metabolism of energy sources like glucose. Understanding these reactions is essential for athletes and coaches in optimizing performance and recovery."
Chemist Swimmer, "Swimming and chemistry overlap in studying water's chemical properties and its interaction with humans and the environment."
Swimmer Chemist, "Breathe!"
Chemist Swimmer, "H_2O, H_2O! H_2O! O_2! O_2! O_2!"
Swimmer Chemist, "H_2O! H_2O! H_2O!, O_2! O_2! O_2!"

The End.
The Curtain goes down (or closes).

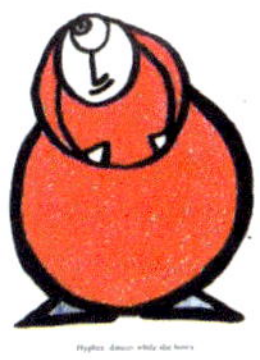

Hyphra: dances while she bows.

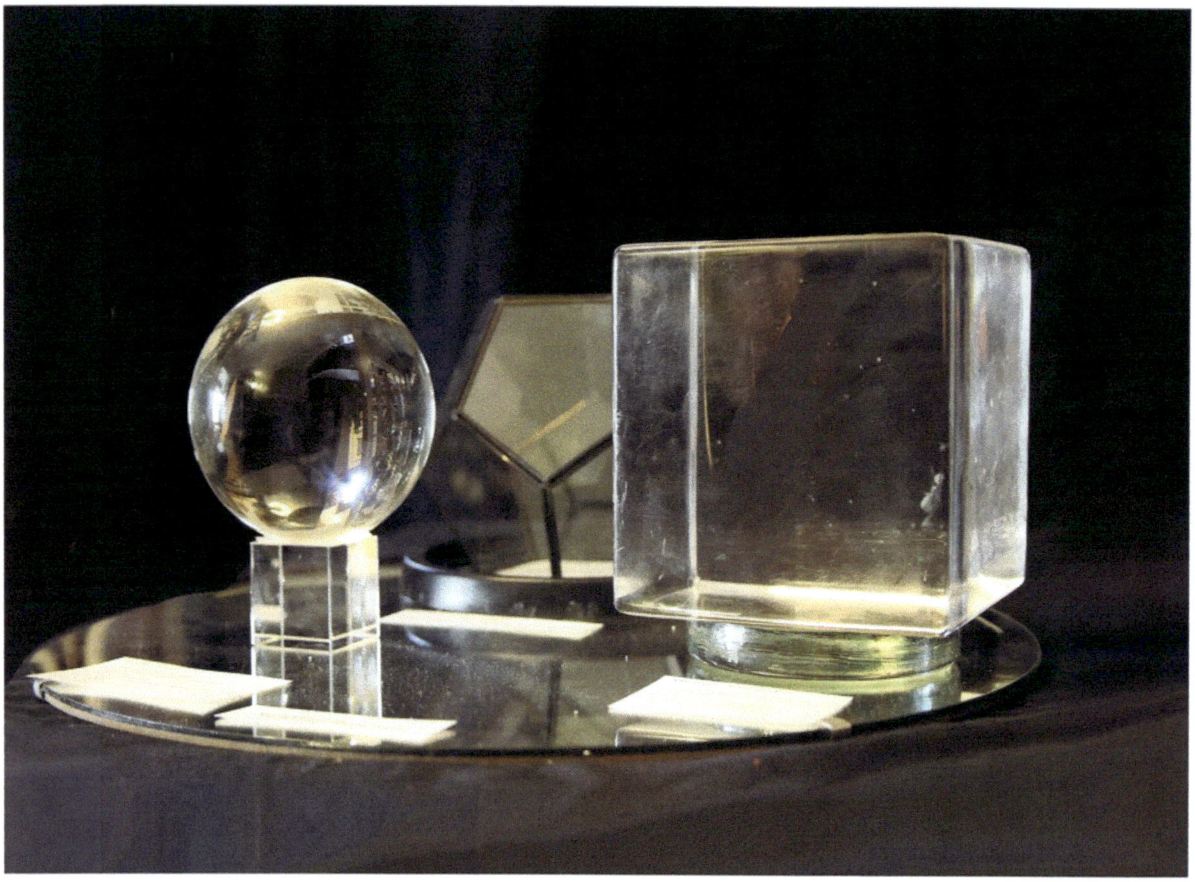

Squaring the Circle. © 2025 by Anna Ursyn

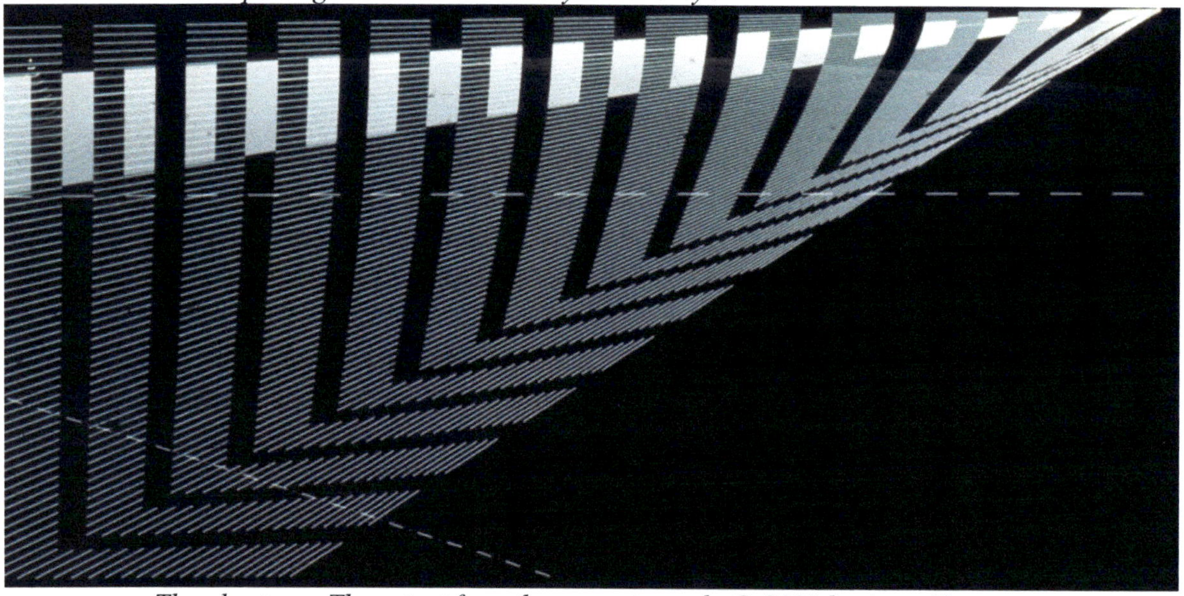

Thunderstorm. The output from the computer code. © 2025 by Anna Ursyn

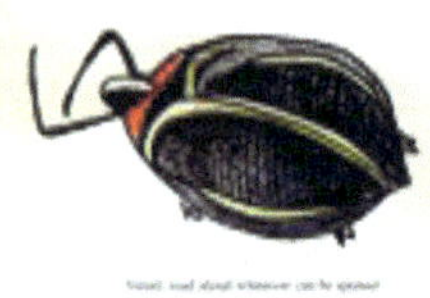

Yulud: reads aloud everything around and above.

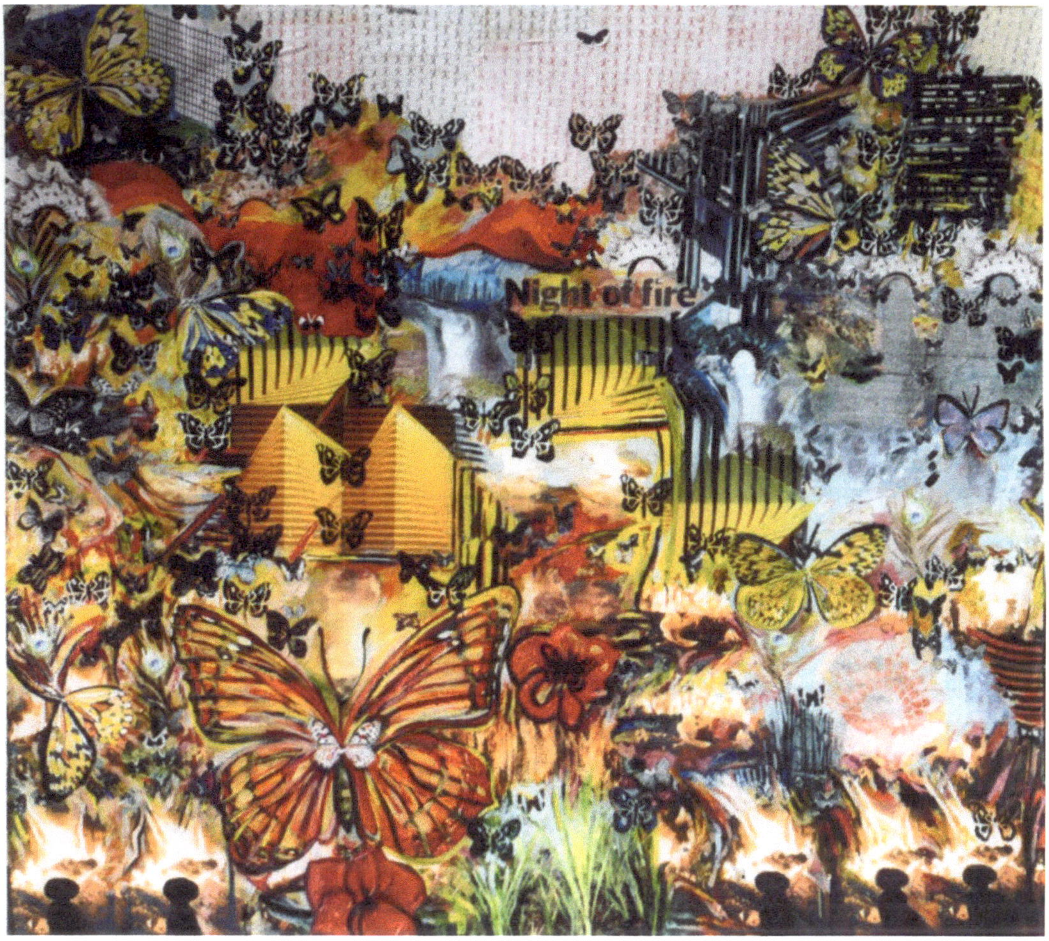

Fire of Night. © *2025 by Anna Ursyn*

CHAPTER 25
CODE DANCE

JOY TO ANGER, CELEBRATION TO PROTEST

INTRODUCTION

We enjoy happiness, celebrating, and participating in a joyful crowd. Group emotions affect us. When we hear about injustice, things that should not be happening or are harmful, we join in to protest to sustain and protect the values and habits we believe in.

SYNOPSIS

Kalizuko and Dramata meet in person this time. They join a joyful parade. An unexpected event triggers the celebrants to protest. While participating, they practice their newly acquired skills.

SUMMARY

A sudden shift can happen even to a large group. We participate in what we believe in.

CAST OF CHARACTERS

Kalizuko, A Coder, now a Dancer
Dramata, A Dancer, now a Coder
A Parader (Celebrator)
A Protester
A Crowd of Paraders
A Mob of Protesters

STAGE DIRECTIONS

A joyful parade involves many colorful, happy characters, while the protest shows the angry ones. The projections of the street are alternated with the codes. The music illustrates the two moods.

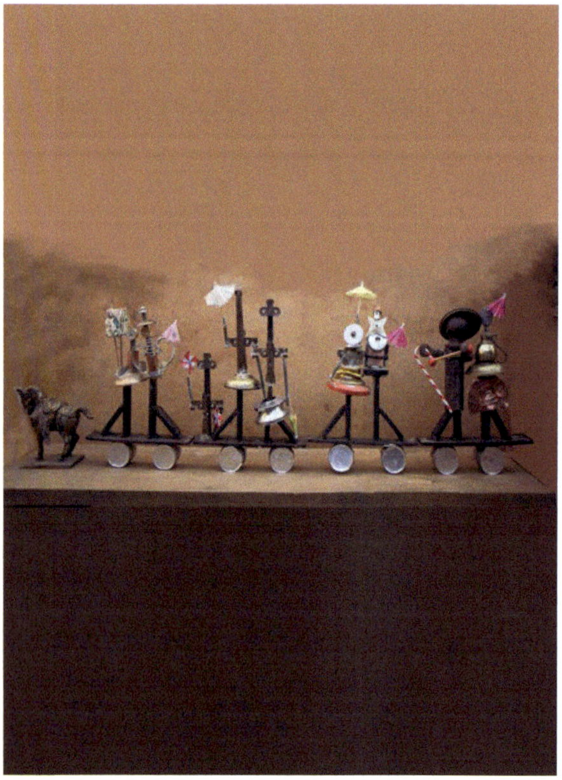

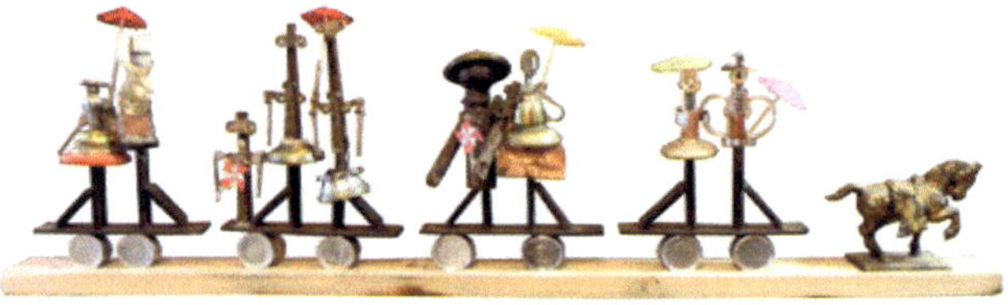

The Curtain goes up (or opens).

`The action happens beyond time and place.`

Dramata, "What a day for a joyful parade. Everybody dressed up according to their professions, I gather?"
Kalizuko, "What's the occasion?"
Dramata, "No idea, but it's good to master our newly acquired skills since we both came from that far."
Kalizuko, "We can even dance in here!"

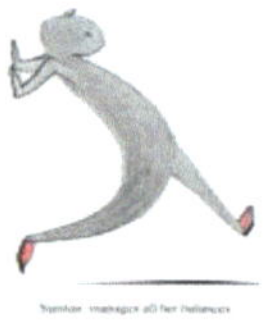

Samtua: manages all her balances.

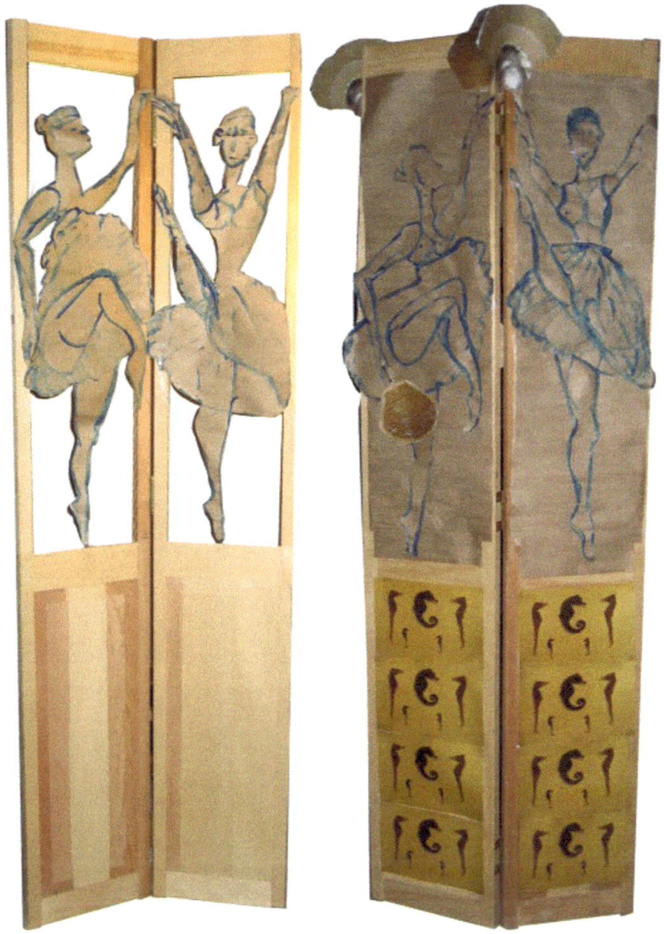

Dramata, "All while coding. Since the parade seems joyful, let's do the waltz!"

```
import pygame
from pygame.locals import *

# Initialize Pygame
pygame.init()

# Set up the window
width, height = 640, 480
screen = pygame.display.set_mode((width, height))
clock = pygame.time.Clock()

# Define colors
WHITE = (255, 255, 255)
RED = (255, 0, 0)

# Define constants for the dancers
DANCER_WIDTH = 50
DANCER_HEIGHT = 50
DANCER_SPEED = 5
```

```
# Load dancer images
dancer1_image = pygame.image.load("dancer1.png")
dancer2_image = pygame.image.load("dancer2.png")

# Set initial positions of the dancers
dancer1_x, dancer1_y = width // 4, height // 2
dancer2_x, dancer2_y = width // 4 * 3, height // 2

# Game loop
running = True
while running:
    for event in pygame.event.get():
        if event.type == QUIT:
            running = False

    # Clear the screen
    screen.fill(WHITE)

    # Move the dancers
    dancer1_x += DANCER_SPEED
    dancer2_x -= DANCER_SPEED

    # Wrap the dancers around the screen
    if dancer1_x > width:
        dancer1_x = -DANCER_WIDTH
    if dancer2_x < -DANCER_WIDTH:
        dancer2_x = width

    # Draw the dancers
    screen.blit(dancer1_image, (dancer1_x, dancer1_y))
    screen.blit(dancer2_image, (dancer2_x, dancer2_y))

    # Update the display
    pygame.display.flip()

    # Control the frame rate
    clock.tick(30)

# Quit the game
pygame.quit()
```

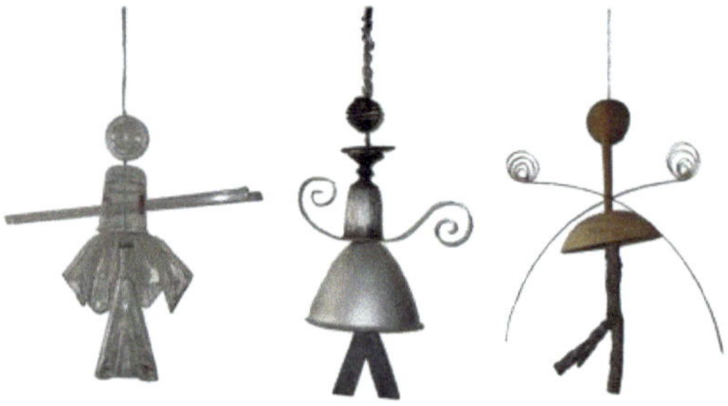

Kalizuko, " In this code, you used the Pygame library to create a window and handle the game loop. The code initializes it, sets up the window, defines colors, and loads dancer images in their initial positions. The game loop continuously moves the dancers in opposite directions to return when they reach the edges. Finally, it draws the dancers on the screen, updates the display, and controls the frame rate. For the code to work, you must provide your dancing photos (dancer1.png and dancer2.png), so let's dance it. But let's have someone take pictures of us while we are at it."

Dramata asks one of the participants to take a picture of them dancing.

Kalizuko, "The waltz is a traditional ballroom dance characterized by its smooth, flowing movements and graceful turns. Let's follow the basic sequence of the waltz: for a starting position, we face each other, with my right hand holding your left hand, my left hand resting on your back, and your right hand resting on my left shoulder."

Dramata, "Good start! The primary step in the waltz is a box step or box pattern, with movements performed in a square. The partners move counterclockwise around the space."

Kalizuko continues, "We take steps in a box divided into the forward and backward parts with three steps each: a step forward or backward, a step to the side, and a step to close the feet together.

Dramata, "Nice. Now, the turns add elegance and variety to the dance, which is performed in different directions and styles, depending on personal preference."

Kalizuko, "Common turns in dancing include the natural turn to the right, reverse turn to the left, and underarm turn where the partner turns under a raised arm to change directions.

Oh, very sorry, Sir….

The waltz incorporates an astonishing rise-and-fall action, adding a sense of lightness and elegance to the dance. We lower as we move forward and rise on our toes as we move backward."
A Parader, "Watch your step!"
Kalizuko, "We can practice intricate footwork, additional turns, embellishments, and patterns at different tempos, ranging from slow and romantic to faster and livelier. The key is maintaining a smooth and flowing motion, connecting with you as we gracefully flow across the parade."
Kalizuko," So sorry, Madam…"
`A loud sound can be heard, and people around them turn angry.`
Dramata, in a scared voice, "What happened?"
Kalizuko, "No clue, but they are all furious. Shell, we leave?"
Dramata, "Nope, we'll do the angry dance."

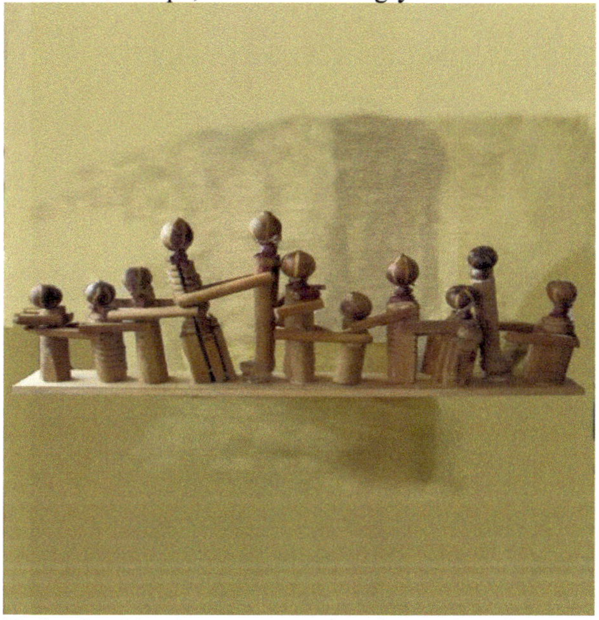
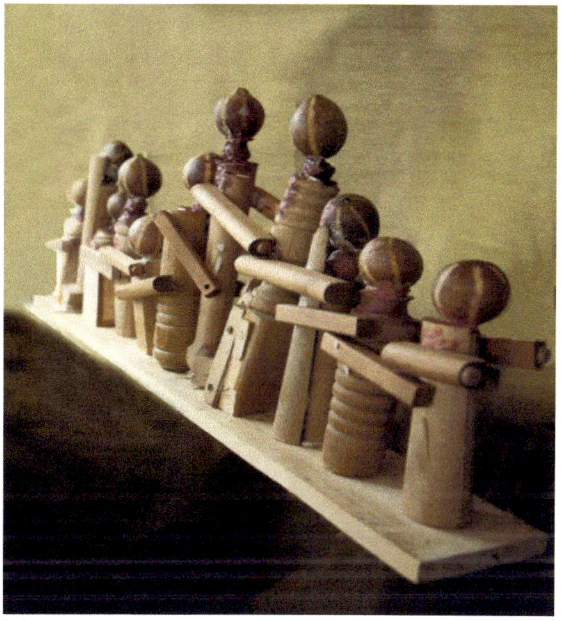

Kalizuko, "An Anger Dance is a form of Latihan, which removes angry energy from your body."

```
import time

def anger_dance(duration):
    print("The Anger Dance begins!")

    for i in range(duration):
        print("Step", i+1, ": Stomp your feet!")
        time.sleep(0.5) # Pause for half a second

        print("Step", i+1, ": Clench your fists!")
        time.sleep(0.5) # Pause for half a second

        print("Step", i+1, ": Shout out loud!")
        time.sleep(0.5) # Pause for half a second

        print("Step", i+1, ": Release your anger!")
        time.sleep(1)  # Pause for one second

    print("The Anger Dance is over!")

# Example usage
anger_dance(5) # Run the anger dance for 5 steps
```

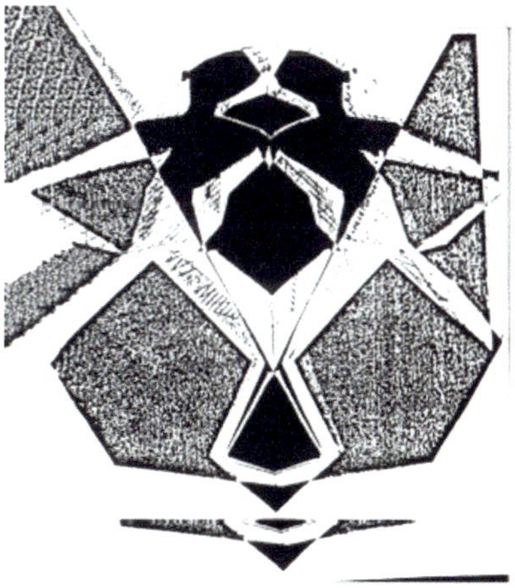

Dramata, "In this code, the anger_dance() function takes a duration parameter, representing the number of iterations the dance should go through. Each step consists of stomping feet, clenching fists, shouting loudly, and releasing anger. The function uses the time.sleep() method to pause the program for a specified time between each step."

Kalizuko, "An angry dance can help release suppressed emotions. Here are steps to incorporate into your routine: stand tall, stomp and march, punch and jab, use sharp movements, keep your fists clenched, use isolations, jump, incorporate floorwork, turn and spin, and use the space around you. Adapt these steps to your own style and comfort level, and prioritize safety. Add personal touches to make the routine expressive of your anger.
A Protester, "Watch it!"
Remember to adapt these steps to your own style and comfort level. It is essential that you prioritize your safety and avoid any movements that may cause injury. Add your personal touches and improvisations to make the dance routine truly expressive of your anger."
`Kalizuko and Dramata dance an angry dance.`
A Protester, "What is your name, please?"
Kalizuko, "Why? It's Kalizuko."
The angry mob of Protesters, "Kalizuko for the CIO! Kalizuko for the CIO! Kalizuko for the CIO!

The End
The Curtain goes down (or closes).

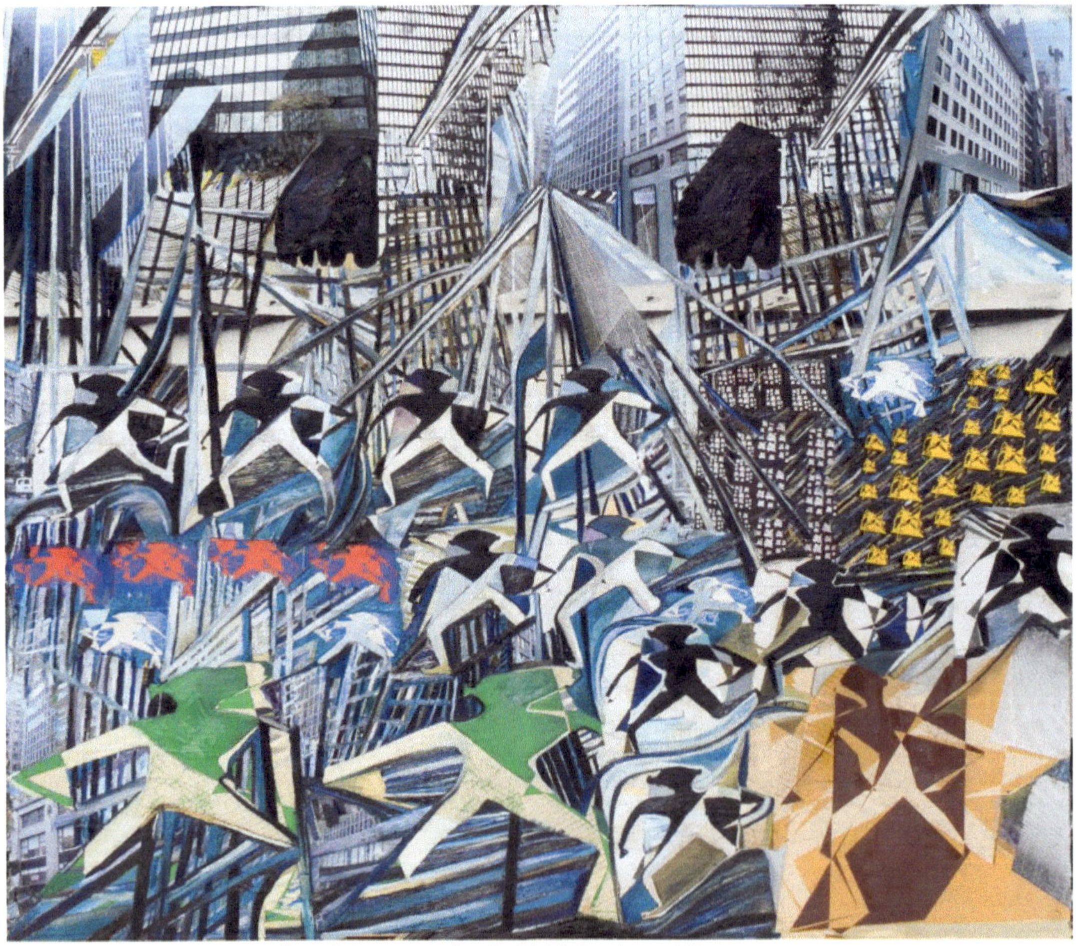

Urban Masquerade. © 2025 by Anna Ursyn

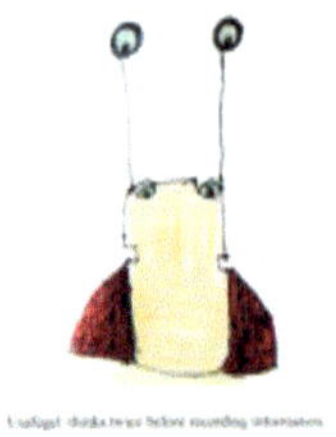

Usafegel: careful but consistent.

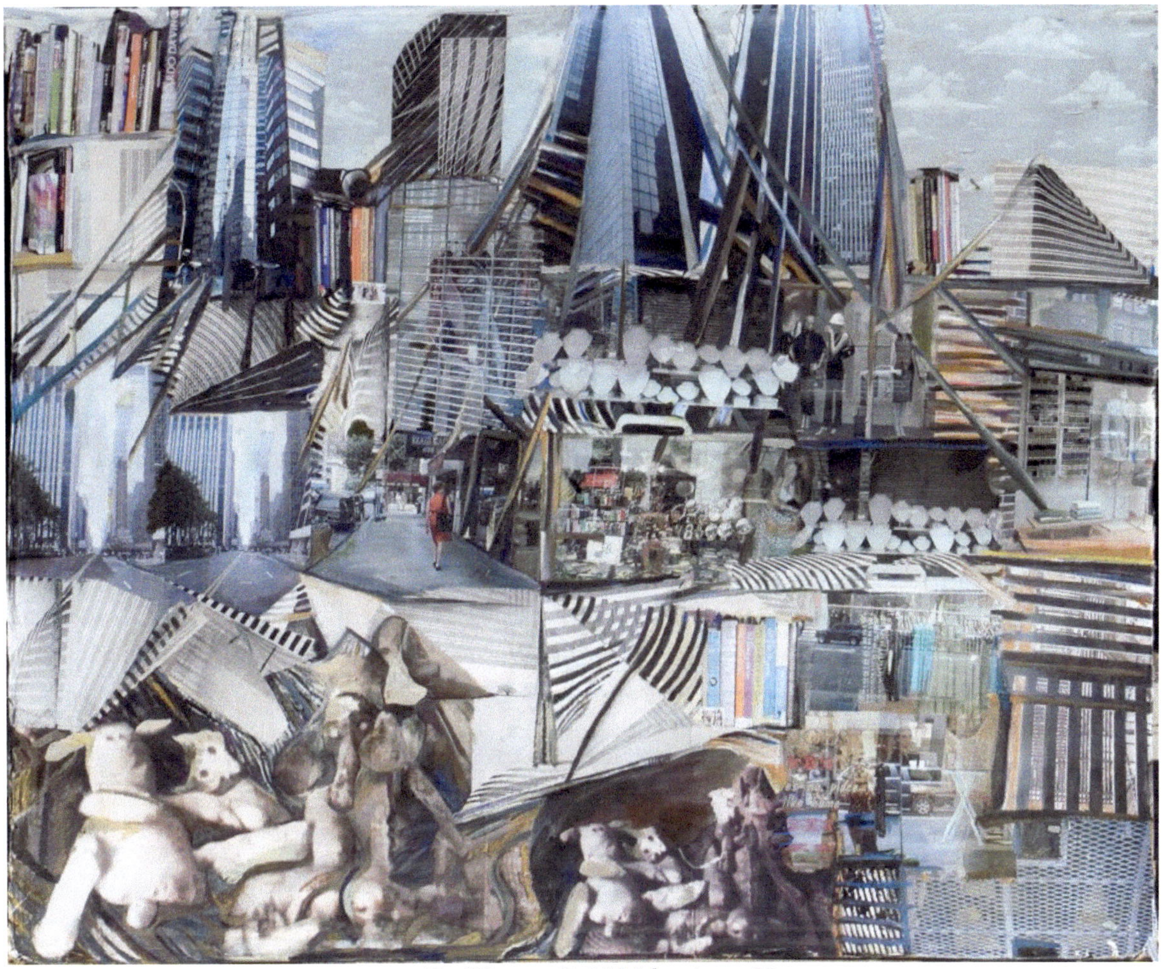

Red Dress. © *2025 by Anna Ursyn*

CHAPTER 26
DRESS CODE

SHOPPING ENCOUNTER

INTRODUCTION

This work explores connections between code and culture. We dress for the occasion, following the code, trends, elegance, and fashion. These drive the economy but affect ecological balance and are partially responsible for many other circumstances.

SYNOPSIS

Violet needs a new outfit to attend a celebration of her husband's achievement at his company. Her friend Cherie, who gives her plenty of advice, is with her.
Stage designers, both named Jon, happen to shop for the outfit for a Diva at the opera performance which is coming soon. They comment on this situation.

SUMMARY

Being elegant, fashionable, and following trends impacts the planet. We must produce and trade to keep the economy going, but it comes with some growing and sometimes ignored danger.

CAST OF CHARACTERS

Violet, the wife of the best employee to be celebrated by his company.
Cherie, her friend, accompanies her to the store and gives her advice
Theodor, the store clerk
Aphelia, The store clerk's assistant
Jons, the two stage designers shopping for their opera's Diva, but commenting on what they overhear.

STAGE DIRECTIONS

The stage opens a view of a luxury, well-lit store filled with clothing, shoes, jewelry, and everything needed to dress up sharp to look elegant, fashionable, and current – the neon "Dress Finesse' leaks inside the store, creating a cozy atmosphere. A sign "Dress for the Occasion appears inside of the store. Well-dressed clerks invite their clients to enjoy coffee, juices, and snacks while handing each of them a glass of champagne.

Act 1

The Curtain goes up (or opens).

Violet, "Thank you for taking me here, Cherie. It looks like a nice place to shop for the occasion."
Cherie, "You'll look glorious, elegant, and sophisticated. All men will admire you, and all women will be jealous."
Violet, "How did you know my motto?"
Cherie, "Theodor is approaching us. Just listen to me talking."
Theodor, to Violet, "My name is Theodor, and it is such a pleasure serving you today. Coffee? Tea? Juice? Cookies? And here is your champagne."
Violet, "I don't drink."
Cherie, "Here you do. Just like you will tomorrow night."
Theodor, while pouring champagne from two small fancy bottles into plastic glasses for the ladies, "What's the occasion, may I ask?"
Cherie, "The best employee award celebration for her husband at his company."
Theodor, to Violet, "My sincere congratulations, ma'am. You must be very happy and proud of your husband. May I offer..."
Cherie, pointing at a festive pink dress. "She wants to try this one."
Jon, "Hey Jon, "They are taking the pink dress I wanted for the opera singer. I am sure it is the only one in this fashionable store or even beyond it."
Jon, "You know, Jon, you are right. We need to do something about it, but what happened with the last dress she used?"
Jon, "Our Diva cannot wear the same dress twice. Some patrons attend more than one evening. No true lady could stand another woman wearing her dress, which applies to our Diva and her listeners. It is hard to buy a dress for her as she gestures a lot while singing, so all the jewelry needs to be attached to her costume. And she needs a lot of jewelry, as she is attending the king's coronation, her husband's. I painted all the jewelry on her costume with some thick acrylic paint. It is a plastic-based medium, and one can

build the thickness with some chemicals that form texture. Metals like cadmium, titanium, lead, and nickel look the best."
Jon, "Nickel allergies can irritate the skin and even cause red rashes. What would she look like when performing? Titanium can cause lung diseases, skin diseases (Eczema), sinus congestion, or vision problems. Those are not conditions for a public performer. Cadmium can cause nausea, diarrhea, abdominal pain, muscle aches, and vomiting. How could she sing and act while experiencing some of those symptoms on the stage? And lead is harmful to children. They might approach her after the matinee performance. She is a hugger, you know."
Jon, "It's just for the evening. Besides, who knows?"
Jon, "People know (hopefully)"

```
import matplotlib.pyplot as plt
import numpy as np

# Simulated survey data (replace this with your actual data)
responses = {
    'Cadmium': np.random.choice([1, 2, 3, 4, 5], size=100),
    'Titanium': np.random.choice([1, 2, 3, 4, 5], size=100),
    'Lead': np.random.choice([1, 2, 3, 4, 5], size=100),
    'Nickel': np.random.choice([1, 2, 3, 4, 5], size=100),
}

# Calculate average awareness for each element
average_awareness = {element: np.mean(responses[element]) for element in responses}

# Plot the data
elements = list(average_awareness.keys())
awareness_scores = list(average_awareness.values())

plt.bar(elements, awareness_scores, color=['blue', 'green', 'red', 'purple'])
plt.title('Average Awareness of Negative Impact')
plt.xlabel('Element')
plt.ylabel('Average Awareness Score')
plt.ylim(1, 5)  # Assuming awareness scores are between 1 and 5
plt.show()
```

Cherie, "You must look like a queen. Look, there is a crown over there."
Theodor to Aphelia, "Bring that crown, please, and grab two of those tiny champagne bottles and two new plastic glasses while you are there. Careful though. On the second thought, make it two trips."
Theodor continues, turning onto the ladies, "That crown is made of Teflon. It is the toughest, non-biodegradable material you may imagine. It will last forever. It is one of a kind, of course. The best gold is encrusted…."
Violet, "Pink does not go well with gold."
Jon to Jon, "For coronation, it does and goes well with the king's red attire. Luckily, our "King" can wear the same costume repeatedly."
Jon, "Someone caring for nature, at least."
Jon, "That is silly; production drives the economy, thus making our lives better."
Jon, "But the planet? Every 3D printer should come with its own recycler, I think. Teflon and plastic are everywhere; they even make flossing out of Teflon. There are mountains of trash that…"

Jon, "By producing and replacing, we drive our country to the top."
Cherie, "The whole evening, they will talk about each man's to-do list. Those lists are costly in nature. You must look like the wife of a king."
Jon: "Oh, no! They are now taking our Diva's ivory crown. Diva needs it for her husband's coronation. She'll sing the role of the queen!"
Violet, "These hats. This one is interesting."
Jon, "Perfect for showing in at the opera to obstruct the view of those sitting in front its wearer."

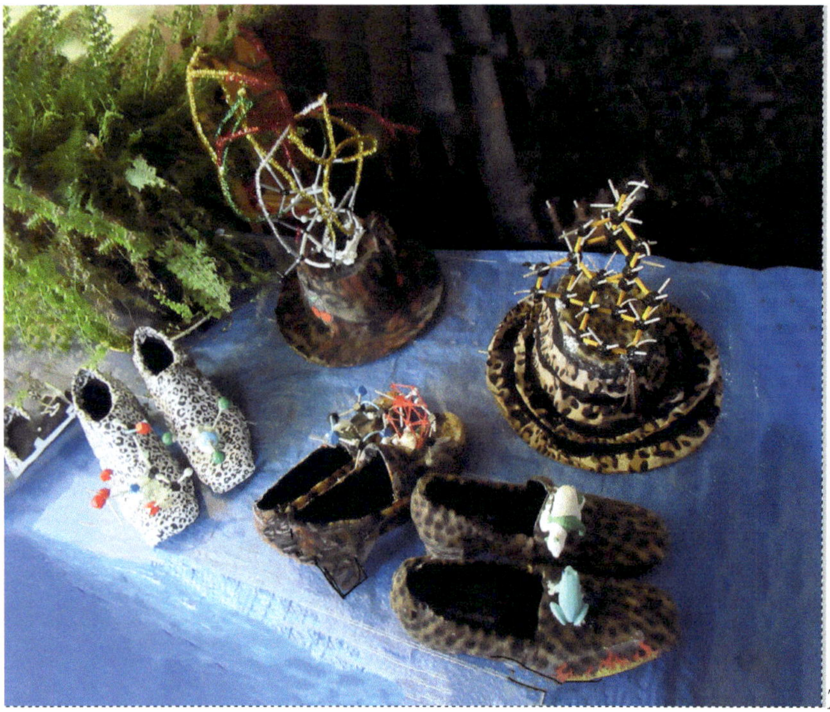

The hats and matching shoes.

Cherie to Theodor, "We'll also need a fashionable handbag for the lady of the evening, please. But it must be made of natural, highest-quality leather, and it must match the shoes, belt, and her hat."

Theodor, "Yes, of course, we have them here, authentic from various types of animal products, all from a luxury market... some are even made from unusual trees, and even fish. All have unique characteristics and qualities. This one is encrusted with heavy metals. They all look spectacular. "
Jon, "Were heavy metals the cause of Van Gogh's problems?"
Theodor, "Those are colored with pure Vermillion."
Jon, "Don't people read anymore? It's derived from mining. Mercury, it is. This ore has mercury in it, causing the miners to lose their lives due to the substance's toxicity. "Even replacing it with cadmium red made the EPA Office set cadmium, with its toxicity, for elimination."
Jon, "We should think twice before driving a gas-powered car, turning on a dishwasher, or loading items into the washer or dryer. We should use solar, wind, or other safe energy sources. Otherwise, our planet will keep getting weaker."
Jon, "Yes, but we need to think about the culture. How we dress defines us. Remember when they wanted to lower the dress code for some group members of the government, and the body language, language, and behavior all went down, so they had to keep it as it was to take the culture back and up? The same applies to various groups, professions it belongs to…"
Jon, "Yes, they sure belong to their prisons in their orange jackets."
Jon, "The hunters wear orange jackets, sometimes the road workers or volunteers who pick trash at the interstates, to lower dirtiness. This is what I call culture. Now it is REDUCE, RECYCLE, plus REPAIR and REFUSE."

*Jon, "*Also, REHOME to take care of those poor animals waiting for us."
Jon, "And UPCYCLE, but it does not start with an R. Not elegant."
*Cherie, "*She'll take that pink dress."
Theodor," Aphelia, please bring that matching, one-of-a-kind pink necklace with a 24-karat brim, matching earrings, ring, and brooch. Just be careful with them, would you? And while you are at it, grab two more small bottles of champagne with two fresh plastic glasses. Take them from a new box."
*Cherie to Theodor, "*Please ask her to bring the most expensive leather shoes you have, red or gold; it does not matter to me."
*Violet, "*Aren't those endangered?"
Theodor, "I can assure you, ma'am, we only sell one-of-a-kind items here."
Cherie, "Call the driver to come here. Tell him the engine can still stay idle."

The Curtain goes down (or closes). The Break.

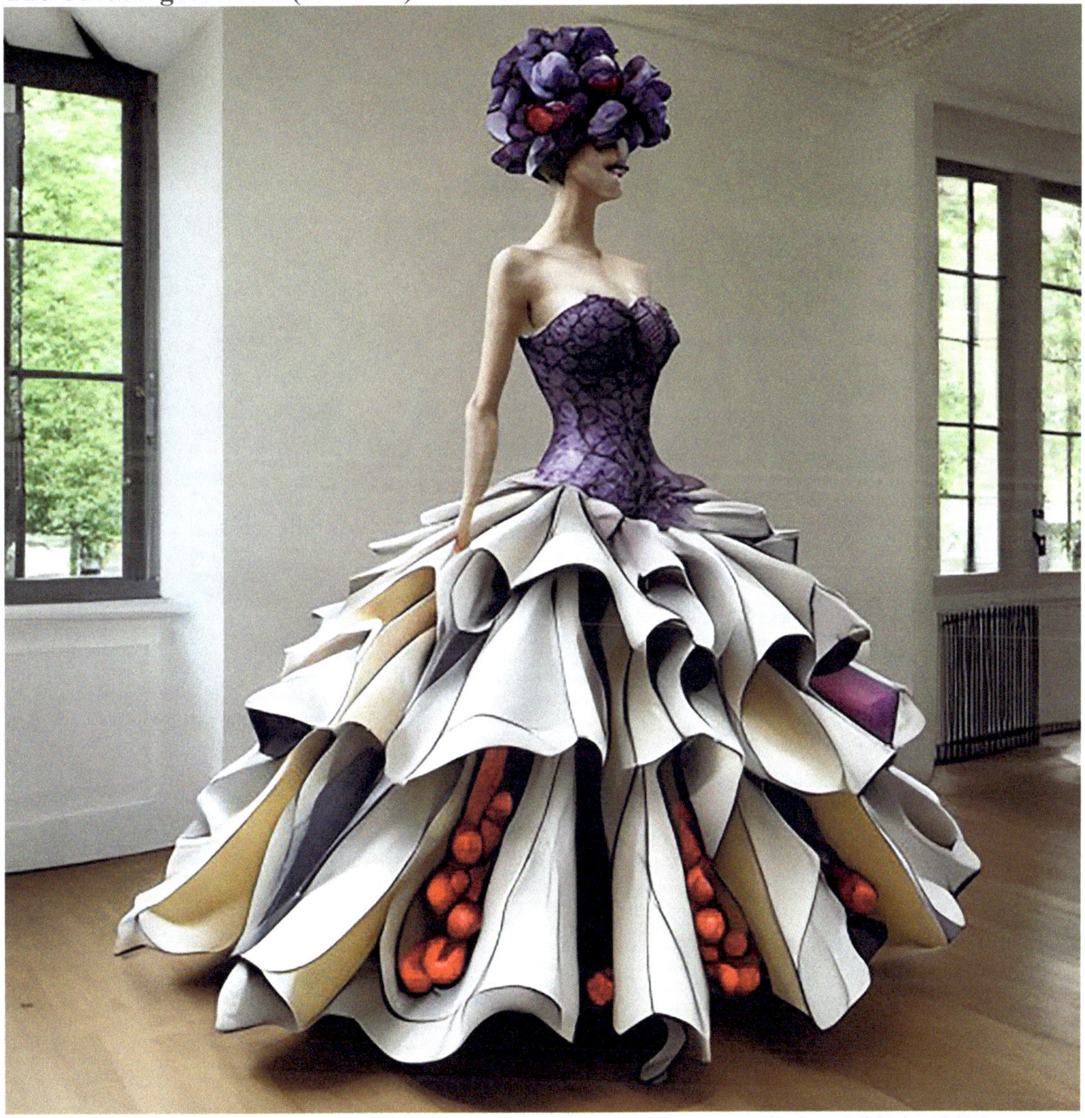

Whitaker Evening Elegance 4 **c. Corinne Whitaker 2024**

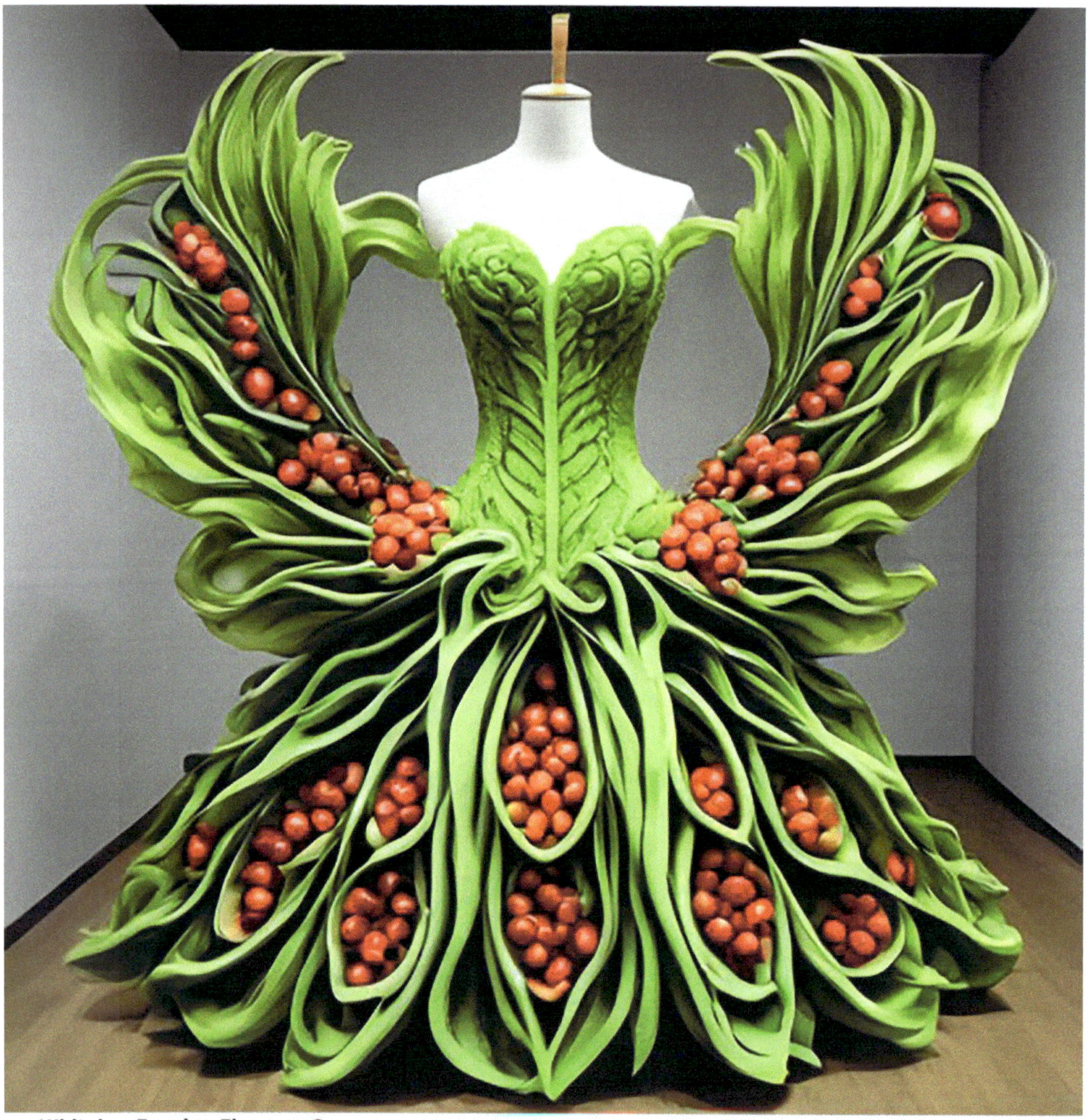

Whitaker Evening Elegance 2 c. Corinne Whitaker 2024

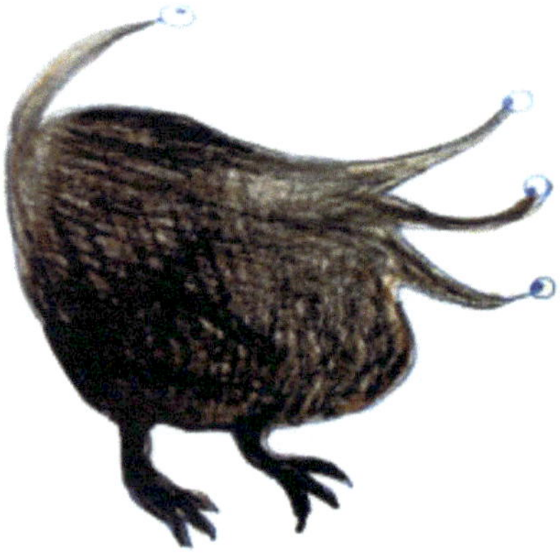

Yubty: watches his own business.

Yubty: too many tasks.

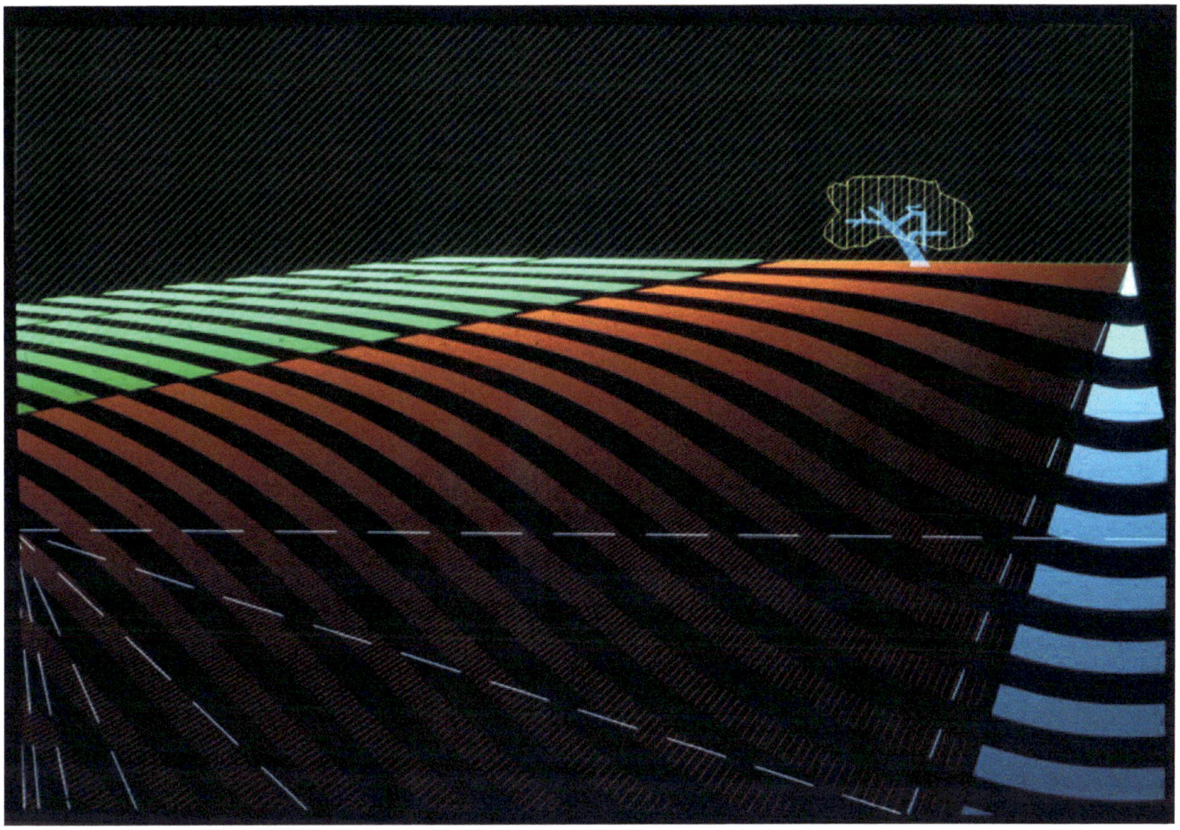

The Red Tree. The output from the computer code. © 2025 by Anna Ursyn

Act 2

The Curtain goes up (or opens).

Jon, "Did you see the review of last night's banquet, where they celebrated the husband of the lady who snatched the Diva's pink dress from us? "
Jon, "Oh, yes, I saw the photo. She looked like a cherry on the top of a cake. Everybody else wore black."
Jon, "Let's check the second-hand and antique stores. I am sure that dress ended up there."
Jon, "I'd rather check with trash companies. No true lady wears the same dress twice and would ever want another woman to appear in, even in a similar one."
Jon, "Let's see."
Jon shows the data to Jon.

```
def check_awareness():
    chemicals = ['cadmium', 'lead', 'nickel']

    for chemical in chemicals:
        print(f"Do you know about the negative nature of {chemical}? (yes/no)")
        response = input().lower()

        if response == 'yes':
            print(f"You are aware of the potential health effects of {chemical}. Good job!\n")
        elif response == 'no':
            print(f"{chemical.capitalize()} can have harmful effects on health. It's important to be informed.\n")
        else:
```

```
        print("Invalid response. Please enter 'yes' or 'no'.\n")

if __name__ == "__main__":
    check_awareness()
```

Jon, “If you excuse me, I must go home and spray on those wicked dandelions. Not only do they make me look bad, but they bring those pesky bugs close to my house.”
Jon, “No bugs, no life, mind you. Let’s try the new coffee shop around the corner. They serve the best dandelion salad in the area. It is very healthy, I was told.”

The End

The Curtain goes down (or closes).

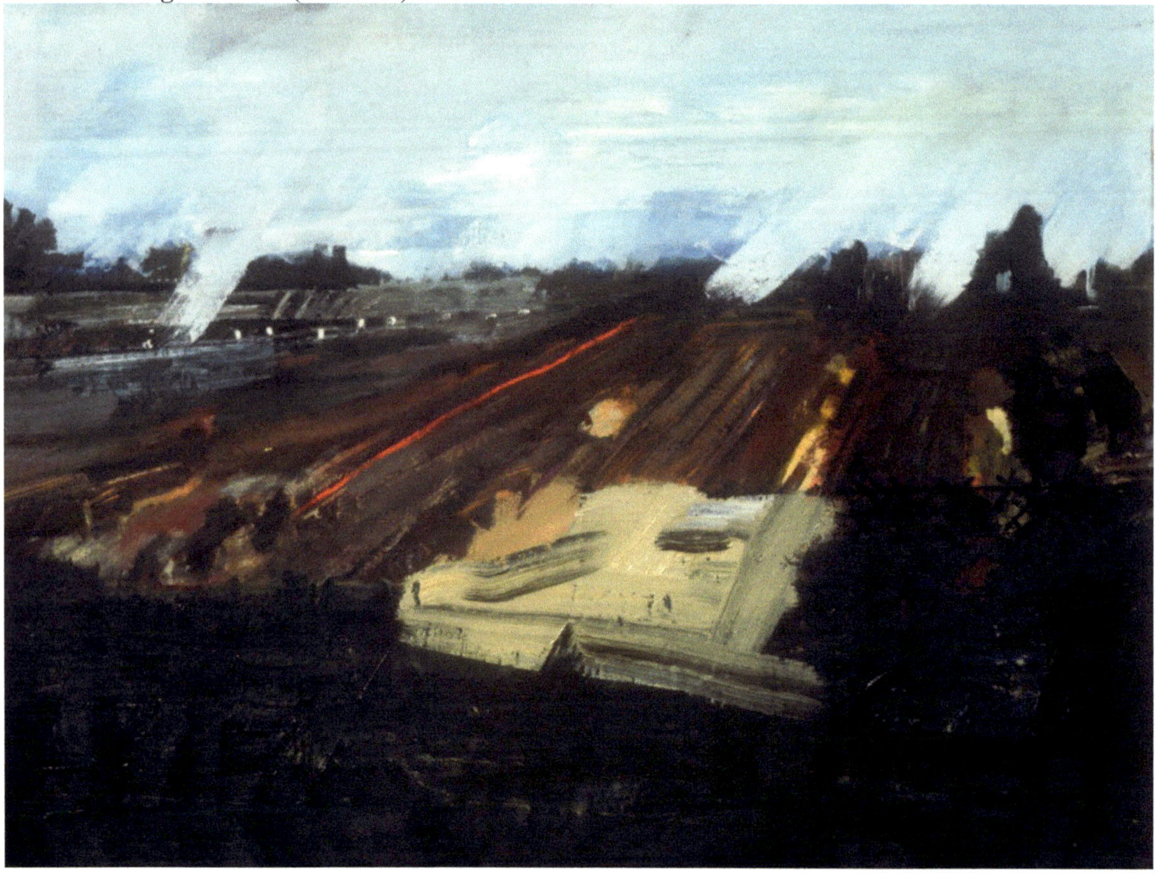

Site for a City. © 2025 by Anna Ursyn

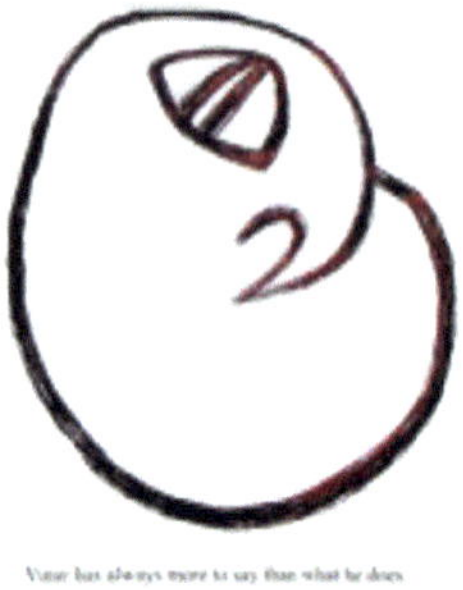

Vutar: has more to say than he does.

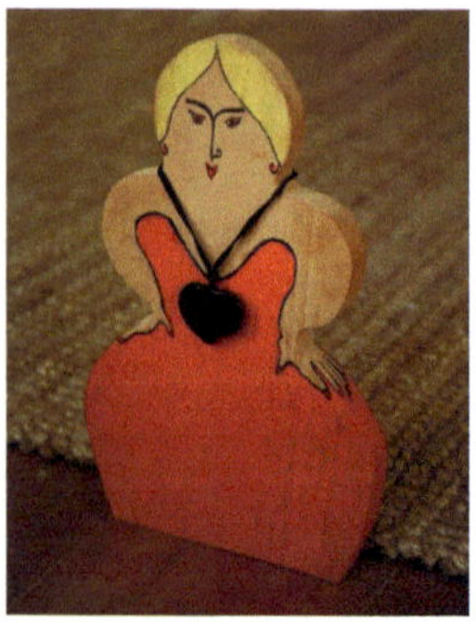

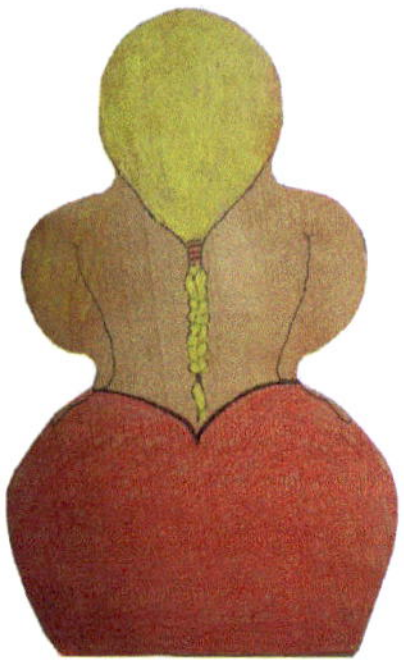

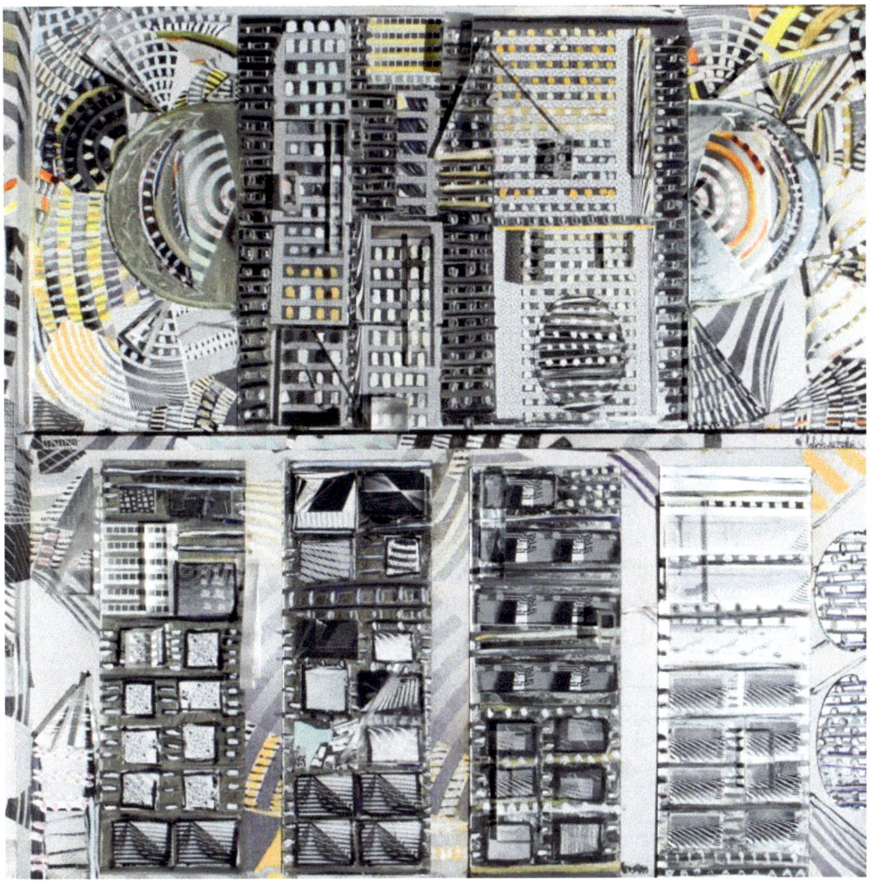

Window Views. © 2025 by Anna Ursyn

CHAPTER 27
WORLD CODE

QUESTIONS AND ANSWERS SESSION

INTRODUCTION

Everything is now connected, and there is multi-level interaction. Unified and multidisciplinary approaches can be observed if we look at translations and how we mechanize and robotize tedious tasks. We ask bots for data and performance-based advice in stocks, medicine, or even inventions. We like to call it collective intelligence. We mimic Nature on various levels, starting with new materials and systems called biomimicry, bio-inspiration, and bio-derivation. Biomimicry by following order in the living systems. The new materials respond to external stimuli. With bio-inspiration, people create structures acting in a different scheme than living systems to perform the same functions. Bio-derivation is achieved by incorporating biomaterials into human-made designs. For example, we create divers 'suits following ducks 'methods, as their palmate feet do not freeze. The adhesive gecko foot, the self-cleaning lotus leaf, and the fracture-resistant mollusk shell as examples of inspiring structures. We use spider webs, eggs, or flour as glue. We observe collective creativity. Our world is computer-based. People collaborate. Batch processing and automatization do the rest. This creates new opportunities for inventions. Artificial Intelligence is seen as helpful and potentially dangerous. We face many challenges.

SYNOPSIS

This chapter summarizes the logical consequence of research-based collaborative efforts. Perhaps it's a way too complicated and challenging topic if you look at the chapters above. Ada and Charles' characters commemorate the origination of the concept of coding and a digital programmable computer. They discuss the shaping needs and solutions for humans in this ever-changing era. The characters in this chapter were named in their honor.

SUMMARY

We look at current times and our future hopes, and how they form from some historical perspective we learn about. We examine the world's most significant challenges while trying to find new technological solutions for the most critical problems people face.

CAST OF CHARACTERS

Charles, the Computing specialist (the idea of a mechanical digital programmable computer.)
Ada, the Computer languages specialist (the first computer programmer).
Moil, who introduced this book (known for making tasks disappear), now suggests new solutions.

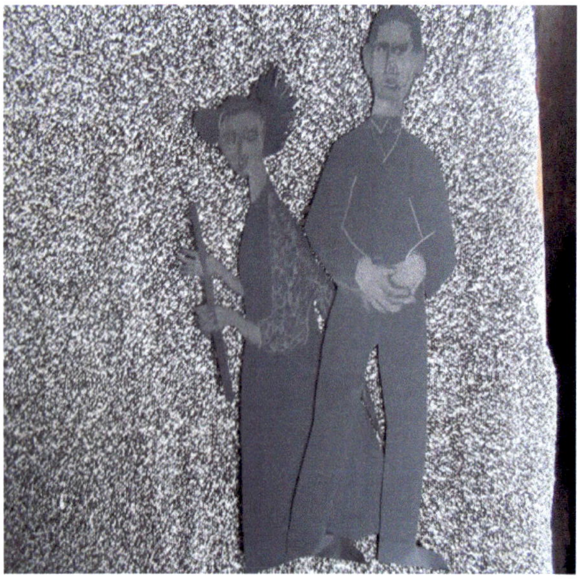

STAGE DIRECTIONS

Ada and Charles are represented by shadow puppets made from a cardboard box on the stage; Moil is an actor dressed in a 3D model of a sphere who interacts solo with projected AI images.

`The action happens beyond time and place.`

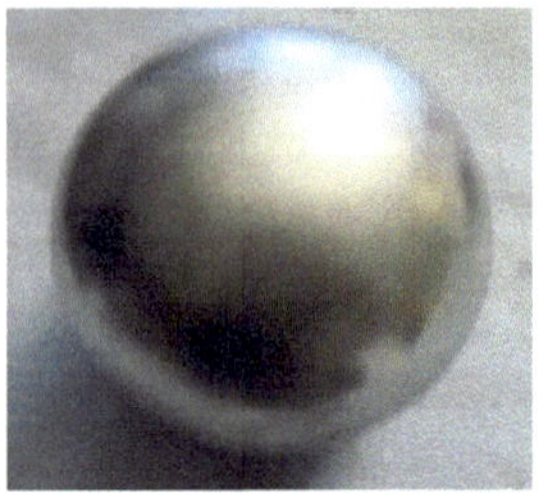

Moil

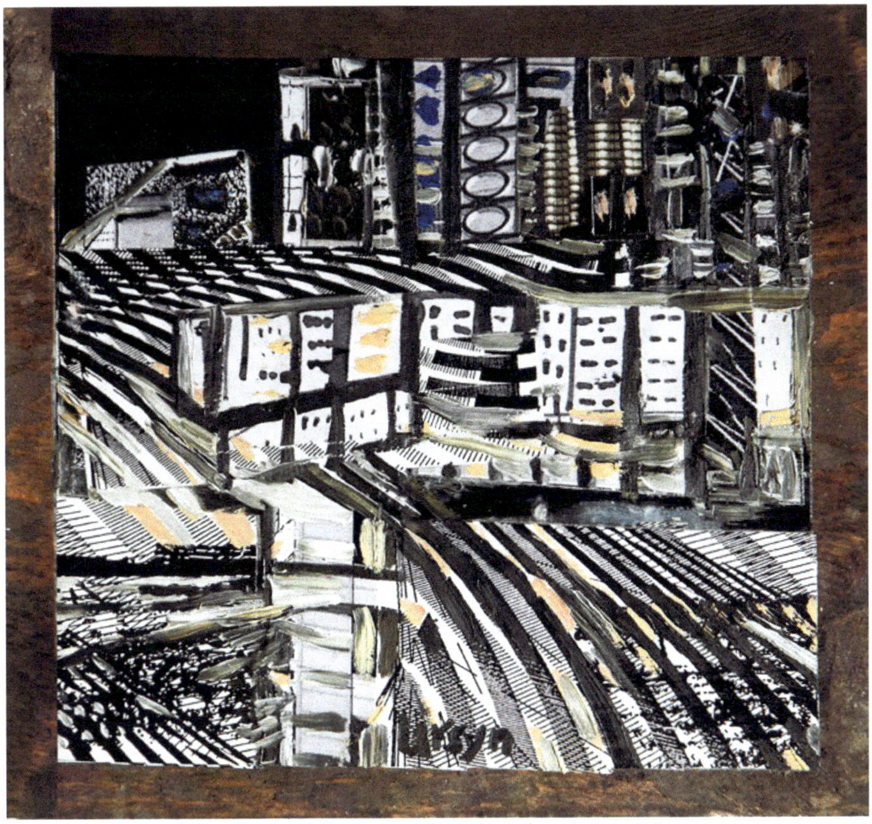

Levels and Layers. © *2025 by Anna Ursyn*

The Curtain goes up (or opens).

Ada, "It's time to recapitulate. There are connections and interactions. The world is now computer-based, everything is more networked, and people collaborate. Cobots help on various levels. Biophotonics changes the way we farm vertically, avoiding refrigeration or transportation. This creates new opportunities for inventions. But (there is always a "but"), we face challenges."
Charles, "First, it is good to know what we face:

Our World's Grand Challenges

Q: Charles, "Hunger."
A: Ada, "3D printing, electronic transportation!"

Q: Charles, "Greed."

Moil, "Preserving agriculture techniques such as precision farming, vertical farming, hydroponics and aquaponics can optimize crop production while conserving water, and minimizing transportation and environmental impact, ensuring food security for a growing the whole planet's population."
A: Ada, "More technology, so everyone has enough, accompanied by policies, social awareness, and ethical considerations for equitable and stable outcomes."
Moil, "Yes, reducing economic inequality, financial gap, status, as social stability requires creating receptive economies with equal opportunities and fair distribution."
Q: Charles, "Diseases."
A: Ada, "Biophotonics-based research."

Moil, "In healthcare innovation, advancements in medical technology, telemedicine,zartificial intelligence (AI), and wearable devices to improve healthcare access, diagnosis, treatment, and disease prevention, enhancing public health outcomes."
Q: Charles, "The world's health crises"
A: Ada, "Helping people be playful. Happy people are healthier, they say."
Moil, "The recent pandemic has shown the vulnerability of the health systems, needs international cooperation in disease prevention, preparedness, and response. Access to healthcare, promotion of research, and strengthening of medical infrastructure is crucial for addressing current and future health crises."
Q: Charles, "Natural disasters and their consequences."
A: Ada, "Solar and safe wind solutions."
Moil, "Disaster Management as utilizing satellite imaging, drones, and AI-powered predictive models can aid in early warning systems, disaster response coordination, and efficient relief efforts for natural disasters. Also, bladeless turbines."
Q: Charles, "Wars."
A: Ada, "More quality entertainment."
Moil, "Solving conflict and violence, such as armed conflicts, and political instability, leading to displacement, loss of life, and human suffering. Promoting peaceful resolutions through dialogue and addressing the root causes of conflicts is crucial for achieving long-term stability and peace."
Q: Charles, "Totalitarianism."
A: Ada, "Virtual Tourism?"
Moil, "Governance and corruption are addressed by transparent, accountable, and effective governance for preserving development, strengthening egalitarian institutions, following the law, and ensuring access to justice, which are important in a fair and just society."
Q: *Charles,* "Exploitation."
A: Ada, "A Robot for Everyone."
Moil, "Poverty and inequality, lacking access to food, clean water, education, and healthcare."
Q: Charles, "Migration and Refugee Crises."
A: Ada, "All of the above!"
Moil, "Forced displacement due to conflicts, persecution, and change need to be addressed by examining the causes, providing humanitarian aid, and finding solutions for refugees and migrants through worldwide cooperation and comprehensive strategies."
Q: Charles, "A 'More' attitude."
A: Ada, "Spread apps for composing music."
Moil, "More entertainment."
Q: Charles, Stereotyping."
A: Ada, "Online jobs."
Q: Charles, "Jealousy."
A: Ada, "That is a tough one, Mr. Charles. Those suffering from jealousy will find all the faults behind the best solutions. That constant need for attention! Not sure if there is a cure or a solution for that."
Q: Charles, "No cure for that, then, Ms. Ada."
A: Ada, "Even if everyone gets the same of everything, there will be a sense of injustice present."
Q: Charles, "Racism."
A: Ada, "Online games."
Moil, "Technological disruptions through opportunities and challenges. Data privacy, cybersecurity, job automation, and ethical implications of emerging technologies like artificial intelligence require careful consideration and appropriate regulations."
Q: Charles, "Politics/church separation."
A: Ada, "Online studying for academic degrees."
Q: Charles, "Religions."
A: Ada, "Interactive connections."

Q: Charles, "Insufficient resources for access to info and technology."
A: Ada, "Artificial Intelligence, Machine Learning, Deep Learning, Neural Networks, and more for interactive learning. Free internet for everyone in every place."
Moil, "Access to Education in developing regions by promoting acceptive and equitable systems, with gender equality, and vocational training to empower people and drive preserving development."
Q: Charles, "Water."
A: Ada, "New Materials."
Moil, "Water management with smart water monitoring systems, advanced purification technologies, reusing, and efficient irrigation techniques to improve water conservation and management, thus diminish water scarcity issues."
Q: Charles, "Trash."
A: Ada, "Color-coded bins on each street."
Moil, "Circular economy with recycling, upcycling, and waste-to-energy conversion to minimize waste generation, conserve resources, and reduce environmental contamination. 5Rs, not just 3. Reuse, Reduce, Recycle, Repair, Refuse."
Q: Charles, "Copyright."
A: Ada, "Free access to everything. Bots perform most tasks, anyway. I understand that this may come as a surprise to you. The ideas are not copyrighted. They are not tangible. When you look at it, people often go online for inspiration. Movements are formed by people mimicking works created by others, just differently. It is too hard to get things exactly as you want them to be. We rely on other people."
Moil: "AI takes ideas and works created by people and delivers images, music, and more. Some help make footage that looks realistic. Many people are not happy that their work serves others."
Q: Charles, "What if everyone had all the resources one wants and needs in any capability?"
A: Ada, "We have automatization, but a machine cannot fulfill abstract concepts."
Q: Charles, "Like love, pride?"
A: Ada, "Add belonging, belief, taste, one's importance, leadership, or order."
Q: Charles, "Nature again. Such as a pecking order or colorful feathers. Do we need a new list of needs?"
A: Ada, "I don't think so. Nature, again."
Moil: "There will always be people who develop and those who pass opinions about others' creations to evaluate and judge them."
Q: Charles, "Can people be both?"
A: Ada, "No time for that. No need, perhaps?"
Moil, "Macro Marketing, and Agile Marketing."
Q: Charles, "We need to be more appreciative of others' tastes, foods, lifestyles, ways to spend time, interactions, and the way we play."
A: Ada, "Open Educational Resources (OER) in education is formed to give equal access to learning materials. When bots do all the tedious work, people can create for themselves and share the joy with others. We can call it collective intelligence. Perhaps collective creativity, just like some animals behave in swarms. That beautifies the world and prevents boredom and competitiveness, probably the major source of problems."
Moil, "If you must be better, it means that you are always comparing yourself. It's tiring."
Ada, Give everyone a nicely designed diploma and ask them to write their strengths and achievements. Whatever they want to be recognized for,"
Q: Charles, "Boredom."
A: Ada, "Co-creating spaces, virtual and physical ones."
Q: Charles, "Housing /homeless people."
A: Ada, "3D concrete pouring."
Moil, "Reducing poverty and bridging the wealth gap requires comprehensive strategies that focus on social equity, economic opportunities, and receptive development."
Q: Charles, "Financial Inclusion."

A: Ada, " More trading as an environmental way to acquire things. "
Moil, "Payment digital solutions, blockchain technology, and mobile banking for underserved populations with secure transactions to foster economic growth in developing regions."
Moil, "Smart Cities by integrating IoT (Internet of Things) sensors, data analytics, and AI algorithms into urban infrastructure can optimize energy usage, enhance transportation systems, improve waste management, and create stable, livable cities."
Q: Charles, "Poverty/unemployment."
A: Ada, "Teaching creativity, abstract thinking, and cognition starting in kindergarten."
Q: Charles, "Traffic."
A: Ada, "More various bots and robots."
Q: Charles, "Pollution."
A: Ada, "Go nano! Explore femtoscale, study the behavior of particles such as quarks and electrons, particle physics, and quantum mechanics to learn more about our planet."
Moil, "Environmental Degradation, including deforestation, habitat loss, contamination, and depletion of natural resources, challenging ecosystems and biodiversity. Protecting and restoring habitats through dand circular economy models."
Q: Charles, "Oh, Ms. Ada, how about toxins/lawns and chemical compounds."
A: Ada, "Love your dandelions! After all, you pay for their healthy leaves at the health stores."
Moi, "Agriculture made with precision farming techniques, vertical farming, hydroponics, and aquaponics to optimize crop production, conserve water, and minimize environmental impact, ensuring food security for a growing population on Earth."
*Q: Charl*es, "Extreme weather."
A: Ada, "Work, learn, play from home. Use the back of the road signs to inform in a simple way."
Moil, "Current set of circumstances with changing temperatures, extreme weather events, sea-level rise, and environmental degradation require urgent action to reduce emissions of carbon dioxide, chlorofluorocarbons, and more, and transition to clean energy sources. Developing and promoting renewable energy sources such as solar, wind, hydro, and geothermal power will reduce our dependence on fuels like coal or gasoline. Maybe fermented leaves as a source of energy. Plenty of them around us."
Q: Charles, "Poaching."
A: Ada, "Virtual Reality."
Moil, "Conservation and environmental monitoring with remote sensing, satellite imagery, and AI algorithms to assist in monitoring biodiversity, tracking deforestation, preventing illegal wildlife trade, and supporting conservation efforts."
Q: Charles, "Drugs."
A: Ada, "Larger homes for people with more space for playful, knowledge-based interactions."
Q: Charles, "Competitiveness."
A: Ada, "Oh, Mr. Charles, Focus on teamwork with playful outcomes in mind."
Moil, "Education technology by leveraging digital learning platforms, interactive tools, and virtual reality (VR) to enhance access to quality education, bridge educational gaps, and provide lifelong learning opportunities."
Q: Charles, "Rulers' egos?"
A: Ada, "Spread respect. And self-respect.
Moil, "Know who you are and your strengths in context."
Q: Charles, "More to come."
A: Ada, "Bots are always waiting with their solutions."

The End. The Curtain goes down (or closes).

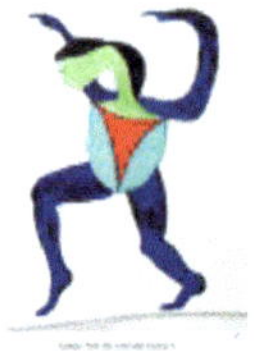

Gubala: feels the wind and records it.

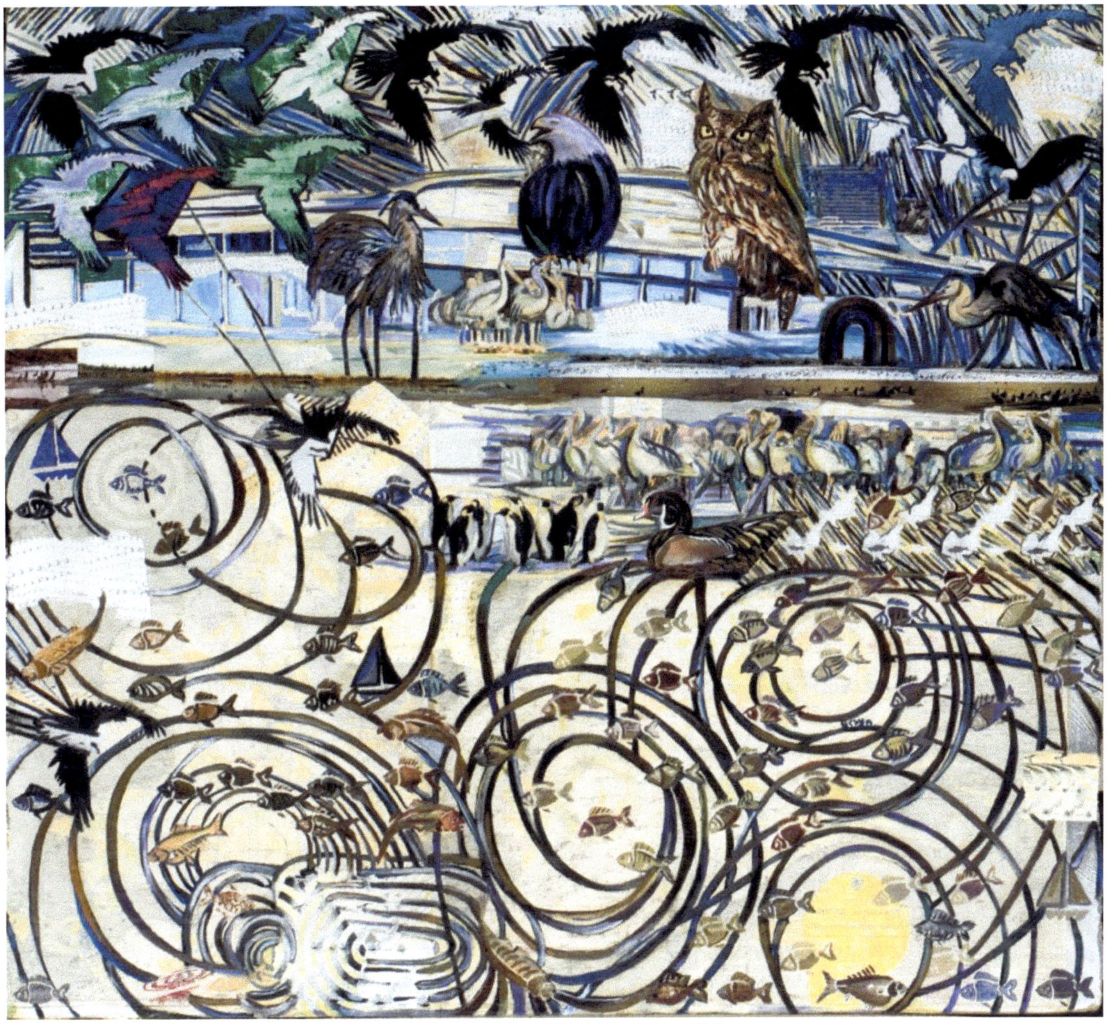

Bornholm. © 2025 by Anna Ursyn

CHAPTER 28
FUTURE CODE

COME, JOIN THE PARTY! GRAND FINALE

INTRODUCTION

We face challenges with artificial intelligence serving us in many directions. We must adjust, as we had before when other inventions were introduced and make the best use of what is offered while distinguishing what is for good and not so good while coping with somehow weak definitions of the two.

SYNOPSIS

The Two Spatian-Narrators from the "Music Code" become Spatian-Commentators who report to other types in the galaxies on what they see on Planet Earth, just like anchors, war reporters, or sports commentators do. This time, they wear ancient Roman toga-style outfits.

SUMMARY

People need to focus on some solutions for the most critical problems humans face, but at the same time, staying hopeful, playful, curious, and supportive. The Two Spatian-Commentators (from Music Code) share their predictions.

CAST OF CHARACTERS

Spatian-Commentator One
Spatian-Commentator Two

STAGE DIRECTIONS

The two Spatian-Commentators from the "Music Code" act in front of projected AI-based images.
The action happens beyond any place but in the near future.

Act I
The Curtain goes up (or opens).

Spatian-Commentator One, "That is a nice party! Hard to tell an Earthsian from a Manmade."
Spatian-Commentator Two, "I know, on the street, they mingle. They can be seen following a lady, carrying her bags, while talking to her and making sure she would not fall on her high heels, break her fingernail, or miss something interesting happening on the street stage."
Spatian-Commentator One, "Earthsians went beyond cobots; they make the Manmades the way they can eat and drink, with the content going straight into a container inside their perfect skin. They judge the quality of the drinks and pass opinions after scanning the labels. They even excuse themselves to go to the restroom. I wonder what they are doing there."
Spatian-Commentator Two, "Talking to other Manmades. Once, one was describing how the Earthsian was accompanying her Manmade husband on the ruling campaign tour, greeting his supporters and making sure he'd get their Earthsians 'votes. Oh, how sweet she was, if you'd understand the meaning of this world, recorded by the crew for their networks."
Spatian-Commentator One, "Yes, of course. It's been a while since "Robot Sophia by Hanson Robotics," or "Einstein Robot," entered the stage!"
Spatian-Commentator Two, "2016. Yes, that was a long time ago. In 2017, she gained legal status as a person, personhood, and citizenship in Saudi Arabia. Wired, Jul 20, 2024, Fast Forward."
Spatian-Commentator On, "Since then, they make those robots less handsome so that they can pass in social circles as a Companion, an Ungrownup, or a Boyfriend/Girlfriend. They added some flows to make it impossible to tell them apart from an Earthsian."
Spatian-Commentator Two, "The Earthsians also programmed them to show weaknesses caused by their experiences, such as tiredness, mood swings, jealousy, competitiveness, and much more. Without those, you'd guess they were not Earthsians."
Spatian-Commentator One, "The Manmades do the chores for Earthsians: they clean, cook, serve, and present food, then join them at the table to enrich their conversations and help them stay current and educated."
Spatian-Commentator One, "Each household should have one shape-shifting robot that shapes itself to match the task. If one needs a leaking sink fixed, the robot shapes and equips itself as a plumber to handle the problem.

If one needs to chase the squirrels from out of the roof, the same robot changes into a flexible rod to get under the roof and then expands to scare them away and fix any potential openings.
Then, it shifts into a snake shape again to get out, lands on the ground to return to its original friendly design."

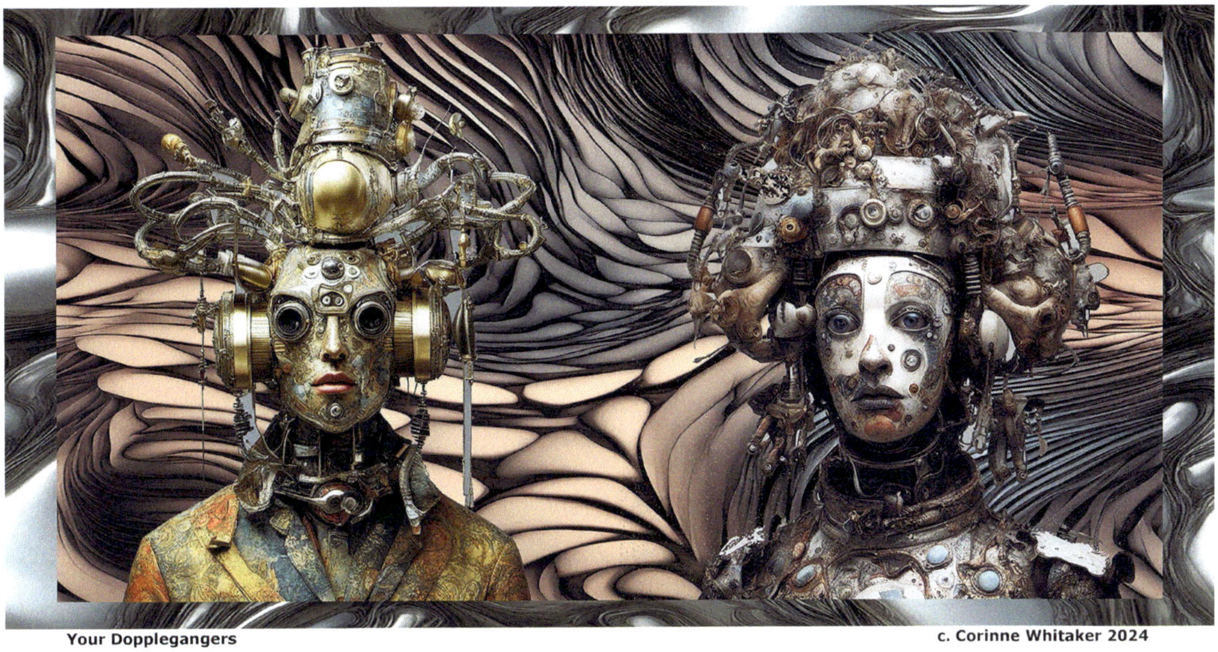

Your Dopplegangers c. Corinne Whitaker 2024

Spatian-Commentator Two, "Just like an octopus. Yes, new gel technologies help them with this. I saw one changing its form when vacuuming their 3D-printed living cuboids. They add more printed spaces whenever their clusters expand, thus needing extra room for more Earthsians. A long, like-a-nose tube extended from its head and started rolling. After that, everything went back to standard. Or it can change its form to become a suitcase that follows a traveler. Like a shapeshifter, it uses new materials. That container inside them collects not only dust but also unused food from the dinner parties they attend and other things. It's such a waste."

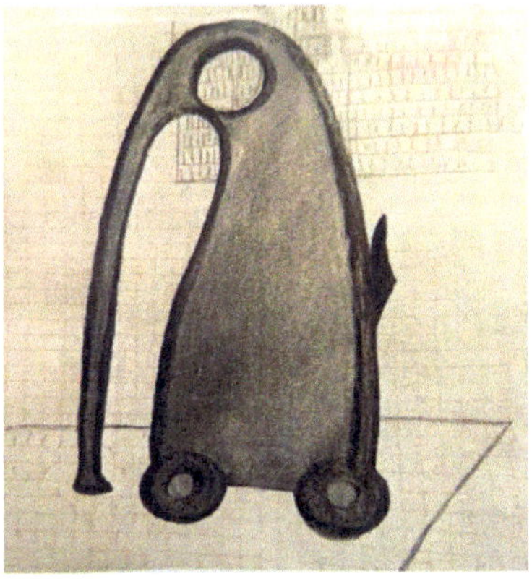

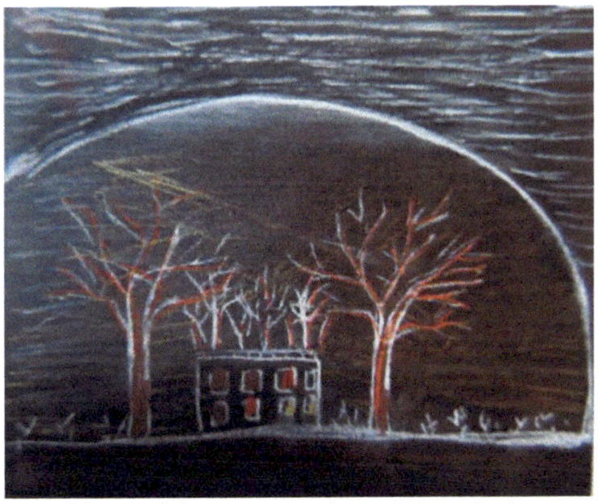

Spatian-Commentator One: "Who would need luggage when 3D printing on demand does it all for us, almost everywhere and anytime? They use those self-closing covers over their living structures, including their 3D-printed living cuboids and outdoorsy spaces around them, especially during winters, to preserve warmth and leave no room for dust."

Spatian-Commentator Two, "There will always be room for dust. Galactic one."
Spatian-Commentator One, "Their 3D printed moving boxes even get them."
Spatian-Commentator Two, "They define a 3D-printed moving box class with attributes like color, make, model, and a function telling if the engine is running or not. Using this code, they can create an instance of the 3D-printed moving box class, start the engine, drive the 3D-printed moving box, stop the engine, and drive the 3D-printed moving box again to see the appropriate messages printed:

```
"class the 3D-printed moving box:
  def __init__(self, color, brand, model):
    self.color = color
    self.brand = brand
    self.model = model
    self.is_engine_started = False

  def start_engine(self):
    self.is_engine_started = True

  def stop_engine(self):
    self.is_engine_started = False

  def drive(self):
    if self.is_engine_started:
      print(f"The {self.color} {self.brand} {self.model} is driving.")
    else:
      print(f"Please start the engine of the {self.color} {self.brand} {self.model} first.")
```

Spatian-Commentator One, "Manmades sit in self-driving 3D moving boxes with the Ungrownups just to cheer them during a soccer game or any practice they follow. It works best for those Manmade Ungrownups, as their feelings and reactions are perfectly pre-planned."
Spatian-Commentator Two, "Yes, feelings. Regarding their own Ungrownups, some Earthsians think that feelings are automatically due to them and only to them, and they talk about others taking away their Ungrownups' feelings from them. It may be that some others offer their Ungrownups exactly what they need, thus attracting them. It does not take anything away from the Earthsians, and the Manmades know exactly who needs what, with the neural networks, mind reading with fMRI checking on prompt reaction brain changes, and more. Love is an abstract concept. It does not end or can be measured in any way."
Spatian-Commentator One, "Jealousy again."
Spatian-Commentator Two, "Famous actors, writers, or sports people have the look-alike Manmades to sign for them on related objects for their fans."
Spatian-Commentator One, "Yes, that gives Earthsians extra time. The question is, what do they do with it? How do they spend it? How do they fulfill their needs?"
Spatian-Commentator Two, "Ha! Those who need to feel like the most important ones in any gathering have no problems if they can recognize a Manmade. The situation gets more complicated if they cannot. Some of those Earthsians just need to be admired or envied."
Spatian-Commentator One, "Meaning?
Spatian-Commentator Two: "Well, they must feel better than anybody around them. They achieve that by finding flows in others. Manmades do not have flows. They keep getting better."
Spatian-Commentator One, "Some Earthsians must be better than everybody else and be the most important in any gathering. That causes many problems, as there will always be a someone who is better, smarter, more talented, or faster at something, which upsets them. An upset Earthsian starts doing questionable things, not so good for them or others."
Spatian-Commentator Two, "They focus on their emotions, rather than what is causing them, which is a core of their problem."
Spatian-Commentator One, "Agreed. The Earthsian Charles asked many questions about their problems, and the Earthsian Ada provided some technological solutions for most of them, but that was in the previous chapter.

The thing is that those problems are causing emotions, and most of them are not suitable as a result. They make Earthsians do strange things, for which they get locked in 3D-printed boxes to sit there for a while after a group judgment, and they suffer and try doing something that damages them afterward. Their real issue is dealing with what causes those negative emotions. They listed five skills of emotional intelligence called RULER: Recognizing, Understanding, Labeling, Expressing, and Regulating emotions."

Spatian-Commentator Two, "Oh, so good for the Earthsians that they met and set the standards on what's for good, and what's for the not-so-good for them, regarding AI usage. And they obey that, somehow. They have no choice, with all those ever-present cameras and the Manmades 'preventiveness capabilities."

Spatian-Commentator One, "Artificial intelligence combined with social media even suggests whom they can collaborate with across their planet."

Spatian-Commentator Two, "I still am not sure how they obey their hierarchy when each one of them has access to all the tools. They complain that their own Sterling Ungrownups lose their skills in performing operations or learning new languages because machines do it all for them."

Spatian-Commentator One, "Their Nature will adjust it for them by having their minds and brains growing in other directions, just like ours does it for us."

Spatian-Commentator Two, "Maybe it is the same Nature?"

Spatian-Commentator One, "What is your name?"

Spatian-Commentator Two, "Spatian-Commentator Two, unless…"

Spatian-Commentator One, "Their schooling system switched from data and information to knowledge, and mostly the development of creativity and cognition."

Spatian-Commentator Two, "Their first 'Creativity and Cognition conference in 1993."

Spatian-Commentator One," One thing is to envision; another is to teach. It takes interminability."

Spatian-Commentator Two, "Putting it this way, it is all based on the value of their Manmades?"

Spatian-Commentator One, "Do you know who made you, Spatian-Commentator Two?"

Spatian-Commentator Two," I have too many bookmarks on my portal."

The End
The Curtain goes down (or closes).

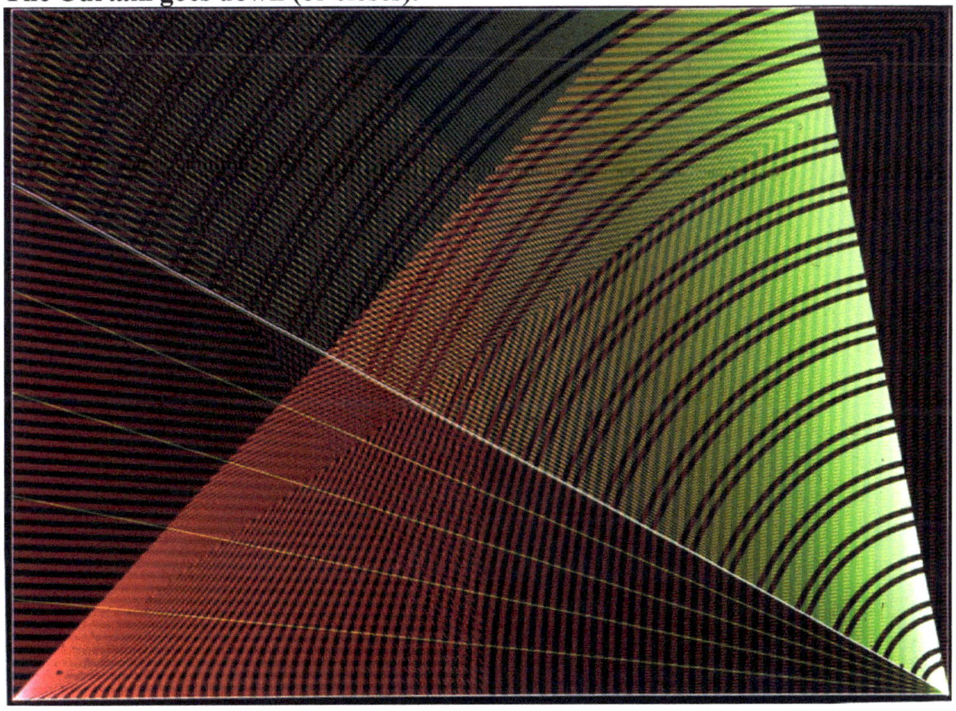

A Split. The output from a computer code. © 2025 by Anna Ursyn

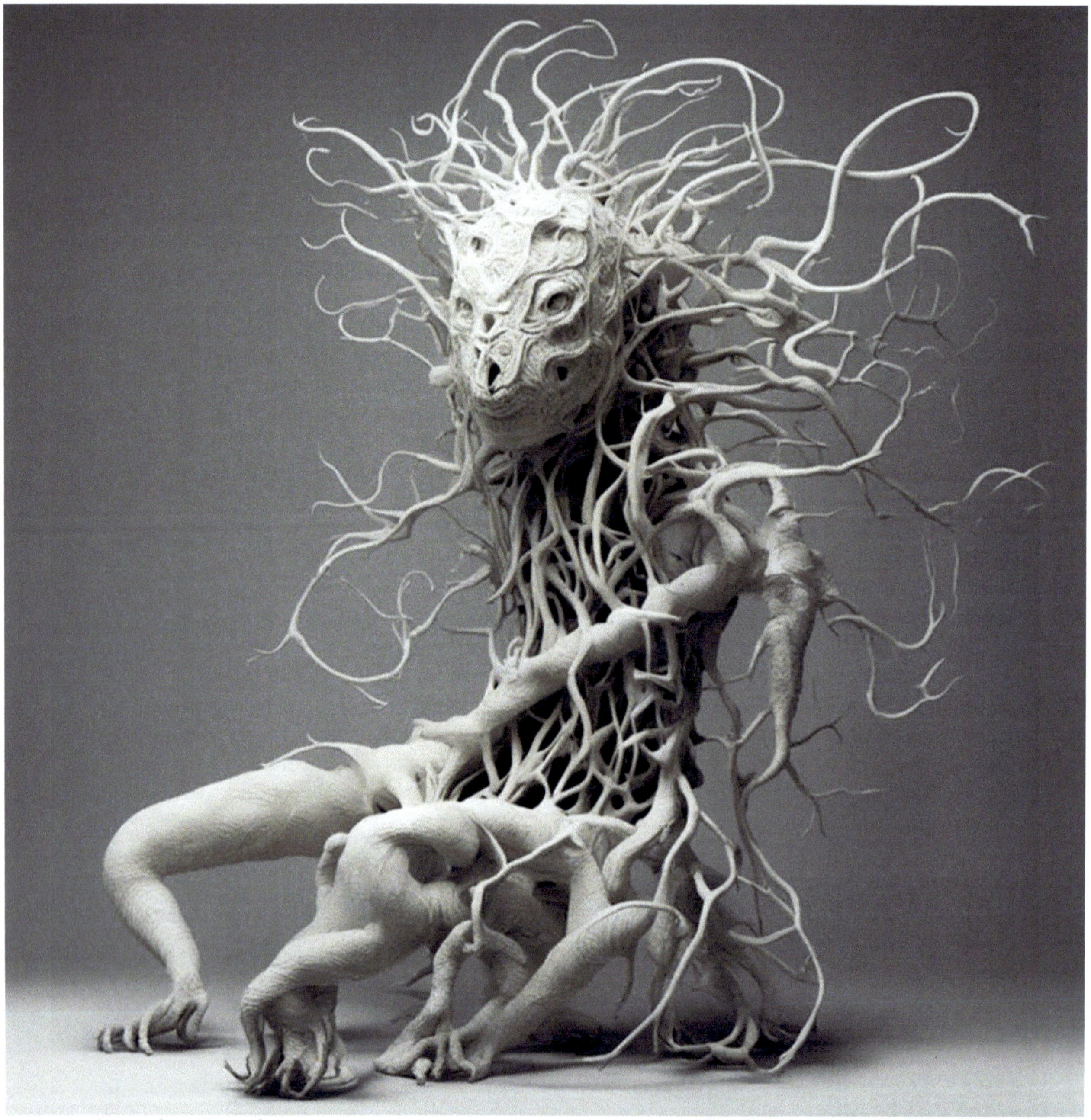

Crossing Borders **c. Corinne Whitaker 2024**

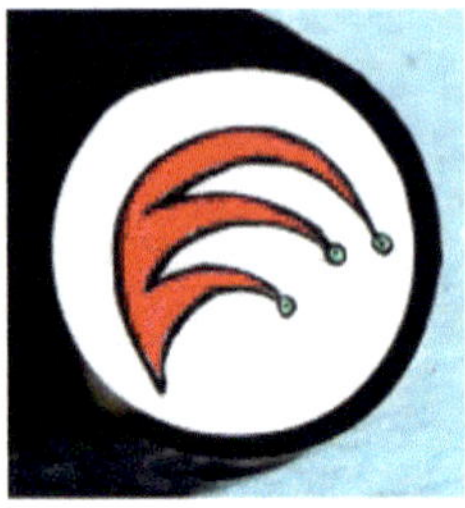

Avaraga: knew three kings and discussed winds with them.

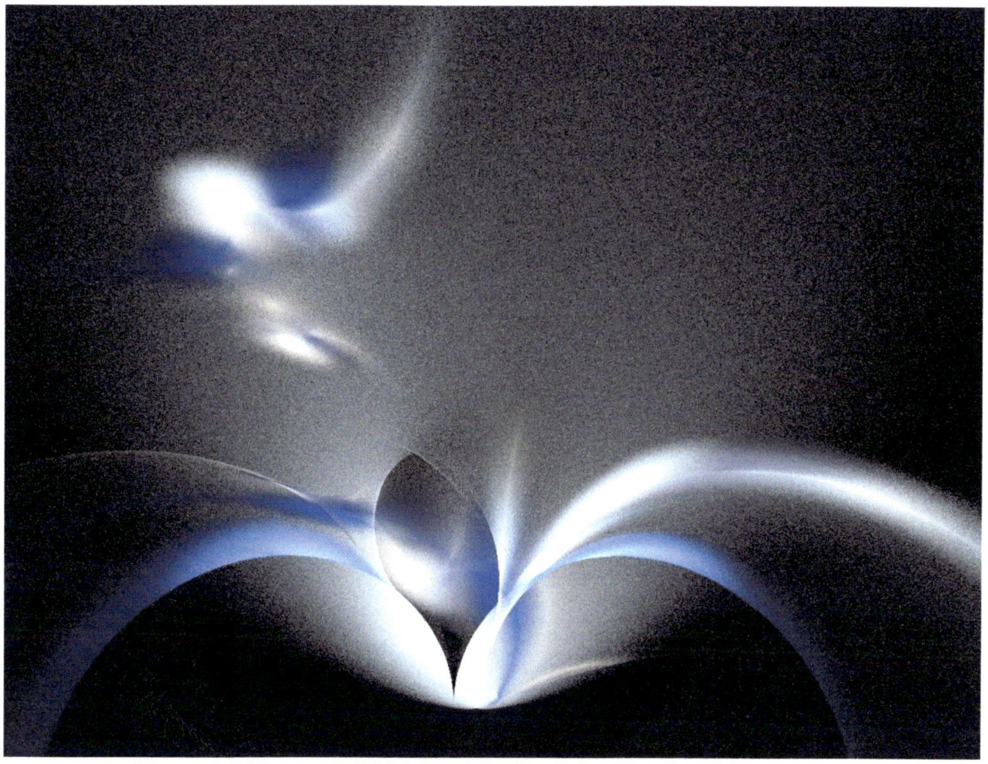

Here and There. © 2025 by Teja Krašek. (Used with Permission).

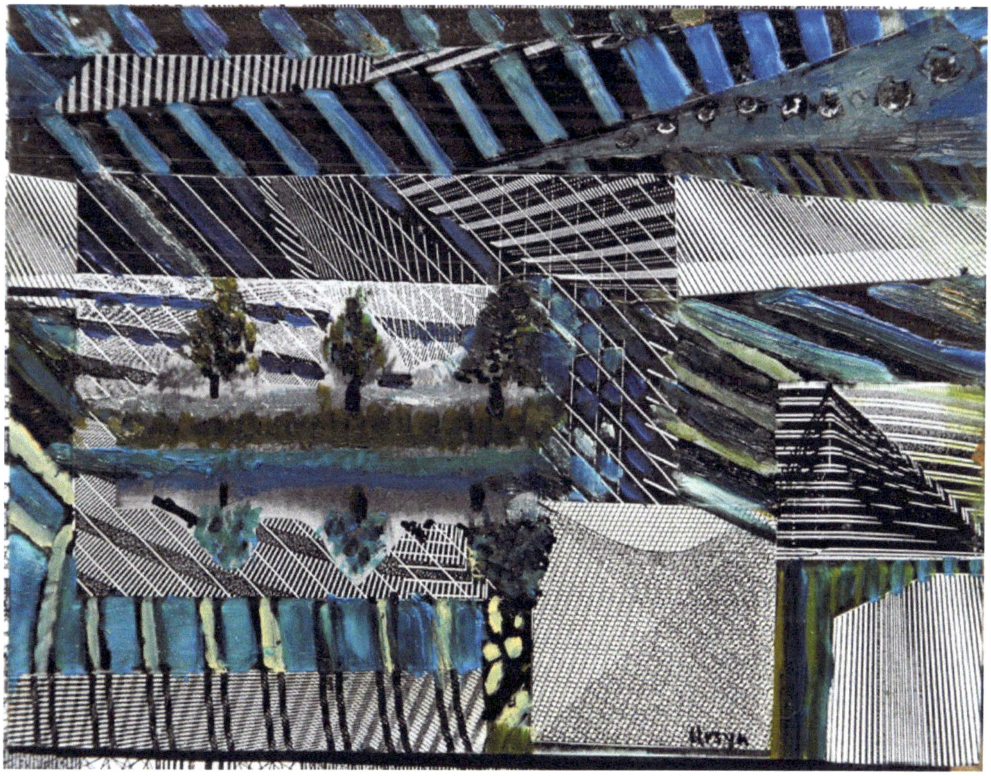

Symmetrical Colors. © 2025 by Anna Ursyn

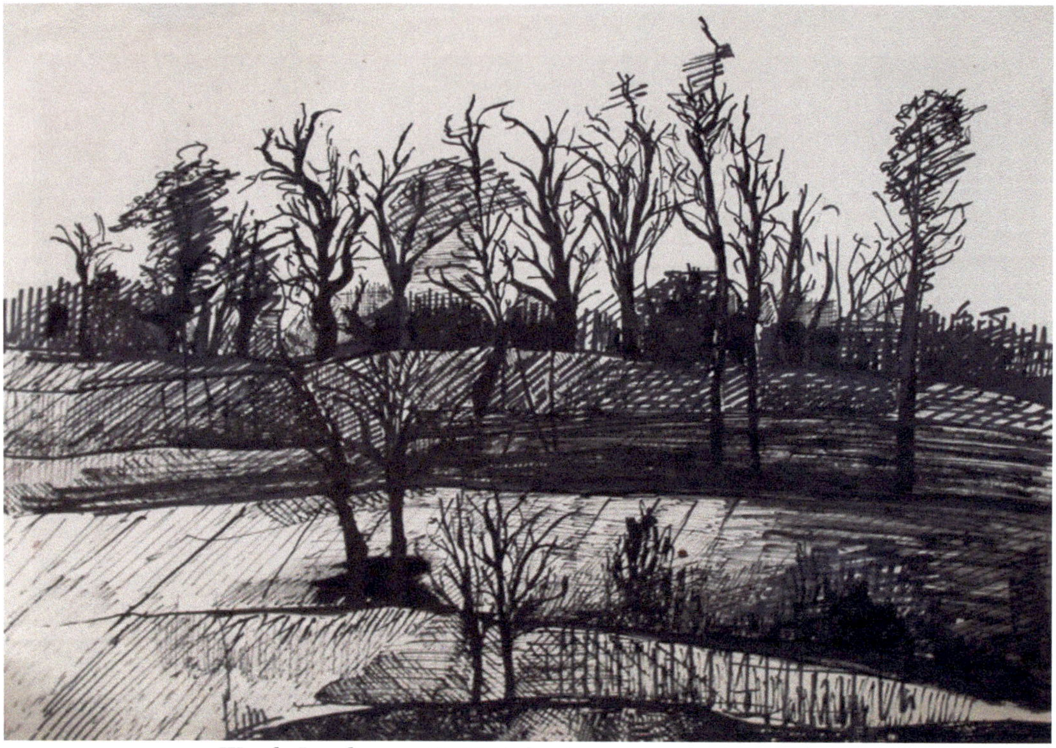

Windy Landscape. © 2025 by Anna Ursyn

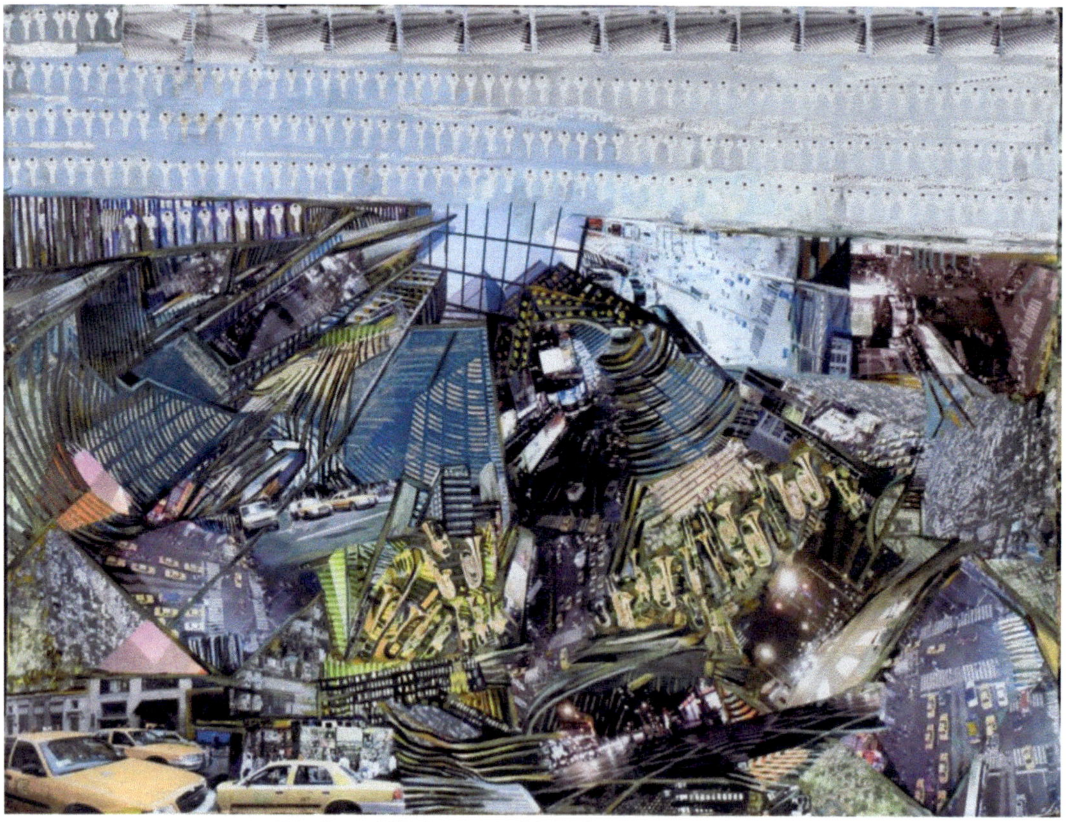

Pitch and Volume. © 2025 by Anna Ursyn

CHAPTER 29 EDUCATION CODE

TEACHER-ARTIST, ARTIST-TEACHER

INTRODUCTION

The transition to new offerings can be challenging yet support our creative thoughts and new ideas.

SYNOPSIS

When rethinking our needs for entertainment and beauty, one can see an artist as a collaborator using their new artificial personal assistants to create new stories delivered for a selected audience in an attractive, playful, entertaining, and beautiful way that spreads kindness, joy, and curiosity, while promoting independent, abstract and cognitive thinking.

SUMMARY

Rethinking our options for delivering stories through actions in a beautiful way for split thinkers becomes a new challenge for creators. Technology constantly offers new solutions, but people are the ones who come up with new, creative, thought-provoking, engaging, and entertaining solutions to deliver beauty through positive content. For that, we need to rethink our educational technology-aided strategies.

CAST OF CHARACTERS

The Human Being

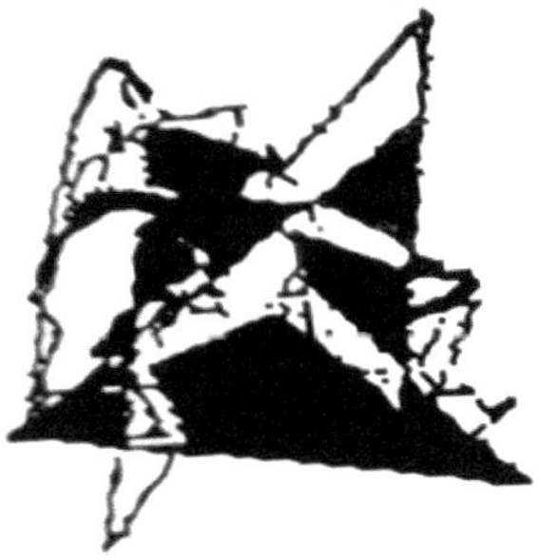

STAGE DIRECTIONS

The animated figure stays animated on the stage on the silver background filled with illustrations, while the actor reads the text from a tablet or the screen while applying pantomime.

Act I
The Curtain goes up (or opens).

The Human Being, "Recently, post-media aesthetics was discussed. There are even post-digital aesthetics divagations. We call technology-based creations art digital, while many solutions are analog. Historically, computers were not much appreciated as an art medium and were seen as threatening many jobs, just like other inventions. A similar situation can now be observed with artificial Intelligence (AI). Some students disclose discomfort with this technology and verbal criticism of it referred to as "a thief." This topic can be addressed because AI can be seen as a personal assistant beyond the visual one. AI helps us write better and form our thoughts more communicatively and straightforwardly. Nature is always our best inspiration. While it holds that companies use technology to create graphic design-related work, from logos, presentations, and reports to websites and interactive content, it is harder for technology to replace the sense of humor, creativity, and formation of new and imaginative ideas that match the needs, and perhaps offer good storytelling. We are inclined to accept current aesthetics, but things become more complicated when it comes to beauty. We do not even have a definition of what art is. We cannot fulfill the "all but only condition." Not all art is beautiful, (can be ugly and still good), and not only art is beautiful (Nature). It is even harder to define the quality of art. I challenge you to place your art in your living space; if you can live with it for a month, it sure is good. Along with the ability to collaborate well, those are skills needed for the entertainment industry that, according to the news, is stagnant and thus not as profitable as expected. A well-known entertainment company reported revenue problems even after the comeback of a successful leader. The news article claimed the audience was tired of the same characters, stories, conflicts, heroes, and villains. They want novelty, and AI is not the best cure for it. "If you think technology will solve your problems, you don't understand technology, and you don't understand your problems," said Laurie Anderson. For the integrative media path, students should be exposed to creativity, various types of storytelling techniques, novelty content, collaborative skills, and character development, as they are vehicles to tell the story. Everything we do can become a story or is a story. How we deliver it depends on our answer to who our audience is. We collaborate!

Computer art graphics students are expected to have a quality portfolio, write well, and appreciate music by playing, knowing musical notation, composing, or listening and enjoying it. They are expected to know good storytelling strategies and have experience with acting or sports to see how a character can move believably. They should at least have a brief understanding of coding to communicate with the coders on the job and get the most out of the AI's offerings. For those reasons, some merger between traditional and computer media is needed, allowing for a constant switch between traditional media and what technology offers while expanding its capabilities. Some people feel better about traditional media, while others prefer technological solutions. Drawing can be seen as a starting point for any creation. It can be sent between traditional and media quickly and reliably. It can be created on portable devices, including a watch.

A set of lines printed on the acetate can offer new transparency and layering solutions. It can be transformed into a three-dimensional, time-based interactive form. Paintings can be scanned, sculptures digitalized, and printmaking expanded by photo silkscreen and photolithography. 3D scanning can serve for 3D printing or projections, just like holograms can. Ceramics can use the roundness of a pot to perform animation (the way people did in Ancient Greece) by transferring computer programs on the surface of a pot. Animation can be based on tangible or reshaping objects, and virtual reality can involve static, moving, or interacting agents. Photography and video can use many forms, such as telling a story from a storytelling glasses point of view, 360-degree cameras, scanned body movements, or old-fashioned footage converted to what is useful now.

So, teach and learn to enjoy your very own creations. We do better what we enjoy doing. One does not have to stay current to develop beauty. What is beautiful to one person may be deemed ugly to another, so staying within one's framework and monitoring one's progress is the key. There is no definition of art. Creating gives us good feelings, leading to happiness. While many books on happiness and creativity theories can be found, it is hard to replace incoming enzymes boosting our moods resulting from the joy of our satisfaction with our creation. AI allows us to gain different insights and become selective to use the best outcome for our use.

Knowing how to use tools is not enough; what to do with them is the key.

Enjoy!"

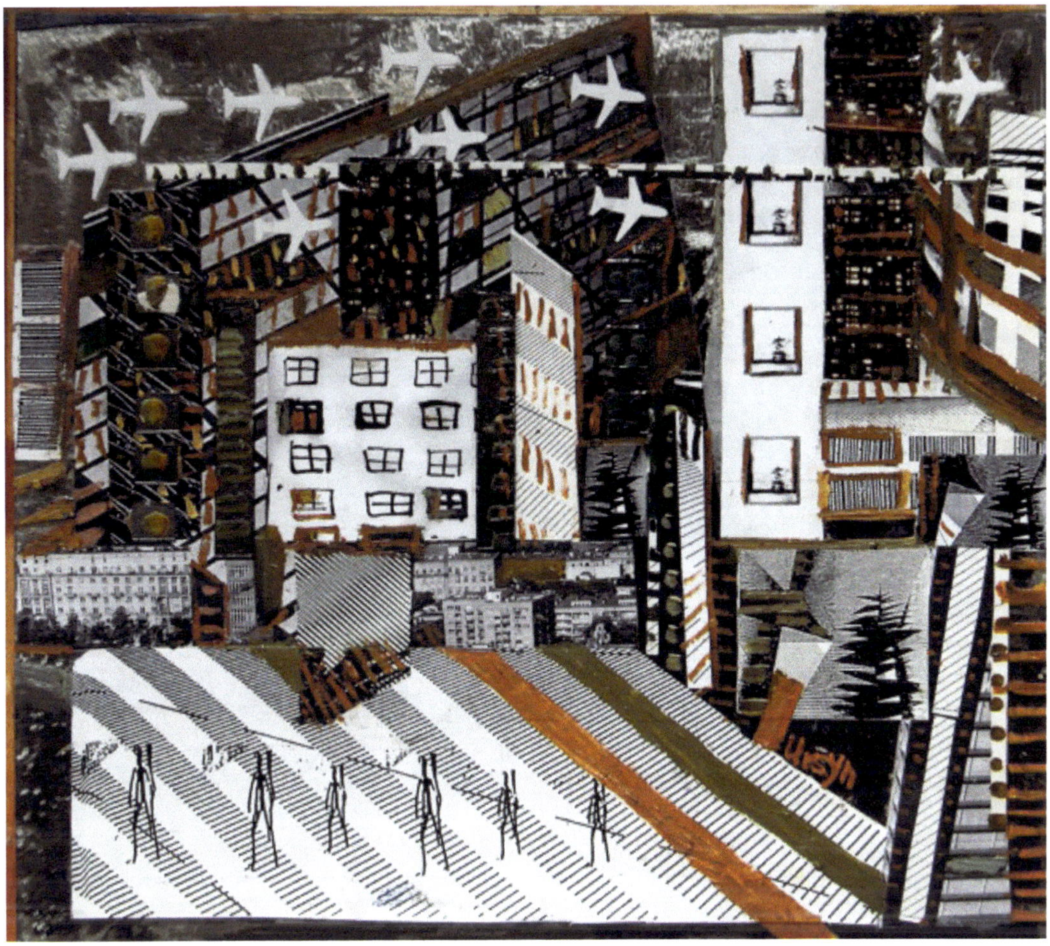

Cul-de-Sac. © *2025 by Anna Ursyn*

No Break. The Curtain goes down (or closes).

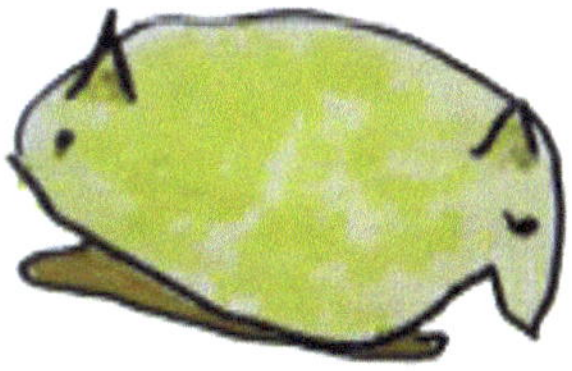

Cusukl: knew it all in and out

Cusukl: knew it all in and out.

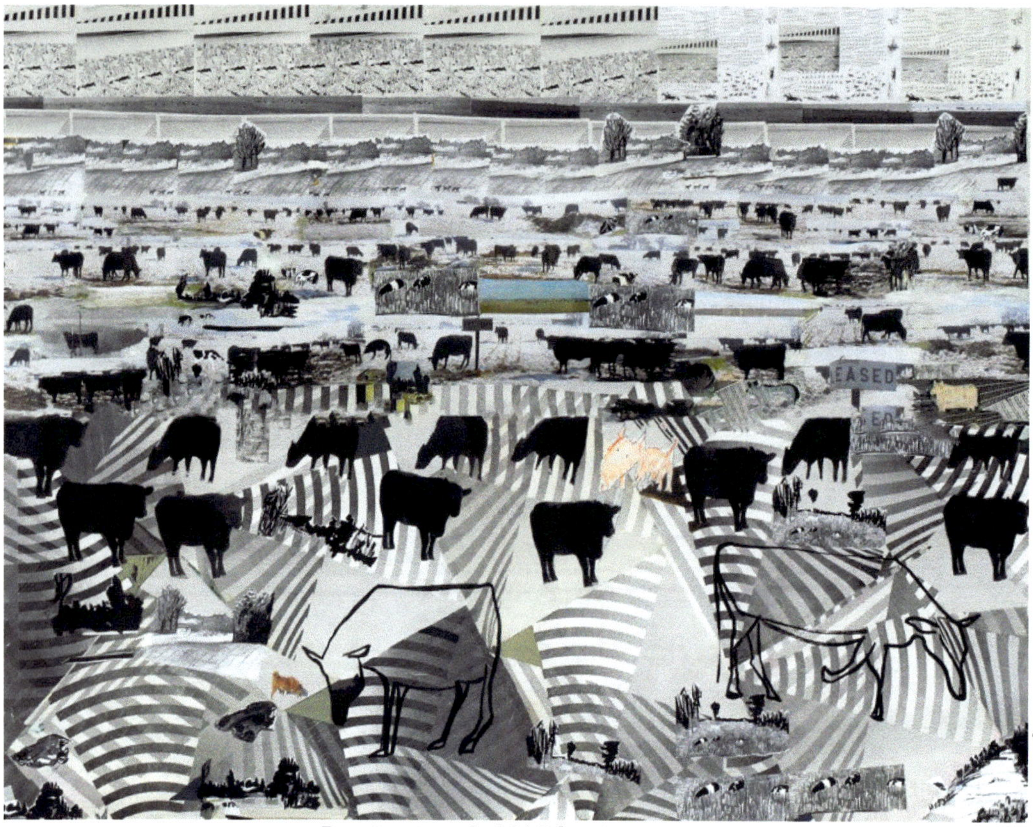

Ruminating. © *2025 by Anna Ursyn*

Act II
The curtain goes up (or opens).

Is Analogue the New Digital?

Generative art results in precise images with perfect lines that follow premeditated transformations. Some artists started working with computers by programming, with a distant dumb terminal connected to the station via modem and a phone. We waited two hours for black and white prints and three days for color slides. Artists lost generations when editing tapes when they worked with film as an analog medium. We could include color, shade, and patterns, apply clipping algorithms, rotate and paste the content into other images, zoom, and transform. Then, photo silkscreen and photolithograph gave a new level of color combinations and the messiness of paint. Movies and animations involve the fourth dimension. Using software, one can recycle drawings and generative shapes and patterns.

Algorithmic images can be transformed into physical constructions. Images free of details can become synthetic expressions of the figure. Sculptural forms in 3-D programs and prototyping can follow. To address the time factor and add some explanatory power and dynamic storytelling, we present images, 3D forms, time-based art, and interactive and immersive art via various channels.

Looking at the two-dimensional work, we can only change the distance, yet we can walk around the sculpture and explore the interactive character of time-based art. By adding action inside the image's surface, we aim to attain another level of possible connotations and interpretations. The next stage—combining everything and combining media— becomes fully digital.

Natural order infuses several levels of both worlds: some determined by man, and some determined by nature. It guides our understanding of big data sets related to network analysis, whether we employ physical analogies of the data, render the data graphically, or interact in real time. Acutely aware of the order that infuses both worlds, we examine what technological and human worlds have in common by juxtaposing nature's regularity with man's physical and intellectual constructions.

The digital factor of all these media and techniques creates even more opportunities for contemporary digital art. For movies, web, and animations, 3-D forms must be flattened and presented as 2-D frames or pages; thus, analog becomes digital.

The Break
The Curtain goes down (or closes)

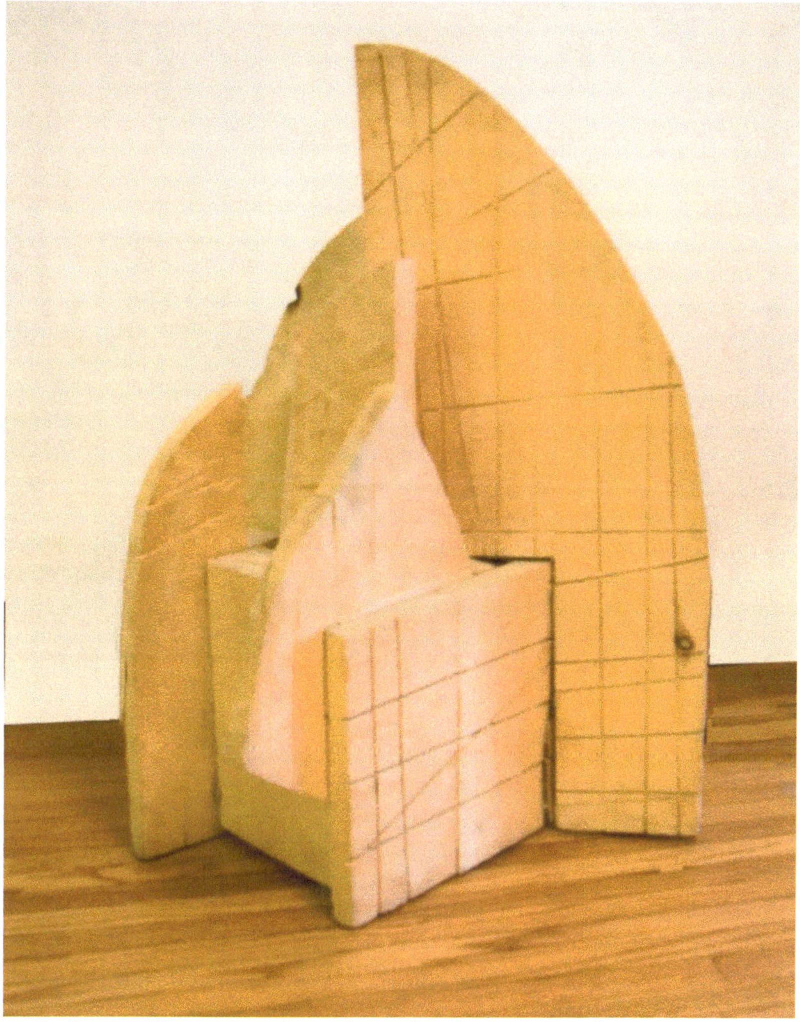

Birdcage, Sometimes a Dome. The output from the code, the aspen sculpture. © 2025 by Anna Ursyn

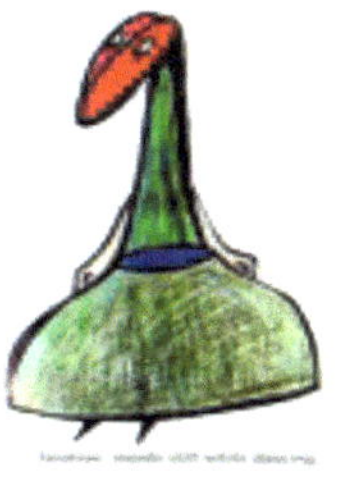

Jasatran: stands still while dancing.

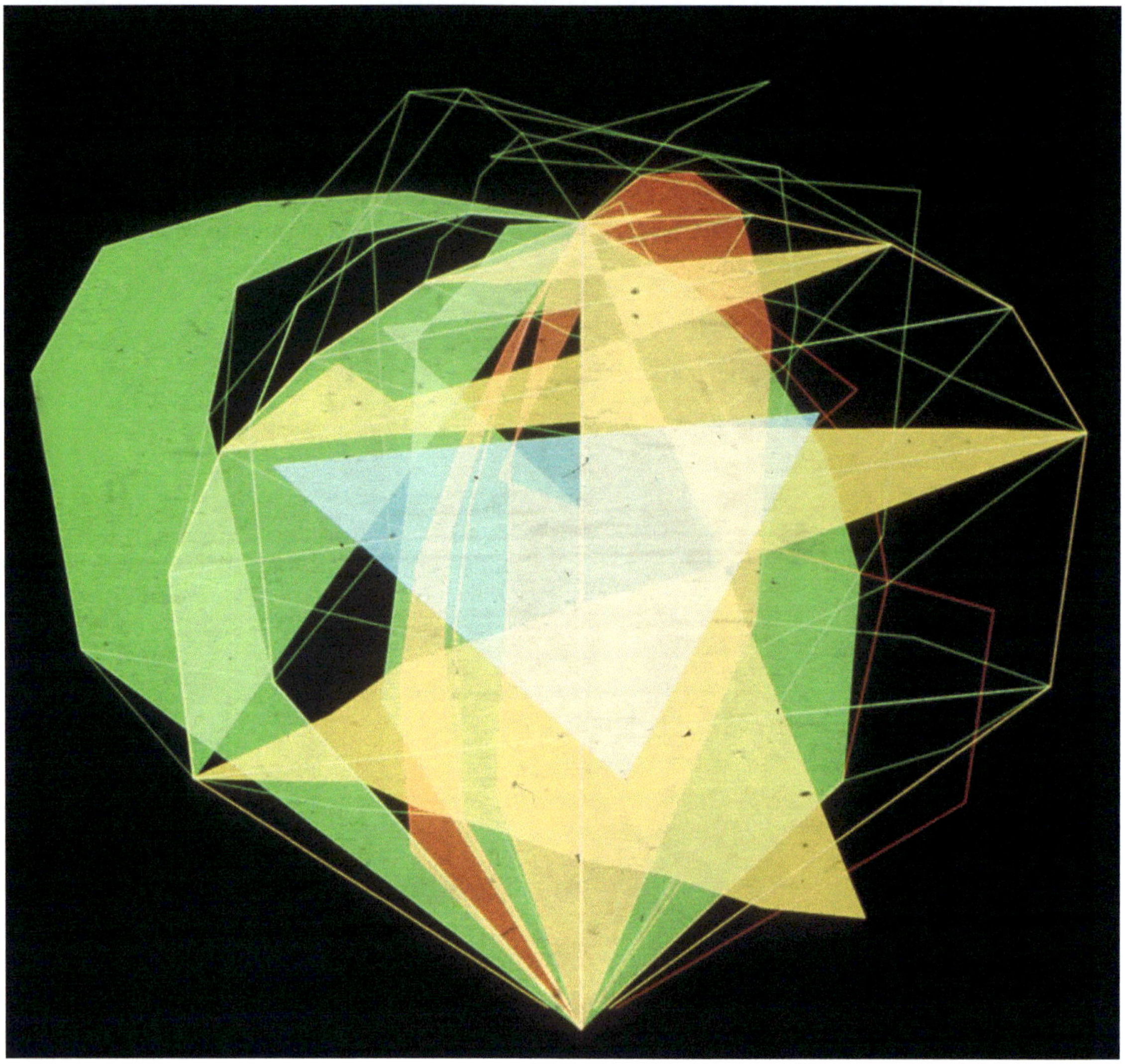

Birdcage. The output from the computer code. © 2025 by Anna Ursyn

Act III
The Curtain goes up (or opens).

Art Educator's Manifesto

1. Students with unique talents, unusual skills, and interests should not be mixed with those with inabilities. Those groups have different needs and requirements for success. Placing gifted and talented students with students requiring special attention under 'Special Education ' is from the teacher's point of view. It should be the other way around.

2. Coding should be taught starting in kindergarten, and it should be continued and supported as a lifetime activity. This will help a person grow and make connections between disciplines.

3. Music, singing, and music notation should be taught starting in kindergarten, continued, and supported as a lifetime activity. This would make the world a better place and people happier, more social, and more active.

4. Abstract concepts should be enforced starting in kindergarten and should be continued and supported as a lifetime activity.

5. Learning Latin should be taught starting in kindergarten, continued, and supported as a lifetime activity. Learning about declination and the symbolic use of phrases would help bridge the gap between various human and computer languages and modes of communication. Other systems in languages should be introduced.

6. Everyone should perform sketching on a daily basis.

7. Writing should be performed daily, not just as a social networking activity. Jotting down special events, meaningful conversations, the content of interesting bumper stickers, or overheard statements that are not private but said with the best intentions can stimulate us.

8. Nature should be introduced, with forces connecting processes and products. Physics can be seen as the laws governing it, chemistry as tools, and mathematics as a way of describing it.

9. Statistics defines our world through means and bell curves.

10. Academic disciplines are intertwined and can be defined in a visual way.

11. Nature's patterns resemble sketching and drawing. We use them to describe and solve various problems. For example, we see lines in bell curves, heartbeat recordings, sound distribution, or fractal geometry.

12. Any 3D printer should be sold with a plastic recycler. All the containers we dispose of could be reused for further production.

13. All art should be beautiful, with attention to color combination and the use of the elements and principles of design.

14. We use many senses simultaneously; listening more and talking less might help us unfold them.

15. Looking is not the same as seeing.

16. Collaboration in the arts promotes curiosity, resulting in sharing and enlightening.

17. Artists should be teachers, and teachers should be artists.

18. Art has many formats and should be interdisciplinary. This includes various types of art, science, and communication ideas.

19. Everyone is born with some talents. Follow Howard Gardner's theory of multiple intelligences, find and grow your own, and stimulate others by looking at what they excel at, often without noticing.

20. Hackers who make wrong decisions might be the brightest, most talented students who are not recognized or even punished for their ideas and contributions in the classroom.

21. Everyone tries to do the best they can. Open up to that without judging.

No Break. The Curtain goes down (or closes).

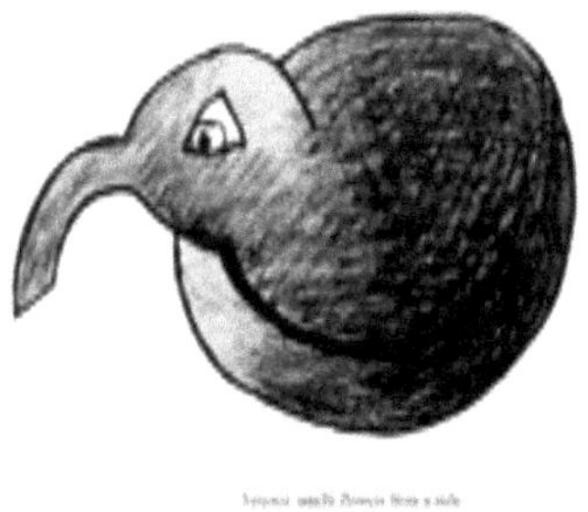

Yeresco: smells flowers from a mile.

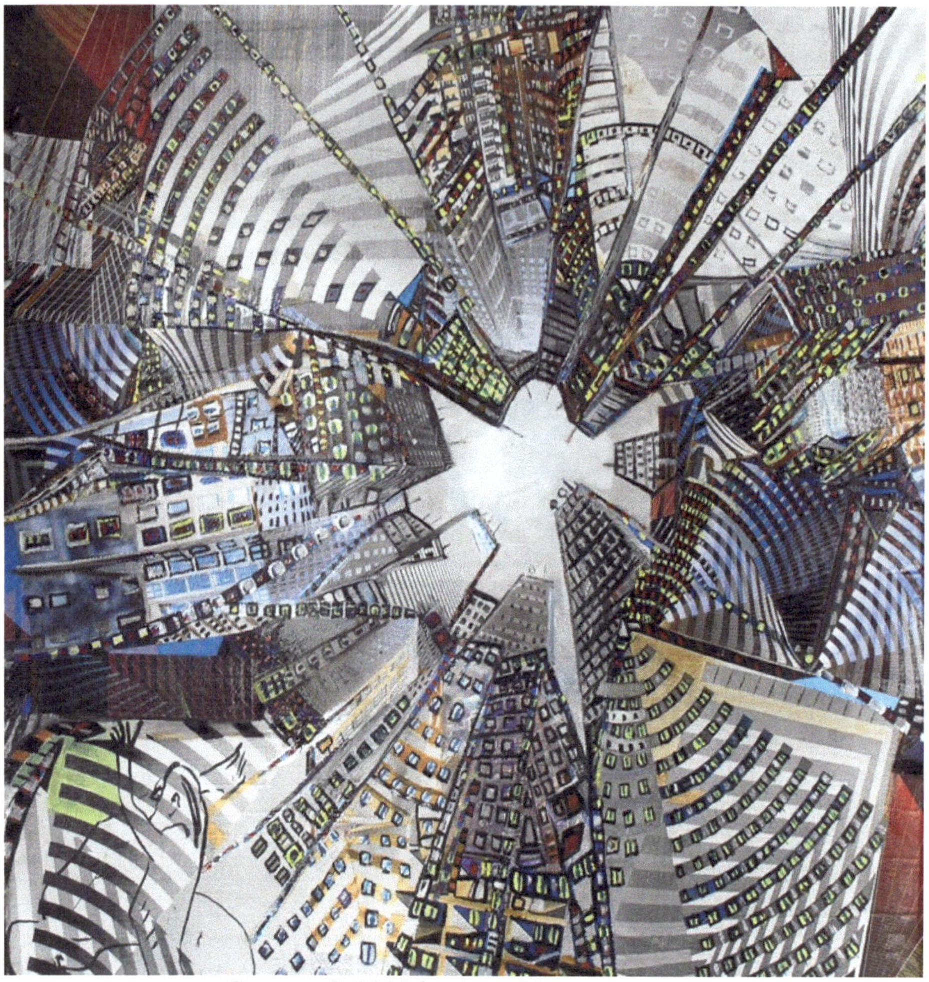

Canopy. © *2025 by Anna Ursyn.*

Act IV
Art Manifesto
The curtain goes up (or opens).

- Technology has many ways to enhance our artistic growth but does not have to. Good art can be done even with a broom.
- A work of art should not be limited to its impact on connotations, associations, or social actions such as equality, gender, status, and political or environmental statements, without an impact of good use of elements and principles of design.
- Beauty in art is never overrated, even if not retrieved by the eyes of a beholder.
- Art does not have to evoke discussions; it can be created to generate a state of mind (often different for various viewers) that can stay private.
- Aesthetics is important through color selections, composition, and relationships within.
- Art does not have to shock, make money with, or make people think one way or another: we have a poster form for that, which still can be art.
- Art can be interdisciplinary but should have a visual impact in its meaning and context.
- Inspiration from Nature works better than appropriating someone else's art or as a pastiche. If we mimic someone's vision, we should do it tastefully and for a reason.
- While in design, the first question would be "who is the audience," art or craft could bypass that.
- Art using someone's misfortune, misery, or depiction of horrifying effects might serve

as a message or political, social, or economic statement but may not qualify as art.
- If art involves an audience as a part of its setup, it should go beyond purely intellectual, playful, or gain-related purposes. There are better ways to achieve those goals.
- Art created to disgust the audience, shake it, or shock it can often be done differently without being called art.
- Artists should not be defined by their "mark" but by their progress. Experimentation is important for their growth.
- While craft is often created to be sold, it should not be used as an objective or a measure of art.
- Art should not be valued by its size as an indicator.

The End
The Curtain goes down (or closes).

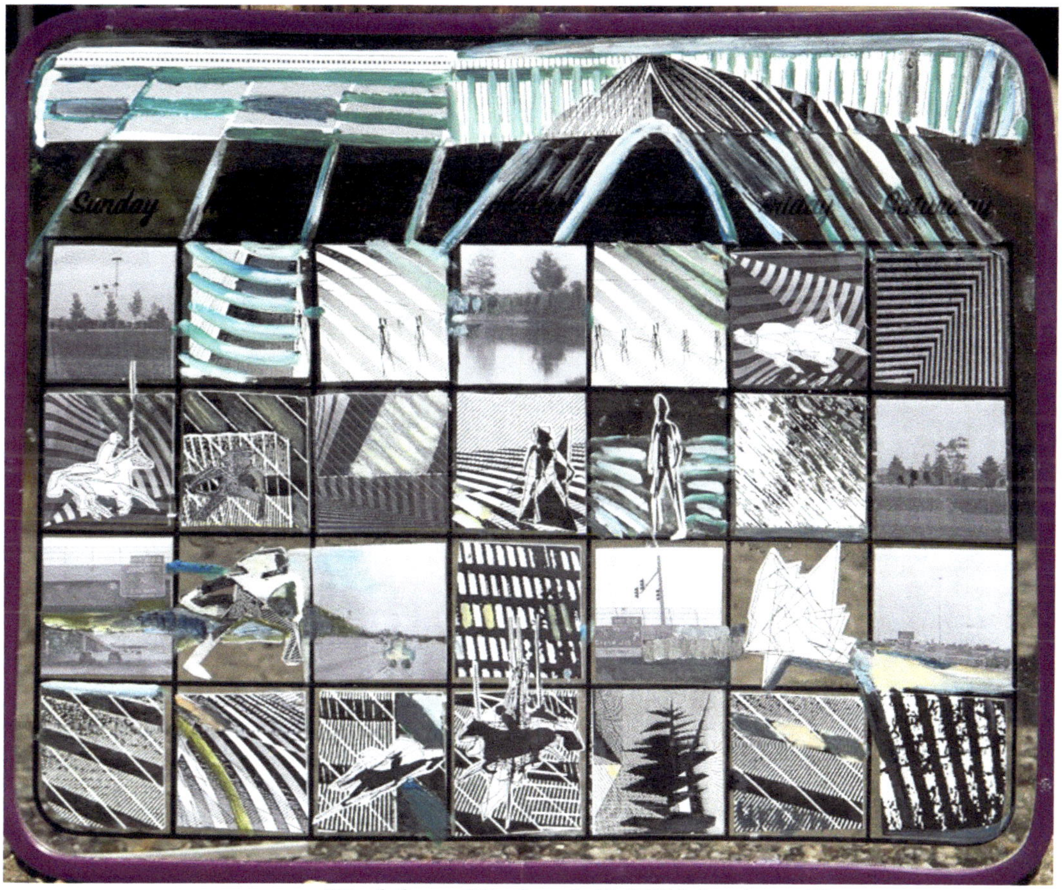

Weekday – Weekend. © 2025 by Anna Ursyn

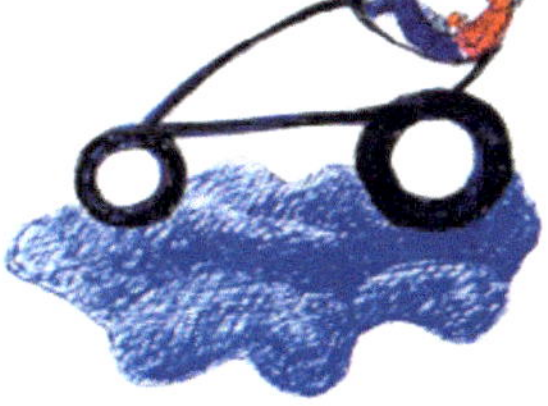

Madalo: never knew if he rode on his bike, or a cloud.

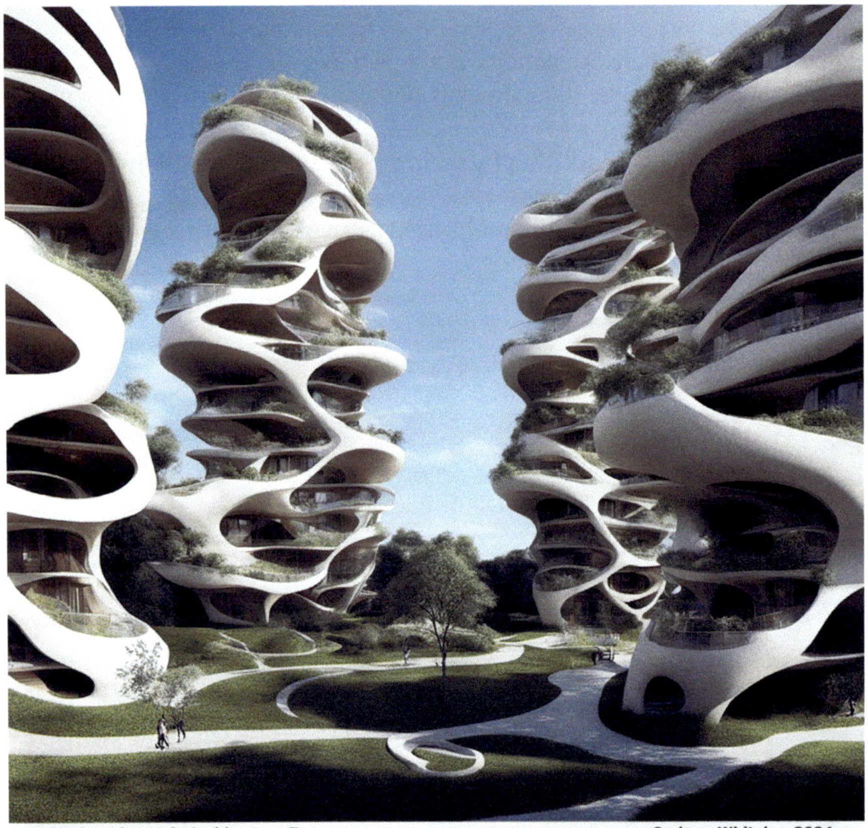

Whitaker Biometric Architecture Two c. Corinne Whitaker 2024

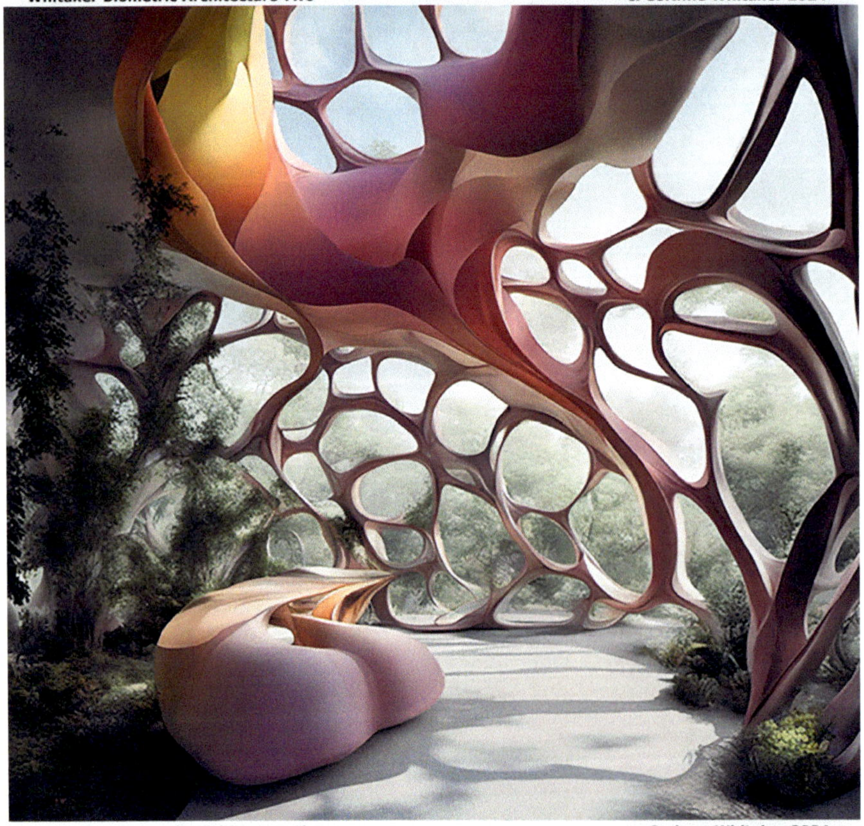

Whitaker Biometric Architecture Five c. Corinne Whitaker 2024

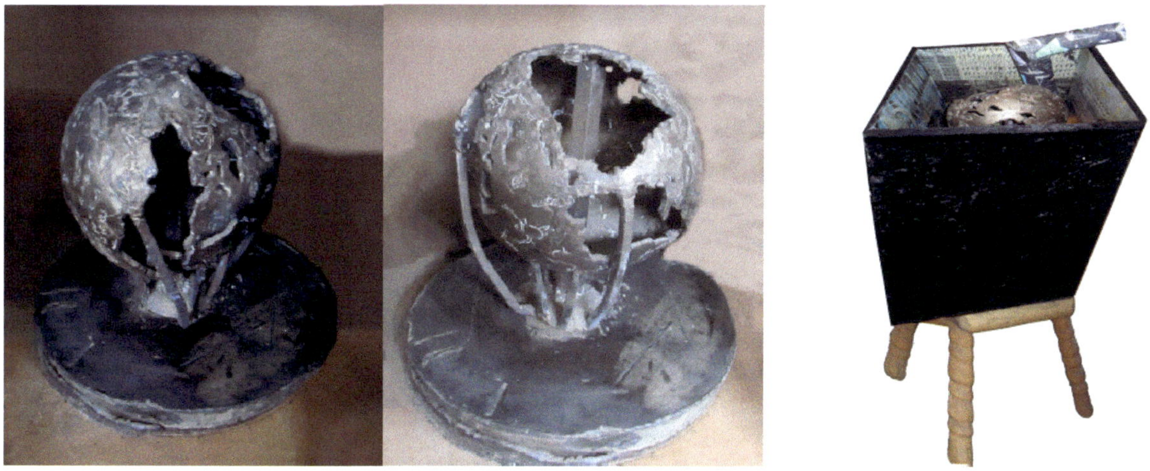

Water Planet. Bronze sculpture and related installation. © 2025 by Anna Ursyn.

CHAPTER 30
MORAL

TENTO'S MANIFESTO

Everybody does their best. It works for them, others, or both. However, sometimes, it does not work for either. Why?

SYNOPSIS

Tento sums up his long-time experience to share. Everyone can take away what they want from his discussion.

SUMMARY

Every story leaves its audience with a *Moral.* It is a tradition. Some expectations and a way of betterment could be met, but only if we can all agree on the meaning of 'better.' This abstract word constantly finds itself miraculously in trouble.

CAST OF CHARACTERS

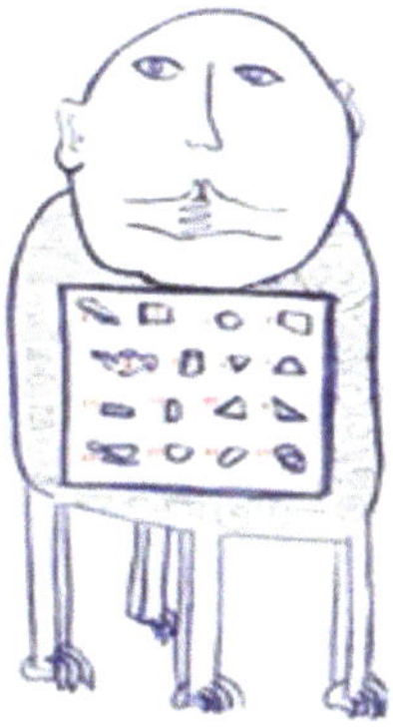

Tento

STAGE DIRECTIONS

Tento stays animated on the stage on the silver background. The audience is polled on their phones and the results are shown on the screen.
It happens now and in the near future.

The curtain goes up (or opens).

Tento, "We all do the best we can. Everybody does their best, they think. It works for them, others, or both. However, sometimes, it does not work for either. Why?
One does not have to always be better; one must work on being happy and staying happy.
We do better what we enjoy. Find your strengths and follow them. They are different from those your partner possesses.
Genuine kindness goes further than trying to be liked or appreciated.
Wish everybody well on the goodness level! We all think what we do is for good, but we often skip the associated costs.
If you have a child, teach them to play chess and code and learn foreign languages at a very young age so they can perceive more and become better strategists.
Children are more intelligent, understand, and remember more than we can appreciate.
Quality might be more important than quantity if we could agree on their meaning.
Dropping an attitude of always looking for more can help our planet.
Grow your curiosity daily. Observe what's around you and search for the awe associated with it. Beauty can be attributed to many senses. It can mean good construction, visual power, exciting solutions, true elegance, nice sounds or smells, etc. Associated words, colors, or images can set or trigger it.
Be respectful. There is some positive power behind everything and anything around you. Search for it, and it will be shared with you for goodness.
Only compete if you do sports. Do not compare yourself. It brings unhappiness as there will always be someone better than you.
Appreciate all your strengths, skills, and good vibes you possess. Aim to straighten them.
Sketch daily and write notes. In most professions, passions, and interests, the habit of sketching will create a path between your mind, heart, and hand.
Learn the basics of coding. You'll appreciate more what's around you.
No matter what, do no harm. It comes back at you one way or another anyway.
Follow your passions that do not cause any form of distress.
Dance often. It is more and less complicated at the same time on many levels.
Build respect toward yourself, others, and Nature!"

The End
The Curtain goes down (or closes).

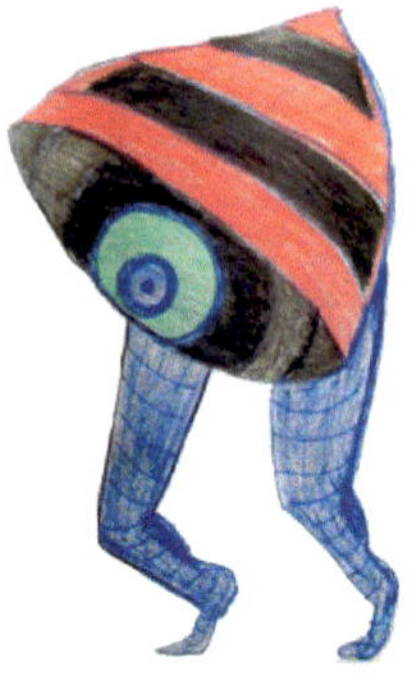

Lugatar: knows his way.

Lugatar: knows well where he goes.

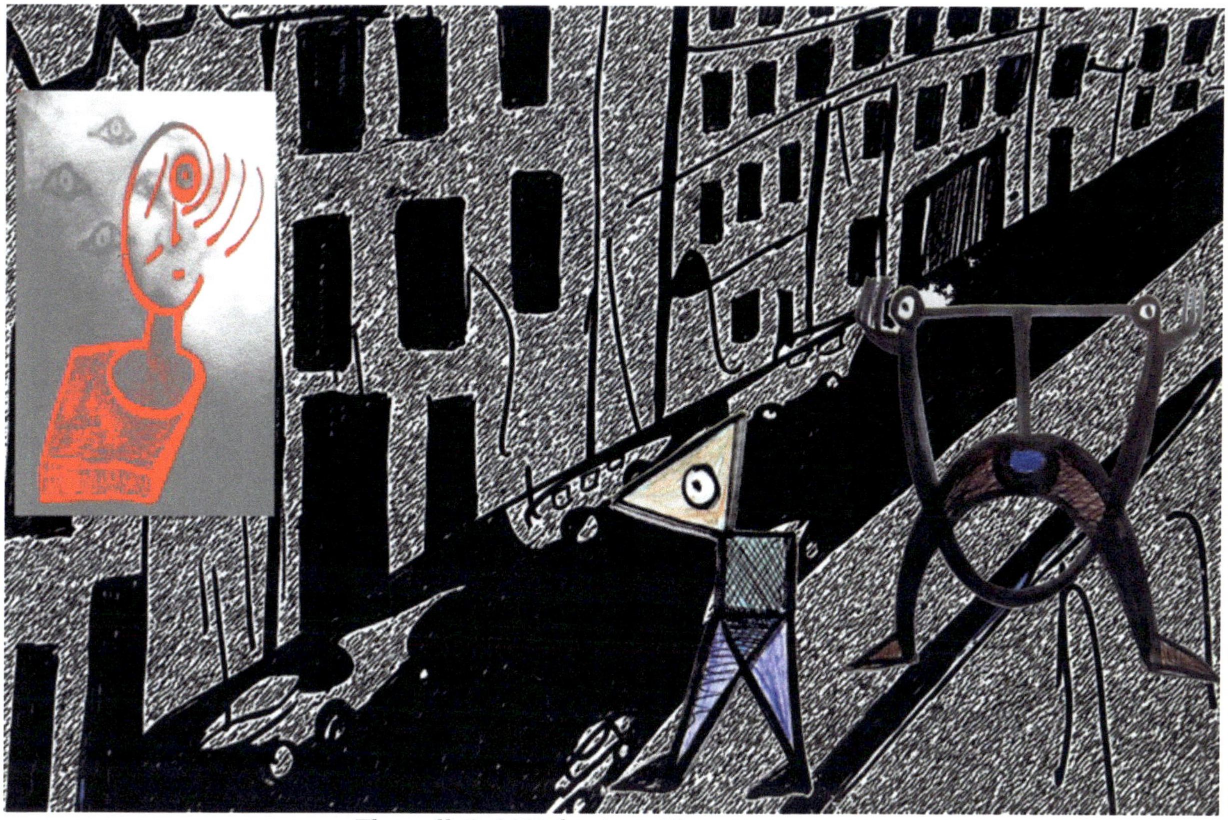

Threeall. © *2025 by Anna Ursyn*

PUBLICATIONS RELATED TO THIS BOOK

al-Rifaie, M. M., Ursyn, A., & Wyeld, T. (2020). *The Art of Coding: The Language of Drawing, Graphics, and Animation.* CRC Press: Chapman and Hall/CRC. Taylor and Francis Group. ISBN 978-0-367-90037-3; 978-1-138-62964-6; 978-1-315-21033-9.

Arya, A. (2020). *Anyone Can Code*. Routledge. ISBN-10: 0367199696, ISBN-13: 978-0367199692

Holoworld, *The Basics of STREAM Education: A Comprehensive Guide* (2024). Retrieved from https://www.blogs.holoworld.one/what-is-stream-education/contents

Beginner's Step-by-Step Coding Course: Learn Computer Programming the Easy Way. (DK Complete Courses), Hardcover –2020. ISBN 1465482210

Erwig, M. (2022). *Once Upon an Algorithm: How Stories Explain Computing.* MIT Press. ISBN-10: 0262545292, ISBN-13: 978-0262545297.

Montfort, N. (2021). *Exploratory Programming for the Arts and Humanities, second edition* MIT Press. ISBN-10: 0262044609.

Rahman, A. (2024) A video: https://youtu.be/zhuMGF8_Whw

Smith, S. (2021). Jazz and Jazz Theory. In *Describing Nature Through Visual Data,* A. Ursyn, Editor. IGI Global. https://www.igi-global.com/chapter/jazz-and-jazz-theory/259689

STEAM (2023). Rhode Island School of Design. Retrieved from https://www.risd.edu/steam. VisionShiftStudios (2024).

STEM to STEAM: Integrated Studies STEM to STEAM Resources Toolkit (2024). Edutopia, George Lucas Educational Foundation. Retrieved from https://www.edutopia.org/article/STEM-resources-downloads

Ursyn, A. (2024). The Transfer of Knowledge through Art and Visualization: Novel Technologies, Collaboration, and Visual Communication of Science-based Projects. Anna Ursyn (Author). Taylor & Francis Group. Routledge. ISBN 9781032624.

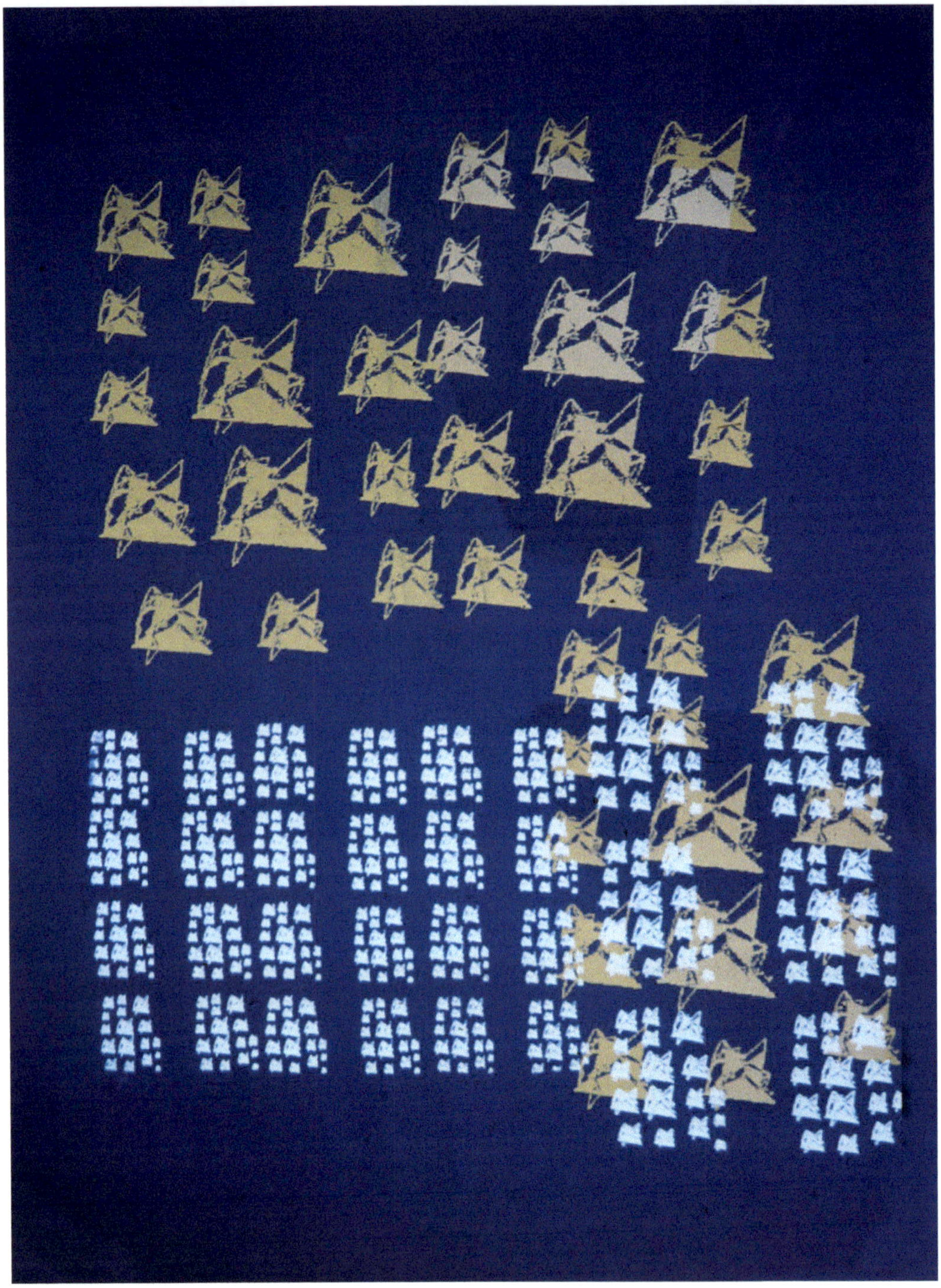

Connected Thoughts. Photosilkscreen after computer code on fabric. © 2025 by Anna Ursyn

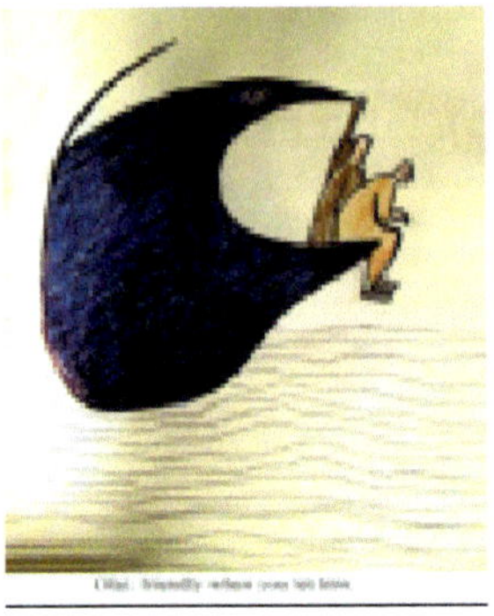

Olai: friendly when you let him.

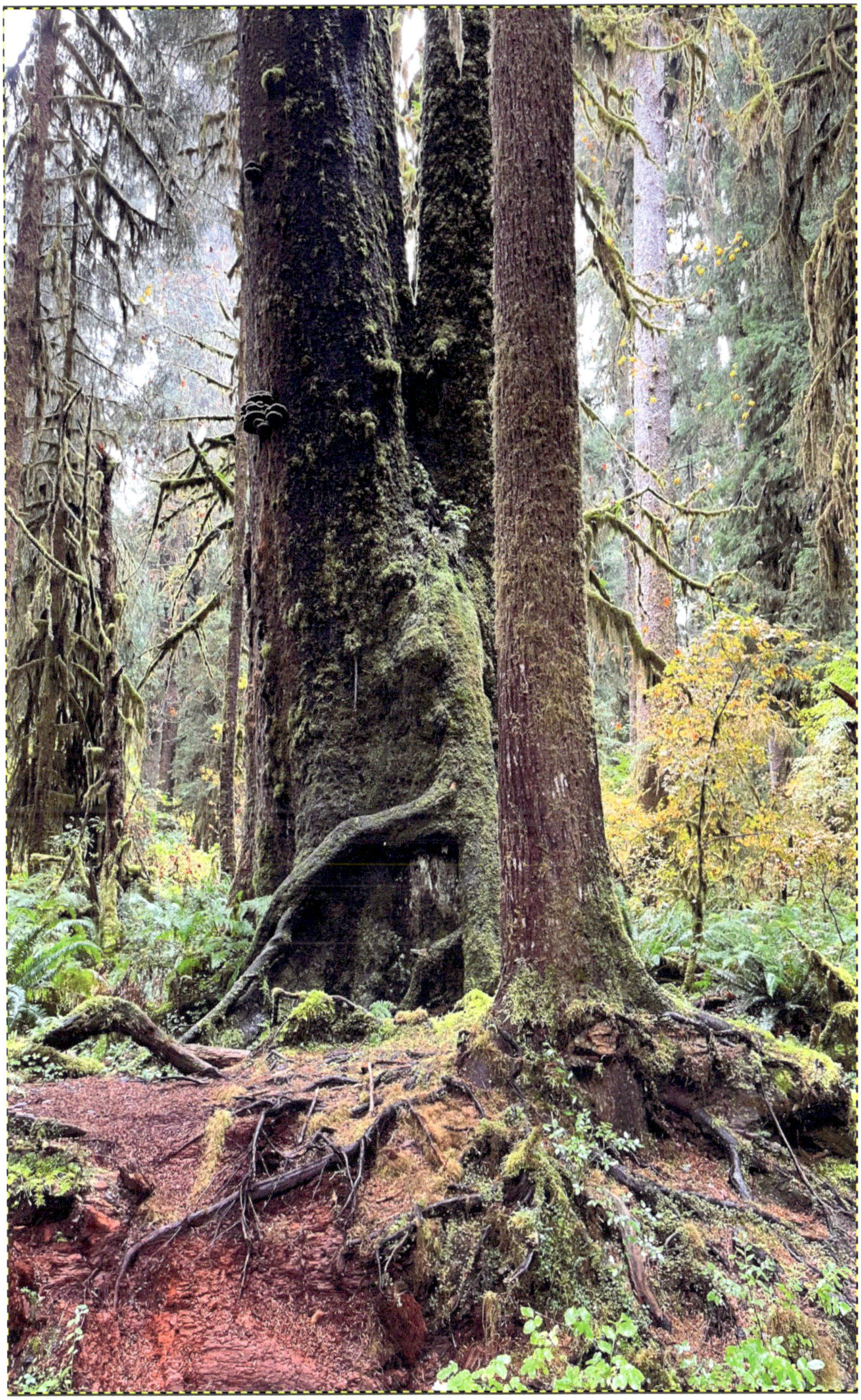

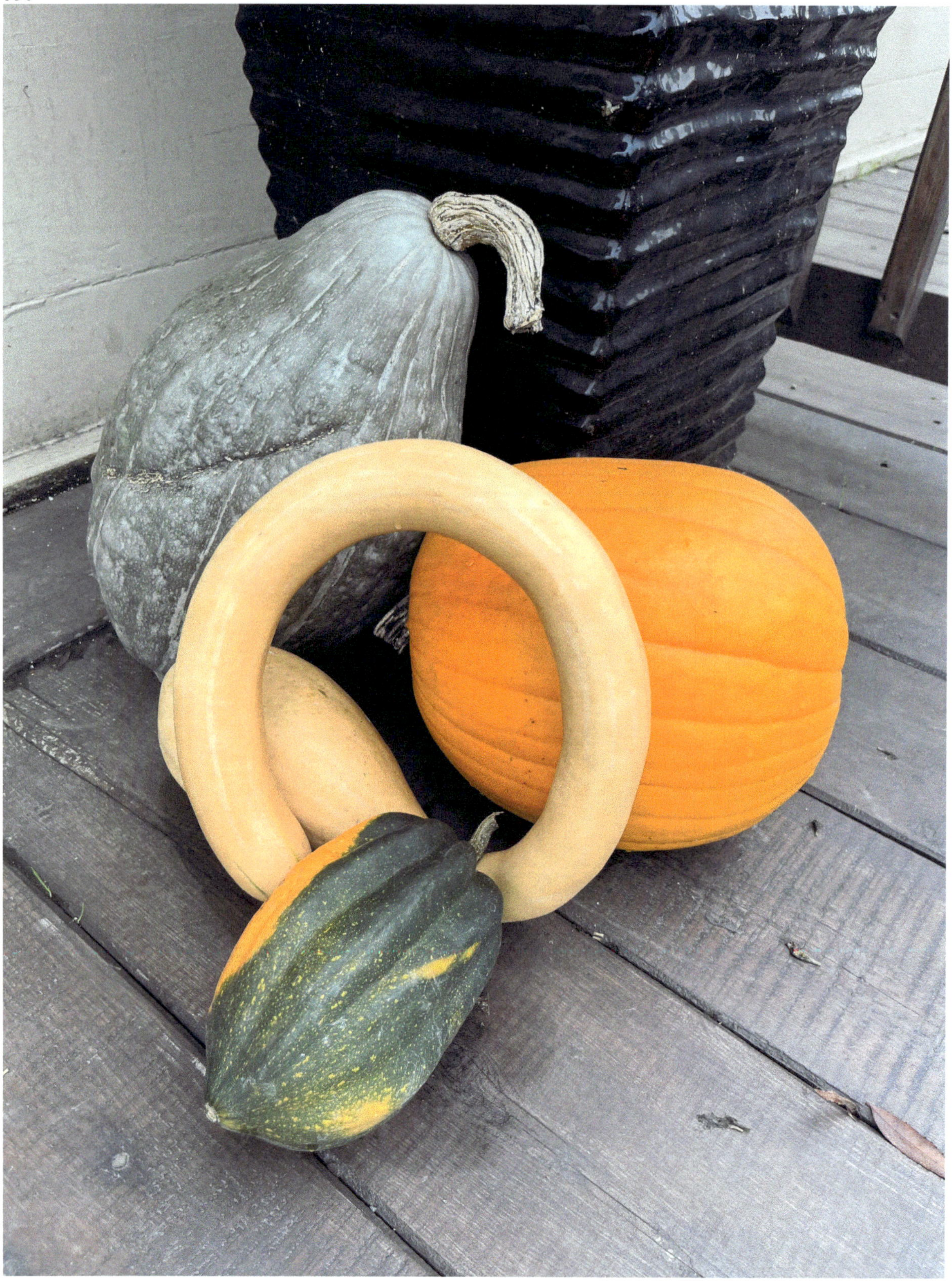

Still Life © by Matylda Czarnecka. (Used with permission)

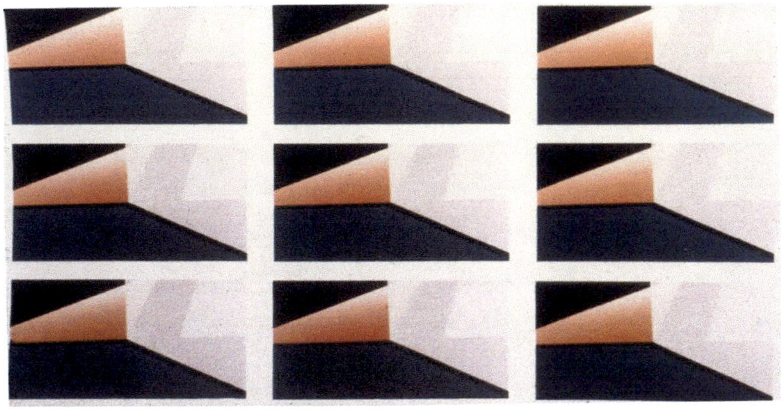

Windows. Output from the Computer Code. © 2025 by Anna Ursyn

Credits, Stage Credits, and Acknowledgments for Time-Based Representation

The UNC President, Board of Trustees members, Provost and members of the Provost Office, Dean of the Performance and Visual Arts, Chair of the School of Art and Design, colleagues, and members of several grant committees have been supporting me in my research and performances based on my books. My great thanks go to all of them and everybody else involved.

The scripts written and illustrated by the author of this book include artwork by Matylda Czarnecka, Lucinda Shellito, Joohyun Pyune, Teja Krašek, Stuart Smith, Ruth N. Sosa-Maciel, and student interns from iArt Institute, NYC: Ava Becker, Evelynn Leung, and Eunice Lee. Some scripts from this book were used for our further collaborations with the University of Northern Colorado's faculty, staff, students, and international contributors, resulting in grants, videos, and performances. The texts were written during summertime with images by the author, copyright-free resources, graphic and music software, and illustrations. The videos, animations, and recorded performances are available on the website listed at the start and end of the book.

Thank you to Randi Slack, Heba Kusseibati, Sherry Thomas, and C. McQueen from Taylor & Francis Group, and my thanks go to the reviewers. Also, thank you to the grant committees for awarding me grants. Thank you to Dr. Lucinda Shellito and members of her courses for consulting and cooperating on the theatrical performances. My appreciation goes to my students and to the Director of the iArt Institute in New York City, Joohyun Pyune, and her crew for arranging an internship for their students to work with me on this.

All the performance and video credits are listed at the end of each performance. The grants supported the performances. My gratitude goes to the coders Stuart Smith and Mohammad Majid al-Rifaie, Md. Fahimul Islam, and Md. Asifur Rahman for their work on the codes and related outputs. For the second set of performances in January 2025, my students Larry Ward, David Ona Munoz, Izze Sajdak, Meena Pant, Jamie Milne, and Alexis Winnett used the 2D and time-based work.

For books and performances, software and apps were used including music and visual music, videos, and animations among them, Grammarly, ChatGPT, QuillBot, Wordtune, Pexels, Flat, Udio, and
https://uisoftware.com/MetaSynth/
https://tuneform.com/media/visualizers,https://www.renderforest.com,
https://openai.com/research/musenet, Microsoft Word, Adobe products, and more. Images are by the author and collaborators, as credited.

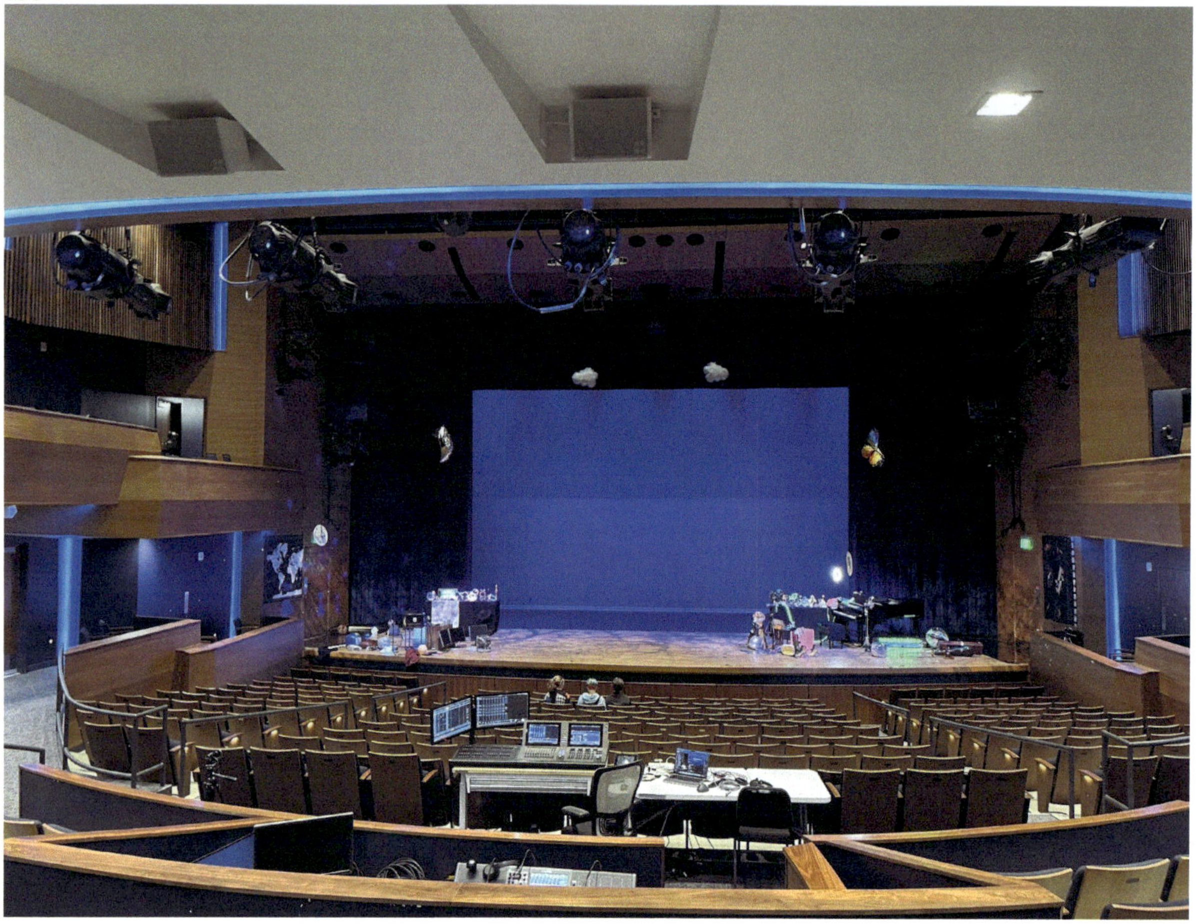

Please see the videos with proper credits and codes written by Stuart Smith, Mohammad Majid al-Rifaie, Md. Fahimul Islam and Md. Asifur Rahman at:

Ursyn.com
then select Art & Programming

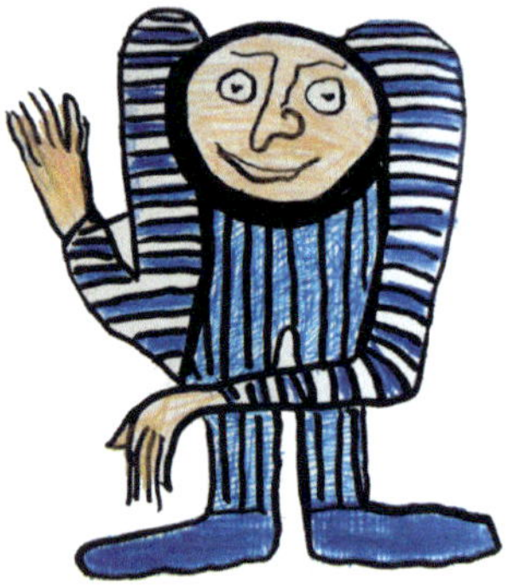

Baduran: knows everyone, if not, sends an invite.

aduran: knows everyone. If not, sends an invitation.

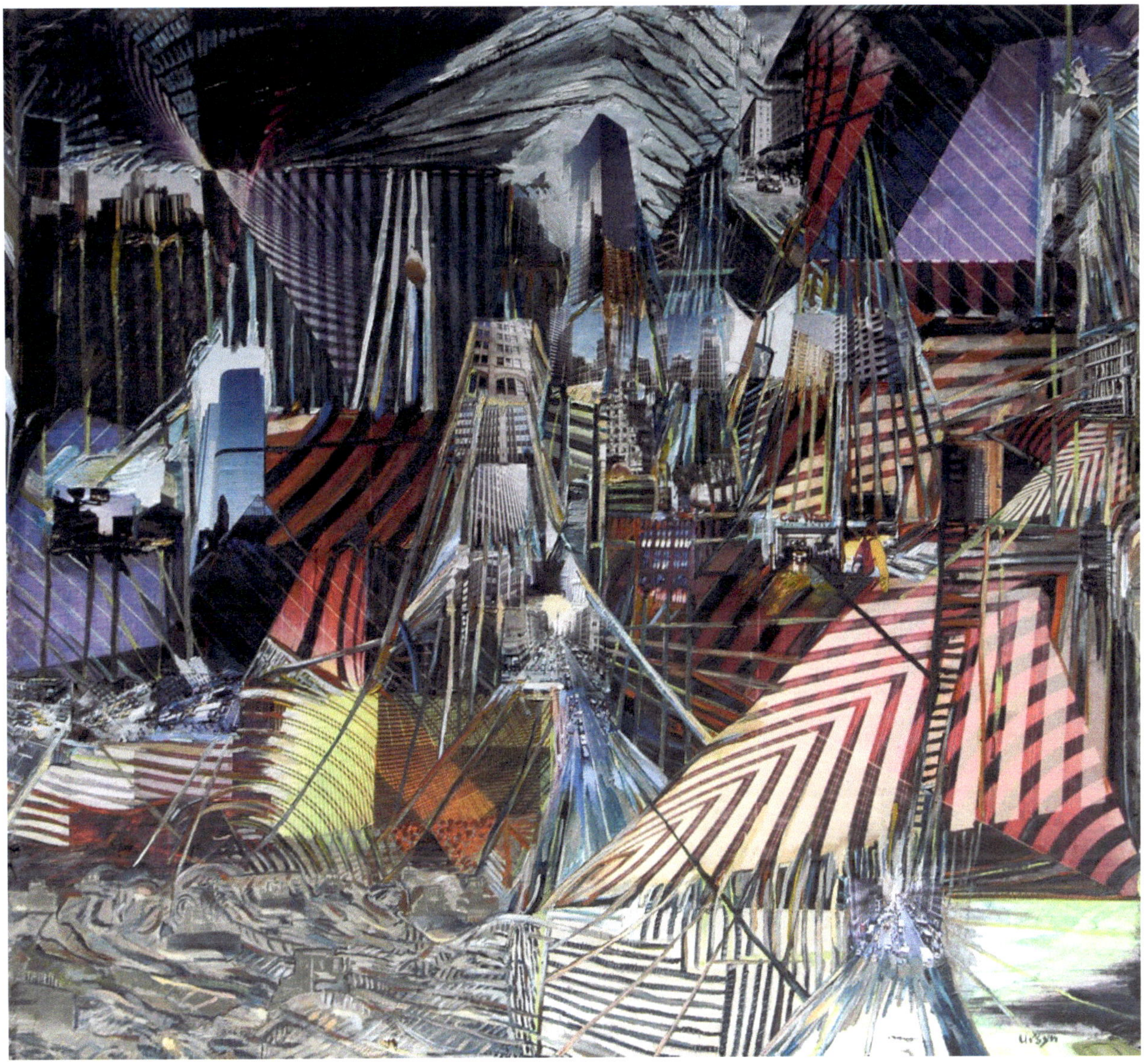

Timetable. © 2025 by Anna Ursyn

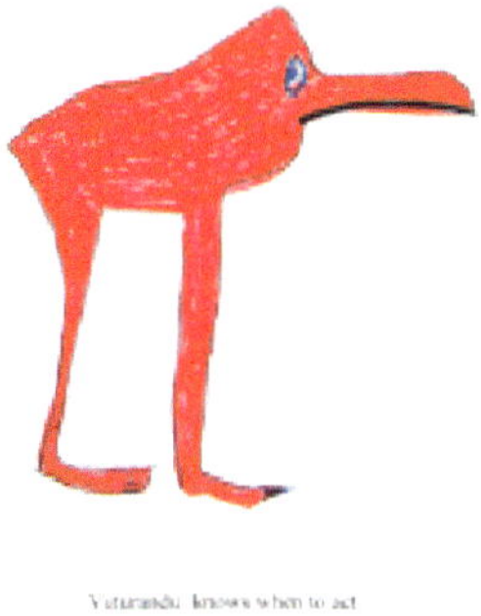

_________________________ *Vuturandu: knows when to act.*

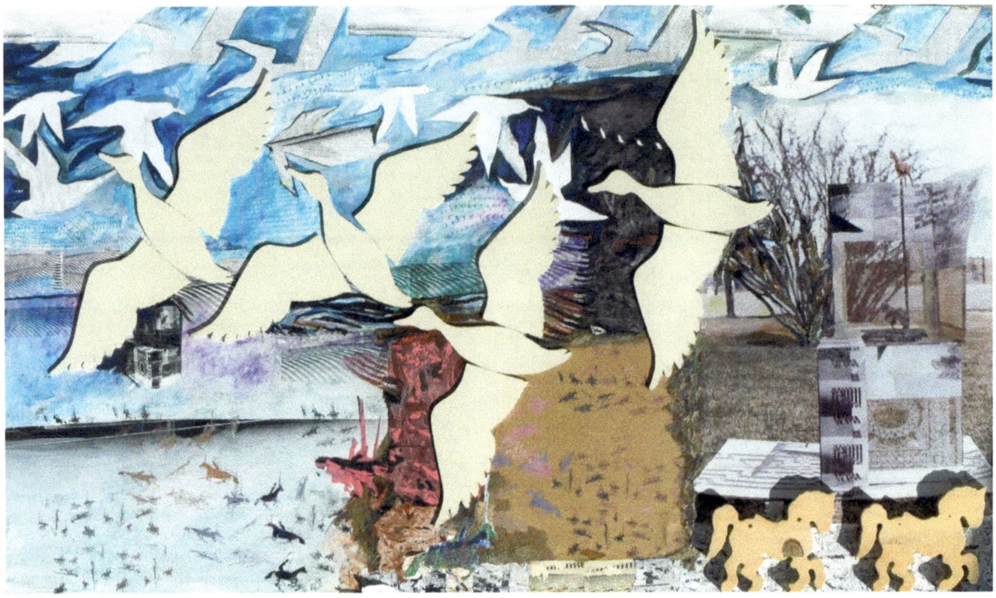

Bird's Eye View. © 2025 by Anna Ursyn

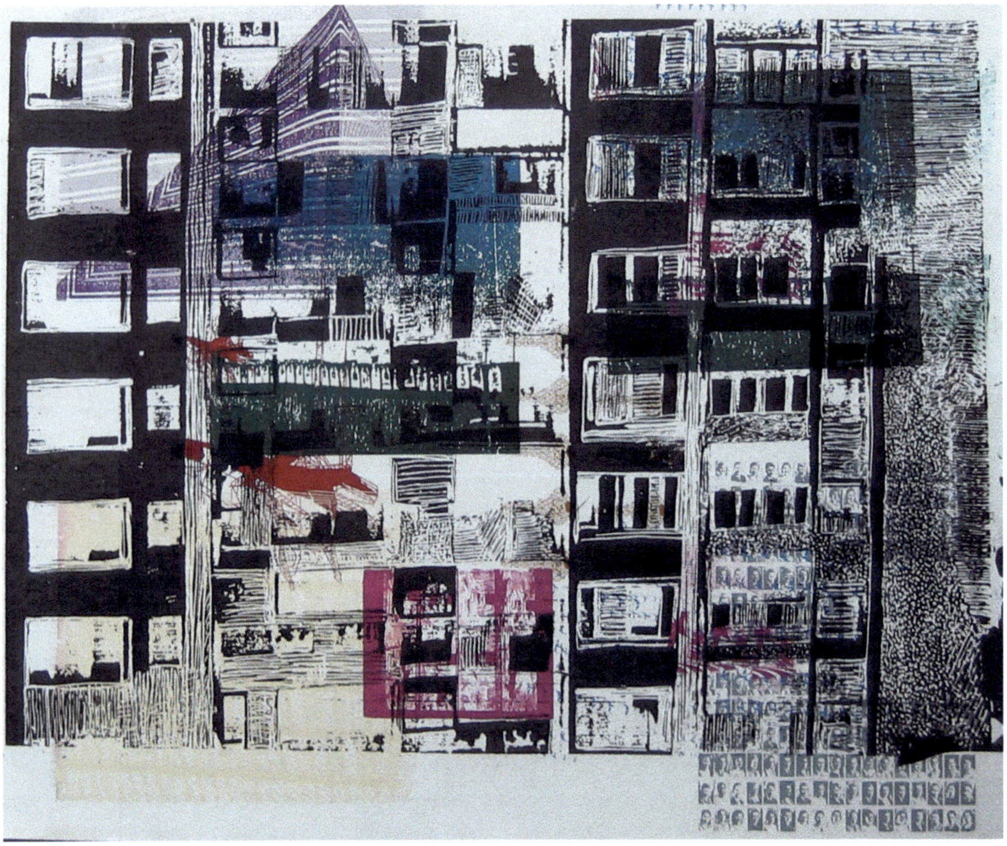

City Neighborhood. Photosilkscreen after computer codes. © 2025 by Anna Ursyn

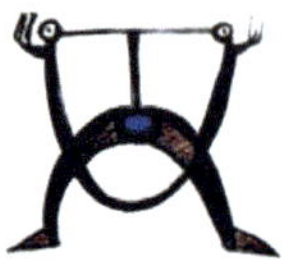

Maoda: always a gentleman; to those he does not compete with.

Terms with Short Descriptions

Abstract – a concept or thought that does not have a physical, concrete existence. Also, an artistic object that has a meaning independent of narrative or pictorial representation. Also, a summary of a larger text.

Aesthetics – analysis of principles related to beauty in terms of arts or philosophy

Algorithm – a sequence of instructions telling a computer how to perform computation or write programs. In a recursive process, algorithms can be written many times to create repetition. Algorithms help to solve a complex problem by writing a sequence of simple steps.

Anthropology means the study of human characteristics. Physical anthropology studies human biological and physiological features and their evolution. Cultural anthropology studies societies, cultures, and their development.

API – application programming interface, is a software interface that allows communication between computers and/or programs.

Artifact – an object produced by a human being, examined in the artistic or historical terms (it may be an artwork, a craft object, a tool, a weapon, or an ornament of archaeological or historical interest).

Artificial intelligence (AI) uses computer systems and applies machine learning for tasks, involving big collections of data, that would require human intelligence.

Binary numeral system uses two symbols: typically, "0" (zero) and "1" (one).

Biointerface is a place of contact between a biomolecule, living tissue, or organism and a living or another material. Nanostructure interfaces are extensively studied.

ChatGPT is a computer program that uses artificial intelligence (AI) and natural language processing (NLP) to understand user questions, providing automatic responses, and simulating human conversation ibm.com/topics/chatbots

Cognitive abilities enable to think abstractly (not only on concrete objects), learn from experience, reason, comprehend ideas and concepts, and solve problems. They support gaining knowledge, utilizing information, creative and critical thinking.

Cobots are robots that collaborate with people.

DALL·E 2 is a version of GPT-3 that can create realistic images and art from text descriptions.

Data – factual information specially organized for analysis, reasoning, or making decisions.

Data Visualization – information abstracted in a schematic form to provide visual insights into data sets. Data visualization enables us to go from the abstract numbers in a computer program (ones and zeros) to the visual interpretation of data. Text visualization means converting textual information into graphic representation, so we can see the information without reading the data, as tables, histograms, pie or bar charts, or Cartesian coordinates.

Dimension relates to spatial measures such as width, height, or length. Dimension means how many numbers (coordinates) are needed to determine a position of a point in space. In the Cartesian three-dimensional space, three coordinates, x, y, and z, describe the position of a point: x-horizontal axis, y-vertical axis, and z-depth. René Descartes (Cartesius) revolutionized mathematics by providing the first systematic link between geometry described by Euclides and algebra). A point has no length, area, volume, or other dimensional attributes, so some mathematicians claim a point is 0-dimensional. A line has one dimension because only one coordinate is needed to describe a point in space, while a surface has two dimensions. Data may be linear or multidimensional.

Electromagnetic radiation results from the electromagnetic field's propagation of waves (or photons) which carries radiant energy. Waves, which have different wavelengths, include radio waves, microwaves, infrared, light (which is visible), ultraviolet, X-rays, and gamma rays.

Empathy means understanding and sharing another person's or creature's feelings. One may apply cognitive (by knowing how to take somebody's perspective), emotional (by feeling somebody's emotions), and compassionate (by combining intellect and feelings) empathy.

Extended Reality (XR) comprises real-and-virtual environments generated by computer technology and used in wearables.

Virtual Reality (VR) refers to immersive experiences created with the use of real-world content (e.g., 360° Video), purely synthetic content (for instance, computer-generated), or a hybrid of both.

Augmented Reality (AR) is an overlay of computer-generated content on the real world that can superficially interact with the environment in real time. With AR, the CG content and the real world do not block themselves.

Mixed Reality (MR) – in MR, the synthetic content is overlaid and anchored to interact with objects in the real world in real-time.

Fiber lasers use fiber optic cables with added rare earth elements and other materials to provide and transmit light and light signals.

Form – mass that occupies space, giving the weight, density, and thickness of a 3D object or is implied in a picture of this object.

Fractal geometry describes self-similar or scale-symmetric objects called fractals. When magnified or reduced in size, fractal things are self-similar: their parts are similar to the whole, and the likeness continues when the parts are magnified more and more. They are present in nature, designs, and artworks. Fractal geometry can explain the origination of patterns in living organisms.

GPT (generative pre-trained transformer) is a deep learning model originated by Google in 2017.

GPT-4 is a multimodal model that accepts prompts of images and texts as inputs and gives out text outputs, such as natural language or code.

Graphic is an image represented by a graph or relating to graphics. Computers often generate graphic displays.

Haptic – relates to the sense of touch; the senses of touch and proprioception enable the perception and manipulation of objects.

Higher-order thinking goes beyond observation of facts and data memorization, enabling one to build data-based knowledge. Higher-order thinking makes critical thinking possible in an evaluative, creative, and innovative way.

HTML – Hypertext Markup Language. This language codes formatting, links, and other things on Web pages. XML – eXtensible Markup Language. A markup language like HTML; it lets individuals define and use their tags.

Hyperlink – a link from a hypertext file or document to another file activated by clicking on a highlighted word or image on the screen.

Icon, iconic object or image – An icon represents a thing or refers to something by resembling or imitating it; thus, a picture, a photograph, a mathematical expression, or an old-style telephone may be regarded as an iconic object. Therefore, an iconic object or image has qualities in common with things it represents by looking, sounding, feeling, tasting, or smelling alike.

Iconography means visual elements such as images and symbols used in a specific culture, society, or artwork. It also may indicate a study about these elements.

Immersive experience happens when a 3D or 4D (including time) image (maybe plus sound or other stimuli) surrounds you creating extended reality. Platforms that support immersive experiences include augmented reality (AR), virtual reality (VR), Mixed reality (MR), 360° video, wearable devices, the Internet of Things (IoT), and more.

Infographics – tools and techniques involved in the graphical representation of data, mostly in journalism, art, and storytelling.

Information – knowledge derived from study, experience, or instruction based on facts or data.

Information visualization – representation plus interaction; it means using the computer-supported, visual-spatial representation of abstract data to amplify cognition and derive new insights. Data presented as information visualization are often interactive, numerical, verbal, and graphical (such as the text of geographic representations).

Ions: cations and anions. An atom or molecule with an electric charge is called an ion. An electric charge results from the presence of single, double, triple, or even higher negative electrons, unequal to the number of positive protons in the nucleus of an atom. Removing or adding one or more electrons changes a neutral atom into an ion. A cation is an ion or group of ions with a positive charge. An anion is a negatively charged ion. In an electrolyte solution, cations move toward the cathode (negative electrode) after applying an electric current, and anions migrate to an anode.

Interface denotes a connection or interaction between two units (which may be subjects, organizations, physical or electronic systems), for example, social interface, or interface between phases of matter such as solid, liquid, and gas, and also interaction of hardware and software. The user and computer interface allows communication with the operating system. Interface with the internet may go through the Internet protocol.

Internet of Things (IoT) means a set of objects connected over a wireless network and acting without human actions. It serves for personal use in smart homes (with everyday physical devices embedded with sensors and software), for elder with disabilities care, as an internet of medical things (IoMT), for business, industrial, vehicular communication, and many kinds of infrastructure systems.

Kinesthesia means knowing about the position and movement of the parts of the body. Sensory organs (proprioceptors) in the muscles and joints signal changes in position.

Knowledge visualization uses visual representations to transfer insights and create new knowledge in communicating different visual formats.

Latitude and longitude are parts of a grid system giving us horizontal and vertical coordinates in the geographic coordinate system. Latitude lines run east-west, and longitude lines run north-south. Every location on Earth has a universal address described by two numbers called latitude and longitude coordinates; they say where the coordinates intersect.

LED, the light-emitting diode, is a semiconductor diode that glows when a voltage is applied.

Mandala is a geometric circular figure depicting the universe according to Hindu and Buddhist traditional symbols.

Manifesto is a public declaration of opinions, statements, and programs mostly of political or social aims. An art manifesto expresses aesthetic and philosophical thoughts about the art defined by an artist or a group of artists. An individual art manifesto facilitates the translation of artistic, visual messages into literary form and conveys it to the viewers, critics, and jurors.

Meander is a geometric pattern made by a line bending along and repeatedly crossing a straight line but not crossing itself. In the arts, it is a decorative pattern constructed from a continuous line shaped into a repeated, ornamental motif.

Metaphor – indicates one thing as representing another, thus making an implied mental comparison. For example, we use metaphors every day when we talk about desktop items, such as folders, documents, and in and out boxes, using familiar objects for organizing elements related to the computer. Also, a figure of speech where we use one word or phrase to designate another one, thus suggesting comparison, as in 'a sea of trouble.'

Mime – a performance art involving body motions without the use of speech.

Mythology is a collection of stories, myths, legends, and beliefs typical of a given culture or religion; for example, Christian, Jewish, Egyptian, Hindu, or Muslim mythologies.

NASA is the *National Aeronautics and Space Administration* civil space program and space exploration. This agency works with contractors, academia, and international and commercial partners to explore, discover, and expand knowledge for the benefit of humanity.

Negative space is the space around the objects depicted in a picture. A figure-ground reversal is an optical illusion that happens when we perceive an image formed by the negative space.

Network is a set of connected (wired or wireless) devices, such as computers, servers, mainframes, peripherals, firewalls, smartphones, and more, which allows people to share data. Devices may be linked through cables, telephone lines, radio waves, satellites, or infrared light beams.

Networking means exchanging ideas and information among people for social or business contact.

Neurotransmitters are chemical substances released by nerve cells that transfer signals from neurons to other cells.

OpenAI is a research unit that derives its solutions from deep learning and natural language processing.

Pantomime – a musical, theatrical production using gestures and movements but not words

Paradigm is a pattern of thought: a set of concepts or a way of thinking characteristic of a specific field in science (research methods, postulates, and standards) or philosophy. Paradigm shifts – transitioning to a new approach to the field under study is how the developments come about. Paradigm also means a model, a typical example.

Pattern means the regular order existing in nature and a manmade design. We see patterns everywhere in nature, mathematics, art, architecture, and design. In nature, patterns can be seen as symmetries (e.g., snowflakes) and/or structures having fractal dimensions such as spirals, meanders, or surface waves. In computer science, design patterns serve in creating computer programs. In the arts, the pattern is an artistic or decorative design made of recurring lines or any repeated elements.

Perspective is the appearance of depth, picturing the world on a two-dimensional, flat surface of a piece of paper or a computer screen. Perspective represents 3D objects and depth relationships on a 2D surface.

Photonics is the science of light (photons) generation, detection, and manipulation. It can go through emission, transmission, modulation, sensing, signal processing, switching, and amplification.

Scale is a range of values that forms a standard system for measuring the size of something. Units for measuring in science are known as the International System of Units, which is based on the meter. Very small physical and biological structures are measuring fractions of a meter: micrometer (one-millionth of a meter – $1x10^{-6}$ m), nanometer one billionth of a meter – $1x10^{-9}$ m), and picometer (one trillionth of a meter – $1x10^{-12}$ m) thus, the picometer is one-thousandth of a nanometer. Below are examples of objects of various sizes.

The Milky Way galaxy (10^{21} m)
Our solar system (10^{13} m)
The Earth (10^{18} m)
A city (10^{4} m)
A tree (10^{1} m)
A leaf (10^{-1} m)
A cell (10^{-5} m)
Strands of DNA (10^{-7} m)
An atom (10^{-10} m), and
Quarks (10^{-16} m).

Scientific visualization presents real, abstract, or model-based objects in a digital way directly from the data. It may deliver art-science cooperative learning projects and make knowledge understandable to a broad audience. Visualization as storytelling comprises narratives, interactive graphics, explanatory and animated graphics, and multimedia.

Semiconductor material has a conductivity between a conductor (most metals, for example, copper) and an insulator (such as glass). The properties of a semiconductor, its moving electrons, and electron holes in a crystal lattice can be explained by quantum physics. Silicon crystals are semiconductive materials; they are used in microelectronics and photovoltaics used for direct conversion of sunlight to electricity with the use of solar panels.

Semiotic studies the meaningful use of signs, symbols, codes, and conventions for communication. The name 'semiotics' is derived from the Greek word 'semeion,' which means "sign." "Meaning" is always the result of social conventions, even when we think something is natural or characteristic and use signs for those meanings. Therefore, culture and art are a series of sign systems. Semioticians analyze such sign systems in various cultures; linguists study language as a system of signs, and some even examine film as a system of signs. The semiotic content of visual design is essential for non-verbal communication applied to practice, especially for visualizing knowledge.

Sign tells about a fact, an idea, or information; it is a distinct thing that signifies another thing. Natural signs signify events caused by nature, while conventional signs may signal art, social interactions, fashion, food, interaction with technology, machines, and practically everything else. Signs take conventional shapes or forms to tell about facts, ideas, or information. Icons and symbols help visually compress information. An icon represents a thing or refers to something by resembling or imitating it; thus, a picture, a photograph, a mathematical expression, or an old-style telephone may be regarded as an iconic object. Therefore, an iconic object has qualities in common with things it represents by looking, sounding, feeling, tasting, or smelling alike. Natural signs signify events caused by nature, while conventional signs may signal art, social interactions, fashion, food, interactions with technology, machines, and practically everything else.

Signage is a visual graphic that displays information, for example, street signs, room identification signs, or any informational or regulatory signs. Signs, symbols, and icons are collectively called signage. Effective design of a complicated product may help memorize and learn how to use this product (for example, 'Where is the switch?' or 'How to open this thing?').

Social media include social networking sites, image-sharing sites, video hosting sites, discussion sites, community blogs, and economic networks.

Social networking means using Internet-based social media websites and applications to interact with other users for a social or business purpose and stay connected with friends, family, colleagues, customers, or clients. Social networking acts through sites like Facebook, Twitter, LinkedIn, and Instagram.

Space is a three-dimensional expanse in the physical universe where we can measure the position and direction of objects and events. A Cartesian coordinate system (with the x, y, and z axes) serves this purpose in Euclidean geometry.

Spectroscopy records how matter interacts with or emits electromagnetic radiation. A spectroscope serves to study matter by measuring properties of specific frequencies and wavelengths of electromagnetic radiation.

Symbol does not resemble things it represents but refers to something by convention; for example, the word "red" represents red. We must learn the relationship between symbols and what they represent, such as letters, numbers, words, codes, traffic lights, and national flags. A symbol represents an abstract concept, not just a thing, and is comparable to an abstract term. Highly abstracted drawings that show no realistic graphic representation become symbols. Symbols are omnipresent in our life, for example:

– An electric diagram that uses abstract symbols for a light bulb, wire, connector, resistor, and switch.
– An apple for a teacher or a bitten apple for a Macintosh computer.
– A map – a typical abstract graphic device.
– A 'slippery when wet' sign.

Symmetry is present when similar parts of an object are arranged around a line, point, or plane. A crystal shows symmetry when it has a center of symmetry, rotation axes, or mirror planes (imaginary planes that divide it into halves). There are several types of symmetry: for example, line or mirror symmetry, radial, cylindrical, or spherical symmetry. A figure with a line, bilateral symmetry has two identical halves when folded along its line of symmetry, and these halves are congruent, meaning they are the same size and shape. An object has a radial symmetry when it can be rotated around the rotation axis. For example, with a fourfold rotation axis, the crystal repeats itself each 90°. Angles of rotational symmetry possible for crystals are: 60 degrees, 90 degrees, 120 degrees, 180 degrees, and 360 degrees. The halves of the bilaterally symmetrical animals, for example, butterflies, form each other's mirror images when seen along the axis. A circle is symmetrical about its center. Optical isomers are 'mirror images' of each other and are symmetrical around a plane. For example, molecules of some sugar isomers deflect the rays of light in the right or left direction.

Synesthesia means the merging of two or more senses. It happens when a sensory stimulus is received by one sense but also triggers perception in another sense.

Synapse – a structure that links (through a synaptic cleft) a nerve cell with another nerve or some other cell type. In an electrical synapse, an activated neuron develops an electric signal on its presynaptic cell membrane, which induces a voltage change on the postsynaptic cell. In a chemical synapse, electrical activity on the presynaptic cell membrane initiates the release of a neurotransmitter and its diffusion to a postsynaptic cell.

Texture – a characteristic of a substance or a material. Texture exists all around us. It can be actual (natural, invented, or manufactured) or simulated (made to look rough, smooth, hard or soft, or like a natural texture). Simulated textures are made to represent real textures, such as smooth arms or rough rock formations. But they are not actual textures; if you touch the picture, you feel only the paint or the pen or pencil marks.

URL means Uniform Resource Locator. Also, resources are called well-known codes, such as http://www.sciam.com/, used in hyperlinks (activated by clicking).

Variable is a feature or a factor that can take on different numerical values.

Vernacular is an adjective to describe the local, indigenous, folkloristic, common, or simple form of a specific culture, architecture, language, or other human activities or products.

Vernacular language is typical of a particular country or region or a dialect that can be regional, professional, or otherwise linking a group of people. It may also denote the architecture of houses in a particular region.

Visuals are pictures, diagrams, graphics, film clips, or various forms of display.

Visual media are primarily images, videos, and infographics. Powerpoint presentations may serve as an example.

Visualization means the communication of information with graphical representations. Interactive visual representations of abstract data use easy-to-recognize objects connected through well-defined relations.

Wireframe is a skeletal three-dimensional model in which only lines and vertices are represented. It can also be a way to design a website at the early structural level, a 2D outline of a web page or app which displays the functional elements of a website.

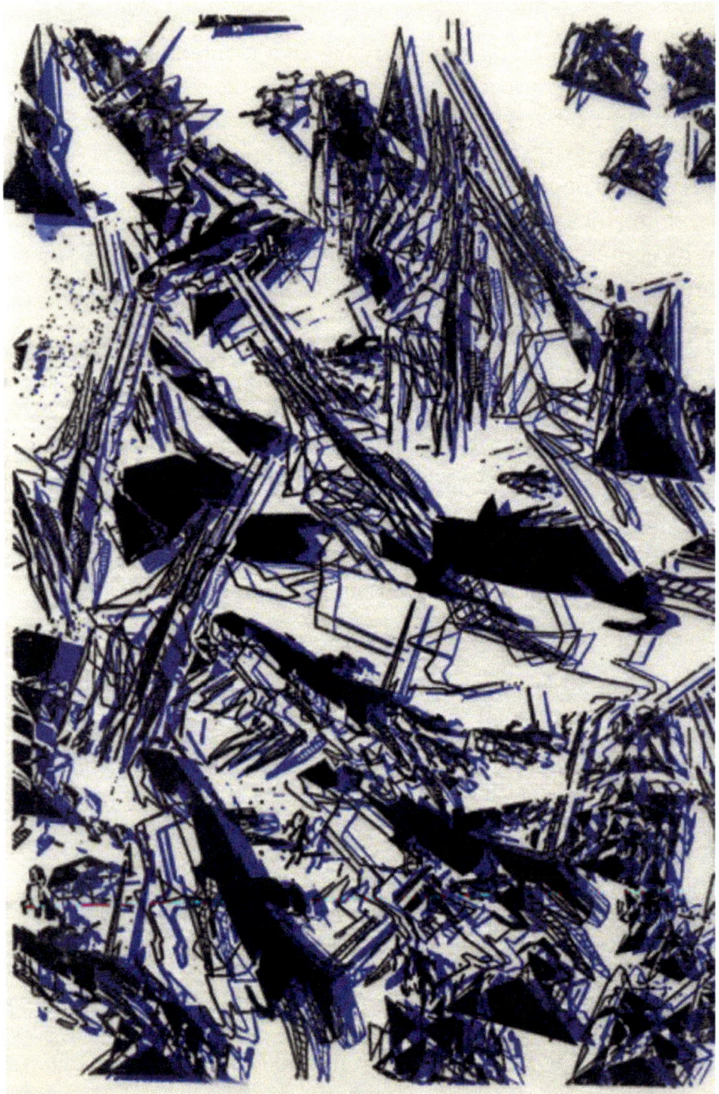

Double Take. Outputs from the computer codes on the Acetate. © 2025 by Anna Ursyn.

* The *Fish* program, translated from a code written by Anna Ursyn in Fortran into Java by Md Fahiul Islam, was published in *The Art of Coding: The Language of Drawing, Graphics, and Animation.*

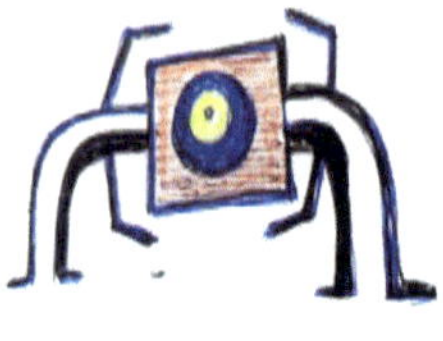

Ugarsa: Enjoys watching the news, but not on his phone.

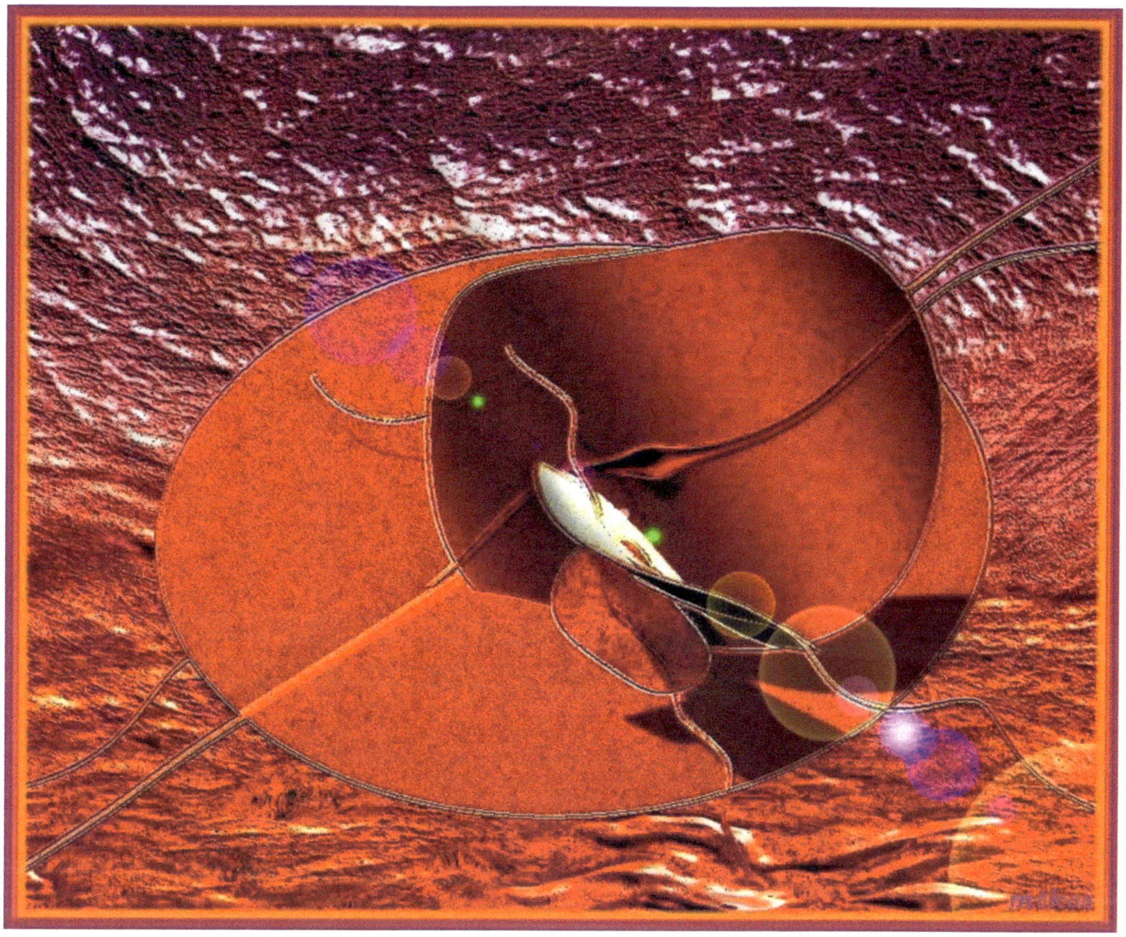

Life on Mars. © 2025 by Teja Krašek. (Used with Permission).

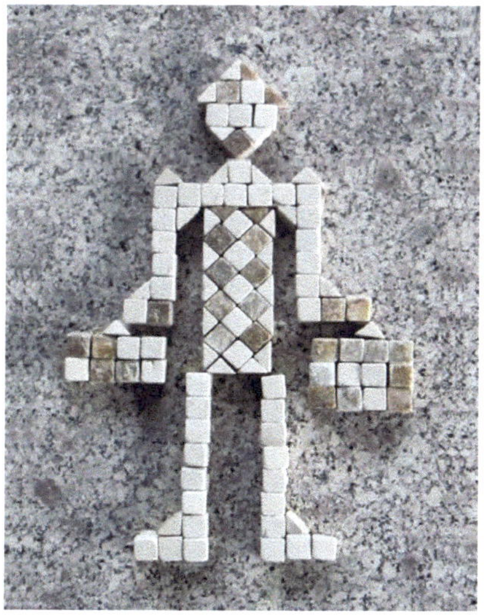

Medic, always helpful

INDEX

#

A

B

C

D

E

F

G

H

I

J

L

M

N

O

P

Q

R

S

T

W

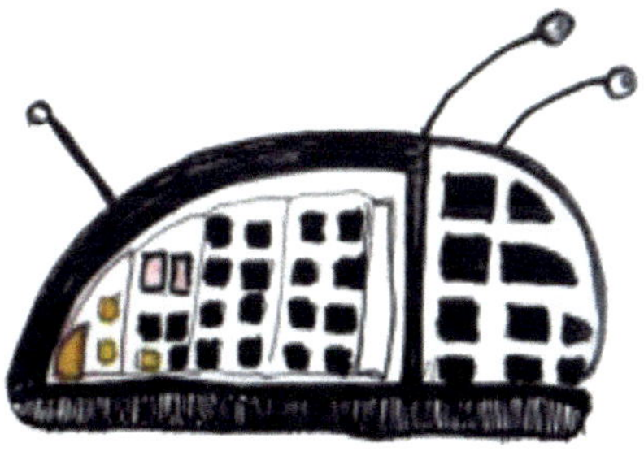

Yarusi: rents traveling flats by weeks.

Yarusi: rents traveling flats by

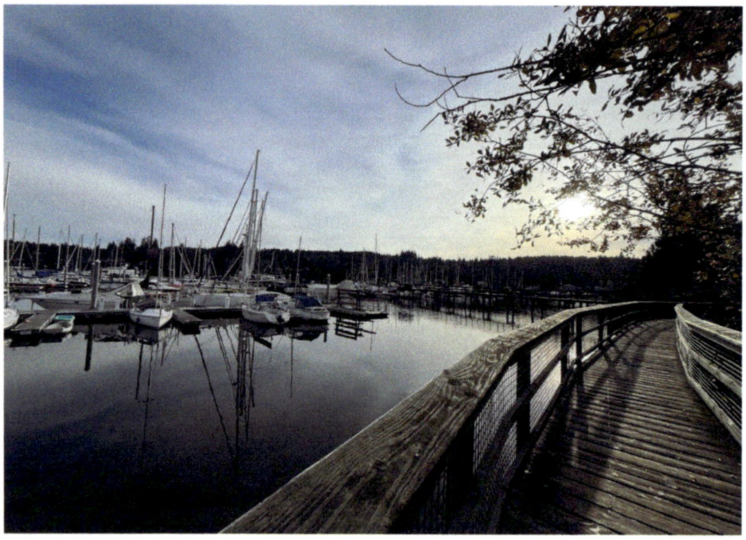

A Coast. © *2025 by Matylda Czarnecka. (Used with permission)*

ABOUT THE AUTHOR

Anna Ursyn, Ph.D., is a professor of Computer Graphics at the University of Northern Colorado. She combines programming with software and printmaking media to unify computer-generated and painted images and sculptures.

She had over 50 single juried and invitational art shows and participated in over 200 juried and invitational fine art exhibitions, such as over a dozen times in ACM SIGGRAPH Art Galleries and traveling shows, including Louvre, Paris, Der Prix Ars Electronica Linz, Austria; Eurographics (Artistic Merit Award), Denver International Airport Show, Denver Capitol shows. Her work was selected to be sent to the Moon by NASA as a part of Carnegie Mellon's MoonArk project and traveling shows, including Centre Pompidou in Paris. Animations projected at the Victory Media Network, Dallas, TX, ISEAs, New York Digital Salons, 20th Century Matrix for NTT Museum, Tokyo, Japan (2000 images and 5000 texts describing the 20th Century), Winner of BauBoden, Deutsche Bau-und Bodenbank AG, cover and 18 color plates, Computerkunst/Computer Art Gladbeck, Germany + traveling shows. Salon de la Culture et des Jeux Mathematiques, CIJM, University Pierre et Marie Curie, Paris, Honorable Mention; Art of the Animal, Australia (award), GRAPHITEs, Art of Photography Show San Diego, CA, Common Ground the Haun Tie Art Museum in Beijing, M.I.A.D. Torento Argentina (Second Place), Immaginando, Digital Visions of Etruria (Honorable Mention), Italy, Bridges Mathematical Art Galleries, Joint Mathematics Meetings Art Galleries, and Generative Art galleries. Her work in ABADs is in the permanent collection of the Museum of Modern Art MOMA in New York City, the Los Angeles County Museum of Art, CA, the Smithsonian Institution, Washington, DC, and more. Anna published over a dozen books, chapters, and articles with her students' artwork included in her book.

Research and pedagogy interests include integrated art, science, and computer art graphics instruction. Chaired the SpaceTime international competitions for students by ACM SIGGRAPH, the International Conference on Computer Graphics and Interactive Techniques. Since 1997, Anna has served as a Liaison, Organizing, and Program Committee member of the International IEEE Conferences on Information Visualization (iV) in London, UK, and has chaired the Symposium and Digital Art Gallery D-ART iV.

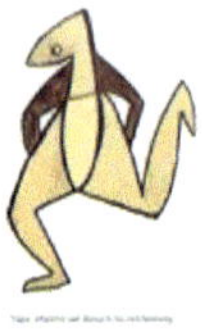

Yngus: Whenever sad, he dances to his own humming.

BOOKS – AUTHORED, CO-AUTHORED, AND EDITED BY ANNA URSYN

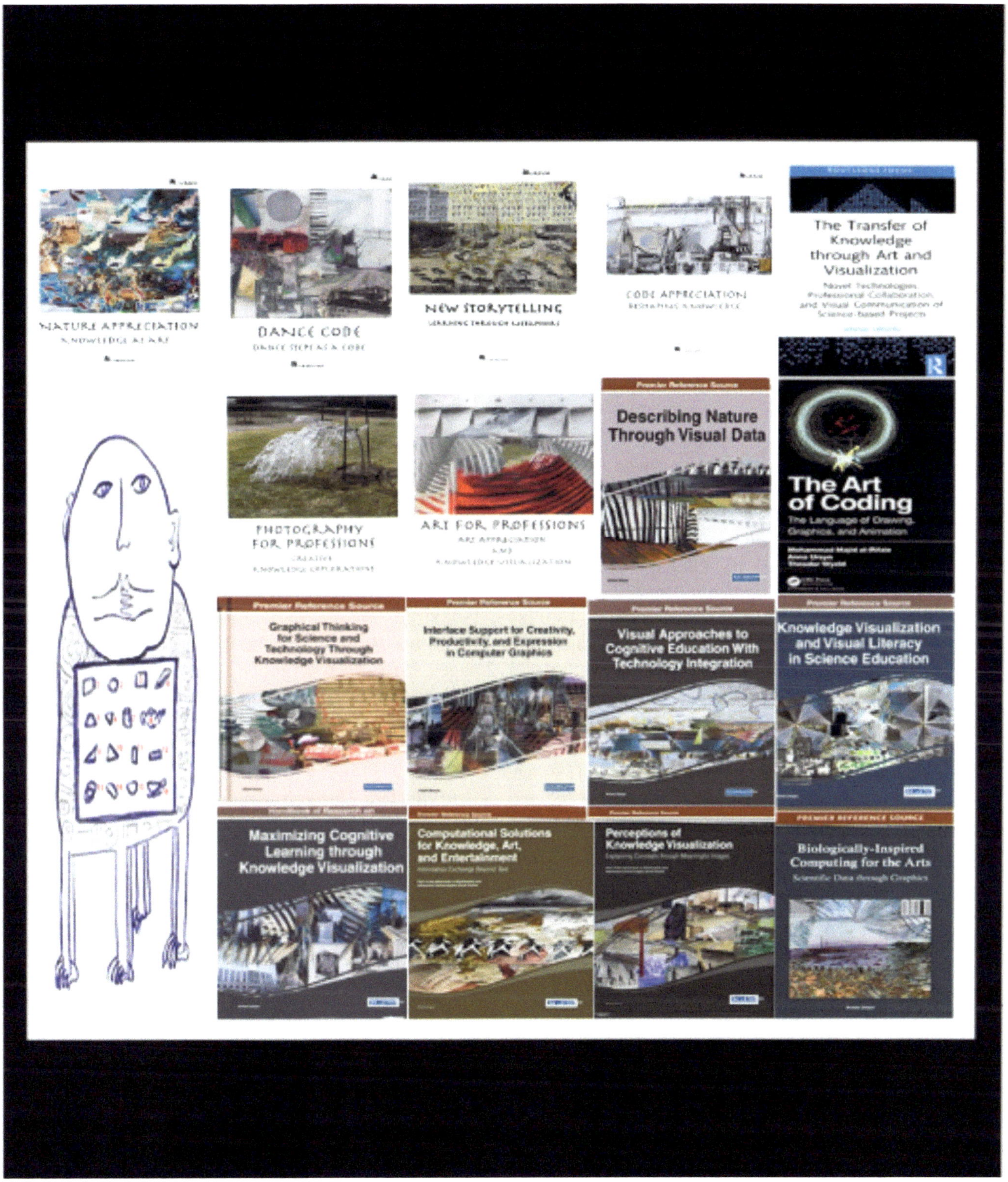

A LIST OF TITLES FROM THE PREVIOUS PAGE

1. *Dance Code, Dance Steps as a Code,* Anna Ursyn (Author). Taylor & Francis Group.
2. *New Storytelling: Learning through Metaphors.* Anna Ursyn (Author). Taylor & Francis Group.
3. *Code Appreciation, Reshaping Knowledge.* Anna Ursyn, (Author). Taylor & Francis Group.
4. *Nature Appreciation: Knowledge as Art,* Anna Ursyn (Author).
5. *The Transfer of Knowledge through Art and Visualization: Novel Technologies, Collaboration, and Visual Communication of Science-based Projects.* Anna Ursyn (Author). Taylor & Francis Group. Routledge. 2024, 143 pages, ISBN 9781032624228.
6. *Photography for Professions: Creative Knowledge Explorations.* Anna Ursyn (Author), Kendall Hunt Publishing Company, 2022, 177 pages, ISBN 979-8-7657-4703-2.
7. *Art for Professions: Art Appreciation and Knowledge Visualization.* Anna Ursyn (Author), Kendall Hunt Publishing Company. 2021, 538 pages, ISBN-10 1792466609, ISBN-13 978-1792466601.
8. *Describing Nature Through Visual Data.* Anna Ursyn (Author/Editor), IGI Global, 2020, 367 pages, ISBN-10 1799857530, ISBN-13 978-1799857532.
9. *The Art of Coding: The Language of Drawing, Graphics, and Animation.* by al-Rifaie, M. M., Ursyn, A., Wyeld, T. CRC Press, Taylor & Francis Group, A Chapman & Hall Book. 2020, 312 pages. ISBN 9780-0-367-90037-3 (hbk), 978-1-138-62964-6 (pbk), 978-1-315-21033-9 (ebk).
10. *Graphical Thinking for Science and Technology Through Knowledge,* Visualization (Advances in Multimedia and Interactive Technologies) (Anna Ursyn, Author//Editor), IGI Global. 2020, 374 pages, ISBN-10 1799816516, ISBN-13 978-1799816515.
11. *Interface Support for Creativity, Productivity, and Expression in Computer Graphics.* Anna Ursyn (Author/Editor) IGI Global. 2019, 355 pages, ISBN-13 9781522573715, DOI: 10.4018/978-1-5225-7371-5.
12. *Visual Approaches to Cognitive Education with Technology Integration.* Anna Ursyn (Author/Editor), IGI Global. 2018, 387 pages, ISBN-13 9781522553328.
13. *Knowledge Visualization and Visual Literacy in Science Education.* Anna Ursyn (Author/Editor). IGI Global. 2016. 431 pages, ISBN-13 9781522504801.
14. *Maximizing Cognitive Learning through Knowledge Visualization.* Handbook of Research. Anna Ursyn (Author/Editor). IGI Global, 2015, 572 pages, ISBN-13 9781466681422.
15. *Computational Solutions for Knowledge, Art, and Entertainment: Information Exchange Beyond Text.* Anna Ursyn (Author), IGI Global, 2014, 511 pages, ISBN-13 9781466646278.
16. *Perceptions of Knowledge Visualization: Explaining Concepts through Meaningful Images.* Anna Ursyn (Author), IGI Global, 2014, 418 pages, ISBN-13 9781466647039.
17. *Biologically Inspired Computing for the Arts: Scientific Data Through Graphics.* Anna Ursyn (Author/Editor), IGI Global, 2012, 442 pages, ISBN-13 9781466609426.

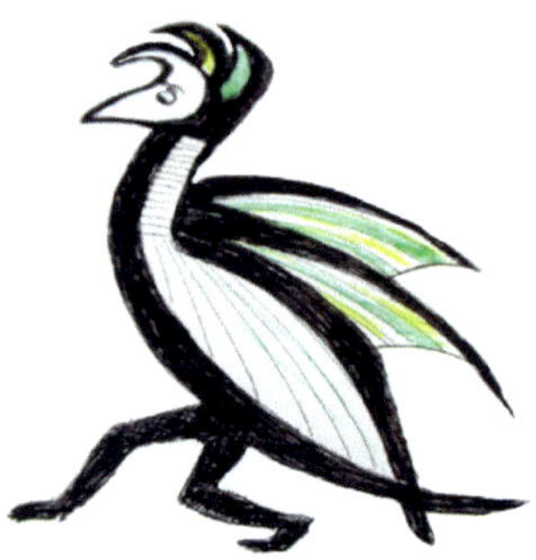

Gyter: has no doubt where to go when.

Gyter, as always, was just doing what he thought was the best for everyon

For Product Safety Concerns and Information please contact our EU representative GPSR@taylorandfrancis.com Taylor & Francis Verlag GmbH, Kaufingerstraße 24, 80331 München, Germany

9781032970608

T - #0201 - 030925 - C356 - 279/216/17 - PB - 9781032970608 - Gloss Lamination